T0181689

Lecture Notes in Computer Science   10908

Commenced Publication in 1973
Founding and Former Series Editors:
Gerhard Goos, Juris Hartmanis, and Jan van Leeuwen

More information about this series at http://www.springer.com/series/7409

Margherita Antona · Constantine Stephanidis (Eds.)

Universal Access in Human-Computer Interaction

Virtual, Augmented, and Intelligent Environments

12th International Conference, UAHCI 2018
Held as Part of HCI International 2018
Las Vegas, NV, USA, July 15–20, 2018
Proceedings, Part II

Springer

Editors
Margherita Antona
Foundation for Research
  and Technology – Hellas (FORTH)
Heraklion, Crete
Greece

Constantine Stephanidis
University of Crete
  and Foundation for Research
  and Technology – Hellas (FORTH)
Heraklion, Crete
Greece

ISSN 0302-9743   ISSN 1611-3349 (electronic)
Lecture Notes in Computer Science
ISBN 978-3-319-92051-1   ISBN 978-3-319-92052-8 (eBook)
https://doi.org/10.1007/978-3-319-92052-8

Library of Congress Control Number: 2018944387

LNCS Sublibrary: SL3 – Information Systems and Applications, incl. Internet/Web, and HCI

Printed on acid-free paper

This Springer imprint is published by the registered company Springer International Publishing AG
part of Springer Nature
The registered company address is: Gewerbestrasse 11, 6330 Cham, Switzerland

Foreword

The 20th International Conference on Human-Computer Interaction, HCI International 2018, was held in Las Vegas, NV, USA, during July 15–20, 2018. The event incorporated the 14 conferences/thematic areas listed on the following page.

A total of 4,373 individuals from academia, research institutes, industry, and governmental agencies from 76 countries submitted contributions, and 1,170 papers and 195 posters have been included in the proceedings. These contributions address the latest research and development efforts and highlight the human aspects of design and use of computing systems. The contributions thoroughly cover the entire field of human-computer interaction, addressing major advances in knowledge and effective use of computers in a variety of application areas. The volumes constituting the full set of the conference proceedings are listed in the following pages.

I would like to thank the program board chairs and the members of the program boards of all thematic areas and affiliated conferences for their contribution to the highest scientific quality and the overall success of the HCI International 2018 conference.

This conference would not have been possible without the continuous and unwavering support and advice of the founder, Conference General Chair Emeritus and Conference Scientific Advisor Prof. Gavriel Salvendy. For his outstanding efforts, I would like to express my appreciation to the communications chair and editor of *HCI International News*, Dr. Abbas Moallem.

July 2018   Constantine Stephanidis

HCI International 2018 Thematic Areas
and Affiliated Conferences

Thematic areas:

- Human-Computer Interaction (HCI 2018)
- Human Interface and the Management of Information (HIMI 2018)

Affiliated conferences:

- 15th International Conference on Engineering Psychology and Cognitive Ergonomics (EPCE 2018)
- 12th International Conference on Universal Access in Human-Computer Interaction (UAHCI 2018)
- 10th International Conference on Virtual, Augmented, and Mixed Reality (VAMR 2018)
- 10th International Conference on Cross-Cultural Design (CCD 2018)
- 10th International Conference on Social Computing and Social Media (SCSM 2018)
- 12th International Conference on Augmented Cognition (AC 2018)
- 9th International Conference on Digital Human Modeling and Applications in Health, Safety, Ergonomics, and Risk Management (DHM 2018)
- 7th International Conference on Design, User Experience, and Usability (DUXU 2018)
- 6th International Conference on Distributed, Ambient, and Pervasive Interactions (DAPI 2018)
- 5th International Conference on HCI in Business, Government, and Organizations (HCIBGO)
- 5th International Conference on Learning and Collaboration Technologies (LCT 2018)
- 4th International Conference on Human Aspects of IT for the Aged Population (ITAP 2018)

Conference Proceedings Volumes Full List

19. LNCS 10919, Design, User Experience, and Usability: Designing Interactions (Part II), edited by Aaron Marcus and Wentao Wang
20. LNCS 10920, Design, User Experience, and Usability: Users, Contexts, and Case Studies (Part III), edited by Aaron Marcus and Wentao Wang
21. LNCS 10921, Distributed, Ambient, and Pervasive Interactions: Understanding Humans (Part I), edited by Norbert Streitz and Shin'ichi Konomi
22. LNCS 10922, Distributed, Ambient, and Pervasive Interactions: Technologies and Contexts (Part II), edited by Norbert Streitz and Shin'ichi Konomi
23. LNCS 10923, HCI in Business, Government, and Organizations, edited by Fiona Fui-Hoon Nah and Bo Sophia Xiao
24. LNCS 10924, Learning and Collaboration Technologies: Design, Development and Technological Innovation (Part I), edited by Panayiotis Zaphiris and Andri Ioannou
25. LNCS 10925, Learning and Collaboration Technologies: Learning and Teaching (Part II), edited by Panayiotis Zaphiris and Andri Ioannou
26. LNCS 10926, Human Aspects of IT for the Aged Population: Acceptance, Communication, and Participation (Part I), edited by Jia Zhou and Gavriel Salvendy
27. LNCS 10927, Human Aspects of IT for the Aged Population: Applications in Health, Assistance, and Entertainment (Part II), edited by Jia Zhou and Gavriel Salvendy
28. CCIS 850, HCI International 2018 Posters Extended Abstracts (Part I), edited by Constantine Stephanidis
29. CCIS 851, HCI International 2018 Posters Extended Abstracts (Part II), edited by Constantine Stephanidis
30. CCIS 852, HCI International 2018 Posters Extended Abstracts (Part III), edited by Constantine Stephanidis

http://2018.hci.international/proceedings

12th International Conference on Universal Access in Human-Computer Interaction

Program Board Chair(s): **Margherita Antona and Constantine Stephanidis,** *Greece*

- João Barroso, Portugal
- Rodrigo Bonacin, Brazil
- Ingo K. Bosse, Germany
- Anthony Lewis Brooks, Denmark
- Laura Burzagli, Italy
- Pedro J. S. Cardoso, Portugal
- Stefan Carmien, UK
- Vagner Figueredo De Santana, Brazil
- Carlos Duarte, Portugal
- Pier Luigi Emiliani, Italy
- Qin Gao, P.R. China
- Andrina Granić, Croatia
- Simeon Keates, UK
- Georgios Kouroupetroglou, Greece
- Patrick M. Langdon, UK
- Barbara Leporini, Italy
- I. Scott MacKenzie, Canada
- John Magee, USA
- Alessandro Marcengo, Italy
- Troy McDaniel, USA
- Silvia Mirri, Italy
- Ana Isabel Paraguay, Brazil
- Hugo Paredes, Portugal
- Enrico Pontelli, USA
- João M. F. Rodrigues, Portugal
- Frode Eika Sandnes, Norway
- Anthony Savidis, Greece
- Jaime Sánchez, Chile
- Volker Sorge, UK
- Hiroki Takada, Japan
- Kevin Tseng, Taiwan
- Gerhard Weber, Germany

The full list with the Program Board Chairs and the members of the Program Boards of all thematic areas and affiliated conferences is available online at:

http://www.hci.international/board-members-2018.php

HCI International 2019

The 21st International Conference on Human-Computer Interaction, HCI International 2019, will be held jointly with the affiliated conferences in Orlando, FL, USA, at Walt Disney World Swan and Dolphin Resort, July 26–31, 2019. It will cover a broad spectrum of themes related to Human-Computer Interaction, including theoretical issues, methods, tools, processes, and case studies in HCI design, as well as novel interaction techniques, interfaces, and applications. The proceedings will be published by Springer. More information will be available on the conference website: http://2019.hci.international/.

General Chair
Prof. Constantine Stephanidis
University of Crete and ICS-FORTH
Heraklion, Crete, Greece
E-mail: general_chair@hcii2019.org

http://2019.hci.international/

Contents – Part II

Intelligent Assistive Environments

Access to the Web, Social Media, Education, Culture and Social Innovation

Contents – Part I

Alternative I/O Techniques, Multimodality and Adaptation

Non Visual Interaction

Designing for Cognitive Disabilities

Virtual and Augmented Reality for Universal Access

Analysis of the Body Sway While/After Viewing Visual Target Movement Synchronized with Background Motion

Nao Amano[1], Hiroki Takada[1(✉)], Yusuke Jono[1], Toru Tanimura[1],
Fumiya Kinoshita[2], Masaru Miyao[3], and Masumi Takada[4]

[1] Department of Human and Artificial Intelligent Systems,
Graduate School of Engineering, University of Fukui,
3-9-1 Bunkyo, Fukui 910-8507, Japan
takada@u-fukui.ac.jp
[2] Toyama Prefectural University,
5180 Kurokawa, Imizu-shi, Toyama 939-0398, Japan
[3] Nagoya Industrial Science Research Institute,
2-10-19 Sakae, Naka, Nagoya 460-0008, Japan
[4] Chubu Gakuin University, 2-1 Kirigaoka, Seki-shi, Gifu 501-3993, Japan

Abstract. Stereoscopic imaging techniques have also become used for not only amusement but also in the industrial, medical care, and educational fields, however, symptoms due to the stereopsis have been reported. In this study, we especially focus on the effect of background motions on the equilibrium function. The body sway was recorded while/after viewing a sphere as a visual target synchronized/unsynchronized with periodic motion of the view point. Statistical analysis was conducted for the stabilograms.

Keywords: Body sway · Total locus length · Area of sway
Total locus length per unit area · Sparse density · Stereopsis
Synchronized/unsynchronized motion

1 Introduction

In these days when developments in the graphical technology has produced an increase in the chance to view 3D video clips, visually induced motion sickness (VIMS) has been widely reported as a negative result from the developments. The onset of the VIMS is explained by some hypothesis; overstimulation theory and sensory conflict theory [1]. The overstimulation theory cannot explain the space motion sickness [2–7] and the simulator sickness with no vestibular stimulation. Along with the later [8–12], disagreement between the convergence and lens accommodation has been pointed out as a cause of visually induced motion sickness (VIMS) with stereopsis [13]. We conducted simultaneous measurements of lens accommodation and the convergence in a dark room >1 lx [14–18]. According to these researches, the time sequences have showed that the lens accommodation also follows the convergence in case of the stereoscopic vision. The lens accommodation is not fixed at the surface of objects/displays. 3D sickness might not be caused by the disagreement between the

© Springer International Publishing AG, part of Springer Nature 2018
M. Antona and C. Stephanidis (Eds.): UAHCI 2018, LNCS 10908, pp. 3–14, 2018.
https://doi.org/10.1007/978-3-319-92052-8_1

convergence and lens accommodation. Also, we investigated the effect of long-term exposure to 3D video clips on the visual function [19] and the body sway [20, 21].

However, the cause of the VIMS does not have been proved yet whereas dizziness and nausea are regarded as symptoms of the VIMS. Previous researches showed that the exposure to blurred/rotational images induces the motion sickness [22] which is also induced while viewing 3D video clips in dark environment on the head-mounted displays [23–26]. The body balance function is affected by the peripheral vision of a 3D video clip compared to a 2D video clip [27]. The authors investigated the effect of the blurred background, especially in the periodic motion, on the equilibrium function [28].

In prior work, background images with 3D images in the peripheral visual field are shown to affect the body's equilibrium system [29]. Furthermore, when viewing images with background instability, the equilibrium system is shown to be affected more when a visual target is present than when there is not [28]. However, the effect on the human body of the connection between visual target movement and background instability is an issue that remains unsolved at present. The objective of the present paper is to study how the body's equilibrium system is affected by background instability in video containing a visual target, that is periodic motion in the backgrounds. A comparative experiment was conducted to experimentally assess the impact on the equilibrium system of the following: video clips with/without a stationary visual target; and video clips that show a spherical visual target moving back and forth quasi-periodically between near and far-distance, while moving from side to side and up and down, showing the visual target movement synchronized with/without the periodic viewpoint changing from side to side (synchronized/unsynchronized movement).

One of the methods to assess motion sickness is stabilometry [30], which is an effective way for the quantitative assessment of the effect of 3D video viewing on the equilibrium system. The present paper therefore makes use of stabilometry.

2   Materials and Methods

The gravicoder was used to record the x-y coordinates for the centre of pressure (CoP) for all sampling times, namely while subjects watched the video clips for 1 min and while they stood with their eyes closed for 2 min in the Experiment 1; and for 1 min in the Experiment 2. CoP data were divided into those for x (right is positive) and y (forward is positive) directions, converted into time series and generated as stabilograms (Fig. 1). The indices; total locus length; area of sway; total *locus length per unit area*; and sparse density were assessed. Total locus length, area of sway and total *locus length per unit area* were used as analytical indices for stabilograms in previous studies, and they have been calculated based on the equations that were defined by the Japan Society for Equilibrium Research as well as in the present paper [31]. Sparse density is an index proposed by Takada *et al.* indicating the density of sampling points distributed in each division on the plane, and is considered to be linked to stability of the body's equilibrium system [32].

(a)

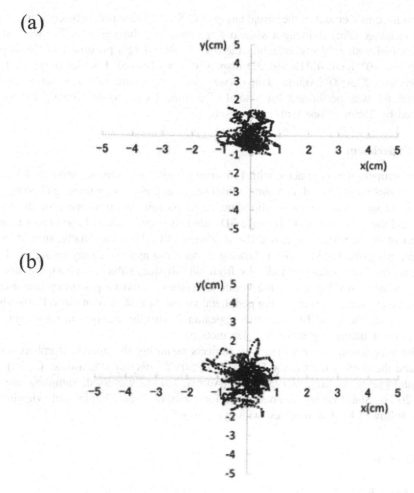

(b)

Fig. 1. Typical example of stabilograms.

2.1   Experiment 1

The experiment was conducted with nine healthy males aged 21–24 years. Consumption of alcohol and caffeine as well as smoking were prohibited for the two hours prior to the experiment, and written consent was obtained upon full explanation of the details of the experiment. Subjects were shown the following sequence with the periodic motion in the backgrounds: a 2D video clip (VC) without a visual target (VC-1); a 3D video clip without a visual target (VC-2); a 2D video clip with a fixed visual target in the centre (VC-3); a 3D video clip with a fixed visual target in the centre (VC-4); a 2D video clip with unsynchronized movement of the visual target (VC-5); a 3D video clip with unsynchronized movement of the visual target (VC-6); a 2D video clip with synchronized movement of the visual target (VC-7); a 3D video with synchronized movement of the visual target (VC-8). Additionally, subjects were shown a control image (Pre) showing a white dot against a gray background. The experiment is performed with subjects assuming the upright Romberg's posture, and the display used is the 40″ KDL-40HX80R 3D display (Sony, Tokyo). For the stabilometry, a *Gravicoder* GS-3000 (Anima, Tokyo) was used. Sampling rate was set at 20 Hz. Stabilometry was performed for a total of 3 min: 1 min while viewing the video, followed by 2 min of rest with eyes closed.

2.2   Experiment 2

This experiment was conducted with 116 subjects, male and female, aged 15–89 years. Three groups were formed, of young, middle-aged and elderly subjects, and compared. They were shown a 3D video clip showing uncoordinated movement of the visual target and the viewpoint (VC-I), and a 3D video showing back and forth (coordinated) movement of the visual target and the viewpoint (VC-II). Additionally, subjects were shown a comparison-video (Pre) showing a white dot against a gray background. By changing the background periodically from side to side, subjects' viewpoint alone is altered without any input into the vestibular system, provoking sensory discordance and increasing the load when using peripheral vision. Specifically in video II, the visual target moving back and forth changes appearance with the changes in viewpoint, and appears to be displaying more complex motion.

The experiment is performed with subjects assuming the upright Romberg's posture, and the display used is the 50″ 3D TH-P50VT5 display (Panasonic, Osaka). For the stabilometry, a *gravicoder* GS-3000 (Anima, Tokyo) was used. Sampling rate was set at 20 Hz. Stabilometry was performed for a total of 2 min: 1 min while viewing the video, followed by 1 min of rest with eyes closed.

3   Results

3.1   Experiment 1

Sway values were obtained from stabilograms while/after viewing video clips (Fig. 2, 3 and 4).

Comparing stabilograms with/without visual target while eyes were open, the value of the total locus length was significantly higher when viewing VC-1 and VC-2 than when viewing the static image (Pre) ($p < 0.05$), and the same statistical tendency was also seen in the sparse density ($p < 0.10$). For the 2 min with closed eyes, the value of the total locus length per unit area tended to be significantly lower when viewing VC-2 compared to the Pre ($p < 0.10$), and significantly lower when viewing VC-4 ($p < 0.05$).

A comparison of the static/dynamic visual target shows that, with their eyes closed for first 1 min, the value of the total locus length was significantly higher in VC-2 compared to VC-4 ($p < 0.05$). With their eyes open, the value of the total locus length was significantly higher while viewing VC-6 than that of the Pre ($p < 0.05$) and tended to be greater while viewing VC-3 and VC-5 ($p < 0.10$). However, no significant results were found when viewing VC-4. Moreover, with their eyes closed for first 1 min, more

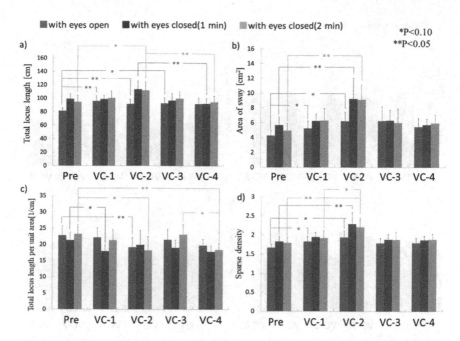

Fig. 2. Sway values while/after viewing a/no visual target with the periodic motion in the backgrounds

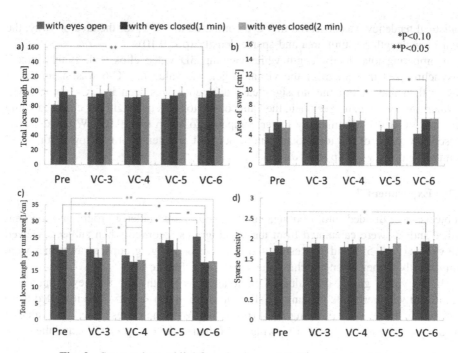

Fig. 3. Sway values while/after viewing a static/dynamic visual target.

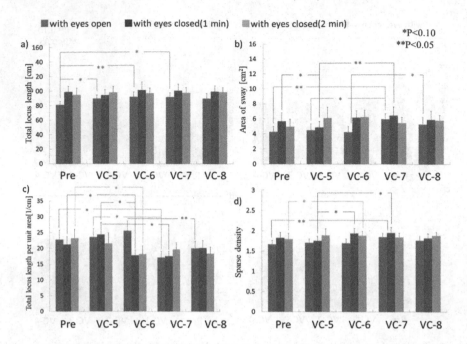

Fig. 4. Sway values while/after viewing visual target movement synchronized with/without a periodic motion of the view point

statistical tendency was observed in VC-6 compared to VC-5, for the area of sway, the total locus length per unit area and sparse density (p < 0.10).

Comparing total locus length while viewing 3D video clips with synchronized/ unsynchronized movement of the visual target, the value in VC-6 was significantly higher than that in Pre but no significant difference was seen in VC-8 (p < 0.05). Furthermore, with their eyes open, the value of the total locus length per unit area while viewing VC-8 was significantly lower compared to VC-6 (p < 0.05). With their eyes closed, the value of the total locus length per unit area tended to be lower for VC-7 compared to for VC-5 (p < 0.10).

3.2   Experiment 2

Subjects were divided into a young, middle-aged and an elderly group, and the analytical indices were calculated from the stabilograms recorded when subjects viewed the videos (Figs. 5, 6 and 7). Results showed that for all age groups, sway values were significantly higher when watching the videos than for the Pre.

In the young group, the value of the total locus length with their eyes open was significantly higher while viewing VC-II than in the Pre (p < 0.05), and it tended to be statistically higher while viewing VC-I (p < 0.10). With their eyes closed, the value of the area of sway was larger after viewing VC-I than in the Pre (p < 0.05), and the value

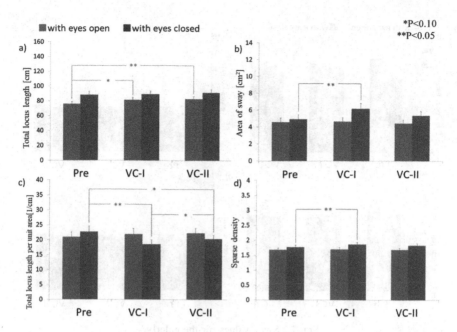

Fig. 5. Sway values for the young.

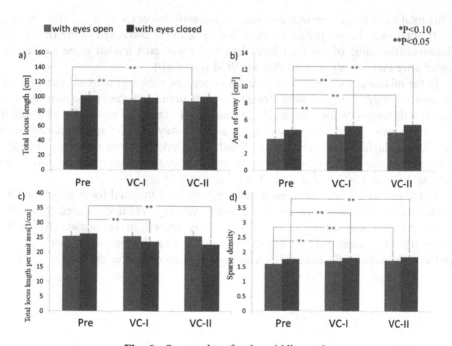

Fig. 6. Sway values for the middle-aged.

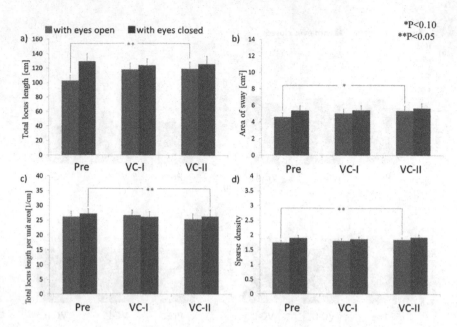

Fig. 7. Sway values for the elderly.

of the total locus length per unit area was significantly lower (p < 0.05). After viewing VC-II, total locus length per unit area tended to be lower compared to Pre (p < 0.10). Moreover, the value of the total locus length per unit area tended to be statistically higher after viewing VC-II than that for VC-I (p < 0.10).

In the middle-aged group, with their eyes open, the values of the total locus length, the area of sway, the *total locus length per unit area*, and the sparse density were significantly higher while viewing VC-I and VC-II compared to the Pre (p < 0.05). With their eyes closed, the values of the area of sway and the sparse density were significantly higher after viewing VC-I and VC-II compared to the Pre (p < 0.05). Moreover, results for the total locus length per unit area were significantly lower after viewing VC-I and VC-II than that of the Pre (p < 0.05).

In the elderly group, with their eyes open, values of the total locus length and the sparse density were significantly higher while viewing VC-II compared to the Pre (p < 0.05), and the value of the area of sway tended to be statistically higher (p < 0.10), With their eyes closed, the value of the total locus length per unit area tended to be statistically lower after viewing VC-II compared to the Pre (p < 0.10).

4 Discussion

4.1 Experiment 1

Since body sway was higher when viewing 3D video clips than when viewing 2D video clips, regardless of a visual target being present in the video or not, it is believed that background instability when viewing 3D video videos impacted more on the equilibrium system. Results were obtained showing that sway values when viewing video clips without a visual target was significantly increased compared to viewing Pre, regardless of solidity of the video clip (2D or 3D) with their eyes open/closed. However, when viewing video with visual targets, no significant differences were seen regardless of the solidity, and thus it is believed that when viewing video with a visual target, the effect due to background instability on the equilibrium system is reduced. We surmise that this may be due to stationary visual targets assisting in balance control in the upright posture. Total locus length when viewing 3D video is shown to be significantly lower after viewing video clip for 2 min with a visual target compared to viewing video without a visual target. Based on this, it can be concluded that, the 3D video clip without a visual target impacts more on the equilibrium than video with a visual target. We surmise that this may be because, since the video clip is in 3D, the visual target is felt to be nearer, thus assisting in balance control in the upright posture.

For viewing the 3D video clip except for the abovementioned comparison, the total locus length results are believed to be more perturbed due to the exposure to the video clips with a visual target. However, since opposite results are found for the area of sway and the total locus length per unit area, we can conclude that although there is an increase in slight sway variation, the range within which the centre of gravity changes has narrowed. It is surmised that this is because controlling one's CoP does not involve an attempt to stay in one spot, but rather it is controlled by swaying within a constant range while matching the movement of the visual target.

Compared to video clips with synchronized movement of the visual target, viewing video with unsynchronized movement of the visual target results in significantly higher total locus length than when viewing Pre. However, based on the results for the area of sway and the total locus length per unit area, statistically increased sway tended to be seen for the exposure to the video clip with synchronized movement of the visual target compared to that with unsynchronized movement. This leads us to conclude that although there is an increase in micro-sway, the range of motion of the CoP has narrowed for the exposure to the video clip with unsynchronized movement. It is believed that this is because, although the total locus length is increased when viewing the unsynchronized movement by swaying the body to match the movement of the visual target, the effect of the exposure to the video clip on the equilibrium system is increased when viewing video clip with the synchronized movement of the visual target.

Compared to video with a static visual target, video clips without a visual target affected the equilibrium system more. Additionally, we can say that the connection between the background and visual target when there is a visual target that functions as an aid to balance control changes the effect on the equilibrium system. This is based on the following: video clips with a moving visual target affected the equilibrium system more than video clips with a static visual target, and it is believed that the impact on the equilibrium system of a moving visual target was severer when viewing video with the synchronized movement of the visual target. Furthermore, in relation to the video clips used in the present paper, motion sickness was more likely to be induced when viewing the visual target movement synchronized with the background motion.

4.2   Experiment 2

Hardly any significant differences were seen between the video clips throughout the age groups. However, regarding the total locus length in the young group, for subjects showing statistical trends when viewing VC-I compared to the Pre, significant differences were seen for VC-II, and for the elderly group no differences were found for viewing VC-I compared to Pre, although significant differences were found in the case of viewing VC-II. Therefore, it is possible that viewing VC-II strongly affects the equilibrium. Since only the young group showed statistical trends between the video clips (Fig. 5c), it is possible that the young group is considered to have sensitive balance function for the VIMS.

In measurements of the middle-aged group, we could find a number of significant differences or statistical tendencies and lack of these in measurements of the elderly group. Deterioration in the stereopsis due to the aging also affect the statistical results in this study.

Acknowledgements. This work was supported in part by the Japan Society for the Promotion of Science, Grant-in-Aid for Research Activity Start-up Number 15H06711, Grant-in-Aid for Young Scientists (B) Number 16K16105, and that for Scientific Research (C) Number 17K00715.

References

1. Reason, J.T., Brand, J.J.: Motion Sickness. Academic Press, London (1975)
2. Homick, J.L.: Space motion sickness. Acta Astronautica **6**, 1259–1272 (1979)
3. Graybiel, A.: Space motion sickness: skylab revisited. Aviat Space Environ. Med. **51**, 814–822 (1980)
4. Talbot, J.M., Fisher, K.D.: Space sickness. Physiologist **27**, 423–429 (1984)
5. Leich, R.J., Daroff, R.B.: Space motion sickness: etiological hypotheses and a proposal for diagnostic clinical examination. Aviat Space Environ. Med. **56**, 469–473 (1985)
6. Oman, C.M., Lichtenberg, B.K., Money, K.E., McCoy, R.K.: MIT/Canadian vestibular experiments on Spacelab-1 mission: 4. Space motion sickness: symptoms, stimuli and predictability. Exp. Brain Res. **64**, 316–334 (1986)
7. Davis, J.R., Vanderploeg, J.M., Santy, P.A., Jennings, R.T., Stewart, D.F.: Space motion sickness during 24 flights of the space shuttle. Aviat Space Environ. Med. **59**, 1185–1189 (1988)
8. Money, K.E.: Motion sickness. Physiol. Rev. **50**, 1–39 (1970)
9. Johnson, W.H., Jongkees, L.B.W., Kornhuber, H.H.: Vestibular system part 2: psychophysics, applied aspects and general interpretations. In: Kornhuber, H.H. (ed.) Motion sickness. Handbook of Sensory Physiology, vol. 6/2. Springer, Heidelberg (1974). https://doi.org/10.1007/978-3-642-65920-1_10

10. Benson, A.J.: Motion sickness. In: Dix, M.R., Hood, J.D. (eds.) Vertigo, pp. 391–426. Wiley, New York (1984)
11. Stott, J.R.R.: Mechanisms and treatment of motion illness. In: Davis, C.J., Lake-Bakaar, G. V., Grahame-Smith, D.G. (eds.) Nausea and Vomiting: Mechanisms and Treatment. Advances in Applied Neurological Sciences, vol. 3. Springer, Heidelberg (1986). https://doi.org/10.1007/978-3-642-70479-6_9
12. Reason, J.T.: Motion sickness: a special case of sensory rearrangement. Adv. Sci. 26, 386–393 (1970)
13. Ukai, K., Howarth, P.A.: Visual fatigue caused by viewing stereoscopic motion images: background, theories, and observations. Displays 29, 106–116 (2008)
14. Shiomi, T., Ishio, H., Hori, H., Takada, H., Omori, M., Hasegawa, S., Matsunuma, S., Hasegawa, A., Kanda, T., Miyao, M.: Simultaneous measurement of lens accommodation and convergence to real objects. In: Shumaker, R. (ed.) VMR 2011. LNCS, vol. 6773, pp. 363–370. Springer, Heidelberg (2011). https://doi.org/10.1007/978-3-642-22021-0_40
15. Shiomi, T., Uemoto, K., Kojima, T., Sano, S., Ishio, H., Takada, H., Omori, M., Watanabe, T., Miyao, M.: Simultaneous measurement of lens accommodation and convergence in natural and artificial 3D vision. J. SID. (2013). https://doi.org/10.1002/jsid.156
16. Kojima, T., Matsuura, Y., Miyao, M., Shiomi, T., Takada, H.: Comparison by simultaneous measurement of lens accommodation and convergence in 3D vision and their distributions. Int. J. Biosci. Biochem. Bioinfo. 3(6), 635–638 (2013)
17. Shiomi, T., Hori, H., Hasegawa, S., Takada, H., Omori, M., Matsuura, Y., Ishio, H., Hasegawa, A., Kanda, T., Miyao, M.: Simultaneous measurement of lens accommodation and convergence to objects. Forma 29(S), S77–S81 (2014)
18. Kimura, R., et al.: Measurement of lens focus adjustment while wearing a see-through head-mounted display. In: Antona, M., Stephanidis, C. (eds.) UAHCI 2016. LNCS, vol. 9738, pp. 271–278. Springer, Cham (2016). https://doi.org/10.1007/978-3-319-40244-4_26
19. Ishio, H., Kojima, T., Oohashi, T., Okada, Y., Takada, H., Miyao, M.: Effects of long-time 3D viewing on the eye function of accommodation and convergence. In: Stephanidis, C., Antona, M. (eds.) UAHCI 2013. LNCS, vol. 8010, pp. 269–274. Springer, Heidelberg (2013). https://doi.org/10.1007/978-3-642-39191-0_30
20. Takada, M., Murakami, K., Kunieda, Y., Hirata, T., Matsuura, Y., Iwase, S., Miyao, M., Takada, H.: Effect of hour-long stereoscopic film on equilibrium function. In: Proceedings of IMID 2011 Digest, pp. 737–738 (2011)
21. Yoshikawa, K., Takada, H., Miyao, M.: Effect of display size on body sway in seated posture while viewing an hour-long stereoscopic film. In: Stephanidis, C., Antona, M. (eds.) UAHCI 2013. LNCS, vol. 8010, pp. 336–341. Springer, Heidelberg (2013). https://doi.org/10.1007/978-3-642-39191-0_38
22. International Standard Organization: IWA3:2005 image safety-reducing determinism in a time series. Phys. Rev. Lett. 70, 530–582 (1993)
23. Takada, H., Fujikake, K., Watanabe, T., Hasegawa, S., Omori, M., Miyao, M.: A method for evaluating motion sickness induced by watching stereoscopic images on a head-mounted display. In: Proceedings of SPIE 7237, Stereoscopic Displays and Applications XX, 72371P (2009). https://doi.org/10.1117/12.807144
24. Fujikake, K., Miyao, M., Watanabe, T., Hasegawa, S., Omori, M., Takada, H.: Evaluation of body sway and the relevant dynamics while viewing a three-dimensional movie on a head-mounted display by using stabilograms. In: Shumaker, R. (ed.) VMR 2009. LNCS, vol. 5622, pp. 41–50. Springer, Heidelberg (2009). https://doi.org/10.1007/978-3-642-02771-0_5
25. Takada, H., Fujikake, K., Miyao, M.: Metamorphism in potential function while maintaining upright posture during exposure to a three-dimensional movie on an head-mounted display. In: Proceedings of 31st EMBS, pp. 4906–4912 (2009)

26. Takada, H., Matsuura, Y., Fujikake, K., Miyao, M.: Bioresponse to stereoscopic movies presented via a head-mounted display. In: Proceedings of the 4th BIOSTEC 2011, pp. 433–437 (2011)
27. Takada, M., Fukui, Y., Matsuura, Y., Sato, M., Takada, H.: Peripheral viewing during exposure to a 2D/3D video clip: effects on the human body. Environ. Health Prev. Med. **20** (2), 79–89 (2015)
28. Amano, N., Kinoshita, F., Takayuki, H., Takada, H.: Mathematical model of equilibrium function while viewing a 3D object in a moving background. Proc. the 81st Sympo. Social Science Format, p. 36 (2016). (in Japanese)
29. Takada, H., Mori, Y., Miyakoshi, T.: Effect of background viewing on equilibrium systems. In: Antona, M., Stephanidis, C. (eds.) UAHCI 2015. LNCS, vol. 9176, pp. 255–263. Springer, Cham (2015). https://doi.org/10.1007/978-3-319-20681-3_24
30. Balaban, C.D., Poster, J.D.: Neuroanatomic substrates for vestibulo-autonomic interactions. J. Vestib. Res. **8**, 7–16 (1998)
31. Japan Society for Equilibrium Research: A standard of stabilometry. Equip. Res. **42**, 367–369 (1983). (in Japanese)
32. Takada, H., Miyao, M.: Visual fatigue and motion sickness induced by 3D video clip. Forma **27**(S), S67–S76 (2012)

Virtual Reality for Pain Management Among Children and Adolescents: Applicability in Clinical Settings and Limitations

Barbara Atzori[1](✉), Laura Vagnoli[2], Andrea Messeri[3], and Rosapia Lauro Grotto[1,4]

[1] Department of Health Sciences, School of Psychology,
University of Florence, Florence, Italy
psicob.atzori@gmail.com, rosapia.laurogrotto@unifi.it
[2] Service of Pediatric Psychology, Meyer Children's Hospital, Florence, Italy
laura.vagnoli@meyer.it
[3] Service of Pain Therapy and Palliative Care,
Meyer Children's Hospital, Florence, Italy
andrea.messeri@meyer.it
[4] Laboratory for Multidisciplinary Analysis of Health Care Relationships
(M.A.H.R.C.), UNISER, Pistoia, Italy

Abstract. Background. In recent years, virtual reality (VR) has emerged as an efficient distraction technique to reduce procedural pain among both adults and children. However, the effectiveness of VR as a distraction technique remains scarcely evaluated during many painful procedures. In many countries, such as Italy, VR analgesia is hardly applied.

Aim. The current study aims to highlight the potentials and the limitations of VR analgesia for children's pain management in clinical settings and to explore the feasibility and the effectiveness of VR distraction in Italy.

Methods. Studies that applied VR analgesia to children and adolescents undergoing painful procedures in clinical settings were included in the analysis. Factors influencing VR analgesia and the effectiveness of VR distraction for pain management were considered. The feasibility and the effectiveness of a low-cost VR system was evaluated for patients undergoing venipuncture in an Italian children's hospital.

Results. Factors influencing VR analgesia are still sparsely investigated, particularly regarding the psychological variables, such as anxiety and coping strategies. Italian patients suffering from cancer and kidney diseases who used VR distraction reported lower levels of pain and higher levels of fun compared with the control group.

Discussion. VR analgesia is destined to be applied more in clinical settings; however, VR systems designed for the specific use of VR analgesia in clinical settings are needed. In the Italian context, VR systems are necessary to improve the knowledge of VR analgesia among physicians, nurses, and clinical psychologists and encourage further research in this field.

Keywords: Virtual reality · Pain · Children · Cancer · Kidney diseases

© Springer International Publishing AG, part of Springer Nature 2018
M. Antona and C. Stephanidis (Eds.): UAHCI 2018, LNCS 10908, pp. 15–27, 2018.
https://doi.org/10.1007/978-3-319-92052-8_2

1 Introduction

1.1 Virtual Reality for Pain Management: How Does It Work?

In recent years, new technologies had a large expansion, not only for entertainment or pleasure, but also as versatile tools applied to improve people's health. Virtual Reality (VR) has probably been one of the most important emerging technologies [1]; it lets people experiment with realistic experiences, overcome their fears, and relax by simply wearing a head-mounted display. The use of VR in clinical settings is not a recent novelty; however, only lately it has been applied in a more extended manner. Healthcare practitioners can use VR to promote patients' health in different directions; one of these methods is VR analgesia, a non-pharmacological technique for pain management that has captured the interest of a growing number of researchers.

VR analgesia is a non-pharmacological technique for pain management based on distraction. Involving the most common distraction techniques (playing with a video game, reading a book, or listening to music), VR analgesia aims to capture the patient's attention to a pleasant activity during painful medical procedures. Generally, the effectiveness of distraction techniques for pain reduction can be explained by Eccleston and Crombez's interruption of attention and pain theory [2]. This interpretive model considers pain a stimulus, such as a sound or an image, that requires attention to be experienced. As personal attentional resources are limited, if a person focuses most of his or her attentive resources on a different stimulus, the person's capability to feel pain would be reduced. This being the case, the techniques for pain management based on distraction should capture the patients' attention by involving them in interesting, age-appropriate, and attention-demanding activities. Generally, the most common distraction techniques are easy to use and require the application of simple tools (i.e., books, toys, and video games) that are well known by patients. However, many other distraction techniques include specific professionals' interventions that involve patients in pleasant activities, such as playing an instrument or having fun with dogs or clowns [3–7]. In this varied scenario, the factor that unifies the most common distraction techniques is that during the painful procedure, although the patient's attention to the painful stimulus is reduced by the activity, the person continues to see and hear what is happening in the room. Indeed, the most widely used distraction techniques can only partially isolate the patient from the real environment (e.g., listening to music or talking with the nurse can occlude the sounds, and playing with video games or reading a book can reduce the visual attention to the painful procedure). On the contrary, while patients are interacting with VR distraction, they wear a head-mounted helmet that physically occludes the possibility to hear and watch the real environment. According to Eccleston and Crombez's interpretive model [2], the high level of isolation from the painful stimulus and the possibility to interact with the VR video game (based on the characteristics of the software) would strongly reduce the attentional resources available to experience pain. Thus, the analgesic effect of VR would be hypothetically stronger compared with the analgesic effect of non-immersive distraction techniques. With respect to this aspect, the pieces of evidence presented in the literature are not uniform, and the superiority of VR analgesia over video games or other distraction techniques is not always supported by proof [8]. These inconsistent results could depend on methodological differences across studies and on individual differences among children.

1.2   Factors Influencing the Effectiveness of VR Analgesia

Presence, Immersion, and Interactivity. *Presence*, described as the psychological illusion of being in the computer-generated world and feeling virtual experience as real [9, 10], seems to play a central role in the user's response to VR stimuli and in the effectiveness of mediated environment applications. Another important factor connected with the effectiveness of VR analgesia is *immersion*, a concept often confused with presence and defined by Slater and Wilbur [11] as the quality of the system's technology and capability to produce a vivid virtual environment. According to the two authors, a deep relationship exists between *presence* and *immersion*; the more immersive the system is, the more likely the user would feel present in the virtual world and the more likely the virtual environment would dominate physical reality in determining the person's response. Regarding the specific field of pain management, it has been demonstrated that patients undergoing thermal pain stimulation while wearing a low-quality helmet reported higher levels of pain compared with patients undergoing the same stimulation but wearing a high-quality helmet and compared with the control group under the no-distraction condition [12]. In another study, Hoffman et al. [13] evaluated the pain ratings of adult volunteers undergoing thermal pain stimulation. The subjects in the "high-tech VR group" (multisensory distraction, helmet, and head-tracking system) reported lower levels of pain and higher levels of *presence* compared with the subjects in the "low-tech VR group" (only visual distraction, eyeglasses, and no head tracking), and the amount of pain reduction (worst pain) was positively and significantly correlated with VR presence levels. In contrast, in a study involving children with burn injuries undergoing a dressing change, the sense of *presence* showed no significant correlation with the patients' pain ratings [14]. Age has been demonstrated to influence the sense of presence, as confirmed by Sharar et al. study [15]. According to their results, *presence* and realism scores were significantly higher among children (6–18 years) than among adults; however, younger patients did not report lower levels of pain compared with adults when interacting with VR. A recent review study that analyzed psychological variables associated with the effectiveness of VR analgesia highlighted that *presence* might not have a direct impact on pain experience *per se*, but it could allow VR to be distractive from a perceptual point of view [16]. However, only a few clinical studies have evaluated the sense of presence among patients undergoing medical procedures, and the role of *presence* in the effectiveness of VR analgesia remains unclear. Other studies comparing VR with video games highlighted better performance when users interacted in a non-immersive setup [17, 18], but these findings were not always confirmed [19]. As for *presence*, the role of *immersion* in the effectiveness of VR as a distraction technique for pain management is not completely clear. Some studies compared pain levels reported by young patients undergoing medical procedures with those under the control condition in which the group was distracted with a desktop video game. The results suggest that immersive systems can produce better analgesia compared with non-immersive systems [20–22]; however, no significant differences have been detected when compared with watching television [23].

Another variable connected with the effectiveness of VR analgesia is *interactivity*. The possibility to interact with the VR environment seems to promote higher pain reduction compared with passive distraction in a laboratory study [24]. This finding supports Eccleston and Crombez's interpretive model [3] and has relevant implications for the realization of VR environments. Passive VR analgesia was compared with interactive VR analgesia among pediatric-age patients in only one clinical study, which supported the results of the laboratory study. However, a significant pain reduction was detected by using a passive VR system compared with watching cartoons among patients undergoing dental care. These findings suggest that interactivity may not make a difference. However, more studies with a larger sample are needed to gain a better understanding of the role played by *interactivity* in the effectiveness of VR analgesia.

Anxiety and Distress. Psychological factors, such as anxiety, could also influence the user's experience during an interaction with VR. Indeed, in a recent study aimed to detect the main difference between VR and a non-immersive video game, significantly higher levels of anxiety emerged when the users interacted with VR compared with the video game [19]. In practical clinics, the deep connection between anxiety and pain is well known, and the literature confirms that anxiety can exacerbate pain perception [25]. For this reason, it can be hypothesized that VR distraction could have a minor analgesic effect if patients report high levels of anxiety. Moreover, high levels of anxiety could influence the patients' capability to focus their attentional resources on the VR environment and limit the levels of presence. To date, no study has directly evaluated the role of anxiety with respect to the effectiveness of VR analgesia [16]; however, Jeffs et al. considered the relationship between anxiety and engagement in the intervention [26]. They highlighted that burn patients' pain ratings were significantly lower in the VR distraction group compared with those in the group that was distracted by watching a video. Moreover, the patients' trait anxiety was negatively correlated with distraction engagement, showing low levels of engagement in distraction when the patients reported high levels of trait anxiety. However, the results of Pallavicini et al. study [19] seemed unconfirmed by clinical studies that evaluated VR as a distraction technique for pain management among children. Indeed, VR analgesia was demonstrated as a useful tool to reduce children's distress in two clinical studies with burn patients [21, 22], and significantly lower levels of anxiety were reported in another research by Hoffman et al. [20].

More studies are needed to understand the factors that can influence VR analgesia in order to evaluate its effectiveness and acceptability compared with other distraction techniques. Indeed, a recent review study highlighted that high-technology distraction techniques (video games and VR) were unable to produce a significantly higher analgesia compared with low-technology distraction techniques (reading a book, blowing bubbles...) during venipuncture [5]. However, these finding should be cautiously interpreted because the quality of the VR systems in the two included studies wasn't indicated and one of the systems was passive [27, 28].

2 Virtual Reality for Children and Adolescents' Pain Management: The State of the Art

VR analgesia has been applied in several clinical settings to improve children's pain management during medical procedures. The first studies included burn patients, who needed numerous painful procedures (such as dressing changes and physical therapy) for the treatment of their wounds [20]. Currently, the evaluation of VR effectiveness for these patients remains the most investigated domain compared with other kinds of diseases and procedures [8]. Little is known about the effectiveness of VR distraction in other invasive procedures, such as needle-related procedures, that are described by young patients as among the most painful and fearful aspects in hospitals [29]. Gold et al. [27] compared VR analgesia to a topical analgesic spray among patients undergoing venipuncture for magnetic resonance. Their results noted a significantly higher satisfaction regarding pain management and lower levels of pain in the VR condition; however, the difference in the pain level was not significant. VR distraction has also been applied to children suffering from cancer during port access and lumbar puncture, two common medical procedures for oncological patients. Significantly lower levels of pain and distress were reported by patients who used VR during port access compared with the control group subjected to the non-distraction condition [30]. However, in Sander Wint's study [28], patients undergoing lumbar puncture in an experimental condition (VR plus pharmacological analgesia) did not report lower levels of pain compared with patients who only received pharmacological analgesia. The inconsistency of these results could depend on the quality of the VR systems used in the studies. Indeed, Sander Wint et al. used a non-interactive VR system (no interactivity and narrow field of view through VR goggles), and the analgesic effect could be reduced for this reason [12, 24]. Moreover, the effectiveness of VR during dental procedures, which often generate anxiety and pain among children [31], is still under-investigated. Only a study involving children undergoing fluoride therapy and restorative treatment found that patients distracted with VR reported significantly lower levels of pain and anxiety compared with the control group that watched cartoons. Interestingly, this study used a passive VR system.

More recently, VR has also been introduced for chronic pain management, but few studies have evaluated its effectiveness among children [32]. In this field, VR could encourage patients to move and experience positive emotions despite their pain [33].

3 Applicability of Virtual Reality Analgesia in Clinical Settings: Specific Aspects, Limitations and Considerations

According to the literature, VR has immense potential as a distraction technique for pain management. However, when planning the use of VR in hospitals and other clinical settings, many aspects connected with the spaces, the hygienic norms, and the specific patients' needs (based on their diseases and own abilities) should be considered. VR analgesia requires the use of at least three elements (a computer, a head-mounted helmet, and a joystick) that need to be connected with a power outlet.

Therefore, the first limitation is that VR distraction can only be used in a room that is large enough and has power outlets Regarding the hygienic norms, the helmet (or the other types of VR goggles) can be easily cleaned with a sanitizing gel, so it can be safely worn by patients in hospitals.

The choice of the most suitable VR system is not easy, neither for the hardware component nor for the software component. On one hand, high-quality VR systems (wide field-of-view helmet, head tracking, and interactive software) should be preferred to promote more realistic experiences, higher levels of presence, and hypothetically better analgesia [12, 24]. On the other hand, low-quality systems (narrow field of view, eyeglasses, and passive software) have also been demonstrated to produce a significant analgesic effect in a limited number of studies. For example, significantly lower levels of pain were reported by pediatric patients who interacted with VR during routine dental care compared with the control group subjected to the no-distraction condition in Aminabadi et al. study [35]. In the VR analgesia condition, patients wore a passive VR system (eyeglasses, no interaction, and unknown diagonal field of view) to watch age-appropriate cartoons. These findings suggest that a low-cost system could be enough to produce an analgesic effect, at least for younger children. Moreover, in some circumstances, high-quality systems should not be recommended due to the charac- teristics of the procedure or specific limitations connected with the clinical environ- ment. For example, patients undergoing dental procedures need to remain still, and a head-tracking system is not recommended because they should move their heads to interact with the system. The ideal VR system should let patients be isolated from the real environment and have multimodal possibilities to be worn and to interact with the virtual scenario. This aspect had been partly considered by Hoffman et al. [13] who implemented a water-friendly VR system that can be used during underwater proce- dures, such as for the wound care for burn patients. However, this revised VR system has never been used with pediatric patients and is more expensive than its classic counterpart.

Regarding the software component, the most applied VR game for pain reduction is Snow World (www.vrpain.com), an ice scenario specifically created for burn pain management. A limited number of other VR environments were used for pain man- agement among children and adolescents, but all of them were designed for burn patients [22] or were not projected for pain reduction [27, 34]. To date, no evidence in the literature has indicated VR objects and scenarios that are more suitable than others for promoting better analgesia. The only suggestion is that age-appropriate software without violence should be preferred for children. In the past, the realization of VR software was expensive, and the availability of serious games (defined by Michael and Chen [34] as "games that do not have entertainment, enjoyment, or fun as their primary purpose") was limited. Currently, it is easier to buy cheap VR video games (created for pleasure and entertainment), which could also be applied to pain management, or to obtain serious video games, specifically designed for health [33]. More studies com- paring different VR environments could help deepen the understanding of how VR analgesia could depend on the kind of VR scenario. Moreover, for some procedures, such as dental ones, images that generate a sensation that is not referred to a cold environment could be preferred.

Psychological aspects should also be considered in the applicability of VR analgesia. One of the most relevant differences between VR and a classic distraction technique is that VR isolates the user from the real environment and blocks the possibility to see and listen to what is happening around the person. Patients undergoing a painful procedure would therefore focus their attentional resources on a pleasant stimulus and avoid watching the procedure. However, wearing the helmet, the patients are also isolated from potentially supporting elements in the real environment that could help them cope with the painful procedure. Indeed, children deal with pain by using different kinds of strategies; some children seek support from their parents during medical procedures, while other patients prefer to maintain their control of the environment rather than be distracted [36]. For patients who require social support or for those who prefer watching the procedure, VR distraction could produce a low analgesic effect, and in the worst case, it could also potentially generate an anxious and more painful experience. On the other hand, for patients who spontaneously use distraction to cope with pain, VR could be particularly indicated and efficient to control their pain. The literature has rarely investigated whether pain-coping strategies could influence the effectiveness of VR analgesia. Only one laboratory study reported that children's coping style would not influence the VR efficacy and that this distraction technique was effective for children who reported both blunting and monitoring coping styles [37]. However, medical procedures are different from simulations in a laboratory setting and these results could in principle be disconfirmed in a clinical study performed during actually painful procedures.

The limitations regarding the applicability of VR distraction also include several contraindications, such as a diagnosis of epilepsy (because the use of VR could induce epileptic seizures) and physical or cognitive disabilities that could impede patients' correct wearing of the helmet or interaction with the VR environment [8, 33]. According to these exclusion criteria, VR analgesia could not be usable by a large number of patients due to their diseases or the need to avoid hypothetical side effects. However, patients affected by different kinds of diseases and undergoing different procedures while distracted by VR did not report side effects in any of the studies [8]. Moreover, patients with intellectual disabilities should not be *a priori* excluded from the possibility to use VR analgesia. In fact, the effectiveness of VR for pain management involving this group of patients has never been investigated.

4   Clinical Applications of Virtual Reality: Our Italian Experience

The research on VR application is quite recent in Italy and has mostly focused on its use in psychotherapy [38, 39] and in training healthcare professionals [40] rather than on VR analgesia. The limited availability of VR systems and the difficulty to find VR head-mounted displays and software have probably made it difficult to introduce VR in Italian clinical settings. In recent years, VR systems have become available at reduced costs, and now, the user has the opportunity to choose among different kinds of VR goggles. However, high- and medium-quality helmets have only recently become accessible in Italy.

Thanks to the collaboration with Professor Hunter Hoffman, Director of the VR Analgesia Research Center at the Human Photonics Lab in the University of Washington, USA, and his collaborators, we recently obtained a VR system. We therefore started a research project aiming to evaluate the feasibility and the effectiveness of VR analgesia for pediatric and adolescent patients undergoing painful procedures in hospitals.

4.1   The Project

Introduction. In our clinical experience, VR analgesia appears to be specifically indicated for pain management during venipuncture. Indeed, this common procedure is particularly fearful and painful for many children in hospitals, including those patients who need to repeat it due to their diseases [29, 41]. Moreover, in Piskorz et al. recent quasi-experimental study [42], VR analgesia emerged as an efficient distraction technique for pain management among patients undergoing blood draw in a pediatric nephrology clinic. Children distracted by VR reported significant lower levels of stress compared with the control group subjected to the no-distraction condition and a 59% reduction in pain intensity in the VR compared with the control group [42]. Our research group decided to promote the clinical use of VR analgesia at A. Meyer Children's Hospital in Florence, Italy. Since 2014, we have introduced the use of VR distraction to the Service of Onco-hematology and the Service of Pediatric Nephrology, in collaboration with the Service of Pain Therapy and Palliative Care and the Department of Health Sciences, University of Florence.

Aim. The project aims to explore the effectiveness of VR as a distraction technique for pain management among pediatric patients undergoing venipuncture and to promote the use of VR analgesia in clinical settings. According to the literature, we expect that patients distracted with VR will report lower levels of pain and will experience the procedure in a non-stressful manner, therefore reporting higher levels of fun in comparison with the control group.

Methods

Study Design. Patients undergoing venipuncture and availing of the Service of Onco-hematology at A. Meyer Children's Hospital in Florence were recruited to participate in a study using a within-subjects randomized design. Patients undergoing venipuncture and availing of the Service of Nephrology were recruited to join a study using a between-subjects randomized design.

In both studies, the patients were selected with the help of a nurse of the hospital service, according to the following inclusion criteria based on the existent literature: children aged 7–17 years old, fluent in the Italian language, and without physical or psychological impediments to be able to use the VR system and complete the tests. Patients with a venous access already inserted in or with a port device, with a diagnosis of epilepsy, who were unaccompanied by parents, and who were over 17 years old or under 7 years old were excluded. Moreover, patients who wanted their own distraction tool (i.e., a book, a video game, or an MP3 player) during venipuncture in the control condition were excluded from the study.

Procedure. The patients meeting the inclusion criteria were approached by a psychologist before the procedure in order to inform their families and obtain the informed consent forms signed by the patients' caregivers. In the between-subjects design, the patients using the Service of Nephrology were randomly assigned to either the control group (No-VR), where they received the standard care pain management (non-medical conversation with the nurse) or the experimental group (Yes-VR), where they were distracted with VR. In the within-subjects design, the patients using the Service of Onco-hematology, who needed to undergo venipuncture twice a year, were assigned to either the control condition (non-medical conversation with the nurse) or the experimental condition (Yes-VR) and repeated the second venipuncture using the distraction technique (VR analgesia or non-medical conversation) that was not used the first time. In both designs, at the end of each procedure, the patients completed a self-report questionnaire to evaluate the quality of their VR experience, fun levels, and nausea.

Measures. Pain levels, the quality of the VR experience, nausea, and fun were measured by using the Italian version of a self-report questionnaire adopted in previous international studies [8], based on the 0–10 graphic rating scale (GRS) [43]. Pain was evaluated in terms of its cognitive component (*time spent thinking about pain*), affective component (*unpleasantness*), and perceptive component (*worst pain*). The quality of the VR experience was investigated in terms of *presence* and the *realism of VR objects*.

The VR system. Our VR equipment consisted of a low-cost VR helmet and the Personal 3D Viewer Sony: HMZ T-2, supported by a laptop that allowed interaction with the VR environment. The helmet had a 45° diagonal field of view, with 1280×720 pixels per eye, and was suitable for both younger and older patients. The VR helmet had two miniature screens, one for each eye of the user, and latex-free earphones to provide acoustic isolation and promote escapism from reality. The VR software used was Snow World, one of the most frequently employed VR environments, specifically designed to promote distraction from procedural pain. In Snow World, patients virtually enter an icy canyon, where they throw snowballs at penguins, snowmen, and other characters in VR, using a wireless mouse with the hand that is not employed in the venipuncture.

4.2 Preliminary Results

In recent years, preliminary results have been presented in occasion of several national and international conferences regarding pain and the care of cancer patients [44]; however, the project is still ongoing.

Service of Onco-hematology Eleven children suffering from cancer and blood diseases (7 males, 4 females; mean age = 10.64, SD = 2.58) underwent venipuncture twice. A *t*-test for paired samples was adopted to compare pain, nausea, and fun levels between the control and the experimental conditions. The patients reported significantly lower levels of *pain unpleasantness* and *time spent thinking about pain* while they underwent venipuncture plus VR analgesia ($p < 0.05$) compared with the group under the control condition, in which they were engaged in non-medical conversation by the nurse. Moreover, the children reported a "strong sense of going inside the computer-generated world" when interacting with VR and experienced significantly higher levels of fun compared with the group under the control condition ($p < 0.05$).

Service of Pediatric Nephrology. The preliminary results were encouraging and followed the predicted direction. The nonparametric Mann–Whitney U test was adopted. Twelve patients (6 females and 6 females, mean age 12,25 years ±2,22) were distracted with VR and 12 patients (6 females and 6 males, mean age 10,42 years ±2,68) received the standard care during the venipuncture. The patients assigned to the experimental group reported significant lower levels of *pain unpleasantness*, and *time spent thinking about pain* ($p < 0,05$). No significant differences were noted for the levels of *worst pain*; however, the patients distracted by VR analgesia reported significantly higher levels of *fun* ($p < 0.05$) compared with their counterparts in the control group. The levels of nausea were negligible in both groups.

4.3 Discussion

This ongoing project represents a contribution to the growing literature that supports the effectiveness of VR as a distraction technique for pain management among children and adolescents. Our preliminary results highlight the huge potential of VR analgesia for pain management among children suffering from onco-hematological and kidney diseases as well. However, our sample, particularly in the study involving patients with kidney diseases, is still rather small. Future research with a larger sample is needed. VR analgesia has been positively evaluated by both the patients and the clinical staff of the hospital, who consider VR distraction a useful tool for pain and anxiety management. In one case, a male patient who used VR analgesia admitted that he had preferred watching the procedure; however, he reported high levels of fun and no pain during the venipuncture. This finding suggests that future studies should evaluate whether the desire to watch the procedure (and other pain-coping strategies) could influence the effectiveness of VR analgesia.

5 Conclusions and Future Perspectives

According to the literature and our clinical experience, VR has immense potential as a distraction technique and can be a useful non-pharmacological analgesic for children's pain management. VR analgesia can help patients experience lower levels of pain and cope with the medical procedure in a non-stressful and safe manner, without side effects. However, more studies are needed to explore in depth the effectiveness of VR during several kinds of procedures and for different types of patients. For example, no study has evaluated the applicability of VR analgesia to patients with special needs or cognitive disabilities. Moreover, little is known about how psychological variables can influence the effectiveness of VR for pain management. Presence plays a central role in the quality of the experience in the VR environment; however, the relationship between presence levels and pain reduction by using VR has not been completely clarified. The analgesic effect of VR could also depend on the patient's wish and capability to be isolated from the real environment. In principle, not all children could benefit from the isolation in a virtual world during a painful procedure.

The drop in the prices of VR systems has facilitated the diffusion of medium/high-quality VR helmets; however, specific VR software developed for children's pain management are still rare. In future studies, different VR scenarios should be considered to evaluate whether specific environments could be preferable to others in order to improve the effectiveness of VR analgesia. Moreover, lightweight and wireless VR helmets should be developed for an easier application in a clinical setting with pediatric patients. Future research could also evaluate how the presence of more users in the same VR environment could improve the analgesic effect of VR. Indeed, a multiplayer software could help patients be isolated from the painful context, but at the same time, the social support of other VR players could improve the analgesic effect of VR. This solution could be particularly useful for those patients who use social support strategies to cope with painful procedures.

With respect to the Italian context, there is the need to improve the knowledge about VR analgesia among physicians, nurses, and clinical psychologists and to encourage research in this field in order to extend the use of VR distraction for pain management in clinical settings.

Acknowledgments. A special thanks to the Cassa di Risparmio Foundation and the Association ATCRUP.

References

1. Heinemann, D.S.: Porting game studies research to virtual reality. New Media Soc. **18**, 2793–2799 (2016)
2. Eccleston, C., Crombez, G.: Pain demands attention: a cognitive-affective model of the interruptive function of pain. Psychol. Bull. **125**, 356–366 (1999)
3. Caprilli, S., Anastasi, F., Lauro Grotto, R., Scollo Abeti, M., Messeri, A.: Interactive music as a treatment for pain and distress in children during venipuncture: a randomized prospective study. J. Dev. Behav. Pediatr. **28**, 399–403 (2007)
4. Koller, D., Goldman, R.D.: Distraction techniques for children undergoing procedures: a critical review of pediatric research. J. Pediatr. Nurs. **27**, 652–681 (2012)
5. Birnie, K.A., Noel, M., Parker, J.A., Chambers, C.T., Uman, L.S., Kisely, S.R., McGrath, P. J.: Systematic review and meta-analysis of distraction and hypnosis for needle-related pain and distress in children and adolescents. J. Pediatr. Psychol. **39**(8), 783–808 (2014)
6. Vagnoli, L., Caprilli, S., Vernucci, C., Zagni, S., Mugnai, F., Messeri, A.: Can presence of a dog reduce pain and distress in children during venipuncture? Pain Manag. Nurs. **16**, 89–95 (2015)
7. Rezai, M.S., Goudarzian, A.H., Jafari-Koulaee, A., Bagheri-Nesami, M.: The effect of distraction techniques on the pain of venipuncture in children: a systematic review. J. Pediatr. Rev. **5**(1), e9459 (2017). https://doi.org/10.17795/jpr-9459
8. Atzori, B., Hoffman, H.G., Vagnoli, L., Messeri, A., Lauro-Grotto, R.: Virtual reality as distraction technique for pain management in children and adolescents. In: Khosrow-Pour, M.: Encyclopedia of Information Science and Technology, 4th edn., Hershey, pp. 5955–5965 (2017)
9. Lee, K.M.: Presence, explicated. Commun. Theor. **14**(1), 27–50 (2004)
10. Bulu, S.T.: Place presence, social presence, co-presence, and satisfaction in virtual worlds. Comput. Educ. **58**, 154–161 (2012)

11. Slater, M., Wilbur, S.: A framework for immersive virtual environment (FIVE): speculations on the role of presence in virtual environments (1997)
12. Hoffman, H.G., Seibel, E.J., Richards, T.L., Furness III, T.A., Patterson, D.R., Sharar, S.R.: Virtual reality helmet display quality influences the magnitude of virtual reality analgesia. J. Pain **7**, 843–850 (2006)
13. Hoffman, H.G., Sharar, S.R., Coda, B., Everett, J.J., Ciol, M., Richards, T., Patterson, D.R.: Manipulating presence influences the magnitude of virtual reality analgesia. Pain **111**, 162–168 (2004)
14. Chan, E.A., Chung, J., Wong, T., Lien, A., Yang, J.Y.: Application of a virtual reality prototype for pain relief of pediatric burn in Taiwan. J. Clin. Nurs. **16**, 786–793 (2007)
15. Sharar, S.R., Carrougher, G.J., Nakamura, D., Hoffman, H.G., Blough, D.K., Patterson, D.R.: Factors influencing the efficacy of virtual reality distraction analgesia during postburn physical therapy: preliminary results from 3 ongoing studies. Archiv. Phys. Med. Rehab. **88**, S43–S49 (2007)
16. Triberti, S., Repetto, C., Riva, G.: Psychological factors influencing the effectiveness of virtual reality–based analgesia: a systematic review. Cyberpsychol. Behav. Soc. Netw. **17**(6), 335–345 (2014)
17. Swindells, C., Po, B.A., Hajshirmohammadi, I., Corrie, B., Dill, J.C., Fisher, B.D., Kellogs, S.B.: Comparing CAVE, wall, and desktop displays for navigation and wayfinding in complex 3D models. In: Proceedings of Computer Graphics International, pp. 420–427. IEEE, New York (2004)
18. Santos, B.S., Dias, P., Pimentel, A., Baggerman, J.W., Ferreira, C., Silva, S., Madeira, J.: Head-mounted display versus desktop for 3D navigation in virtual reality: a user study. Multimed. Tools Appl. **4**, 161–181 (2009)
19. Pallavicini, F., Ferrari, A., Zini, A., Garcea, G., Zanacchi, A., Barone, G., Mantovani, F.: What distinguishes a traditional gaming experience from one in virtual reality? An exploratory study. In: Ahram, T., Falcão, C. (eds.) AHFE 2017. AISC, vol. 608, pp. 225–231. Springer, Cham (2018). https://doi.org/10.1007/978-3-319-60639-2_23
20. Hoffman, H.G., Doctor, J.N., Patterson, D.R., Carrougher, G.J., Furness III, T.A.: Virtual reality as an adjunctive pain control during burn wound care in adolescent patients. Pain **85**, 305–309 (2000)
21. Gershon, J., Zimand, E., Pickering, M., Rothbaum, B.O., Hodges, L.: A pilot and feasibility study of virtual reality as a distraction for children with cancer. J. Am. Acad. Child Adolesc. Psychiatr. **43**, 1243–1249 (2004)
22. Hua, Y., Qiu, R., Yao, W., Zhang, Q., Chen, X.: The effect of virtual reality distraction on pain relief during dressing changes in children with chronic wounds on lower limbs. Pain Manag. Nurs. **16**(5), 685–691 (2015)
23. Van Twillert, B., Bremer, M., Faber, A.W.: Computer-generated virtual reality to control pain and anxiety in pediatric and adult burn patients during wound dressing changes. J. Burn Care Res. **28**, 694–702 (2007)
24. Wender, R., Hoffman, H.G., Hunner, H.H., Seibel, E.J., Patterson, D.R., Sharar, S.R.: Interactivity influences the magnitude of virtual reality analgesia. J. Cybertherapy Rehab. **2**, 27–33 (2009)
25. Ploghaus, A., Narain, C., Beckamm, C.F., Clare, S., Bantik, S., Wise, R., Matthews, P.M., Rawlins, J.N.P., Tracey, I.: Exacerbation of pain by anxiety is associated with activity of hippocampal network. J. Neurosci. **21**, 9896–9903 (2001)
26. Jeffs, D., Dorman, D., Brown, S., Files, A., Graves, T., Kirk, E., Meredit-Neve, S., Danders, J., White, B., Swearingen, C.: Effect of virtual reality on adolescent pain during wound care. J. Burn Care Res. **35**, 395–407 (2014)

27. Gold, J.I., Kim, S.H., Kant, A.J., Joseph, M.H., Rizzo, A.: Effectiveness of virtual reality for pediatric pain distraction during IV placement. Cyberpsychol. Behav. **9**, 207–212 (2006)
28. Sander Wint, S., Eshelman, D., Steele, J., Guzzetta, C.E.: Effects of distraction using virtual reality glasses during lumbar punctures in adolescents with cancer. Oncol. Nurs. Forum **29**, E8–E15 (2002)
29. Caprilli, S.: I bambini non devono provare dolore. Giornale Italiano di Scienze Infermieristiche e Pediatriche **2**, 44 (2010)
30. Wolitzky, K., Fivush, R., Zimand, L.H., Hodges, L., Rothbaum, B.O.: Effectiveness of virtual reality distraction during a painful medical procedure in pediatric oncology patients. Psychol. Health **20**, 817–824 (2005)
31. Guelman, M.: Dental fear in children may be related to previous pain experience during dental treatment. J. Evid. Based Dent. Pract. **5**(3), 143–144 (2005)
32. Shahrbanian, S., Ma, X., Aghaei, N., Korner-Bitensky, N., Moshiri, K., Simmonds, M.J.: Use of virtual reality (immersive vs. non immersive) for pain management in children and adults: a systematic review of evidence from randomized controlled trials. Eur. J. Exp. Biol. **2**, 1408–1422 (2012)
33. Won, A.S., Bailey, J., Bailenson, J., Tataru, C., Yoon, I.A., Golianu, B.: Immersive virtual reality for pediatric pain. Children **4**(7), 52 (2017). https://doi.org/10.3390/children4070052
34. Michael, D., Chen, S.: Serious games: games that educate, train, and inform. Thomson Course Technology, Boston (2006)
35. Aminabadi, N.A., Erfanparast, L., Sohrabi, A., Oskouei, S.G., Naghili, A.: The impact of virtual reality distraction on pain and anxiety during dental treatment in 4–6 year-old children: a randomized controlled clinical trial. J. Dent. Res. Dent. Clin. Dent. Prospects **6**, 117–124 (2012)
36. Axia, G., Bonichini, S.: La valutazione delle strategie di coping al dolore fisico nei bambini di età scolare. Psicologia Clinica dello Sviluppo **1**, 97–123 (2000)
37. Sil, S., Dahlquist, L.M., Thompson, C., Hahn, A., Herbert, L., Wohlheiter, K., Horn, S.: The effects of coping style on virtual reality enhanced videogame distraction in children undergoing cold pressor pain. J. Behav. Med. **6**(4), 117–124 (2012)
38. Riva, G., Bacchetta, M., Baruffi, M., Rinaldi, S., Molinari, E.: Virtual reality based experiential cognitive treatment of anorexia nervosa. J. Behav. Ther. Exp. Psychiatr. **30**(3), 221–230 (1999)
39. Riva, G.: Virtual reality: an experiential tool for clinical psychology. Br. J. Guid. Counc. **37**(3), 335–343 (2009)
40. Mantovani, F., Castelnuovo, G., Gaggioli, A., Riva, G.: Virtual reality training for health-care professionals. Cyberpsychol. Behav. **6**(4), 389–395 (2003)
41. Bisogni, S., Dini, C., Olivini, N., Ciofi, D., Giusti, F., Caprilli, S., Lopez, J.R.G., Festini, F.: Perception of venipuncture pain in children suffering from chronic diseases. BMC Res. Notes **7**, 735–739 (2014)
42. Piskorz, J., Czub, M.: Effectiveness of a virtual reality intervention to minimize pediatric stress and pain intensity during venipuncture. J. Spec. Pediatr. Nurs. **23**, e12201 (2018). https://doi.org/10.1111/jspn.12201
43. Gracely, R.H., McGrath, F., Dubner, R.: Ratio scales of sensory and affective verbal pain descriptors. Pain **5**, 5–18 (1978)
44. Atzori, B., Hoffman, H.G., Vagnoli, L., Messeri, A., Alhalabi, W., Patterson, D., Lauro Grotto, R.: Virtual Reality pain management for children with onco-hematological diseases undergoing venipuncture. In: 18th International Psycho-oncology Society Congress, 17th–21st October 2016, Dublin, Ireland (2016)

Virtual Reality Based Assessment of Static Object Visual Search in Ocular Compared to Cerebral Visual Impairment

Christopher R. Bennett[1](✉), Emma S. Bailin[1], Timothy K. Gottlieb[1], Corinna M. Bauer[1], Peter J. Bex[2], and Lotfi B. Merabet[1]

[1] The Laboratory for Visual Neuroplasticity,
Department of Ophthalmology, Massachusetts Eye and Ear Infirmary,
Harvard Medical School, Boston, MA, USA
Christopher_bennett@meei.harvard.edu
[2] Department of Psychology, Northeastern University, Boston, MA, USA

Abstract. Virtual reality (VR) can provide robust assessment of cognitive spatial processing skills in individuals with visual impairment. VR combined with objective measures of behavioral performance, such as eye and hand tracking, affords a high degree of experimental control, task flexibility, participant engagement, and enhanced data capture. Individuals with visual impairment typically have difficulties identifying objects in a cluttered environment. Furthermore, these difficulties may differ depending on the type of visual impairment. Specifically, individuals with cortical/cerebral visual impairment (CVI) may show a greater sensitivity to visual task complexity compared to those with ocular based visual impairment (OVI). We have developed a VR environment with integrated eye and hand tracking to simulate exploring a toy box to assess performance on a static object-based visual search task. A grid of toys was displayed for a brief duration while participants found and fixated on a specific toy hidden among others. For a given trial, we manipulated multiple factors: the number of unique distractor toys, a color/theme matched toy, and the background clutter. Results to date show that both visually impaired groups demonstrate increased variability in search patterns and reaction times as compared to controls. Additionally, performance of the CVI group fluctuates greatly as a function of task difficulty. Findings from the current work demonstrate a successful interaction between individuals with visual impairments and VR simulations in assessing high level visual function. Further studies will serve as theoretical foundation for the creation of new assessment and training paradigms for visually impaired individuals.

Keywords: Virtual reality · Visual search · Visual impairment
Eye-Tracking · Hand-Tracking · Spatial processing

© Springer International Publishing AG, part of Springer Nature 2018
M. Antona and C. Stephanidis (Eds.): UAHCI 2018, LNCS 10908, pp. 28–38, 2018.
https://doi.org/10.1007/978-3-319-92052-8_3

1 Introduction

The present work presents a novel application of virtual reality (VR) environments for assessing and comparing visual search performance and spatial processing in individuals with visual impairment.

The combination of VR usage with objective measures of behavioral performance affords a high degree of experimental control, task flexibility, participant engagement, and enhanced data capture and characterization. Specifically, parameters of task difficulty, experimental factors, and environmental complexity can all be manipulated, along with the immediate capture of multiple behavioral performance outcome parameters [1–3]. Recent enhancements in VR technology, including device miniaturization, ease of implementation, increasing realism, and relatively low cost, give the possibility of developing more mobile platforms for the testing of individuals outside of the research laboratory and clinical settings.

Previous research has shown that with regards to tasks requiring visual spatial knowledge acquisition, individuals showed equivalent performance and preferences when conducting testing within the real world and in virtual simulations [4, 5]. Thus, VR can negate any conflicting demands related to physical exertion for participants, while incorporating objective performance measures like eye and hand tracking for naturalistic data collection. In essence, as long as the participant understands the nature and demands of the task, VR based assessments can be very useful in assessing behavioral performance even in individuals with physical or developmental disabilities [6].

One arena in which VR based environments could show great utility is in the assessment of cognitive spatial processing of individuals with visual impairment. Specifically, standard clinical testing measurements of visual acuity and visual field perimetry are inherently limited in that they fail to fully capture and characterize visual functional deficits associated with higher level visual processing, particularly in complex real world situations [7]. As an example, individuals with visual impairments often have difficulties recognizing familiar objects while viewing complex visual scenes. Furthermore, the nature of the visual impairment may also impact upon the type and degree of functional visual deficit observed [8].

We conducted a focus group study (see Design section for further details) that revealed that visually impaired children and adolescents often have trouble locating and identifying their favorite toy when it is in close proximity to other toys, but they can locate the same toy easily when it is in isolation. For example, individuals with ocular visual impairment (OVI) (e.g. ocular albinism) often have reduced visual acuity and impaired oculomotor function (i.e. nystagmus) and thus may take longer to find a target object when searching in a complex and cluttered visual scene. In contrast, individuals with developmental damage to visual processing areas of the brain (referred to as cortical/cerebral visual impairment, or CVI) may miss a visual target entirely, despite having the necessary visual acuity to perform the task and unimpaired eye movements. These observations highlight potential differences in visual search and spatial processing strategies related to task demand, as well as the type of visual impairment. While there is extensive research investigating perceptual abilities in ocular based visual impairments, the CVI population remains relatively understudied despite being the leading cause of congenital visual impairment in children in developed countries [9]. Furthermore, there is a growing need to develop novel methods to better characterize visual perceptual deficits beyond what can be achieved with standard clinical testing.

In this direction, we developed a VR testing environment called the "virtual toy box". This VR platform creates a realistic simulation and testing environment in which a participant is instructed to find a target toy within a grid of other toys. Firstly, by exploiting the aforementioned advantages of VR, factors related to cognitive spatial processing of object complexity and clutter can be experimentally manipulated to characterize their individual effects on visual search performance. Secondly, integrated data capture methods obtained from eye and hand movement tracking provide realistic and objective measures of behavioral performance. Lastly, the flexibility and range of testing parameters mean that the same environment can be used to assess performance across different types of visual impairments.

2 Methodology

2.1 Participants

Preliminary data presented here include three participant groups: individuals with normally developed sight (controls), ocular visual impairment (OVI), and cortical/ cerebral visual impairment (CVI). A total of 9 participants highlight the study design and methodology of the current research. Age of participants ranged from 14 to 28 years of age (Control mean = 18.3, OVI mean = 25.0, CVI mean = 18.7). All participants had at least a high school level education and were right handed. Ocular and cortical/cerebral visual impaired groups had comparable visual acuity albeit reduced compared to controls. However, all individuals possessed sufficient acuity for the present task (Snellen visual acuity range between 20/20 to 20/80).

2.2 Hardware and Software

An Alienware Aurora R6 with an Intel i5 processor, NVidia GTX 1060 graphics card, and 32 GB of ram (Alienware Corporation ©) was used for development and execution of the experiment. A ViewSonic 27″ Widescreen 1080p (1920 × 1080 resolution) LED monitor (ViewSonic Corporation ©) displayed the testing environment. A Tobii 4C Eye Tracker (90 Hz sampling rate) (Tobii AB ©) recorded the eye movements. A Leap Motion (120 Hz sampling rate) tracked hand motion (Leap Motion, Inc. ©). The testing platform was created in the Unity 3D game engine version 5.6 (Unity Technologies ©). The 3D object models were created using the modeling software Blender (Blender Foundation ®).

2.3 Design and Procedure

A focus group survey was conducted with teachers of the visually impaired prior to the development of the current iteration of the testing platform. The goal of this focus group study was to ensure that the final design of the testing platform accurately addressed the problem of visual search, spatial processing, and visual scene complexity, by taking into consideration the opinion of experts possessing extensive experience working with these visually impaired individuals. After viewing a video that highlighted the VR environment and current design features, six focus group participants rated their responses (using a 7 point Likert scale, with 1 meaning strongly disagree and 7 strongly agree) to a series of predetermined statements (e.g. rating the realism of 3D object models) and also open ended questions (e.g. listing additional factors for consideration). The results were overwhelmingly positive for scores of realism (5.7 out of 7) and feature importance (6.8 out of 7). Open ended feedback was used to improve/modify the design of the tested factors (e.g., addition of a "catch trial" containing a color/theme matched distractor). The survey results revealed unmet needs related to the assessment of visual performance and key factors of interest related to the VR environment realism and effectiveness for further consideration.

Prior to the experimental run, eye tracking calibration was performed for each participant using the Tobii Eye Tracking Software v2.9 calibration protocol, which took about 30 to 45 s. Participants then viewed and selected their favorite toy (i.e. target of interest, or "target toy") for the search task. There were three possible toys to choose from that varied in color and theme: a blue truck, orange basketball, and yellow duck. Participants viewed each target toy in isolation as it rotated around the Y-axis before choosing. Toy selection was done to enhance the immersive feel of the task and ensure that the participant was able to correctly identify a target of interest.

After selecting the target toy, the experimental program began. Participants viewed a toy box from an overhead perspective to simulate looking down into the box (see Fig. 1). Trials started with the box covered and only a fixation point displayed. The cover disappeared after 2 s and revealed a 5×5 grid of toys. Each toy within the grid was presented in a conical view (see Fig. 1). Participants had 4 s to visually locate and fixate on the target toy before that trial ended. The cover and fixation point reappeared between each trial of a new grid of toys. The primary factor of interest was the number of other unique toys filling the grid (ranging from 1 to 9 unique toys) to test the effect of multiple distractors (Fig. 1A and B). As a secondary factor of interest, a color/theme matched toy within the grid (presented in 25% of the trials) served as "catch trials" designed to test how participants were identifying the target toy (Fig. 1C). An additional factor of interest, a background layer of toys, was present in 50% of the trials to test the effect of background visual complexity (Fig. 1D).

Unique distractor numbers were classified into three levels: "Low" (1 to 3 unique toys), "Medium" (4 to 6 unique toys), and "High" (7 to 9 unique toys), with each group representing 33% of the trials. The color/theme matched distractor varied based on the selected target toy with the goal of not only presenting a toy with the same color but also the same categorical theme of the target. For example, if a participant selected the blue truck, the color/theme matched toy appeared as a blue helicopter (same color and transportation category – see Fig. 1C).

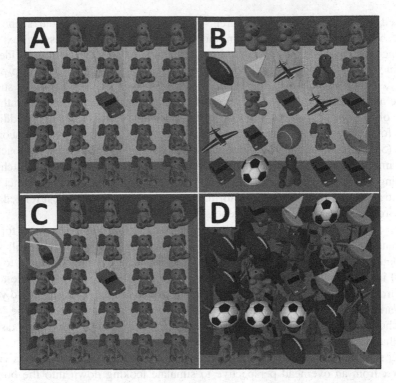

Fig. 1. Visual demonstration of various levels of the experimental factors. (A) example trial with minimum number of unique distractors (low), (B) trial with highest number of unique distractors (high), (C) trial with color/theme matched distractor (circle), and (D) trial with background toys enabled. (Color figure online)

Participants completed a total of 35 trials per run with 3 runs overall. A run lasted approximately 3.5 min with a brief rest between each run. Response collection was done entirely through eye tracking, as participants were instructed to visually locate and fixate on the target toy with their eyes. The eye tracker collected the (X, Y) coordinate position of the gaze point on the screen at any given moment. The Tobii Unity SDK mediated data collection and data was sampled at the tracker's default refresh rate of 90 Hz.

Two additional runs mimicked the main experiment but also had the participants reaching for the target toy. Hand position tracking by the Leap Motion hand tracker provided free physical movement and ran in parallel with eye tracking system. The goal was to elucidate potential differences between visual and kinesthetic/haptic/physical search patterns as well as observe visuo-motor coordination. Figure 2 shows a picture of a participant using the system.

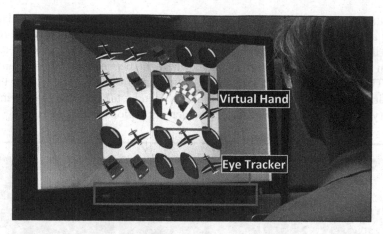

Fig. 2. Photo of practice trial with participant. Eye tracker and virtual hand are highlighted.

3 Results and Discussion

3.1 Eye Gaze Data: Heatmaps

The raw coordinate gaze data were smoothed and aggregated over time using Gaussian filtering and histogram regional binning to generate heatmaps [10]. The varying colors in these heatmaps represent differing levels of gaze data density across spatial regions of the screen space, with each color being a ratio of point density. Yellow indicates that a participant spent more time looking in that area whereas blue indicates that a participant spent far less time there. There is approximately a 9:1 ratio of point density between yellow and blue. Given that the target location on the screen changed per trial, gaze data had to be offset on an individual trial basis to center the data from all the trials into one central region of interest. Due to this centering correction, the toy box image displayed behind the following heatmap data is merely a representation of a given condition or factor manipulation and not the actual position of the toy for a given trial. Portions of the images that do not show any color indicate a lack of sufficient data points to meet a minimum data capture threshold and are not indicative of a complete lack of gaze points. The data in the heatmaps are representations of hundreds of trials of eye gaze data. Overall distribution area and color scaling of the heatmap regions signify increased visual searching.

Figure 3 contains heatmaps for two categories of unique distractors (low and high) for each of the three participant groups as a visual demonstration of the collected eye tracking gaze data. The control group, regardless of unique distractors, showed a tight clustering of gaze points. The minimal spread of eye data suggests that the control participants found the target quickly on each trial and maintained their focus on that target. In contrast, the ocular visual impaired group (OVI) showed a more scattered search pattern with less defined gaze density regions that was comparable for both levels of unique distractors. The large spread of gaze data reflected decreased performance as compared to the control group, suggesting slower reaction times, less success finding the target, and fewer periods of strong fixation. The CVI group data also reflected an increased area of gaze data, revealing longer search patterns and reduced focus on the target location during trials as compared to controls. For the given task and condition levels, the CVI group fell somewhere in between the sighted and OVI groups. There was also a noticeable loss in definition of the eye gaze data for the CVI group during the high unique distractor trials, as seen by the decrease in high intensity regions (yellow colors) and increase of low density regions (blue colors).

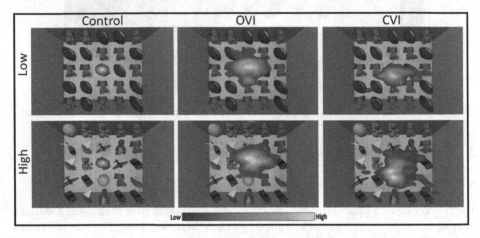

Fig. 3. Heatmaps for the Control, OVI, and CVI groups for "low" and "high" number of unique distractors. (Color figure online)

3.2 Eye Gaze Data: Confidence Ellipses

Ellipses of best fit from the eye gaze data further quantified task performance. The area of these ellipses represented a 95% confidence interval for the contained input data based on percentage of viewing screen (see Fig. 4). Both visually impaired groups showed worse performance than the control group across each number of unique distractors. At the highest level, however, the CVI group exhibited the largest change in performance, indicating that these individuals were more affected by the number of unique distractors around the target object. Confidence ellipse area data also revealed that the threshold for impaired performance rests somewhere between the medium and high number of unique distractors.

Similar results are displayed for "catch trials", when the color/theme-matched distractor was present. Figure 5 shows the effect on confidence ellipse areas for trials with and without the matched distractor for the three study groups. The control group performance was noticeably better than both the visually impaired groups and was relatively consistent between trial types. The OVI and CVI groups demonstrated performance changes, but in opposite directions (increased and decreased performance in relation to the presence of the color/themed matched distractor, respectively). The CVI group showed the largest effect, indicating that the presence of the matched distractor was disruptive to their search patterns.

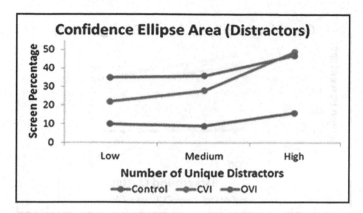

Fig. 4. Graphical representation of the area of 95% confidence ellipses generated from gaze data. (Color figure online)

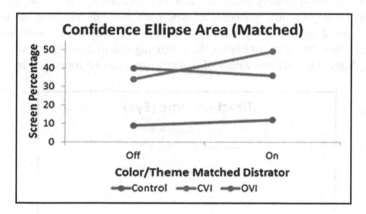

Fig. 5. Confidence ellipse area averaged for the three groups for color/match trials. (Color figure online)

Results for background enabled versus disabled trials are shown in Fig. 6. While the control group was unaffected by a background within the toy box, the OVI and CVI groups both showed improvement in performance. Early participant feedback may help provide an explanation for this difference, as multiple individuals reported that the background helped provide a feeling of greater depth and separation of the toy grid from the box.

3.3 Reaction Times

For each trial, there were two separate reaction time metrics. The first time that the participant's eyes came into contact with the target toy on the screen was treated as an initial "hit" reaction. A second "fixate" reaction time was determined after the participant's eyes remained in contact with the target for 300 ms. The "fixate" reaction

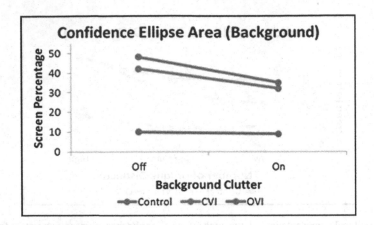

Fig. 6. Confidence ellipse area averaged for the three groups for background trials.

time was measured separately as an indicator of sustained fixation rather than simply identifying the target at first glance. If a participant was still searching the screen but had not identified the correct toy, passing over the target may be erroneously scored as an extremely fast "hit". For this reason, the following results detail the "fixate" reaction time data. A graphical representation of reaction time can be found in Fig. 7.

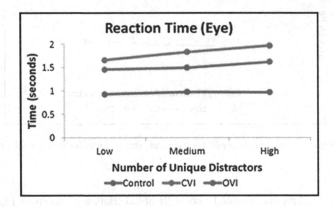

Fig. 7. Graphical representation of 'fixate' reaction time data for all three participant groups.

The control group was the quickest to locate and fixate on the target toy for all three levels of unique distractors. Additionally, the CVI group data reflected a discernible effect of increasing difficulty, similar to that observed with the visual search area quantified by the confidence ellipse area (compare with Fig. 4).

Reaction time data for all three groups based on color/theme match and background (results not shown) followed a similar pattern as the unique distractor data. Performance did not change strikingly with regards to manipulation of both factors. However, the group distinctions observed in the previous measures persisted. Controls consistently found the target toy quicker than both groups with visual impairment, while the OVI group was quicker than the CVI group.

Finally, reaction time for hand tracking data is presented in Fig. 8. The following data represent the time it took the participants to reach for and virtually touch the target toy. Controls reached for the target faster than both visually impaired groups and did not display much of an effect of unique distractor level. The CVI reaction time decreased at the highest number of unique distractors. During debriefing, multiple participants noted that they were using the virtual hand as a reference to help them search the area when the trials became increasingly difficult. This may translate to a real-world training strategy, where the individual uses their physical hand to help parse a complex visual scene. Overall, reaction times were slower when compared to the "fixate" reaction times for eye tracking data of both the visual impaired groups. This was expected given the physical time required for executing the reaching movements.

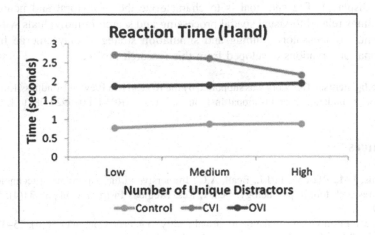

Fig. 8. Hand data reaction time for the three groups at each level of unique distractors.

4   Conclusions and Future Work

The present work demonstrates the successful development of a VR testing environment designed to assess and compare object visual search in both cerebral and ocular based types of visual impairment.

The design and development process directly involved input from experts in the field to create a novel assessment method that goes beyond what is typically evaluated in the standard clinical setting. Results thus far illuminate what we learned from our focus group study in that individuals with visual impairment have difficulties identifying familiar objects when placed in a cluttered and complex environment. Furthermore, difficulties were related to the type of visual impairment. Specifically, performance of the group with cortical/cerebral visual impairment (CVI) compared to the group with ocular visual impairment (OVI) worsened at higher levels of task difficulty, but OVI performance was more stable across task difficulty. Overall, individuals with CVI also took longer to find target objects than both control and OVI participants when task difficulty was highest.

It is important to consider that there is currently no cure for CVI, as the visual deficits are due to early developmental brain damage. Therefore, work such as outlined in the current study is paramount to understanding the underlying cognitive and behavioral mechanisms associated with this type of visual impairment. Further, this same approach may serve as a platform for the further development of novel training and rehabilitation techniques. The visuo-motor coordination deficits associated with CVI furthers the demand for combined eye and hand tracking data collection. Combining VR along with eye and hand tracking technologies can provide for an entirely novel and more realistic assessment and training toolkit for clinical and behavioral sciences.

Future work will continue to collect data to validate currently observed behavioral trends while exploring other means of data collection and technologies (e.g. combined electroencephalogram (EEG) recordings and immersive visual presentation with head mounted displays). The end goal is to characterize the behavioral and neurological underpinnings related to visual spatial processing and search in individuals with visual impairment. Compensatory training and simulation strategies may emerge from the foundational observations developed from this research project.

Acknowledgements. This work was supported by the Research to Prevent Blindness/Lions Clubs International Foundation to and National Institutes of Health (R01 EY019924-08) to L.B.M.

References

1. Loomis, J.M., Blascovich, J.J., Beall, A.C.: Immersive virtual environment technology as a basic research tool in psychology. Behav. Res. Methods Instrum. Comput. **31**(4), 557–564 (1999)
2. Zyda, M.: From visual simulation to virtual reality to games. Computer **38**(9), 25–32 (2005)
3. Bennett, C.R., Corey, R.R., Giudice, U., Giudice, N.A.: Immersive virtual reality simulation as a tool for aging and driving research. In: Zhou, J., Salvendy, G. (eds.) ITAP 2016. LNCS, vol. 9755, pp. 377–385. Springer, Cham (2016). https://doi.org/10.1007/978-3-319-39949-2_36
4. Richardson, A.E., Montello, D.R., Hegarty, M.: Spatial knowledge acquisition from maps and from navigation in real and virtual environments. Mem. Cogn. **27**(4), 741–750 (1999)
5. Kuliga, S.F., et al.: Virtual reality as an empirical research tool—exploring user experience in a real building and a corresponding virtual model. Comput. Environ. Urban Syst. **54**, 363–375 (2015)
6. Parsons, T.D., et al.: Virtual reality in paediatric rehabilitation: a review. Dev. Neurorehab. **12**(4), 224–238 (2009)
7. Merabet, L.B., et al.: Disentangling How the Brain is "Wired" in Cortical/Cerebral Visual Impairment (CVI). Seminars in Pediatric Neurology (2017)
8. Martín, M.B., et al.: Cerebral versus ocular visual impairment: the impact on developmental neuroplasticity. Front. Psychol. **7**, 1958 (2016)
9. Kong, L., et al.: An update on progress and the changing epidemiology of causes of childhood blindness worldwide. J. Am. Assoc. Pediatr. Ophthalmol. Strabismus **16**(6), 501–507 (2012)
10. Gibaldi, A., et al.: Evaluation of the Tobii EyeX Eye tracking controller and Matlab toolkit for research. Behav. Res. Methods **49**(3), 923–946 (2017)

3D Spatial Gaming Interaction to Broad CS Participation

Santiago Bolivar(✉), Francisco R. Ortega, Maia Zock-Obregon,
and Naphtali D. Rishe

Florida International University, Miami, FL 33196, USA
{sboli001,mzock001}@fiu.edu, {fortega,rishen}@cs.fiu.edu

Abstract. We propose a 3D environment in the form of a video game where the main idea is to increase Computer Science (CS) interest. We believe that by providing software that can be used by everyone, we can spark more interest in CS. We created a simple prototype emulating an Escape Room with the idea to attract individuals of any age range with a fun learning activity, but our primary focus is on teenagers and young adults. The puzzles in the game engage the player by giving them challenges that can be completed optimally by using computer science concepts. However, the game is presented as a typical puzzle game to avoid scaring away players who may have preconceived notions of computer science. The aim is to engage players through the puzzles to promote further interest in CS concepts.

1 Introduction

Statistics show that Computer Science is a field that is highly in demand not only with regards to industry but also when considering Academia [1]. Even with the heightened demand, the amount of people that graduate from CS majors is significantly lower than the number of students that initially enrolled. Also, computer science has traditionally been less diverse than other fields. Minorities comprise less than one-fourth of all students that enroll in a bachelor of Computer Science [2].

Current institutional practices still offer standard methodologies when attracting and educating CS students. Students present a diverse population, and some may require extended time and other educational aids to learn a new subject as they may experience difficulties when using traditional techniques. Most science related classes require substantial problem-solving skills and math backgrounds. Even though these skills can be taught and learned, these requirements drive away students from pursuing any science, technology, engineering, or mathematics (STEM) majors [3].

Even though public education is free for most people, graduation rate from public education is quite low. When an individual finishes high-school most of them do not pursue higher education of any kind [4].

It is important to create ways in which students not only care about education but also promotes and encourages a desire to reach higher educational goals.

© Springer International Publishing AG, part of Springer Nature 2018
M. Antona and C. Stephanidis (Eds.): UAHCI 2018, LNCS 10908, pp. 39–47, 2018.
https://doi.org/10.1007/978-3-319-92052-8_4

Many of today's graduates are passionate about their education, and this is a trend which we hope proceeds to grow.

As technology continues to progress, new types of learning can also be applied to motivate retention and inclusion. It is imperative to understand that many individuals have a better chance of being attracted to something by using visuals rather than narratives [5], everyone gets steered away by the common misconception of "difficult" classes such as calculus, physics, and programming. Most people have difficulty understanding CS because they view it as a singular, monolithic, and complex topic when in actually most CS concepts are simple when viewed individually. Computers are also comparable to the human mind. This idea is what we are trying to convey in the game. Allowing the user to see how their everyday actions are the same simple actions carried by a computer and hence the foundation of computer logic [6].

1.1 Contribution

Even though the game has been designed for high-school Juniors and/or Seniors, it can easily be played by K-12 children or older adults. Our contribution can be break into four ideas:

1. Help students better understand concepts of Computer Science.
2. Increase interest in Computer Science after anyone plays the game, especially teenagers and young adults.
3. Create an entertaining medium capable of reaching broad audiences while making the game entertaining.
4. Increase enrollment and graduation numbers of minorities.

1.2 Motivation and Challenges

The number of high-school graduates that pursue higher education is low. Compounding this issue, the amount of minorities that go to college or university is low as well. Once students start their college career, many of them will not go on to complete their degree according to recorded statistics. These numbers can be predicted based upon high-school graduation rates.

By generating early interest in Computer Science, we can help students identify and focus on the attributes required for a successful college career. When attempting to generate this interest, it is vital to recognize how influential video games can be when trying to reach an audience comprised of young adults [7].

2 Background

It is critical to understand that the concept of higher education is highly conflated with money and socioeconomic status. Many students desist going to college because they lack interest in higher learning and there is also a social stigma regarding how students pay for their education. Moreover, if the few students that decide to enroll, do not generate an interest in learning through their college career, the rate of graduation can be further reduced [6].

It is demonstrated that teenager and young adults can display great abilities when playing video games.

Young adults and teenagers have shown an aptitude for completing complex tasks when playing video games. This aptitude exists because as video games have become more popular, modern examples offer a small learning curve and many interactions share common standards across the industry. Even though different types of video games are developed constantly by various companies, any person eager to play a video game can pick up a controller or keyboard and start enjoying these adventures. Games not only entertain the player but also release dopamine which can also generate an addiction to the game itself [8]. If these attributes are taken into consideration when developing games, the retention, and attention that the player will allocate while playing can also generate great opportunities for learning.

Research has shown that there is a quantifiable benefit when humans play video games. For example, benefits include areas such as rehabilitation, motor skills, ability to react and there have even been benefits to counseling [9]. By including learning concepts in a video game, we can not only help individuals learn new concepts, but we can also change the negative outlook given to video games [10].

Current educational video games fail to generate interest whereas most of the industry is successful in this aspect. The games that are currently being used are either simulators or tutorials of how to learn something new. As good as the concepts seem, they create a sterile environment instead of a naturally interactive one which strips the game of its critical component, fun. Players want to discover, be challenged and obtain rewards for their work.

The average household owns a computer, smartphone, and a console gaming device. By creating software that does not require an extra purchase, it is easier to reach a broader population. By making video games that can teach or spark interest in computer science, we are bridging the gap between individuals and their fear of it. It is essential to include these concepts early in the developmental process preferably introducing the concepts to children but also to teenagers and older. This inclusion will assist in generating interest in STEM that can carry over to adulthood [11].

3 CScape 3D: Discover CS by Playing

3.1 Objective

We developed a video game that imitates the concept of an Escape Room. Regular games always provide a challenge and a reward system where the player strives to complete it. On CScape 3D the player needs to find the correct combination of objects to open the door and be able to escape the room. We also decided on using the concept of an Escape room to spike even more interest into picking up the game and playing it.

3.2   Concept

The Game was developed using Unreal Engine and Visual Basic Studio. It combined the use of Unreal's Blueprint system, along with C++. The current room was a prototype to test the level of interest in the game. Many of the assets used were borrowed from the Unreal Library Starter content pack. The next step was to add functionality to the room. This functionality was achieved by creating three trigger volumes that would only interact with movable objects. Meaning that only some objects from the room can be used and that not all the objects can be moved. Each plate has special activation method. Thanks to the Unreal Engine, the game physics mimic real-world physics to a close level (see Fig. 1).

For the first room, all volumes share a common concept: IF STATEMENTS.

The way each plate was programmed was using the basic concept of decision making. The yellow plate will only be activated by adding objects that only add up to a total weight of forty five kilograms (see Fig. 2). The green plate will only be activated by only adding at least four objects (see Fig. 3). The white plate can only be activated by adding the object with the specific name (see Fig. 4).

Once the player activates the three switches (see Fig. 5), and the player leaves the room, they will be greeted with a notification congratulating the escape of the room, followed by an explanation of how he/she escaped. A small explanation about IF Statement and its use in Computer Science will follow the previous explanation.

Fig. 1. Top Side view of environment on Unreal Engine

(a) Empty Yellow Trigger Volume   (b) Solved Puzzle for Yellow Area

Fig. 2. Yellow Puzzle (Color figure online)

(a) Empty Green Trigger Volume   (b) Solved Puzzle for Green Area

Fig. 3. Green Puzzle (Color figure online)

(a) Empty White Trigger Volume   (b) Solved Puzzle for White Area

Fig. 4. White Puzzle (Color figure online)

(a) Door Will Remain Closed Until All Puzzles   (b) Door Opens After All The Puzzles Are
Are Solved   Solved

Fig. 5. Door States

By showing this information to the player, we are rewarding the player and
also showing that subconsciously he or she already knows how to use concepts of
Computer Science. It is known that learning by doing is an effective tool towards
memory retention and learning. By utilizing this technique on a subconscious
level with the game, we can stimulate and engage more interaction with the
player.

3.3   Controls

The system uses a basic control scheme shared among many video games. Using
the keyboard, the player can use the W Key and Up-arrow to move forward, S
Key and Down-arrow key to move backward, A Key and the Left-Arrow key to
move to the left and D Key and the Right-Arrow key to move to the left (see
Fig. 6).

To minimize the player's learning curve, there is only one interaction with the
environment. This interaction is the grab action, which allows the user to pick up
and move an object from its current position to the new desired location. This
action can be activated by using the mouse left click. The grab action utilizes the
hold/release actions. These actions, require that the user hold down the left mouse
button which is an interaction already known from their computer usage 7).

It is important to understand that when users are presented with a complicated control scheme. Frustration can occur, but by providing a simpler control
scheme, the experience of the game can be more fluid and enjoyable [12].

3.4   Camera View

The camera is set to a first-person perspective. This perspective helps the player
to immerse themselves in the game. To move the camera, the user only needs to
move the mouse around giving 360° of freedom. Also, this camera can be easily
reused for Virtual Reality and Augmented Reality environments, giving the user

Controls

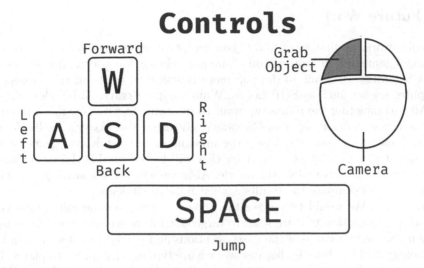

Fig. 6. Basic control system

Fig. 7. Object being held by user using Grab command

a better sense of spatial location. Currently, the game is being deployed to the traditional desktop only. This deployment allows a reduction of motion sickness that the player may experience as he or she plays the game. The game can be ported into Virtual Reality to allow the increase of interest in players but at the same time reducing the number of possible players due to limited access to VR devices in the current market.

4 Future Work

In future work, we first want to test how receptive are individuals to the idea of playing a game to spark interest on Computer Science. Moreover, after surveying non-CS majors, we want to develop more rooms that cover other concepts of computer science such as FOR Loops, While Loops, Arrays, and Nodes.

After completing the rooms, we want to run some test on how much interest the game sparked for any non-CS gamer. By using the player's feedback, we can reshape the game to enhance the amount of interest it can generate for subsequent players. One of the metrics that will be collected is the total time it took each player to complete the puzzle. Also, we will run a control group with CS students to compare the results against non-CS students.

Moreover, We would like to see the impact of the game on minorities. One important population that we want to target for future studies would be non-cs women. Not only because of the misconceptions and perception of women in the technology field [13] but also because women are typically less prone to play video games or even be considered as a target audience by the gaming industry [14].

5 Conclusion

We propose a video game that resembles an Escape room. The purpose of this game is to offer the same level of entertainment as any other game but at the same time generate interest in Computer Science. The player will be immersed in this game and progressively learn more and more about the basic concepts of Computer Science. The concepts are presented to the player as an achievement system to develop a feeling of accomplishment.

Future work will include the addition of more rooms and more complex puzzles. Furthermore, porting the game to mobile phones such as iPhone and Android. The last addition will be to port the game to Virtual Reality to attract even broader audiences. We want to put the game within reach of every demographic to see the impact of gaming when promoting higher education. Finally, our principal goal is to show that computer science is a field that can be learned from an early age and does not require high levels of education.

Acknowledgments. Support provided by the National Science Foundation: I/UCRC IIP-1338922, III-Large IIS-1213026, MRI CNS- 1429345, MRI CNS-1532061, MRI CNS-1532061, MRI CNS-1429345, RAPID CNS-1507611, DUE-1643965. U.S. DOT Grant ARI73. Also, we acknowledge Daniel Perez and Armando Carrasquillo.

References

1. USDL: Computer and information technology occupations, January 2018
2. NCES: Bachelor's degrees conferred to females by postsecondary institutions, by race/ethnicity and field of study: 2014-15 and 2015-16, August 2017
3. Rheingold, H.: Virtual Reality: Exploring the Brave New Technologies. Simon & Schuster Adult Publishing Group, New York (1991)

4. NCES: Public high school graduation rates, April 2017
5. Felder, R.M., Silverman, L.K.: Learning and teaching styles in engineering education. Eng. Educ. **78**, 674–681 (1988)
6. Carter, L.: Why students with an apparent aptitude for computer science don't choose to major in computer science. SIGCSE Bull. **38**, 27–31 (2006)
7. Papastergiou, M.: Digital game-based learning in high school computer science education: Impact on educational effectiveness and student motivation. Comput. Educ. **52**(1), 1–12 (2009)
8. Gentile, D.: Pathological video-game use among youth ages 8 to 18: a national study. Psychol. Sci. **20**(5), 594–602 (2009). PMID: 19476590
9. Barko, T., Sadler, T.D.: Practicality in virtuality: finding student meaning in video game education. J. Sci. Educ. Technol. **22**, 124–132 (2013)
10. Funk, J.B.: Reevaluating the impact of video games. Clin. Pediatr. **32**(2), 86–90 (1993). PMID: 8432085
11. DeJarnette, N.: America's children: providing early exposure to stem (science, technology, engineering and math) initiatives. Education **133**(1), 77–84 (2012)
12. Cummings, A.H.: The evolution of game controllers and control schemes and their effect on their games. In: The 17th Annual University of Southampton Multimedia Systems Conference (2007)
13. Falkner, K., Szabo, C., Michell, D., Szorenyi, A., Thyer, S.: Gender gap in academia: perceptions of female computer science academics. In: Proceedings of the 2015 ACM Conference on Innovation and Technology in Computer Science Education, ITiCSE 2015, pp. 111–116. ACM, New York (2015)
14. Funke, A., Berges, M., Mühling, A., Hubwieser, P.: Gender differences in programming: research results and teachers' perception. In: Proceedings of the 15th Koli Calling Conference on Computing Education Research, Koli Calling 2015, pp. 161–162. ACM, New York (2015)

Using Immersive Virtual Reality Serious Games for Vocational Rehabilitation of Individuals with Physical Disabilities

Lal "Lila" Bozgeyikli[1(✉)], Evren Bozgeyikli[1], Andoni Aguirrezabal[1],
Redwan Alqasemi[1], Andrew Raij[2], Stephen Sundarrao[1],
and Rajiv Dubey[1]

[1] University of South Florida, Tampa, FL 33620, USA
lboz@email.arizona.edu
[2] University of Central Florida, Orlando, FL 32816, USA

Abstract. This paper presents a system for vocational training and assessment of individuals with severe physical disabilities using immersive virtual reality. The system was developed at the University of South Florida's Center for Assistive, Rehabilitation, and Robotics Technologies (CARRT). A virtual and physical assistive robot was used for the remote-control skills training. After going through several iterations, the system was tested by a total of 15 participants along with professional job trainers. The results were encouraging in further exploration of virtual reality as a promising tool in vocational training of individuals with severe physical disabilities.

Keywords: Virtual reality · Vocational training · Physical disabilities
Robotics · Serious games

1 Introduction

It was reported recently that there are 34.8 million individuals with severe disabilities in the U.S. [1]. A severe disability can be described as a disability that limits one or more functional capabilities of individuals, such as mobility, self-care, or employment [2]. Individuals with severe disabilities face difficulties in employment for various reasons, such as difficulty in performing some tasks due to limited abilities, predetermined or subconscious biases of employers about the possible challenges they may face, resulting in avoiding such individuals altogether [3]. It is intuitive that the most effective job training can be gained at the physical job site. However, due to the reasons mentioned above, many employers would hesitate to accept giving job training to individuals with severe disabilities at such sites, without prior training that is enough to handle the equipment at these places. This may create dangerous situations for both the trainee and the workers as injuries due to misuse of mechanical equipment may occur. With this motivation, we believe that virtual reality (VR) can be a strong alternative to job site training. Virtual reality offers many advantages over direct job site training that both speaks to the characteristics of specific disability groups and eliminates the possible hazardous outcomes of the physical job site training for them. These

© Springer International Publishing AG, part of Springer Nature 2018
M. Antona and C. Stephanidis (Eds.): UAHCI 2018, LNCS 10908, pp. 48–57, 2018.
https://doi.org/10.1007/978-3-319-92052-8_5

advantages can be summarized as follows: safe training in a controlled environment, gradual increase in level complexity, customizable virtual scenarios, real time feedback, prompts and distractions, repetitive automated training, no time constraint on training, automated data collection, focusing on the performed task by isolation from the surroundings, no severe consequences for mistakes, system scalability, automated assessment and reporting, reduced transportation costs, and overall low cost training due to the virtual reality systems becoming more affordable in recent years [4, 5].

With these in mind, we proposed an advanced immersive virtual reality system we call 'VR4VR' that aims to train and assess individuals with severe disabilities on vocational skills. The VR4VR project was funded by the Florida Department of Education. Immersive virtual reality can be described as a system that makes the user feel like they have stepped into the virtual world. This can be achieved by a few ways: incorporating motion of the user into interaction via real-time motion tracking, providing a head mounted display that renders the virtual environment based on user's head movements, and using seamless projections on large displays. The VR4VR caters for three disability groups: autism spectrum disorder (ASD), traumatic brain injury (TBI) and severe mobility impairment, such as spinal cord injury (SCI), and is composed two main components: cognitive disabilities training system and physical disabilities training system. This paper focuses on the physical disabilities training system which caters for the severe mobility impairment population. The physical disabilities modules offer training on manipulating an assistive physical robot to move and manipulate boxes or smaller objects (camera control, base motion, single arm, dual arm, and gripper operations). Main components of the VR4VR system's physical disabilities modules are: Baxter physical robot, Razer Hydra user controller, virtual replicas of the Baxter robot and the Razer Hydra controller, wireless remote-control panel, and a large screen. To train individuals with severe physical disabilities on using an assistive robot, several modules were implemented. These modules included tasks that aim to teach users how to use the Baxter/PowerBot assistive robot for manipulating and moving objects. Users were first trained in the virtual reality system and they then performed the same tasks using the physical robot.

This paper presents and discusses the user study results of 15 individuals (10 neurotypical, 5 severe physical disabilities) who used the VR4VR system's physical disabilities modules. Challenges faced during the design, development and user study phases and implications of the user study results are also discussed, which we believe will benefit future virtual reality studies for vocational rehabilitation. Finally, future research directions are presented.

2 Related Work

Using virtual reality for vocational training of individuals with disabilities have become an emerging area in recent years, due to the advantages it offers and the prevalence of low cost new generation virtual reality systems. In this section, we present the key previous works in the area of using virtual reality for vocational training of adults with disabilities.

Smith et al. assessed the feasibility and efficacy of a virtual reality job interview training system for individuals with Autism Spectrum Disorder (ASD) [6]. The system included job interview simulations with a virtual character. Users who were trained with the virtual reality system showed greater improvement than the traditionally trained users. In addition, users found the virtual reality system enjoyable and easy to use. The authors concluded that the results indicated evidence on the system's feasibility and efficacy. A follow-up study revealed that the participants who trained with the system had increased chances of receiving job offers in the next 6 months [7]. Wade et al. developed a virtual reality driving training system for individuals with ASD [8]. The system utilized gaze information of users to adaptively change the virtual environment accordingly. User study results indicated that the system was beneficial in training users on driving skills. Tsang and Man proposed a virtual reality vocational training system for individuals with schizophrenia and measured its effectiveness [9]. Results indicated that the performance of individuals who were trained with the virtual reality system was improved more than the individuals who were trained by the conventional methods. Virtual reality training was more effective in improving the individuals' self-efficacy as well. The authors indicated that virtual reality was an effective tool in vocational training of individuals with schizophrenia. Yu et al. proposed a virtual reality system for training hearing impaired individuals on CNC machine operation skills [10]. The usability test results were promising in terms of effective training. The system is currently under iteration and is planned to be evaluated with a user study in the future.

As our VR4VR system is compared to the previous works in the emerging area of vocational rehabilitation using virtual reality, the following main differences can be listed: (1) utilizing and seamlessly integrating several immersive components such as motion tracking, head mounted display, curtain display, tangible object interaction, a haptic device and an assistive robot, (2) Offering training in a wide range of vocational skills, (3) Catering to three main disability groups.

3   The VR4VR System

Our VR4VR system is composed of several components. In this section, we present the design and implementation of the main components of the system and parts that are specific to the physical disabilities training system.

3.1   Hardware

Several hardware components were used in the VR4VR system. In the physical disabilities training system, a large 50″ TV was used as the display. Baxter robot was used [16] with PowerBot mobile platform [17]. Razer hydra controllers were used for controlling the physical and virtual replica of the robot [18]. Software was custom developed with the Unity game engine [19] and C# programming language.

3.2   Physical Disabilities Training System

To train individuals with severe physical disabilities on using an assistive robot, several modules were implemented. These modules included tasks that aim to teach the users using the Baxter/PowerBot assistive robot on manipulating and moving objects. The users were first trained in the virtual reality system and then performed the tasks using the physical robot. The modules were designed as follows: (1) camera control module that teaches the user how to switch between the cameras and how to perform basic functions such as zooming and panning, (2) base control module that teaches the user how to move the PowerBot base platform of the robot around inside the virtual environment, (3) using the controls taught in the previous two modules in tandem in order to navigate around a cluttered environment, (4) arm control module that teaches the user how to use the two included hand tracking motion controllers in order to control the robot's hands and arms, (5) a module that combines all of the skills learned in the previous modules into one cohesive test of matching both the base platform and hand configuration of a semitransparent robot silhouette in the virtual environment, (6) gripper operations module that teaches the user how to use the motion controllers to control the operation of the robot's dual parallel grippers, (7) dual arm control module that teaches the user how to move both hands on the robot simultaneously, using only one motion controller, and (8) a test module for the dual arm control system that requests the user to retrieve an item from within a warehouse environment and bring it to the delivery area located at the front of the warehouse. The Physical disabilities training system is presented in Fig. 1.

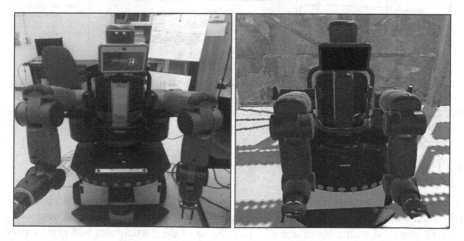

Fig. 1. Physical skills training modules of the VR4VR system. Left: The physical robot. Right: The virtual replica of the physical robot in a virtual warehouse environment.

Completing the components of a task would raise the user's score, to a maximum of 100 points. Failing to complete a component within the time constraints, dropping an object, or positioning it in an incorrect location would result in that component being skipped and those points lost. Colliding with objects in the robot's workspace, including other objects, tables and shelves would result in a deduction of 5 points. Colliding with environmental objects, such as walls, doors, and other static objects would result in a deduction of 10 points. The following equation shows how scores were calculated, where γ denotes the progress of the user (out of 100), α denotes the number of scene object collisions, and β denotes the number of environment object collisions: Score = $\gamma - (\alpha(30) + \beta(20))$.

The controls for the physical disabilities modules were the same when using the physical robot and the virtual robot. A special control program retrieved the current state information from either the virtual robot running inside of the VR4VR Simulation, or the physical robot. The input from the user's controller was sent to the control program and were used in conjunction with the state information to generate the motion of the robot's base and arms. The control program would then execute these motions on either the virtual robot or the physical robot. Finally, the user was presented either the live camera feed from the physical robot's cameras, or the virtual camera feed from the virtual robot's cameras within the simulation. The virtual robot had been modeled after the physical robot and emulated the physical robot's specifications. An overview of the control system can be seen in Fig. 2.

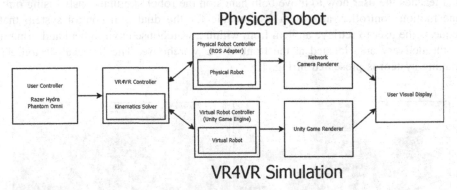

Fig. 2. Overview of the physical disabilities training system showing the integration of the controls with the virtual robot and the physical robot.

4   User Study

A user study was performed for the physical disabilities training system with a total of 15 participants (10 neurotypical, 5 severe physical disabilities). All users were older than 18 years old with a mean age of 26.88. None of the participants had prior virtual reality experience. Participants with disabilities were clients of the Florida Vocational Rehabilitation (VR) program and were job seekers. Professional job trainers accompanied the participants with disabilities during the testing sessions. The testing took two and a half hours in total per participant: one-hour virtual reality training module testing, 15 min break time and survey filling, one-hour physical robot testing, followed by survey filling. The user study was performed under the IRB #Pro00013008.

5 Results

Level scores for the physical disabilities training modules are presented in Fig. 3 for the virtual reality training and in Fig. 4 for the physical robot used for neurotypical individuals and individuals with physical disabilities. Level scores were out of 100 with possible deductions from the following: collisions with the environmental props and walls, and dropping items onto the floor.

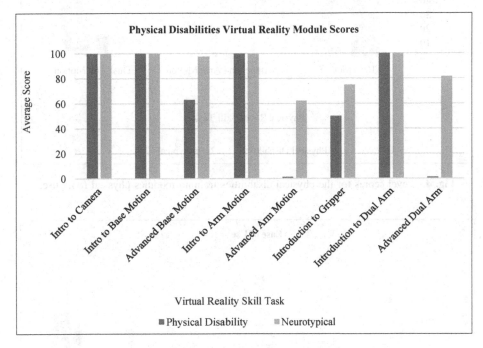

Fig. 3. Level scores for the physical disabilities training modules virtual reality training.

Ease of interaction scores for the physical disabilities training modules are presented in Fig. 5. These scores were out of 5 with answers ranging on a 5-point Likert scale. For the Physical Disability training module, when asked the question "Would you come back to train with us again?" 14 of the participants answered "Yes.", and 1 participant answered "No."

As the job trainers were interviewed about the physical disabilities training modules, they stated that the virtual reality training would be beneficial for the job seekers. However, they indicated that the training would be challenging for individuals with limited gripping abilities due to the joystick controllers used in the module. They also emphasized that the training time in the virtual reality module was not sufficient to prepare the users for using the physical robot. They suggested repeating the virtual reality training module at least three times before letting the users operate the physical robot.

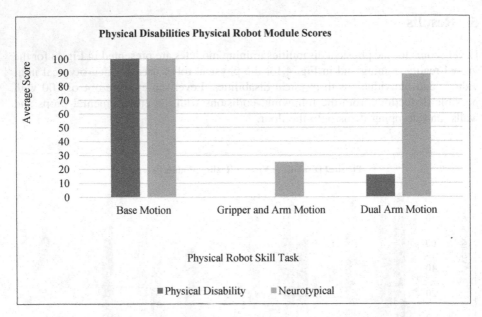

Fig. 4. Level scores for the physical disabilities training modules physical robot use.

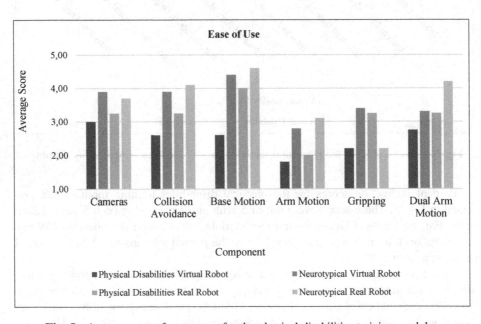

Fig. 5. Average ease of use scores for the physical disabilities training modules.

6   Discussion

The results for the physical disabilities training modules were lower than expected, especially for the arm control and gripper. Ease of use scores were also low for these two components. The participants gave lower scores for the ease of use of the virtual reality module than the physical robot. As we investigated the possible reasons behind this by interviewing the participants and the job trainers, they stated that it was easier to operate the robot when they saw it in the real world, instead of seeing the virtual robot on a monitor through cameras. The additional camera manipulation in the virtual reality training was found difficult to operate by the users. In addition to this, the users stated that understanding the depth was more challenging in the virtual reality training as compared to seeing the physical robot in the real world. To remedy these, camera controls will be automatized and more cues to help in understanding the depth will be added.

The participants stated that the sensitivity of the controls, the large number of controls and comprehending the orientation of the robot's components took time to get used to. The most common problem was in the gripping of the objects. It required the users to orient the arm accurately and grasp small objects such as a water bottle. The users had difficulty in fine tuning the motion and some users were confused about remembering the controls.

Another reason behind the low scores of the participants with physical disabilities was the secondary cognitive disabilities, although not severe, which were existing in some of the participants. The instructions of the physical disabilities modules were not prepared to accommodate for the cognitive disabilities, hence it was observed to be a bit overwhelming for these participants to comprehend the controls in the allocated time.

For both user groups, the comprehension needed in order to fully operate the robotic platform both in virtual reality and on the physical robot was an issue. Since there was no direct mapping between the users' motion and the corresponding robot's motion, users had to adapt their motion through the controller to achieve the desired robot motion. This was observed to be counterintuitive for some participants, therefore additional training sessions and more in-depth explanation of the control system and its' limitations need to be added in order to facilitate easier comprehension.

Another challenge was maintaining the accuracy of the virtual test environment through the physical robot test environment. One of the problems encountered was in the object grasping task. In this task, the users needed to grasp a water bottle. However, the water bottles in the virtual environment were more difficult to knock over than the water bottles in the real environment. This was observed to make this particular task much more difficult to perform on the physical robot.

Even though they weren't completely comfortable in controlling the physical robot, most of the participants were pleased to be able to control an advanced physical robot with an hour of virtual reality training. Most of the participants stated that more training time would prepare them better for controlling the physical robot.

Overall, although virtual reality training partially prepared the users to operate the physical robot, they gained a baseline understanding and were able to perform simple tasks with the physical robot which they had no prior training to operate. We think that this makes virtual reality a platform that is worth further exploration in vocational training of individuals with physical disabilities.

7   Conclusion

In this paper, we presented the physical disabilities component of the VR4VR system that aims to train and assess individuals with severe disabilities on vocational tasks. A total of 15 individuals (neurotypical and with physical disabilities) participated in testing the system with accompanying professional job trainers. The results encouraged that virtual reality is a promising tool in vocational training of individuals with physical disabilities. Future work will include iterating the system according to the feedback from the participants and the job trainers and perform a second user study with more participants.

Acknowledgment. The authors would like to thank the Florida Department of Education for funding the VR4VR project.

References

1. Brault, M.W.: Americans with disabilities: 2010. US Census Bureau, Census Brief. https://www2.census.gov/library/publications/2012/demo/p70-131.pdf. Accessed 23 Feb 2018
2. U.S. Bureau of Reclamation: Rehabilitation Act of 1973. http://www.usbr.gov/cro/pdfsplus/rehabact.pdf. Accessed 05 Nov 2016
3. America's Heroes at Work, Traumatic Brain Injury (TBI) & Post-Traumatic Stress Disorder (PTSD): Do's and Don'ts for Employers & Hiring Managers. http://www.brainlinemilitary.org/content/2013/04/hiring-veterans-with-traumatic-brain-injury-and-post-traumatic-stress-disorder-dos-and-donts-for-employers-and-h.html. Accessed 23 Feb 2018
4. Schultheis, M.T., Rizzo, A.A.: The application of virtual reality technology in rehabilitation. Rehabil. Psychol. **46**, 296 (2001)
5. Cherniack, E.P.: Not just fun and games: applications of virtual reality in the identification and rehabilitation of cognitive disorders of the elderly. Disabil. Rehabil. Assist. Technol. **6**, 283–289 (2011)
6. Smith, M.J., Ginger, E.J., Wright, K., Wright, M.A., Taylor, J.L., Humm, L.B., Olsen, D.E., Bell, M.D., Fleming, M.F.: Virtual reality job interview training in adults with autism spectrum disorder. J. Autism Dev. Disord. **44**(10), 2450–2463 (2014)
7. Smith, M.J., Fleming, M.F., Wright, M.A., Roberts, A.G., Humm, L.B., Olsen, D., Bell, M. D.: Virtual reality job interview training and 6-month employment outcomes for individuals with schizophrenia seeking employment. Schizophr. Res. **166**(1), 86–91 (2015)
8. Wade, J., Zhang, L., Bian, D., Fan, J., Swanson, A., Weitlauf, A., Sarkar, M., Warren, Z., Sarkar, N.: A gaze-contingent adaptive virtual reality driving environment for intervention in individuals with autism spectrum disorders. ACM Trans. Interact. Intell. Syst. (TiiS) **6**(1), 3 (2016)
9. Tsang, M.M., Man, D.W.: A virtual reality-based vocational training system (VRVTS) for people with schizophrenia in vocational rehabilitation. Schizophr. Res. **144**(1), 51–62 (2013)

10. Yu, S., Ryu, J., Han, I., Kim, M.: Developing a 3D virtual environment for hearing impaired learners' learning of CNC machine operation. In: Society for Information Technology and Teacher Education International Conference, vol. 2016, no. 1, pp. 2450–2454 (2016)
11. Rethink Robotics. http://www.rethinkrobotics.com/baxter/. Accessed 23 Feb 2018
12. Adept Mobile Robots. http://www.mobilerobots.com/ResearchRobots/PowerBot.aspx. Accessed 23 Feb 2018
13. Sixense. http://sixense.com/hydra_faq. Accessed 05 Nov 2016
14. Unity. https://unity3d.com/. Accessed 23 Feb 2018

Virtual Reality Interaction Techniques for Individuals with Autism Spectrum Disorder

Evren Bozgeyikli[1]([⊠]), Lal "Lila" Bozgeyikli[1], Redwan Alqasemi[1], Andrew Raij[2], Srinivas Katkoori[1], and Rajiv Dubey[1]

[1] University of South Florida, Tampa, FL, USA
evren@mail.usf.com
[2] University of Central Florida, Orlando, FL, USA

Abstract. Virtual reality (VR) systems are seeing growing use for training individuals with Autism Spectrum Disorder (ASD). Although these systems indicate effective use of VR for training, there is little work in the literature evaluating different VR interaction techniques for this audience. In this paper, different VR interaction techniques are explored in the Virtual Reality for Vocational Rehabilitation (VR4VR) system and additional data analysis on top of our previously published preliminary results [1] was performed via a user study with nine individuals with ASD and ten neurotypical individuals. The participants tried six vocational training modules of the VR4VR system. In these modules, tangible object manipulation, haptic device, touch and snap and touchscreen were tested for object selection and manipulation; real walking and walk-in-place were tested for locomotion; and head mounted display and curtain screen were tested for display. Touchscreen and tangible interaction methods were preferred by the individuals with ASD. The walk-in-place locomotion technique were found frustrating and difficult to perform by the individuals with ASD. Curtain display received higher preference scores from individuals with ASD although they accepted the HMD as well. The observations and findings of the study are expected to give insight into the poorly explored area of experience of individuals with ASD with various interaction techniques in VR.

Keywords: Virtual reality · Vocational rehabilitation · Interaction techniques Autism spectrum disorder

1 Introduction

Autism spectrum disorder (ASD) is a lifelong developmental disability that may impact people's understanding of their environment. It can result in difficulties with social relationships, communication and behavior [2]. The latest studies by U.S. Department of Health and Human Services show that today, about 1 in 68 children is identified with ASD [3]. Attention to this specific group and applications for them has increased recently because of an increase in the awareness of prevalence of ASD. According to the Centers for Disease Control and Prevention, National Center for Health Statistics, prevalence of autism has increased by 289.5% from 1997 to 2008 [4]. The three most significant impairments that are associated with autism are listed as; social interaction,

© Springer International Publishing AG, part of Springer Nature 2018
M. Antona and C. Stephanidis (Eds.): UAHCI 2018, LNCS 10908, pp. 58–77, 2018.
https://doi.org/10.1007/978-3-319-92052-8_6

communication and behavior [5]. Because of these impairments, individuals with autism often have difficulty in their daily lives, especially while interacting with others. Because of the limiting properties of ASD, it is usually harder for individuals with autism to find jobs and succeed in them without proper training.

There are several advantages of using virtual reality over traditional training methods, such as active participation in accurately represented real-life like situations, opportunities for repetitive practice on simulators, unique training experiences with suitable and customizable difficulty levels, consistent and real time feedback, and opportunity for users to train and correct errors without severe consequences [6]. Due to these positive properties, virtual reality has been used in many different training applications for neurotypical individuals, such as training federal law enforcement agents on interrogation methods [7] and primary care physicians to perform intervention to treat alcohol abuse [8]. Virtual reality is found to be especially useful for populations with ASD, since virtual reality training offers several aspects that resonate with their characteristics, such as the predictability and the ability to repeat the exercises with adjusted difficulty levels until the user feels ready for the task to be performed [9].

There have been many scientific studies for training of individuals with ASD using virtual reality. These studies showed that virtual reality is an effective tool in training individuals with ASD [10, 11]. However, there has been little work to understand which virtual reality locomotion and interaction techniques are useful for individuals with ASD. Although there are many possible advantages of using virtual reality systems for job training, effective interaction techniques should be implemented for the users to truly benefit from the advantages of virtual reality. Since the perception and behaviors of individuals with ASD can be different from neurotypical individuals, using the same interaction techniques that work well for neurotypical individuals may not be a good practice. To bridge this gap, in this study, we examined different virtual reality interaction techniques for individuals with ASD. For this purpose, several different interaction techniques for object selection and manipulation (tangible object manipulation, haptic device, touch and snap, and touchscreen) and locomotion (real walking and walk-in-place) that have been implemented in different modules of the Virtual Reality for Vocational Rehabilitation (VR4VR) system were explored. VR4VR is a highly immersive virtual reality system for vocational rehabilitation of individuals with disabilities. The interaction techniques along with the two different display methods (head mounted display and curtain screen) were explored based on different aspects such as; the ease of interaction, level of enjoyment, frustration, dizziness, nauseousness, tiredness, and user statements.

2 Related Work

Several studies show that advances in technology have been used for assisting individuals with ASD for a long time. Goldsmith et al. collected and published the early examples of the technologies that were used for children with ASD [12]. In general, the developed systems were using an interaction technique that seemed to be the most suitable by the authors for the application and using that technique was rarely justified in the publications. Interaction techniques are one of the most important elements of virtual reality systems since they are directly related to the user's experience with the system. Existing systems support a variety of interaction techniques for different platforms and input devices, from conventional devices such as mice or joysticks, to modern devices such as touch gestures, speech-recognition devices, and digitally augmented environments. Interaction techniques may affect several aspects of the user experience such as presence, enjoyment, frustration, and tiredness [13].

Most of the precious assistive training applications were implemented using a single interaction technique. The recent applications usually used touchscreen devices since they are easy to use, affordable and available. Furthermore, one of the recent studies showed that the tablet applications with multi touch interactions could make children with ASD more verbally and physically engaged as compared to the traditionally performed similar activities [14]. In a study conducted by Madsen et al., the researchers developed touch screen applications for teaching children with ASD to recognize facial expressions [15]. In this study, lessons learned about the software and hardware design of touch screen applications for this specific population were shared very briefly. In a study on developing an expression recognition game for individuals with ASD using touch enabled mobile devices, the research team has studied the previously existing popular ASD games and tried to consolidate guidelines for designing user interfaces for children with autism [16].

Another popular approach in designing applications for individuals with ASD is using touchless interactions. The availability of the depth sensors, such as Microsoft Kinect and their usage for skeleton tracking made this technique easily usable and popular. Moreover, some researchers suggest not to use wearable sensors since some individuals with ASD may not prefer to wear any sensors on them [17]. A study made on five children with ASD showed that games with touchless interaction helped in improving the attention skills for children with autism. However, the authors stated that the interaction technique was not tested on being appropriate or not for this special user group [18]. Another recent study for individuals with ASD was aiming at improving their motor skills [19]. With this goal, the researchers developed a motion based touchless application and tested the results. This study focused on the importance of physical activity, but did not justify why the authors chose to use this interaction technique while developing the application.

There were also some applications that used more than one interaction technique simultaneously. One study focused on full body interaction techniques for low functioning children with ASD [20]. An environment similar to a virtual reality cave was developed with surrounding projectors, cameras and sensors. Some touchless interaction techniques as well as touch-based interaction techniques were implemented, and the children's acceptance of the system was discussed. Most of the children accepted the system and used it effectively.

With the emerging technology of virtual reality, some researchers have been integrating virtual reality interaction techniques into training applications for people with ASD. In a study, researchers used a virtual reality system to teach street-crossing skills to children with ASD [10]. The results showed that training in virtual reality improved the related skills of those children. In another study, a virtual reality driving training system was developed [11]. In this system, gaze tracking was implemented to track where the users looked during the training sessions since individuals with ASDs' gaze positions were reported to be different from neurotypical individuals. The users were trained to look at the important regions such as traffic lights, traffic signs and pedestrians. The results showed that effective training was achieved using the developed virtual reality system with the incorporation of gaze positions.

Although many studies focused on using only one interaction technique per application, there have been some studies in the literature that used two different interaction techniques in the same application or in different applications that were developed for the same purpose for individuals with ASD. One example was a study that aimed at increasing the social engagement of children with ASD [21]. Two different games were used with two different interaction techniques. One was using multiple mice while the other was using a Diamond touch surface. The study did not test the differences observed while using these interaction techniques and did not make any suggestions for researchers. There was a detailed study on a computer-based training system for children with ASD [22]. In the study, a tangible user interface design was compared with the traditional mouse-based approach. The results of the study showed more learning progress using the tangible user interface. Another recent study showed observations on the usability of basic 3D interactions such as translation and rotation for the adolescents with ASD [23]. The authors aimed at finding the differences in the usage of 3D user interaction techniques between neurotypical individuals and individuals with autism. The results showed that the deficits in hand-eye coordination of individuals with ASD caused some difficulties in using the 3D interaction techniques. The authors suggested that developers should add some assistive cues to aid individuals with ASD with the hand-eye coordination.

Although different interaction techniques and their effects have been thoroughly examined for neurotypical individuals; so far, only limited research in this area has been explored for individuals with ASD. The existing studies briefly include a specific interaction technique or two basic interaction techniques. But virtual reality interactions can be more complicated since they are often (but not always) made as similar to real life as possible to increase the immersiveness. In our study, we explored several different immersive virtual reality interaction techniques with user studies and shared the results that may be beneficial for future virtual reality studies that focus on individuals with ASD.

3 Interaction Techniques

In our VR4VR system, there are six modules that were developed for the training of six different transferrable vocational skills: shelving, cleaning, environmental awareness, loading the back of a truck, money management, and social skills. In each different skill, the most convenient interaction technique to be tested was decided by literature review and discussions with the professional job trainers of individuals with ASD. These job trainers have been training individuals with ASD professionally for vocational rehabilitation for a long time and are highly experienced in this area.

To implement the locomotion and interaction techniques, the Unity game engine [24] and MiddleVR software [25] were used. The implemented software was run on a desktop computer with the following specifications: AMD FX-8150 3.61 Ghz Eight-Core CPU, AMD FirePro W600 GPU and 16 GB RAM. For motion tracking, the OptiTrack [26] V100R2 FLEX optical motion tracking system with 12 cameras was used in a 2 m × 2 m tracked area.

3.1 Object Selection and Manipulation

In the VR4VR system, different object selection and manipulation techniques were implemented and used in different skill modules. The interaction techniques were selected according to the requirements of the task and inputs received from the professional job trainers.

For object selection and manipulation, four different interaction techniques were implemented and explored: tangible object manipulation, haptic device, touch and snap, and touchscreen. These were used in different skill modules for interacting with the virtual world. These interaction techniques have been used in different skill modules of the VR4VR system. All interaction techniques and the skill modules they were tested in the VR4VR system along with the relevant interaction tasks are presented in Table 1.

Tangible Object Manipulation. In this interaction technique, two types of real tangible objects were tracked and represented in the virtual world: (1) identical looking real boxes that were shown in the virtual world with different textures or labels, and (2) a broomstick handle that was represented as a vacuum cleaner or a mop that the user used for cleaning the virtual environments.

In the shelving skill module, there were two physical shelves and one physical table in the real-world environment. The virtual conjugates of those objects were created and placed at the same positions in the virtual world. Furthermore, there were four real boxes that were identical in appearance with reflective markers placed on top of each (for infrared camera tracking). The virtual conjugates of the boxes were created and placed at the same positions in the virtual world with different virtual textures projected on them.

An immersive tangible object manipulation technique was implemented and tested. With this technique, the users could move and rotate the real tangible boxes in the tracked area (see Fig. 1). This enabled a tactile feedback during the interaction, which was expected to increase the presence for the users. Head mounted display (HMD) was used along with hand bands with reflective markers. This enabled real time head and hand tracking. The user was able to see two virtual hands in the virtual world approximately at the same position and orientation with their real hands. We used virtual hand models representing real hands of users since it was reported to increase the realism and the immersiveness in virtual reality applications [27] and help users to better understand virtual distances.

A different tangible interaction method was implemented in the form of a tangible broomstick that was used for controlling a virtual vacuum cleaner and a virtual mop. The real broomstick handle was replaced with a virtual vacuum cleaner or a virtual mop in different tasks (see Fig. 2). To be able to track the real stick by the optical cameras in real-time, three pieces of reflector marker tape were attached around

Table 1. The interaction and locomotion techniques and the displays in the VR4VR system. The skill modules they were implemented in and the tasks that were used within these modules.

Category	Interaction technique	Skill module	Interaction tasks
Object selection and manipulation	Tangible object manipulation (real boxes)	Shelving	• Rotating the boxes • Placing the boxes
	Tangible object manipulation (real broomstick)	Cleaning	• Vacuuming • Mopping
	Haptic device	Loading	• Moving the boxes inside the back of a truck
	Touch and snap	Cleaning	• Litter collection
	Touchscreen	Cash register	• Selection on a touchscreen tablet computer
locomotion	Real walking	Shelving	• Rotating the boxes • Placing the boxes
	Walk-in-place	Cleaning	• Vacuuming • Mopping • Litter collection
	Walk-in-place	Environmental awareness	• Walking to destination points
Display Methods	Head mounted display	Shelving	• Rotating the boxes • Placing the boxes
	Head mounted display	Cleaning	• Vacuuming • mopping • litter collection
	Head mounted display	Environmental awareness	• Walking to destination points
	Curtain screen	Loading	• Moving the boxes inside the back of a truck
	Curtain screen	Cash register	• Selection on a touchscreen tablet computer
	Curtain screen	Social	• Talking with virtual people

the cylinder. Since the cylinder was symmetric along its longitudinal axis, we used software calculations to visualize the cleaning head (nozzle or mop) according to the angle between the cylinder and the ground. This time, in addition to HMD and hand bands, feet bands with reflective markers were also worn by the user. This enabled real time head, hand and feet tracking. The user was able to see two virtual hands and feet in the virtual world.

Fig. 1. Tangible box manipulation in the VR4VR system. The user is rotating a real box. The curtain screen displays the user's view through the HMD.

Fig. 2. Tangible stick manipulation in the VR4VR system. Real broomstick handle with virtual representations of (left) a vacuum cleaner and (right) a mop.

Haptic Device. Haptic devices utilize force feedback to create a tactile sense of touch. In this module, Phantom Omni® haptic device by SensAble Technologies [28] was used for interacting with the virtual world. Phantom Omni® haptic device created a sense of weight for the users so that they could feel if they were interacting with a light or heavy object. This was expected to help in increasing the immersion. The working area of the haptic device was restricted to a planar surface that was parallel to the display area. This helped the users to relate the haptic device input to the visual output easily and removed the ambiguity coming from the extra degree of freedom for the sake of this task.

The buttons on the haptic device handle were assigned for specific commands (see Fig. 3). One of the buttons was used to hold the boxes similar to the vastly used mouse gesture for drag and drop. The other button was used to rotate the boxes by 90° counter clockwise.

Touch and Snap. Touch and snap interaction technique is often used in existing virtual reality applications. In this technique, a virtual object is snapped to a moving object, which usually is selected to be the virtual hand of the user. To trigger the release of the snapped object, different techniques can be used, such as time triggering, position triggering or gesture triggering.

In our implementation, user's hands were equipped with reflective markers to be tracked in real time by the optical tracking system cameras. Those positions were used to place the virtual hands into the virtual world. Virtual litter object was snapped to the

Fig. 3. The haptic device interaction in the VR4VR system. (a) The user controls the cursor in the virtual world by using the haptic device. (b) Haptic device with two buttons on the handle.

user's virtual hands when the user bended and their hands came close to the litter. Users carried the litter objects in the virtual world and once the litter arrived in the vicinity of a trash bin, it disengaged from the hand and fell into the trash bin (see Fig. 4).

Fig. 4. Left: The touch and snap interaction in the VR4VR system. The user is (left) grabbing a virtual litter and (right) releasing their hand to throw the litter into a green virtual trash bin (right). Right: The touchscreen interaction in the VR4VR system. The digital cash register interface implemented on a touchscreen tablet computer. (Color figure online)

Touchscreen. With the increasing number of mobile devices such as smart phones and tablet computers, touch interaction became one of the most popular and prevalent interaction techniques in daily lives of users. Nowadays, even some personal computers, televisions and projectors are currently using this technique. Since the visual output and the touch input are aligned perfectly, this interaction method is thought to be very intuitive and easy to use.

In the VR4VR project, a touchscreen ASUS T100 10-in. display tablet computer was used as another interaction method in the form of a digital cash register (see Fig. 4). In this module, only the single touch static touching technique was used instead of the more complicated dynamic or multi touch interactions. A touchscreen keypad similar to the real cash register keypads was presented to the user.

3.2 Locomotion

Locomotion techniques are used for moving viewpoint (and avatar, if used) of users in virtual world. There are many different techniques for locomotion in virtual reality. In this user study, two locomotion techniques were implemented and explored: real walking and walk-in-place.

Real Walking. To move the avatar in the virtual world with this locomotion technique, the user really walks in the tracked area, as they would do in real life. Although this is a very intuitive method, there is the significant restriction of the limited tracked area. In our implementation, the user was equipped with reflective markers on their hands and head, so that the real position of the user was approximated by these tracked position values and transferred to the virtual world. The virtual world was viewed inside from a virtual camera that was attached to the position of the virtual head and this view was rendered to the HMD. The movement and the rotation of the real head affected the virtual camera's position and rotation, so that a realistic view of the virtual world could be displayed inside the HMD.

Since this technique is restricted with a limited tracking area, the user was surrounded by two physical shelves and one desk. All the tasks were designed so that they could be performed inside that limited tracked area (see Fig. 5). The design of the module allowed for the use of a limited tracking area and real walking as the locomotion method.

Fig. 5. Left: Picture of the real walking locomotion technique in the VR4VR system. The user walks inside the tracked area in the shelving module. Right: Pictures of the walk-in-place locomotion technique in the VR4VR system. The user navigates in the virtual world by walking in place in the real world. (left) Cleaning module, (right) environmental awareness module.

Walk-in-Place. If the real tracked area is smaller than the virtual world, then real walking technique may not be an effective choice due to the size restriction. To overcome this limitation, walk-in-place technique is commonly used in virtual reality implementations. In this technique, the user marches in the same place while the virtual avatar walks in the virtual world in the direction the user faces. This way, the limitation of the physical tracking area can easily be overcome. But this comes with the additional gesture of walking in place instead of real walking. In our VR4VR system, the implementation of this technique included different walking speeds, depending on the speed of walking in place gesture, so that the user could adjust the virtual speed of the avatar by modifying their marching speed in the real-world. The walking direction of the virtual avatar was controlled by the head direction of the user (see Fig. 5). We assumed that the head of the user was aligned with the user's body orientation, and the neck of the user was not rotated. If the user turned their head to the left while their body was front facing and marched in place, they would have moved towards the left in the virtual world, where their head was facing.

To be able to detect the walk-in-place gesture, a marker set was attached to the same position on top of the user's both feet. The difference of the heights (h0) of the left and the right foot markers (h0 = hr − hl) was calculated in each cycle of the program. If the difference of the heights of the foot markers became higher than a threshold (ht), the system entered the ready state for a possible walking action. In a specific time interval (Δt), if the difference of the heights of the foot markers (h1) became higher than a threshold again, but this time in the opposite direction, the walking action was triggered. The walking speed was calculated by collecting the time between the two triggers, and dividing the average step length to the collected time. After each trigger, the system looked for another trigger in a specific time interval. If another trigger occurred, the walking speed was updated, and walking proceeded. If no trigger was initiated in that time interval, the walking was ended.

3.3 Display Methods

Different locomotion and interaction techniques were implemented in different modules of the VR4VR system. Each implemented locomotion and interaction technique was decided to be more suitable for a specific display method following literature review and discussions with the professional job trainers. In this project, head mounted display and a 180° curved screen were used as the available display methods. In the study, the most suitable display method was selected for each locomotion interaction technique and the user preference on the display methods were explored.

Head Mounted Display. Using head mounted display is an immersive way of displaying the virtual world to the user. A pair of digital displays is placed in front of the user's eyes so that the user sees the virtual world through them. In our study, VR2200 head mounted display with high resolution XGA (1024×768) was used. The main reason for selecting this HMD was to provide individuals with ASD with empty space around their heads since the professional job trainers stated that covering all of their view with the HMD might create a sense of feeling trapped and disconnected from the real world. The job trainers also stated that having open space in the HMD would make sure that they still had some connection with the real world and provide a more comfortable training experience for individuals with ASD. Hence, instead of using a highly immersive HMD that surrounds the user's whole vision, we preferred to use a more open spaced HMD that could be flipped up when not in use.

Curtain Screen. For the interaction techniques that were implemented from a stationary point of view of the virtual world, a 180° large curved curtain screen with two projectors were employed in our VR4VR system. The curved screen had 3.5 m diameter and 2.4 m height, and its surface was white fabric to make the projections easily visible. This way, possible discomfort of users while using the HMD could be eliminated and two different display methods could be explored.

4 User Study

Ten neurotypical individuals (10 males, aged between 21 and 50) and nine individuals with high functioning ASD (7 males and 2 females, aged between 20 and 41) participated in the user study. Although there may be different definitions of neurotypical in the literature, a commonly used description would be indicating a typical neurological development and not being on the Autism spectrum [29]. In our study, we defined neurotypical individuals as not having any form of disability. All participants with ASD were previously diagnosed as high functioning by medical professionals. The participants with ASD came to our research facility to try all six modules of the VR4VR system with their professional job trainers. Within subjects experiment was performed. The users completed the skill modules in two different sessions that were scheduled on two different days. Each session was approximately two hours long and there were at least three days between the consecutive sessions. The order of the modules was assigned randomly with counterbalancing. At the end of each skill module, the users were asked to fill out a questionnaire about their experience with the VR4VR system. After completing the final skill module of the system, the users were asked to fill out a general questionnaire including questions about their preferences on different components of the system. Other than these methods of data collection, we also asked the users' opinions about the interaction techniques during the breaks between the consecutive sessions in the form of interviews. The user study was performed under the IRB with the identification number Pro00013008.

The questions that were asked after each skill module were about the users' experience with the interaction techniques and the display methods. The questions were about how easy it was to interact with the system, and how much they enjoyed, got frustrated or tired while interacting with the system. We used the answers to these questions to explore the used interaction and locomotion techniques, since they were one of the major differences between the six modules besides the tasks in our VR4VR system. The users were asked to choose from available answer choices based on a five-level Likert scale [30]. The users were also asked if they felt dizzy or nauseous, during and/or after the virtual reality training. In addition, the users were asked to select their preferred interaction technique and their preferred display method after completing all of the modules. The users were also asked to state their own opinions about these explored aspects.

5 Results

The results obtained from the participants are presented in this subsection to provide a general idea on the preference of a cohort of users with autism on several virtual reality locomotion and interaction techniques. However, since our VR4VR system was not designed with the aim of comparing virtual reality locomotion and interaction techniques, these results are only expected to give a general idea instead of generalizable powerful conclusions. Error bars on the charts represent standard errors calculated by dividing standard deviation with square root of sample size.

5.1 Selection and Manipulation Techniques

The results obtained from the users for the four different selection and manipulation techniques –tangible object manipulation, haptic device, touch and snap, and touchscreen– are presented in this sub-subsection. Figure 6 shows the average scores for the neurotypical users, whereas Fig. 7 shows the average scores for individuals with ASD. A score of 1 represents very little, while a score of 5 represents very much of the related aspect. Tiredness and frustration scores were low for all interaction techniques. On the other hand, for ease of interaction, enjoyment and immersion; the averages were above 3.0. The users with ASD found the haptic device hard to interact as compared to the other interaction techniques. Touchscreen interaction received the best results for the ease of interaction, enjoyment, and immersion aspects as compared to the other three interaction techniques for individuals with ASD.

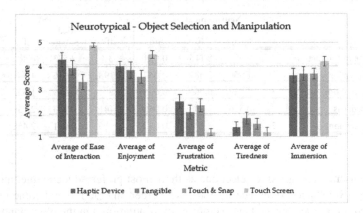

Fig. 6. Survey results for the selection and manipulation techniques in the VR4VR system for neurotypical individuals.

Statistical analysis was performed on the collected data using the IBM SPSS Statistics 23 software. The results of One Way ANOVA with repeated measures with manipulation technique as 4-level factor and alpha value 0.05 showed that there were significant differences for the ease of interaction for both population groups ($F(3, 27) = 8.115$, $p = 0.001$ for the neurotypical individuals and $F(3, 24) = 4.406$, $p = 0.026$ for the individuals with ASD). Mauchly's test was used to test the data for sphericity. If the data was not spherical, Greenhouse-Geisser correction was made. Detailed ANOVA results can be seen in Table 2. For further exploration, a Tukey post hoc test was also performed. For the users with ASD, the haptic device was found to be significantly hard to interact as compared with the touchscreen.

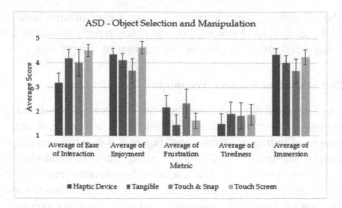

Fig. 7. Survey results for the selection and manipulation techniques in the VR4VR system for individuals with ASD.

Table 2. One Way ANOVA with repeated measures with manipulation technique as 4-level factor and alpha value 0.05 results for selection and manipulation techniques.

| | | Neurotypical | | | | ASD | | | |
		df	Mean Square	F	Sig.	df	Mean Square	F	Sig.
Object Selection and Manipulation	Ease of Interaction	3	4.396	8.115	0.001	3	2.533	4.406	0.026
	Enjoyment	3	1.556	2.881	0.057	1.198	0.616	1.341	0.314
	Frustration	3	3.630	6.066	0.003	3	0.379	1.625	0.236
	Tiredness	3	0.546	3.006	0.050	1.441	0.973	2.139	0.201
	Immersion	3	0.785	2.404	0.092	1.116	0.661	2.458	0.186

As the users were asked to select one as their most preferred technique, most of the users with ASD stated preference for the touchscreen interaction and some users with ASD stated preference for the tangible object manipulation. On the other hand, most of the neurotypical users preferred tangible interaction. None of the users stated preference over the haptic device or the touch and snap interaction. A chart of the results is presented in Fig. 8.

5.2 Locomotion Techniques

The results for the two different locomotion techniques; real walking and walk-in-place, are shown in Fig. 9 for neurotypical individuals and individuals with high functioning ASD. Real walking received higher scores for the ease of interaction, enjoyment and immersion as compared to walk-in-place for both populations. The results for the two locomotion techniques were quite similar for the tiredness aspect. Both user groups found the walk-in-place locomotion technique more frustrating as compared to the real walking. Paired samples t-tests with alpha 0.05 showed that

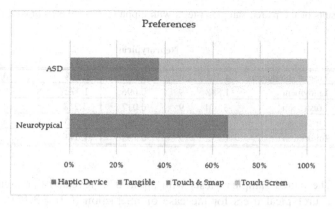

Fig. 8. Preference of the two user groups on the selection and manipulation techniques in the VR4VR system.

walk-in-place locomotion method was significantly harder to use (t(9) = 4.714, p = 0.002), and introduced significantly more frustration (t(9) = −3.001, p = 0.017) for the neurotypical users as compared to the real walking. Detailed results of these paired samples t-tests are presented in Table 3. No significant difference was found for the data of the individuals with ASD. However, during the breaks, some of the users with ASD complained about the difficulty of walking-in-place while trying to concentrate on the tasks and they stated that they liked the real walking much more than the walk-in-place technique.

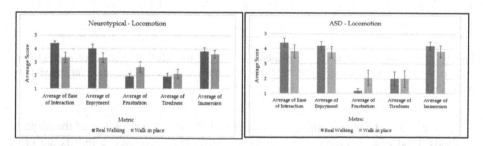

Fig. 9. Left: Survey results for the locomotion techniques in the VR4VR system for neurotypical individuals. Right: Survey results for the locomotion techniques in the VR4VR system for individuals with ASD.

5.3   Display Methods

The average results for the different display methods are presented in Fig. 10 for neurotypical users and individuals with ASD. Curtain display received higher scores for the ease of interaction for both population groups. The tiredness values were lower for the curtain display for both user groups. This was a predicted result since the tasks performed with curtain display required low or no effort, as they didn't involve

Table 3. Results of the paired samples t-tests with alpha 0.05 for the locomotion techniques.

		Neurotypical			ASD		
		t	df	Sig.	t	df	Sig.
Locomotion Techniques	Ease of Interaction	4.714	9	0.002	0.598	8	0.582
	Enjoyment	1.888	9	0.096	1.372	8	0.242
	Frustration	-3.001	9	0.017	-1.218	8	0.290
	Tiredness	-1.155	9	0.282	0.180	8	0.866
	Immersion	1.152	9	0.138	1.633	8	0.178

locomotion. The paired samples t-tests with alpha 0.05 revealed that significant differences for neurotypical users for the ease of interaction (t(9) = 3.121, p = 0.012), enjoyment (t(9) = 2.502, p = 0.034), frustration (t(9) = −2.954, p = 0.016) and tiredness (t(9) = −5.679, p = 0.000) aspects. No statistically significant difference was found for the participants with ASD. Detailed results of the paired samples t-tests for the display methods can be seen in Table 4.

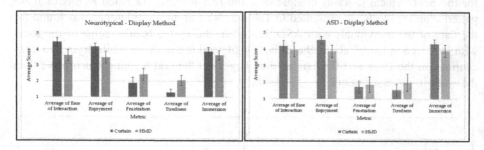

Fig. 10. Left: Survey results for the display methods in the VR4VR system for neurotypical individuals. Right: Survey results for the display methods in the VR4VR system for individuals with ASD.

At the end of the testing, the users were asked about their preference of the display methods: head mounted display and curtain screen. These preference results are presented in Fig. 11. Most of the participants with ASD stated preference for the curtain display. For the neurotypical users, the preference results indicated the opposite.

As the individuals with ASD were asked about their opinions on the HMD display, only one of them stated that they did not like the concept of the HMD due to its resemblance to a television that was placed very near to their eyes. Other than that, no users with ASD stated any negative comments about the HMD. We did not observe any problems in the individuals with autism's acceptance of the HMD during the user studies. All users with ASD made positive comments about the curtain display method and its ease of use.

Table 4. Results of the paired samples t-tests with alpha 0.05 for the display methods.

		Neurotypical			ASD		
		t	df	Sig.	t	df	Sig.
Display Methods	Ease of Interaction	3.121	9	0.012	1.481	8	0.189
	Enjoyment	2.502	9	0.034	2.300	8	0.061
	Frustration	-2.954	9	0.016	-0.547	8	0.604
	Tiredness	-5.679	9	0.000	-1.980	8	0.095
	Immersion	1.441	9	0.183	1.787	8	0.539

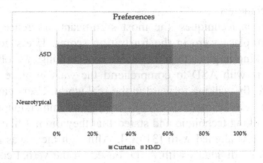

Fig. 11. Preference of the two user groups on the display methods in the VR4VR system.

6 Discussion

Among the selection and manipulation techniques, touchscreen received the highest score from the users with autism for the ease of interaction aspect, whereas haptic device received the lowest score. We interpret that this may be caused by the users' previous experience. None of the users with ASD were familiar with the haptic device whereas all of them stated that they used touch enabled devices regularly on a daily basis. We observed that most of our participants with ASD were interacting with their touchscreen phones during the breaks of the user study sessions. The same fact might also be the reason of touchscreen's receiving the best results for the enjoyment, frustration, and presence aspects. Since we were not expecting the touchscreen to get high presence scores, we asked the users with ASD about the reason behind giving higher scores for this aspect. The participants expressed the reason as the touchscreen's not requiring any extra thinking or effort for them to use it and hence feeling intuitive. Tangible object manipulation and touch and snap were found to be the most tiring interaction techniques. Those results were expected, since these techniques required more physical activities such as carrying the boxes and bending. The users with ASD stated positive comments about the tangible object manipulation technique. Some of the users stated that it was much easier for them to interact with the tangible objects in virtual reality than the virtual ones. Some users also stated that the tangible boxes gave them physical cues and made the tasks easier to perform for them.

None of the users stated preference over the haptic device or touch and snap. We did not observe any difficulties in using the touch and snap interaction. However, the users with ASD found the haptic device difficult to interact as compared to the other interaction techniques. We observed some difficulties in some users with ASD's using the haptic device. It took longer for the individuals with ASD to get comfortable with using this interaction technique as compared to the other interaction techniques.

In overall, most of the users with ASD preferred the touchscreen interaction over all of the other techniques tested. In light of these results, user comments and our observations, we interpret that it is better to implement selection and manipulation techniques that utilize commonly used real life interactions as much as possible for the effective use of individuals with autism in virtual reality applications, such as tangible and touchscreen techniques.

For the locomotion techniques, the most significant difference between the real walking and walk-in-place were in the frustration scores. Users got more frustrated while they were walking-in-place than they were real walking. We observed that it was difficult for the users with ASD to comprehend the walk-in-place gesture and keep doing that without really walking forward in the real world. Users gave better scores to real walking for the ease of interaction, enjoyment, and immersion aspects. The users preferred the real walking technique and stated that they did not like the walk-in-place technique. These results aligned with [31–33]. Although there was no significant difference in the data of individuals with ASD, based on the verbal comments and their preference indications, we interpret that walk-in-place may be a questionable loco-motion technique to be used for individuals with ASD in virtual reality applications. On the other hand, we interpret that real walking can be considered as a suitable method for virtual reality implementations for individuals with autism. Of course, real walking locomotion is not easy to achieve due to the limitation imposed by the motion tracking cameras but as a solution, the tasks in the virtual world would be designed such that the users do not need to go outside the physical tracked area, such as the shelving module of our VR4VR system.

As the display methods were explored, most of the users with ASD preferred the curtain screen over the head mounted display. But as they were interviewed, only one user with ASD stated negative comments about the view through the HMD, mostly about the tired eyes. There weren't any acceptance or adjustment problems, thus we interpret that both the curtain display and the HMD might be used as virtual reality viewing tools for users with ASD. The neurotypical users stated preference for the HMD over the curtain screen. The results were in alignment with [33, 34].

7 Limitations

The user study was performed with nine individuals with high functioning autism. Thus, it should be avoided to generalize these results. The results may not be applicable for the medium or low functioning individuals with ASD. This study was not designed for a thorough evaluation of different interaction, locomotion and display methods. An existing system was utilized to explore the use of interaction, locomotion and display methods in virtual reality by individuals with ASD with the aimed outcome of providing some insight in this area. These techniques were not examined in isolation, but within a larger scope tasks, hence might have been affected by other factors such as the task design and different virtual environments. In the data analysis, univariate analysis of variance (ANOVA) was performed since not all variables were dependent or correlated. However, some variables such as enjoyment and frustration can be considered as dependent, and a multivariate analysis of variance (MANOVA) could give different results. The study results, interpretations and conclusions were not based on solid data, but mostly on the verbal user statements and observations during the user study sessions. Even still, the long hours of testing sessions with the participants gave us the opportunity to observe, discuss and have an initial idea on the suitability of the several virtual reality interaction, locomotion and display methods for the use of individuals with autism.

8 Conclusions

This study aims at exploring different virtual reality interaction techniques for individuals with autism within the VR4VR system. Several interaction techniques of object selection and manipulation, locomotion and display methods were implemented and tested in different contexts. User experience with these interaction techniques were explored with a user study of ten neurotypical individuals and nine individuals with high functioning ASD. For the object selection and manipulation; touchscreen and tangible interaction methods were preferred by the individuals with ASD. The walk-in-place locomotion technique were found frustrating and difficult to perform by the individuals with ASD. Curtain display method received higher preference scores from the individuals with ASD although they accepted the HMD as well. Based on our observations during the user study sessions and the verbal comments made by the participants, we interpret that users with autism are likely to prefer the most realistic and real life linkable interaction techniques while having some difficulties with the gesture based and more abstract ones. Although not based on data analysis results, we still believe that these insights may benefit future VR studies focusing on individuals with ASD.

Future work will consist of implementing several isolated modules for evaluation of different virtual reality interaction and locomotion techniques for individuals with autism. After the modules are implemented, a user study with more individuals with autism will be performed with the aim of revealing suitable virtual reality interaction and locomotion techniques for this group of individuals.

Acknowledgment. The authors would like to thank the Florida Department of Education, Division of Vocational Rehabilitation for funding the VR4VR project.

References

1. Bozgeyikli, E., Bozgeyikli, L., Raij, A., Katkoori, S., Alqasemi, R., Dubey, R.: Virtual reality interaction techniques for individuals with autism spectrum disorder: design considerations and preliminary results. In: Kurosu, M. (ed.) HCI 2016. LNCS, vol. 9732, pp. 127–137. Springer, Cham (2016). https://doi.org/10.1007/978-3-319-39516-6_12
2. Ward, K.: Teaching Students with Autism Spectrum Disorders. Book 9 in the Programming for Students with Special Needs Series. Alberta Learning, Edmonton (2003)
3. Centers for Disease Control and Prevention: Prevalence of Autism Spectrum Disorder among Children Aged 8 Years - Autism and Developmental Disabilities Monitoring Network, 11 Sites, United States, 2010. MMWR Surveillance Summaries 63, SS-2 (2014)
4. Boyle, C.A., Boulet, S., Schieve, L.A., Cohen, R.A., Blumberg, S.J., Yeargin-Allsopp, M., Visser, S., Kogan, M.D.: Trends in the prevalence of developmental disabilities in US children, 1997–2008. Pediatrics **127**, 1034–1042 (2011)
5. Hendricks, D.: Employment and adults with autism spectrum disorders: challenges and strategies for success. J. Vocat. Rehabil. **32**, 125–134 (2010)
6. Barry Issenberg, S., Mcgaghie, W.C., Petrusa, E.R., Lee Gordon, D., Scalese, R.J.: Features and uses of high-fidelity medical simulations that lead to effective learning: a BEME systematic review. Med. Teach. **27**, 10–28 (2005)
7. Hubal, R.C., Frank, G.A.: Interactive training applications using responsive virtual human technology. Children **21**, 25 (2001)
8. Fleming, M., Olsen, D., Stathes, H., Boteler, L., Grossberg, P., Pfeifer, J., Schiro, S., Banning, J., Skochelak, S.: Virtual reality skills training for health care professionals in alcohol screening and brief intervention. J. Am. Board Fam. Med. **22**, 387–398 (2009)
9. Smith, M.J., Ginger, E.J., Wright, K., Wright, M.A., Taylor, J.L., Humm, L.B., Olsen, D.E., Bell, M.D., Fleming, M.F.: Virtual reality job interview training in adults with autism spectrum disorder. J. Autism Dev. Disord. **44**, 2450–2463 (2014)
10. Josman, N., Ben-Chaim, H.M., Friedrich, S., Weiss, P.L.: Effectiveness of virtual reality for teaching street-crossing skills to children and adolescents with autism. In. J. Disabi. Hum. Dev. **7**, 49–56 (2008)
11. Wade, J., Bian, D., Fan, J., Zhang, L., Swanson, A., Sarkar, M., Weitlauf, A., Warren, Z., Sarkar, N.: A virtual reality driving environment for training safe gaze patterns: application in individuals with ASD. In: Antona, M., Stephanidis, C. (eds.) UAHCI 2015. LNCS, vol. 9177, pp. 689–697. Springer, Cham (2015). https://doi.org/10.1007/978-3-319-20684-4_66
12. Goldsmith, T.R., LeBlanc, L.A.: Use of technology in interventions for children with autism. J. Early Intensive Behav. Interv. **1**, 166 (2004)
13. Hale, K.S., Stanney, K.M.: Handbook of Virtual Environments: Design, Implementation, and Applications. CRC Press, Boca Raton (2014)
14. Hourcade, J.P., Williams, S.R., Miller, E.A., Huebner, K.E., Liang, L.J.: Evaluation of tablet apps to encourage social interaction in children with autism spectrum disorders. In: Proceedings of the ACM SIGCHI Conference on Human Factors in Computing Systems, pp. 3197–3206 (2013)
15. Madsen, M., El Kaliouby, R., Eckhardt, M., Hoque, M.E., Goodwin, M.S., Picard, R.: Lessons from participatory design with adolescents on the autism spectrum. In: Proceedings of ACM CHI 2009 Extended Abstracts on Human Factors in Computing Systems, pp. 3835–3840 (2009)
16. Harrold, N., Tan, C.T., Rosser, D.: Towards an expression recognition game to assist the emotional development of children with autism spectrum disorders. In: Proceedings of the Workshop at ACM SIGGRAPH Asia, pp. 33–37 (2012)

17. Kientz, J.A., Hayes, G.R., Westeyn, T.L., Starner, T., Abowd, G.D.: Pervasive computing and autism: Assisting caregivers of children with special needs. IEEE Pervasive Comput. **6**, 28–35 (2007)
18. Bartoli, L., Corradi, C., Garzotto, F., Valoriani, M.: Exploring motion-based touchless games for autistic children's learning. In: Proceedings of the ACM 12th International Conference on Interaction Design and Children, pp. 102–111 (2013)
19. Garzotto, F., Gelsomini, M., Oliveto, L., Valoriani, M.: Motion-based touchless interaction for ASD children: a case study. In: Proceedings of the ACM 2014 International Working Conference on Advanced Visual Interfaces, pp. 117–120 (2014)
20. Parés, N., Carreras, A., Durany, J., Ferrer, J., Freixa, P., Gómez, D., Kruglanski, O., Parés, R., Ribas, J.I., Soler, M., Sanjurjo, À.: Starting research in interaction design with visuals for low-functioning children in the autistic spectrum: a protocol. Cyberpsychol. Behav. **9**, 218–223 (2006)
21. Bauminger-Zviely, N., Eden, S., Zancanaro, M., Weiss, P.L., Gal, E.: Increasing social engagement in children with high-functioning autism spectrum disorder using collaborative technologies in the school environment. Autism **17**, 317–339 (2013)
22. Sitdhisanguan, K., Chotikakamthorn, N., Dechaboon, A., Out, P.: Using tangible user interfaces in computer-based training systems for low-functioning autistic children. Pers. Ubiquit. Comput. **16**, 143–155 (2012)
23. Mei, C., Mason, L., Quarles, J.: Usability issues with 3D user interfaces for adolescents with high functioning autism. In: Proceedings of the 16th International ACM SIGACCESS Conference on Computers and Accessibility, pp. 99–106 (2014)
24. Unity Game Engine. https://unity3d.com/. Accessed 23 Feb 2018
25. MiddleVR Middleware. http://www.middlevr.com/. Accessed 23 Feb 2018
26. OptiTrack Motion capture systems. http://optitrack.com/. Accessed 23 Feb 2018
27. Rosenberg, M., Vance, J.M.: Virtual hand representations to support natural interaction in immersive environments. In: Proceedings of the ASME 2013 International Design Engineering Technical Conferences and Computers and Information in Engineering Conference, pp. V02BT02A028–V002BT002A028 (2013)
28. Sensable. http://www.sensable.com/haptic-phantom-omni.html. Accessed 13 June 2016
29. Loftis, S.F.: Imagining Autism: Fiction and Stereotypes on the Spectrum. Indiana University Press, Bloomington (2015)
30. Likert, R.: A technique for the measurement of attitudes. Arch. Psychol. **140**, 5–55 (1932)
31. Slater, M., Usoh, M., Steed, A.: Taking steps: the influence of a walking technique on presence in virtual reality. ACM Trans. Comput. Hum. Interact. (TOCHI) **2**, 201–219 (1995)
32. Usoh, M., Arthur, K., Whitton, M.C., Bastos, R., Steed, A., Slater, M., Frederick P., Brooks, J.: Walking > walking-in-place > flying, in virtual environments. In: the Proceedings of the 26th Annual Conference on Computer Graphics and Interactive Techniques, pp. 359–364 (1999)
33. Zanbaka, C., Babu, S., Xiao, D., Ulinski, A., Hodges, L.F., Lok, B.: Effects of travel technique on cognition in virtual environments. In: Proceedings of IEEE Virtual Reality, pp. 149–286 (2004)
34. Zanbaka, C., Lok, B.C., Babu, S.V., Ulinski, A.C., Hodges, L.F.: Comparison of path visualizations and cognitive measures relative to travel technique in a virtual environment. IEEE Trans. Visual Comput. Graphics **11**, 694–705 (2005)

Analysis of Human Motion and Cognition Ability with Virtual Reality System

Basic Mechanism of Human Response

Kouki Nagamune[(✉)] and Keisuke Takata

Graduate School of Engineering, University of Fukui, Fukui, Japan
nagamune@u-fukui.ac.jp

Abstract. When grasping an object, a human needs to recognize the object. In general, after the center of gravity of the object is recognized from the object shape, the human grasps a position close to the center of gravity. This research analyzes the relationship between the object shape and the sight trajectory until grasping. The proposed method traces finger motions when grasping the virtual 3D objects displayed on a screen by using finger motion capture device. In the motion, the sight trajectory is also measured and analyzed by using the eye tracking device. We conducted experiments with five subjects and analyzed the relationship between the variation of the line of sight trajectory and the size of the grasped object.

Keywords: Virtual reality · Rehabilitation · Motion

1 Introduction

The number of persons who has handicap or paralysis in daily living motion is increasing with years. As one of the reason, an increasement of the survival rate in stroke patients can be considered. In Japan, the survival rate was doubled in the past five decade [1, 2]. This results in that patients would have paralysis in the after-effect of the stroke. However, the paralysis has a variety. Daily motion consists of recognition, judgement, and reaction. Usually, only the reaction relating with motor function is focused as the target of rehabilitation. Recognition function is often ignored for grasping motion. The purpose of this study is to reveal the relationship of recognition and reaction. Especially, this study focuses on response time of recognition and reaction.

The target motion is to grasp objects. Grasping is an important motion in daily life, therefore, many researchers reports many kinds of rehabilitation for the grasping [3–5]. However, studies relating with recognition ability is rare [6, 7]. In the grasping motion, we firstly recognize the target. Then, we secondly grasp the target. If the reaction ability is low, naturally, success rate of the grasping might be low. But, we assume that the recognition ability also effects the success rate of the grasping. Therefore, we propose an evaluation system for recognition and motor functions in grasping motion.

© Springer International Publishing AG, part of Springer Nature 2018
M. Antona and C. Stephanidis (Eds.): UAHCI 2018, LNCS 10908, pp. 78–86, 2018.
https://doi.org/10.1007/978-3-319-92052-8_7

2   Method

Human motion consists of recognition and motor functions. They firstly recognize an environment, then secondly move their body according with the environment. However, human motion ability decreases with aging called as sarcopenia. Generally, sarcopenia is thought to be with motor function. The relation with sarcopenia and recognition function is unclear. This study aims to reveal the relationship by using virtual reality system. This study focuses on recognition and motion times in grasping.

Unity (Unity 5.5.1.f1(64 bit), Unity Technologies Inc.) is used for constructing a virtual 3D environment as shown in Fig. 1. Eye tracker (Steel Series Sentry Gaming Eye Tracker 69041,) is used for measuring eye motion as shown in Fig. 2. Leap Motion (Leap Motion Controller, Leap Motion Inc.) is used for measuring finger motion as shown in Fig. 3.

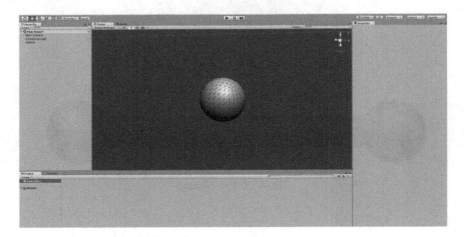

Fig. 1. Unity

In the experiment, subjects first calibrate Eye tracker. After that, on Unity, display the hand obtained from Eye tracker and the position obtained from LeapMotion. Both of them are checked to be correctly reflected in Unity. The experiment is measured from the state in which the subject gazes at the center point on Unity. Let the object (Fig. 4) appear three seconds after the start of measurement. The subjects move the line of sight and hand so that the hand on Unity grasps the object. After grasping, lowers the hand and gazes at the first center point. This is the experimental procedure. The x-y coordinate system (Fig. 5) of the eye motion and the bending angle of the finger were measured from the start to the end of the experiment.

Since it is necessary for the subject to recognize and recognize the object and perform the actions to grasp naturally, the object is hide before starting measurement. The appearance position was also changed every time, and the object itself was also grasped in the same way with the original angle and rotated by 90° around the z axis as shown in Fig. 6. The shape of the target object adopts the shape of the iron dumbbell of

Fig. 2. Eye tracker

Fig. 3. Leap motion

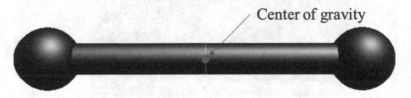

Center of gravity

Fig. 4. Target object

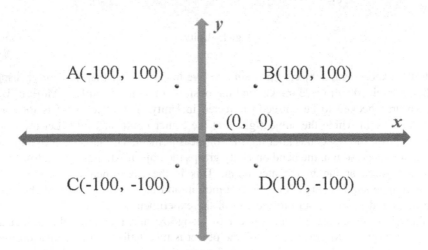

Fig. 5. Coordinate system

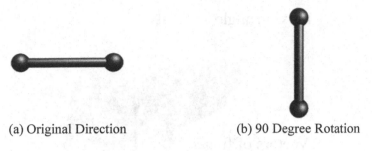

(a) Original Direction   (b) 90 Degree Rotation

Fig. 6. Iron dumbbell direction

a shape that the appearance seems to be heavy and easy to hold since the process until the subject guesses and grasps its center of gravity is important. The radius The x-y coordinates of the measured line of sight has the center point as (0, 0), with the upper right as positive and the lower left as negative. Also, let the coordinates of the movement of the center of gravity of the object be A (−100, 100), B (100, 100), C (−100, −100), D (100, −100) [mm]).

The virtual hand is displayed on the monitor with virtual display environment developed by Unity as shown in Fig. 7. The virtual hand moves real user hand by capturing the motion with Leap Motion. Leap Motion can obtain the 3D position of each joint of the hand. The obtained joint information can make the bending angle in grasping motion. The bending angle of the finger is obtained from the angle between the base phalanx of the middle finger and the metacarpal bone as shown in Fig. 8. By this way, time series data while grasping the objects is obtained.

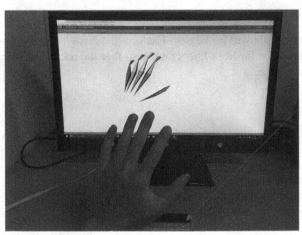

Leap Motion

Fig. 7. Virtual hand

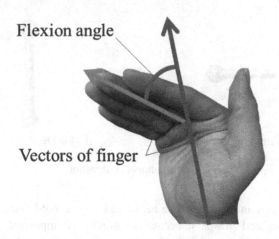

Fig. 8. Bending angle

3 Experiments

3.1 Subjects

Experiments were conducted with five healthy volunteers (23 ± 1 year old, right handed), and each one had four positions of the 3D object (upper left, lower left, upper right, lower right on the display screen), two orientations (horizontal and Vertical direction) in total 8 times. The order of measurement was randomized to minimize the learning process.

3.2 Measurement Environment

Measurement environment is shown in Fig. 9. Each parameters are tabulated in Table 1. Leap Motion is set to be far from Eye Tracker so that the user hand does not prevent from tracking eye motion.

3.3 Measurement Items

This study performs two experiments. The first one is to check characteristics eye motion without target. In this experiment, let subjects to look at the center of display. The second one is to track eye and grasping motions.

4 Results

4.1 Eye Motion Without Target

The result is shown in Table 2. This value shows the distance from the center of the display. A direction dependency to x and y axes was not observed. The maximum and minimum distances are 34.359 mm and 12.191 mm, respectively.

Eye Tracker

Leap Motion

Fig. 9. Measurement environment

Table 1. Measurement parameters

Height of chair [mm]	400
Height of desk [mm]	700
Distance to display screen [mm]	500
Distance to Leap Motion [mm]	200

Table 2. The result of eye motion without target

Subjects	X (mm)	Y (mm)	Distance (mm)
#1	18.894	16.133	24.845
#2	11.173	4.876	12.191
#3	4.400	34.076	34.359
#4	14.897	9.965	17.923
#5	12.007	17.161	20.944

4.2 Eye Motion and Finger Motion

The average of the time (t_1) from the appearance of the object of each subject to fixation and the average of the time (t_2) from fixation to grasp are calculated as shown in Fig. 10. The average of the errors of the x and y coordinates of the center of gravity of the first fixed fixture and the center of gravity of the object and t_1 for each of the x and y coordinates. Each response time of all the data is tabulated in Table 3. Table 4 shows the difference between target direction. Figures 11 and 12 show the distributions in 0° angle and 90° angle, respectively.

About the errors in the coordinates of fixation and the coordinates of the center of gravity of the object, we can see that the first gazing coordinates are focused on the hand position of the object regardless of the orientation of the object. In response to this change, the object to be held was changed to a spherical object with no concept of

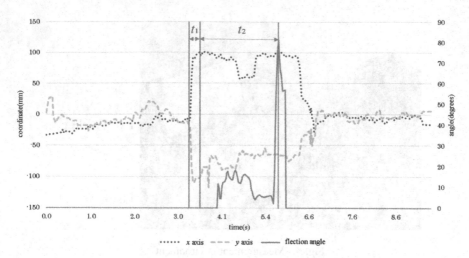

Fig. 10. An example of the motion data

Table 3. The results of response time

Subjects	t_1 (s)	t_2 (s)
#1	0.300	1.721
#2	0.222	1.795
#3	0.383	1.958
#4	0.677	2.001
#5	0.224	2.120

Table 4. The difference between target direction

Rotation angle (degree)	Coordinate system	t_1 (s)	Distance between fixation and the center of gravity of the object
0	x	0.395	25.497
	y	0.229	19.877
90	x	0.264	7.732
	y	0.594	25.596

orientation, and the same process as the experiment of this time was carried out to the subject. As for the result, the coordinates which fixed to the center of the object also concentrated here. From this result, when a person tries to grasp, he sees the center of the target object. After that, it can be inferred that after moving the line of sight, obtaining information such as the size of the object, the center of gravity, and so forth, it moves to the grasping action. The time during which the information at this time is obtained corresponds to t_2. Moreover, since the vertical direction of the vertical direction is longer than the value of t_1 in the vertical direction and the horizontal

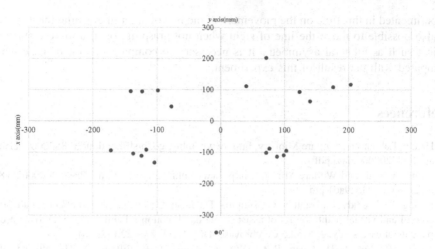

Fig. 11. The distribution of fixation in 0°

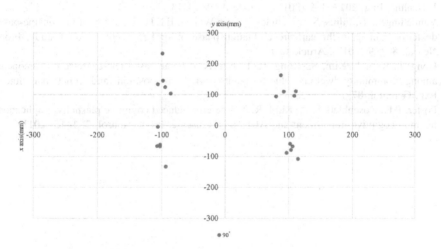

Fig. 12. The distribution of fixation in 90°

direction, it is consistent with the theory that human eyes are more likely to enter the field of view than in the vertical direction.

5 Conclusion

As a future work, in the eye gaze measurement, the Eye tracker was calibrated for each subject at the beginning of the experiment, but a deviation of about several millimeters was confirmed at Unity's operation confirmation. In the future, improvement of the experimental environmental equipment can be mentioned to improve the accuracy. Although the gaze point coordinates of the object to be gripped have been experimented in this time on the movement of the line of sight in grasping the object, it is also possible to move the line of sight when not grasping, or to a more distinctive object such as bilateral asymmetry It is necessary to compare motion of gaze when compared with the result of this experiment.

References

1. Health, Labour and Welfare Ministry. http://www.mhlw.go.jp/stf/houdou/2r9852000002iau1-att/2r9852000002iavi.pdf
2. Health, Labour and Welfare Ministry. http://www.mhlw.go.jp/stf/shingi/2r98520000029a85-att/2r98520000029ad1.pdf
3. Huang, X., Naghdy, F., Naghdy, G., Haiping, D., Todd, C.: The combined effects of adaptive control and virtual reality on robot-assisted fine hand motion rehabilitation in chronic stroke patients: a case study. J. Stroke Cerebrovasc. Dis. 27(1), 221–228 (2018)
4. Yeh, S.-C., Lee, S.-H., Chan, R.-C., Wu, Y., Zheng, L.-R., Flynn, S.: The efficacy of a haptic-enhanced virtual reality system for precision grasp acquisition in stroke rehabilitation. J. Healthc. Eng. 2017, 1–9 (2017). Article ID 9840273
5. Vanbellingen, T., Filius, S.J., Nyffeler, T., van Wegen, E.E.H.: Usability of videogame-based dexterity training in the early rehabilitation phase of stroke patients: a pilot study. Front. Neurol. 8, 1–9 (2017). Article 654
6. Hong, J., Kim, J., Kim, S., Kong, H.-J.: Effects of home-based tele-exercise on sarcopenia among community-dwelling elderly adults: body composition and functional fitness. Exp. Gerontol. 87, 33–39 (2017)
7. Foster, P.P., Rosenblatt, K.P., Kulji, R.O.: Exercise-induced cognitive plasticity, implications for mild cognitive impairment and Alzheimer's disease. Front. Neurol. 2, 1–15 (2011)

Effectiveness of Virtual Reality Survival Horror Games for the Emotional Elicitation: Preliminary Insights Using Resident Evil 7: Biohazard

Federica Pallavicini[✉], Ambra Ferrari, Alessandro Pepe,
Giacomo Garcea, Andrea Zanacchi, and Fabrizia Mantovani

Department of Human Sciences for Education "Riccardo Massa",
University of Milan Bicocca, Milan, Italy
federica.pallavicini@gmail.com

Abstract. Survival horror games played in virtual reality can trigger intense fright and anxiety in the players. Such unique characteristics can thus be exploited not only as a source of entertainment, but also as a tool for both emotion elicitation and emotional training. However, studies investigating the players' experience and the emotional activation while playing virtual reality video games are still very limited and horror games represent an even more limited number of these. Within this context, this study was aimed to compare a horror game Resident Evil 7: Biohazard, experienced through virtual reality as opposed to a non-immersive display modality (i.e. console system), and exploring differences in the usability and the emotional activation. In order to answer to such objectives, the game was played by a sample of 26 young adults, half of which played using Playstation VR, while the other half through a more traditional non-immersive console setup (PS4 Pro). The usability and the emotional impact of the game was assessed through self-report questionnaires and the recording of physiological indexes (heart rate, skin conductance response). Results showed that: (a) playing a horror video game in virtual reality was not more difficult than playing in a non-immersive display modality; (b) players showed an increased perceived anxiety both after playing the horror video game in virtual reality and playing in a non-immersive display modality; interestingly, the perceived sense of happiness significantly increased only after playing in virtual reality; finally the sense of presence resulted to be greater in virtual reality as opposed to the non-immersive condition.

Keywords: Virtual reality · Video games · Survival horror games
Emotion

1 Introduction

1.1 Virtual Reality and Survival Horror Video Games

In the last years, virtual reality has become a booming trend in the video game and entertainment industry [1, 2]. Starting from 2016, in particular, there has been an actual

© Springer International Publishing AG, part of Springer Nature 2018
M. Antona and C. Stephanidis (Eds.): UAHCI 2018, LNCS 10908, pp. 87–101, 2018.
https://doi.org/10.1007/978-3-319-92052-8_8

breakthrough in the gaming business, thanks to the entry in the mass market of several commercial head mounted displays, including Oculus Rift (Oculus), HTC Vive (HTC and Valve corp.), and PlayStation VR (Sony corp.). Only in 2017 over 7249 games developed for virtual reality have been released on the Steam platform [3], while Sony Corp, by June 2017, had already sold more than one million units of its virtual reality headset globally [2].

Among the most successful video games developed for virtual reality, horror games constitute one of the most played genres in 2017 [4]. One of the best-selling games of this genre is Resident Evil 7: Biohazard (Capcom, 2017), the last chapter of the renowned saga that first introduced the term "survival horror" with Resident Evil (Capcom, 1996), and that, by November 2017, achieved an impressive number of 307,884 VR users, comprising 11.55% of the total Resident Evil 7: Biohazard player base [5].

Survival horror games played in virtual reality, thanks to a high level of immersion, defined as a "quantifiable description of a technology, which includes the extent to which the computer displays are extensive, surrounding, inclusive, vivid and matching" [6], can trigger real fright in the players, who are required to actively decide how and when to respond to such threats and manage to survive [7]. Compared to non-immersive display modalities that use a monitor as a graphical interface for users, through virtual reality the player can perform as an actor [6], and actually feel an intense sense of presence, namely "the extent to which a user feels present in a virtual environment [8]", allowing real emotions to be activated by such environment [9, 10].

In virtual reality horror video games, such unique characteristics of "mediated fright" can thus be exploited not only as a source of entertainment, but also as a therapy tool: as a feeling of fear comparable to what is experienced in the real world can be obtained in a realistic yet safe environment, this kind of games can have important applications for both emotion elicitation and emotional training, including the assessment and training of emotional skills (such as stress management and emotional regulation skills), as well as for the therapy of anxiety disorders and phobias [7, 11].

Previous studies suggested in fact that virtual reality is more emotion-inducing than content presented with less immersive technologies (e.g., video, audio) [12], and that it can induce emotional and behavioral responses similar to those that occur in the real world [13, 14]. In addition, studies have reported that commercial video games combining the horror genre and biofeedback techniques could be useful stressors to practice stress management skills [15]. Furthermore, players' fright reactions and coping strategies in an immersive virtual reality horror game have recently been investigated [7], showing that this kind of games provides an excellent means to simulate close-rangephysical threats, and consequently are proven to be useful tools through which toobserve how people react to, and cope with, such fearful stimuli

Despite such interesting results, studies investigating the players' experience and the emotional activation while playing virtual reality video games are still very limited [e.g., 16–18], and studies concerning survival horror games represent an even more limited number of these [i.e., 7]. A deep scientific understanding of the characteristics of virtual reality video games compared to games delivered through non-immersive modalities and of what and how elements elicit effective mediated frights in virtual reality horror games could be fundamental for theoretical contributions and practical implications for entertainment, as well as for the assessment and training of emotional skills [19].

1.2 Aim of the Study

Within the context described above, this study was aimed to compare the usability of acommercial survival horror video game, Resident Evil 7: Biohazard (Capcom 2017), experienced through virtual reality as opposed to a non-immersive display modality (i.e., console system), and to explore differences in the emotional activation while playing the horror video game in the two experimental conditions, and to explore differences in the emotional activation while playing the horror video game in virtual reality or through console. In order to answer to such objectives, Resident Evil 7: Biohazard was played by a sample of 26 young adults, half of which played with a virtual reality device (Playstation VR, Sony Corp.), while the other half through a more traditional non-immersive console setup (PS4 Pro, Sony Corp.). The players' experience has been evaluated in terms of performance, usability, and emotional impact through both self-report questionnaires and the recording of physiological indexes (heart rate and skin conductance response).

More in detail, the main hypotheses explored by the research were:

- (H1) No differences in performance and usability between the two versions of the game: while in the past most video games research has focused on understanding outcomes of playing games [e.g., 20, 21], recently there has been a shift towards understanding how specific game features, especially display devices (virtual reality vs. non-immersive ones, such as desktop modality) can affect the player experience [22–24]. Despite scientific literature exploring the differences between virtual reality video games and non-immersive ones is still limited [17, 18, 24, 25], on the basis of a previous exploratory study we can hypothesize that no differences in performance and usability will be found between the two conditions of the game (virtual reality opposed to non-immersive console setup) [18].
- (H2) The horror game is able to elicit in the players a sense of anxiety, both innon-immersive modality [e.g., 15, 26, 27] and in virtual reality [7]: in particular we hypothesize that such anxious response will be accompanied by a positive emotional response [28–31], and an increased sense of presence [12, 32, 33] when compared to a game experienced in a non-immersive modality (i.e., console).

2 Methods

2.1 Participants

26 participants - 7 females (26.9%) and 19 males (73.1%); age m = 22.65 (SD = 2.54); years of education m = 15.2 (SD = 3.2) - were recruited among students and personnel of the University of Milano-Bicocca and of other universities in Milan. No credits (ECTS) nor economic rewards were provided during the research. In order to be included in the study, individuals had to meet the following criteria: (1) age between 18 and 35 years old; (2) no major medical disorders (heart disease or high blood pressure, neurological disorders, epilepsy); (3) no left-handed; (4) no presence of pharmacotherapy (psychoactive drugs, anti-hypertensive, anti-depressants); (5) no significant visual impairment (all with normal or corrected-to-normal visual acuity).

Before participating, all participants were provided with written information about the study and were required to give written consent in order to be included. The study received ethical approval by the Ethical Committee of the University of Milano-Bicocca. The research was conducted in accordance to American Psychological Association [34] ethical principles and code of conduct.

2.2   Measures

A multi-trait (i.e. focused on both psychological constructs and physiological measures of users' experience) and multi-method (i.e. based on the integrated use of different technical and methodological solutions) approach has been used, previously tested during pilot studies conducted by the researchers involved in this empirical experimentation [18, 35].

In particular, the following self-report questionnaire was given to the participants at the start of the experimental session:

- *Demographics, gaming habits and virtual reality knowledge:* individuals were asked to indicate their gender (female/male), age (years old), their gaming habits (mean hours spent gaming per week), their previous experience with Resident Evil 7: Biohazard (yes/no). In addition, they were asked to assess their knowledge of virtual reality on a 7-point Likert scale.

Furthermore, the following self-administered questionnaires were used to measure the subjective indexes concerning individuals' emotional state:

- *State-Trait Anxiety Inventory, Form-Y2 (STAI-Y2)* [36]: A validated and widely used measure of trait anxiety (STAI-Y2). Individuals are asked to specify to which extent, on a 4–point Likert scale (from "not at all" to "very much"), they usually perceive each of the 20 indicated feelings;
- *Visual Analogue Scale for Subjective Feelings of Anxiety (VAS-A)*: an horizontal line, 100 mm in length, anchored by word descriptors at each end. Participants mark on the line the point that they feel to visually represent their perception of their current level of anxiety;
- *Visual Analogue Scale for Subjective Feelings of Happiness (VAS-HP), and Surprise (VAS-SP):* Participants mark on the line the point that they feel to visually represent their perception of their current level of happiness (VAS-HP), and Surprise (VAS-SP).

Finally, after the game, the following self-administered questionnaires were used to measure the subjective indexes concerning the gaming experience:

- *Slater-Usoh-Steed Presence Questionnaire (SUS-II)* [37]: a custom questionnaire concerning the perceived sense of presence, divided into 6 items on a 7-point Likert scale. A single total score is obtained;
- *System Usability Score (SUS)* [38]: a reliable tool for measuring the usability. It consists of a 10-items questionnaire with five response options for respondents (from "strongly agree" to "strongly disagree"), concerning the ease of use or the difficulties encountered by the participant while using the system.

Psychophysiological Assessment. Physiological data can be valuable in helping to read the emotional state of game players [e.g., 39, 40]. For this reason, in this study at the beginning of the experimental session and during the gaming experience, the following psychophysiological data were recorded: Heartbeat (HR), measured with Electrocardiogram (ECG), and Skin Conductance Response (SCR). In particular, HR mean value, measured in Beats per Minute (BMP), was calculated through R-to-R peak detection. The physiological signals have been acquired using a ProComp Infiniti device from Thought Technology, including Biograph Infiniti 5.0.2 software to record and export all raw signals. Every signal was exported at a 256 Hz sampling rate.

Video Game (Resident Evil 7: Biohazard). A first-person survival horror game, the seventh chapter of the Resident Evil saga, one of the best-selling and most famous series of this genre. In Resident Evil 7: Biohazard (Capcom, 2017), the player assumes the role of Ethan, a man who receives an unexpected email from a woman claiming to be his wife Mia, who however has been presumed dead for several years. The gameplay experience proposed during the experiment has been selected among the initial phases of the game. The players will find themselves in an abandoned mansion, in particular in a corridor with three doors, one of which leads back to the basement from which the main character came. After exploring the corridor and the bathroom, the players have to retrace their steps to the basement, where a short cut-scene (a non-interactive scene that breaks up the gameplay) begins. The players will be attacked by a monstrous version of Mia and will have to press the R2 button repeatedly in order to free themselves from the attacking woman, who will regain awareness for a short moment, then collapse on the floor. It takes approximately 4 min to complete this gameplay. The game's difficulty has been set on standard, which is the difficulty Resident Evil 7: Biohazard is automatically set at the beginning of a new game.

Experimental Design. A between-subjects design has been used to compare emotional responses and usability of the two experimental conditions. Specifically, the study compared the following conditions:

- *Virtual Reality (Immersive) Condition.* Participants were seated at a desk and were asked to wear the PlayStation VR (Sony Corp.), connected to a PS4 Pro (Sony Corp.) on which they played the selected game. After a brief training about the PlayStation VR's controls, participants started to play the game using the standard wireless controller of the PS4 (Sony Corp.);
- *Console (Non-immersive) Condition.* Individuals were seated at a desk on which a PS4 Pro (Sony Corp.), and a 32" TV monitor (Samsung HD Flat Series 4 K4100) were positionedat a distance of about 1.5 m from the monitor. Participants were asked to play thegame using the standard wireless controller of the PS4 (Sony Corp.).

Procedure. Participants were randomly assigned to the condition, counterbalanced for the total individuals through an established randomization scheme obtained from http://www.randomizer.org/. At the start of the experimental session, individuals were asked to complete the self-report questionnaire about their demographics, gaming habits and virtual reality knowledge, the STAY-Y2, VAS-A, VAS-HP, VAS-SP. Participants were then connected with biosensors to record their HR and SCR. A baseline measure of these signals was registered for 3 min in rest condition, with eyes opened. Once the physiological baseline was recorded, the experimental session started, and psychophysiological signals were recorded while the participants completed the game. After completion, participants answered the following self-reported questionnaires: VAS-A, VAS-HP, VAS-SP, SUS-II, and SUS.

Strategy of Data Analysis. Data were analyzed by mean of a set of multivariate statistical tests. First, common assumptions (normality, homogeneity of variance, and homoscedasticity) for multivariate analysis were assessed and procedures of data cleaning (missing values analysis, detection of uni- and multi-variate outliers) were conducted. In general, major violation to assumptions were not found and a multi-variate outlier was skipped. Then, first-order correlation analysis, controlled for the effect of condition, among scores were conducted in order to check the viability of other analysis.

With the aim of verifying the comparability of the sample divided into the two experimental groups, Chi-square tests of independence and independent sample t-tests were calculated on the demographic statistics and on the state characteristics (using both self-report questionnaires and physiological indicators) previous to the gameplay experience.

In line with the epistemological framework of hypothesis 1, plain t-test analyses was conducted in order to test potential differences about the two condition with regards of performance and usability scores. In order to support research hypothesis 2, a series of Generalized Linear Model (GLM) for repeated measures were computed. Such kind of analysis is useful in measuring the effect of a "treatment" at different time points and in different groups. Furthermore, GLM allowed to evaluate the main effect within and between the subjects as well as interaction effects between factors. Finally, GLM estimated the magnitude of effect sizes for all variables. In the present study, the GLM model were in such a way that pre/post measures were the within-subject factor (i.e. two levels) whereas the condition (Virtual Reality vs Console) was the between-subject factor. The interactive effect within*between was included into the model.

3   Results

3.1   Demographics

A Chi-square test of independence was calculated in the two experimental conditions comparing gender and participants' previous experience with Resident Evil 7: Biohazard. No statistically significant differences were found (see Table 1).

Independent sample t-tests revealed no statistically significant differences in participants' age, years of education, hours spent gaming per week, knowledge of videogames, and knowledge of virtual reality (see Table 2).

Similarly, independent sample t-tests revealed no differences between the two experimental conditions in the participants' characteristics, as assessed by STAY-Y2 (Virtual Reality: m = 44.1; SD = 10.1, Console: m = 40.5; SD = 8.56; t(24) = −.967;

Table 1. Chi-square test of independence on gender, and previous experience with Resident Evil 7: Biohazard in the two experimental conditions (Virtual Reality, N = 13; Console, N = 13)

Variable		Virtual Reality	Console	Chi-square	gl	p
Genre	Female	3	4			
	Male	10	9	.195	1	.658
Previous experience with Resident Evil 7: Biohazard	Yes	3	2			
	No	10	11	.248	1	.619

Table 2. Independent sample t-tests on age, years of education, hours spent gaming per week, knowledge of videogames, and knowledge of virtual reality in the two experimental conditions (Virtual Reality, N = 13; Console, N = 13)

Variable	Condition	m	SD	t	gl	p
Age	Virtual reality	23.4	2.87	1.67	24	.107
	Console	21.8	1.95			
Years of education	Virtual reality	14.6	2.06	−.916	24	.561
	Console	15.7	4.04			
Hours spent gaming per week	Virtual reality	13.7	9.4	−.345	24	.733
	Console	15	10.9			
Knowledge of virtual reality	Virtual reality	3.69	1.97	−.102	24	.920
	Console	3.77	1.87			

p = .343), VAS-A (Virtual Reality: m = 24.6; SD = 25.9, Console: m = 26; SD = 32.2; t(24) = −.122 p = .904), VAS-HP (Virtual Reality: m = 67.5; SD = 20.6, Console: m = 68.3; SD = 16.3; t(24) = −.101; p = .921), VAS-SP (Virtual Reality: m = 43; SD = 35.7, Console: m = 26.7; SD = 23.8; t(24) = 1.36; p = .185), HR (Virtual Reality: m = 80.4; SD = 13.4, Console: m = 83.3; SD = 12.1; t(24) = −.579; p = .568), and SCR (Virtual Reality: m = 11.1; SD = 5.71, Console: m = 8.21; SD = 7.88; t(24) = 1.1; p = .282).

3.2 Hypothesis 1

An independent sample t-test was conducted to compare participants' performance in Virtual Reality and Console conditions. Results revealed that there was not a statistically significant difference in the total time required to complete the game for Virtual Reality (m = 226, SD = 49.7) and Console (m = 230, SD = 68.7) conditions; t(24) = .160, p = 87. In a similar way, the condition (m = 80.4, SD = 7.96; m = 83.67, SD = 11.7) seemed to not affect scores on SUS (t(24) = .830, p = .87). The analysis provide support to the first hypothesis of the study and no effect sizes were found.

3.3 Hypothesis 2

Generalized Linear Model for repeated measures was used to test whether and to what extent the pre-post differences on psychometric (VAS-A, VAS-HP, VAS-SP) and psychophysiological (HR and SCR) scores on emotional activation were related to Virtual Reality or Console conditions.

First of all, regarding the self-report questionnaires, the model testing scores on VAS-A resulted statistically significant ($F(1, 24) = 4.51$, $p < .05^*$, $\eta^2 = .170$) meaning that, regardless the condition ($F(1, 24) = 0.13$, $p = .99$, $\eta^2 = .004$), participant feelings of anxiety were high at the end of the experience. In contrast, VAS-HP revealed a different dynamics (see Fig. 2). In fact, the GLM suggested that at the end of the experience, scores on happiness in Virtual Reality condition had grown, whereas in Console condition had decreased ($F(1, 24) = 4.28$, $p < .05^*$, $\eta^2 = .152$). Finally, the model testing scores on VAS-SP did not revealed a statistical significance $F(1, 24) = 2.89$, $p = .10$, $\eta^2 = .023$.

With regards to physiological measures, the results of GLM revealed a large main effect of the pre/post factor ($F(1, 24) = 23.26$, $p < .05^*$, $\eta^2 = .50$) in relation to mean of heart beats. Such effect was not detected in relation to the condition ($F(1, 24) = .61$, $p = .44$, $\eta^2 = .025$). A similar large and statistically significant main effect was also found in relation to skin conductance ($F(1, 24) = 50.77$, $p < .05^*$, $\eta^2 = .68$) regardless the condition $F(1, 24) = .26$, $p = .61$, $\eta^2 = .011$). Means and standard deviations for all variables in each condition were summarized in Table 3.

Finally, an independent sample t-test was used to compare participants' scores at SUS-II after the two experimental conditions. Results revealed a statistically significant difference in the feeling of presence for Virtual Reality (m = 26.9, SD = 6.91) and Console (m = 20.6, SD = 7.8) conditions; $t(24) = 2.18$, $p < .05^*$, $\eta^2 = .50$ (Fig. 2).

4 Discussion

The purpose of this study was to compare the effectiveness of emotional induction caused by virtual reality horror video games if compared to non-immersive ones, such as console games. As such, we want to extend the currently existing academic knowledge about the possible effectiveness of commercial virtual reality video games, in particular of the horror genre, and their possible use as tools for both emotion elicitation and emotional training. Seen video games' intrinsic characteristics of being motivating, engaging, and easily accessible [41], combined with the characteristics of virtual reality as an interactive and deeply immersive instrument [42, 43], virtual reality video games represent potentially useful, low cost, and easily accessible tools to be used in the treatment of anxiety disorders and phobias, as well as to assess and train the healthy individuals' emotional skills.

Starting form the first main hypothesis of this study, we confirmed that playing the horror video game Resident Evil 7: Biohazard (Capcom 2017) in virtual reality did not result to be more complex than playing the classic version of the game (i.e., on the console). Data showed in fact no statistically significant differences between the virtual

Table 3. Summary of VAS-A, VAS-HP, VAS-SP, heart beats (HR) and skin conductance response (SCR) scores in different experimental conditions (Virtual Reality, N = 13; Console, N = 13)

Variable	Condition	Time	m	SD
VAS-A	Virtual reality	Pre	21.7	21.6
		Post	31.1	21.5
	Console	Pre	18.3	23.8
		Post	27.8	14.2
VAS-HP	Virtual reality	Pre	67.5	20.6
		Post	75.9	18.1
	Console	Pre	68.3	16.3
		Post	59.6	20.8
VAS-SP	Virtual reality	Pre	43.1	35.7
		Post	57.1	35.3
	Console	Pre	26.7	23.9
		Post	32.2	21.5
HR	Virtual reality	Pre	80.4	13.4
		Post	92.4	10.7
	Console	Pre	83.3	12.1
		Post	91.9	18.2
SCR	Virtual reality	Pre	11.1	5.71
		Post	15.7	6.01
	Console	Pre	8.21	7.88
		Post	13.4	9.3

reality and console version of the horror video game in terms of total time required to complete the gameplay, and of usability, assessed through the SUS questionnaire [38].

These results seem to be in line with what has been observed in a previous exploratory study [18], in which playing a first-person shooter game Smash Hit (Mediocre 2014) in virtual reality did not result to be more difficult than playing the same video game on a non-immersive mobile device (i.e., the iPad). It is interesting to note that in both studies the majority of the sample population presented a low previous knowledge of virtual reality, possibly suggesting that naive users as well perceive this technology as pleasant and easy to use. VVirtual reality video games, however representing a new or not well-known game experience for the majority of the players, characterized by deeply different characteristics if compared with non-immersive set ups (e.g., PC, console or mobile gaming) [18, 44], do not result to be perceived as more complex compared to more traditional non-immersive gaming modalities.

Results obtained from past experiments comparing non-immersive to virtual reality display modalities reported a different global tendency, stating that individuals tend to perform better when using traditional systems [17, 45, 46]. Nonetheless, it is important to underline that such experiments, when compared to the present one, did not use commercial virtual reality video games as stimuli, but game-like situations (i.e., navigation and wayfinding tasks), and virtual reality hardware systems that are very

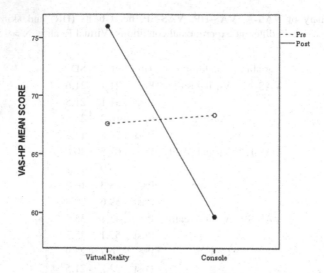

Fig. 1. Generalized Linear Model for repeated measures on the VAS-HP scores before and after the two experimental conditions. Scores in Virtual Reality condition had grown, whereas in Console condition had decreased (F(1, 24) = 4.28, p < .05*, η^2 = .152).

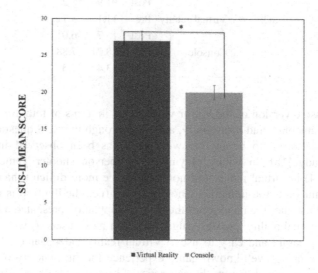

Fig. 2. Independent sample t-test on participants' scores at SUS-II after the two experimental conditions Results revealed statistically significant values, in particular an increased feeling of presence for Virtual Reality if compared to Console conditions; t(24) = 2.18, p < .05*.

different from what is commercially available nowadays. These elements could explain the differences between what emerged from the present study and previous results. However, future studies are needed to investigate the differences in players' experience between video games presented through virtual reality compared to non-immersive devices, in order to better understand the relationship between interactivity, the intensity of emotional response, and players' performance.

Secondly, the survival horror video game was confirmed to be effective in eliciting anxious emotional responses in individuals, similarly to what has been observed in previous studies, both in non-immersive [15, 26, 27], and immersive set ups [7]. In particular, results showed a significant increase of perceived anxiety as assessed with self-report questionnaires (VAS-A) and with physiological indexes (heart rate and skin conductance response) after playing the survival horror game, without significant differences in the intensity of the anxious response between the two conditions.

Interestingly, statistically significant differences were instead observed in relation with the users' self-reported feeling of happiness, assessed through the VAS-HP. In particular, results revealed that, while the perceived feeling of happiness increased after the virtual reality game experience, the opposite result was obtained after the console gameplay, namely a decrease in the sense of happiness in comparison to the baseline.

Such results seem to be consistent with previous literature: virtual reality has already been demonstrated to successfully induce positive moods [28–31]. In particular, studies showed that it is possible to evoke positive emotions with virtual reality in healthy individuals [e.g., 30], to the point that participants tend to prefer virtual contents rather than traditional non-immersive techniques [29]. This has been confirmed by many other previous studies: for instance, joy and relaxation were induced by virtually walking into a park designed ad hoc in virtual reality by researchers [28], and a virtual environment specifically designed for chronic pain patients increased their mood state, positive emotions, motivation, and self-efficacy [31]. What emerges from our study shows, interestingly and differently from previous studies, that not only virtual reality contents specifically created for emotional induction, but also a commercial virtual reality game, specifically an horror game among the most popular and best-selling ones as Resident Evil 7: Biohazard, can effectively induce a feeling of anxiety in people, combined to a positive emotional state.

Moreover, in relation to these outcomes, it appears even more interesting to underline the final result obtained by this study: namely, as hypothesized, players reported a statistically larger sense of presence after the virtual reality horror video game experience if compared to the level of presence perceived after the non-immersive (desktop console setup) experience. Such results corroborate what has been observed in previous studies about the possibility for people to "be in the game" thanks to the virtual reality technology [47], and, thanks to the plausibility illusion mechanism [6], to personally face immediate threats, actively deciding how they will react to such threats and manage to survive [7].

Virtual reality has been found to be able to elicit frights similar to those perceived in real events [9] and to be effective in anxiety and phobia treatments, as well as for the stress management training [12, 18, 48]. Triggering real fright in a simulated virtual environment could have important consequences not only on the design of video games that are more and more effective in eliciting emotions in players, but also for emotional assessment and treatment programs. On the one hand, in fact, this kind of video games played in virtual reality, and consequently eliciting an intense emotional response, could become assessment tools for people's emotional skills when confronting dangers or stressful situations. For instance, recording the performance, as well as the subjective physiological and emotional response during such type of video game, could offer relevant data about the individual's reaction modalities in similar situations. On the other hand, acquiring the psychological skills to cope with frights or stress in a "safe" virtual environment, during a game experience that qualifies as entertaining and highly motivating [49], could represent an effective, low-cost and easily accessible tool for the training of emotional skills (i.e. emotional regulation, stress management), as well as for the rehabilitation of anxiety disorders or phobias.

Although the results of the present study could be interesting for their possible applications, this research has some important limitations that could affect the generalizability of the results or that may have influenced the findings. The main issues are related to the small sample size and the specific sample included in the study, who were young adults, played often (several hours per week) and had a low knowledge of virtual reality systems. In particular, on the basis of the results obtained by previous studies [7, 30, 49], it could be interesting to examine differences in the virtual reality video game experience, in relation with particular users' characteristics such as gender and age.

Another limitation lies in the fact that interesting variables such as the cybersickness experienced by players were not assessed. As it has been observed in previous studies [e.g., 24], in fact, differently from what usually happens while playing non-immersive console games, a particular type of motion sickness occurs when the person is immersed in a virtual environment through an head mounted display, including symptoms such as discomfort, nausea, headache, and dizziness [50]. Cybersickness can therefore negatively affect the users' experience of virtual reality contents, and for this reason it is important to better investigate such aspect, with the objective to limit the negative effects.

Finally, it would be interesting to use other physiological indexes related to the emotional activation, such as the facial electromyography (fEMG), that is considered a good measure of negative emotional state [51, 52], and the electroencephalography (EEG), which has already been used in a previous study about horror games [52].

Despite these limitations, the present exploratory study found that: (a) playing a commercial horror video game in virtual reality was not more difficult than playing in a non-immersive modality, such as console; (b) players showed an increased perceived anxiety both after playing the horror video game in virtual reality and after playing through the console; interestingly, however, the perceived sense of happiness significantly increased only after playing in virtual reality; finally, the sense of presence resulted to be greater in virtual reality as opposed to the console modality.

References

1. Yee, M.: 50+ new PlayStation VR games coming this year and into early 2018. https://blog.eu.playstation.com/2017/10/13/60-new-playstation-vr-games-coming-this-year-and-into-early-2018/. Accessed 21 Feb 2017
2. Reuters: Sony's PlayStation VR headset sales top 1 million units. https://www.cnbc.com/2017/06/07/sonys-playstation-vr-headset-sales-top-1-million-units.html. Accessed 21 Feb 2017

3. Kain, E.: The Most Disappointing Video Games of 2017. https://www.forbes.com/sites/
   erikkain/2017/12/19/the-top-11-most-disappointing-video-games-of-2017/#1b2595fc76c6.
   Accessed 21 Feb 2017
4. Shuman, S.: The Scariest PS4 and PS VR Horror Games of 2017. https://blog.us.playstation.
   com/2017/10/29/the-scariest-ps4-and-ps-vr-horror-games-of-2017/. Accessed 21 Feb 2017
5. Hills-Duty, R.: One Year on: Resident Evil 7 Biohazard Still Drawing in New Players.
   https://www.vrfocus.com/2018/01/one-year-on-resident-evil-7-biohazard-still-drawing-in-
   new-players/. Accessed 21 Feb 2017
6. Slater, M.: Place illusion and plausibility can lead to realistic behaviour in immersive virtual
   environments. Philos. Trans. R. Soc. Lond. 364(1535), 3549–3557 (2009)
7. Lin, J.H.T.: Fear in virtual reality (VR): fear elements, coping reactions, immediate and
   next-day fright responses toward a survival horror zombie virtual reality game. Comput.
   Hum. Behav. 72, 350–361 (2017)
8. Riva, G.: Is presence a technology issue? Some insights from cognitive sciences. In: Virtual
   Reality, pp. 159–169 (2009)
9. Parsons, T.D., Rizzo, A.A.: Affective outcomes of virtual reality exposure therapy for
   anxiety and specific phobias: a meta-analysis. J. Behav. Ther. Exp. Psychiatry 39(3), 250–
   261 (2008)
10. Price, M., Mehta, N., Tone, E.B., Anderson, P.L.: Does engagement with exposure yield
    better outcomes? Components of presence as a predictor of treatment response for virtual
    reality exposure therapy for social phobia. J. Anxiety Disord. 5(6), 763–770 (2011)
11. Opriş, D., Pintea, S., García-Palacios, A., Botella, C., Szamosközi, Ş., David, D.: Virtual
    reality exposure therapy in anxiety disorders: a quantitative meta-analysis. Depress. Anxiety
    29(2), 85–93 (2012)
12. Pallavicini, F., Cipresso, P., Raspelli, S., Grassi, A., Serino, S., Vigna, C., Triberti, S.,
    Villamira, M., Gaggioli, A., Riva, G.: Is virtual reality always an effective stressors for
    exposure treatments? Some insights from a controlled trial. BMC Psychiatry 13, 52 (2013)
13. Gorini, A., Griez, E., Petrova, A., Rivam, G.: Assessment of the emotional responses
    produced by exposure to real food, virtual food and photographs of food in patients affected
    by eating disorders. Ann. Gen. Psychiatry 9, 30 (2010)
14. Villani, D., Riva, G.: Does interactive media enhance the management of stress? Suggestions
    from a controlled study. Cyberpsychol. Behav. Soc. Netw. 15(1), 24–30 (2012)
15. Bouchard, S., Bernier, F., Boivin, E., Morin, B., Robillard, G.: Using biofeedback while
    immersed in a stressful videogame increases the effectiveness of stress management skills in
    soldiers. PLoS One 7(4), e36169 (2012)
16. Munafo, J., Diedrick, M., Stoffregen, T.A.: The virtual reality head-mounted display Oculus
    Rift induces motion sickness and is sexist in its effects. Exp. Brain Res. 235(3), 889–901
    (2017)
17. Sousa Santos, B., Dias, P., Pimentel, A., Baggerman, J.W., Ferreira, C., Silva, S., Madeira,
    J.: Head-mounted display versus desktop for 3D navigation in virtual reality: a user study.
    Multimedia Tools Appl. 41(1), 161–181 (2009)
18. Pallavicini, F., Ferrari, A., Zini, A., Garcea, G., Zanacchi, A., Barone, G., Mantovani, F.:
    What distinguishes a traditional gaming experience from one in virtual reality? An
    exploratory study. In: Ahram, T., Falcão, C. (eds.) AHFE 2017. AISC, vol. 608, pp. 225–
    231. Springer, Cham (2018). https://doi.org/10.1007/978-3-319-60639-2_23
19. Baas, J.M., Nugent, M., Lissek, S., Pine, D.S., Grillon, C.: Fear conditioning in virtual
    reality contexts: a new tool for the study of anxiety. Biol. Psychiat. 55(11), 1056–1060
    (2004)

20. Anderson, C.A., Shibuya, A., Ihori, N., Swing, E.L., Bushman, B.J., Sakamoto, A., Rothstein, H.R., Saleem, M.: Violent video game effects on aggression, empathy, and prosocial behavior in Eastern and Western countries: a meta-analytic review. Psychol. Bull. **136**(2), 151–173 (2010)

21. Ferguson, C.J.: The good, the bad and the ugly: a meta-analytic review of positive and negative effects of violent video games. Psychiatric Q. **78**(4), 309–316 (2007)

22. Hou, J., Nam, Y., Peng, W., Lee, K.M.: Effects of screen size, viewing angle, and players' immersion tendencies on game experience. Comput. Hum. Behav. **28**(2), 617–623 (2012)

23. McMahan, R.P., Bowman, D.A., Zielinski, D.J., Brady, R.B.: Evaluating display fidelity and interaction fidelity in a virtual reality game. IEEE Trans. Visual Comput. Graph. **18**(4), 626–633 (2012)

24. Merhi, O., Faugloire, E., Flanagan, M., Stoffregen, T.A.: Motion sickness, console video games, and head-mounted displays. Hum. Factors **49**(5), 920–934 (2007)

25. Sharma, H.N., Toups, Z.O., Dolgov, I., Kerne A., Jain A.: Evaluating display modalities using a mixed reality game. In: Proceedings of the 2016 Annual Symposium on Computer-Human Interaction in Play - CHI PLAY 2016, pp. 65–77. ACM Press (2016)

26. Perron, B.: Sign of a threat: the effects of warning systems in survival horror games. In: COSIGN 2004 (2004)

27. Vachiratamporn, V., Legaspi, R., Moriyama, K., Fukui, K., Numao, M.: An analysis of player affect transitions in survival horror games. J. Multimodal User Interfaces **9**(1), 43–54 (2015)

28. Baños, R.M., Botella, C., Rubió, I., Quero, S., García-Palacios, A., Alcañiz, M.: Presence and emotions in virtual environments: the influence of stereoscopy. CyberPsychol. Behav. **11**(1), 1–8 (2008)

29. Baños, R.M., Etchemendy, E., Farfallini, L., García-Palacios, A., Quero, S., Botella, C.: EARTH of well-being system: a pilot study of an information and communication technology-based positive psychology intervention. J. Positive Psychol. **9**(6), 482–488 (2014)

30. Felnhofer, A., Kothgassner, O.D., Schmidt, M., Heinzle, A.K., Beutl, L., Hlavacs, H., Kryspin-Exner, I.: Is virtual reality emotionally arousing? Investigating five emotion inducing virtual park scenarios. Int. J. Hum. Comput. Stud. **82**, 48–56 (2015)

31. Herrero, R., García-Palacios, A., Castilla, D., Molinari, G., Botella, C.: Virtual reality for the induction of positive emotions in the treatment of fibromyalgia: a pilot study over acceptability, satisfaction, and the effect of virtual reality on mood. Cyberpsychol. Behav. Soc. Netw. **17**(6), 379–384 (2014)

32. Diemer, J., Alpers, G.W., Peperkorn, H.M., Shiban, Y., Mühlberger, A.: The impact of perception and presence on emotional reactions: a review of research in virtual reality. Front. Psychol. **6**, 26 (2015)

33. Riva, G., Mantovani, F., Capideville, C.S., Preziosa, A., Morganti, F., Villani, D., Gaggioli, A., Botella, C., Alcañiz, M.: Affective interactions using virtual reality: the link between presence and emotions. CyberPsychol. Behav. **10**(1), 45–56 (2007)

34. American Psychological Association: 2010 amendments to the 2002 "Ethical Principles of Psychologists and Code of Conduct." American Psychologist, vol. 71, p. 900 (2010)

35. Pallavicini, F., Toniazzi, N., Argenton, L., Aceti, L., Mantovani, F.: Developing effective virtual reality training for military forces and emergency operators: from technology to human factors. In: 14th International Conference on Modeling and Applied Simulation, MAS 2015, pp. 206–210 (2015)

36. Spielberger, C.D.: State-Trait Anxiety Inventory. Wiley, London (2010)

37. Slater, M., Usoh, M., Steed, A.: Depth of presence in virtual environments. Presence Teleoperators Virtual Environ. **3**(2), 130–144 (1994)

38. Brooke, J.: SUS-A quick and dirty usability scale. Usability Eval. Ind. **189**(194), 4–7 (1996)
39. Grimshaw, M., Lindley, C., Nacke, L.: Sound and immersion in the first-person shooter : mixed measurement of the player's sonic experience. In: Audio Mostly, Piteå, pp. 22–33, October 2008
40. Moffat, D.C., Kiegler, K.: Investigating the effects of music on emotions in games. In: Audio Mostly, pp. 7–41 (2006)
41. Granic, I., Lobel, A.E.C.M., Engels, R.C.M.E.: The benefits of playing video games. Am. Psychol. **69**(1), 66–78 (2014)
42. Freeman, D., Reeve, S., Robinson, A., Ehlers, A., Clark, D., Spanlang, B., Slater, M.: Virtual reality in the assessment, understanding, and treatment of mental health disorders. Psychol. Med. **47**(14), 2393–2400 (2017)
43. Riva, G., Baños, R.M., Botella, C., Mantovani, F., Gaggioli, A.: Transforming experience: the potential of augmented reality and virtual reality for enhancing personal and clinical change. Front. Psychiatry **7**, 164 (2016)
44. Heineman, D.S.: Porting game studies research to virtual reality. New Media Soc. **18**(11), 2793–2799 (2016)
45. Swindells, C.B.A., Hajshirmohammadi, I., Corrie, B., Dill J.C., Fisher, B.D., Booth, K.B.: Comparing CAVE, wall, and desktop displays for navigation and wayfinding in complex 3D models. In: IEEE Proceedings Computer Graphics International, pp. 420–427 (2004)
46. Yeh, M., Wickens, C.D., Merlo, M.A.J., Brandenburg, D.L.: Head-up vs. head-down: effects of precision on cue effectiveness and display signaling. In: 45th Annual Meeting of the Human Factors and Ergonomics Society, pp. 1–6 (2001)
47. Lott, A., Bisson, E., Lajoie, Y., McComas, J., Sveistrup, H.: The effect of two types of virtual reality on voluntary center of pressure displacement. CyberPsychology **6**(5), 477–485 (2003)
48. Pallavicini, F., Argenton, L., Toniazzi, N., Aceti, L., Mantovani, F: Virtual reality applications for stress management training in the military. Aereospace Med. Hum. Perfor. **87**(12), 1–10 (2016)
49. Rosa, P.J., Morais, D., Gamito, P., Oliveira, J., Saraivam, T.: The immersive virtual reality experience: a typology of users revealed through multiple correspondence analysis combined with cluster analysis technique. Cyberpsychol. Behav. Soc. Netw. **19**(3), 209–216 (2016)
50. Larsen, J.T., Norris, C.J, Cacioppo, J.T.: Effects of positive and negative affect on electromyographic activity over zygomaticus major and corrugator supercilii. In: Psychophysiology, pp. 776–785 (2003)
51. Dimberg, U., Thunberg, M.: Rapid facial reactions to emotional facial expressions. Scand. J. Psychol. **39**(1), 39–45 (1998)
52. Garner, T.: Identifying habitual statistical features of EEG in response to fear-related stimuli in an audio-only computer video game. In: Proceedings of the 8th Audio Mostly Conference on AM 2013, pp. 1–6. ACM Press, New York (2013)

Mobile Augmented Reality Framework - MIRAR

João M. F. Rodrigues[1]([✉])(iD), Ricardo J. M. Veiga[1], Roman Bajireanu[1],
Roberto Lam[1](iD), João A. R. Pereira[1], João D. P. Sardo[1],
Pedro J. S. Cardoso[1](iD), and Paulo Bica[2]

[1] LARSyS (ISR-Lisbon) and ISE, University of the Algarve, 8005-139 Faro, Portugal
{jrodrig,rlam,pcardoso}@ualg.pt, ricardojorge@martinsveiga.com,
romanmsn.com@hotmail.com, jandrepereira00@gmail.com, joao_dps@outlook.com
[2] SPIC - Creative Solutions, Loulé, Portugal

Abstract. The increasing immersion of technology on our daily lives
demands for additional investments in various areas, including, as in the
present case, the enhancement of museums' experiences. One of the technologies that improves our relationship with everything that surrounds
us is Augmented Reality. This paper presents the architecture of MIRAR,
a Mobile Image Recognition based Augmented Reality framework. The
MIRAR framework allows the development of a system that uses mobile
devices to interact with the museum's environment, by: (a) recognizing
and tracking on-the-fly, on the client side (mobile), museum's objects,
(b) detecting and recognizing where the walls and respective boundaries
are localized, as well as (c) do person detection and segmentation. These
objects, wall and person segmentation will allow the projection of different contents (text, images, videos, clothes, etc.). Promising results
are presented in these topics, nevertheless, some of them are still in a
development stage.

Keywords: Augmented reality · Object recognition
Wall detection · Human detetion · HCI

1 Introduction

Augmented Reality (AR) [2] is a technology that, thanks to the mobile devices
increasing hardware capabilities and new algorithms, quickly evolved in the
recent years, gaining a huge amount of users. AR empowers a higher level of
interaction between the user and real world objects, extending the experience
on how the user sees and feels those objects by creating a new level of edutain-
ment that was not available before. The M5SAR: Mobile Five Senses Augmented
Reality System for Museums project [48] aims for the development of an AR system that acts as guide for cultural, historical and museum events. This is not
a novelty, since almost every known museum has its own mobile applications
(App), e.g. [31,57]. While the use of AR in museums is much less common, it

© Springer International Publishing AG, part of Springer Nature 2018
M. Antona and C. Stephanidis (Eds.): UAHCI 2018, LNCS 10908, pp. 102–121, 2018.
https://doi.org/10.1007/978-3-319-92052-8_9

is also not new, see e.g. [25,44,54,59]. The novelty in the M5SAR project is to extend the AR to the human five senses, see e.g. [48] for more details.

This paper focus on MIRAR, Mobile Image Recognition based Augmented Reality framework, one of the M5SAR's modules. MIRAR focuses on the development of a mobile multi-platform AR [2] framework, with the following main goals: (a) to perform "all" computational processing in the client-side (mobile device), minimizing, this way, costs with server(s) and communications; (b) to use real world two- and three-dimensional (2D and 3D) objects as markers for the AR; (c) to recognise environments, i.e., walls and its respective boundaries; (d) to detect and segment human shapes; (e) to project contents (e.g., text and media) onto different objects, walls and persons detected and displayed in the mobile device's screen, as well as enhance the object's displayed contents, by touching on the device's screen regions on those objects; and (f) to use the mobile device's RGB camera to achieve these goals. A framework that integrates these goals is completely different from the existing (SDK, frameworks, content management, etc.) AR systems [1,8,32,33,40].

The MIRAR sub-module for object recognition and environment detection presented in this paper is AR marker-based, often also called image-based [9]. AR image-based markers allow adding pre-set signals (e.g., from paintings, statues, etc.) easily detectable in the environment, and the use computer vision techniques to sense them. There are many image-based commercial AR toolkits (SDK) such as Catchoom or Kudan [8,32], and AR content management systems such as Catchoom or Layar [8,33], including open source SDKs [1]. Each of the above solutions have pros and cons. Between other problems, some are quite expensive, others consume too much memory (it is important to stress that the present application will have many markers, at least one for each museum piece), and others take too much time to load on the mobile device.

The increasing massification of AR applications brings new challenges to the table, such as the demand for planar regions detection ("walls"), with the more popular being developed within the scope of Simultaneous Localization And Mapping (SLAM) [4,12]. Usually, the common approach for image acquisition of 3D environments uses RGB-D devices or light detection and ranging (LIDAR) sensors [30,47,55,60]. There are also novelty advances within environment detection, localization or recognition, either using Direct Sparse Odometry [13], or using descriptors, like ORB SLAM [37] or even Large-Scale Direct Monocular SLAM [14]. However, as mentioned, the MIRAR framework focuses on mobile devices with only monocular cameras. Following this, an initial study of an environment detection sub-module was presented in [43], being the purposed method a geometric approach to the extracted edges of a frame. It should be considered that a frame is always captured from a perspective view of the surrounding environment, with the usual expected environment being characterized by the existence of numerous parallel lines which converge to a unique point in the horizon, called vanishing point [11,53].

The last topics addressed in the MIRAR framework regards the detection of human shapes in real world conditions. This continues to be a challenge in computer vision due to the existence of multiple variants, e.g., object obstructions, light variations, different viewpoints, the existence of multiple humans (occlusions), poses, etc., nevertheless, the detection of human shapes is an area with many studies and developments [17,39,52,56,61].

In summary, the MIRAR's object recognition sub-module uses images from the museum's objects, and the mobile device's camera to recognise and track on-the-fly, on the client-side, the museum's objects. The environment detection and recognition sub-module is supported upon the same principles of the object's recognition, but uses images from the environment, walls, to recognise them. Finally, the human detection and segmentation uses Convolutional Networks for the detection and an image processing algorithm for foreground (person) extraction. The main contribution of this paper is the integration of these three topics into a single mobile framework for AR.

The paper is structured as follows: The MIRAR framework and architecture is introduced in Sect. 2. Section 3 presents the main MIRAR's sub-module, namely the object detection, followed by the wall detection sub-module in Sect. 4 and the human shape detection in Sect. 5. The paper concludes with a final discussion and future work, Sect. 6.

2   MIRAR Framework

Before detailing the MIRAR framework it is important to give a brief overview of the M5SAR system, shown on top of Fig. 1. On the figure's left side, the basic communications flow between the server and mobile device is outlined (a detailed description is out of the scope of this paper) and, on the right side, the simplified diagram of the mobile App and the devices "connected" (via bluetooth) with the mobile device is shown. The displayed Beacons [16] are employed in the user's localisation and the Portable Device for Touch, Taste and Smell Sensations (PDTTSS) [51] used to enhance the five senses. In summary, the M5SAR App architecture is divided into three main modules: (A) Adaptive User Interfaces (AUI), see [48]; (B) Location module, a detailed explanation is out of this paper's focus, and (C) MIRAR module (see Fig. 1 bottom).

The MIRAR has four main features: (a) the detection and recognition of museum objects, triggering a card in the (M5SAR) App [48]; (b) the detection, recognition and tracking of objects as the user moves along the museum, allowing to touch different areas of the objects displayed in the mobile screen and showing information about that region of the object, MIRAR sub-module (i); (c) detection and modelling of the museum walls, and projecting information into the detected walls (e.g., images, movies, text) related with the recognized object's epoch, sub-module (ii); (d) detection of persons that are moving in the museum, and, for instance, to dress them with clothes from the object's epoch, sub-module (iii).

Sub-modules (i) and (ii) need to communicate with the server, i.e., the MIRAR module sends the user's position to the server, based on the previous object detections and the localisation given by the beacon's signals. From the

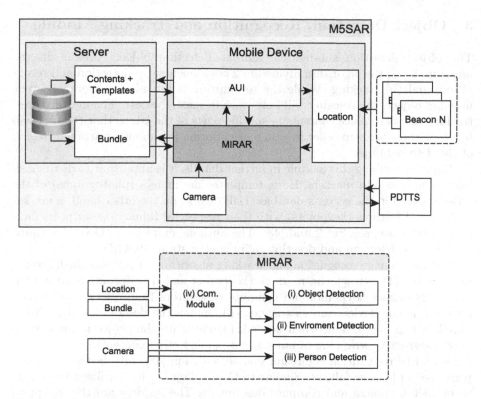

Fig. 1. Top: overall simplified system architecture. Bottom: MIRAR block diagram.

server, the MIRAR module receives a group of object markers (image descriptors; see next section), here called bundles, that contain all the objects available in the located room or museum section. In a way to minimise communications, the App stores in the memory (limited to each device's memory size) the bundles from the previous room(s), museum section(s), and as soon as it detects a new beacon signal it downloads a new bundle. Older bundles are discarded in a FIFO (first in, first out) manner.

It is also important to stress that, since the sensor used to acquire the images from the environment is the mobile's camera, in order to save battery, the camera is only activated when the AR option is selected in the UI. When the activation occurs, the user can see the environment in the mobile screen and effectuate the previously mentioned actions. As an additional effort to save battery, the device will enter a low-power state if the user turns the phone upside down, by dimming the phone's screen and interrupting the processing.

As final remarks, the App was implemented using Unity [58], the computer vision algorithms were deployed using the OpenCV [38] library (Asset) for Unity, and tests and results consider that the mobile device is located inside a museological space. The next section will present the object detection and tracking module.

3 Object Detection, Recognition and Tracking Module

The object detection sub-module aim at detecting objects present in the museum, being the algorithm divided in 2 components: (a) detection and recognition, and (b) tracking. While the recognition is intended to work on every museum object, the tracking will only work in masterpieces[1]. The masterpieces' tracking allows to place contents in specific parts of the UI, so that the user will touch on those areas in order to gain more information about a particular region of the detected object.

Before describing this module in further details, it is important to distinguish from templates and markers. Here, templates are images (photographs) of the objects stored in the server's database (DB) while, on the other hand, a marker is the set of features (keypoints) with their respective (binary) descriptors for a certain template, see Fig. 2 and [43]. The authors' employ the ORB descriptor for keypoint detection and descriptors implementation [19,43,50].

A generic image recognition and tracking algorithm for AR has the following main steps: (1) extract the markers (keypoints and descriptors) from a template; (2) extract keypoints and compute descriptors from query images (i.e., for each mobile device camera's frame); (3) match the descriptors of both the template and query; and, when needed, (4) calculate the projection matrix to allow perspective wrapping of images, videos, and other contents.

An initial recognition algorithm was presented in [48], with further advances presented in [43], as follows. Similar to [3], in Step (1) it is utilised the image to extract keypoints and compute descriptors. The borders are the exception (e.g., the painting frame) which were removed, since usually there is no relevant information in those areas. Nevertheless, the templates are processed in different scales (image sizes): starting at the pre-defined camera frame size, 640×480px (pixels), the templates are scaled up and down (by a $1/3$), resulting in a total of 3 scales per template. To further increase the framework's performance, these markers continue to be created on a server and sent to the client (mobile device) on demand, to be de-serialized. Step (2) from the frame acquired by the camera, the keypoints are simply extracted and their respective descriptors computed (using the ORB descriptor).

Regarding Step (3), the query image descriptors are (3.1) brute-force matched, using K-Nearest Neighbours (KNN), with $K = 2$, against the descriptors of the available markers. Next, (3.2) the markers' descriptors are matched to the query's descriptors. Following, (3.3) a ratio test is performed, i.e., if the two closest neighbours of a match have close matching distances (65% ratio), then the match is discarded [3], because this would be an ambiguous match. This ratio evaluation is the test where most matches are removed. For this reason, this test is performed first to improve performance later on. Then, (3.4) it is performed a symmetry match where only the matches resulting from the KNN in (3.1) that are present in (3.2) are accepted. After this, a (3.5) homography refinement is

---

[1] Masterpieces are objects that have an enlarged (historical and cultural) value in the museum's collection.

Fig. 2. Top: Example of existing objects in Faro Municipal Museum. Bottom: examples of detected and tracked markers with the corresponding axis.

applied. This refinement uses the RANSAC method to verify if the matched keypoints in the query image maintain the same configuration between them (same relative position) as they had in the template image. If any of the keypoints stay out of this relation, then they are considered outliers and removed from the match set. (3.6) If after all of these refinements there are at least 8 matches left, then it is considered as a valid classification.

In the (3.6.i) classification stage the query image is compared using Brute-Force (BF) to all marker scales for each of the available templates. This, in turn, returns a classification based on the count of (filtered) matches, when there are at least 8 descriptors matches. The marker that retrieved the most number of matches is considered the *template to be tracked*. Afterwards (3.6.ii), if the tracking stage is necessary, i.e., if a masterpiece is present, the matching only occurs with the markers of the 3 scales of the *template to be tracked* previously selected in classification phase. If the object (*template to be tracked*) is not visible in the scene for 1 second then it is considered lost and the recognition process initiates again. Last, but not least, Step (4) of the generic algorithm is done using perspective wrapping (pose estimation) in order to place content on the same plane as the detected image (marker).

Figure 2 bottom shows some examples of tests done in the Faro Municipal Museum where the classification number is shown in red. For more algorithm details and results see [43].

4   Environments Detection

As previously mentioned, the objective of this sub-module is to be able to discern the location and position of the walls of a given environment, and afterwards replace them with other contents. The algorithm presented here does not yet supports our investigation over this subject mentioned in [43], although it will eventually merge with the preceding work. In the present case, similar to Sect. 3 markers are used (keypoints and descriptors) for each template, with the bundles being previously generated. For this sub-module, the templates are of the entire walls, and not only of the museum's object, see Fig. 3 top row, which allows for the retrieval of the expected wall shape using a pose estimation algorithm. Various implementations of pose estimation have already been presented for 3D objects using RGB-D sensors [6] or through monocular images [46], and urban environments [22]. The main contribution of this sub-module is the initial implementation of the wall estimation for primarily indoor detection and recognition while the user navigates through museums, which are presented in this paper, with a future user localization feature already being developed. Regarding our implementation of wall estimation, it is important to note that the aim for this sub-module is a seamlessly fully integrated AR application for mobile devices; therefore, the presented algorithm is focused and adjusted for performance on smartphones.

Fig. 3. Top: Example of templates. Bottom: Extracted keypoints location for each template.

Contrary to what was presented for the object detection, instead of using ORB descriptors, we found that BRISK [34] descriptors perform better for this task, which will be explained later in Sect. 4.1. For comparison between markers, not only Brute-Force was tested, but also the *Fast Library for Approximate Nearest Neighbours* (FLANN) [36]. The necessity of evaluating both matchers for this task will be posteriorly explained.

The current algorithm, after the bundle has been created and loaded, is applied to each frame from the mobile device camera as follows: (1) A number of the most significant keypoints are retrieved (filtered) and the respective descriptors computed; (2) Optimal matches are found and filtered; (3) Pose estimation is performed after discarding the defective homography; (4) Polygons corresponding to the matched templates are superimposed on the frame.

Beginning with Step (1), all the keypoints (using the BRISK keypoint detector) found from the frame provided are ordered by their response, which defines the ones with stronger information, and only an amount of keypoints is maintained, which in our case was $Num_{KP} = 385$ (this number was empirically computed, see Sect. 4.1). More keypoints will not improve results and it increases computational time. If this number is decreased significantly, many "template (wall) - frame" matches are lost. Afterwards, the respective descriptor for each keypoint is computed using the BRISK descriptor.

In Step (2), before searching through all the stored templates, it is verified if the location of the user is known through the previous frames, thus allowing for the matching search to begin with the surrounding templates. The method used for matching was K-Nearest Neighbours (the same as in Sect. 3), with $K = 2$, either by BF matching, or using FLANN. While the BF compares all the retrieved markers' descriptors from the frame with the stored markers from the templates, it was created an index with FLANN that uses multi-probe LSH [35]. The parameters used were 6 hash tables, with 12 bits hash key size, and 1 bit to be shifted to check for neighbouring buckets. The number of times we defined for the index to be recursively traversed was 100, as we observed a good balance between additional processing time and the increased precision. It is important to refer that, as opposed to BF, FLANN does not return a complete matching between the markers, but instead it gives an approximate correspondence. The remaining matches are filtered through the Lowe's ratio test, where we discard the pairs with close matching distances (65% ratio), allowing only the more distinct ones to remain. Subsequently, if at least 10 good matches are found, then the perspective transform is retrieved through the homography refinement using the RANSAC method, where the original pattern of keypoints from the templates are compared with the ones from the frame, considering the ones with the same configuration as inliers, and the others as outliners.

Regarding Step (3), for the pose (wall) estimation templates to be properly found, the perspective matrix must be found valid. It should be noted that the existing planes across the provided frames will be randomly presented with acute perspective angles, or at deeper distances. Concerning the templates' format, for this sub-module we chose to include the desired full wall delimitations to be found, even if the regular walls did not offer relevant information to be retrieved, with the keypoints gathered in clusters along the museums' objects, see in Fig. 3.

The chosen template format after the pose estimation returned the approximated horizontal limits of the walls. In order to improve accuracy and performance, it was necessary to discard the non relevant perspective matrices. To do so, we analysed the matrix extracted from the homography and applied a group of tests. We calculated the determinant of the top left 2×2 matrix and limited the output between 1 and 100, given that, with the perspective transform, if the values of said determinant were to be negative there would be an inversion, and as the templates were created for the expected projection, there should be none. The limit of 100 was imposed because in case there was a large value for the determinant, then the aspect ratio would have been overly deformed. Furthermore, after finding the coordinates, their order is compared against the original template, e.g., if the (x_0, y_0) of the template is on the top left and the (x_1, y_1) on the lower left; then, after the perspective transform, this orientation should remain. Afterwards, it is verified if the angles between each 3 points are not overly convex, as they are expected to be nearly perpendicular. Finally, as the environment/room is "regular", which means the presence of vertical walls without deformations (no circular walls) or extensive 3D artwork, all the non vertical resulting polygons with and error of 15% are discarded.

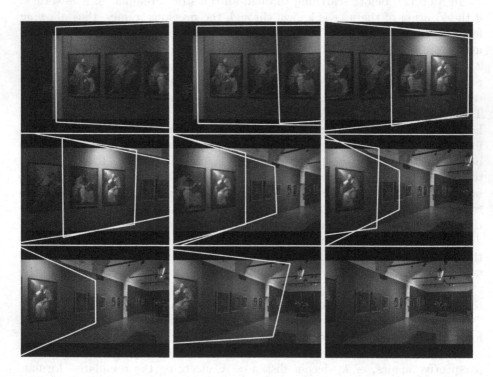

Fig. 4. Example of a sequence of frames with matched templates. See also Fig. 6.

The last Step (4), the retrieved coordinates are converted into polygons that are superimposed upon the original frame for each of the matched templates, corresponding to the expected surface of the wall in the environment; a sequence of the output results can be seen in Fig. 4. With this outcome it is possible to project content not only replacing the walls, as presented before in [43], but also to present floating AR content. It is important to stress that when the angle between the wall and the mobile user is "too sharp" is not yet possible to find the boundaries of the wall, which can be shown if Fig. 4 bottom row.

4.1   Tests

In order to test de reliability of the algorithm, test were done before converting the algorithm to the mobile platform; nevertheless, all the videos used for the tests were acquired by mobile devices (smartphones and tablets). The tests were done using a desktop computer with an Intel CPU i5-6300 running at 2.4 GHz with the algorithm limited to run in single-thread. The videos consisted on a total amount of 4.306 frames of expected user navigation through the museum, with both the horizontal and vertical orientations used. An additional video containing persons in between the camera and the walls also showed good results, as seen in Fig. 6. It is important to note that it is expect that this sub-module will not always detect and recognize the environment in all the frames; therefore, the most important measure of success is the amount of frames with valid matches found.

The tests were conducted in following ways: the templates' width size between 320px and 640px; the frame's width size between 640, 480 and 320px; and increasing the number of minimal good matches, starting with 10 and using steps of 5. All the tests were performed using BF and FLANN.

Regarding the variation of the minimal good matches between markers to begin the template matching, as expected, with the increase of this threshold the amount of frames with a found template match were dramatically reduced, while it was observed the maintenance of a similar processing time, either for each frame as for each matched frame, showing little to no variation. The results in terms of "pose" estimation of the polygons over the output frame were also improved. Upon reviewing this results we decided to use the minimal value of 10, given that it returned the highest number of frames matched without overly increasing the undesired results; for example, changing this value to 15 reduced the frames matched by $35 - 40\%$. With the variation of the templates width size, it was expect to add additional detected matches for when the wall is distant and is presented smaller on the frame. The results showed that even when it occasionally happens, it doesn't justify adding different scales of templates for this sub-module at the current version in exchange of processing time performance, as it was presented in [48].

The obtained processing times for the current algorithm, while reducing the templates and frames width, decreased from $28, 3 \pm 13, 8$ms to $17, 9 \pm 5, 9$ms with BF, and from $33, 2 \pm 14, 2$ms to $24, 1 \pm 17, 8$ms. Even though it presented some improvement on the time performance, the amount of frames matched dropped $73 - 63\%$ respectively.

Considering the necessity a higher rate of matching, the performance of different templates and frames sizes were compared. The illustration in Fig. 5 presents the amount of frames matched with the colour black within the total frames of different expected user interaction videos. On the left is shown the frame number (1,..., 4306), and on the right, the histogram of matched template-frame along the different widths and matching algorithms, namely FLANN and BF. The intent of this comparison, other than reporting the total of matched frames for each different test, was to analyse if the scale factor would introduce new

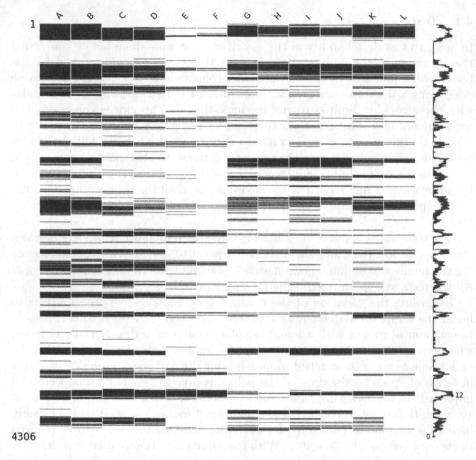

Fig. 5. Illustration of the number of matched frames (in black) with templates, changing the widths of both, i.e., from A-F is shown for each pair Flann (A, C and E) and BF (B, D and F) the matched templates with a width of 640px, the frames' width varies from 640 (A and B), to 480 (C and D) and 320px (E and F). From G-L the same but now with the template with the width of 320px. At right, an histogram of the total of matches for each frame is shown.

results, either by reducing the frame width while retaining a larger template width, which is shows from A-F, or by reducing the template width, while again changing the size of the frame, as can be seen from G-L, with a template width of 320px. The test were also divided in FLANN (A, C, E, G, I and K) and BF (B, D, F, H, J and L). The variation of frames' width is organized as 640 (A and B), 480 (C and D) and 320px (E and F), with the same from G-L.

Using the illustration shown in Fig. 5 it becomes easier to analyse the effect of the different parameters, being one of the main comparisons the use of FLANN or BF for feature matching. Is it relevant to note that, as BF needs a complete certainty for matching, which would be achieved more easily if the desired matching template was in full frame, FLANN does not, which introduces the possibility of the existence of false positives. As a continuous outputs of false positives from the same template is uncommon, it became easier to discard them. Although FLANN versus BF is usually restricted to a large amount of keypoints, in our case for 640px templates the average was 384.5 ± 119.48 keypoints per image, where FLANN surpasses BF in processing time performance, for our case it was primarily used with the intend of retrieving additional matched frames. Regarding the obtained results, FLANN returned additional matched frames with 38% of the total number of 4.306 frames matched, and BF returned 32% for 640px templates, while for 320px we obtained 20% and 15%, respectively. Although there is an increase in processing time for FLANN in order of 17% facing BT, when analysing the results shown in Fig. 5, it is possible to verify a more sparse occurrence of matched frames for FLANN versus BF, allowing for a higher probability of matching while the user navigates the museum, which will be used in order to recalibrate (in the future) the user localization and focus, improving the projection of content tracking and stability.

Focusing on the 640px width templates, it is possible to observe the expected lower matching while reducing the frames' width, for the total of available markers for each frame was reduced against the templates average number of extracted keypoints. With the 320px templates, the results showed a different outcome. While the total matched frames was also reduced, it became almost invariable across the tests, which means that with a lower processing time the same results would be achievable. One interesting point is noticeable near the medium point, where there was more matched frames acquired with lower templates' width. This is explained with the distance of the matching template, i.e., if the frame's width is 640px and the templates' 320px, if the respective location of the template is inside the frame at distance, it will be closest to the lower templates' width than the larger, and as we are using BRISK descriptors, even if they are invariant to scale, there is a threshold to the maximum of that invariance. In conclusion, for these results it can be seen that in the future the implementation of different scales of templates to improve the localization tracking may be needed.

As referred before, for this module a BRISK descriptor was used instead of ORB. Although the amount of frames with matched templates was similar in between, ORB performed slightly better, with 771 frames with match against 726 of BRISK, from a total amount of frames of 1.857. The outcome of said matches presented worse projected polygons, meaning that even with the homography additional sanity tests, the occurrence of bad homographies increased. Furthermore, an increase in the occurrence of false positives with a factor of ten times between ORB and BRISK was observable, which largely contributed to the bad homographies received. The performed times from ORB to BRISK lowered from 37.8 ± 9.5ms to 27.1 ± 10.4ms while using FLANN, and 36.7 ± 9.6ms to 26.0 ± 8.5ms with BF. Is important to observe that for our tests using ORB, FLANN does not seem to affect the performance times. Lastly, the amount of average keypoints retrieved from the templates actually decreased from ORB to BRISK, with a total of 5.824 keypoints, with an average of 485.3 ± 24.4 keypoints per template, to a total of 4.614 keypoints, with an average 384.5 ± 119.5, which shows ORB being more consistent than BRISK for the amount retrieved, although it did not prove that with the additional keypoints the results would improve.

As the objective of this sub-module is the recognition and detection of the walls throughout the visit within some rooms of the museum, it is expected a loss of tracking/recognition and its recovery at a slightly different location or angle, which demands that the recognized template shape be the as close as possible to the desired, every time there is a match within frames. Since the amount of good expected results with BRISK surpassed the ORB descriptor, we decided to perform the current algorithm using only the BRISK descriptor, while the algorithm for object detection shown at Sect. 3 remains using ORB. The different outcomes between both the descriptors for this challenge could be due to the fact that the BRISK descriptor is invariant to scale, while the ORB is not. Furthermore, while for object detection we used scaled versions of the templates for matching, as the object is expected to fill the screen of the mobile device, with this module there was an additional inclusion of different scales, as it should be considered that the user will be navigating the different rooms of the museum; therefore, the templates, in this case the walls, will appear on the mobile device with different geometric shapes and distances; see also [43].

Additional examples of results obtained can be observed in Fig. 6, where is possible to see on top the algorithm working with vertical frames and some of the still occurring bad outcomes retrieved from faulty perspectives transforms from the homography. On the 2nd row, results of the current algorithm can be observed, while the view is partially obstructed with people. Additionally, it is important to remark that this module is being ran only from the frames obtained, without additional sensors or 3D information, an so, the results obtained with obstructed views are a welcoming result for the current implementation.

In Fig. 6 bottom row it is possible to observe the results of part of the former algorithm [43] applied to the retrieved frames. While with the former implementation the process would begin by elimination of all non relevant lines, or in our former case, all the non vertical, horizontal and vanishing lines, the future fusion of both developments will be more focused in only retrieving the nearest lines to the already extracted polygons through the Hough Transform [26], improving the polygons veracity to the actual walls' shapes and adding a level of longer distance detection, either by additional calculations through the use of the vanishing point together with the vertical and horizontal lines, as can be seen in [43], or with an eventual introduction of a pre-known room shape, which, combined with the user localisation, would achieve better results, presenting the opportunity for the use of indoor 3D models, further increasing the user immersion with AR.

On the next section we introduce an initial study for the detection and segmentation of the human shape.

Fig. 6. Top row, examples of different vertical matching outcomes. Middle row, initial results of matching while the view is obstructed by persons. Bottom row, examples of the Hough Transform [26] applied to different frames.

5   Human Shape Detection

Human shape detection, as mentioned in the Introduction, already presents its challenges; furthermore, for this sub-module we have to consider the detection in real-time on a mobile device, while the user is moving trough six degrees of freedom (6DOF), which will increase the level of complexity [5,42]. Recent researches approach the human shape detection either by a top-down or a bottom-up method. Top-down means that the persons' shape are first detected and afterwards an estimation of their poses is achieved [23,24,41], while with bottom-up the humans' limbs are individually detected, generating groups of body parts in order to form humans' poses [7,17]. For the initial study of this module we used a top-down approach, being the objective the detection and segmentation of the humans' shapes, allowing for the projection of AR content over it, as for example, the ability "to dress" the museums' users with clothes corresponding to the desired surrounding epoch of the museums' objects.

In order to overcome the complex challenges imposed by the detection of human shapes in video, captured by a moving camera of a mobile device, we used a convolutional neural networks (CNN), built in TensorFlow [21]. To detect human shapes in a video feed with reasonable rate of *fps* we used a single shot

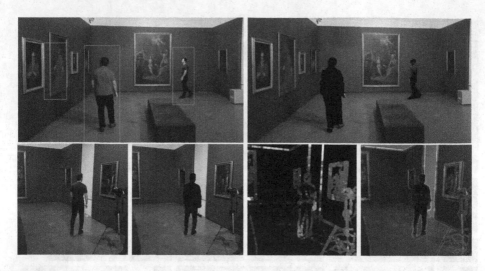

Fig. 7. Top row-left, example of human detection with SSD-Mobilenet. Right, the result of human segmentation by GrabCut. Bottom row, from left to right, original image (frame), human segmentation, computed optical flow of two consecutive frames and overlap of segmentation and optical flow (the two former images).

detection (SSD) network, and we used the MobileNet model for the neural network architecture; as its name suggests, it is designed for mobile applications [27]. The other technique used in the process of human detection/segmentation is the GrabCut algorithm [42]. It has a limitation where it needs to define the foreground and background areas; hence, we propose a fully-automatic human segmentation method by using the bounding box as a basis for the foreground and background areas.

The algorithm for this module is executed for each frame following these steps: (1) Apply SSD-Mobilenet [29], used for human detection, which outputs a bounding box around the detected humans (see Sect. 5.1 for the justification). (2) Resize the extracted bounding box by an increase of 10%; the original bounding box would cut some parts of the human shape in some image conditions, thus this improves the foreground precision. Step (3) follows with a cut of the input image, the cut is made with twice (2x) the size of the initial bounding box, with the same centre, and inside, the cropped area is used as background. Finally, (4) we use the GrabCut [49] algorithm for human shape segmentation.

5.1 Tests

Three models were tested in the mobile device for the human shapes detection, SSD-Mobilenet [28], YOLO [45], and DeepMultiBox [15]. Empirical tests were done in a Museum (Faro Municipal Museum) using an ASUS Zenpad 3S 10 tablet, showing that in real world conditions the SSD-Mobilenet presented a better accuracy and speed, validating what is mentioned in [28]. Initially, we used COCO [10] frozen pre-trained weights for SSD-Mobilenet. The evaluation setup, as mentioned, consisted on a ASUS Zenpad 3S 10 tablet and a windows machine with an Intel i7-6700 CPU @ 3.40 GHz. A total of 86 frames of data were run 15 times through the network, with their performance being recorded. The resolution of the input frames was 640px and the spatial size of the convolutional neural network was 320px. To filter out weak detections we use a confidence threshold of 0.25. Our tests for this model, using the tablet, returned an average processing time of 346.0ms, while the computer achieved 33.7ms, being these values only regarding Step (1).

After the human detection, and for the remaining Steps (2–4) in our algorithm, with the use of GrabCut for segmentation, we achieved an average processing time of 127.3ms using the computer. In Fig. 7 top row is possible to observe the output frame showing promising results regarding human segmentation. An observable disadvantage for this module within the museum environment can also be observed with a painting of a person being detected as living person. Although it is a good feature, for this task it is an undesirable result. Furthermore, in Fig. 7 bottom row is possible to inspect that, when the conditions provide a discriminative foreground and background areas, the GrabCut algorithm can perform with high precision.

To solve the problem caused by mis-segmentation of the limbs of a segmented person, as for example in the left image, where the arms are indistinguishable from the torso, we started to apply Gunnar Farneback?s algorithm to compute dense optical flow between two consecutive frames [18,20]. This allows to complement the GrabCut segmentation process by using the consistency of pixel values in two frames. Using Farneback?s algorithm allows to estimate the optical flow in a sequence of frames, and it is possible to use it to locate the borders of limbs that do not appear in the GrabCut segmentation. The algorithm shows an optical flow field with distinguished values between torso and arms because they have different speed movements, see Fig. 7 bottom right.

6   Conclusions

This paper presents the current Mobile Image Recognition based Augmented Reality (MIRAR) framework architecture. Even in its current state, MIRAR had already presented good results in the object detection, recognition, and tracking sub-modules. The integration with the new approach for the wall detection and recognition shows satisfactory results, taking in consideration that it is still a work in progress. For the human shapes detection, initial results were shown; nevertheless, more consistent tests need to be performed in different museum conditions.

For future work, the recognition of 3D objects is an immediate focus in terms of creating a robust bank of tests, and so is the refinement of the object recognition and tracking module. This can be achieved by refining the matches with homography and trying to find an optimised set of keypoints from multiple scales. For the wall detection, the focus will be on improving the stability and further filtering the occasional bad results, introducing pre-tuned templates to increase the range of detection, while preserving performance, the inclusion of a tracking system, and a merger with the previous work presented on edges detection for geometric prediction to stabilise the resulting polygons, reaching for a predictive localization of the surrounding indoor environment. The current different choices of descriptors between objects and wall detection will also be addressed.

For the human shapes detection, the segmentation done with the use of the GrabCut algorithm needs to be complemented in order to acquire a good human segmentation, since it will allow the projection of contents onto those shapes/persons. In the future we plan to use optical flow estimation (with initial results already shown) in the final segmentation process in order to improve the segmentation results. Additional work needs to be done to reduce the execution times of the detection and segmentation.

As a final conclusion, the MIRAR shows, even in this current stage, promising results, and it is expected to be an excellent tool to give a more impactful relation between the museum's user and the museum's objects.

Acknowledgements. This work was supported by the Portuguese Foundation for Science and Technology (FCT), project LARSyS (UID/EEA/50009/2013), CIAC, and project M5SAR I&DT nr. 3322 financed by CRESC ALGARVE2020, PORTUGAL2020 and FEDER. We also thank Faro Municipal Museum and the M5SAR project leader, SPIC - Creative Solutions [www.spic.pt].

References

1. Artoolkit.: ARtoolKit, the world's most widely used tracking library for augmented reality (2017). http://artoolkit.org/. Accessed 16 Nov 2017
2. Azuma, R., Baillot, Y., Behringer, R., Feiner, S., Julier, S., MacIntyre, B.: Recent advances in augmented reality. IEEE Comput. Graph. Appl. **21**(6), 34–47 (2001)
3. Baggio, D.L.: Mastering OpenCV with Practical Computer Vision Projects. Packt Publishing Ltd, Birmingham (2012)
4. Bailey, T., Durrant-Whyte, H.: Simultaneous localization and mapping (SLAM): part II. IEEE Robot. Autom. Mag. **13**(3), 108–117 (2006)
5. Bhole, C., Pal, C.: Automated person segmentation in videos. In: 21st International Conference on Pattern Recognition (ICPR), pp. 3672–3675. IEEE (2012)
6. Buch, A.G., Kraft, D., Kamarainen, J.-K., Petersen, H.G., Krüger, N.: Pose estimation using local structure-specific shape and appearance context. In: IEEE International Conference on Robotics and Automation (ICRA), pp. 2080–2087. IEEE (2013)
7. Cao, Z., Simon, T., Wei, S.E., Sheikh, Y.: Realtime multi-person 2D pose estimation using part affinity fields. In: CVPR, vol. 1, no. 2, p. 7 (2017)
8. Catchoom.: Catchoom (2017). http://catchoom.com/. Accessed 16 Nov 2017
9. Cheng, K.-H., Tsai, C.-C.: Affordances of augmented reality in science learning: suggestions for future research. J. Sci. Educ. Technol. **22**(4), 449–462 (2013)
10. COCO.: COCO - common objects in context (2018). http://cocodataset.org/. Accessed 14 Jan 2018

11. Duan, W.: Vanishing points detection and camera calibration. Ph.D. thesis, University of Sheffield (2011)
12. Durrant-Whyte, H., Bailey, T.: Simultaneous localization and mapping: part I. IEEE Rob. Autom. Mag. **13**(2), 99–110 (2006)
13. Engel, J., Koltun, V., Cremers, D.: Direct sparse odometry. IEEE Trans. Pattern Anal. Mach. Intell. **40**(3), 611–625 (2017)
14. Engel, J., Schöps, T., Cremers, D.: LSD-SLAM: large-scale direct monocular SLAM. In: Fleet, D., Pajdla, T., Schiele, B., Tuytelaars, T. (eds.) ECCV 2014. LNCS, vol. 8690, pp. 834–849. Springer, Cham (2014). https://doi.org/10.1007/978-3-319-10605-2_54
15. Erhan, D., Szegedy, C., Toshev, A., Anguelov, D.: Scalable object detection using deep neural networks. In: Proceedings of the IEEE Conference on Computer Vision and Pattern Recognition, pp. 2147–2154 (2014)
16. Estimote.: Create magical experiences in the physical world (2017). https://goo.gl/OHW04y. Accessed 04 Apr 2017
17. Fang, H., Xie, S., Lu, C.: RMPE: Regional multi-person pose estimation. arXiv preprint (2017)
18. Farnebäck, G.: Two-frame motion estimation based on polynomial expansion. In: Bigun, J., Gustavsson, T. (eds.) SCIA 2003. LNCS, vol. 2749, pp. 363–370. Springer, Heidelberg (2003). https://doi.org/10.1007/3-540-45103-X_50
19. Figat, J., Kornuta, T., Kasprzak, W.: Performance evaluation of binary descriptors of local features. In: Chmielewski, L.J., Kozera, R., Shin, B.-S., Wojciechowski, K. (eds.) ICCVG 2014. LNCS, vol. 8671, pp. 187–194. Springer, Cham (2014). https://doi.org/10.1007/978-3-319-11331-9_23
20. Fleet, D., Weiss, Y.: Optical flow estimation. In: Paragios, N., Chen, Y., Faugeras, O. (eds.) Handbook of Mathematical Models in Computer Vision, pp. 237–257. Springer, Boston (2006). https://doi.org/10.1007/0-387-28831-7_15
21. Google.: TensorFlow - an open-source machine learning framework for everyone (2018). https://www.tensorflow.org/. Accessed 14 Jan 2018
22. Hallquist, A., Zakhor, A.: Single view pose estimation of mobile devices in urban environments. In: 2013 IEEE Workshop on Applications of Computer Vision (WACV), pp. 347–354. IEEE (2013)
23. He, K., Gkioxari, G., Dollár, P., Girshick, R.: Mask R-CNN. In: IEEE International Conference on Computer Vision (ICCV), pp. 2980–2988. IEEE (2017)
24. Hernández-Vela, A., Reyes, M., Ponce, V., Escalera, S.: Grabcut-based human segmentation in video sequences. Sensors **12**(11), 15376–15393 (2012)
25. HMS.: Srbija 1914/augmented reality exhibition at historical museum of Serbia, Belgrade (2017). https://vimeo.com/126699550. Accessed 04 Apr 2017
26. Hough, P.V.: Method and means for recognizing complex patterns. Technical report (1962)
27. Howard, A.G., Zhu, M., Chen, B., Kalenichenko, D., Wang, W., Weyand, T., Andreetto, M., Adam, H.: Mobilenets: Efficient convolutional neural networks for mobile vision applications. CoRR, abs/1704.04861 (2017)
28. Huang, J., Rathod, V., Sun, C., Zhu, M., Korattikara, A., Fathi, A., Fischer, I., Wojna, Z., Song, Y., Guadarrama, S., et al.: Speed/accuracy trade-offs for modern convolutional object detectors. arXiv preprint arXiv:1611.10012 (2016)
29. Huang, J., Rathod, V., Sun, C., Zhu, M., Korattikara, A., Fathi, A., Fischer, I., Wojna, Z., Song, Y., Guadarrama, S., et al.: Speed/accuracy trade-offs for modern convolutional object detectors. In: IEEE CVPR (2017)

30. Hulik, R., Spanel, M., Smrz, P., Materna, Z.: Continuous plane detection in point-cloud data based on 3D hough transform. J. Vis. Commun. Image Represent. **25**(1), 86–97 (2014)
31. InformationWeek.: Informationweek: 10 fantastic iPhone, Android Apps for museum visits (2017). https://goo.gl/XF3rj4. Accessed 04 Apr 2017
32. Kudan.: Kudan computer vision (2017). https://www.kudan.eu/. Accessed 16 Nov 2017
33. Layar.: Layar (2017). https://www.layar.com/. Accessed 16 Nov 2017
34. Leutenegger, S., Chli, M., Siegwart, R.Y.: BRISK: binary robust invariant scalable keypoints. In: IEEE International Conference on Computer Vision (ICCV), pp. 2548–2555. IEEE (2011)
35. Lv, Q., Josephson, W., Wang, Z., Charikar, M., Li, K.: Multi-probe LSH: efficient indexing for high-dimensional similarity search. In: Proceedings of the 33rd International Conference on Very Large Data Bases, pp. 950–961. VLDB Endowment (2007)
36. Muja, M., Lowe, D.G.: Fast matching of binary features. In: 2012 Ninth Conference on Computer and Robot Vision (CRV), pp. 404–410. IEEE (2012)
37. Mur-Artal, R., Montiel, J.M.M., Tardos, J.D.: ORB-SLAM: a versatile and accurate monocular slam system. IEEE Trans. Rob. **31**(5), 1147–1163 (2015)
38. OpenCV.: OpenCV (2017). http://opencv.org/. Accessed 04 Apr 2017
39. Ouyang, W., Wang, X.: Joint deep learning for pedestrian detection. In: 2013 IEEE International Conference on Computer Vision (ICCV), pp. 2056–2063. IEEE (2013)
40. Pádua, L., Adão, T., Narciso, D., Cunha, A., Magalhães, L., Peres, E.: Towards modern cost-effective and lightweight augmented reality setups. Int. J. Web Portals (IJWP) **7**(2), 33–59 (2015)
41. Papandreou, G., Zhu, T., Kanazawa, N., Toshev, A., Tompson, J., Bregler, C., Murphy, K.: Towards accurate multiperson pose estimation in the wild. arXiv preprint arXiv:1701.01779, 8 (2017)
42. Park, S., Yoo, J.H.: Human segmentation based on grabcut in real-time video sequences. In: IEEE International Conference on Consumer Electronics (ICCE), pp. 111–112. IEEE (2014)
43. Pereira, J.A.R., Veiga, R.J.M., de Freitas, M.A.G., Sardo, J.D.P., Cardoso, P.J.S., Rodrigues, J.M.F.: MIRAR: mobile image recognition based augmented reality framework. In: Mortal, A., Aníbal, J., Monteiro, J., Sequeira, C., Semião, J., Moreira da Silva, M., Oliveira, M. (eds.) INCREaSE 2017, pp. 321–337. Springer, Cham (2018). https://doi.org/10.1007/978-3-319-70272-8_27
44. Qualcomm.: Invisible museum (2017). https://goo.gl/aS0NKh. Accessed 04 Apr 2017
45. Redmon, J., Farhadi, A.: Yolo9000: better, faster, stronger. arXiv preprint arXiv:1612.08242 (2016)
46. Riba Pi, E.: Implementation of a 3D pose estimation algorithm. Master's thesis, Universitat Politècnica de Catalunya (2015)
47. Ring, J.: The laser in astronomy. New Sci. **18**(344), 672–673 (1963)
48. Rodrigues, J.M.F., Pereira, J.A.R., Sardo, J.D.P., de Freitas, M.A.G., Cardoso, P.J.S., Gomes, M., Bica, P.: Adaptive card design UI implementation for an augmented reality museum application. In: Antona, M., Stephanidis, C. (eds.) UAHCI 2017. LNCS, vol. 10277, pp. 433–443. Springer, Cham (2017). https://doi.org/10.1007/978-3-319-58706-6_35
49. Rother, C., Kolmogorov, V., Blake, A.: Grabcut: Interactive foreground extraction using iterated graph cuts. In: ACM Transactions on Graphics (TOG), vol. 23, no. 3, pp. 309–314. ACM (2004)

50. Rublee, E., Rabaud, V., Konolige, K., Bradski, G.: ORB: an efficient alternative to SIFT or SURF. In: Proceedings of International Conference on Computer Vision, pp. 2564–2571. IEEE (2011)
51. Sardo, J.D.P., Semião, J., Monteiro, J.M., Pereira, J.A.R., de Freitas, M.A.G., Esteves, E., Rodrigues, J.M.F.: Portable device for touch, taste and smell sensations in augmented reality experiences. In: Mortal, A., Aníbal, J., Monteiro, J., Sequeira, C., Semião, J., Moreira da Silva, M., Oliveira, M. (eds.) INCREaSE 2017, pp. 305–320. Springer, Cham (2018). https://doi.org/10.1007/978-3-319-70272-8_26
52. Sermanet, P., Kavukcuoglu, K., Chintala, S., LeCun, Y.: Pedestrian detection with unsupervised multi-stage feature learning. In: IEEE Conference on Computer Vision and Pattern Recognition (CVPR), pp. 3626–3633. IEEE (2013)
53. Serrão, M., Shahrabadi, S., Moreno, M., José, J.T., Rodrigues, J.I., Rodrigues, J.M.F., du Buf, J.M.H.: Computer vision and GIS for the navigation of blind persons in buildings. Univ. Access Inf. Soc. 14(1), 67–80 (2015)
54. SM.: Science museum - atmosphere gallery (2017). https://vimeo.com/20789653. Accessed 04 Apr 2017
55. Sousa, L., Rodrigues, J.M.F., Monteiro, J., Cardoso, P.J.S., SemiãO, J., Alves, R.: A 3D gesture recognition interface for energy monitoring and control applications. In: Proceedings of ACE 2014, pp. 62–71 (2014)
56. Tian, Y., Luo, P., Wang, X., Tang, X.: Deep learning strong parts for pedestrian detection. In: Proceedings of the IEEE International Conference on Computer Vision, pp. 1904–1912 (2015)
57. TWSJ.: The wall street journal: Best apps for visiting museums (2017). https://goo.gl/cPTyP9. Accessed 04 Apr 2017
58. Unity.: Unity3D (2018). https://unity3d.com/pt. Accessed 10 Jan 2018
59. Vainstein, N., Kuflik, T., Lanir, J.: Towards using mobile, head-worn displays in cultural heritage: user requirements and a research agenda. In: Proceedings of the 21st International Conference on Intelligent User Interfaces, pp. 327–331. ACM (2016)
60. Xiao, J., Zhang, J., Adler, B., Zhang, H., Zhang, J.: Three-dimensional point cloud plane segmentation in both structured and unstructured environments. Rob. Auton.Syst. 61(12), 1641–1652 (2013)
61. Zhang, L., Lin, L., Liang, X., He, K.: Is faster R-CNN doing well for pedestrian detection? In: Leibe, B., Matas, J., Sebe, N., Welling, M. (eds.) ECCV 2016. LNCS, vol. 9906, pp. 443–457. Springer, Cham (2016). https://doi.org/10.1007/978-3-319-46475-6_28

Effect of Controlled Consciousness on Sense of Presence and Visually Induced Motion Sickness While Viewing Stereoscopic Movies

Akihiro Sugiura[1]($\boxtimes$), Kunihiko Tanaka[1], Kazuki Ohta[1],
Kazuki Kitamura[1], Saki Morisaki[1], and Hiroki Takada[2]

[1] Department of Radiological Technology, Gifu University of Medical Science,
Seki, Japan
asugiura@u-gifu-ms.ac.jp
[2] Graduate School of Engineering, University of Fukui, Fukui, Japan

Abstract. In our previous study, we found it is possible to have an effect of change in the condition of consciousness (allocation of consciousness) on visually evoked postural response (VEPRs) Then, in this study, we verified effect of controlling consciousness on VEPRs, visually induced motion sickness (VIMS), a sense of presence while viewing 3D movies. Participants watched 3D movie consisted of several colored balls sinusoidal moving at 0.25 Hz in the depth direction for 3 min each under condition following pre-instruction. The detail of the pre-instruction were "sway body in a parallel/opposite direction". The position of the body sway center of pressure was continuously recorded. As subjective evaluation, participants completed a simulator sickness questionnaire and reported three feelings (the sense of presence, motion and interactive) by using a visual analog scale. The results clearly showed that (1) The influence of pre-instruction appeared much stronger than that of VEPRs, and (2) The relationship between change in body sway and degree of VIMS or the feeling of presence do not always match under the situation included multi factors related to sense information or the condition of consciousness.

Keywords: Visually Evoked Postural Response (VEPR) · Body sway
Visually Induced Motion Sickness (VIMS) · Sense of presence
Consciousness

1 Introduction

With recent advances in display technologies, users can enjoy virtual experiences that provide feeling of presence defined as "sense of being there," [1] whether at home or at amusement parks. As a result, there has been an increase in the presentation of symptoms similar to motion sickness, often referred to as visually induced motion sickness (VIMS) or cybersickness [2, 3], which are experienced by users during or after enjoying these virtual activities. Stanney reported that 88% of virtual environment participants developed VIMS when viewing virtual reality movies for an hour [4]. Thus, in their current state, virtual experiences with the purpose of amusement often become stressors instead.

© Springer International Publishing AG, part of Springer Nature 2018
M. Antona and C. Stephanidis (Eds.): UAHCI 2018, LNCS 10908, pp. 122–131, 2018.
https://doi.org/10.1007/978-3-319-92052-8_10

The pathogenic mechanism of VIMS and the reasons for the onset of its complex symptoms are not sufficiently understood. However, one of the leading hypotheses involves sensory conflict theory, which suggests that the complex symptoms are caused by the presence of conflicts among the afferent inputs of the sensory modalities (vision, equilibrium sense, somatosensation) and the subject's perception [5, 6]. In particular, VIMS is evoked when information relayed by the visual system is contradictory to information from the other senses.

Postural responses that are induced by visual information, such as motions or gradients, are called visually evoked postural responses (VEPRs) [7] and are among the body responses related to VIMS or feeling of presence [8, 9]. Although there are various theories as to the reason for the appearance of VEPRs, our past study suggested the possibility that VEPRs were a conflict correction response aimed at matching the information from the other senses [10]. If the conclusions of the past study are correct, imposing suppression or acceleration of the conflict correction response (VEPRs) may be a method of preventing VIMS. Moreover, control of VEPRs might be useful for adjustment of the feeling of presence. In our previous study, we found it is possible to have an effect of change in the condition of consciousness (allocation of consciousness) on VEPRs [11]. In a similar example, Hoshikawa reported that when subjects devoted more attention to their own bodies, body sway induced by a visual stimulus lessened [12]. In this study, we verified the effect of controlling consciousness on VEPRs, VIMS, a sense of presence while viewing stereoscopic movies.

2   Material and Method

2.1   Participants

Seven university students (2 males and 5 females; 21–22 years old) who did not have vision or equilibrium problems participated in this study. The study was approved by the Research Ethics Committee at Gifu University of Medical Science. Oral and written consent was obtained from the participants after the purpose and significance of the study and the nature and risk of the measurements were explained. In addition, the study was conducted in accordance with the 1964 Declaration of Helsinki and its later amendments or comparable ethical standards.

2.2   Visual Stimulation

A screenshot of the movie as visual stimulation used in this study is shown in Fig. 1. The visual stimulation was delivered via a movie created using 3ds Max 2017 computer graphics software (Autodesk, San Rafael, CA, USA). The movie consisted of several colored balls displayed at random positions. We designed the movie with the balls sinusoidal moving at 0.25 Hz in the depth direction and was generated by moving camera-simulated ocular globes (the balls themselves did not move). The amplitude of the sinusoidal motion was set to 200 as the software setting.

The experimental setup utilized in this study is shown in Fig. 2. We performed the experiments in a controlled environment (illuminance: under 10 lx) in order to limit the

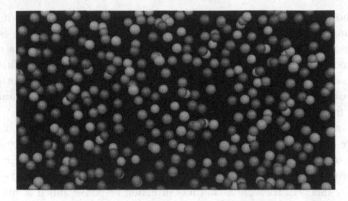

Fig. 1. Screenshot of the movie used in this study. A large number of balls were located at random positions, The motion in the movies was sinusoidal at 0.25 Hz in the depth direction.

variations to visual input. The movie was displayed on an LCD monitor (42LW5700, LG, Seoul, Korea) 50 cm in front of the participant. The displayed movie size was 99.30 cm × 52.62 cm with a resolution of 1,920 × 1,080. The participants watched the experimental 3D movies using circularly polarized glasses.

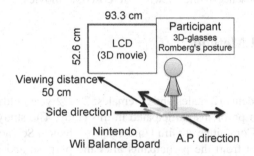

Fig. 2. Experimental session diagram. The movie was displayed on an LCD monitor 50 cm in front of the participant. The participants watched the experimental 3D movies using 3D-glasses. In order to measure the position of the center of pressure (CoP), participants were asked to stand on a Wii Balance Board with Romberg's posture. Points to the left or posterior to CoP were expressed as negative values.

2.3   Procedure and Design

The study protocol is shown in Fig. 3. For Task 1, a participant stood on the Wii Balance Board and watched a static (nonmoving) movie for 1 min as the pretest. Task 2 was divided into three tasks, For Task 2-A, participants watched the motion movie for 3 min under uncontrolled their consciousness. For Task 2-B, participants watched that for 3 min based on a pre-instruction (sway your body in a parallel direction with ball moving phase while maintaining Romberg's posture). For Task 2-C, participants watched that for 3 min based on the pre-instruction (sway your body in a opposite direction with that while maintaining Romberg's posture). Participants performed the three tasks (Task 2-A to 2-C) in a random sequence to avoid the order effect. Task interval was set at more than 5 min.

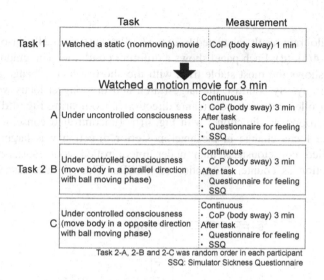

Fig. 3. Study protocol and measurements.

2.4 Measurement and Analysis

The position of the body sway center of pressure (CoP) was continuously recorded with the Wii Balance Board using stabilometry software custom-built with WiimoteLib in each Task. The CoP measurements were recorded at 20 Hz, which is a basic sampling setting in clinical gravimetric tests. The continuous CoP data were separated by intervals of 1 min of viewing time to analyze each time segment. CoP data were analyzed for instability of postural maintenance and body sway periodicity. Area and total locus length were measured as indexes of the postural instability, and the power spectral density (PSD) at 0.25 Hz in depth direction calculated from a fast Fourier transform with a Hamming window assessed the body sway periodicity. Wilcoxon signed-rank tests with Šidák correction were performed using ORIGIN Pro 8.5 (OriginLab, Corporation, Northampton, MA, USA) among each Task 2 in same time segment.

As VIMS symptoms, participants completed a simulator sickness questionnaire (SSQ) after each Task 2. The total score and three subscores (nausea, oculomotor discomfort, disorientation) were calculated. Then, Wilcoxon signed-rank tests with Šidák correction were performed among each Task 2.

As the sense of presence, participants reported three feelings (the sense of presence, motion and interactive) as that word or similar meaning words) by using a visual analog scale (VAS) that ranged from 0 to 10 after each Task 2 after the sensory scale was explained (0: not at all, 10: very much). Then, Wilcoxon signed-rank tests with Šidák correction were performed among each Task.

3 Results

A typical stabilogram result calculated from the CoP data (from a 21 year-old female) is shown in Fig. 4(a)–(d). Each panel shows a different condition. The graph in Fig. 4(a) (nonmoving) shows the most stable trial, with the shortest locus change and smallest area of body sway. By contrast, the largest area and the longest locus were found in Fig. 4(c) (controlled consciousness (same direction)). Comparing Fig. 4(d) (controlled consciousness (opposite direction)) with Fig. 4(b) (uncontrolled consciousness (same direction)), the locus change in the anteroposterior direction was larger in the trial under controlled consciousness than under uncontrolled consciousness despite of opposite direction as counter instruction to VEPRs. Thus, it was assumed that the

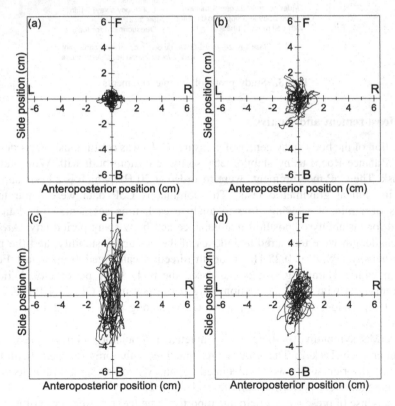

Fig. 4. A typical stabilogram result (21 year-old female). "F, B, R, and L" in each stabilogram represent "front", "back", "right", and "left", respectively. (a) Task 1: nonmoving (pretest), (b) Task 2-A: uncontrolled consciousness, (c) Task 2-B: controlled consciousness (same direction), and (d) Task 2-C: controlled consciousness (opposite direction).

pre-instruction has an especially strong influence, comparing information from other senses.

Figure 5 shows the change in postural instability at different the pre-instruction. Figure 5(a) and (b) show area and total locus length, respectively, and Fig. 5(c) shows the power spectral density (PSD) at 0.25 Hz as index of body sway periodicity, which were obtained from the frequency analysis. These results indicated similar tendencies. The results of the controlled consciousness (same direction) task showed the highest postural instability and the body sway periodicity among all tasks, and the results of the uncontrolled consciousness were lowest. Then, compared with the uncontrolled consciousness task, both of the controlled consciousness tasks indicated significantly increases in postural instability and body sway periodicity ($P < 0.05$). Moreover, temporal change in the index was only seen in the same direction task.

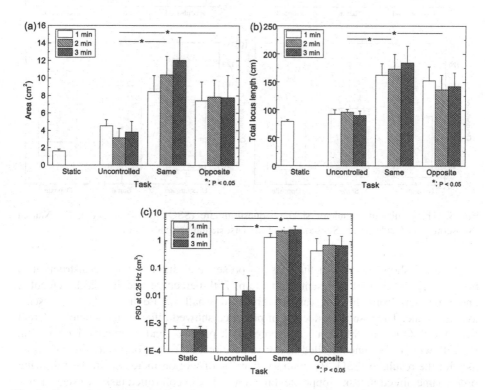

Fig. 5. Postural instability and body sway periodicity at different the pre-instruction and temporally changes. (a) Area, (b) Total locus length, and (c) PSD at 0.25 Hz

Figure 6 shows SSQ results (total score and three subscores) at different the pre-instruction as box plot. Each box plot represents maximum, 75th-percentile, median, 25th- percentile and minimum from the top, respectively, and small square in the box represents average score. All SSQ scores indicated the same tendencies, regardless of kind of SSQ score. First, median score and 75th-percentile value increased in the following order: uncontrolled task < same direction task < opposite direction task. However, significantly changes in all SSQ scores were not found in between tasks. Second, individual bias of SSQ score was large in all tasks.

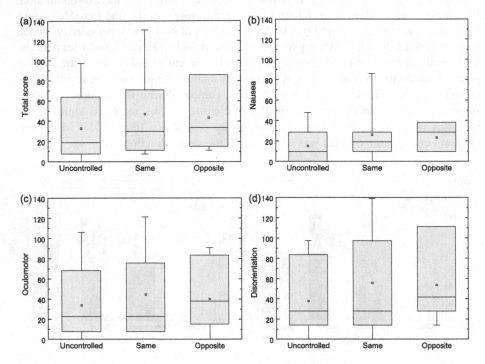

Fig. 6. The results of Simulator sickness questionnaire (SSQ). (a) Total score, (b) Nausea (Subscore), (c) Oculomotor (Subscore), and (d) Disorientation (Subscore)

Figure 7 shows results for the sense of presence at different the pre-instruction as box plot. Each box plot represents maximum, 75th-percentile, median, 25th-percentile and minimum from the top, respectively, and small square in the box represents average value. The results for feeling of presence showed different tendencies different from the SSQ results. Median VAS scores both presence and interactive increased in the following order: uncontrolled task < same direction task < opposite direction task, as with the results of SSQ. By contrast, that for of motion increased in the following order: same direction task < opposite direction task < uncontrolled task. All sense items (presence, motion and interactive) also had huge individual bias.

4   Discussion

In this study, we verified the effect of controlling consciousness on VEPRs, VIMS, the sense of presence while viewing 3D movies with the balls sinusoidal moving at 0.25 Hz in the depth direction. For the controlling consciousness, we instructed that maintaining Romberg's posture under uncontrolled consciousness, that under

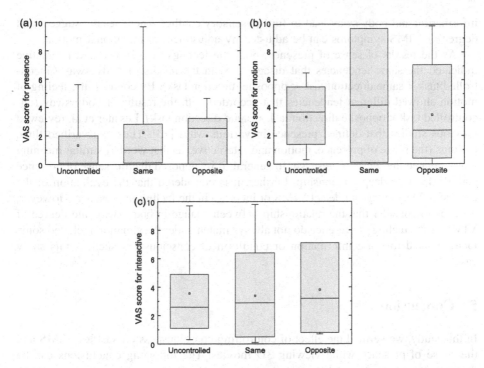

Fig. 7. The results for the sense of presence. (a) feeling of presence, (b) feeling of motion, and (c) feeling of interactive.

controlled consciousness (sway your body in a parallel direction with ball moving phase), or that under controlled consciousness (sway your body in a opposite direction with that) while viewing the experimental movie in each Task. The results of sta-bilogram, indexes of the postural instability such as area and total locus length and the frequency analysis showed increase in locus length and area as indexes of postural instability and body sway periodicity following order: same direction task > opposite direction task > uncontrolled task. The influence of pre-instruction appeared much stronger than that of VEPRs because the results related measurement of body sway in opposite direction task were larger than that in the uncontrolled direction task. In the opposite direction task, these results assumed that VEPRs had counter role to the intentional body sway under control. Thus, the pre-instruction had strong influence. In other words, the condition of consciousness (allocation of consciousness) was important factor for the relationship between vision and equilibrium sense.

As the results of SSQ, all SSQ scores indicated the same tendencies that disagreed with the results of body sway, although individual variation existed (uncontrolled task < same direction task < opposite direction task). Compared to the uncontrolled task, the task with controlled consciousness increased in the sensory conflict because participant swayed advisedly based on the pre-instruction. In same direction task, participant swayed larger than their supposition because VEPRs were added to body sway evoked the pre-instruction. In opposite direction task, increase in conflict between vision information and body sway lead to further sensory conflict. These results suggest that degree of VIMS symptoms can be adjusted by adjustment of intentional motion.

As the results of sense of presence, both the feelings of presence and interactive indicated the same tendencies that disagreed with the results of body sway (uncontrolled task < same direction task < opposite direction task). By contrast, the feeling of motion showed different tendencies that accorded with the results of body sway (uncontrolled task < opposite direction task < same direction task). Lessiter et al. reviewed previous studies that defined presence in various ways [13]. Thus, we verified three feelings (the sense of presence, motion and interactive) as that word or similar meaning words related the sense of presence. In general, it is supposed that the sense of presence and VIMS have deep relationship. Further, it is considered that the evaluation of the change in body sway can detect VIMS or increase in the feeling of presence. However, it needs to consider that the relationship between change in body sway and degree of VIMS or the feeling of presence do not always match under the situation included some factor related to sense information or condition of consciousness such as this study case.

5 Conclusion

In this study, we verified the effect of controlling consciousness on VEPRs, VIMS and the sense of presence while viewing 3D movies. The following conclusions can be drawn:

1. The influence of pre-instruction appeared much stronger than that of VEPRs because the results related measurement of body sway in the opposite direction task were larger than that in the uncontrolled task. The pre-instruction had strong influence to the relationship between vision and equilibrium sense.

2. The relationship between change in body sway and degree of VIMS or the feeling of presence do not always match under the situation included multi factors related to sense information or the condition of consciousness such as this study case.

Acknowledgments. We would also like to thank the participants who participated in this experimental study. This work was supported by a JSPS KAKENHI Grant-in-Aid for Scientific Research (C), 15K00702 and 17K00715.

References

1. Bowman, D.A., Mcmahan, R.R.P., Tech, V.: Virtual reality: how much immersion is enough? Comput. (Long. Beach. Calif.) **40**, 36–43 (2007)
2. Kennedy, R.C.S., Drexler, J., Kennedy, R.C.S.: Research in visually induced motion sickness. Appl. Ergon. **41**, 494–503 (2010)
3. Stanney, K.M., Kennedy, R.S., Drexler, J.M., Harm, D.L.: Motion sickness and proprioceptive aftereffects following virtual environment exposure. Appl. Ergon. **30**, 27–38 (1999)

4. Stanney, K.M., Kingdon, K.S., Kennedy, R.S.: Dropouts and aftereffects: examining general accessibility to virtual environment technology. In: Proceedings of the Human Factors and Ergonomics Society Annual Meeting, pp. 2114–2118. SAGE Publications (2002)
5. Oman, C.M.: Motion sickness: a synthesis and evaluation of the sensory conflict theory. Can. J. Physiol. Pharmacol. **68**, 294–303 (1990)
6. Reason, J.T.: Motion sickness adaptation: a neural mismatch model. J. R. Soc. Med. **71**, 819–829 (1978)
7. Bronstein, A.M.: Suppression of visually evoked postural responses. Exp. Brain Res. **63**, 655–658 (1986)
8. Stoffregen, T.A., Smart, L.J., Stofregen, T.A., Smart, L.J.: Postural instability preceedes motion sickness. Brain Res. Bull. **47**, 437–448 (1998)
9. Rebenitsch, L., Owen, C.: Review on cybersickness in applications and visual displays. Virtual Real. **20**, 101–125 (2016)
10. Sugiura, A., Tanaka, K., Wakatabe, S., Matsumoto, C., Miyao, M.: Temporal analysis of body sway during reciprocator motion movie viewing. Nihon Eiseigaku Zasshi **71**, 19–29 (2016)
11. Sugiura, A., Akachi, K., Ito, A.Y.C., Kondo, S., Tanaka, K., Takada, H.: Experimental study on control of visually evoked postural responses by galvanic vestibular stimulation. In: 2017 12th International Conference on Computer Science and Education (ICCSE), pp. 77–82. IEEE (2017)
12. Hoshikawa, T.: Effects of body control and attention on body sway induced by a tilting room. Jpn. J. Psychol. **69**, 310–316 (1998)
13. Lessiter, J., Freeman, J., Keogh, E., Davidoff, J.: A cross-media presence questionnaire: the ITC-sense of presence inventory. Presence Teleoperators Virtual Environ. **10**, 282–297 (2001)

Exploring Virtual Reality to Enable Deaf or Hard of Hearing Accessibility in Live Theaters: A Case Study

Mauro Teófilo[✉], Alvaro Lourenço, Juliana Postal, and Vicente F. Lucena Jr.

SIDIA - Samsung Research Institute, Federal University of Amazonas, Manaus, Brazil
{mauro.t,alvaro.abl,j.postal}@samsung.com, vicente@ufam.edu.br

Abstract. Recent advancements in Virtual reality (VR) have made them a potential technology to improve speech understanding for deaf or hard of hearing (DHH). We want to extend this commodity to live communication in theater plays, which has not been investigated so far. For this, present study evaluates the efficiency of a language processing system, which makes use of VR technology combined with AI implementations for automatic speech recognition (ASR), sentence prediction and spelling correction. A quantitative and qualitative study was performed and demonstrated good overall results of the system regarding DHH understanding and satisfaction along entire play sessions. *abstract environment.*

Keywords: Virtual reality · Accessibility
Deaf or hard-of-hearing people · Captioning system
Subtitle display · Speech transcription

1 Introduction

In the last years, a rising number of researches around virtual environments (VE) has been scoping its possible benefits to compensate people for hearing disadvantages by improving their autonomy. In a previous study, VR technology has proved efficiency in helping impaired people [27], and with increased availability and public interest around virtual/augmented reality topic (VR/AR) [19,20], a number of authors started working on automated transcriptions for deaf or hard-of-hearing (DHH) people, attacking the matter from a number of models with different levels of success [3,22,24]. The overall approach leverages VR and AR capabilities of attaching message to objects in real-time [3] to improve usability within many specific contexts: from silent to noisy environments [19,20], single educational material [24] to entire library spaces and other indoor positioning systems [18].

When put in perspective, these works reveal a common consensus about the need for accuracy and the stratification of concerns that potentially solves the whole problem. Some argue of error suppression and its relevant impacts over

© Springer International Publishing AG, part of Springer Nature 2018
M. Antona and C. Stephanidis (Eds.): UAHCI 2018, LNCS 10908, pp. 132–148, 2018.
https://doi.org/10.1007/978-3-319-92052-8_11

understandability [10]; others of the composition with further technology such as text-to-speech (TTS), automatic speech recognition (ASR) and audio-visual speech recognition (AVSR) [19,20]; all trying to reach a better transcription, caption, and signal language performance across many scenarios. Approaches measured confidence and reliability of display styles, output latency and precision of on-screen subtitles; observed and interviewed DHH users; and also inspected final levels of understanding with results ranging around 60 and 80%, without however declaring a gold standard to address one mainstream user experience [3,10,20,22,24].

1.1   VR and the Accessibility Research Field

The use Virtual Reality (VR) for DHH and other recent accessibility research for the inclusion of impaired people comes from a resourceful research sprint that ranges at least two strong decades. Within this time, plentiful reports applied the technology to a wide range of accessibility topics, targeting from those with learning disabilities to others with anxiety and phobias, other times leveraging mobility and life quality for spinal cord injured patients and those fighting along post strokes. Just recently, as more authors are following the fresh possibilities of the renewed generation of pervasive and popular technologies, a newer thread have been targeting the benefits of virtual accessibility to socialize the visual and auditory impaired people.

Before hitting the inclusion topic, however, this ever growing legacy for accessibility fields ranged at least three major research groups: Autism Spectrum Disorders (ASDs) [7], happening around 1996, continuing across 2005 with Physical Rehabilitation, and in later years with reports about VR therapies to ease Parkinson Disease (PD) and Traumatic Brain Injury (TBI) symptoms. Along the years, analysis of the VR benefits often included the improved safety and adherence to programs, the documentation and individualization capabilities, and of course some hard and better results.

Autism Spectrum Disorders. In autism, psychology authors considered that VR may provide improvements to the treatment of ASDs (Autism Spectrum Disorders) by increasing frequency and customization of role-playing tests while demanding less resources (e.g. teachers, parents, schools) [23]. Although theorized to offer enhanced results for ASD therapies, these methods were not tested so far [21]. Proponents of methodologies such as the 'Behavioral' and 'Theory of Mind' (ToM) discuss the different approaches and results for the topic, mainly arguing around the cost and outcomes in terms of learning and generalization. While the first offers better promises, it does so at more expensive school and structure requirements. ToM in the other hand focuses on teaching straightforward behaviors with the expense of less resources, with unfortunately lesser ambitions in terms of recovering children from their generalization handicaps. Acting in a position to overcome structure investments, some authors consider VR technology capabilities to automate and personalize therapies, and therefore improve final results.

Physical Rehabilitation. For motor rehab, compared studies between traditional and VR based therapies had consistently reported the VR superiority in a number of programs ranging from bicycle exercises to occupational therapy [28]. The studies generally presents the opportunity for automatic movement analysis and progressive challenge updates, while reducing boredom, fatigue and lack of cooperation with an acute increment of patients motivation [1,4]. So far, these studies managed to improve posture, balance control, velocity and path deviation on bicycle exercises, inspecting increased pain tolerance levels, distance, duration, and energy consumption [12]. Similarly, studies on the field of occupational therapy also managed to inspect greater gains of dynamic standing tolerance in geriatric patients by using the VR technology. Studies of virtual therapies for traumatic brain injury and orthopedic appliances stated substantial improvements of patient enthusiasm [9,17,25,26], confidence and motivation [5,13], even when in absence of better hard performance indicators.

Parkinson Disease. Improvements on the negative impacts of Parkinson disease (PD) over patients cognitive and motor functions were also reported in 2010, succeeding to apply VR to exceed traditional treadmill training (TT) outcomes in aspects such as attention management, gait speeds, stride lengths, with additional development of cognitive strategies to navigate throughout virtual obstacles [14]. Results were inspected and proven to be retained after therapy sessions, being thoroughly scrutinized during and after program administration, confirming the retention and the occasional improvement of therapy gains in the months after. Authors assumes that TT with VR technology can actually relief cognitive and motor malfunctions of patients with PD, delivering better attention levels with the development of new strategies to overcome virtual obstacles.

1.2 Research Context

With a DHH population of 9 million people and a rich cultural environment, Brazil presents a challenging yet resourceful landscape for accessibility systems to be introduced and matured. Majority of impaired people in the country are unable to attend at theaters due to the lack of even basic accessibility services such as stage live-action subtitles and professional interpreters. All this poses Brazil as a good research lab to start and scale production of VE methods abroad, later hitting the impressive global DHH population of 5% [10].

From this scenario, our study takes advantage of Samsung Research efforts in Brazil to add more findings on this research thread. With first results publicized through "Theater for All Ears" campaign[1], the research underneath attempted to spot improvement venues for HCI in VE, inspecting challenges of DHH theater accessibility to propose a new concept that exceeds the efficiency and scalability results of traditional interpreters and stage captioning systems. We started from basic speech transcription models to inquire more than 40 users across 10 semi-controlled experiments that happened between May and July 2017, on

---

[1] https://vimeo.com/217227242.

weekly theater sessions in São Paulo, Brazil. Then we assessed new opportunities based on collected results and explored progressive models to improve accuracy of captioning systems using ASR, natural language processing (NLP), and artificial intelligence (AI); tame key usability factors; and achieve new state of art technology for better accessibility in live theaters.

In Sect. 2, we present related works that also scoped the automatic generation of subtitles for DHH people, followed by the proposal of a new IA based approach for language processing in Sect. 3. Our experiment methodology and results are discussed in Sect. 4, with conclusions further planned steps in Sect. 5.

2   Related Work

The use of Augmented Reality to improve communication with DHH people in real-time is a chance for research with strong social impacts as it enables the social inclusion of impaired people in theater entertainment, conferences and all sorts of live presentations. In this section we highlight related works that followed this important thread.

Mirzaei et al. [19] solution improves live communication between deaf and ordinary people by turning ordinary people's speech into text in a device used by the deaf communicator. In this situation, the deaf also can write texts to be turned back into speech, so the ordinary people can understand. The solution is composed by a device and a software in which narrator (ordinary person) speech is captured by ASR or AVSR (Audio-Visual Speech Recognition) and turned into text, the Joiner Algorithm uses the text generated by ASR or AVSR and creates an AR environment with the image of narrator and text boxes of his speech. TTS engines are used to convert texts written by deaf people into speech for the narrator, making possible a two-way conversation. The results pointed that the average processing time for word recognition and AR displaying is less than 3 s using ASR mode, and less than 10 s for AVSR mode. To evaluate the solution, they conducted a survey with 100 deaf people and 100 ordinary people to measure the interest rate of using technological communication methods between them and 90% of participants agreed that the system is really useful, but there's still opportunity for improvements with AVSR mode, which is more accurate in noisy environments.

Berke [3] believes that providing word and its confidence score in a subtitle using AR environment, in order to give more information about the narrators speech, will improve deaf people understanding of a conversation. The method proposal consists in a captioning which words generated by speech to text are displayed with its score of confidence in the subtitle and different colors are given for more confident and less confident words. These scores are calculated based on how sure speech to text algorithm are about the match of voice captured and the acoustic model of a word. The author also wants to study a way to present these information without confuse or make more difficult for the deaf to read the subtitle and pay attention on the narrator.

Piquard-Kipffer et al. [22] made a study to evaluate the best way to present the text generated by speech to text algorithm in French language. The study covered 3 display modes: Orthographic, where recognized words are written into orthographical form; International Phonetic Alphabet (IPA), which writes all the recognized words and syllables in phonetic form by using the International Phonetic Alphabet, and lastly a Pseudo-phonetic where recognized words and syllables are written into a pseudo-phonetic alphabet. Some problems that challenge automatic subtitle systems such as noises captured by the device's unsophisticated microphones, implied in an incorrect word generation by ASR as reported in [19] thus flawing message understanding in deaf people's side. To minimize this negative, they included additional information about converted text within the subtitle for all display modes - like a confidence value for each word as proposed in [3, 22]. Experiments with 10 deaf persons found best reviews when using a confidence score to format correct words in bold while presenting the incorrectly recognized ones in pseudo-phonetic mode; and suggested that preceding training phase for the experiment would be necessary to make participants more familiar with pseudo-phonetic reading. All participants manifested interest for such a system and thought that it could be helpful.

Hong et al. [6] propose a scheme to improve the experience of DHH people with video captions, called Dynamic Captioning. It involves facial recognition, visual saliency analysis, text-speech alignment and other techniques. First, a script-face matching is done to identify which people the subtitles belong to in the scenes, this is based on face recognition, then a non-intrusive area is chosen in the video so that the caption can be positioned to avoid occlusion of important parts of the video and compromise the understanding of its content, the display of the caption emphasizing word for word is done through script-speech alignment and finally a voice volume estimation is done to display the magnitude indicator of the character's voice in the video. In order to validate the solution, the authors invited 60 hearing impaired people to an experiment that consists of watching 20 videos where some metrics such as comprehension and impression about the videos would be evaluated, in this experiment 3 captioning paradigms were tested: No Captioning, Static Captioning and Dynamic Captioning. The results showed that the No Captioning paradigm presented a poor experience for users, Static Captioning contributed to user distraction and 93.3% of users preferred Dynamic Captioning.

Beadles et al. [2] patent propose an apparatus for providing closed captioning at a performance comprise means for encoding a signal representing the written equivalent of spoken dialogue. The signal is synchronized with spoken dialog and transmitted to wearable glasses of a person watching the performance. The glasses include receiving and decoding circuits and means for projecting a display image into the field of view of the person watching the performance representing at least one line of captioning. The field of view of the displayed image is equivalent to the field of view of the performance. A related method for providing closed captioning further includes the step of accommodating for different interpupillary distances of the person wearing the glasses.

Luo et al. [15] designed and implemented a Mixed Reality application which simulates in-class assistive learning and tested at Chinas largest DHH education institute. The experiments consisted in let these DHH children study a subject that is not in their regular curriculum and verify if the solution can improve the learning process. The solution has two main components, one component is the assisting console controlled by a hearing student, the other component is the virtual character displaying viewport which fulfills assistance. Both components use a dual-screen setup, within each component, one of the screens displays lecture video and the other screen displays mixed reality user interaction or rendering content. Videos on the screens of both components are synchronized in time. The hearing impaired student side of the system has a virtual character shown on the user content screen which can take predefined actions, while the hearing student side of the system has a control UI shown on the user content screen to manipulate virtual character at the other end to perform such actions. Results showed that the experience of being assisted by a virtual character were mostly very positive. Students rated this approach as novel, interesting and fun. 86,7% of them felt that with such help, it was easier to catch the pace of the lecture, understand the importance of knowledge points, and keep focused across the entire learning session.

Kercher and Rowe [11] propose a design, prototyping and usability testing of an AR head-mounted display system designed to improve the learning experience for the deaf, avoiding the attention split problem common among DHH people in learning process. The solution is focused in child's experience in a planetarium show. Their solution consists in three parts: Filming of the interpreter in front of a green screen, use a server to communicate the interpreter video to the headset and user interface for testing headset projection manipulation and optimization, then the interpreter will be always in the field of view of DHH spectator as it can also look freely to all directions and enjoy the show. The authors expect in the end of 3 years of research to not only help young children to have better experience in planetarium show but contribute in major changes in the experiences of the deaf in a variety of environments including planetariums, classrooms, museums, sporting events, live theaters and cinemas.

In our solution we present different strategies to deal with these problems, as detailed in the following section.

3   System Overview

This section presents a solution which uses speech recognition and AI to retrieve the correct subtitle of live play scenes using text from play script. Figure 1 hows the concept model for system's architecture.

3.1   The Actor Module

In Actors device module, a speech-to-text algorithm for Portuguese language converts recorded voice into text, using the first few words to retrieve the correct play speech using a sentence prediction algorithm before communicating it to server. The sentence prediction workflow is presented in Fig. 2. When the device

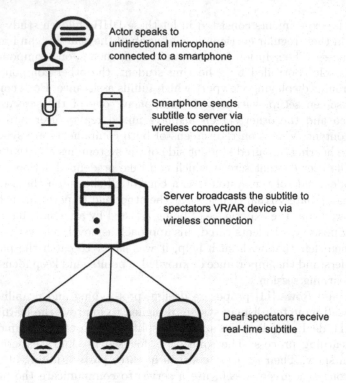

Actor speaks to
unidirectional microphone
connected to a smartphone

Smartphone sends
subtitle to server via
wireless connection

Server broadcasts the subtitle to
spectators VR/AR device via
wireless connection

Deaf spectators receive
real-time subtitle

Fig. 1. System architecture.

application starts, play script is submitted to Ngram algorithm which counts and calculates probabilities for all sets of N sentences, building a data table that serves as language model which can be queried with first N words converted from speech-to-text as key, and returning the most probable sentence.

Sentence prediction will ensure the behavior of retrieving subtitles in real-time while scene performance is occurring. If a search for speech play retrieves no match, system realizes that there is an impromptu occurring, and if needed it passes raw converted words to a word correction algorithm, which then communicates with the server. As demonstrated by Fig. 3, word correction algorithm verifies if the words are present in Portuguese dictionary. If they are it skips correction, otherwise it searches for the most similar word in dictionary based on edit distance, and then overwrites those incorrect with similar words. Incorrect words are saved to be used as data for word correction retraining, as well as words captured from impromptu, which can be used in future sentence prediction retrain. Subtitles sent to server contain actor's character identification, line of speech identification and the subtitle itself. Server uses these line values to broadcast subtitles in the correct order. Lines for impromptu messages receives an special value.

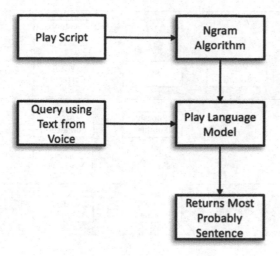

Fig. 2. System's sentence prediction.

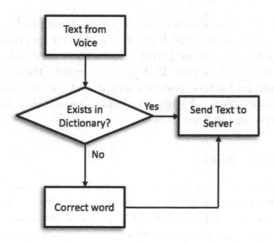

Fig. 3. System's word correction.

3.2   The Server Module

All performing actors in stage for the play carried a unidirectional microphone connected to a Samsung S8 device. Unidirectional microphones prevented undesired recording of noises from environment and voices from other actors. Each device had a copy of the play script to support the task of retrieving actor's speech as text. Actors voices were continuously recorded by their devices and no further interaction was required to operate the application.

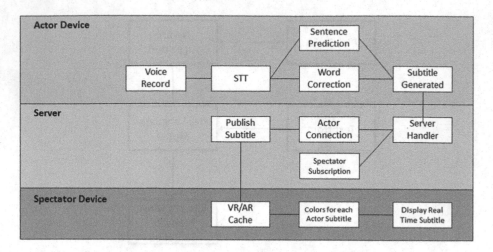

Fig. 4. System solution.

All actors and spectator's device connections are managed by a single server, which broadcasts subtitles received from all actors to all spectators. The first few words converted into text are used to search for the exact play speech using IA before communicating it to server. If there is no match, the system understand it as an impromptu, and starts sending every word to server as soon as they are converted from actor's voice. Figure 4 presents the solution and explain more specifically how system modules work.

3.3 The Spectator Module

Server have handlers for actor devices connections, disconnections and subtitle communication. Each actor's device has its own connection which remains open until application closes. In the other side, spectator devices do not send messages to server, using only available subscription services. For each subscribed spectator, server broadcasts every received subtitle until unsubscription request happens. When subtitles are received by AR/VR application, they are added to a queue and wait to be displayed. The application renders each actor's subtitles with a distinct color that is consistent during all play. When presenting these, a calculation is made to verify whether text fits in the UI space, and if they don't, subtitle gets split and displayed by parts. Then a comfortable time estimation is given based in each subtitle's size, defining when it will be overwritten by the next subtitle. When there is no subtitles in queue, application simply listens for upcoming server subtitles until the end of the play. Figure 5 shows an demonstration of how subtitle is in VR environment.

Fig. 5. Subtitle in gear VR.

4   Experiment and Results

In 2017, from May 12th to July 23rd, we conducted 10 user testing (UT) sessions in two mainstream theaters in São Paulo city, Brazil. Structured data and qualitative insights were collected from 43 DHH attendants over weekly performances of 'O Pai' play - 'The Father', from the original French 'Le Père'.

Fig. 6. User's test participants and instructors.

Writer	Florian Zeller
Director	Léo Stefanini
Translators	Carolina Gonzalez and Lenita Aghetoni
Cast	Fulvio Stefanini, Carol Gonzalez, Lara Córdulla, Carol Mariottini, Paulo Emilio Lisboa and Wilson Gomes

Fig. 7. Cast actors and information about the play "O Pai".

The Fig. 6 shows participants using Gear VR after the play in Fernando Torres theater.

Figure 7 shows the cast of play 'O Pai' and summarizes the technical information about play staged during tests.

4.1   User Test Method

Participants were selected with aid from regional Deaf association. Before play, participants were trained by supervisors about how to use the app on the VR device (Gear VR + Galaxy S7), eventual experiment issues and quick fixes, in case they occur. Figure 8 shows the DHH participants watching the play through Gear VR.

After play, participants answered 4 structured questions about image/display, subtitle, understanding and satisfaction using Likert-scale (1 poor to 5 best):

Fig. 8. DHH users watching the play.

- Image/display: whether they could see actors and stage with desired quality
- Subtitle: if they could read transcriptions with proper timing and readability
- Understanding: whether they could get the entire stream of speeches and emotions
- Satisfaction: how pleasant and rewarding it was to use the VR captioning system

The answers are summarized in the Boxplot chart showed in Fig. 9 and finally, participants went into an interview that collected qualitative insights about their experience along the play.

4.2   Results

Evaluation of Image/Display. Most participants had neutral to bad opinion about image provided by Gear VR + Galaxy S7, thus image/display was the worst factor of all analysis, mainly due to its inability to manage light intensity and to provide required definition. By sitting afar from stage, participant camera was unable to capture enough pixels to render details from actor's facial expressions, suffering severe interference from stage lights, which sometimes added just too much brightness to final rendered image. Some users suggested the addition of features such as zoom, focal adjustments, and brightness control.

Evaluation of Subtitles. Subtitles had some dispersion on votes, but a consistent amount of these were around a good opinion, it means that subtitles may performed well, but there is still much room for improvements. There were

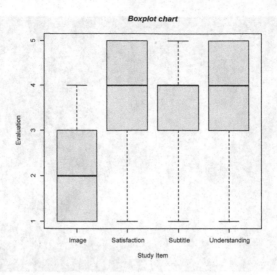

Fig. 9. Results from structured questions.

one relevant complaint about caption synchronization, and a minor critic about recognition errors. Users also suggested additional features to regulate caption size, adjust its placement and contrast on-screen.

Evaluation of Understanding and Satisfaction. Overall understanding and satisfaction were good, understanding were well voted by participants, that means they could follow all the play and be aware of surrounding spectators emotions, many participants freely stating that not only the technology helped on understanding but also that it was better than using professional interpreter services. Votes for satisfaction had similar distribution, this may suggest that understanding positively influences satisfaction.

Evaluation of Technical Setup. Technical setup, however, suffered from some issues during UT sessions. A third of users complained about head or eye strain during the play, most accusing solution from being too bright and Gear VR from being too heavy; Nearly 30% of users opted to remove the device at least once during play to take of the device to accommodate, clean their correction glasses or complained about image quality; It was necessary to replace devices some times along sessions due to overheating and some other unidentified application malfunction; And finally, 10% of users reported that technical breaks compromised the understanding at some extent.

4.3   Experiment Limitations

All participants were invited by Samsung (free of charge); We noticed some observer-expectancy effect; It is still important to test the device in different plays styles.

4.4   Improvement Chances

Great majority of issues seems to have an integrated solution with the adoption of lighter and unobtrusive AR glasses instead of Gear VR: from light intensity to image definition, facial expressions, inadequate rendering of stage lights, excessive brightness, head and eye strain, and excessive device weight. All seem to be easily solved by most of AR concepts available and probable to come.

Some other issues, however, can yet be discussed for further optimization: better software validation, overheating and simultaneous use of correction glasses.

5   Conclusion

Captioning system empowers DHH people by translating people's voice into text and then turning it into subtitles. This work extended this convenience to live theaters, by proposing a specific application that has not been investigated so far. Systems like this are far from optimal with many unsolved challenges for bullet-proof subtitle generation that ensures understanding and participation for DHH people in any live event. However, with the increasing interest of research community on the topic, authors and solutions tend to improve over time.

Current solutions for captioning in theaters which involves specialized sound equipment and professional typists raises two main problems:

- *Contract specialized sound and caption systems are expensive:*
  There is a complex sound setup to support the typists because of special equipment to treat the sound (avoid noise in sound signal and enhance the voice of actor), the hiring of professional typist itself and also the softwares used to generate and send subtitles and to manage the connections of typists and Spectators Gear VR through the server. This condition may result in higher theater tickets prices that could discourage DHH people to attend the show or theater itself to no more provide this accessibility.
- *Typists cause delay in subtitles:*
  Typists need to listen to all actors speech before typing the subtitle, so it means that subtitles will come always after the scene is already passed.

Despite the problems, our experiments to verify if DHH people found such system useful in this case of study of a live theater situation leveraged knowledge about usability of this special class of people and we were able to propose an improvement for current solution based on collecting their insights and improvement suggestions. Thus, knowing the problems and collecting suggestions we proposed a new solution that uses a combination of AI implementations for language modeling and transcription for VE that exempts traditional human interpreter or typist work.

UT pointed that participants could follow the entire play with good understanding of both scene rationale and crowd emotion, with results pointing that these two components are crucial drivers for user overall satisfaction. Subtitles had good reviews with lesser complaints about subtitle synchronization, but it was expected once we knew that the typist would influence in this point and images had bad reviews mostly because of camera and hardware limitations.

In general, subtitle systems for theaters are well accepted by DHH spectators and we believe that a new version supported by our proposed technology, can improve DHH people experience watching the play. This points VR and AR devices as cost reduction alternatives for accessibility in theaters and possibly other live events.

5.1 Future Works

With results reveling opportunity for improvements in subtitles and image areas, we will conduct new UT sessions using proposed solution of Sect. 4 to test the main hypothesis of AR devices performing better and overcoming most of current image limitations, because usage of AR device will prevent any smartphones camera issues, eye strain and less concern about how stage lighting influences in camera, so DHH users will be able to see the show as it is, and the only virtual object will be the subtitle, this is a more natural and less tiring type of interaction, so in these new tests, participants will no longer watch the play having a device's camera projection as medium, but the real play itself.

Subtitles will become the sole virtual component in the scene, improved by yet another AI implementation that replaces the need for a typist. Delays and synchronization issues will be improved by an ASR word sequencing system that overcomes human listening and typing speeds. And finally, we will refine the N values when querying the language model to reach better accuracy, sentence prediction and spelling correction, reducing misinterpreted subtitles to a minimum and ensuring clear contexts for DHH spectators. Also, we want to build a more complete accessibility software that helps DHH people not only in theaters but in many other tasks of their daily lives and to improve their communication and interaction with hearing people.

Acknowledgments. The Authors would like to express their gratitude to Leo Burnett company staff and also Samsung Institute Research in São Paulo (SRBR) for the collaboration in some parts of the project.

References

1. Arthur, E., Hancock, P., Chrysler, S.T.: The perception of spatial layout in real and virtual worlds. Ergonomics **40**(1), 69–77 (1997)
2. Beadles, R.L., Ball, J.E.: Method and apparatus for closed captioning at a performance. US Patent 5,648,789, 15 July 1997
3. Berke, L.: Displaying confidence from imperfect automatic speech recognition for captioning. ACM SIGACCESS Accessibility Comput. **117**, 14–18 (2017)
4. Cromby, J., Standen, P., Brown, D.: The potentials of virtual environments in the education and training of people with learning disabilities. J. Intellect. Disabil. Res. **40**, 489–501 (1996)
5. Rivaetal, G.: Virtual reality in paraplegia: a VR-enhanced orthopedic appliance for walking and rehabilitation. Stud. Health Technol. Inform. **58**, 209–218 (1998)
6. Hong, R., Wang, M., Xu, M., Yan, S., Chua, T.S.: Dynamic captioning: video accessibility enhancement for hearing impairment. In: Proceedings of the 18th ACM International Conference on Multimedia, pp. 421–430. ACM (2010)
7. Howlin, P.: Autism: Preparing for Adulthood (1997)
8. Huang, X.D., Ariki, Y., Jack, M.A.: Hidden Markov Models for Speech Recognition (1990)
9. Inness, L., Howe, J.: The community balance and mobility scale (cbm) an overview of its development and measurement properties, vol. 22, pp. 2–6 (2002)
10. Kafle, S., Huenerfauth, M.: Effect of speech recognition errors on text understandability for people who are deaf or hard of hearing. In: Proceedings of the 7th Workshop on Speech and Language Processing for Assistive Technologies, INTERSPEECH (2016)
11. Kercher, K., Rowe, D.C.: Improving the learning experience for the deaf through augment reality innovations. In: 18th International ICE Conference on Engineering, Technology and Innovation (ICE), 2012, pp. 1–11. IEEE (2012)
12. Kim, N., Yoo, C., Im, J.: A new rehabilitation training system for postural balance control using virtual reality technology. IEEE Trans. Rehabil. Eng. **7**, 482–485 (1999)
13. Kizony, R., Katz, N., et al.: Adapting an immersive virtual reality system for rehabilitation. Comput. Anim. Virtual Worlds **14**(5), 261–268 (2003)
14. Jones, L.E.: Does virtual reality have a place in the rehabilitation world? Disabil. Rehabil. **20**, 102–103 (1998)
15. Luo, X., Han, M., Liu, T., Chen, W., Bai, F.: Assistive learning for hearing impaired college students using mixed reality: a pilot study. In: International Conference on Virtual Reality and Visualization (ICVRV) 2012, pp. 74–81. IEEE (2012)
16. Mays, E., Damerau, F.J., Mercer, R.L.: Context based spelling correction. Inf. Process. Manage. **27**(5), 517–522 (1991)
17. Mc Comas, J., Sveistrup, H.: Virtual reality applications for prevention, disability awareness, and physical therapy rehabilitation in neurology: our recent work. J. Neurol. Phys. Ther. **26**, 55–61 (2002)
18. Meredith, T.R.: Using augmented reality tools to enhance childrens library services. Technol. Knowl. Learn. **20**(1), 71–77 (2015)
19. Mirzaei, M.R., Ghorshi, S., Mortazavi, M.: Combining augmented reality and speech technologies to help deaf and hard of hearing people. In: 14th Symposium on Virtual and Augmented Reality (SVR) 2012, pp. 174–181. IEEE (2012)
20. Mirzaei, M.R., Ghorshi, S., Mortazavi, M.: Using augmented reality and automatic speech recognition techniques to help deaf and hard of hearing people. In: Proceedings of the 2012 Virtual Reality International Conference, p. 5. ACM (2012)

21. Scherer, M.J.: Virtual reality: consumer perspectives. Disabil. Rehabil. **20**, 108–110 (1998)
22. Piquard-Kipffer, A., Mella, O., Miranda, J., Jouvet, D., Orosanu, L.: Qualitative investigation of the display of speech recognition results for communication with deaf people. In: 6th Workshop on Speech and Language Processing for Assistive Technologies, p. 7 (2015)
23. Sanchez, J., Lumbreras, M.: Usability and Cognitive Impact of the Interaction With 3-D Virtual Interactive Acoustic Environments by Blind Children, pp. 67–73 (2000)
24. Sudana, A.K.O., Aristamy, I.G.A.A.M., Wirdiani, N.K.A.: Augmented reality application of sign language for deaf people in android based on smartphone. Int. J. Softw. Eng. Appl. **10**(8), 139–150 (2016)
25. Sveistrup, H., McComas, J., Thornton, M., Marshall, S., Finestone, H., Mc-Cormick, A., Babulic, K., Mayhew, A.: Experimental studies of virtual reality-delivered compared to conventional exercise programs for rehabilitation. Cyber Psychol. Behav. **6**, 243–249 (2003)
26. Sveistrup, H., Thornton, M., Bryanton, C., Mc Comas, J., Marshall, S., Finestone, H., McCormick, A., McLean, J., Brien, M., Lajoie, Y., Bisson, Y.: Outcomes of Intervention Programs Using Flat Screen Vitual Reality, pp. 4856–4858 (2004)
27. Teofilo, M., Vicente J., Lucena, F., Nascimento, J., Miyagawa, T., Maciel, F.: Evaluating accessibility features designed for virtual reality context. In: 2018 IEEE International Conference on Consumer Electronics (ICCE) (2018 ICCE), Las Vegas, USA, January 2018
28. Witmer, B., Bailey, J., Knerr, B.: Virtual spaces and real world places: transfer of route knowledge. Int. J. Hum. Comput. Stud. **45**, 413–428 (1996)

Use of 3D Human-Computer Interaction for Teaching in the Architectural, Engineering and Construction Fields

Shahin Vassigh[1](✉), Francisco R. Ortega[2], Armando Barreto[3],
Katherine Tarre[2], and Jose Maldonado[2]

[1] Department of Architecture, Florida International University,
Miami, FL 33199, USA
svassigh@fiu.edu
[2] School of Computer and Information Sciences,
Florida International University, Miami, FL 33199, USA
fortega@cs.fiu.edu, {ktarr007,jmald045}@fiu.edu
[3] Electrical and Computer Engineering Department,
Florida International University, Miami, FL 33199, USA
barretoa@fiu.edu

Abstract. In this paper, we outline the development of SKOPE VR, a system for immersive interaction within a 3-Dimensional Virtual Reality(VR) Environment designed to teach of architecture, engineering and construction (AEC) students. The paper presents the potential capacity of immersive and interactive tools for teaching and will discuss the key challenges for creating 3-D environments with embedded interactivity. Then, the solution proposed in the SKOPE-VR system will be discussed in terms of its rationale and its development process. Finally, some of the advantages of using immersive technologies for teaching future AEC professionals will be discussed.

Keywords: 3-D interaction · Virtual reality · Oculus Rift
Navigation in virtual environments · Virtual learning environments

1 Introduction

The use of visualization tools has been native to Architecture. For the past decades Architects have used 3D modeling and visual simulations as a main design vehicle to better understand building performance. More recently the use of VR has enabled architects to improve their designs by engaging clients or potential users in realistic walkthroughs of proposed buildings and alter the design according to their feedback [1].

In the past few years, the use of VR in construction and engineering has also become prevalent. VR-based training for creating safer construction sites, site analysis and planning, and visualizing construction scenarios for decision making are becoming increasingly widespread.

As virtual immersive environments become easier and cheaper to produce, more practical and useable, their educational use will follow. This paper discusses a project

© Springer International Publishing AG, part of Springer Nature 2018
M. Antona and C. Stephanidis (Eds.): UAHCI 2018, LNCS 10908, pp. 149–159, 2018.
https://doi.org/10.1007/978-3-319-92052-8_12

which develops a prototype VR environment to teach architecture, engineering and construction (AEC) students lessons on building sciences.

2   Benefits and Challenges of Immersive 3-D VR Navigation

The adoption of the new technologies that allow a user to be fully immersed in a 3-dimensional virtual world for the purpose of AEC education opens up a wide array of potential benefits, but it also presents with important challenges. In the following sections we will summarize the benefits and challenges most relevant to the application of BVR to AEC education.

2.1   Benefits

Virtual reality technology mainly draws its novel benefits from its robust and innovative human-computer interaction framework. Contemporary technology such as the Oculus Rift can provide developers and users with low latency 360-degree view of a virtual environment, as well as accurate and robust hand tracking and control. These features, verified in previous research, present a wide variety of benefits for education. Such as:

Immersion - Virtual reality's main feature is its ability to completely immerse users in a virtual environment, leading to a sustained period of focus [2]. Previous studies have shown that immersion plays a critical role in education, as a user focuses on interacting, absorbing and applying concepts presented in the virtual world [3, 4]. The result is a Virtual Learning Environment (VLE) that provides a focused space to analyze and explore concepts separate from the real world and its limitations.

Interaction - Virtual environment interaction is fundamental to VR design. Novel VR control and tracking systems have been recently introduced by devices such as Oculus Rift, HTC Vive and Windows Mixed Reality. Through these novel controls, users can physically interact with the virtual world as we can with the real world which provides a sense of familiarity [5]. Pan explains this interactive component of VLE's as "Active Action" which allow learners to act in their learning environment effectively [6].

Display of Information - While immersion and interaction are the most commonly attributed benefits in VLE's, the method and techniques we use to display information in these immersive worlds are just as important. Learning takes place in a structured environment where information is easily accessible and analyzed. Virtual Reality provides the benefit of a virtual 3-Dimensional world space to structure and organize information for learning [7]. The inherent and beneficial capability to represent concepts in 3D is well documented, as users can analyze a concept in a wider range of views [4]. In this paper the focus is on this benefit and the associated challenges that arise when we seek to apply VR/VLE's in education.

2.2 Challenges

Immersion and interaction are highly beneficial to the user in VR applications to education, however, our current methodology for displaying information and interacting with it in an immersive environment has limited the usability VLE's. While the display of concepts in a 3D space takes advantage of both immersion and interactivity, it also brings complexity [5]. Users now must take into consideration the extra dimension provided by VR, which with poor design, often leads to confusion and frustration. Simply put, users won't be able to access the immersive and interactive features of a VLE effectively.

When we consider the applications of VR for education, we must also consider the pedagogical approach we want to translate to a Virtual Environment [4]. As stated by Vassigh and Huang, understanding and defining a solid pedagogic framework is fundamental to the design of such virtual experience [8]. Effectively using such a framework brings complexity to a VLE's design, and presents its own set of challenges.

3 Rationale and Development of SKOPE VR

As discussed in the previous section, 3D brings an extra dimension of complexity to the design and use of a VLE. The placement of information (whether it be a 3D model or text) is critical to how the user experiences this information (i.e., absorb it, analyze it, etc.). Current VLE designs often overwhelm users with confusion, and degrade the immersive character of the VLE experience.

If we look closely, we see that while VLE's place users in a 3D space like the real world, we do not usually have standardized tools to help users interact with a virtual world's information in a concentrated and intuitive fashion [2]. What do we mean by this? In the real world, books and computers are examples of tools that help us understand the information around us in a "concentrated" fashion. VLE's lack these tools, and thus make it difficult for the user to experience the information in a VLE in an efficient and enjoyable way.

An example of a VR application that attempts to solve this issue is Google Tilt Brush. Tilt Brush presents the user with an open Virtual Environment in which they can draw in 3 Dimensions with a wide variety of colors, shaders and effects. While drawing might not seem like much, Google tilt brush supports all the functionality (or even more) that a program like MS Paint would provide. Google Tilt Brush successfully deals with complexity by creating a user tool that centralizes all user decisions and interaction with the virtual world. These tools are in the user's hands, which use VR's interaction benefits such as hand tracking and gesture control.

We believe that the philosophy utilized in Tilt Brush can be beneficial for a variety of VLEs. Using the same idea, we could possibly use VR's interaction benefits to create a centralized "Hub" tool of experiences and decision making in a VLE. This will improve a user's experience with the information around them, removing unnecessary complexity to the user. This is a step in the right direction; however the efficiency of the approach may depend significantly on the actual contents displayed in this "Hub" tool. In other words, what information should the concentrated "Hub" tool inherently display?

3.1   Pedagogical Framework

While most studies agree on the VLE's potential benefits in education, they all suggest the importance of building the VLEs on a solid pedagogical framework [4]. Pedagogical frameworks provide an in depth theoretical view of teaching and learning. By choosing a solid pedagogical framework, we could start building VLEs based on these frameworks and add structure to our experiences [8].

There are a variety of different pedagogical frameworks, but Constructivism is one of the most frequently frameworks used in similar research efforts [4, 8]. This is because Constructivism uses VLE benefits from immersion, interaction and display of information. For example, constructivism treats the user as an active learner who not only absorbs information, but also builds upon and connects previous knowledge to construct new knowledge through active interaction. Constructivism also encourages the construction of learning environments rather than instructional sequences to reinforce authentic knowledge in the user [4]. At its core, Constructivism promotes active experiences to construct knowledge in an immersive and interactive approach.

Through constructivism, we can introduce experiences that will be useful for our user in our theoretical experience "hub". We can also define how the user will interact with different concepts in our VLE through Constructivism to ensure a consistent and focused learning approach.

3.2   Development of SKOPE VR

In summary, the critical concepts that we kept under consideration as we planned the development of SKOPE VR were:

- Information vs. Experience
- VLE inherent Benefits: Immersion, Interaction, Display of Information.
- VLE inherent Challenges: 3D complexity and Pedagogical framework implementation.
- Information Perception and Centralization in a 3D Virtual Environment
- Constructivism pedagogical framework and Information Structure

Based on this information, we found a need for two tools that will separately handle experiences and information in the virtual environment. This will provide a user with a consistent set of controls to use in the VLE:

- Pointer
- Hub

3.3   Pointer (Information)

The pointer's focus is to enable user interaction with information in a VLE. As the name suggests, the user will use this virtual pointer tool to select information presented to the user and trigger some experience for the selected information (Fig. 1). This approach takes advantage of the VLE interaction benefit and reduces complexity in selecting information of interest. For example, access to a wide variety of experiences can be achieved by pointing and selecting environment buttons using the pointer.

Fig. 1. Pointer

The Pointer also serves as a tool for locomotion around a VLE, as it can be used to point to the next desired location of the user in the virtual world and (upon pressing a button in the controls) "move" or "teleport" the user to that desired location. Figures 2a and b show this user translation mechanism. This facilitates efficient user access to information and the exploratory capabilities around a 3D world space. Mikropoulos suggests that navigation around a 3D world space can provide natural semantics for users, and avoid complicated and hard to remember symbolism and controls, further improving the user learning experience [2].

a. The pointer points to the next desired user location

b. Upon pressing a button the user is translated to the desired location

Fig. 2. Use of the pointer for changing the position (point of view) of the user within the virtual environment.

3.4 Hub (Experience)

The Hub (Fig. 3) is the centralized point of experience for the user. Its primary focus is to provide an appropriate experience for a selected piece of information by the Pointer. For example, let's assume we want to find out more about a 3D cube in a virtual environment. Once selected by our pointer as information of interest, our hub will display relevant information to have the appropriate experiences about the selected object. In order to display an appropriate experience, the hub contains three separate panels each dedicated to a different aspect of the user experience in a VLE. These are:

Fig. 3. Hub

Map Panel

The Map Panel in the hub is responsible for providing position feedback from the user's environment location, as well as providing the location of a VLE's experiences. Ultimately, the map panel aims at reducing the complexity of accessing information and experiences in the VLE alike. Furthermore, the map panel incentivizes user exploration around the virtual environment which improves a user's sense of immersion (Fig. 4).

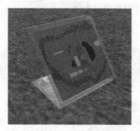

Fig. 4. Map panel

Options Panel

The Options Panel is responsible for displaying relevant options that are available to the user in a given experience. That is, information in a VLE might contain a set of options that will trigger a corresponding experience. Furthermore, the Options Panel takes advantage of the interaction and display of information benefits while reducing complexity and centralizing both areas. This allows the implementation of pedagogical frameworks like Constructivism, which demand active learning, in VLE's (Fig. 5).

Fig. 5. Options panel

Info Panel

The Info Panel is used to provide relevant information in a given experience. This will enable a user to establish focus on a given experience while providing adequate background information. This is especially important when we adopt a Constructivism framework for the design and implementation of a VLE. Building new knowledge based on previous knowledge and experiences can be tricky in a virtual environment, so the Info Panel aims at reducing this inherent complexity while improving the user learning experience (Fig. 6).

Fig. 6. Info panel

3.5   SKOPE VR Implementation

The implementation of the form of interaction described above used the Oculus Rift (headset and touch controllers) and its most recent Software Development Kit (SDK). The virtual environment was developed using Unity 3D and Visual Studio 2017. The virtual world was rendered on a computer running Windows 10. 3D Studio Max was used for editing the models used in the project.

Figure 7 shows a user fitted with the Oculus Rift head set and both touch controllers in his hands. The headset provided the stereoscopic display of the virtual world and sensed the changes of orientation of the user's head to modify the stereoscopic display accordingly. The left hand controller was used to manipulate a selected hub. Its thumbstick provided the mechanism to rotate the selected hub on its x-axis, so that the desired panel would be presented to the user. The right hand controller was utilized to manipulate the pointer, using the "A button" to execute the teleport (move) operation, and the trigger as a general selection control.

Figure 8 illustrates the basic organization followed in the design of the system, outlining the interplay between the actual physical controls, the user interface element (the hub, with its three panels), and the user experiences. It is worthwhile noting the types of experiences developed for this particular architectural application: *Light-Changes*, *RemoveWalls*, *InspectMechanics*, etc.

Figure 9 shows some sample screenshots of user experiences. These correspond to two alternative views of the building housing the School of International and Public Affairs (SIPA) at Florida International University.

Fig. 7. User wearing the Oculus Rift and the touch (hand) controllers

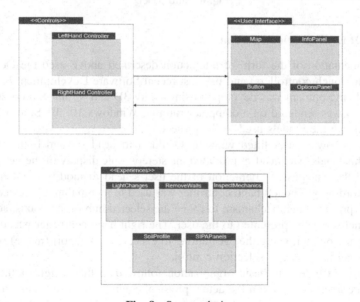

Fig. 8. System design

4 Advantages of Using Immersive Interaction for Teaching Building Sciences

VR has the potential to expand and transform learning in building sciences because of the two distinctive features described earlier. First, is its capacity to support interactivity. Steuer defines interactivity "as the extent to which users can participate in

Fig. 9. Sample displays of user experiences viewing the FIU SIPA building: (a) (top) default view; (b) (bottom) *InspectMechanics* view.

modifying the form and content of a mediated environment in real time" [9]. Interacting with a responsive environment where the user can navigate and modify the learning context is a powerful aspect of VR technology. Interactive 3D environments can also produce game-like experiences that are truly engaging.

For teaching AEC students, interactivity could be used to enable students to change the parameters of their learning. While text, visuals, and animations can describe a building's performance, properties, structure, and construction details, the ability to change the existing parameters provides additional opportunities to better understand the content and be able to predict the behavior of the building.

Consider a student walking around a virtual building able to interact with objects within the environment. She can touch a wall and activate an animation showing its construction process, access metrics on the building envelope's thermal resistance, learn about the material properties used in its construction, and get information on the cost of its assembly.

VR environments could also recreate many processes that are not assessable in real-time. Example of this include building energy performance in various seasons, water collection and flow around the building site in various conditions, and structural materials' behavior. Using the interactivity features of the VR, students can change the season or the date to observe heat loss and heat gain through building walls, visually locate thermal breaks, and gauge natural lighting of the building interior in different time of the day.

Finally, interactivity affords another benefit. Hoffman and Vu describe that interactivity afforded by the VR environments reduces "cognitive overhead," allowing the users to focus attention on the content rather than the semantics of the computer interface [10]. VR offers a direct way of engaging the content.

Second feature of the VR is its immersive capacity. Bryson describes immersion as the sense that the "user's point of view or some parts of the user's body is contained within the computer generated-model [11]. Immersion can provide realistic experiences, where knowledge is produced through experience. By becoming part of a phenomenon learners gain direct experiential intuitions about how the various components of buildings work. Through using multisensory immersion in VR customized for students, complex and abstract scientific concept can be understood at an intuitive level [12].

In the context of building sciences, the experience of being inside a virtual building can provide a powerful way of learning. A virtual walkthrough of a building can equip the viewer with an almost x-ray vision, enabling her to see through the walls to examine the structural components, look through the ground plane to see the building foundation, and look through the ceiling to examine the building's mechanical systems.

5 Conclusion and Future Work

Virtual Learning Experiences (VLEs) show increasing promise to improve the educational experience for everyone, and hold a particularly strong promise for enhancing architecture, engineering and construction education. As with any new technology, VLEs possess inherent benefits, challenges and complexity that must be handled accordingly to implement them in an effective manner. Through the theoretical examination of information perception/centralization and appropriate pedagogical frameworks, we presented a novel user interaction approach to tackle VLEs challenges and complexities in hope to improve the user learning experience.

Acknowledgements. This research was supported by National Science Foundation grants under award IUSE-1504898, HRD-0833093 and CNS-1532061.

References

1. Bouchlaghem, D., Shang, H., Whyte, J., Ganah, A.: Visualisation in architecture, engineering and construction (AEC). Autom. Constr. **14**(3), 287–295 (2005)
2. Mikropoulos, T.A., Natsis, A.: Educational virtual environments: a ten-Year review of empirical research (1999–2009). Comput. Educ. **56**(3), 769–780 (2011). https://doi.org/10.1016/j.compedu.2010.10.020

3. Paes, D., et al.: Immersive environment for improving the understanding of architectural 3D models: Comparing user spatial perception between immersive and traditional virtual reality systems. In: Automation in Construction, vol. 84, pp. 292–303, (2017). https://doi.org/10.1016/j.autcon.2017.09.016

4. Huang, H.-M., Rauch, U., Liaw, S.-S.: Investigating learners' attitudes toward virtual reality learning environments: Based on a constructivist approach. Comput. Educ. **55**(3), 1171–1182 (2010)

5. Erra, U., et al.: A methodological evaluation of natural user interfaces for immersive 3D graph explorations. J. Vis. Lang. Comput. **44**, 13–27 (2017)

6. Pan, Z., et al.: Virtual reality and mixed reality for virtual learning environments. Comput. Graph. **30**(1), 20–28 (2006)

7. Merchant, Z., et al.: Effectiveness of virtual reality-based instruction on students' learning outcomes in K-12 and higher education: a meta-analysis. Comput. Educ. **70**, 29–40 (2014)

8. Vassigh, S., et al.: Collaborative learning in building sciences enabled by augmented reality. Am. J. Civil Eng. Archit. **2**(2), 83–88 (2014)

9. Steuer, J.: Defining virtual reality: dimensions determining telepresence. J. Commun. **42**(4), 73–93 (1992). P. 14

10. Hoffman, H., Vu, D.: Virtual reality: teaching tool of the twenty-first century? Acad. Med. J. Assoc. Am. Med. Coll. **72**(12), 1076–1081 (1997). p. 1077

11. Bryson, S.: Approaches to the successful design and implementation of VR applications. In: Virtual Reality Applications, pp. 3–15 (1995)

12. Dede, C., Salzman, M.C., Loftin, R.B.: ScienceSpace: virtual realities for learning complex and abstract scientific concepts. In: Proceedings of the IEEE 1996 Virtual Reality Annual International Symposium, 1996, pp. 246–252. IEEE, March 1996. P. 1

The Formulation of Hybrid Reality: Pokémon Go Mania

Chih-yuan Wang[1] and Chen-li Kuo[2]([✉])

[1] National Sun Yat-sen University, Kaohsiung City, Taiwan
chihyuan.wang@cm.nsysu.edu.tw
[2] Chang Gung University, Taoyuang City, Taiwan
chenli.kuo@mail.cgu.edu.tw

Abstract. This paper investigates the formulation of hybrid reality via game play experience. The once world popular Pokémon Go is the research context, which is a great example of a hybrid reality game that mixes physical and virtual elements. In order to investigate the complex process of the shaping of hybrid reality, self-ethnology and interpretative phenomenology are used as the research methods. Although rules and goals have been provided by game developers, we found that the actual rules used are co-created by both the designer and individual players. New player experience could be created through "drawing on the spot" and borrowing. Furthermore, organizing resources about the game playing through interaction with other players contribute to the formulation of hybrid reality as well. The findings suggest the system functionality is not the most important element of a hybrid reality game. Game developers should provide flexibility on the storyline, allow the players to further develop their own unique experience. In addition, developers should consider cooperate with third-party application developers to enable rich and diverse hybrid reality.

Keywords: Pokémon Go · Hybrid reality · Player experience

1 Introduction

Pokémon Go is a mobile game featuring location-based technology and augmented reality developed by Niantic. Since the launched of the game in July 2016, the game has broken the record of downloads in the first week on both Apple Store and Google Play. On top of this achievement, Pokémon Go hit the headlines of international and national news media wherever there are players. This game does not only attract one particular type of players, but a group of heterogeneous players. Despite the game system incorporates a set of rules, functionality and storyline, each player seem to be playing and enjoying the game in different ways.

The concept of hybrid reality has been proposed by scholars, including de Souza e Silva [3], de Souza e Silva and Sutko [5], where the elements of physical reality and virtual reality represented in a digital game are intertwined. What players experience in this type of games no longer determined largely by the game designers, but the complex interactions with different spaces that the player situated in. The previous studies endeavored to depict what are different spaces in this hybrid reality, but ignore

© Springer International Publishing AG, part of Springer Nature 2018
M. Antona and C. Stephanidis (Eds.): UAHCI 2018, LNCS 10908, pp. 160–170, 2018.
https://doi.org/10.1007/978-3-319-92052-8_13

the formulation of this reality from a digital game. The purpose of this study is to look at the shaping for the hybrid reality through playing Pokémon Go. To investigate how mobile game players' experience shape their hybrid reality, the current authors adopt self-ethnology as the research method to collect data and use hermeneutic phenomenology as the method to analyze the collected data. The discussion of the results intends to shine a light on the future development of hybrid reality games.

The organization of this paper is as the following. Section 2 reviews the concepts of playability, player experience and hybrid reality in digital games. Section 3 introduces data collection and analysis methods in addition to the research context in this study, Pokémon Go. Section 4 presents the findings of the research. The last section discusses the findings and provides practical implications to game developers.

2 Literature Review

2.1 Playability and Player Experience

For any game developers, it is important to design a game what will attract players and keep the players playing the game. A digital game usually incorporates a set of rules and a storyline designed by the developers. Through the game, the player gain enjoyable experience. To keep the player stick to the game, the game developer must strive to provide appealing experience [7].

Experts in the field of human-computer interface tried to apply the concepts of usability proposed by Nielsen [14] to digital games in order to guide the first few phases of the game development. They quickly realized that the concepts such as "easy to learn" and "efficient to use" might not suitable for every type of games: some games typically attract players who consider themselves tech-savvy [13]. In addition, what have been considered in the usability engineering are insufficient for game assessment, since the main objective of using an information system is to complete a task efficiently and correctly, while game players are seeking enjoyment and entertainment, or in Sánchez et al. [16] words "to make the player feel good when playing it". The term playability emerges to coin the concept of "a set of properties that describe the Player Experience using a specific game system whose main objective is to provide enjoyment and entertainment, by being credible and satisfying, when the player plays alone or in company" [16]. This definition recognizes elements other than the software program itself, like player's company, as part of the playability. Some of the attributes considered as playability are associated with player experience, e.g. emotion and motivation; others are associated with the design of the game, e.g. learnability and effectiveness. Despite the effort to elaborate what to consider when developing a digital game, Sánchez et al. [16] did not explain how playability affects player experience.

Nacke et al. [12] provided another model to analyze player experience. They considered playability determined by the game design and the game itself, and the player experience is derived from the player's interaction with the game. In other words, the game is an object that provides playability through storylines, rules and the functions of the software, and player experience is based on the provided playability. The question is, do players create new properties of playability that are not intended by the game designers? It is not uncommon to use third-party applications to gain advantage while playing a digital game despite being disapproved by developers in many of the cases, as elaborated by Banks and Humphreys [1]. In addition, the nature of hybrid reality discussed in the next subsection might have contributed to playability that is not designed.

2.2   Hybrid Reality and the Digital Games

The latest technology used in digital games allows players to mix the real environment with digital objects. Scholars refer this broad concept as augmented reality. Milgram and Colquhoun [11] further distinguished three different levels of augmented reality discussed in literatures: (1) using head-mounted or head-up display to see the real world with digital data attached; (2) any case the real environment is augmented by virtual objects, e.g. computer-generated images are superimposed on a real image; (3) cases involving any mixture of real and virtual environment. The broadest definition of augmented reality is coined by Milgram and Colquhoun [11] as "mixed reality". In the mixed reality, the boarder of real and virtual is blurring, and there is no predominance of either side of the elements. Unlike the first two types of augmented reality where the virtual elements are attached to the real ones, the distinction of real and virtual elements in the mixed reality might easily be ignored by the users or players.

Game players are not always playing alone, and not always playing in the same place, in particular when the use of Internet and location-based technology is ubiquitous. As de Kort and Ijsselsteijn [2] pointed out, player experience is a type of situated experience affected by social and spatial factors. The player experience develops from the hybrid spaces incorporating the connected spaces, mobile spaces, and social spaces, where the connected spaces refer to the connections between the physical and digital spaces, mobile spaces refer to networked social spaces defined by using portable interfaces, and social spaces refer to the communities derived from the game playing [3].

The mixture of the social spaces is particular interesting in the emerging hybrid reality games which contain mobile activities, collaborative actions among many users, and the merge of physical and the digital spaces [5]. This type of games drive digital game players out of the dens where computers or game consoles might be the center of the private rooms and participating different mobile activities and perhaps gain opportunities of face-to-face interactions. In this hybrid reality, players experience the physical reality and virtual reality intertwined [10, 18]. Once the game player experience is no longer confined in the representation of the game design, the players might have different perception of the experience, because the context of the game is more complex than the game system itself [13]. In addition, the player will further influence the context of the game by adding personal experience and preference and make the game customize for him/her which is different from the default storyline and the rules set by the game developers.

3 Methodology

3.1 Data Collection and Analysis

The purpose of this paper is to use Pokémon Go as an example to explore how mobile game players' experiences shape the hybrid reality. We use self-ethnology as the research method to collect data, and use hermeneutic phenomenology as the research to analyze data.

Self-ethnology, also known as auto-ethnology, is a research method requiring researchers acting as participants. Researchers, under these circumstances, immerse in the research context. Hence, it is more suitable for explore the meaning behind experience [6]. As this paper is about the shaping of players' experiences, self-ethnology is a suitable research method to collect data.

The authors start to collect data from August, 2016 until July, 2017 in Taiwan. Both of us downloaded the Pokémon Go game and play it. On the course to become Pokémon Masters, we interacted with other players, observed them, and keep our field notes. Additionally, we produced our self-narrative weekly. We also kept an eye on the Pokémon Go related Internet forums. These sources of data give us a clear view of Pokémon Go communities.

The collected data was then analyzed with hermeneutic phenomenology approach. This approach is developed by Martin Heidegger based on Edmund Husserl's phenomenology. Phenomenology is about the study of lived experience or the life world. In Husserl's view, phenomena appear through consciousness, and minds and objects both occur within experience, thus eliminating mind-body dualism. Like phenomenology, hermeneutic phenomenology is about the life world or human experience as it is lived. However, Compared to Husserl's approach, Heidegger's hermeneutic phenomenology focused on 'Dasein', which is "the mode of being human" or "the situated meaning of a human in the world". Understanding is a basic form of human existence, and interpretation is critical to the process of understanding. Hermeneutics is about human cultural activity as texts, with a view towards interpretation to find intended or expressed meanings [8].

During the analyzing phase, we authors separately read all the field notes, self-narratives, and communications of Internet forums, developed our first-level coding and themes based on the spirit of hermeneutic phenomenology, and then compare our findings, and repeat the process until we both reach agreement.

3.2 Research Context: Pokémon Go

Pokémon Go is a mobile game, licensed by Pokémon Company, and developed by Niantic. This game is based on the Pokémon card game, developed by Nintendo, and its spin-off anime. With the slogan of "gotta catch'em all" and supported by locational and augmented technologies, this game enables players to play the role of trainers, like Ash or Missy. Players may meet different Pokémons in different physical locations (based on locational technology) and see Pokémons mixed with the real world from their screen (based on augmented technology). They could catch these Pokémons with Pokéballs, or use their Pokémons to fight other Pokémons in gym battles.

Pokémon Go was released in New Zealand and Australia on July, 6, 2016 and gradually released in other regions. This game soon became the most downloaded mobile game on Apple's App Store and Google's Google Play. It has been downloaded more than 750 million times until June, 8, 2017[1]. In April, 2017, there are around 5 million daily active users and 65 million month active users globally. A high proportion of players are aged between 18 and 35. These players were the audience of Pokémon anime or players of Pokémon Gameboy version[2]. In the meantime, there are a significant number of players with no previous knowledge of Pokémon stories. And the older players, aged above 40 are the die-hard players who continue to play the game one year after the game's release[3].

The Pokémon Go game starts with players act as Pokémon trainers searching for Pokémons, wining gym battles, and collecting medals in different physical locations. At the beginning, players will meet three "first" Pokémons – Bulbasaur, Charmander, and Squirtle, see Fig. 1. After he or she catches one of them, their trainer careers begin. Pokémons with different attributes would appear in different types of physical locations. Players could collect different Pokémons by visiting these places and catching them, or by hatching eggs when they walk for a certain distance. When they encounter a Pokémon, they could see this Pokémon on the screen with AR function turned on, as shown in Fig. 2-1. They may also visit some places labeled as gyms to challenge other players and earn some Pokécoins, as shown in Fig. 2-2, the token used in game to exchange for tools. When players complete certain tasks, such as catching a particular type of Pokémons or winning a certain number of gym battles, they could get medals, as shown in Fig. 2-3. Moreover, they could get stardust and candies if they catch Pokémons, win a gym battles, or hatch eggs. Players can also accumulate their experience points by participating in these activities, and level up their status.

Fig. 1. First Pokémons

---

[1] From http://expandedramblings.com/index.php/pokemon-go-statistics/, Accessed August 8, 2017.

[2] From http://www.adweek.com/digital/joan-daly-gotham-pr-guest-post-pokemon-go/, Accessed August 22, 2017.

[3] From https://www.valuesccg.com/knowledge/report/marketing/034/, Accessed February 23, 2018.

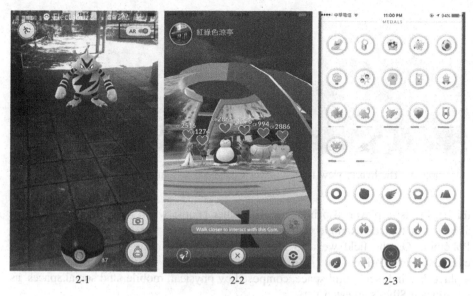

Fig. 2. Screenshots of Pokémon Go. 2-1. Catching Pokémon in AR mode; 2-2. Gym Battle; 2-3. Medals.

4 Findings

4.1 Pokémon Go as a Hybrid Reality Game

Despite of being marketed as an augmented reality (AR) game, Pokémon Go is also a hybrid reality (HBR) game in essence. Hybrid reality is the reality in hybrid spaces. According to de Souza e Silva, Hybrid spaces combine the physical and digital spaces in a social environment. Such a space is enabled by the advent of mobile technology. Hybrid reality is the experience of user in such an environment [3, 5]. From a player's perspective, what he/she experienced is a hybrid reality.

"When I am in this location, I can see the top of gym emitting blue light."
-    Discussion with Player A

Inside the Pokémon Go game, players can see the location of gym or Pokéstop on the map. When a player arrives this location, what he/she actually see is the real scene, but in his/her mind, the scene appears to be the combination of the real world and the digital world, as shown in Fig. 3. The quotation above reflects such an image. In other words, the reality in the player's mind is the hybrid of physical spaces and the digital spaces on his/her mobile phone.

"Where is the Dragonite, did you see it?"
A conversation between the author and Player B

The hybrid reality within a player's mind does not limit to the intersection between physical and digital space: the social environment is blended in. The interesting part of

Fig. 3. The hybrid view from a player's perspective Source: http://ift.tt/2tkrZOM

this reality is: a player also interacts with other people when playing. The quotation above is a typical example that two players exchange the whereabouts of a rare Pokémon. On the field we also found a group of youngsters meeting in the park everyday, having dinner, and catching Pokémons together. In other words, the image in a player's mind is a hybrid space, composed by physical, mobile, and social spaces, as de Souza e Silva suggested [4].

4.2   The Shaping of Players' Experiences

From a game developer's perspective, he/she may want to create a reality for players to enjoy by applying the state-of-art technology, fascinating graphics, and meticulous game rules. However, such an effort may be in vein because players may not simply follow the rules. Instead, they may set up their own rules to play the game with any tools at their disposal.

4.2.1   Rules of the Game is Co-constructed by Developers and Players

"This game is like the real life. We need to work hard, apart by pure luck. If we do so, we definitely can be great Pokémon trainers."
                                        -    From a player refection on an Internet forum

Although Pokémon Go is based on the story of Pokémon amine, not all players are familiar the story. Some of them may have played the Gameboy version Pokémon, or watched Pokémon amine; others are new to the Pokémon world. The game developer may have some default settings, such as how to create a level system to distinguish trainers, medal system, etc. Players may not simply play for those achievements, and have their own ways to play the game and set their own goals to achieve. The key message we could grasp from the quotation above is the personalized experience. There is no well-defined ending of this game. This allows players to set up their personal goals. Some players want to collect all the available Pokémons; some just want to see all Pokémons in Pokédex without actually catching them; others may just catch Pokémons without real targets and claim he/she is just playing for personal health. Moreover, the personal goal of this game is changeable, as shown in the following conversation.

"Will you keep playing if you catch the remaining two Pokémons?"
"Probably yes. Because I am getting old now, keeping playing can prevent me from developing Alzheimer's."

- A conversation between the author and Player C

Apart from setting personal goals, players have many ways to create their personal experiences. First, many Pokémon Go players are not familiar with the Pokémon story. Hence, they use their own way to name their Pokémons. For example, some players named Abra as "Little Fox" because of the appearance. Some players named their Pokémon as Dra_A15D15S14CH to present its attribute levels and skillset in order to choose the most appropriate Pokémons in gym battles.

Second, Pokémon Go players would choose which game function to be on or off when gaming. Despite acclaimed as the best designed AR mobile game, many Pokémon Go players soon turn off the AR functions because it is energy-consuming and not easy to catch Pokémons under AR mode. Players may also use third-party apps to assist the process of game. They may use third-party tools to check the potential of their Pokémons, or use other messaging tools to communicate with other players.

Finally, players may create their own rules. Some players see the nearby gyms as their own turf. If you occupied a gym for a certain period of time, you will be awarded Pokécoins. However, if players always initiate gym battles, no one could accumulate enough time to claim their reward. Hence, some players reach gentleman's agreement to allocate time slot for players from different teams, as shown in the following dialogue.

"Hi, mate, this is our time slot. You blue team should only battle for the gym AFTER 11pm. Go away!"

- Dialogue of player D

4.2.2 Drawing on the Spot and Borrowing – Ways to Create Experiences

Player's gaming experience is not affected by how they interact with the game, but also influenced by their life experience [13]. Hence, player experience is personal and could be created through drawing on the spot and borrowing.

Drawing on the spot can be defined as players use tools developed for other purposes in the gaming activities. For instance, they may exchange the locations of some rare Pokémons with existing messaging apps.

Borrowing can be defined as players search for inspiration from other experience in order to solve the problems they encounter in gaming. From the previous sections, we can find that players name their Pokémons based on the appearance of animals they are familiar with. In order to secure the maximum of Pokécoins, they borrow the concept of "turf" like gangsters. These are typical examples of borrowing.

Both "drawing on the spot" and "borrowing" are crucial ways for players to create their gaming experiences. The reality they experienced is not simply as what game developers designed. Rather, it is up to their ingenuity to use what is available to satisfy their needs.

4.2.3   Gaming as Organizing Resources

Although on the screen players could only see themselves, it does not mean they are alone. In the process of the game, players have to organize their resources within their social network. For instance,

> "Grandpa, how do you learn to use this app to check the potential of your Pokémons?"
> "My grandson taught me. I told him my bag is too small to carry more Pokémons. He just installed this app for me and asked me to check which Pokémons could be deleted on my own".
>
> - A conversation with player E

In this example, we can see grandson became a resource to solve player E's issues.

> "Where did you find the Snorelax? I cannot find it."
> "Near the 7-11 down there. I have seen Snorelax there several times"
>
> - A conversation with player F

This is another example. Players exchange the whereabouts of Snorelax, a rare Pokémon, when they display their trophies.

These examples demonstrate that players may interact with others to exchange information. Sometimes, they may interact with total strangers in order to achieve certain goals. For instance, it is very common for one experienced player to give "orders" to other players in order to defeat legendary Pokémons.

In short, players need to organize his resources through social interaction when playing Pokémon Go game. It is very similar with de Souza e Silva's idea of "social spaces" [4].

5   Discussion

The advance of technology has brought many new possibilities to game developers to create games with many fancy functions. For instance, players in the 1990s could only stay in an indoor space to play game on their own. In the 2000s onwards, the diffusion of Internet technology enabled players play game online and interact with each other, and the advent of mobile and location-based technologies further allowed gamer walking on the street and gaming outdoors [9, 19].

In the meantime, how to create a different gaming experience has become a challenge for game developers, even with so many new technologies at their disposal. Nacke *et al.* [12] pointed out that game developer could affect the playability through game design, but game design could not translate into player experience directly. The real experience of a player is the interplay between technical experience, individual experience, and context experience [13]. Hence, gaming experience is a personal experience, and may be out of the hands of game developers.

Pokémon Go is a very good example. Marketed as a mobile game with AR technology, most players do not actually experience its AR functions for most of the playing time. What players experienced is a hybrid reality, which is a reality combined with physical, mobile, and social spaces [4]. As this study showed, players' experiences are not provided by game developer alone. Players actually used their ingenuity to create such a hybrid reality by "drawing on the spot", "borrowing", and "organizing resource socially". In other words, player experience is co-created by players and game developers [1].

Acceptability, accessibility, simplicity, and flexibility may be the good measurement for evaluating game design [7], but these criteria should not be interpreted as functionality. Learning within game is a source of attractiveness of game [17]. The sense of learning is embedded in the storyline of the game [15]. Hence, when creating a game with high playability, a good storyline is necessary.

What is a good storyline of a game? Based on the example of Pokémon Go, it has provided enough space for players to set their personal goals and rules. Moreover, the gaming experience is also affected by players' abilities to "draw on the spot" and "borrowing". How to create an environment for players and third-party app developers is equally important.

References

1. Banks, J., Humphreys, S.: The labour of user co-creators. Convergence **14**, 401–418 (2008). https://doi.org/10.1177/1354856508094660
2. de Kort, Y.A.W., Ijsselsteijn, W.A.: People, places, and play: player experience in a socio-spatial context. Comput. Entertainment **6**, 1–11 (2008). https://doi.org/10.1145/1371216.1371221
3. de Souza e Silva, A.: From cyber to hybrid. Space Culture **9**, 261–278 (2006). https://doi.org/10.1177/1206331206289022
4. de Souza e Silva, A.: Pokémon Go as an HRG: mobility, sociability, and surveillance in hybrid spaces. Mob. Media Commun. **5**, 20–23 (2017). https://doi.org/10.1177/20501579 16676232
5. de Souza e Silva, A., Sutko, D.M.: Playing life and living play: how hybrid reality games reframe space, play, and the ordinary. Crit. Stud. Media Commun. **25**, 447–465 (2008). https://doi.org/10.1080/15295030802468081
6. Foster, K., McAllister, M., O'Brien, L.: Extending the boundaries: autoethnography as an emergent method in mental health nursing research. Int. J. Mental Health Nurs. **15**, 44–53 (2006). https://doi.org/10.1111/j.1447-0349.2006.00402.x
7. Kultima, A., Stenros, J.: Designing games for everyone: the expanded game experience model. In: Proceedings of the International Academic Conference on the Future of Game Design and Technology, Vancouver, British Columbia, Canada, 06 May 2010–07 May 2010, pp. 66–73. ACM (2010). 1920788. https://doi.org/10.1145/1920778.1920788
8. Laverty, S.M.: Hermeneutic phenomenology and phenomenology: a comparison of historical and methodological considerations. Int. J. Qual. Methods **2**, 21–35 (2003). https://doi.org/10.1177/160940690300200303
9. Licoppe, C., Inada, Y.: Emergent uses of a multiplayer location-aware mobile game: the interactional consequences of mediated encounters. Mobilities **1**, 39–61 (2006). https://doi.org/10.1080/17450100500489221

10. Mäyrä, F.: Pokémon GO: entering the ludic society. Mob. Media Commun. **5**, 47–50 (2017). https://doi.org/10.1177/2050157916678270

11. Milgram, P., Colquhoun Jr., H.: A taxonomy of real and virtual world display integration. In: Ohta, Y., Tamura, H. (eds.) Mixed Reality: Merging Real and Virtual Worlds, pp. 5–28. Springer, New York (1999)

12. Nacke, L., et al.: Playability and player experience research. Paper presented at the Proceedings of DiGRA 2009: breaking new ground: innovation in games, play, practice and theory, London (2009)

13. Nacke, L.E., Drachen, A.: Towards a framework of player experience research. In: Proceedings of the Second International Workshop on Evaluating Player Experience in Games. In: The Second International Workshop on Evaluating Player Experience in Games at FDG, Bordeaux, France (2011)

14. Nielsen, J.: Usability Engineering. Academic Press, Cambridge (1993)

15. Rouse III, R.: Game Design: Theory and Practice. Jones & Bartlett Learning, Sudbury (2005)

16. Sánchez, J.L.G., Zea, N.P., Gutiérrez, F.L.: Playability: how to identify the player experience in a video game. In: Gross, T., Gulliksen, J., Kotzé, P., Oestreicher, L., Palanque, P., Prates, R.O., Winckler, M. (eds.) INTERACT 2009. LNCS, vol. 5726, pp. 356–359. Springer, Heidelberg (2009). https://doi.org/10.1007/978-3-642-03655-2_39

17. Shiratuddin, N., Zaibon, S.B.: Mobile game-based learning with local content and appealing characters. Int. J. Mob. Learn. Organ. **4**, 55–82 (2010). https://doi.org/10.1504/ijmlo.2010.029954

18. Sicart, M.: Reality has always been augmented: play and the promises of Pokémon GO. Mob. Media Commun. **5**, 30–33 (2017). https://doi.org/10.1177/2050157916677863

19. Soh, J.O.B., Tan, B.C.Y.: Mobile gaming. Commun. ACM **51**, 35–39 (2008). https://doi.org/10.1145/1325555.1325563

Accessibility Guidelines for Virtual Environments

Breno Augusto Guerra Zancan[1(✉)], Guilherme Corredato Guerino[1],
Tatiany Xavier de Godoi[2], Daniela de Freitas Guilhermino Trindade[1],
José Reinaldo Merlin[1], Ederson Marcos Sgarbi[1],
and Carlos Eduardo Ribeiro[1]

[1] Center of Technological Sciences,
State University of Paraná, Bandeirantes, Paraná, Brazil
brenozancan@gmail.com, guilherme.guerinosi@gmail.com,
{danielaf,merlin,sgarbi,biluka}@uenp.edu.br
[2] Computer Department, Federal Technological University of Paraná,
Cornélio Procópio, Paraná, Brazil
tatigodoi_11@hotmail.com

Abstract. The technological advances resulting from the Digital Revolution have enabled the growth of virtual spaces, of the most varied types and for various purposes, facilitating access to information, as well as communication between people. However, a large number of people cannot enjoy these benefits because they face difficulties related to accessibility in these environments. In this scenario, the objective of this work is to present a conceptual framework, which contain a set of Web accessibility guidelines to allow a greater number of people to take advantage of the resources and facilities provided by virtual environments, regardless of their physical or functional limitations. In addition, it should be emphasized that the present research is not intended the presentation of a rigid guide or a step by step, but rather a suggested model, composed of recommendations that represent a compilation of different surveys and that intends to offer a direction to developers in creating Web environments with better accessibility.

Keywords: Accessibility guidelines · Virtual environments
Conceptual framework · Physical differences

1 Introduction

The great changes caused by the so-called Digital Revolution had an impact on society as a whole, affecting political and economic aspects as well as social and cultural aspects. According to [12], by January 2017, the number of existing sites exceeded 1.8 billion. However, if on the one hand, there is an increase in the number of virtual environments and people who benefit from them, on the other hand there are individuals who, due to physical or functional limitations, cannot access the content and information provided by those environments

© Springer International Publishing AG, part of Springer Nature 2018
M. Antona and C. Stephanidis (Eds.): UAHCI 2018, LNCS 10908, pp. 171–183, 2018.
https://doi.org/10.1007/978-3-319-92052-8_14

According to a World Report on Disability, released by [20] in 2011, more than 1 billion people in the world live with some type of disability; in addition, according to another report released by [20] in 2014, the number of older people should double, reaching 2 billion by 2050. These figures only corroborate the concern about creating Web spaces as inclusive as possible.

In the literature, it is possible to find different works with a focus on Web accessibility. However, research related to this topic usually deals with specific issues, which involve only one type of disability, or some accessibility recommendations for a particular type of environment. In this scenario, the objective of this work is to present a conceptual framework, which contain a set of Web accessibility guidelines to allow a greater number of people to take advantage of the resources and facilities provided by virtual environments, regardless of their physical or functional limitations. According to [22], by improving Web access and its resources, people with some type of limitation are allowed to participate more actively in society.

In order to elaborate the guidelines, this research used the following methodological steps: (i) diagnosis of the characteristics and elements that compose the virtual environments; (ii) selection of works related to Web accessibility, according to their relevance (main recommendations for users with different types of physical or functional limitation); (iii) selection of works related to the use of the user's natural interface; (iv) compilation of accessibility guidelines to support the creation of more accessible virtual environments.

2 Digital Accessibility

The concept of accessibility is very broad, and according to [5], involve physical-spatial factors such as distance, displacement and comfort, as well as political, social and cultural aspects.

Article 3th of [3] defines accessibility as "[...] possibility and scope for the safe and autonomous use of spaces, urban equipment, buildings, transportation, information and communication, including its systems and technologies, as well as other services and facilities open to the public, for public use or private for collective use, both in urban and rural areas, by persons with disabilities or with reduced mobility."

Therefore, according [5], the concept of accessibility involves the practice of social inclusion of citizens, because it is related to the possibility of their participation in society, so that there are conditions of equality. In this context, [11] defines the goal of accessibility as guaranteeing a better quality of life for people, and especially for people with disabilities, who face the greatest difficulties.

Regarding these difficulties, [13] states that functional weaknesses considered as characteristics of individuals with special needs can be divided into the following general categories:

- Visual impairment: people with reading difficulties of very small texts or of a particular color, or even may need visual information to be converted to oral or Braille speech;

- Hearing impairment: people who have difficulty hearing or recognizing audible signals as acoustic warning signs (beep);
- Movement impairment: people with difficulties that prevent them from using the keyboard or mouse;
- Cognitive impairments: people differences in perception or language impairments.

Regarding Web accessibility, it is necessary to highlight the contributions made by the World Wide Web Consortium (W3C), which is an international organization in which affiliated companies, full-time teams, independent organizations and public work together to develop standards for the Web. One of the contributions by the [21] was the creation of the Web Accessibility Initiative (WAI), which seeks to develop strategies, guidelines and resources that help make the Web accessible to people. According to [22], Web accessibility makes it possible for people with disabilities, as well as those who may have had some loss of ability (such as older people) to perceive, understand, navigate, interact and even contribute with the Web.

In addition, [21] has developed the Web Content Accessibility Guidelines (WCAG). This set of guidelines provides recommendations that seek to standardize the accessibility of Web content. In doing so, by following these guidelines, Web content becomes accessible to a wider range of people with disabilities, including blindness and low vision, deafness and hearing loss, learning disabilities, cognitive limitations, limited movements, speech deficiencies, photosensitivity, and individuals with combinations of these characteristics, besides users in general.

Also related to [21] contributions, this consortium has the Web Accessibility Working Group (Web Accessibility WG), which was created in March 2012 and meets periodically to plan actions to be carried out in Brazil. The WG Brazil highlights that people with disabilities are the biggest beneficiaries of a more accessible Web, because a virtual environment with low accessibility can harm these users or even prevent their access. On the other hand, good accessibility allows people with disabilities to enjoy all the information and services available on the web.

Also with regard to Web accessibility, it is possible to cite the Modelo de Acessibilidade em Governo Eletrônico (eMAG) or Accessibility Model in Electronic Government, created by the Brazilian federal government. The [7] helps professionals in the development, alteration and/or adaptation of pages, Websites and portals, in order to do them accessible to a larger number of individuals, thus increasing digital inclusion and, consequently, social inclusion. For their conception, experts contributed, taking into account the latest research related to the area of Web accessibility, in addition to the recommendations of [19].

Moreover, one point that deserves to cite is the relationship between usability and accessibility. According to the [21], usability and user experience enable to design products to be effective, efficient, and satisfying. Additionally, according to [8], usability is the "[…] extent to which a product can be used by specified users to achieve specified goals with effectiveness, efficiency and satisfaction in a specified context of use". [14] define usability as being the speed with which users can learn to use something, their efficiency in using it, as well as how much they can remember and enjoy using it.

[18] present the following usability principles: Error prevention and handling; Consistency; Feedback; Control; Efficiency and efficacy; Easy learning; Flexibility; Visibility; Compatibility; Easy Memorization; Prioritization of Functionality and Information; Equitable Use; Affordance; Help; Shortcuts; Low Physical Effort; Restrictions; Reversal of Actions; Subjective Satisfaction; and Security.

The concept of usability can be related to accessibility, according to [21], since basic accessibility is a prerequisite for usability. In this way, accessibility can be considered a subset of usability. Therefore, it is probable that, satisfying some usability principles, some characteristics related to accessibility are met. In addition, a virtual environment with better usability will possibly help your users navigate with greater satisfaction and want to return to that Web page.

3   Conceptual Model for Supporting the Creation of Virtual Environments with Focus on Accessibility

This work is part of a study by the HCI group of the State University of Paraná, which develops two complementary studies, one focusing on natural interfaces and the principles of usability, interactivity and communicability for a specific type of environment, the Virtual Museums, and the other focusing on the accessibility aspects of Virtual Environments in general. Thus, to reach the objective of this work, which is to propose accessibility guidelines through a conceptual framework, first will be presented the concepts related to framework and conceptual framework.

[17], in his master's thesis, defines a framework as "a generic project in a domain that can be adapted to specific applications, serving as a template for the construction of applications". Thus, according to [2], a framework has as main idea, to enable the use of a set of common resources, allowing its reuse in the development of new applications.

Consequently, it is possible to facilitate one of the frequent situations faced by system developers, which is the need to use similar resources for the development of new programs. In view of this, [17] emphasizes that the reuse provided by a framework becomes a necessary condition for achieving a productivity gain, for software development.

With respect to the conceptual framework, [9] defines as being a network of interconnected concepts that, because they are together, provide a comprehensive understanding of one or more phenomena. The author also clarifies that, instead of offering a theoretical explanation, as well as the quantitative models, a conceptual framework provides understanding, and it can be developed and constructed through a process of qualitative analysis. For [15] the objective of a conceptual framework is to "[…] provide a class diagram that can be used as a basis for modeling application domain classes."

3.1   Conceptual Model

To create the conceptual framework, researches were carried out that involved several types of virtual environments, as well as the main difficulties encountered by its users. From this, and based on the main factors of the design of interactive systems proposed by [1] and the contributions of [16], a conceptual model was proposed, which served as support for the creation of the final conceptual framework.

As can be seen in Fig. 1, the conceptual model presents, for virtual environments, three main elements in its structure: (i) People; (ii) Components; and (iii) Activities. It should be noted that each of these elements may have subelements, which may also have their unfolding, and so on. The segmentations from the first level seek to reflect the specificities of each type of virtual environment. For example, a Virtual museum, can present as Functions of element People: administrator, curator, specialist and visitor; a real estate site, in turn, can present for this same element, the functions of administrator, multimedia expert and visitors; therefore, subelements may vary, but they will come from a common element.

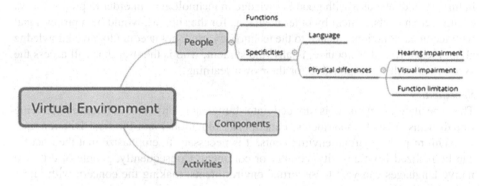

Fig. 1. Conceptual model to support the creation of the conceptual framework.

Below, each element and its sub-elements will be explained in more detail.

People
The People element is divided into Functions, which represent the types of people that will interact with the virtual environment; and Specificities, which has the Language in which the environment will be created, as well as the physical and psychological differences of the various users that can access the virtual space.

Functions
Types of users that will interact with the virtual environment, from different forms. Two examples will be presented below, in order to present possible functions related to two different types of environments: a virtual museum and a distance learning system. It is hoped, with these examples, to show that, because of there are different types of virtual spaces, the definition of roles will depend on the needs and objectives of each environment.

In a virtual museum, it is possible there are the functions of administrator, curator, computer graphics specialist and visitor. Thus, the administrator would be responsible for determining what information will be available in the museum, by selecting and requesting content that can be created and/or adapted by a curator and/or computer graphics expert; curator, according to [6], is anyone who participates in a curatorial process, which includes collection, research, safeguarding (museological conservation and documentation) and communication (exhibition and education); a computer graphics expert, in turn, is a generic definition for the person in charge of tasks involving the use of technology to make the content, determined by a curator, for later display in the virtual museum; finally, a visitor is any individual who accesses the virtual museum in search of information, knowledge and learning.

Another example of defining functions may be in relation to the creation of a distance learning system. In this system, the functions could be module coordinator, mentoring coordinator, tutor, support and student. In this way, the module coordinator would be responsible for the organization and administration of the course, being a professional in the teaching area of the course; as for the mentoring coordinator, would be a professional in the area of education that manages the way tutors work; the tutor, in turn, would be a user with good knowledge in technologies, in order to propose ways of interaction of its content by other media; as for the support, would be a professional with technical functions, related to the technology used, not needing to have knowledge about the subject of the course; finally, the student, who is the user that will access the system and will be responsible for their own learning.

Specificities
The Specificities element is divided into Language, Physical differences (Hearing Impairments, Visual Impairments, Functional Limitations) and Physical Differences.

With respect to virtual environments, it is necessary to emphasize that their access can be realized from any city, country or continent. Consequently, people of different native languages can visit these virtual environments, making the concern with idiom an important issue in their creation.

As for the physical differences between the various visitors of a virtual environment, the [21] says that the Web must be accessible to provide equal opportunities to people with diverse abilities, which range from users without physical limitations to those who may have some kind of disability, such as hearing, visual or physical. These deficiencies can affect a person from birth or be acquired and/or developed during their lifetime, in the event of accidents, illnesses and even the advancing age.

Furthermore, it is necessary to consider possible psychological differences between the different visitors, which includes different cognitive capacities. For example, according to the [21], an elderly user may have reduced cognitive abilities, affecting their short-term memory and ability to concentrate, and consequently impairing their Web browsing.

Components
In the Components element, there are subelements that can be part of a virtual environment. Thus, as in the case of the Functions subelement, the composition of the Components element will depend on the purpose of the virtual environment created.

Typically, a virtual environment may have components such as:

- Text: presentation of textual information, available to the visitor, which can be related to the details of an item, how space is used, data about the authors, among others.

- Video: material that can be used to explain certain content present in the environment; may contain subtitles or be also available in other languages, such as sign language of deaf communities.
- Audio: audio is a more dynamic and effective way of transmitting information. It can be an explanatory audio, about a certain item present in the environment in order to improve the accessibility of the virtual environment.
- Image: can be captured images (photo) or digitally generated images.
- Object: three-dimensional objects, related to the environment theme, which can be available to the user's touch for manipulation and observation.
- External Link: used to access information from other pages, inside or outside the virtual environment, such as news or additional information related to the subject or to some element of the environment
- Navigation Map: virtual environment plan, serving as reference so that the visitor can be located inside the museum and better understand how the site is organized.

It should be noted that for creating a virtual environment, it is not necessary for all components presented to be part of the space created or, still, other components may be present. However, by using a greater number of elements, the environment tends to be more diverse, attractive, interactive and accessible. In addition, combining the natural user interface with these components, it is possible to further facilitate the accessibility to the environment content, since, according to [10], this type of interface focuses on the natural abilities of being human such as touch, vision, voice, movement, and cognitive functions such as expression, perception, and recall. Access to an image (when available) can use, for example, touch commands in order to zoom in it on and manipulate it; also, searching for certain information may use voice commands, assisting users with limitations that difficult their use of mouse and/or keyboard.

Activities

The Activities element is related to what each of the functions will perform during their interactions with the virtual environment. For a better understanding, the possible activities related to the two examples already discussed will be presented: virtual museum and distance learning system.

In a virtual museum, an administrator may be responsible for the inclusion, alteration and exclusion activities of a curator and a computer graphics expert, in addition to being able to approve/refuse and include/exclude content made available by a curator; a curator is responsible for organizing and validating content related to the theme of the virtual museum; as for the computer graphics specialist, is responsible for tasks that involve the use of computational resources, working in partnership with the curator, in order to diversify the content made available by a virtual museum; the visitor, in turn, is anyone who can visit the virtual museum, searching and accessing a specific object, visiting the virtual rooms and/or accessing details about an object.

In the case of a distance education system, there is the coordinator of the module, responsible for the organization, coordination and administration of the course, approving the didactic material and the contents to be taught during a given course; in relation to the mentoring coordinator, is responsible for the pedagogical tools, as well as for the coordination of the work of the tutors; as for the tutor, it is responsible for the interaction between the student and the teaching platform, becoming very important in the success and motivation of the distant students; in relation to a support professional, is responsible for maintenance, improvements and other issues related to the technical part of the system; finally, a student, has as possible activities, access to the system and material made available, as well as resolution and sending of tasks, as well as other.

Therefore, each of the elements of the conceptual model presented will depend directly on the objectives, contents, user types, technical needs and other peculiar factors of the virtual environment to be developed. However, in all cases, one should try, to the maximum, to facilitate accessibility to the various types of users who will have access to the system. In Sect. 3.2, below, guidelines will be presented that can assist in improving accessibility for virtual environments.

3.2   Accessibility Guidelines

In this section, some accessibility guidelines will be presented, based on the proposed conceptual model. These guidelines are intended to contribute improve accessibility in virtual environments, especially for users with some type of disability, physical or cognitive limitation, as well as their activities in the use of virtual environments.

Establishing a relation with the conceptual model, considering that the People present some specificities as to their physical or cultural conditions, guidelines will be presented, which are intrinsically linked to the Components that the environment may have (contents, images, alternative media, among others) to that the Activities can be developed by all People, regardless of their culture or physical differences.

Regarding the criteria used to select the accessibility recommendations in virtual environments, were used researches based on the four principles of accessibility that constitute the [21]: perceivable, operable, understandable and robust. In addition, some of the recommendations presented come from research that was based on works by different scholars on accessibility, as well as recommendations that integrate the [7] or that are in line with some of the usability principles already presented.

Table 1 is related to improved accessibility for blind or vision impaired users, referred to in the table by the letter "B", as well as improved accessibility to deaf or hearing impaired users, referred to in the table by the letter "D". For the elaboration of the table, were used the researches carried out by [4], whose objective was to evaluate the accessibility of deaf people in Websites, taking into account the view of different authors. Also for the creation of Table 1, the work of [11] which evaluated the accessibility of the visually impaired in virtual practice communities, was used as a basis, showing a series of relevant aspects in the creation of these virtual environments, some of them very important for creating virtual environments in general.

It is possible to notice, in Table 1, that the attention given in the creation of the different aspects presented, can help certain types of users, which are represented by different letters. Therefore, these aspects cover different elements and subelements elucidated by the conceptual model presented in the previous section.

Thus, by following the guidelines associated with these aspects, it is possible to favor the improvement of accessibility of users with different types of disabilities. Therefore, it is verified that the improvement of accessibility in virtual environments can result from the exploration of different elements of the proposed conceptual model.

Table 1. Accessibility recommendations for blind or vision impaired users and for deaf or hearing impaired users.

Aspects		Guidelines	Benefited users
Content Creation	Content Language	Page title should be simple and clear	B
		Headings and labels should describe the topic or the topic purpose	
		Position the labels in order to make clear what elements they refer to	
	Language	Indicate the language to the user, both in the interface and in the encoding	B, D
	Visual Representation	Separate foreground from background, for easy navigation via keyboard	B
Communication Mediation	Mediation of Interpreters	Provide a language interpreter for sign language mediation	D
User Navigation	Alternate Text for Links, Images and Elements	Provide textual alternative to link, image or any type of non-textual elements by means of the 'alt' attribute	B
		Provide a simple description of the images, in order to facilitate the understanding of the users	B, D
	Keyboard Use	Provide all functionality and shortcuts through the keyboard to make it easy to use screen readers	
		Provide Help About the Virtual Environment	
	Links destination	Indicate, clearly and succinctly, where the links are pointing	
Technologies and Alternatives for Time-Based Media	Technologies Used in Videos	For visually impaired people with blindness, all possible information must be passed through audio	B
		Ensure understanding rate of the deaf for visual detection of hand movements and facial expressions	D
		The delay of the image should be less than 1.2 s to enable the video feature of signal language	
	Media Time	Provide the user with control over the executions of the media, such as: start, stop, resume and others	B
		Provide video description of audio information and allow the user to control the speed of content that "moves"	D

Source: Adapted from [4] and [11].

Table 2, in turn, contains recommendations from studies by [18]. These studies involved researches based on the work of different authors, resulting in a table that relate some of the usability principles already presented, with recommendations that may help both usability and accessibility in the development of digital information environments for the elderly.

It is important to highlight that, although Table 2 emphasizes the benefits provided to elderly users, who tend to present greater physical and cognitive difficulties, the presented guidelines can also help the accessibility of people with less experience of using virtual environments, as well as experienced users who do not have any cognitive and/or physical loss.

Table 2. Essential usability and accessibility recommendations for digital information environments for the elderly.

Principles	Guidelines	Authors
Error prevention and handling	Provide clear messages to the user about an error of his own in the execute of a certain task or even a system error	Nielsen (2002); Zaphiris et al. (2007)
Consistency	Layout, navigation and lettering/terminology should be simple, clear and consistent	Zaphiris et al. (2007)
	Exhibit information (messages, icons, labels, etc.) and interaction objects (edit field, command button, etc.), repeated on different pages of the site, in consistent positions and shapes	Zaphiris et al. (2007); Sales and Cybis (2009)
Feedback	Provide confirmation for tasks performed by the user	Zaphiris et al. (2007)
Control	Do not use pull-down menus and Promote enough time to read the information	Zaphiris et al. (2007); Sales and Cybis (2009)
	Do not provide options that require double-clicking	Zaphiris et al. (2007).
	Avoid the automatic scrolling feature unless can be simple way disable it	Sales and Cybis (2009)
	"Click here" and "read more" links are highly accessible by this audience, as its direct them to actions they may not be able to visualize	Vechiato (2007); Vechiato and Vidotti (2008)
Easy Learning	Use color distinction for visited and unvisited links	Nielsen (2002); Zaphiris et al. (2007)
	The icons should be simple and meaningful	Zaphiris et al. (2007); Sales e Cybis (2009)

(continued)

Table 2. (*continued*)

Principles	Guidelines	Authors
Visibility	Use uppercase and lowercase letters; avoid the use of long phrases with uppercase letters	Zaphiris et al. (2007); Sales and Cybis (2009); Echt (2002).
	Provide descriptions (in full, in captions, etc.) of abbreviations or acronyms and highlight them when they occur on their first occurrence on each page	Sales e Cybis (2009)
Prioritization of Functionality and Information	Highlight for the most important information	Zaphiris et al. (2007); Sales and Cybis (2009)
	Information should be concentrated in the center of the page	Zaphiris et al. (2007)
Affordance	Provide clues to users about where they are located on a Web page at the time of access	Zaphiris et al. (2007); Sales and Cybis (2009)
Low Physical Effort	Facilitate interaction between the user and the page, preventing repetitive actions	Sales and Cybis (2009)

Source: Adapted from [18].

3.3 Application of the Conceptual Framework

In order to verify the possible benefits to accessibility in virtual environments, some of the recommendations proposed in this research were applied in the development of a virtual museum. This museum aims to present the history of the municipality of Bandeirantes, located in the northern part of the state of Paraná (region known as Pioneer North) in Brazil.

For the creation of this virtual museum, some recommendations related to the creation of content were followed, such as use clear and simple titles to identify a page, position the labels appropriately, indicate the language of the page to the users, both in the interface and in the encoding. Some recommendations were also followed regarding user navigation, providing alternative texts for images and elements, as well as trying to clearly indicate where the available links point to.

Also, some usability principles, and their respective recommendations, were opportune for the created environment. In this way, a layout was created for a simple and clear navigation, aiming to result in a consistent museum. Also, were avoided options that require double click, as well as automatic scrolling of text and, on the other hand, links of the type "click here" and "read more" were placed in prominence, trying to meet the principle of control. In relation to links, were distinguished the visited ones of those not yet visited. In addition, acronyms used were described, in addition to prioritizing information in the center of the pages and providing tasks with low physical effort.

4   Conclusion

It is hoped that with this research, it will be possible to contribute to the elaboration of more accessible virtual environments, through the conceptual framework presented, directing, in this way, the development most varied types of virtual spaces, such as institutional, advertising, studies, art, culture, e-commerce, etc. It is also hoped that this study may also serve as a reference or help for future research which has the idea of improving the framework proposed by this work or even creating a new model.

For this reason, the present study should not be interpreted as a rigid or step-by-step guide, but rather as a suggested model, composed of recommendations that represent a compilation of different researches and are intended to serve as a basis, or, at least, offer a direction on developers to create more accessible virtual environments.

In addition, proposing a conceptual framework with a focus on accessibility, can collaborate not only for more virtual environments to be developed, but can also serve as a support for a greater variety of users to access and enjoy these virtual spaces, the which tend to grow, both in terms of quantity and content.

References

1. Barbosa, S.D.J., Silva, B.S.: Interação Humano-Computador, 1st edn. Campus, Rio de Janeiro (2010)
2. Barros Filho, E.M.: Um Framework para o Desenvolvimento de Treinamentos em Dispositivos Móveis Utilizando Realidade Virtual (Computer Science Master's thesis). Federal University of Ceara, Fortaleza (2005)
3. Brazil, Law n°. 13,146 of July 6, 2015: Brazilian Law on the Inclusion of Persons with Disabilities (Statute of Persons with Disabilities). http://www.planalto.gov.br/ccivil_03/_ato2015-2018/2015/lei/l13146.htm. Accessed 08 Feb 2018
4. de Araújo Cardoso, M.E., de Freitas Guilhermino, D., da Silva Neitzel, R.A.L., Garcia, L.S., Junior, R.E.: Accessibility in E-commerce tools: an analysis of the optical inclusion of the deaf. In: Antona, M., Stephanidis, C. (eds.) UAHCI 2015. LNCS, vol. 9175, pp. 162–173. Springer, Cham (2015). https://doi.org/10.1007/978-3-319-20678-3_16
5. Cardoso, E., Santos, S.L.D., Silva, F.P.D., Teixeira, F.G., Silva, T.L.K.D.: Tecnologias Tridimensionais para Acessibilidade em Museus. In: Proceedings of the XVII Conference of the Iberoamerican Society of Digital Graphics: Knowledge-based Design, Blucher, São Paulo, pp. 444–448 (2014)
6. Cury, M.X.: Novas perspectivas para a comunicação museológica e os desafios da pesquisa de recepção em museus. Proceedings, Porto, pp. 270–279 (2009)
7. e-MAG. Modelo de Acessibilidade em Governo Eletrônico (Accessibility Model in Electronic Government), http://emag.governoeletronico.gov.br. Accessed 08 Feb 2018
8. ISO. International Organization for Standardization: Ergonomic requirements for office work with visual display terminals. 1st edn. (1998)
9. Jabareen, Y.: Building a conceptual framework: philosophy, definitions, and procedure. Int. J. Qual. Methods 8, 49–62 (2009). International Institute for Qualitative Methodology (IIQM). University of Alberta, Canada
10. Liu, W.: Natural user interface - next mainstream product user interface. In: IEEE 11th International Conference on Computer-Aided Industrial Design & Conceptual Design, vol. 1, Yiwu, pp. 203–205 (2010)

11. Marques, L.F.C., Freitas Guilhermino, D., de Araújo Cardoso, M.E., da Silva Neitzel, R.A. L., Albano Lopes, L., Merlin, J.R., dos Santos Striquer, G.: Accessibility in virtual communities of practice under the optics of inclusion of visually impaired. In: Antona, M., Stephanidis, C. (eds.) UAHCI 2016. LNCS, vol. 9737, pp. 14–26. Springer, Cham (2016). https://doi.org/10.1007/978-3-319-40250-5_2

12. Netcraft, January 2017 Web Server Survey. https://news.netcraft.com/archives/2017/01/12/january-2017-web-server-survey.html. Accessed 08 Feb 2018

13. NETO, C. M. Ergonomia de Interfaces WWW para Cidadãos com necessidades Especiais. In: 3rd Symposium Investigation and Development of Educational Software. Universidade de Évora, Évora (1998). http://www.minerva.uevora.pt/simposio/comunicacoes/ergoweb. Accessed 08 Feb 2018

14. Nielsen, J., Loranger, H.: Usabilidade na web, 1st edn. Elsevier, Rio de Janeiro (2007)

15. Rocha, L.V., Edelweiss, N.: GeoFrame-T: A temporal conceptual framework for data modeling. In: Proceedings of the 9th ACM International Symposium on Advances In Geographical Information Systems, ACM-GIS, Atlanta (2001)

16. Schneider, C. A. SAMVC – Sistema de Autoria de Museus Virtuais Colaborativos (Electrical Engineering Master's thesis). Federal University of Rio Grande do Norte, Natal (2011)

17. Souza, C.R.B.: Um framework para editores de diagramas cooperativos baseados em anotações (Computer Science Master's thesis). State University of Campinas, Campinas (1998)

18. Vechiato, F.L., Vidotti, S.A.B.G.: Recomendações de usabilidade e de acessibilidade em projetos de ambientes informacionais digitais para idosos. In: XIII Encontro Nacional de Pesquisa em Ciência da Informação, pp. 1–21. Fiocruz (2012)

19. WCAG. Web Content Accessibility Guidelines 2.0. https://www.w3.org/TR/WCAG20. Accessed 08 Feb 2018

20. WHO. World Health Organization. www.who.in. Accessed 08 Feb 2018

21. W3C. World Wide Web Consortium. http://www.w3.org. Accessed 08 Feb 2018

22. W3C/WAI. Web Accessibility Initiative. http://www.w3.org/WAI. Accessed 08 Feb 2018

Intelligent Assistive Environments

Ambient Assisted Living and Digital Inclusion: Overview of Projects, Services and Interfaces

Alessandro Andreadis[✉] and Riccardo Zambon

Department of Information Engineering and Mathematical Sciences,
University of Siena, Siena, Italy
{andreadis,zambon}@unisi.it

Abstract. The last decades have been characterized by great advances in the field of information and communication technologies and innovative applications and services have been developed in all sectors. People who are more familiar with Internet technologies can take full advantage of the benefits brought by the new systems to everyday life, but, at the same time, if services are not carefully designed, they contribute to augment the digital gap between "info-skilled" users and people who are not acquainted with the new technologies. This paper provides an overview of interesting projects developed with the aim to favor social inclusion and to tear down barriers posed by digital technology, by supporting people with special needs (e.g., elderly and people with different impairments) in the fruition of e-services through easy forms of interactions. The study is restricted to solutions that envisage the TV device as the main user interface for supporting Ambient Assisted Living. From the survey, a basic set of services and interfaces, here described, appear to be fundamental for improving digital and social inclusion, but the design methodology for developing TV-based interfaces and services must be carefully chosen to reduce social marginalization.

Keywords: Ambient assisted living · TV interface · Inclusion

1 Introduction

In these last years, ageing of population and the percentage of elderly people with respect to the entire population are constantly growing, as well as the digital gap between them and *Information and Communication Technology* (ICT) society; this fact is leading to a new type of social marginalization in the era of digital communications.

The concept of social inclusion is strictly correlated with digital inclusion notion, intended as the way to overcome the digital gap between people who are familiar with the fruition of Internet technologies ("info-skilled") and people who are not ("info-marginalized"). Such technologies can provide a huge support to social inclusion, helping elderly or people with special needs to live like others. Although the implementation of ICT services could solve some social marginalization issues for impaired people, the introduction of several services with low usability could limit the number of people accessing them.

© Springer International Publishing AG, part of Springer Nature 2018
M. Antona and C. Stephanidis (Eds.): UAHCI 2018, LNCS 10908, pp. 187–200, 2018.
https://doi.org/10.1007/978-3-319-92052-8_15

A key issue to favor social inclusion is the provision of e-services through easy forms of interaction, so as to allow elderly or disable people with different impairments (i.e. vision, hearing, mobility, dexterity) to access ICT services without being marginalized by information society. To achieve this goal, specific services and interfaces should be designed and implemented by starting from user perspective and understanding their needs and criticalities.

In this work, we provide an overview of e-service provisioning models, aimed at enhancing digital and social inclusion through the implementation of accessible and usable television-oriented interaction interfaces. Such interfaces are aimed to involve elderly, disabled and their caregivers and other info-marginalized people into the benefits of the ICT society. Specifically, human-machine interfaces towards an easier and more familiar user interaction are described, focusing on their adoption by info-marginalized people.

The paper is organized as follows. Section 2 provides an overview of several projects adopting the TV in *Ambient Assisted Living* (AAL) scenarios. The main concepts of these framework are introduced and discussed, in order to highlight their differences and characteristics. Starting from the outcomes of such projects, Sect. 3 describes platforms, interfaces and services designed to ease the access of info-marginalized users to the ICT society. Available services and user interfaces are introduced, focusing on innovation provided on the digital and social inclusion field. Finally, Sect. 4 presents the concluding remarks.

2   Overview of TV-Centric Projects

Several projects are intended to face critical issues such as to increase independent living or to implement a comprehensive assisted living scenario. This section provides a brief overview of interesting solutions introduced by some projects adopting the TV interface to interact with users.

2.1   T-Seniority

The T-Seniority EU project [1] focuses on the prevention and early action on care for elders, by improving quality of life and social independence through innovative ICT services, delivered on different digital TV technologies. It enabled a replicable solution across Europe within digital services area for the improvement of the quality of life and social care of ageing population.

The system offers a set of integrated care e-services delivered throughout TV and it is basically composed as explained in the following (see Fig. 1).

From the T-Seniority server side, all the information technology infrastructure and support tools necessary to deliver the service reside in a central server hosting a data center. Services are then delivered through the Internet, according to a *Software as a Service* (SaaS) model. All the back-office functionality is included as well.

As regards the channel used by T-Seniority platform to reach end-users, it is convenient to make a distinction among the following television technologies:

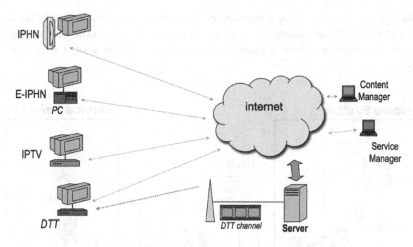

Fig. 1. T-Seniority architecture

- *Digital Terrestrial TV* (DTT), with a basic interaction due to very simple set-top-boxes;
- *Internet Protocol TV* (IPTV), delivered through the Internet as for multimedia content;
- *Internet Protocol Home Networking* (IPHN) with media consoles as interaction devices, such as Nintendo Wii;
- *Enhanced-IPHN* (E-IPHN), added in a second phase, providing a hidden pc as a central device for enhancing usability and accessibility.

The care e-services delivered by the system are composed of several functionalities (i.e. video conferencing, forms, picture books, etc.) that will be available on a specific TV technology, depending on the level of interactivity of the selected TV delivery mechanism. However, a basic set of e-care services are available on all TV technologies on T-Seniority platform, adopting the same user-friendly interfaces which take into account the impairments in vision, hearing, mobility or dexterity.

Concerning tests, several pilots have been arranged in different geographical sites, in order to prove concepts, applications, services, devices and technologies, as well as to gather continuous feedback from users. In particular, seven test sites have been established at partners locations in Spain, Italy, Greece, UK, Finland, France and Cyprus.

2.2   Oldes

OLDES (*Older People's e-services at home*) [2] is an EU co-funded project under the IST Programme that offers new technological solutions to improve quality of life of older people, through the development of very low cost and easy-to-access thematic channels and forums supported by animators.

The system includes wireless environment and medical sensors, linked via a contact center to social services and health care providers for remote monitoring.

The system (see Fig. 2) is composed of a computer installed at user's home and connected to a TV set displaying info provided by the platform via a simplified graphical user interface; access contents are selected by means of a simple remote control.

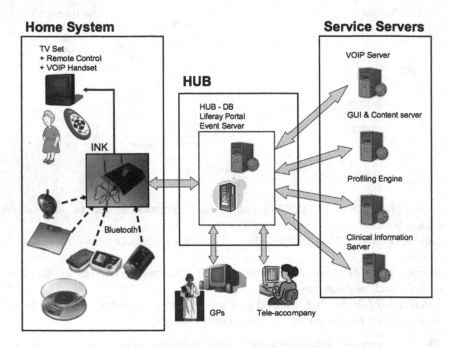

Fig. 2. OLDES architecture (Source: [2])

The system allows users to access audio and video contents and, through an adapted handset connected to the computer, they can actively participate in discussion groups with an animator or call their relatives and friends through VoIP calls.

Concerning health monitoring, a local hub communicates with wireless connection to several medical devices for the telemedicine aspects involving diabetic and cardiopathic patients: an adapted version of sphygmomanometer for obtaining elderly blood pressure, a fingertip pulse oximeter for monitoring SpO2, ECG for measuring heart rate and R-R, a glucose meter for blood glucose level, together with scales for weight check and daily diet. Moreover, some ambient monitoring systems (for patient's home temperature and humidity) have been tested, in order to check patients' living conditions, mainly in summer periods, when raising temperatures may cause serious rebounds to elderly health.

Health services and physicians are therefore able to receive, store and compare medical data and, in case of need, they can promptly respond to raising alarms.

2.3   Soprano

SOPRANO (*Service Oriented PRogrammable smArt enviroNments for Older Europeans*) [3] is an European project aimed to design a system able to assist older people with comfort and safety during everyday life, through integrated delivery of high quality support and care. SOPRANO develops and adapts to normal home environments a sophisticated range of suitably unobtrusive components, seamlessly linked to external service provision, thus enabling elderly users to live independently in society.

A major objective of SOPRANO is to take a leap forward in the way users can interact with and take charge of their living environment, as well as to develop the way professional care personnel can support the SOPRANO users when called on to do so.

Three main focuses of research and development are involved:

- Stand-alone assistive technology: products designed to compensate for motor, sensory and cognitive difficulties, frequently affecting older adults;
- Smart home technology: ICT networking in the home environment, with the integration of appliances and devices to provide control of the entire living space;
- Tele-care services: applications addressing care-related needs prevalent among older people, with ICT used to enable support from professionals and informal carers.

SOPRANO technical architecture enables pro-active assistance, by interpreting information gathered by the system about a user's situation. Responses must follow agreed rules and seamless access provided to external professionals. Safety and security is strongly enhanced with adherence to stringent reliability standards.

To ensure that services fully meet user needs, developers worked with users of SOPRANO system throughout the project lifecycle, from user requirements, through iterative prototyping, validation of concepts and functionality and usability tests involving users in their own homes.

2.4   MonAMI

The objective of the MonAMI (*Mainstreaming on Ambient Intelligence*) [4] project is to demonstrate that accessible, useful services for elderly and disabled persons living at home can be delivered in mainstream systems and platforms, by cooperating with those users and by involving key mainstream actors in the whole process.

MonAMI focuses on an open services architecture, where both services and applications are developed with a Design for All approach involving potential users.

Services are implemented in five thematic sets:

- comfort applications: home control, personalized communication interface, activity planning;
- health: monitoring, medication;
- safety and security: safety at home, visitor validation;
- activity detection;
- communication and information (Fig. 3).

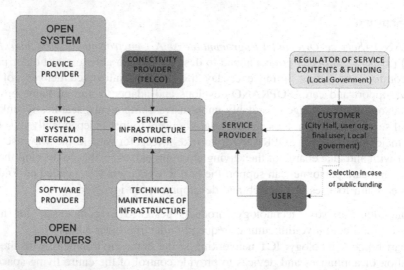

Fig. 3. MonAMI Architecture for open AAL service value chain (Source: [4])

These services were first tested to be feasible, usable and appropriate to user needs in feasibility and usability centres with laboratory conditions, then a living-scale field trial was carried out in Slovakia, Spain and Sweden at users' homes.

This project is an important proof of concept concerning open service provision architecture, implying in the service provision chain primary stakeholders (carers and beneficiaries) and also political institutions, raising awareness on the ambient assisted living solutions for elderly at home.

2.5   Vital

The VITAL (*Vital Assistance for the Elderly*) [5] project uses a combination of technologies and platforms for assisting remotely the elderly users in their home environment, through their most familiar devices, specifically designed for them (mainly TV, but also mobile phones for applications on the run).

The platform of ICT services offered by VITAL is focused on needs which are not limited to traditional assistance, but extend to inter-personal communication, education, personal advice, leisure, entertainment, integration into the information society and to their need of feeling safe while moving in the physical environment.

One of most interesting characteristics of the VITAL project is that it aims at tearing down the barriers which currently impede elderly users from accessing information and infrastructures; it supports elderly people to achieve an active life and to take care of themselves inside and outside their living environment.

2.6   Care@Home

Care@Home [6] project designs and develops an open platform able to provide services to elderly for fostering independent living and, at the same time, to notify caregivers about information on elder's health when needed, in order to prevent health diseases.

As for previously described projects, it encloses the social support system for the elderly, in the form of personalized communication and service channel in their home. It offers not only a two-way communication system for family, friends and caregivers, but also entertainment and additional services (i.e., enabling empowerment, wellness and social care, household, shopping and community information).

Care@home platform takes advantage of the adoption of sensors, wireless communications and multimedia. However, all such complex technologies and functionalities are combined to integrated products and services, in a personalized and easy-to-use approach. Services are delivered through interactive multimedia television, based on the 'design platform' of the Philips Smart TV, so as to be easily accessible and familiar for the user.

2.7 iTVCare

iTVCare [7] is a technological platform based on interactive television, aimed to provide seniors with support for challenging everyday activities, such as medication intake and reminders of medical appointments. It points to improve the quality of life of older adults in non-clinical settings, such as home and public nursing homes. The key challenge of this work is to determine if a television set is suitable and accepted by older people, for reminding to take their medications and doctor appointments, in order to help improving their quality of life

This project concerns the creation of an improved platform of interactive television, based on Google/Android TV technology. It envisages an open platform, built on the Android operating system including Google Chrome and applications developed with Android SDK (*Software Development Kit*).

The system architecture is shown in Fig. 4 and is composed of the following elements:

- iTVCare: a Google TV representing the home system of the user (TV, set-top-box, controller);
- Database: containing information related to medical appointments and medicine intakes;
- Android SDK: embedded in the set-top-box, enabled to execute the applications;
- Services to be consumed by iTVCare;
- Medication intakes and alert generation manager;
- Medical appointments manager;

Basically, users receive the information visually from the TV screen, by interacting through the remote control and a keyboard.

This project carried out also an evaluation of acceptance of the TV technology by the elderly, showing that users have good attitude and strong intention to use this platform, thanks to its ease of use and usefulness.

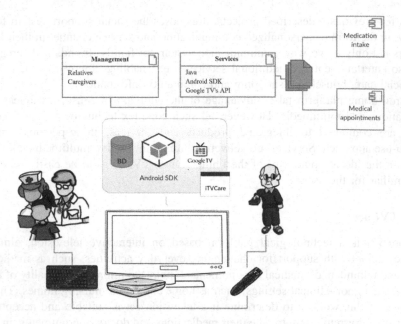

Fig. 4. iTVCare Architecture (Source: [7])

2.8 A Smart TV System for e-Health Services

Work described in [8] introduces and discusses a system for providing a set of e-health services through the smart TV interface. It implements a cloud- based service for remote access to personal medical records and it envisages a local service which allows to monitor health-related parameters, gathered through NFC-enabled medical devices, and to manage reminders for medicines

As shown in Fig. 5, a software application resident within the smart TV is the link between local and remote services. It is also responsible to provide the user's interface to the entire system.

To perform health monitoring, a microcontroller board endowed with Ethernet and NFC modules is used to collect health-related data from medical devices. The NFC reader allows to easily acquire parameters and to store the measures in a database, making them accessible in any moment through the TV application.

Usability tests were performed in laboratory settings, involving elderly people with no experience with smart TV. Results highlighted the usability of the system, showing that users could take advantage of the application and of its functionalities and they could successfully carry out the process of health parameter measurements.

2.9 Other Works

The projects described in this section refer to monitoring platform solutions, not involving TV as service delivery interface for the elderly/patient. They have been added here for providing a wider vision of Ambient Assisted Living concept.

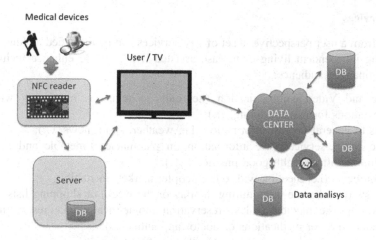

Fig. 5. Overall architecture

Reference [9] describes the design and implementation of an integrated system which collects data from different sensors, placed in a house of a person having dementia, and transmits them to a cloud system, so as to detect the daily activities of the patient and to make them available to remote caregivers.

Seven kinds of sensors are positioned in key places inside the house (i.e. flame sensor, rain sensor, temperature sensor, force sensitive, light sensitive, reed, infrared motion sensor).

Notifications from any IoT device are stored chronologically in the database, and the detection of an activity is determined by triggering a specific set of the sensors. All configurations are analyzed by the software, which enables correct interpretation of the activity in the specific context of the scenario. Consequently, it is possible to identify specific activities and their logical consequences (i.e. interrupted actions, forgotten issues, open doors) and to remind them to the patient or to his caregiver/doctor.

The work in [10] describes a system designed for passive care: it monitors several parameters through a personal area network, composed by a wrist-wearable wireless sensor node and a mobile platform. The system monitors vital parameters (i.e. temperature, accelerometer for falls, heart rate), in order to detect variations on user's status when they are at home. It directly communicates with the user through natural language and it currently accepts simple responses (i.e., Yes or No through voice recognition module) and a more specific limited vocabulary which is tailored to both the user and its general application for the elderly.

3 Services and Interfaces

This chapter summarizes the key elements (services and interfaces) that have been highlighted in the previous projects overview. The main lines of in-depth analysis and research in the sector of ambient assisted living are identified, and specific attention is given to the adoption of the TV terminal as the interface for the fruition of services.

3.1 Services

Starting from a user perspective, a set of key services can be identified as fundamental to prolong independent living or to ease assisted living and to enhance inclusion of info-marginalized audience:

- Voice and Video communication (i.e. calls to relatives, messaging with care organizations for assisted living, ...);
- access to general interest information (i.e. weather, sport, news, ...);
- public care e-services (i.e. information on pharmacies timetable and locations, hospital facilities, health good practices, ...);
- appointments (i.e. meeting with other people, market timetable, ...);
- task lists (to schedule tasks during the day or the week) or shopping lists;
- reservations (i.e. medical analysis reservation, movie/theater ticket reservation, ...);
- reminders (i.e. for medications or doctor appointments);
- fall detection algorithms, integrated with specific devices;
- exercises at home: showing exercises, motivating users for physical and cognitive stimulation;
- tele-presence (i.e. for fighting loneliness, psychological help)
- tele-monitoring of independent living, available both to external supervision by formal carers or public administration carers, or to the elderly (e.g., firing or fall alerts, ...);
- tele-monitoring of vital parameters through specific devices and sensors.

3.2 Interfaces

User interfaces are mechanisms for mediating user interaction with the system and provide different types of interaction with the user, depending on the adopted device [11]:

- *Graphical User Interface* (GUI), a visual way of interacting with computer systems, based on elements presented in a specific device [12] (i.e., desktop computers, television, mobile devices);
- *Web User Interface* (WUI), allowing interactions similarly to GUI, but focused on the Web page standards [12];
- *Tangible User Interface* (TUI), characterized by design retaining the richness of physical interaction, thus involving physical objects [13];
- *Natural User Interface* (NUI), enabling interactions with devices by using human natural resources, like gestures or voice;
- *Multimodal Interaction* (MI), combining natural input modes in a coordinated manner with multimedia systems output [14], through the integration of different categories of user interfaces.

We provide below an overview of the input and output user interfaces which can help to overtake the barriers of common hardware/software; such interfaces, available through different technological solutions, are described for both input and output modes.

Input mode:

- new devices enriching input modalities with easier forms of interaction: Wiimote-like devices [15] and 3D mouses [16] for more intuitive interactions [17];
- an on-screen *qwerty* keyboard, designed to be easily typed through the given controller (or touchscreen if provided) and introducing word prediction algorithms for minimizing typos [18];
- speech commands and tools for content reading (e.g., reading louder for hearing impairments);
- easy user identification, through several biometric techniques such as fingerprinting, hand-palm/iris/voice recognition, or specific movements [19–21], or by adopting smartcards or RFID cards, Quick Response (QR) codes [22] or barcodes.

Output mode: the special needs of older people make it necessary to comply with design guidelines created to support their specific needs.

Some of these guidelines [23–25] were used to design a low-fidelity prototype of iTVCare. The more relevant features are summarized below:

- minimize steps to reach a given screen/option/information;
- avoid scrolling;
- use of tree menus with an intuitive navigation menu;
- show same set of options in the same order, to enhance information consistency.
- reduce the information (i.e. short sentences), avoiding irrelevant content for memory impaired;
- clear indication of the current selection, in order to avoid elderly to get lost when browsing.
- use meaningful and big icons and labels for vision impairment
- prefer graphic symbols to words;
- present clear error messages, only if necessary;
- adopt large font type, high contrast and easy to read font family

Note that "elderly-centered" interface characteristics are based on the technology capabilities in relation with the end user needs. Although different media and technology adopted for service providing and/or application implementation are constantly evolving and improving, Ambient Assisted Living environments should adopt a "common interface": it should be intuitive, easily understandable and familiar for end users, in order to improve their acceptance of technology and to enhance their learning, understanding and usage of value added services [26].

3.3 Design Process

To obtain better results in terms of usability, accessibility and, consequently, digital inclusion, all services and interfaces must be designed focusing on the real user needs [27].

The design phase should be based on the user perspective and should involve users in the implementation and test phase, according to a user-centered design approach [28], as detailed below:

- Specify the usage context: identify people that will use the product, what their goals are when using it, and under which circumstances they will use it.
- Specify requirements: identify all the requirements and the users' objectives that are needed to achieve success with the product.
- Produce design solutions: this part must follow an iterative process, starting from a low fidelity prototype and evolving to a high-fidelity prototype.
- Evaluation: this phase is the most important part of the process and it must be (ideally) executed through tests with real users.

4 Conclusions

In this work we provide a survey on some interesting solutions which envisage the TV terminal as the main user-interface for supporting Ambient Assisted Living.

From these works, carried out within European Community research projects, it can be pointed out how important is the adoption of the TV screen as the main interface for presenting information to info-marginated people (i.e., elderly, impaired ...). In fact, many elderly and disabled users are not familiar, and hence not well disposed, with the use of computers or mobile devices, like smartphones or tablets.; on the contrary, the television terminal allows to enhance their willingness towards the fruition of applications, specifically designed for monitoring and supporting an active every-day life, thus contributing to increase digital inclusion.

This survey points out that some types of interfaces are in common to many of the analyzed works; this happens because they are endowed with an ergonomic level and an ease of use, which permit the fruition of crucial services and complex functionalities by persons not acquainted with interaction modalities and information fruition that are typical of ICT channels.

Additionally, it emerges that a set of basic services can be considered as fundamental in the sector of Ambient Assisted Living, towards the improvement of social inclusion and monitoring elderly users and people with impairments in general. Particular attention should be paid to the choice of design methodology and the development of interfaces and services. User-centered design or, in general, participatory design methodology, where users are directly involved in the design phase and provide their feedback to researchers, has been demonstrated to represent the best way to achieve intuitive, familiar and simple interactions for info-marginated people.

We hope that this paper can provide basic indications to whom is involved in the design and implementation of services for disadvantaged users; the key concepts related to interfaces and services for TV-centric systems can be adopted for delivering more accessible information contents, coming also from Internet of Things and innovative sensors scenarios.

References

1. Moumtzi, V., Farinos, J., Wills, C.: T-Seniority: an online service platform to assist independent living of elderly population. In: Proceedings of the 2nd International Conference on Pervasive Technologies Related to Assistive Environments, PETRA 2009, 9–13 June, Corfu, Greece (2009)
2. OLDES (Older People's e-services at home). http://www.oldes.eu/home.html. Accessed 01 February 2018
3. SOPRANO - 045212 - (Service Oriented PRogrammable smArt enviroNments for Older Europeans). http://cordis.europa.eu/project/rcn/80527_en.html. Accessed 25 January 2018
4. Roy, A., Artigas, J., Lain, L., Vaquerizo, E., Falco, J., Ibarz, A.: MonAMI: mainstream on ambient intelligence. e-inclusion living scaled field trial experience in Spain. J. Res. Pract. Inform. Technol. 45(2), 133–149 (2013)
5. VITAL (Vital Assistance for the Elderly) Contract Type: Specific Targeted Research Project. http://cordis.europa.eu/project/rcn/80735_en.html. Accessed 25 January 2018
6. Care@Home. http://www.aal-europe.eu/projects/carehome/. Accessed 25 January 2018
7. Santana-Mancilla, P., Anido-Rifón, L.: The technology acceptance of a TV platform for the elderly living alone or in public nursing homes. Int. J. Environ. Res. Public Health 14(6), 617 (2017)
8. Raffaeli, L., Spinsante, S., Gambi, E.: Integrated smart TV-based personal e-Health system. Int. J. E-Health Med. Commun. 7, 48–64 (2016)
9. Demir, E., Köseoğlu, E., Sokullu, R., Seker, B.: Smart home assistant for ambient assisted living of elderly people with dementia. Procedia Comput. Sci. 113, 609–614 (2017)
10. Winkley, J., Jiang, P., Jiang, W.: Verity: an ambient assisted living platform. IEEE Trans. Consum. Electron. 58(2), 364–373 (2012)
11. Bittencourt, I.I., Baranauskas, M.C., Pereira, R., et al.: A systematic review on multi-device inclusive environments. Univ. Access Inf. Soc. 15, 737 (2016)
12. Newell, A.F., Gregor, P., Morgan, M., Pullin, G., Macaulay, C.: User sensitive inclusive design. Univ. Access Inf. Soc. 9, 235–243 (2010)
13. Sommerville, I.: Software Engineering, 9th edn. Addison-Wesley, Reading (2010)
14. Pereira, R., Miranda, L.C., Baranauskas M.C.C., Piccolo, L.S.G., Almeida, L.D., Reis, J.C.: Interaction design of social software: clarifying requirements through a culturally aware artifact. In: Proceedings of the International Conference on Information Society, pp. 310–315 (2011)
15. Wii (Nintendo): http://wiiportal.nintendo-europe.com/. Accessed 25 January 2018
16. Logitech MX Air Mouse: https://support.logitech.com/it_it/product/mx-air-rechargeable-cordless-air-mouse. Accessed 25 January 2018
17. Martins, M., Cunha, A., Oliveira, I., et al.: Usability test of 3Dconnexion 3D mice versus keyboard + mouse in Second Life undertaken by people with motor disabilities due to medullary lesions. Univ. Access Inf. Soc. 14, 5 (2015)
18. Badr, G., Raynal, M.: Optimized interaction with word prediction list. In: Proceedings of the Association for the Advancement of Assistive Technology in Europe, Florence, Italy, p. 871 (2009)
19. Shirali-Shahreza, M.: Login to internet websites by next generation game console. In: Proceedings of IEEE/IFIP International Conference in Central Asia on Internet, Tashkent, Uzbekistan, pp. 1–4 (2006)
20. Akhteruzzaman, M., Alam, M.S.: Real time fingerprint identification. In: Proceedings of IEEE National Aerospace and Electronics Conference, NAECON, Tuscaloosa, Alabama, USA, pp. 433–440 (2000)

21. Alonso, J.B., Ferrer, M.A., Rafael Diaz, M., Travieso, C.M.: Biometric system based in the feature of hand palm. In: Proceedings of the International Carnahan Conference on Security Technology (2004)
22. ZXing, Z.: Crossing: http://code.google.com/p/zxing/. Accessed 25 January 2018
23. Johnson, J., Finn, K.: Designing User Interfaces for an Aging Population: Towards Universal Design. Elsevier, Amsterdam (2017)
24. Loureiro, B., Rodrigues, R.: Design guidelines and design recommendations of multi-touch interfaces for elders. In: Proceedings of the 7th International Conference on Advances in Computer-Human Interactions, Barcelona, Spain, 23–27, pp. 41–47 (2014)
25. Nunes, F., Kerwin, M., Silva, P.A.: Design recommendations for TV user interfaces for older adults: findings from the eCAALYX project, p. 41. ACM Press, New York (2012)
26. Wills, C., Moumtzi, V., Vontas, A.: A real case study of assistive living ecosystems. In: Proceedings of 4th IEEE International Conference on Digital Ecosystems and Technologies (2010)
27. Dewsbury, G., Rouncefield, M., Sommerville, I., et al.: Designing technology with older people. Univ. Access Inf. Soc. **6**, 207 (2007)
28. Bevan, N., Bogomolni, I.: Incorporating user quality requirements in the software development process. In: Proceedings of 4th International Software & Internet Quality Week Conference (QWE2000), Brussels, Belgium (2000)

Intelligent Driver Profiling System for Cars – A Basic Concept

Nermin Caber(✉), Patrick M. Langdon, and P. John Clarkson

Engineering Design Centre, University of Cambridge,
Department of Engineering, Trumpington Street, Cambridge CB2 1PZ, UK
{nc501,pml24,pjcl0}@cam.ac.uk

Abstract. Many industries have been transformed by the provision of service solutions characterised by personalisation and customisation - most dramatically the development of the iPhone. Personalisation and customisation stand to make an impact on cars and mobility in comparable ways. The automobile industry has a major role to play in this change, with moves towards electric vehicles, autonomous cars, and car sharing as a service. These developments are likely to bring disruptive changes to the business of car manufacturers as well as to drivers. However, in the automobile industry, both the user's preferences and demands and also safety issues need to be confronted since the frequent use of different makes and models of cars, implied by car sharing, entails several risks due to variations in car controls depending on the manufacturer. Two constituencies, in particular, are likely to experience even more difficulties than they already do at present, namely older people and those with capability variations. To overcome these challenges, and as a means to empower a wide car user base, the paper here presents a basic concept of an intelligent driver profiling system for cars: the system would enable various car characteristics to be tailored according to individual driver-dependent profiles. It is intended that wherever possible the system will personalise the characteristics of individual car components; where this is not possible, however, an initial customisation will be performed.

Keywords: Automotive engineering and technology
Advanced driver assistance systems · Car driver profiling · Customisation
Personalisation · Inclusive design · Human factors and ergonomics

1 Introduction

With the move to increased usage of car sharing services, it is crucial to reflect on the factor of transportation safety. Every day about 3,000 people are killed in road traffic crashes, resulting in up to 1.8 million deaths per year according to the World Health Organization [1]; a majority of these accidents can be attributed to human errors [2]. Since car manufacturers lack sufficient data, knowledge and understanding concerning users' motor, sensory and cognitive capabilities and limitations, they complicate driving for the majority of users and, thus, help facilitate those kinds of errors. However, technology is now at a stage where it may accommodate the wide range of diversity among car users, leading to increased safety. This becomes even more important when people use different vehicles with varying controls, as is the case with

© Springer International Publishing AG, part of Springer Nature 2018
M. Antona and C. Stephanidis (Eds.): UAHCI 2018, LNCS 10908, pp. 201–213, 2018.
https://doi.org/10.1007/978-3-319-92052-8_16

car sharing services, and, thus, do not have previous experience of the car they use. In cases where fundamental controls for driving differ, such as the utilisation of wind-screen wipers or the reverse gear, a considerable effect on safety can be expected.

In every sector, whether that of smartphones, computers, furnishings or cars, the importance of customisation and personalisation is increasing significantly; people prefer, as far as possible, to have products perfectly tailored to their demands and needs [3–6]. This can be done either by customisation or by personalisation; while in cus-tomisation the user decides on product characteristics, in personalisation this is derived from information gathered about the user. Amazon, utilising user data to make per-sonalised product suggestions, is a good example for personalisation, while Dell, enabling their customers to customise their computer, is an example for customisation [4]. Within the car industry, the circumstance of users wanting personalised features is gaining importance as engineering progress begins to allow autonomous driving. In consequence, this is radically changing Human Machine Interface (HMI) as both customisation and personalisation are further driven by the continuing growth of car sharing, a growth which can partly be attributed to the car's decreasing importance as a social status symbol for most people [7–10]. In the future, there may be less privately owned cars and more shared ones. Mobility may become a service, often called 'Mobility as a Service' (MAAS), and might change the business model of car manu-facturers significantly.

Today, the ability to select different driving modes already allows a driver to customise various characteristics of the car such as the suspension, the response qualities of the engine and the gearbox, the steering, and advanced driver assistance systems (e.g. Electronic Stability Control (ESC)). Several such characteristics, including steering wheel and seat position, only have to be adjusted once as they can be memorized by the car and associated with the car keys, making readjustment, e.g. after someone else has driven the car, unnecessary. Most of these systems are able to save multiple drivers, generally up to three, per key. However, this single modal approach is extremely sensitive to errors since, e.g. in corporate automobile fleets or families, several people often use the same car and share keys thus leading to false customisation of the car. For use in car sharing those systems have to be based on the user's card applied to unlock the car; to the best knowledge of the authors, such a system has not been applied yet. Nevertheless, these systems cannot be termed intelligent, are mostly based on customisation, and tailor only a small scope of areas.

To meet all these challenges, it is proposed that a system be developed, which goes a step further than current systems and implements automatic personalisation in all feasible areas of a car; if personalisation is not achievable, a driver-dependent cus-tomisation is intended. More precisely, the research, this paper is based on, aims to conceptually design an intelligent driver profiling system for cars through trials of alternative techniques fulfilling a specific sub-function, as well as of integral concepts, and through the usage of an inclusive design approach ensuring the inclusion of a wider population. By considering a wider population, including the elderly and those with capability variations, such a system will empower car users and, as a consequence, will constitute a profound solution for the safety problem since this system is able to facilitate driving for a majority of people and, as a result, be safer. Such a system, moreover, paves the way for MAAS and, thus, will increase customer satisfaction due to the preference for personalised and customised items [6]. Both car manufacturers and society benefit from this; car manufacturers are able to increase business and society enjoys higher satisfaction alongside safer driving.

This paper introduces the topic of an intelligent driver profiling system for cars by presenting the state of the art in this field as well as related ones, and by elaborating a basic concept for such a system.

2 State of the Art

Although several adjustments in current cars can be memorised and recalled based on the driver's key or profile, the intended system aims at extending this customisation approach and adding personalisation in all feasible areas. Contemporary cars already utilise various applications potentially helpful for the development of such an intelligent driver profiling system for cars. Some of these systems can constitute potential sub-systems adapted by and implemented in the driver profiling system, or the sensors used by these systems to fulfil their task can be helpful in creating profile data necessary for other profile-based adjustments.

2.1 Automotive Sensors

Modern cars are equipped with a huge amount of sensors measuring several parameters within chassis, body, and power train areas; for instance, contemporary luxury cars are equipped with more than 100 sensors per vehicle [11]. Generally, two kinds of sensors are distinguished: proprioceptive measuring in-vehicle data and exteroceptive, such as video, lidar, or radar, observing vehicle environment [9]. While in the first half of the 20th century cars did not have any kind of sensors, in the 1970s car companies started to implement sensor equipment and increased the amount significantly over the years; this growth is driven by rising requirements in several fields [12]. Sensors in power train systems ensure optimal car performance and the compliance with statutory provisions, e.g., emission restrictions. In chassis systems, sensors mainly serve safety, stability, weight reduction, and legislation reasons; for example, the United States government demands, since September 2007, a Tire Pressure Monitoring System (TPMS), which uses a pressure sensor on each wheel to detect a possible pressure drop in the tires, in all new cars. Body sensors generally aim for increased security, occupant safety, comfort and convenience by, for example, applying night vision sensors which detect potential hazards beyond the lighting range of the car's headlights and, thus, support driver's awareness. All current safety systems such as Electronic Stability Control (ESC), Antilock Brake System (ABS) and advanced airbags use multiple sensors; some of the collected data can be useful for the intended driver profiling system, as in the case of advanced airbags [11, 13, 14]. In this case, sensors measure the seat position, the seatbelt tension, and the seated weight, to derive specific information about the driver [11]. This example already indicates the potential of in-vehicle sensor data gathering; a thorough analysis in this area in further research will reveal a variety of data enabling to derive various driver characteristics.

2.2   Advanced Driver Assistance Systems

Advanced driver assistance systems aim to increase safety and support drivers by supplying relevant information about the environment, providing warnings in risky situations and automating some driving tasks to excuse the driver from manual control [15]. In other words, while some ADAS only provide visual, haptic or audible warnings, other ADAS actively intervene in control when a potential risk is detected [16]. Research conducted on the effectiveness of semi-autonomous ADAS demonstrated the safety improvement in emergency situations [17].

All that started back in 1978 with the production of the Antilock Braking System (ABS) invented by Bosch, the first actively engaging assistance system. Since then multiple ADAS such as ESC, Parking Assistance Systems, Adaptive Cruise Control, Forward Collision Prevention Systems, Lane Departure Warning (LDW) Systems, and Traffic Jam Assistance Systems have been introduced to the market [9]. In the next step, these systems are combined with a driver status monitoring system to enable an automated activation in the case of an abnormal driver's state [18].

Up to date, most ADAS operate autonomously without communicating with ADAS from other cars or the road infrastructure; however, in the future a cooperative approach is sought, enabling continuous Car2Car and Car2X communication. Such cooperative driving permits the exchange of information to communicate, for example, slowdowns or congestions to rear traffic which is not aware of the hazard; in this way, information not measurable with in-vehicle sensors can be gathered [9, 15]. The usage of such ADAS in the context of an intelligent driver profiling system for cars allows, on the one side, to support drivers with specific limitations, and, on the other side, to tailor these systems to the driver's profile so that an even greater safety benefit and customer satisfaction can be achieved [5]. ESC, for example, can already be customised in modern cars by authorising the driver to choose between specific system settings, such as normal, sport, and race mode.

2.3   Driver Behaviour Profiling

The state of the art in driver behaviour profiling focuses on the use of in-vehicle and in some cases external sensors, such as smartphones, to analyse driver behaviour; these systems try to detect risky or aggressive drivers in order to support fleet management targeting to reduce fleet degradation and costs, insurance companies aiming for driver-dependent premiums, and economical as well as safe driving [19, 20]. When using in-vehicle sensors most approaches rely on Controller Area Network Bus (CAN Bus) data to retrieve proprioceptive as well as exteroceptive measurements and to fuse this data [21–24]. Gathering a variety of data allows to more precisely judge the risk of a certain driving behaviour [25]. In the case of the application of external sensors, the same method of broad gathering is applied [26, 27]. Another possibility of data gathering is the installation of an external data recording system. Many insurance companies use these devices to enable driver dependent premiums [28, 29]. The calculation of such a driver behaviour profile delivers valuable data that can be used for the computation of the more comprehensive driver profile aimed at by the intended system. In contrast to driver behaviour profiling, the intended system suggested in this paper aims to implement a broader system that not only analyses driver's behaviour but also takes into account driver's capabilities, needs, schedule, preferences, state and so on; the goal is a highly tailored car allowing optimal utilisation of MAAS and enhanced user satisfaction and safety.

2.4   Driver State Monitoring

Since multiple fatalities are caused by driver's inattention, a wide range of research has been performed on implementing a driver state monitoring system, also known under the terms driver impairment monitor, driver inattention monitor or driver vigilance monitoring; the term driver state includes all kinds of distraction or fatigue possibly occurring. In autonomous cars currently used indirect inattention systems measuring driving performance metrics will no longer be feasible, making the investigation of new direct approaches essential. Promising approaches observe the driver and assess, based on distinct visual, auditory, mechanical and cognitive characteristics, whether the driver is distracted or fatigued. Most of these systems use modern camera technology and image processing in order to evaluate possible distraction based on eye and head movement [30–36]. The next level of state monitoring does not only include the further improvement of general distraction or fatigue assessment but goes one step further and aims to detect complex mental states [37]. Such systems are crucial for a potential intelligent driver profiling system for cars since the information provided is required to enable car characteristic adjustments based on the driver's physical as well as mental conditions. Fusing the data gathered by the driver state monitoring system with additional profile based information about the user, such as age, diseases, biometrics and capabilities, enables a more robust and earlier detection.

3   Basic Concept

3.1   Motivation

It is believed that the way people travel will change significantly within the next decades; the majority of people will switch from privately owned to shared or rented cars. Whenever people plan to travel, they will book a car and use this to get from one place to the other instead of utilising their own car; already in large cities, cars provided by car sharing services may be found within a short walking distance from nearly every point. Some car manufacturers have already started to offer car sharing services (see DriveNow (BMW MINI & Sixt) and Car2Go (Daimler)) since they are aware of the trend towards MAAS, especially, within the younger generation for whom cars do not represent an important social status symbol. A consequence of this shift is a frequent change of the cars people drive; accordingly, people will drive cars they are not familiar with resulting in potential safety hazards. Up to date, even for some fundamental controls, such as the use of windscreen wipers or the reverse gear, no standard has been implemented. For example, when a car sharing customer drives a car he is not familiar with on the highway and a sudden shower of rain appears, he must know how to activate the windscreen wipers because otherwise the driving performance is deteriorated significantly. Another example is the case of older people who have driven a special car brand perhaps for decades and, therefore, are used to the controls of this car brand; they probably will experience severe difficulties when faced with divergent controls in a shared car. Although people will learn the utilisation of controls depending on the car brand, this process can be annoying for the user and is prone to failure. Consequently, an intelligent driver profiling system for cars identifying the user and adjusting car characteristics based on the user's preferences can increase safety as well as customer satisfaction and gives the car manufacturers implementing such a system first a competitive advantage. Therefore, in the long run this research aims to deliver and trial different techniques for and concepts of an intelligent driver profiling system for cars in order to contribute to MAAS and to increase safety, comfort and customer satisfaction [19, 20]. Thereby, car manufacturers as well as society benefit from such a system.

3.2 Remit and Research Approach

The aspiration here is a device or system able to adjust car characteristics perfectly to the user's preferences, capabilities and limitations; the system shall be able to transmit the profile information between cars in order to be car-independent. Based on personalisation and customisation, the system shall tailor the car as the user approaches it. Any technical solution is likely to be based around elements of the vehicle control system. Based on current knowledge and research, the following remit can be derived:

1. Identifying the user
2. Gathering data from the vehicle about the user
3. Allowing customisation of areas by data obtained from direct user input during use
4. Calculating a profile based on the data gathered as well as on the user's customisation
5. Tailoring all adjustable car characteristics based on the profile
6. Updating the profile continuously based on new data gathered or entered by a customer
7. Storing the data

In this research project the inclusive design approach is equated with the human-centred design approach since it is understood that these two approaches mainly differ in their scope; while human-centred design focuses on the potential target users, inclusive design extends this idea and aims to target the widest possible audience including people with capability impairments, perhaps as a result of ageing [38–40]. Since a great part of the population drives and, therefore, only few people can be expelled, the design process in this research pursues such an inclusive design approach; this ensures that user experience is considered a crucial part of design [1, 38]. As a consequence, user acceptance as well as the perceived benefit of an intelligent driver profiling system for cars are increased. In this way, it is ensured that especially those people, who experience most difficulties when driving, are considered in the design. Accordingly, establishing the needs, wants and expectations of possible end-users, including those who have no experience of personalised devices and possibly no needs for such features, will be an important part of this research.

The prospective research in this field aims to handle this challenge by answering the central research question:

How is it possible to improve user satisfaction and performance using an intelligent driver profiling system for cars based on customisation and personalisation?

The process to answer this research question and to achieve the conceptual design of an intelligent driver profiling system for cars mainly comprises eight key work packages: (1) ascertainment of the current state of the art, (2) identification of end-user's requirements and needs, (3) clarification of hypotheses and research questions, (4) development of a research methodology, (5) definition of a hypothetical intelligent driver profiling system for cars, (6) development of a design specification, (7) development of a detailed conceptual design, and (8) the evaluation of the design's benefits. With this approach mainly the following research sub-questions are addressed:

– What is the current state of the art?
– What are the end-users' needs, preferences, wants, limitations, characteristics and capabilities?
– What does a hypothetical intelligent driver profiling system for cars look like?

3.3 Visualisation of Intended System

To visualise the remit and objective of the intended system, a juxtaposition of the present and the prospective human-car-interaction is sketched, using the example of a car rental scenario. Based on the Hierarchical Task Analysis of Driving (HTAoD) developed by [41] and personas, the tasks to be fulfilled are addressed and examined successively from a present and a future perspective in order to give an overview of the system's functions and potential benefits. Personas constitute detailed caricatures facilitating the visualisation of user's needs, demands, capabilities, and limitations, and are a common methodology applied in human-centred design [38].

Richard, a 67-year-old German man, and his wife, Gudrun (65 years old), are travelling to Majorca. Both retired last year from their jobs and want to enjoy their new freedom; Richard worked as an electrical engineer while Gudrun was a language teacher. They have driven Mercedes-Benz cars over decades and are used to its controls; currently, they drive a 2017 Mercedes-Benz C220d. They are both afflicted with age related long sightedness. Although both have got a smartphone, they are not exceptionally interested in digital technology and find it difficult to learn how to use sophisticated interfaces or interfaces not meeting their expectation. The couple have never been to Majorca before and are, consequently, unfamiliar with the airport and the destination. After arriving at the airport, they hire a car to get to their hotel. During this trip they meet several challenges.

After getting the key from the customer service, Richard and Gudrun, at first, have to find their rental car in a multi-storey car park. The customer service assistant told them the registration number, the storey the car is parked on, and the brand and model of the car; however, since the couple do not know how a Jaguar XF looks like they only can focus on the registration number to find the car on the specific storey. Under current circumstances, this task is annoying and time-consuming. Richard and Gudrun run all over the place and use the opening and closing buttons of the car key to observe opening and/or closing indication and, in that way, to facilitate the search for the car.

In the next step, after entering the car, Richard has to adjust the driver's seat and the mirrors to his preferences. Richard hunts for the controls to adjust the longitudinal position, the backrest, and the head restraint of the seat; however, he cannot find the controls. What Richard does not realise is that, in contrast to his Mercedes-Benz where the power seat control switches are placed at the door panel, the control switches of the Jaguar are located on the side of the seat valance. In order to adjust his seat, Richard calls the customer service assistant for help; the assistant helps him to adapt the seat position as well as the mirrors. Although Richard behaves properly in this situation and asks for help, the chance of someone relinquishing the seat adjustment and driving without accurately adjusted seat and mirrors is high; this constitutes a severe driving risk.

After adjusting seats and mirrors, Richard tries to start the Jaguar XF. Based on experience with his current Mercedes-Benz and the cars before it, he hunts for the ignition switch barrel to put the car key into it; however, he is not able to find it since the Jaguar is equipped with keyless entry. After a while Gudrun brings the 'Start Engine Stop' button to Richard's attention and he presses the button to start the engine. While the engine does not start, Richard notices a message in the dashboard he cannot read and asks Gudrun for his reading glasses. When reading the message, Richard realises that the language is Spanish and asks Gudrun for help to translate it. Since the car asks Richard to press the brake pedal, he does that and, concurrently, pushes the 'Start Engine Stop' button to start the engine. Although in this example the information presented in the dashboard is not correlated to safety and the car does not move, in other examples, such as driving on a highway and loosing pressure in one tire, not being able to read a warning message informing the driver, for example about a tire pressure drop, can, indeed, deteriorate the driving safety.

Since Richard and Gudrun have not been to Majorca, yet, they are frightened of not being able to handle the navigation system of the Jaguar XF. Nevertheless, they try to enter the address of their hotel into the navigation system. Out of habit, he spins the rotary control knob on the transmission hump to scroll through the menu. Because of flashing up symbols on the dashboard, he, immediately, realises that he operates the automatic gear box instead of the infotainment system. In consequence of this confusion, they, based on their experience with smartphones, try to handle the infotainment system by touching the display and discover that it works. Now, they are able to enter their hotel address into the navigation system although the different menu structure and Spanish address format confuse them and make the task time-consuming and annoying.

On their route to the hotel Richard notices his increasing fatigue and deteriorating awareness since he and Gudrun have already travelled for several hours since leaving their home in Germany. In the same moment the driver condition monitoring system warns Richard against his drowsiness. Therefore, Richard and Gudrun decide to take a break before continuing their journey and to exchange positions. After adjusting her seat and the mirrors, Gudrun takes over control and drives them safely to the hotel. Although current driver drowsiness warning systems function well, they cannot detect drowsiness until the driving performance has deteriorated already.

Such a scenario occurs every day in the world and exacerbates people's journeys. Especially older people and those with capability variations are afflicted by these challenges. However, even younger and/or intellectual people sometimes struggle with tasks due to disinterest or lack of knowledge in the specific field. Without further discussion, we can agree that such a scenario is not desirable. Hence, the question arises how it might look like with an intelligent driver profiling system.

After getting the key from the customer service, Richard and Gudrun, at first, have to find their rental car in a multi-storey car park. The customer service assistant told them the registration number, the storey the car is parked on, and the brand and model of the car. When arriving at the correct floor, the intelligent driver profiling system guides Richard and Gudrun directly to the car. This might be by voice and/or visual instructions performed by either a car key or a customer's smartphone. Besides displaying the visual instruction on the screen of the car key or smartphone, the device may be able to display the instructions on the floor and to tell them the exact position of the car by, for example, saying 'Your Jaguar XF is parked in the fourth parking on the left side'. When approaching the car, it indicates its location visually as well as aurally and opens automatically for the couple.

In the next step, when entering the car, Richard realises that the seat is reversed and starts adjusting to his preferred position as he sits down; he immediately feels extremely comfortable. Based on the profile which might know about Richard's anthropometry, the car adjusts the seat and the mirrors fitting Richard's preferences. Moreover, since the system is familiar with the age of Richard and Gudrun, it reverses the seats to facilitate the entry before it moves them into driving position. If Richard decides that the seating position is not optimal, he is able to adjust the seat by, for example, voice control and the system might align his anthropometry information in the deposited profile. At first use, the question arises whether to acquire the anthropometry by sophisticated sensors scanning the user, this means personalisation, or by an initial manual data input performed directly by the user, this means customisation. This question has to be explored in prospective research. After adjusting seats and mirrors, Richard tries to start the Jaguar XF. The intelligent driver profiling system communicates to Richard how to start the engine by, for instance, voice and/or visual instructions and, in that way, helps him to understand the system. With ease Richard starts the engine. Understandably, the system uses visual as well as voice instructions in English; the visual instructions, furthermore, are in a readable font size for Richard, making use of reading glasses unnecessary. An exemplary instruction might be 'Richard, please press the brake pedal and then press the "Start Engine Stop" button positioned on the transmission hump and highlighted by a pulsating red circle'. All this might be possible since the profile is aware of the user's capabilities and personalises the adaptive interface accordingly. The intended system will try to avoid any complex information procurement and misunderstanding in order to facilitate the driving task and, in consequence, to increase user satisfaction.

Since Richard and Gudrun have not been to Majorca, yet, they are frightened of not being able to handle the navigation system of the Jaguar XF. However, after starting the car Richard and Gudrun are asked visually and aurally whether they want to be guided directly to their hotel or whether they want to render an intermediate stop. They decide to drive to the hotel directly; therefore, the system automatically enters the address of the hotel into the navigation system. The intelligent driver profiling system may be connected to their smartphones and, thus, be aware of Richard's and Gudrun's destination. If they had wanted to render an intermediate stop, the system would have asked for the new destination, elucidated the Spanish address format, explained how to use the infotainment system, and adjusted the adaptive interface. The adjusted interface looks familiar and comparable to Richard's and Gudrun's Mercedes-Benz and uses a large enough font size making it easily readable for Richard and Gudrun.

On their route to the hotel the intelligent driver profiling system warns Richard about his fatigue and deteriorating awareness before he is aware of it and asks him to take a break and/or to let Gudrun drive the rest of the route. After a small break, Gudrun sits down on the driver's seat, which immediately adjusts to her preferences, and drives them to the hotel. The system is aware of Richard's and Gudrun's departure time and physical conditions, and, consequently, warns Richard without allowing any deterioration of driving performance. To calculate physical conditions, the system may monitor driver characteristics, such as gaze direction, blinking, heart rate, and body posture, and may combine these with general physical conditions, such as age, diseases, and exhaustion. The departure time is known to the profiling system since it might be connected to Richard's and Gudrun's smartphones and might share several information with them, such as schedule, health data, and movement profile. The automatic seat adjustment after Gudrun sits down on the driver's seat might function based on a facial recognition system identifying Gudrun and automatically initiating adjustments.

This scenario illustrates the potential of an intelligent driver profiling system for cars. Richard and Gudrun experience a less stressful and less exhausting journey. Thus, they are a lot more motivated to undertake another trip in near future. In conclusion, the intended system may facilitate driving an unfamiliar car enormously and, hereby, smooth the way for MAAS where driving unfamiliar cars will be the rule rather than the exception.

4 Summary and Conclusion

A large amount of ADAS is already available in current high-end cars and these systems will distribute even further within the next several years [9]. This paper presents a basic concept of an intelligent driver profiling system for cars as an additional assistance system that customises and personalises car features and other ADAS. First, a short introduction to the state of the art of the areas automotive sensors, ADAS, driver behaviour profiling, and driver state monitoring, is given. Their importance and potential application for the intended system is outlined and, in this way, the framework of the profiling system is illustrated. Subsequently, the motivation of the system is pointed out; the move towards MAAS is inevitable and will change the way people use cars. A profiling system assists this shift and increases business as well as customer satisfaction and safety. The main functions of the intelligent driver profiling system are to identify the user, to create a profile based on entered settings and gathered data, and to tailor all adjustable areas of a car based on this profile. The goal of the profiling system is visualized by using a persona and presenting challenges faced in current cars which, however, can be met with an intelligent profiling system.

An intelligent driver profiling system for cars has great potential to benefit customers as well as manufacturers and should therefore be researched further. Identifying adjustable areas in the car, testing adjustments, and evaluating their performance will constitute important parts of further research. After identification of beneficial areas of adjustment, a thorough analysis of automotive sensors must be performed to define personalisable areas and the extent of personalisation in these areas. A compromise between personalisation and customisation has to be elaborated to ensure robustness and proper functioning. Following this, a testing platform will be created to run early stage trials for acceptance, usability and preferences. The findings will be analysed and modelled to generate design guidance material supporting the detailed creation of an intelligent driver profiling system for cars which is based on personalisation and customisation.

References

1. Green, P.: Motor vehicle driver interfaces. In: Sears, A., Jacko, J.A. (eds.) Computer Interaction Handbook: Fundamentals, Evolving Technologies, and Emerging Applications, 2nd edn., pp. 701–719. Lawrence Erlbaum Associates, New York (2008)
2. Treat, J.R., Tumbas, N.S., McDonald, S.T., Shinar, D., Hume, R.D., Mayer, R.E., Stansifer, R.L., Castellan, N.J.: Tri-level study of the causes of traffic accidents - final report. 82 (1979)
3. Riemer, K., Totz, C.: The many faces of personalization. The Customer Centric Enterprise. Advances in Mass Customization and Personalization, pp. 35–50. Springer, Heidelberg (2003). https://doi.org/10.1007/978-3-642-55460-5_3
4. Arora, N., Dreze, X., Ghose, A., et al.: Putting one-to-one marketing to work: personalization, customization, and choice. Mark. Lett. 19, 305–321 (2008)
5. Moniri, M.M., Feld, M., Müller, C.: Personalized in-vehicle information systems: building an application infrastructure for smart cars in smart spaces. In: Eighth International Conference Intelligent Environments, pp. 379–382. IEEE (2012)
6. Wockatz, P., Schartau, P.: IM travellers needs and UK capability study: supporting the realisation of intelligent mobility in the UK. Transport Systems Catapult, Milton Keynes, UK (2015)
7. Shaheen, S., Cohen, A.: Growth in worldwide carsharing: an international comparison. Transp. Res. Rec. J. Transp. Res. Board 1992, 81–89 (2007)
8. Martin, E., Shaheen, S., Lidicker, J.: Impact of carsharing on household vehicle holdings: results from North American shared-use vehicle survey. Transp. Res. Rec. J. Transp. Res. Board 2143, 150–158 (2010)
9. Bengler, K., Dietmayer, K., Färber, B., Maurer, M., Stiller, C., Winner, H.: Three decades of driver assistance systems: review and future perspectives. IEEE Intell. Transp. Syst. Mag. 6, 6–22 (2014)
10. Fagnant, D.J., Kockelman, K.M.: The travel and environmental implications of shared autonomous vehicles, using agent-based model scenarios. Transp. Res. Part C Emerg. Technol. 40, 1–13 (2014)

11. Fleming, W.J.: New automotive sensors - a review. IEEE Sens. J. **8**, 1900–1921 (2008)
12. D'Orazio, L., Visintainer, F., Darin, M.: Sensor networks on the car: state of the art and future challenges. In: Design, Automation & Test in Europe Conference & Exhibition (DATE), pp 1–6. IEEE (2011)
13. Fleming, W.J.: Overview of automotive sensors. IEEE Sens. J. **1**, 296–308 (2001)
14. Abdelhamid, S., Hassanein, H.S., Takahara, G.: Vehicle as a mobile sensor. Procedia Comput. Sci. **34**, 286–295 (2014)
15. Piao, J., McDonald, M.: Advanced driver assistance systems from autonomous to cooperative approach. Transp. Rev. **28**, 659–684 (2008)
16. Ziebinski, A., Cupek, R., Erdogan, H., Waechter, S.: A survey of ADAS technologies for the future perspective of sensor fusion. In: Nguyen, N.-T., Manolopoulos, Y., Iliadis, L., Trawiński, B. (eds.) ICCCI 2016. LNCS (LNAI), vol. 9876, pp. 135–146. Springer, Cham (2016). https://doi.org/10.1007/978-3-319-45246-3_13
17. Itoh, M., Horikome, T., Inagaki, T.: Effectiveness and driver acceptance of a semi-autonomous forward obstacle collision avoidance system. Appl. Ergon. **44**, 756–763 (2013)
18. Sun, B., Akamatsu, K., Nagai, T.: Advanced driver assistance system for vehicle. 18 (2016)
19. Lorber, A.: Driver profiling. 16 (2012)
20. Castignani, G., Derrmann, T., Frank, R., Engel, T.: Driver behavior profiling using smartphones: a low-cost platform for driver monitoring. IEEE Intell. Transp. Syst. Mag. **7**, 91–102 (2015)
21. Van Ly, M., Martin, S., Trivedi, M.M.: Driver classification and driving style recognition using inertial sensors. In: Intelligent Vehicles Symposium IV 2013 IEEE, Australia, pp 1040–1045. IEEE (2013)
22. Carmona, J., García, F., Martín, D., Escalera, A., Armingol, J.: Data fusion for driver behaviour analysis. Sensors **15**, 25968–25991 (2015)
23. Meiring, G., Myburgh, H.: A review of intelligent driving style analysis systems and related artificial intelligence algorithms. Sensors **15**, 30653–30682 (2015)
24. Joubert, J.W., de Beer, D., de Koker, N.: Combining accelerometer data and contextual variables to evaluate the risk of driver behaviour. Transp. Res. Part F Traffic Psychol. Behav. **41**, 80–96 (2016)
25. Jelbert, R., Heavyside, G.: Driver profiling system and method. 29 (2017)
26. Castignani, G., Frank, R., Engel, T.: Driver behavior profiling using smartphones. In: Proceedings of the 16th International IEEE Annual Conference on Intelligent Transportation Systems, ITSC 2013, pp. 552–557. IEEE, The Hague (2013)
27. Engelbrecht, J., Booysen, M.J., van Rooyen, G.-J., Bruwer, F.J.: Survey of smartphone-based sensing in vehicles for intelligent transportation system applications. IET Intell. Transp. Syst. **9**, 924–935 (2015)
28. Toledo, T., Musicant, O., Lotan, T.: In-vehicle data recorders for monitoring and feedback on drivers' behavior. Transp. Res. Part C Emerg. Technol. **16**, 320–331 (2008)
29. Musicant, O., Bar-Gera, H., Schechtman, E.: Electronic records of undesirable driving events. Transp. Res. Part F Traffic Psychol. Behav. **13**, 71–79 (2010)
30. Boverie, S., Giralt, A.: Driver vigilance diagnostic based on eyelid movement observation. In: Proceedings of the 17th World Congress International Federation of *Automatic* Control, Seoul, Korea, pp. 12831–12836 (2008)
31. May, J.F., Baldwin, C.L.: Driver fatigue: the importance of identifying causal factors of fatigue when considering detection and countermeasure technologies. Transp. Res. Part F Traffic Psychol. Behav. **12**, 218–224 (2009)
32. Rauch, N., Kaussner, A., Krüger, H.-P., Boverie, S., Flemisch, F.: The importance of driver state assessment within highly automated vehicles. In: Proceedings of the 16th ITS World Congress (2009)

33. Friedrichs, F., Yang, B.: Camera-based drowsiness reference for driver state classification under real driving conditions. In: 2010 IEEE Intell. Veh. Symp. San Diego, California, USA, pp 101–106 (2010)

34. Dong, Y., Hu, Z., Uchimura, K., Murayama, N.: Driver inattention monitoring system for intelligent vehicles: a review. IEEE Trans. Intell. Transp. Syst. **12**, 596–614 (2011)

35. Horrey, W.J., Lesch, M.F., Dainoff, M.J., Robertson, M.M., Noy, Y.I.: On-board safety monitoring systems for driving: review, knowledge gaps, and framework. J. Saf. Res. **43**, 49–58 (2012)

36. Gonçalves, J., Bengler, K.: Driver state monitoring systems– transferable knowledge manual driving to HAD. Procedia Manuf. **3**, 3011–3016 (2015)

37. Ma, Z., Mahmoud, M., Robinson, P., Dias, E., Skrypchuk, L.: Automatic detection of a driver's complex mental states. In: Gervasi, O., Murgante, B., Misra, S., Borruso, G., Torre, C.M., Rocha, A.M.A.C., Taniar, D., Apduhan, B.O., Stankova, E., Cuzzocrea, A. (eds.) ICCSA 2017. LNCS, vol. 10406, pp. 678–691. Springer, Cham (2017). https://doi.org/10.1007/978-3-319-62398-6_48

38. Maguire, M.: Methods to support human-centred design. Int. J. Hum-Comput. Stud. **55**, 587–634 (2001)

39. Langdon, P., Thimbleby, H.: Inclusion and interaction: designing interaction for inclusive populations. Interact. Comput. **22**, 439–448 (2010)

40. Clarkson, P.J., Coleman, R.: History of inclusive design in the UK. Appl. Ergon. **46**, 235–247 (2015)

41. Walker, G.H., Stanton, N.A., Salmon, P.M.: Human factors in automotive engineering and technology. Ashgate, Farnham Surrey, England, Burlington, VT (2015)

Development of an Energy Management System for the Charge Scheduling of Plug-in Electric Vehicles

Dario Cruz[1], Nelson Pinto[1], Jânio Monteiro[1,2(✉)],
Pedro J. S. Cardoso[1,3], Cristiano Cabrita[1,4], Jorge Semião[1,2],
Luís M. R. Oliveira[1,5], and João M. F. Rodrigues[1,3]

[1] ISE, University of Algarve, Faro, Portugal
{dmcruz,nfpinto,jmmontei,pcardoso,ccabrita,jsemiao,
lolivei,jrodrig}@ualg.pt
[2] INESC-ID, Lisbon, Portugal
[3] LARSyS, Lisbon, Portugal
[4] Centre of Intelligent Systems, IDMEC, IST, Lisbon, Portugal
[5] CISE - Electromechatronic Systems Research Centre, Covilhã, Portugal

Abstract. As the number of Plug-In Electric Vehicles continues to rise, existing electrical grids need to adapt to support the expected charging demand of such vehicles. Fortunately, a growing number of renewable energy sources are also being introduced in current electrical grids, reducing the dependency on fossil fuels. Leveraged by the self-consumption legislation in several countries, the introduction of renewable energy sources continue to happen well beyond the end of the feed-in tariff rates. However, due to their variable nature, renewable energy sources are frequently characterized as intermittent resources, which cause mismatches in the required equilibrium between production and demand. In this scenario, the role of end users is very important, since they are not only required to participate in energy generation - becoming the so-called prosumers – but also they should allow the adjustment of the consumption, according with the generation levels. Plug-In Electric Vehicles, due to their power requirements, just exacerbate this problem. Following our previous work concerning scheduling algorithms for self-consumption scenarios, in this paper we describe the implementation of an Energy Management System for the charge scheduling of Electric Vehicles. The proposed system considers several requirements, including electrical grid limitations, present time and subsequent tariff costs, actual and predicted renewable energy generation levels, and user preferences. It then runs an optimization algorithm that decides when the charging of such vehicles should happen and controls the power delivered to charge them, accordingly.

Keywords: Plug-in electric vehicles · Load scheduling

© Springer International Publishing AG, part of Springer Nature 2018
M. Antona and C. Stephanidis (Eds.): UAHCI 2018, LNCS 10908, pp. 214–225, 2018.
https://doi.org/10.1007/978-3-319-92052-8_17

1   Introduction

Electrical grids are undergoing a process of transformation that result, among others, from an increasing integration of renewable energy sources at the distribution level. In many countries, legislation nowadays allow end users/companies to produce electricity from renewable energy sources and consume it, or sell it, while they are still connected with the utility operator.

The introduction of such Distributed Generation (DG) sources (Shen 2012), however, requires the implementation of methods capable of ensuring the mandatory real time balance between consumption and production - a challenge magnified by the variable nature of renewable energy sources.

In this context, users play a critical role (Monteiro et al. 2014). In order to use the energy that is produced at a certain time instant, users need to allow the adjustment of the working periods of their electrical appliances. This can be done through a manual control of each equipment, machine or lighting system, or preferably through an Energy Management System (EMS) that automates the whole process. EMSs perform the control of electrical devices, reducing user intervention by running an optimization algorithm that decides when electrical devices should work. In order to do it, EMSs take into account several factors, including: (1) user restrictions, (2) generation levels, (3) tariff rates, (4) contracted power level and (5) electrical circuit limitations (Monteiro et al. 2014). Based on these parameters and restrictions, EMSs then run scheduling algorithms that identify solutions aiming to either minimize costs or maximize profits. While EMSs can potentially simplify power management, reducing the weight of individual on/off control of electrical devices, they are also a complex solution that require a combination of Information and Communication Technologies (ICT), Internet of Things (IoT), Human Computer Interaction (HCI) and Operational Research techniques.

At a certain level, Electric Vehicles (EVs) can be seen as another electrical load that require significant amounts of energy and power in the charging process. In the context of Smart Grids, the increasing capacities of their batteries also make them an ideal storage solution capable of accommodating the overproduction, whenever the power generated surpasses the consumption levels. Thus, even without considering reverse charging, EVs can not only be seen as a problem, but also, as part of the solution.

Since EV parking facilities will likely play an important role in the charging process, in this paper we focus in building an EMS for these infrastructures (see Fig. 1). Given the current legislation regarding self-consumption and the current perspectives about the introduction of renewable energy sources, in this paper we consider that the electrical grid of such park is, at the same time, connected to the utility grid and generating electricity for their own consumption. Thus the energy can either be bought from the utility company or sold.

For this type of scenario, in (Monteiro and Nunes 2015, Cruz and Monteiro 2017) we have defined and tested different algorithms for charge scheduling of EVs. Particularly in (Cruz and Monteiro 2017) the EV scheduling algorithm was adapted to consider different charging powers, as happens with EVs. Based on these improvements we have then tested the enhanced versions of the scheduling algorithms

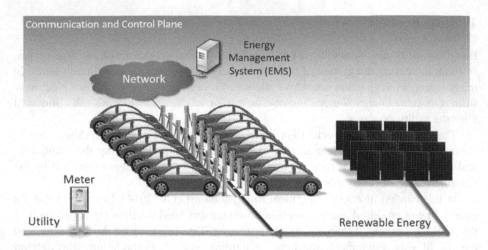

Fig. 1. Scenario considered in this paper.

considering real generation data and dynamic tariff values of several days in different months of the year, with very distinct generation conditions. In this paper we extend the work previously done, by describing the implementation of an EMS and Electric Vehicle Supply Equipment (EVSE) that use these algorithms to manage charging stations.

The rest of this paper has the following structure. Section 2 presents the current state of the art in terms of standards for EV charge control and algorithms for the charge scheduling of EVs. Section 3 presents the results of a survey that analyzed user preferences concerning the scheduling of electric vehicles. Section 4 presents the implemented elements comprising the EMS and EVSE. Section 5 concludes the paper, pointing out some future developments of this work.

2 State of the Art

2.1 Standards for EV Charge Control

Several standards have been defined for the interoperation between electric vehicles and electrical grids (Schwarzer and Ghorbani 2015). One of such standards is the International Electrotechnical Commission standard IEC-62196 that defines the conductive charging processes of electric vehicles. Particularly, the IEC International Standard 62196-1 (2014) defines the general requirements that apply to plugs, socket-outlets, vehicle connectors, vehicle inlets and cable assemblies for electric vehicles, incorporating control solutions and having a rated voltage not exceeding: (1) 690 V AC, 50–60 Hz, with a rated current not exceeding 250 A; or (2) 600 V DC, with a rated current not exceeding 400 A.

The international standard IEC 61851 defines conductive charging systems based on AC or DC, and defines the charging modes for electric vehicles and their respective EVSE. As defined in the IEC International Standard 61851-1 (2017) the defined modes are: Mode 1 - Slow charging through normal household outlets; Mode 2 - Slow charging through standard household outlets, but with a cable protection unit; Mode 3 - Slow or fast charging with a specific outlet, with protection and control functions; and Mode 4 - Quick Charging, using an external charger.

Signalling pins that allow status information to be conveyed between the EV and EVSEs have been defined in the standard SAE J1772-2001, and later on, included in both IEC 61851 and IEC 62196-2 standards. In addition to the power pins and Protective Earth, all types of IEC 62196-2 connectors have two additional pins: the Control Pilot (CP, pin 4) and the Proximity Pilot or Plug Presence (PP, pin 5). Together they allow a basic control and communication between the EV and the EVSE regarding the charging process. For instance, in Mode 3, EVSEs are able to inform EVs about the maximum current that they are allowed to get from the electrical grid, using a PWM signal in the CP.

Another standard that is currently under definition for the vehicle-to-grid communication interface (V2G CI) is ISO 15118. It complements the IEC 61851-1 standard, providing Internet Protocols (IP) bi-directional digital communications. It also defines the data and message format of the V2G CI. Thus, the aim of the standard is to establish a more advanced and autonomous charge control mechanism between EVs and charging infrastructures (Schmutzler et al. 2012; Käbisch et al. 2010). Currently, ISO 15118-1 (2013) standard concerning the general information and use case definition, ISO/IEC 15118-2 (2014) regarding network and application protocol requirements and ISO/IEC 15118-3 (2015) that includes the physical layer and data link layer requirements have already been issued as international standards. The rest of the list of ISO/IEC 15118 international standards, namely: 15118-4 (network and application protocol conformance test); 15118-5 (physical and data link layer conformance tests); 15118-6 (general information and use case definition for wireless communication); 15118-7 (Network and application protocol requirements for wireless communication); and 15118-8 (physical layer and data link layer requirements for wireless communication), are currently under definition.

While these standards support the communication between EVSEs and EVs, other mechanisms are needed to schedule the charging process of these vehicles. In the following we describe some of these solutions.

2.2 Algorithms for Charge Scheduling of Electric Vehicles

Given an EV parking facility, consisting of several EVSEs and/or plugs, which integrates renewable energy generation under a self-consumption scenario, several algorithms can be used to schedule their charging periods. Basically these algorithms can be classified into two types: predictive versus non-predictive solutions.

Predictive scheduling algorithms decide when loads should work taking into consideration future variables, like for instance the future (i.e. predicted) generation levels or the subsequent tariff rates. Using an objective function, optimization algorithms are used to either minimize costs, or maximize profits. Several predictive scheduling solutions can be used, as exemplified next.

The Earliest Departure First (EDF) (Chen et al. 2012) is an algorithm that schedules the charging of electric vehicles according with the associated time of departure. So

EVs that leave sooner, will have a higher priority. While EDF was adapted to EV scheduling in (Chen et al. 2012), the proposed EDF algorithm did not consider self-consumption scenarios and thus the variability of renewable sources could lead to the non-completions of the charging process, so penalties were considered when a request was not assured. Since the variability of the renewable energy sources does not fit well in strict models that assures all the energy that is requested by car owners, in (Monteiro and Nunes 2015) the algorithm was changed to consider two charging components, one mandatory and the other optional. Given the fact that EVs tend to have battery capacities well beyond the required for daily usage, the model considers that drivers will tend to allow their cars to serve as storage units whenever the generation levels surpass the consumption ones. Yet, this assumption was not validated. This last model, was called Adapted EDF (AEDF). AEDF was compared with other scheduling solutions (Monteiro and Nunes 2015), namely Linear Programming (LP), First Come First Served (FCFS) and with an algorithm that charges conversely in respect of tariff rates (so called gradual). Later in (Cruz and Monteiro 2017), the model was improved and further tested in different scenarios.

In terms of non-predictive solutions, one implementation that has gained some relevance is PowerMatcher. PowerMatcher combines power distribution systems with a communication protocol to create a unique and flexible Smart Grid. This technology allows the adjustment of the operation of loads according with the production from both renewable and conventional energy sources. It also applies demand and supply market laws. These algorithms were adapted to consider EV charging, as in (Bliek and Van Den Noort 2010) and (Kamphuis et al. 2013). Also, in (Kempker et al. 2015), a stochastic dynamic programming strategy is used to perform the load scheduling in PowerMatcher, with the objective of minimizing the total cost of charging EVs, within a given time interval. For this, an optimum control rule was used to determine the amount of energy that can be charged in a given period of time.

Among all the above explained solution only the proposed LP and AEDF algorithms perform a predictive type of scheduling. The results obtained in (Monteiro and Nunes 2015) demonstrate that these predictive algorithms are able to achieve better results when compared with non-predictive options, like the FCFS and Gradual model. Still, while LP has demonstrated in (Monteiro and Nunes 2015, Cruz and Monteiro 2017) to be able of achieve the best results, AEDF obtained similar results with much lower computational costs. Thus in the following we will select the AEDF algorithm as the optimization mechanism of the Energy Management System.

3   Evaluation of User Preferences in the Scheduling of Electric Vehicles

As already explained the AEDF model assumes that the vehicle owner will be available or willing to participate in demand response, by adjusting the charging level of the EV according with the generation levels. However this assumption was not previously validated. In order to assess it, we started by conducting a survey. In it, among other questions, we asked assessors about their availability in adjusting the charging level of their Electric Vehicle according with the level of power generated locally. The survey was made available online, resulting in a total of 364 assessments. Table 1 summarizes the main characteristics of the evaluation panel.

Table 1. Description of the evaluation panel in terms of: Gender; Education; Age group; Number of persons in the household; and Number of vehicles in the household

Gender	[%]	Age	[%]	Persons in the household	[%]	Vehicles in the household	[%]
Female	50.6	18 – 25	5.1	1	13.6	1	24.8
Male	49.4	26 – 30	7.3	2	27.1	2	58.0
		31 – 35	12.0	3	28.8	3	13.2
		36 – 40	10.7	4	26.6	4	2.5
Education	[%]	41 – 45	22.6	5	3.6	5	0.6
Basic	0.3	46 – 50	19.2	6	0.3	6	0.3
Secondary	8.0	51 – 55	12.0			7	0.0
Bachelor	31.6	56 – 60	6.4			8	0.6
Master	23.8	61 – 65	3.4				
Phd or above	36.3	66 – 70	0.9				
		71 – 75	0.4				

The large majority of assessors stated that they would be available to adjust the charging of their EV according with the generation levels (only 4.2% of assessors answered no). Among those that responded this question: (1) 57.5% answered that they would be available to do it, but just if the system would guaranty them a minimum level of charge, and thus autonomy; (2) 36.8% answered that they would be willing to charge with energy coming from renewable energy sources, regardless of the economic benefit they would get from it, while (3) 26.4% answered that they would be available to do it, if they could get some economic benefit from it; finally (4) 26.1% answered that they would be available to do it, but only if the system was automated, and thus not relying in their interaction.

When asked about the relevance of having a system in their homes capable of lowering the electricity costs by automatically managing the charging periods of their future electric vehicle(s) (according with the tariff rates, renewable energy generated, and/or avoiding to pay more for the contracted power), 73.2% of answered positively.

These results show that most of the persons consider it relevant to have a device that is capable of managing the charging process of their EVs, and to use them as storage units, as long as it respects some conditions like: minimum autonomy of the EV, economic benefit, and/or simplicity of usage.

4 Development of the Electric Vehicle Scheduling Device

Given the aforementioned results we now proceed to describe the implementation of the Energy Management System. We start by describing the renewable aware model for the scheduling of EVs, followed by the description of the implemented system.

4.1   Charge Scheduling Algorithm

The EMS schedules EV charging times in accordance with a model that was firstly proposed and described in (Monteiro and Nunes 2015). It considers that the total energy requested by each EV (E_{Tv}) can be obtained through two components, a Guaranteed Energy (E_{Gv}) part and Non-Guaranteed (E_{Nv}) one.

The Guaranteed Energy part reflects the minimum energy required by the user/owner to charge a specific EV, whose fulfilment until the end of the charging period, is mandatory. This energy in turn can be obtained from two power components, namely the utility grid (C_{vt}) or local renewable sources $\left(P_{gvt}\right)$.

As for the non-Guaranteed Energy component, it can only use power generated locally $\left(P_{nvt}\right)$ using renewable energy sources and therefore it completely depends in its availability. When there is no spare energy, the non-Guaranteed Energy component will not be fulfilled. However if, at any given instant, the power generated surpasses the Guaranteed Energy part, EVs will start to be used as storage units. This can be an advantage to parking facilities that, by this way, are able to avoid selling the energy at a very low rate (as for instance 0.045 € per kWh in Portugal), as long as they are able to sell it to car owners by any value higher than that. This would also result in an advantage to car owners since they would probably pay more at their own facilities if they buy it from the utility.

From the point of view of the electrical grid, the non-Guaranteed Energy component gives an additional degree of freedom to the system, introducing a flexibility in the charging process that aims to compensate the intermittent nature of renewable energy sources.

The total energy requested for an EV (E_{Tv}) is thus given by the sum of the two energy components, as shown in Eq. (1).

$$E_{Tv} = E_{Gv} + E_{Nv} \tag{1}$$

In (Cruz and Monteiro 2017), the AEDF algorithm was improved when compared with the one presented in (Monteiro and Nunes 2015). Not only allows charging of EV batteries with different power levels, but also accounts for the economic return obtained from selling the surplus photovoltaic production to the utility grid, in accordance with a self-consumption legislation. The algorithm aims at minimizing the cost of buying energy from the utility and maximize the profit that will be obtained from the energy regulator.

For each EV, starting with the ones that leave sooner, the algorithm selects as charging intervals, the subsequent periods of time that show lowest tariff costs. In addition, if there is local generation, the purchase cost and sale revenue of the renewable energy produced are compared, and the lowest cost (highest profit) is selected.

The EV allocation is done according to:

- For each non allocated EV, allocate renewable energy for the Guaranteed part (E_G) until exhaustion;

- For each non allocated EV, allocate power from the utility grid for the Guaranteed part (E_G) starting with the lowest available costs;
- For each non allocated EV, allocate renewable energy for the Non-Guaranteed part (E_N) until exhaustion.

Please see (Cruz and Monteiro 2017) for further details regarding the AEDF scheduling algorithm.

4.2   Implementation of the Energy Management System

Figure 2 shows the general architecture of the implemented energy management system, including the communication interfaces between several modules. The system is divided into four units, namely the Energy Management System (EMS), Human Machine Interfaces (HMI), Machine to Machine (M2M) and Operations Management System (OMS). Each of these units encompasses several modules responsible for a specific function.

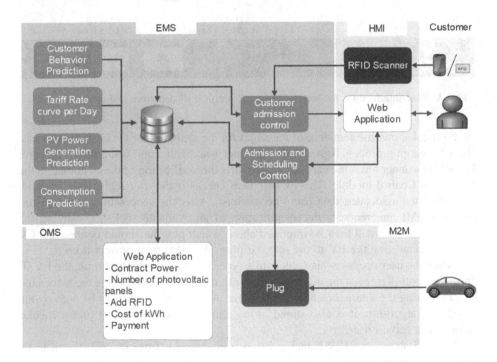

Fig. 2. System architecture of the energy management system.

When accessing the system for the first time, the user communicates with the EMS using an Web interface. An RFID card in then associated to his account. In the Web interface he will be able to insert the expected time of departure and the assured (Guaranteed) and optional (non-Guaranteed) charging levels, as shown in Fig. 3. After this initial configuration, the system will try to minimize repeated user intervention by learning from his daily routines. Still, subsequent changes to these values can always be made online, from any computer or smartphone.

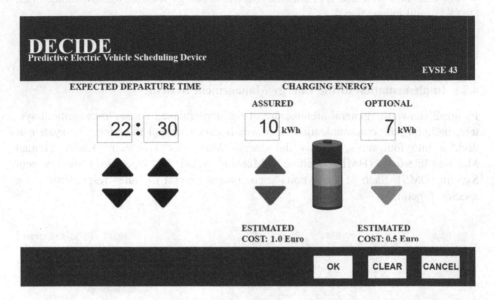

Fig. 3. User Interface for the selection of expected time of departure and charging values.

Figure 4 shows the sequence of messages for the setting up of the charging process. The EV charging process begins with Customer's authentication using the RFID card. The RFID scanner reads the card ID and requests the verification of the customer, to the Admission Control module. This module then checks if the user registration is valid, requesting the associated data from the database. After the successful client registration, the HMI unit requests the identification of an available socket, consulting the database. The user will then be informed about which plug he should connect his EV to. After connecting the EV to the selected plug, the HMI then powers it up.

When the user connects his vehicle to a type 2 socket for the first time, the EVSE Protocol Controller reads the maximum power that can be used to charge the associated EV, measuring the internal resistor of the cable. As this value will later be used by the scheduling algorithm, it is also stored in the database, as a feature of that particular vehicle of a certain user.

Figure 5 shows the EVSE that is being implemented, from the 3D design to its internal structure.

5   Conclusions and Future Work

In this article, we describe the development of an EMS and EVSE that implement the scheduling of electric vehicles in a charging facility/park. The implementation is based on an optimization model that was previously tested.

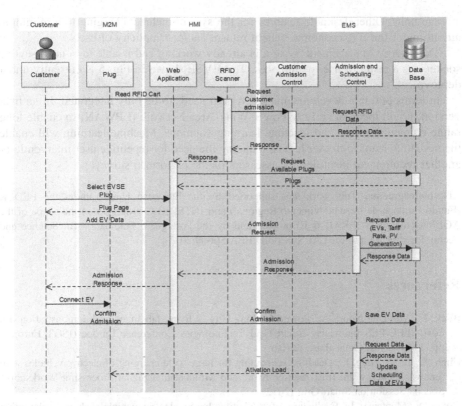

Fig. 4. Sequence diagram for the communication steps during the process of charge setup.

Fig. 5. 3D modeling of the EVSE (left and central images) and its current internal implementation (right side images).

The relevance of the proposed system, and developed model, was validated using a survey. In it, assessors considered it relevant to have a system like the one proposed in this paper, i.e. capable of managing the charging process of EVs and to use them as storage units. Other desirable features for the system include: charging to a minimum autonomy of the EV, economic benefit return, and/or simplicity of use.

The Energy Management System is already working and is able to control several sockets, as a result of user preferences. The EVSE shown in Fig. 5 is currently under deployment.

In terms of future developments the system needs to be fully integrated. In its final version, it will incorporate Low-Power Wide-Area Network (LPWAN) to enable long range communications, and machine learning solutions. Machine learning will enable the system to learn from user habits, reducing the need for repetitive user intervention - another requirement identified by assessors of the performed survey.

Acknowledgments. This work was supported by the European Union, under the FEDER (Fundo Europeu de Desenvolvimento Regional) and INTERREG programs, in the scope of the AGERAR (0076_AGERAR_6_E) project, and by the Portuguese Foundation for Science and Technology (FCT), project LARSyS (UID/EEA/50009/2013).

References

Bliek, F., Van Den Noort, A.: PowerMatching City, a living lab smart grid demonstration. In: 2010 IEEE PES Innovative Smart Grid Technologies Conference Europe (ISGT Europe), pp. 1–18. IEEE, Gothenburg (2010)

Chen, S., Ji, Y., Tong, L.: Deadline scheduling for large scale charging of electric vehicles with renewable energy. In: IEEE Sensor Array and Multichannel Signal Processing Workshop - Special Session on Smart Grid (2012)

Cruz, D., Monteiro, J.: Evaluation of predictive based electric vehicle's charge scheduling algorithms in self-consumption scenarios. In: Proceedings of International Conference on Engineering and Sustainability (INCREaSE 2017). Springer, Cham, 11–13 October 2017

IEC International Standard 61851-1: Electric vehicle conductive charging system - Part 1: General requirements. International Electrotechnical Commission (2017)

IEC International Standard 62196-1: Plugs, socket-outlets, vehicle connectors and vehicle inlets - Conductive charging of electric vehicles - Part 1: General requirements. (ed3.0). International Electrotechnical Commission (2014)

ISO 15118-1: Road vehicles - Vehicle to grid communication interface - Part 1: General information and use-case definition. International Organization for Standardization (2013)

ISO 15118-2: Road vehicles - Vehicle-to-Grid Communication Interface - Part 2: Network and application protocol requirements. International Organization for Standardization (2014)

ISO 15118-3: Road vehicles - Vehicle to grid communication interface - Part 3: Physical and data link layer requirements. International Organization for Standardization (2015)

Käbisch, S., Schmitt, A., Winter, M., Heuer, J.: Interconnections and Communications of Electric Vehicles and Smart Grids. In: First IEEE International Conference on Smart Grid Communications (SmartGridComm), pp. 161–166 (2010)

Kamphuis, R., Macdougall, P., Van der Veen, W., Bakker, E., Van de Vel, J.: Constrained capacity management and cost minimisation of EV-charging in a parking garage. In: PowerTech (POWERTECH), pp. 1–5. IEEE, Grenoble (2013)

Kempker, P., Van Dijk, N.M., Scheinhardt, W.R.W., Van der Berg, J.L., Hurink, J.L.: Optimization of charging strategies for electric vehicles in PowerMatcher-driven smart energy grids. In: Proceedings 9th EAI International Conference on Performance Evaluation Methodologies and Tools, pp. 1–8. Valuetools, Berlin, Germany (2015)

Monteiro, J., Cardoso, P.J.S., Serra, R., Fernandes, L.: Evaluation of the human factor in the scheduling of smart appliances in smart grids. In: Proceedings of 16th International Conference on Human-Computer Interaction, pp. 537–548 (2014)

Monteiro, J., Eduardo, J., Cardoso, P., Semião, J.: A distributed load scheduling mechanism for micro grids. In: Proceedings of IEEE International Conference on Smart Grid Communications (IEEESmartGridComm), pp. 1–2. IEEE (2014)

Monteiro, J., Nunes, M.: A renewable source aware model for the charging of plug-in electrical vehicles. In: Proceedings of the 1st International Conference on Vehicle Technology and Intelligent Transport Systems, Lisbon, pp. 51–58 (2015)

Schmutzler, J., Wietfeld, C., Andersen, C.A.: Distributed energy resource management for electric vehicles using IEC 61850 and ISO/IEC 15118. In: Vehicle Power and Propulsion Conference (VPPC), pp. 1457–1462. IEEE (2012)

Schmutzler, J., Wietfeld, C., Jundel, S., Voit, S.: A mutual charge schedule information model for the vehicle-to-grid communication interface. In: IEEE Vehicle Power and Propulsion Conference (VPPC), pp. 1–6, 6–9 (2011)

Schwarzer, V., Ghorbani R.: Current state-of-the-art of EV chargers (2015). http://evtc.fsec.ucf.edu/publications/documents/HNEI-01-15.pdf. Accessed 02 2018

Shen, X.S.: Empowering the smart grid with wireless technologies [Editor's note]. IEEE Netw. **26**(3), 2–3 (2012)

Designing IoT Solutions for Elderly Home Care: A Systematic Study of Participatory Design, Personas and Semiotics

Renata de Podestá Gaspar[1($\boxtimes$)], Rodrigo Bonacin[1],
and Vinícius P. Gonçalves[2]

[1] Faculdade de Campo Limpo Paulista, Campo Limpo Paulista, SP, Brazil
repodesta@gmail.com, rodrigo.bonacin@gmail.com
[2] University of Brasília, Brasília, DF, Brazil
vpg.vinicius@gmail.com

Abstract. Population aging is one of the most difficult challenges in the next years. The increase of life expectancy is one of the most important human achievements in the 21st century. Despite this achievement, it is also an important technological innovation to ensure the wellbeing of this new generation. The Internet of Things (IoT) is a technological revolution that aims to connect electronic devices used daily through the internet. This occurs thanks to advances and innovation in smart spaces such as wireless sensors, artificial intelligence, nanotechnology, and information security. Technology can be a key ally to Home Care, by generating solutions for Ambient Assisted Living (AAL). AAL combined with the IoT is a promising solution for the elderly public, promoting more autonomy, security, and quality of life. However, the design of technological solutions that consider the opinion and needs of the elderly is still a problem to be researched. Given this context, this article presents a systematic study of publications from 5 scientific databases. The aim is to identify the participatory methods used in the design of IoT solutions for elderly Home Care, as well as how Personas and Semiotics methods were used in this context. The results include a consistent analysis that aims to assist designers, researchers, and developers in future solutions for Home Care and AAL for elderly people.

Keywords: Participatory Design · IoT · Elderly · Home Care
Personas · Semiotics

1 Introduction

According to the World Health Organization (WHO) records, the world's population is aging faster than in the other moments [1]. Thus, aging is an important subject of many academic areas. Aging also became an important theme in Human Computer Interaction (IHC) studies [2].

The WHO defines elderly people as individuals over 60 years old in developing countries, and over 65 years old in developed countries [3]. However, the use of chronological age as the unique criteria for classification is insufficient, once health status and the ability for independence may have a strong influence on the lives of individuals of the same age. According to [4, p. 403] "older people are not a homogeneous group: they do not live in the same place, they do not have access to the same resources, they do not have the same abilities. They are not, in short, a 'they' at all".

At the same time as there are needs for increasing care, security, and social inclusion of the elderlies, there is the need for more autonomy. These needs boost the innovation of products and services to promote and to support self-realization and independent living. Reference [5] names this new reality as Active Ageing. In this sense, the problem in focus is not aging in and of itself, but aging without quality.

The use of technology in elderly's healthcare solutions allows for the more accurate diagnosis and effective treatments of a large number of diseases [6]. The technical approach in the health sector aims to monitor and improve the individual's health, as well as improve their independence, mobility, security, and sociability.

There are numerous challenges in designing technologies that really support elderly people or those directly connected to their care. Some of these challenges are connected to the heterogeneity of this group. Thus, Participatory Design (PD) techniques, Personas and Semiotics are valuable tools for designing individualized solutions. This article presents a systematic study aiming to identify the use of techniques and theories in the design of solutions in Internet of Things (IoT) for Home Care of elderly people. We focus in how PD, Personas and Semiotics have been used in this context.

We performed structured searches of articles between 2010 and July/2017 in 5 scientific databases (ACM Digital Library[1], Springer Link[2], IEEE Xplore Digital Library[3], Google Scholar[4] and Science Direct[5]). We obtained 135 results, which we then applied selection criteria in order to identify 30 primary studies for comparative analysis. Section 2 presents the background of this review, Sect. 3 presents the methods, results, and a comparative analysis of the identified studies, and Sect. 4 presents the final remarks of this paper.

2   Theoretical Basis and Background

2.1   The Concept of Home Care, AAL and IoT

Home Care is a broad term, which describes health services performed exclusively in the home environment. The WHO defines Home Care as a series of health and social care services provided to clients in their own house [7]. Home Care is comprised of interdisciplinary work by health professionals integrated with the family. This work can involve doctors, nurses, psychologists, physiotherapists, among other health professionals. In this context, the term Ambient Assisted Living (AAL) can be understood as

---

[1] https://dl.acm.org/.

[2] http://link.springer.com/.

[3] http://ieeexplore.ieee.org/Xplore/home.jsp.

[4] https://scholar.google.com.br/.

[5] http://www.sciencedirect.com.

the use of intelligent technologies to build safe Home Care environments to provide health care and support to patients so that they may keep an independent lifestyle [8].

AAL is not restricted to those that need intensive care in their houses. When considering the context of the elderly, AAL may also refer to the technological resources that allow for the most possible independent and comfortable lifestyle in their homes [9]. AAL can be an important resource provided to the elderly in order to guarantee active aging [5].

According to [10], AALs can be divided as follows: daily task facilitation, mobility assistance, health care and rehabilitation, and social inclusion and communication. Thus, AAL uses innovative computing concepts, such as intelligent sensors network, ubiquitous pervasive computing, and robotics, among others. The integration of these technologies may allow personalized services to elderly people, with the objective of attending to different expectations and needs.

According to [11], IoT integrates the concepts of Ubiquitous Computing, Pervasive Computing, and Intelligent Environment. The integration of such concepts to that of context-awareness proves to be a compilation of the most innovative and recent ideas regarding ubiquity and mobility. The IoT provides internet connection and computational capabilities to the objects in our daily life. This connection allows for users to control these objects remotely, accessing them as services, as well as transforms such objects into smart objects [12].

By linking the concept of AAL to IoT technology, we have a powerful tool to increase the independence, and promote the participation of the elderly as well as people with disabilities [10].

2.2   User-Centered Design, Participatory Design and Personas

According to [13], elderly people are among the most demanding stakeholders for the development of Information Technology (IT). Therefore, it is important to understand their real needs, which can be achieved by involving the elderly and supporting stakeholders (e.g., family members, caregivers, and health professionals) during the design process. HCI Researchers have explored many design alternatives, such as User-Centered Design (UCD) and PD, to improve acceptance and efficiency rates.

Reference [9] presents several UDC techniques that are appropriate in each phase of the design of technological solutions, such as: scenario analysis, questionnaire, interview, workshop, brainstorm, storyboard, video analysis, and others. Design Thinking (DT) is valuable method for UCD. According to [14], DT has a set of UCD techniques and tools that provide for an interactive design process, producing inovative solutions to real problems.

PD can be defined as a design process *with* the user, rather than *for* the user [15]. In other words, the user must be involved in various phases of the system's development. This type of participation presupposes the need to give voice to the users, rather than users just serving as a source of information or observation. Reference [16] argues that the development of a single method has not been the goal of PD; rather, it aims to provide a systematic organization of design practices with a coherent set of tools and techniques.

The Personas technique proposes the fictitious representation of a user [17]. It is a valuable alternative to enhance user participation during design activities. Personas allow for a greater coverage of the participatory method, since it personifies the solution, allowing the user to come closer to the solution; therefore, breaking barriers, generating empathy, and increasing users' engagement during the design process.

2.3   Organizational Semiotics

Organizational Semiotics (OS) is a discipline based on Semiotics (science that studies signs). OS applies Semiotics principles to study organizational processes. It studies the nature, characteristics, function, and effect of information and communication in organizational contexts.

According to OS's perspective, an organization is a social system in which people behave in an organized manner and in accordance to a set of norms. These norms describe behavior and perception patterns, and other aspects [18, 19]. Thus, according to this perspective, a population of heterogeneous users can be studied as an organization [20, 21].

OS has been contributing to the design of computational systems in many ways, such as by improving the system's efficiency and its acceptance by the users [13]. For instance, OS methods provide the means to carry out a thorough examination of information and communication aspects that occur during the interaction of elderly users with AAL systems. This may include the description of human-human and human-system interaction.

3   Review Methodology

Our review methodology is adapted from the systematic review method suggested by [22]. Thus, there is a concern to include as many studies as possible, as well as to avoid biases that can lead to erroneous conclusions [23]. Therefore, as mentioned above, we performed structured searches in 5 scientific databases.

According to [22], the review process involves a series of well-defined activities divided into 3 phases: planning, execution, and outcome analysis. In order to inform our planning phase and to investigate the viability of the methodology, we developed a preliminary review, presented in [24].

3.1   Planning

The planning phase is important to define how the systematic review will be performed, and to define the inclusion and exclusion criteria adopted in the review [25]. Thus, we defined that this review aims to answer the following question: (MQ) "Which of the studies on IoT solutions for elderly home care use at least one of the following approaches, and how: Participatory Design, Personas and Semiotics?"

Sub-questions were elaborated in order to structure the interpretation of the results, and to support the MQ analysis, as follows:

- Q1: Which elderly care needs are addressed by the analyzed literature?
- Q2: Which IoT technologies are employed in home care solutions for the elderly?
- Q3: How are the users engaged in the design process?
- Q4: How are Personas construed and used?
- Q5: What is the role of Semiotics in the design process?

As shown in Table 1, we defined search parameters based on these questions.

Table 1. Search parameters

Strategy	Articles available from 2010 to July 2017 published in journals and conferences in English and Portuguese.
Research databases	IEEE Xplore Digital Library, ACM Digital Library, Springer Link, Google Scholar and Exploratory Study (exploratory research carried out on the web, including Science Direct base)
Keywords	Participatory Design, Internet of Things (IoT), Home Care, Elderly

There are several ways in which to express the keywords related to our research; therefore, it was necessary to use various synonyms to increase the search results. Table 2 presents a list of adopted synonyms for each main keyword.

Table 2. Synonyms list

Keyword	Synonyms in English	Synonyms in Portuguese
Elderly	elderly person, old person, old adult, aged person, elderly people, old people, aged people	*terceira idade, velhice, senior*
IoT	ubiquitous computing, internet of things, web of things	*computação ubíqua, internet das coisas, web das coisas*
Home Care	Home Care, ambient assisted living	Home Care, *assistência domiciliar*
Participatory Design	collaborative design	*design colaborativo*
Personas	–	–
Semiotic	–	–

In order to obtain a first selection from the databases, we performed 3 main tasks: definition of the search strings, execution of the searches, and preliminary selection of the studies. The main search string is defined as follows (in simplified syntax):

(Participatory Design OR Personas OR Semiotics) AND IoT AND Home Care AND Elderly

We then defined the inclusion and exclusion criteria (Table 3). Initially, these criteria were applied to the **Title, Summary, and Keywords** of each article. The studies that fit the criteria were selected and categorized as a Primary Study. Subsequently, we read the Primary Studies' entire text and once again applied the inclusion or exclusion criteria. The three authors of this paper revised the selected studies, and selected papers based on consensus.

Table 3. Selection criteria: inclusion and exclusion

Criteria	ID	Description	Weight
Inclusion	I1	Studies involving elderly people	3
	I2	Studies presenting Home Care alternatives for the elderly	2
	I3	Studies using PD techniques with the elderly	2
	I4	Studies that use Personas technique for the elderly	2
	I5	Studies that use Semiotics based design process	1
	I6	Studies with IoT solutions (quoted implicitly or explicitly) for Home Care of the Elderly	1
Exclusion	E1	Articles not in English or Portuguese languages	–
	E2	Articles with the same content, in different databases	–
	E3	Articles with unavailable full text	–
	E4	Studies restricted (only) to IoT technical issues (operating systems, network protocols, etc.)	–
	E5	Studies not directly related to the elderly and at least 2 related topics (IoT, Home Care, PD, Personas or Semiotics)	–
	E6	Studies restricted (only) to medical issues, i.e., not related to technological issues	–
	E7	Articles selected using Portuguese in the search engines with main text that was not in the Portuguese language	–
	E8	Doctoral and masters dissertations	–

3.2 Execution

We initially obtained **427 studies** from the database search, of which **135** were considered as valid results. Among these, **45 studies were considered Primary Studies and 90 studies were disregarded,** according to the selection criteria. We excluded **15 studies** during the process of reading the article's full text and, therefore, **30 Primary Studies** remained to be analyzed in this study. In summary, from the initial set of **135 valid results from the database search, 30 articles were considered as Primary Studies** (Table 4) and **105 excluded**. Figure 1 depicts quantitative data on the Primary Studies in two charts: one with the scientific databases used, and the other with the status of the identified articles.

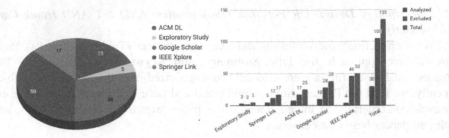

Fig. 1. Total primary studies categorized by databases and status

Table 4. Primary studies, inclusion criteria and weight

Ref.	Year	Source	Criteria	Weight
[26]	2014	Google Scholar	I1, I2, I3, I4, I6	10
[27]	2013	ACM	I1, I2, I3, I6	8
[17]	2016	ACM	I1, I2, I3, I6	8
[28]	2016	ACM	I1, I2, I3, I6	8
[29]	2013	ACM	I1, I2, I3, I6	8
[9]	2017	Exploratory Study	I1, I2, I3, I6	8
[30]	2015	IEEE	I1, I2, I3, I6	8
[31]	2017	Springer	I1, I2, I3, I6	8
[32]	2014	Google Scholar	I1, I2, I3, I6	8
[33]	2012	Google Scholar	I1, I2, I3, I6	8
[34]	2016	Google Scholar	I1, I2, I3, I6	8
[35]	2013	ACM	I1, I2, I3	7
[36]	2016	ACM	I1, I2, I3	7
[37]	2017	ACM	I1, I2, I3	7
[38]	2016	ACM	I1, I2, I3	7
[39]	2016	Exploratory Study	I1, I2, I4	7
[40]	2010	IEEE	I1, I2, I3	7
[41]	2013	IEEE	I1, I2, I3	7
[42]	2011	Springer	I1, I2, I3	7
[43]	2011	Springer	I1, I2, I3	7
[44]	2011	Springer	I1, I2, I3	7
[45]	2013	Google Scholar	I1, I2, I3	7
[46]	2011	Google Scholar	I1, I2, I5, I6	7
[47]	2011	Google Scholar	I1, I2, I3	7
[48]	2010	Google Scholar	I1, I2, I3	7
[5]	2017	Google Scholar	I1, I2, I3	7
[9]	2015	Exploratory Study	I1, I2, I6	6
[49]	2012	IEEE	I1, I2, I6	6
[50]	2015	Springer	I1, I2, I6	6
[13]	2011	Google Scholar	I1, I2, I5	6

Table 4 presents the Primary Studies selected for analysis (reference and year), the scientific database in which we found the article, the respective inclusion criteria applied, and the sum of the weights of the inclusion criteria.

3.3 Result Analysis

We performed a comparative analysis with the objective of answering the main research question (MQ). This analysis was structured according to Q1, Q2, Q3, Q4 and Q5, as follows:

Q1: Which elderly care needs are addressed by the analyzed literature?

Aiming to facilitate the analysis, we categorized the care need and AAL solutions into 8 major groups. Table 5 shows the analyzed studies grouped by category, which was devised based on the home care monitored in the AAL solutions. According to this analysis, the most frequents categories of care in the observed studies are *health* and *safety*, followed by *communication* and *dementia*. Post-fall *rehabilitation* [40], promotion of *independence* using robots [30], and controlling the *location* of the elderly person [29] was addressed by one study each. Around 8 studies address Home Care in a comprehensive way, *i.e.,* without focusing on a specific care.

Table 5. Results of the care analysis monitored in each home care study

Category	Monitored Care	Articles
Not specific	Article does not address a specific care; several possibilities are mentioned in the article without focusing on one specific category	[5, 8, 9, 26, 27, 34, 37, 48]
Health	Health and wellness prevention, monitoring diseases and vital signs, and medical emergencies. Ex: heart rate monitoring, medication control, nutritional monitoring, health monitoring, and well-being in general	[18, 33, 35, 43, 44, 46]
Safety	Fall prevention, fire safety, kitchen care, and general housing monitoring	[10, 13, 31, 32, 38, 47]
Communication	Solution monitors the exchange of information between the elderly, family members, caregivers, and/or healthcare professionals. Article aims to improve the interaction, organization, and control of daily activities	[28, 42, 45]
Dementia	Specific monitoring of the elderly with dementia, including well-being, safety and/or communication	[15, 36, 39, 41]
Location	Monitoring elderly location, inside and outside their homes	[29]
Independence	Use of robotics to assist the elderly in their daily activities, promoting greater independence and support at home	[30]
Rehabilitation	Technology used for post-fall rehabilitation of elderly people, including health-related situations, promoting monitoring, and supporting the return to a normal life	[40]

The most observed challenges in studies regarding the use of AAL solutions include: elderly people's difficulties to deal with changes [27], elderly people's difficulty in dealing with new technologies [27, 42], as well as ethical issues related to information security [28] and privacy [15, 47].

According to [35], the technology, by itself, is not enough to support preventive health self-monitoring. Therefore, it is necessary to better understand the elderly, and be more aware of their role as "informed and active patients" within their homes.

We also observed the increase in the use of AAL technology for Home Care. Ubiquitous and pervasive technologies are used to promote a ubiquitous context, facilitating the elderly's independence and their well-being [28].

Q2: Which IoT technologies are employed in home care solutions for the elderly?

During the analysis of the studies, it was observed that the term IoT is not frequently used in the articles: 14 studies (46.7%) do not mention the term IoT, 12 studies (40.0%) mentioned the term indirectly, and only 4 studies (13.3%) mention IoT explicitly. Table 6 summarizes the IoT solutions adopted in the 4 studies that mention it.

Table 6. Articles that mention IoT explicitly, the type of monitored care, and the proposed IoT solution

Ref.	Monitored Care	Proposed IoT solution
[9]	Not specified	This study addresses various types of technology, including IoT, and uses intelligent components and sensors that detect motion, emotions, biological, among others, in order to serve as a tool that assists, is preventive and rehabilitates
[10]	Not specified	This study briefly discusses IoT technology proposals that implement AAL with IoT, and categorizes them into following categories: daily task facilitation, mobility assistance, health care and rehabilitation, social inclusion and communication
[34]	Not specified	This study proposes a distributed system to support the elderly's autonomy in their home, including sensors, actuators, and IoT devices connected in a middleware. This system is designed to adapt to the user's needs and routines by means of a machine-learning component
[26]	Not specified	This study reinforces the importance of implementing solutions that allow for recreation, occupation, healthcare, and independent living. These must be easy to install, using sensors and network actuators, including wearable devices, home automation technologies, and robotic mechanisms

12 articles do not explicitly mention the term IoT, but include related technologies, such as: sensors (environment, movement, emotion), RFID, ubiquitous and pervasive computing and wearables. Thus, as shown in Table 7, they include indirect solutions that can be considered as partial IoT solutions with respect to elderly home care.

Table 7. Articles that mention terms/technologies related to IoT

Ref.	Proposed solutions	Technologies
[27]	Platform that allows for the integration of several independent Home Care devices	RFID (wireless sensors), and biometry
[17]	Identify behavioral, environmental and physiological signs, aiming to alert caregivers of possible hazards faced by people with dementia	Built-In sensors everywhere in the house, often hidden from view
[28]	Communication between elderly people and caregivers through sensors input into the mobile devices in order to capture emotion and movement. Alerts in visual display in the family's home	Remote sensors for emotion and movement, electrocardiogram, and GSR (Galvanic Skin Response sensor)
[29]	Track the location of the elderly, inside and outside of their homes	Vital sensors, GPS, and accelerometer, web server, and anomaly detector
[30]	Care-o-Bot: a robot designed to make life easier for the elderly at home	A robot that provides information about the elderly and their home; interface in Tablet to control the robot
[49]	An e-health system to support health care of the elderly at home using wearable sensors, including data record (activity routine and frequency of heart rate) for medical evaluation	Wearable sensors, automatic alerts, environmental sensors, and machine learning
[42]	Exchange text messages between family members and caregivers through an intelligent system using sensors and ubiquitous computing	RFID, augmented binder, pen Anoto (digitally writing record), and voice notification
[31]	Increase the safety of healthy older people through the use of sensors, aiming to promote greater independence within their homes	Network of environmental sensors, Backend (set-top box android), and Frontend (TV connected to Internet)
[50]	The e-wall system uses a network of environment and health sensors to monitor the elderly. The objective is to allow remote management, treatment, and rehabilitation of illnesses inside and outside the home. A backboard that allows for the family to manage risk, safety, lifestyle, and Health	Environmental and health sensors, personalization techniques, ubiquitous interaction, infrastructure in the cloud, and decision support technology
[32]	A system to support safety in the kitchen with sensors, and a central of intelligent processing for promoting interoperability between household appliances, emergency detection, analysis of data collected, and corrective measures	Sensors, RFID, and e-Servant (in-core intelligence for decision making)

(*continued*)

Table 7. (*continued*)

Ref.	Proposed solutions	Technologies
[46]	The telecare system aims to provide home care services, to monitor with sensors, and to trigger health professionals in case of emergency.	Sensors, Ubiquitous computing, and Environment Sensors
[33]	The OLDES telecare system remotely monitors the health and wellbeing of the elderly. It has an intelligent system of entertainment and decision making, with a Web Portal for system administration	Tele-Health, decision making (diffuse logic, machine learning), and Bluetooth

In 14 articles the term IoT was not mentioned explicitly nor indirectly. These studies often covered alternatives of ubiquitous and pervasive computing, robotics, network sensors, GPS monitoring or augmented reality. Although these are IoT related technologies, these studies were not considered by the evaluators as typical IoT solutions. They do not include intelligent decision making, and are frequently restricted to information gathering.

The key challenges identified by the analyzed studies regarding Q2 are: integration of sensors due to the lack of a common protocol, the applications' and devices' code are not open source, and compatibility with existing equipment [27].

According to [28], the sensors' safety is an aspect to be improved. Despite their advantages, this is a more critical aspect in wearables. In addition, [38] highlights that there is a great challenge in the interpretation of the primary data obtained from the sensors. Such an analysis can be done by means of rules defined by a formal specification, or by means of machine learning techniques and datamining.

Reference [46] emphasizes that intelligent capabilities can make simple utensils too expensive. To avoid this, they suggest the development of a responsible central intelligence entity. Reference [49] suggests that the house must support a layered infrastructure, which allows for the easy installation (plug-and-play) of sensors and network actuators of various types.

Q3: How are the users engaged in the design process?

As shown in Fig. 2, 6 studies do not mention the use of PD directly, while 5 studies mentioned user participation in their design process but do not detail how the users participated of the design. 6 studies partially detail the participation process, and 13 studies present the participation process completely. That is, 24 studies (80%) use some method to support users' participation in their design process.

Although some studies do not characterize themselves as PD studies, Table 8 presents methods adopted by articles that mention the process of developing the design with users. This Table also includes articles that do not give all the details as to how the participation occurred. An article can contain more than one method.

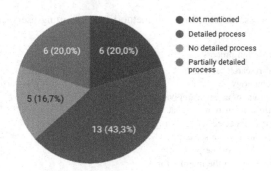

Fig. 2. Distribution of articles based on the user participation model

Table 8. Methods for supporting design activities with the users

Methods for supporting user participation	# of Articles
Workshop	12
Scenarios	11
Brainstorm	2
Design Thinking/Service Design	2
Thinking Aloud	2
Co-construction of Stories	1
Wizard of Oz	1
Brainwriting	1
Design Studio	1
Interactive Posters	1
Day Reconstruction Method (DRM)	1
Several, without detailing	1

By analyzing the results presented in Table 8, we highlight:

- A workshop with a multidisciplinary focus group is the most common participation format, and, in general, the studies did not mention the use of single method to encourage participation;
- User scenarios in narrative form or video (11 studies) was the second most common format. According to [39], a scenario can be presented in the form of a narrative to make the Persona's experience explicit;
- Reference [17] also emphasizes the importance of using Personas to complement the PD, giving greater comprehensiveness to the process.

Table 9 presents a summary of the 13 Primary Studies that detail the design process, the stakeholders, and the method used for supporting the users' participation.

According to [17], the PD process allows for the breaking down of barriers and generates empathy, consequently increasing the engagement of the elderly. According to [46], the evaluation of AAL systems with real users is a challenging task and some aspects must be considered: (1) the methodology used to integrate both qualitative and

Table 9. Design process, stakeholders, and method for supporting users' participation used in the analyzed studies

Ref.	Summary of the design process	Stakeholders	Method
[17]	1- Literature and research review regarding the technology 2- Definition of group of actors: caregivers 3- Future scenario construction: ("What if...?" and (What is expected...? ") 4- Choice of the intermediate scenario (neither the pessimistic nor the positive) 5- Conducting research on the internet for scenario validation and reduction of 'bias'	Caregivers, People on Internet	Scenarios (Design Fiction Probe)
[35]	1- Interview 2- Focal group choice 3- Workshops 4- Prototyping 5- Search for prototype feedbacks	Elderly and a Nurse	Workshop (including Day Reconstruction Method)
[28]	1- Brainstorming to develop concepts and ideas 2- Workshop: user study 3- Co-Construction of Stories 4- Individual interviews 5- Thematic analysis of results to identify pattern	Researchers (electrical and biomedical engineers, computer scientists, psychologists), Elderly, Caregivers	Co-Construction of Stories and Brainstorm
[29]	1- Experimental analysis with users, for definition of product accuracy 2- Group questionnaire, to assess service needs to be monitored * Late user participation (evaluation)	Elderly and Family	Workshop (questionnaire survey)
[37]	1-Workshop with a brainstorm of the problems faced in the AAL Project, categorization, prioritization by relevance, and analysis of solutions 2- Interactive Posters in a congress	Professionals from different areas with experience in AAL projects (electrical engineers, computer scientists, sociologists and business experts)	Workshop, Brainstorm and Interactive Posters
[30]	Video-scenario workshops (3) to evaluate: 1- Familiarization: GUI assessment 2- Affective Space: Interaction with the robot 3- Expression Analysis: evaluation of empathy and robot familiarization	Elderly and Youth	Scenarios (video-scenario and games)
[43]	1- Participants recruitment 2- Cognitive test 3- Scenario analysis 4- Analysis of the prototypes' usability (low, medium and high fidelity) 5- Comparative study with Google Health	Elderly, Caregivers, and Doctors	Scenarios (prototypes reviews)
[45]	1- Visit to the elderly's home 2- Visit to the caregiver's office 3- Use of the ethnographic method and interviews 4- PD Workshops (4)	Family and Caregivers	Workshop

(*continued*)

Table 9. (*continued*)

Ref.	Summary of the design process	Stakeholders	Method
[13]	1- Product demonstration 2- Free trial interface, in order to evaluate the acceptance of interface symbols and icons 3- Analysis of scenarios to improve interfaces: questionnaires and informal discussion	Elderly	Scenarios (Questionnaires and informal discussion)
[32]	1- Personas definition 2- Classification of users into Personas 3- User selection for validation 4- System presentation 5- Execution of tests by the users 6- Final Quiz * Late PD for solution evaluation.	Elderly, Caregivers, and Family	Scenarios (Use Cases)
[33]	1- Telecare and AAL research 2- Insights about "Digital Experience" 3- Ethnographic observation technique 4- Interviews 5- Focal group activity (Workshop) 6- Laboratories for system use 7- Telephone and personal questionnaires 8- Prototype for proposal validation	Elderly and IT Professionals	Workshop and Scenarios
[47]	1- Workshop with focus group (ideation) 2- Presentation of research carried out 3- Prototype development 4- Evaluation of prototype usability through the use of a focal group	Elderly	Workshop (Focal group, questionnaires and prototype)
[34]	1- PD workshops with researchers (Future Workshops) 2- PD for ideation of solutions 3- Interviews with the elderly 4- Categorization and selection of the best solutions	Researchers (HCI, computer science, health and social sciences); elderly only interviews	Workshops, Brainwriting, Design Studio (Ideation)

quantitative instruments; (2) the final users' and caregivers' engagement in design and evaluation activities; and, (3) the provision of sufficient training before the activities.

Reference [30] suggests the need to diversify the artifacts (e.g., videos, images, colored pens, post-it, and posters) in order to improve the elderly's engagement in the process. While [48] proposes the combination of several current concepts, such as: Experience Design, which can be used to think about the interactions between the user and the product or service; DT which can be used to produce innovation guided by direct observation of behavior, preferences, needs and desires; and Lean Startup to provide short feedback cycles. Reference [37] highlights the main causes of failures in AAL design: the caregivers' needs are not properly evaluated, reliability, usability, lack of inclusion of partners in the project, use of technologies that are not affordable to the users, and the adoption of a stereotyped view of older people.

Q4: How are Personas construed and used?

From the 30 Primary Studies analyzed, only 4 have cited the use of Personas: 3 studies mention the use of Personas, however, without presenting details as to how the Personas models were created [15, 26, 39]; i.e., only 1 study details the process of creating Personas [32].

In [32] 10 models of Personas are presented. They were created based on European statistics, including attributes of age, education, work, family situation, deficiencies, and technological background. In [32] the users' profile aims to consider cognitive and sensory abilities, and they were defined through the use of Personas.

Reference [26] identifies and characterizes a large number of stakeholders, such as: caregivers, informal caregivers, service users, and others. During DP for Services' activity, several sessions were held to identify the needs and characteristics of each Person, as well as how they interact with each service.

References [15, 39] emphasize the use of Personas as a tool to support the analysis of scenarios. Reference [17] complements these articles by describing that the use of Personas gives more flexibility to the design process, by exposing daily situations. This is especially interesting for the analysis of delicate scenarios (such as financial matters and death), avoiding that people become intimidated or emotionally involved.

Q5: What is the role of Semiotics in the design process?

Only 2 articles mention Semiotics. These studies include the analysis of signs to improve system acceptance [13], and the use of norms to describe behaviors and system-user interactions [46].

Reference [13] reinforces that the use of semiotic can increase efficiency, acceptance, and intuition. The semiotics' analysis of interfaces, and the design of icons capable of representing concepts, can improve the system's usability [13].

Reference [46] emphasizes that it is important to consider the user's emotions, attitudes, and preferences. This is particularly important to improve the acceptance of technical solutions in AAL. The norm analysis is used to capture interactions and structure them, thus, allowing for a better acceptance of Home Care systems. The norm analysis has 2 objectives in [46]: to describe the human-human and human-system interaction, and to describe the system's behavior by means of actions [46].

4   Final Remarks

Table 10 shows the consolidated results of the Systematic Review, containing the 12 most relevant studies according to our MQ. These studies use participatory methods for defining AAL using IoT. This table includes the type of care monitored, participatory method, IoT Technology, and whether Semiotics and Personas were used or not in the study.

This systematic review identifies that there are many challenges and opportunities to be considered in the design of Home Care and AAL technology for the elderly. In this context, IoT is still an unexplored technology, since only 12 articles present solutions based on IoT for Home Care, and only 4 studies explicitly mention IoT.

Table 10. Summary of the 12 most relevant studies according to the MQ

Ref	Care monitored	IoT technology	Participatory method	Semiotics personas
[32]	Security	Sensors, RFID, decision making	Scenarios	No
[26]	Several	Does not address a specific solution	DT	Personas
[42]	Communication	RFID, Augmented binder, Anoto pen, PressToTalk	Workshop Scenarios	No
[31]	Security	Environment Sensors, Set-top box android, TV connected to internet	Scenarios	No
[28]	Communication	Ubiquitous and pervasive computing, Sensors of emotion and movement in the cell, Electrocardiogram, visual alert display	Co-construction Brainstorm	No
[30]	Independence	Robot that provides information about the elderly and their home, tablet interface for Robot control	Scenarios	No
[33]	Health	Tele-Health System, diffuse logic, machine learning, Bluetooth	Workshop Scenarios	Personas
[29]	Localization	Vital sensors, GPS and accelerometer; Web server; Anomaly detector	Workshop	No
[17]	Dementia	Monitoring technologies of behavioral, environmental, and physiological signs	Scenarios	No
[9]	Several	Sensors (used, deployed, environment), social media, bio-robotics, RFID (not detailed)	Several, without detailing	No
[34]	Several	Distributed system, sensors, actuators and IoT devices, connected by a shared middle-ware, machine learning	Brainwriting Design Studio Workshop	No
[27]	Nonspecific	RFID, Biometry	Workshop	Personas

Thus, the ubiquity of IoT may increase the potential for acceptance of innovative technologies among elderly users.

Safety and health are the most addressed topics in the AAL studies. Therefore, IoT solutions that explore ubiquitous computing associated with such topics might have a greater acceptance.

Many articles emphasize that user participation in the design process can bring the elderly and family members closer to the proposed solution, by breaking barriers and generating empathy. However, more than half of the articles do not detail the used participation method; such information could be of great value in future researches. The majority of the studies (that described the participation method) mentioned "scenarios" (videos and narratives) as a participation strategy. Scenario-based methods were used in the ideation of a solution, in the requirements gathering, specification, construction, and validation of prototypes. The use of prototypes, even those with low fidelity, proved to be fundamental, once they allow for a better understanding of the design alternatives by the elderly.

The DT process with different stakeholders, including the elderly, is presented as a powerful tool to achieve effectiveness in the solution's design. The DT is a promising method to be evaluated in future researches. Results suggest that using various alternatives and materials (videos, images, colored pens, post-it and others) can improve the engagement and participation of the elderly in the process. This can make the design more playful and easy to carry out through gamification [30].

Another investigated aspect is the use of Personas. The combination of Personas with scenario-analysis is shown to be a powerful tool [15, 39]. This is especially important in the analysis of delicate scenarios (e.g., financial issues and death), once it helps to avoid that people become intimidated or emotionally involved. Besides, Personas support the characterization of different groups, facilitating the definition of Home Care technology for each of their needs.

Few studies have associated Semiotic with user participation in the analyzed review (just 2 articles mention its use). The use of norms, for instance, might contribute to the scenarios and interaction analysis.

We expect that this research contributes to the field by providing a review of state of the art studies of the researched topics, and by presenting how PD can contribute to the development of innovative solutions in the context of this work. In the next step of this research, we plan to extend this review to other design methods, as well as to perform long-term practical evaluations of the design of Home Care solutions using PD, Personas, and Semiotics based methods.

References

1. World Health Organization: Data and Statistics on World Ageing (2011). http://www.who.int/research/en/
2. Vines, J., Pritchard, G., Wright, P., Olivier, P., Brittain, K.: An age-old problem: examining the discourses of ageing in HCI and strategies for future research. ACM Trans. Comput.-Hum. Interact. (TOCHI) 22(1), 2 (2015)
3. Simões, C.C.S.: Relações entre as Alterações Históricas na Dinâmica Demográfica Brasileira e os Impactos Decorrentes do Processo de Envelhecimento da População. Instituto Brasileiro de Geografia e Estatística, Rio de Janeiro (2016)
4. Blythe, M.A., Wright, P.C., Monk, A.F.: Little brother: could and should wearable computing technologies be applied to reducing older people's fear of crime? Pers. Ubiquit. Comput. 8(6), 402–415 (2004)
5. Talamo, A., Camilli, M., Di Lucchio, L., Ventura, S.: Information from the past: how elderly people orchestrate presences, memories and technologies at home. Univ. Access Inf. Soc. 16(3), 739–753 (2017)
6. Magjarevic, R.: Home care technologies for ambient assisted living. In: Jarm, T., Kramar, P., Zupanic, A. (eds.) 11th Mediterranean Conference on Medical and Biomedical Engineering and Computing 2007. IFMBE Proceedings, vol. 16, pp. 397–400. Springer, Heidelberg (2007). https://doi.org/10.1007/978-3-540-73044-6_101
7. Knight, S., Tjassing, H.: Health care moves to the home. World Health 4, 413–444 (1994)
8. Gonçalves, V.P., et al.: Enhancing intelligence in multimodal emotion assessments. Appl. Intell. J. (APIN) 46, 470–486 (2016)

9. Spinsante, S., Stara, V., Felici, E., Montanini, L., Raffaeli, L., Rossi, L., Gambi, E.: Ambient Assisted Living and Enhanced Living Environments: Principles, Technologies and Control, pp. 61–85. Elsevier (2017). Chap. 4

10. Li, R., Lu, B., McDonald-Maier, K.D.: Cognitive assisted living ambient system: a survey. Digit. Commun. Netw. 1(4), 229–252 (2015)

11. Mano, L.Y., Faiçal, B.S., Nakamura, L.H., Gomes, P.H., Libralon, G.L., Meneguete, R.I., Geraldo Filho, P.R., Giancristofaro, G.T., Pessin, G., Krishnamachari, B., Ueyama, J.: Exploiting IoT technologies for enhancing health smart homes through patient identification and emotion recognition. Comput. Commun. 89, 178–190 (2016)

12. Mancini, M.: Internet das Coisas: História, Conceitos, Aplicações e Desafios. Revista MundoPM (2017)

13. Holzinger, A., Searle, G., Auinger, A., Ziefle, M.: Informatics as semiotics engineering: lessons learned from design, development and evaluation of ambient assisted living applications for elderly people. In: Stephanidis, C. (ed.) UAHCI 2011. LNCS, vol. 6767, pp. 183–192. Springer, Heidelberg (2011). https://doi.org/10.1007/978-3-642-21666-4_21

14. Soledade, M., Freitas, R., Peres, S., Fantinato, M., Steinbeck, R., Araújo, U.: Experimenting with design thinking in requirements refinement for a learning management system. Anais do Simpósio Brasileiro de Sistemas de Informação, pp. 182–193 (2013)

15. Kuhn, S., Winograd, T.: Participatory design. In: Winograd, T. (ed.) Bringing Design to Software, pp. 273–289. ACM Press, New York (1996)

16. Kensing, F., Blomberg, J.: Participatory design: issues and concerns. Comput. Support. Coop. Work (CSCW) 7(3–4), 167–185 (1998)

17. Schulte, B.F., Marshall, P., Cox, A.L.: Homes for life: a design fiction probe. In: Proceedings of the 9th Nordic Conference on Human-Computer Interaction, p. 80. ACM, October 2016

18. Liu, K.: Semiotics in Information Systems Engineering. Cambridge University Press, Cambridge (2000)

19. Stamper, R.K., et al.: Measur: method for eliciting, analizing and specifying user requirements. In: Computerized Assistance During the Information Systems Life Cycle. Elsevier Science Publishers, North-Holland (1988)

20. Baranauskas, M.C.C., Bonacin, R.: Design indicating through signs. Des. Issues 24, 30–45 (2008)

21. Gonçalves, V.P., et al.: Assessing users' emotion at interaction time: a multimodal approach with multiple sensors. Soft Comput. J. (SOCO) 1, 1–15 (2016)

22. Kitchenham, B.: Procedures for performing systematic reviews. Keele, UK, Keele Univ. 33 (2004), 1–26 (2004)

23. Gonçalves, V.P., Neris, V., Morandini, M., Nakagawa, E.Y., Ueyama, J.: Uma revisão sistemática sobre métodos de avaliação de usabilidade aplicados em software de telefones celulares. In Proceedings of the 10th Brazilian Symposium on Human Factors in Computing Systems and the 5th Latin American Conference on Human-Computer Interaction, pp. 197–201. Brazilian Computer Society, October 2011

24. Podestá, R.G., Catini, R.C.: Design Participativo na Identificação de Soluções IoT no Homecare de Idosos - Uma Revisão Sistemática. XIII WCF Faccamp (2017)

25. Biolchini, J., Mian, P.G., Natali, A.C.C., Travassos, G.H.: Systematic review in software engineering. System Engineering and Computer Science Department COPPE/UFRJ, Technical report ES, 679(05), 45 (2005)

26. Camarinha-Matos, L.M., Ferrada, F., Oliveira, A.I., Rosas, J., Monteiro, J.: Care services provision in ambient assisted living. IRBM 35(6), 286–298 (2014)

27. Wagner, S., Hansen, F.O., Pedersen, C.F., Memon, M., Aysha, F.H., Mathissen, M., Nielsen, C., Wesby, O.L.: CareStore platform for seamless deployment of ambient assisted living applications and devices. In: 2013 7th International Conference on Pervasive Computing Technologies for Healthcare (PervasiveHealth), pp. 240–243. IEEE, May 2013
28. Davis, K., Feijs, L., Hu, J., Marcenaro, L., Regazzoni, C.: Improving awareness and social connectedness through the social hue: Insights and perspectives. In: Proceedings of the International Symposium on Interactive Technology and Ageing Populations, pp. 12–23. ACM, October 2016
29. Ouchi, K., Doi, M.: Smartphone-based monitoring system for activities of daily living for elderly people and their relatives etc. In: Proceedings of the 2013 ACM Conference on Pervasive and Ubiquitous Computing Adjunct Publication, pp. 103–106. ACM, September 2013
30. Marti, P., Iacono, I.: Social and empathic behaviours: novel interfaces and interaction modalities. In: 2015 24th IEEE International Symposium on Robot and Human Interactive Communication (RO-MAN), pp. 217–222. IEEE, August 2015
31. Cozza, M., De Angeli, A., Tonolli, L.: Ubiquitous technologies for older people. Pers. Ubiquit. Comput. 21(3), 607–619 (2017)
32. Blasco, R., Marco, Á., Casas, R., Cirujano, D., Picking, R.: A smart kitchen for ambient assisted living. Sensors 14(1), 1629–1653 (2014)
33. McLoughlin, I., Maniatopoulos, G., Wilson, R., Martin, M.: Inside a digital experiment. Scand. J. Inf. Syst. 24(2), 3–26 (2012)
34. Stein, M., Boden, A., Hornung, D., Wulf, V., Garschall, I.M., Hamm, T., Müller, C., Neureiter, K., Schorch, M., van Velsen, L.: Third spaces in the age of IoT: a study on participatory design of complex systems. In: Symposium on Challenges and Experiences in Designing for an Ageing Society, 12th International Conference on Designing Interactive Systems (COOP) (2016)
35. Grönvall, E., Verdezoto, N.: Understanding challenges and opportunities of preventive blood pressure self-monitoring at home. In: Proceedings of the 31st European Conference on Cognitive Ergonomics, p. 31. ACM, August 2013
36. Wan, L., Müller, C., Randall, D., Wulf, V.: Design of A GPS monitoring system for dementia care and its challenges in academia-industry project. ACM Trans. Comput.-Hum. Interact. (TOCHI) 23(5), 31 (2016)
37. Haslwanter, J.D.H., Fitzpatrick, G.: Issues in the development of AAL systems: what experts think. In: Proceedings of the 10th International Conference on PErvasive Technologies Related to Assistive Environments, pp. 201–208. ACM, June 2017
38. Bianco, M.L., Pedell, S., Renda, G.: Augmented reality and home modifications: a tool to empower older adults in fall prevention. In: Proceedings of the 28th Australian Conference on Computer-Human Interaction, pp. 499–507. ACM, November 2016
39. Phull, R., Liscano, R., Mihailidis, A.: Comparative analysis of prominent middleware platforms in the domain of ambient assisted living (AAL) for an older adults with dementia (OAwD) scenario. Procedia Comput. Sci. 83, 537–544 (2016)
40. Aarhus, R., Grönvall, E., Kyng, M.: Challenges in participation. In: Pervasive computing technologies for healthcare (PervasiveHealth), 2010 4th International Conference on-NO PERMISSIONS, pp. 1–4. IEEE, March 2010
41. Jordan, P., Silva, P.A., Nunes, F., Oliveira, R. mobileWAY–a system to reduce the feeling of temporary lonesomeness of persons with dementia and to foster inter-caregiver collaboration. In: 2013 46th Hawaii International Conference on System Sciences (HICSS), pp. 2474–2483. IEEE, January 2013

42. Christensen, L.R., Grönvall, E.: Challenges and opportunities for collaborative technologies for home care work. In: Bødker, S., Bouvin, N., Wulf, V., Ciolfi, L., Lutters, W. (eds) ECSCW 2011: Proceedings of the 12th European Conference on Computer Supported Cooperative Work, 24–28 September 2011, Aarhus Denmark. pp. 61–80. Springer, London (2011). https://doi.org/10.1007/978-0-85729-913-0_4

43. Siek, K.A., Khan, D.U., Ross, S.E., Haverhals, L.M., Meyers, J., Cali, S.R.: Designing a personal health application for older adults to manage medications: a comprehensive case study. J. Med. Syst. **35**(5), 1099–1121 (2011)

44. Menschner, P., Prinz, A., Koene, P., Köbler, F., Altmann, M., Krcmar, H., Leimeister, J.M.: Reaching into patients' homes–participatory designed AAL services. Electron. Mark. **21**(1), 63–76 (2011)

45. Bossen, C., Christensen, L.R., Grönvall, E., Vestergaard, L.S.: CareCoor: augmenting the coordination of cooperative home care work. Int. J. Med. Inf. **82**(5), e189–e199 (2013)

46. Chidzambwa, L., Michell, V., Liu, K.: Applying Semiotics in Configuration of Home Telecare Devices in Ambient Assisted Living Environments, 8 p. University of Reading. http://www.academia.edu/1384496/Applying_Semiotics_in_Configuration_of_Home_Telecare_Devices_in_Ambient_Assisted_Living_Environments. Accessed 01 Feb 2017

47. Caine, K.E., Zimmerman, C.Y., Schall-Zimmerman, Z., Hazlewood, W.R., Camp, L.J., Connelly, K.H., Sulgrove, A.C., Huber, L.L., Shankar, K.: DigiSwitch: a device to allow older adults to monitor and direct the collection and transmission of health information collected at home. J. Med. Syst. **35**(5), 1181–1195 (2011)

48. Camilli, M., Di Lucchio, L., Malakuczi, V., Salvetti, A.: A cross-disciplinary approach to design ICTs enabling active ageing and social inclusion. In: 7th Conference on Euro-Mediterranean Public Management Dialogue, 08–10 October, Rome, Italy, 15 p.

49. Ugulino, W., Ferreira, M., Velloso, E., Fuks, H.: Virtual caregiver: a system for supporting collaboration in elderly monitoring. In: 2012 Brazilian Symposium on Collaborative Systems (SBSC), pp. 43–48. IEEE October 2012

50. Kyriazakos, S., Mihaylov, M., Anggorojati, B., Mihovska, A., Craciunescu, R., Fratu, O., Prasad, R.: eWALL: an intelligent caring home environment offering personalized context-aware applications based on advanced sensing. Wirel. Pers. Commun. **87**(3), 1093–1111 (2016)

Participatory Design Approach to Internet of Things: Co-designing a Smart Shower for and with People with Disabilities

Mexhid Ferati$^{(\boxtimes)}$, Ayesha Babar, Kanani Carine, Ali Hamidi, and Christina Mörtberg

Informatics Department, Linnaeus University, Växjö, Sweden
{mexhid.ferati,christina.mortberg}@lnu.se,
{ab223yc,kc222df,ah223vd}@student.lnu.se

Abstract. Smart home products are becoming widespread aiming to increase people's independence, especially for the elderly and people with disabilities. In order to design them suitably for this community, their involvement in the requirement gathering and design process is particularly important. In this paper, we report a study we conducted with six people having various disabilities. The aim was to identify the type of smart product that mostly increases their independence at home. We used three requirement gathering methods in a participatory fashion, namely, cartographic mapping, future workshop, and cultural probe. The outcome of the study revealed that participants mostly needed a product for a bathroom, specifically a smart shower. The initial prototype design of the product was developed together with participants. Researchers further investigated the prototype design using littleBits electronic modules. The smart shower is anticipated to have the most effect in increasing not only user independence, but also privacy.

Keywords: Cartographic mapping · Future workshop · Cultural probe
Prototyping · Participatory design · LittleBits · Smart home · Internet of Things
Disability · Elderly

1 Introduction and Background

The quality of life is steadily improving leading to an increase in life expectancy, which will result in the number of the elderly rising in the coming years. Demographers predict that the number of the elderly will increase to 30% by 2060, compared to 17% in 2009 [1]. Surveys show that 80% of the current elderly people suffer from at least one chronic disease [2]. In addition, the World Health Organization reports that 15% of world's population lives with some sort of disability [3], 3.8% of whom are people over 15 years old with considerable physical movement challenges. This trend shows that it will be difficult for this community to independently live alone.

The technology has the potential to help such community to increase or maintain their independence [4]. By using mobile technology and wireless integration, the cost of care for the elderly and people with disabilities can be reduced [5, 6]. Examples of such developments are many. For instance, there are systems developed that enable

© Springer International Publishing AG, part of Springer Nature 2018
M. Antona and C. Stephanidis (Eds.): UAHCI 2018, LNCS 10908, pp. 246–261, 2018.
https://doi.org/10.1007/978-3-319-92052-8_19

users to urgently communicate with their healthcare provider using pre-recorded audio messages that can be easily activated using a mobile device interface [7]. Since the elderly typically suffer from health issues due to their age, health care providers monitor their real-time condition using wearable technologies [8, 9].

According to Pew Research, 83% of experts claim that by 2025, Internet of Things (IoT) will be ubiquitous and positively affect people's everyday life [10]. The advantage of using IoT is their ability to communicate with one another to orchestrate and address user needs in a smooth manner, contributing to enhancing productivity and ease of life [11]. The proliferation of IoT devices has potential to help the elderly and people with disabilities to continue living independently in their preferred environment, such as, their home. Moreover, research shows that the transition from home to the health care facilities may cause increase in anxiety for the elderly and people with disabilities [12].

Examples of using IoT to help the everyday lives of the elderly and people with disabilities include medication reminder devices that help patients keep track of their pill taking routines [13]. In scenarios with blind people, an IoT-based indoor navigation is helping such users to easily find their way throughout large building facilities, which is the case with healthcare centers and hospitals [14].

IoT have also been proposed as a requirement gathering methodology to complement traditional methods when access to participants is difficult, such as people with disabilities [15]. Several other studies report a type of participatory design where participant requirements are collected by using sensors that passively collect data from an elderly person [16, 17]. Gkouskos and Burgos [18] have observed a difference between how participatory approaches differ depending on the field. The design fields have long tradition of participatory approaches and hence involve people through traditional methods, such as workshops, testing probes, and prototyping. On the other hand, health and engineering fields typically rely on technology-based user participation for data gathering, which has gained more importance with the introduction of IoT. In any case, extensive research shows that user participation helps build better usable systems [19]. Because of that, there are studies within the field of Ambient Assisted Living (AAL) that use participatory development approach for their solutions [19, 20]. Many other studies report the use of participatory approaches by involving primary users, caregivers [21], psychiatric patients [22], and the use of an interactive dollhouse for residential monitoring [23].

To make use of IoT and understand how those can benefit the elderly and people with disabilities, in this paper we report a study that we conducted following a participatory design approach. Our aim was to understand the everyday tasks and experiences at home of the elderly and people with disabilities in order to understand their needs. Especially, we wanted to explore how IoT devices could make people's lives easier, comfortable and more independent.

In order to identify common needs of our potential users, the requirements gathering was done by using various participatory design methods, such as, cartographic mapping, cultural probes, future workshop and prototyping. Participants' highest needs were linked to bathroom and kitchen activities. We focused on the bathroom scenario considering the importance of privacy related to activities typically conducted in such setting. This, likely also has a greater impact in user's independence.

2 Participatory Design

The application domain of IoT is evolving, but it is still dominated by a technical focus. Koreshoff et al. [24:365] discuss how HCI can be more deeply engaged in IoT "to ensure that people, their particular needs, contexts, situatedness and interests" are included in IoT. To bridge the gap between a technical orientation and human-oriented approaches, they argue that Participatory Design (PD) as a design approach can include human-centred concerns to IoT [24]. Following this suggestion, we included PD to give space to persons with impairments and to their wishes and demands to facilitate their everyday lives using digital services (IoT applications). Hence, the project revolved around PD values such as co-design, participation, cooperation and situatedness [25]. Therefore, we used three different participative methods to involve participants in co-design sessions: cartographic mappings, future workshop, and cultural probe. In total, six participants were involved in several of the methods, but not in all. Table 1 gives an overview of the methods in which each participant took part, along with other details, such as, age, gender and the type of disability.

Table 1. List of participants

Participant	Age	Gender	Type of disability	Participation session
A	30	Male	Paraplegic	Cartography, probes, future workshop, prototyping (paper, GUI)
B	40	Male	Paraplegic	Cartography, probes, future workshop, prototyping (paper, GUI)
C	20	Female	Paraplegic	Probes
D	87	Female	Arthritis, paralyzed	Cartography
E	33	Female	Cognitive, paraplegic	Future workshop, prototyping (paper, GUI)
F	28	Male	Blind, paraplegic	Probes, future workshop

2.1 Cartographic Mappings

Cartographic mapping is a participative method to visualize people's activities and doings in their everyday lives. The method is simple and does not demand any preparations in advance. By using only materials familiar to all, such as images, paper, post-it notes, and pencils, participants are encouraged to start telling their stories and to visualize their experiences and wishes [26, 27]. Two sessions, involving three persons with physical impairment (refer to Table 1), were conducted in two different ways; one participant via skype and two other participants in a face-to-face group meeting.

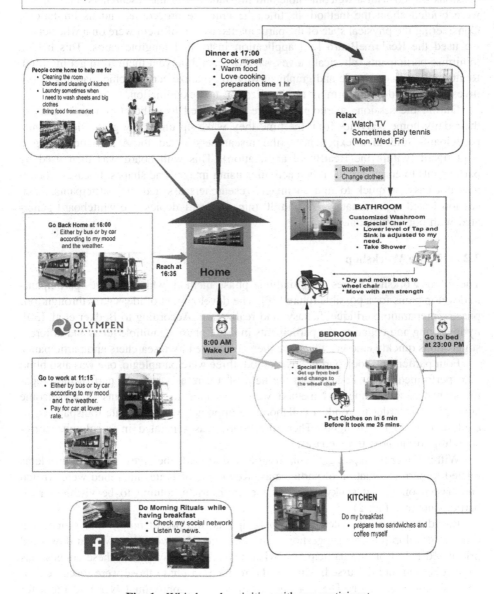

Fig. 1. Whiteboard activities with one participant.

The activities were titled "I, my home and daily activities from morning till night". Sessions started with a welcome note and introduction of the researchers. Participants were briefed about the method, its title, the aim, the procedure, and its limitations. Considering the physical state of the participants, as two of them were on a wheelchair, we used the RealtimeBoard [28] application instead of tangible cards. This helped minimise participants' physical moves, save time, and prevent them from getting tired. RealtimeBoard is a simple and graphical way to organize cartographic mappings from investigation and brainstorming to visualization and examination.

During the sessions, participants were encouraged to elaborate on and visualize their daily home activities from the time they wake up until they go to sleep. While participants told their experiences, the researchers noted those activities using a whiteboard (within the RealBoard application). This whiteboard was then used by participants to enrich the identified activities using images and shapes. In cases when it was not easy or quick to find an image, researchers assisted the participants. Each session lasted approximately 1 h and 30 min. Figure 1 depicts the whiteboard generated with one participant.

2.2 Future Workshop

The future workshop represents a multiple phase method, which involves participants to develop plans for a possible future [29]. The development of ideas goes through four phases: preparation, critique, fantasy, and realization. According to Bødker et al. [30], by involving and engaging the participants in these phases, multiple ideas and different suggestions quickly emerge, which are then considered by researchers and participants.

Four participants took part in this method, three were paraplegic, one was also blind who performed the workshop with the help of a care assistant. As part of the preparation phase, the theme and method were presented to participants in a welcome atmosphere in order to conduct collaborative approach with adequate transparency to explore participants thoughts. Then, the board was separated in 3 columns corresponding to the next three phases.

Within the critique phase, the discussions led towards the investigation of problems related to current situation of participants. Keywords of issues identified were written and pasted on post-it sticky notes on the appropriate column to be visible for all participants (see Fig. 2).

Based on priorities stated by the participants, the post-it notes were grouped in order to develop possible suggestions. These suggestions were then written down and prioritized based on the participants' wishes. In the fantasy phase, these suggestions were reviewed and discussed, while in the realization phase those were discussed for possible implementation. The workshop completed in approximately 2 h (30 min for each phase) and finalized with 15 min concluding discussion.

Fig. 2. Future workshop post-it sticky notes.

2.3 Cultural Probes

Cultural Probes can be defined as *'collections of evocative tasks meant to elicit inspirational responses from people'* [31:53, [32]. This method helps in understanding and gathering rich information about a setting or situation by user participation [33]. It was also chosen because access to homes of participants with disabilities was not possible.

For this method, four participants (refer to Table 1) were involved. In a period of two weeks the probes method was completed including delivering and collection of packages. The probe package contained task cards and few reminiscent images about daily activities at home. The packages were personally delivered to and collected from three participants, and emailed to the fourth person. Also, a short introduction stating 'this kit is a way to get to know your needs better' was given before handing over the probe kit.

The probe package was designed keeping in mind the common interests and constraints to support various needs of participants with disabilities so that they could give inspirational suggestions within the comfort of their homes. Simple instructive words were used on the task cards to enable participants understand and complete the tasks without researcher's guidance. Task cards also included images to allow participants enough space and possibilities when providing suggestions. The materials were in English based on the preference stated by participants when consent was received.

In total, there were seven inspirational task cards along with seven images portraying all rooms that a typical apartment has. The tasks contained daily activities that are typical for a home setting. Participants were supposed to look at each image and write answers at the back of the card (Fig. 3).

Fig. 3. Cultural probe inspirational cards.

3 Lessons Learned

The outcome from the three participatory design sessions revealed that participants priorities and needs were related to bathroom and kitchen. Initially, the use of cartographic mappings enabled us in a co-design fashion together with participants to restructure the study and learn how to systematically map and understand participant's activities. The analysis of the activities revealed that despite all participants being on a wheelchair and having the same daily routine, they handled them in different ways. For instance, one participant takes off his shoes and socks himself while the other one needs help.

The future workshop revealed and demonstrated many issues participants had related to physical activities, such as, opening and closing a door, clipping the nails, brushing teeth, and putting shoes on and off. In the kitchen, the position and location of different equipment and objects presented a problem. For instance, the height of cupboards and fridge shelves were not suitable for participants that use a wheelchair. Activities related to cooking were also found difficult for participants, such as, stoves and other food preparation devices. In the bathroom, participants noted that showering demanded immense effort. Particularly, issues were related to shower seat, shower jet adjustment, control of temperature and water pressure, and moving from the wheelchair to the shower seat. When participants took a shower alone, often they felt the need to contact an assistant to help them with reaching the shower head or the soap. Since typically they did not bring their phone in the shower cabin or simply forgot to do so, often they were forced to move out of the shower, to put clothes on, and use the wheelchair to reach for the phone. All these issues made participants tired when taking a shower.

The probe method revealed the difficulties participants faced during their everyday chores at home. It provided rich data, which helped us understand how participants moved around the house, and what were the key areas that they needed most assistance. Several different ideas and opinions emerged after the analysis of responses on the images. For instance, one participant stated that he felt most comfortable in his bedroom, however he was not happy with his wardrobe as he faced problems when reaching the clothes because the closet was not customized or adjusted to his height.

This method formed a basis and helped researchers to narrow the collection of ideas received from analysis of all methods leading towards creating a smart device for the people with disabilities. It also aided the researchers to get acquainted with the homes of participants and provide a rich picture to inspire the design of a device.

Ultimately, a smart shower, smart refrigerator, and a smart oven were three proposed devices after conducting the participatory methods. Based on various aspects, such as feasibility of the production, processes and the cost of the device, the smart shower device was mutually chosen by researchers and participants. Considering the cost aspect for instance, the device is likely to have an overall lower cost compared to other proposed devices, due to their complexity features.

4   Prototype Development

Following the requirements gathering phase using three participatory design methods, we were ready to explore and design the product that our participants mostly preferred. We continued to involve participants in the design of initial prototypes; we used three participants that also participated in requirements gathering methods [33] (refer to Table 1). The prototype design went through three phases; (1) paper prototype using sketching, (2) digital prototype using Photoshop PS6, and (3) an advanced prototype using littleBits [35]. Participants were involved only in the first two phases.

4.1   Paper Prototype

Taking in consideration the participants' physical disabilities and special needs, we found that the use of paper prototyping should be an appropriate and easy way to make a prototype in a short time frame [34]. Additionally, Lowgreen and Stolterman [36] argue that using low tech prototypes helps to generate more comments and discussions, since participants get the impression that they can contribute easily to an early stage prototype rather than a refined version. The prototype was created using white papers, coloured pencils, markers, eraser, ruler, scissor and tape. With the paper prototype, participants were able to envision their original ideas about the design of the device and customize it according to their wishes and demands.

Initially, participants were informed about the overall purpose of this workshop and the goals to be met. In previous sessions, we had decided about designing a smart shower, while now we started by brainstorming of ideas on how to design the smart shower. Device options, such as, buttons, screen, mic, speaker, colours, were discussed. We then proceeded in discussing the physical aspects of the device including its size, shape, and placement of the device in a bathroom. Although participants had no sensory disability, such as, sight and hearing, they were reminded that the device should also be used by people with such disability.

With the occasional help from researchers or facilitators, participants started to cut the white papers in different sizes that they imagined the device size. The participants were asked to think about the key features to be placed on the device. Various features were suggested and the most important ones were decided, which included the water temperature control, pressure control, and the assist alert button. One participant stated that *"the shape of the buttons for every function should be different to make it easier to find and work with"*. Hence, the buttons were designed to have distinctive shape, colour, and dimension in order to be accessible and usable by people with visual impairment. Other features, such as, voice interaction and language options, were discussed to be important to be included into the design. The design process with participants took approximately one hour. In the days that followed, researchers refined the paper prototype and it finally looked as in Fig. 4.

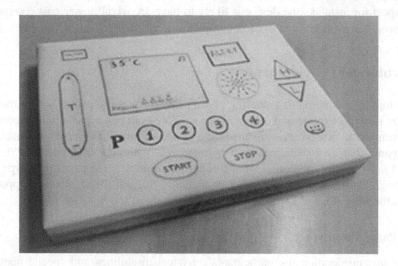

Fig. 4. Final paper prototype.

4.2 Graphical User Interface Prototype

A week after the paper prototype session, the same participants were invited again to take part in designing a digital prototype. The session started by showing them the improved paper prototype, to confirm their vision. Participants continued to discuss and provide their suggestions, while two researchers implemented those on a computer using the Photoshop PS6 application. Besides providing enhancements regarding its look and feel, the digital prototype also was used to explore how the device would be used.

The device is envisioned to be operated using two interaction modes; by pressing the buttons or by voice commands. The device is turned on when the user sits on the washing chair, which activates the pressure sensor. A blue light then comes out from the device along with a greeting message. By pressing the Start Shower button, the water will start pouring and a voice feedback is heard stating "Shower is On". The user then can adjust the water temperature and pressure either by pressing the appropriate buttons or using voice commands. The device is paired with care assistant's mobile phone, which notifies her via a text message that the person is in the shower. This will keep the assistant aware in case the user needs any help. If such cases arise, the user presses the alert button, which sends a message to the care assistant stating "I need your help". The response from the care assistant is displayed on the device screen along with a voice message coming out of the speaker. If the alert button is pressed once, a message is sent; if it is pressed twice, a call will be initiated to care assistant's mobile phone (Fig. 5).

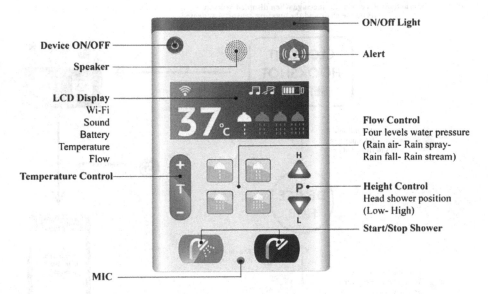

Fig. 5. Finalized digital prototype of device.

Other relevant buttons are also designed on the device that provide several functionalities. The position of the shower head can be adjusted using triangle shaped buttons labelled with letters "H" and "L" for high and low, respectively. The temperature control button is denoted by "T" and "+" and "−" can be used to increase or decrease the water temperature respectively. At the center of the device, four squared buttons are placed to regulate the typology of the water flow. Besides the speaker that provides auditory feedback, the device also has a display to show the temperature degrees, jet flow type, battery level, Wi-Fi connection, and music on/off.

Lastly, the shower can be turned off by pressing the dark grey button with head shower icon on the bottom. This will stop the water flow and an audio feedback is heard from the speaker stating 'Shower is Off, Thank You!'. At the same time, the care assistant is notified via a text message.

4.3   Prototype Using LittleBits

Considering the hardware aspects of the smart shower, such as pressure and temperature sensors, we explored the idea of enriching the prototype using electronic building blocks called littleBits [35]. These electronic components are attached together in order to perform a function. To illustrate it simply, for instance, a component with a button could be attached to another component with a light, and a simple function could be that the light will turn on, when the button is pressed.

USING THE CLOUDBIT WITH IFTTT: Device On

Bit to web interaction: Receive a text message when disabled person
sits on the chair and the pressure sensor is activated

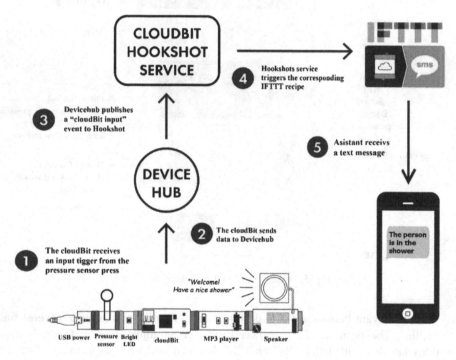

Fig. 6. IFTTT, sending message to a care assistant when the device turns on.

For the prototype, two services, Devicehub and Hookshot, are used to connect the cloudBit and register the webhooks. The different functions of the prototype are implemented using IFTTT [37] app recipes and the cloudBit. With the help of cloudBit, a wireless enabled module (component), enables the prototype to be connected to the internet to perform functions. Once the connection is established, simple "If This Then That" code recipes via the IFTTT app are used to trigger actions that perform various functions. Some of the features of the smart shower device that were developed using the littleBits kit are: turn the device on, simulation of shower on and off, temperature

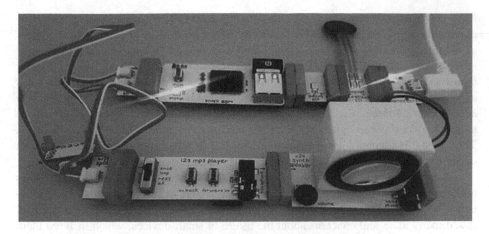

Fig. 7. Device On implementation using littleBits.

display, and alert notification. The IFTTT route of 'device switched on' function that sends an alert to a care assistant when a person is in the shower, is illustrated in Fig. 6 and its littleBits prototype is shown in Fig. 7.

During this study, due to limitations and some restrictions of using littleBits, several functions were not implementable like two-way communication using mic, height adjustment, pressure buttons, temperature increase and decreases as well as voice recognition functions.

5 Discussion

The contribution of this study lies in bringing the human-centred design approach to Internet of Things. Involving participants in the requirements gathering methods helped us understand their ways of doing things in their homes. Each requirement gathering method inadvertently served a different role. The cartographic mapping was useful to understand the differences among our participants, even those with the same disability. This indicates that people of similar disabilities should not be treated homogeneously as their wishes and issues might differ. The future workshop provided a full cycle of the design process, from identifying details about the issues, prioritizing among those presented, and all the way to giving suggestions about their implementation. Moreover, using this method, we were able to more accurately pinpoint what activities and in which settings provided most challenge for participants; which was the kitchen and bathroom. Finally, the cultural probes offered a richer context of the issues people faced, perhaps because they had more time to complete it (two weeks) and by asking their comments on the type of activities people conducted in each room of their homes.

Another important aspect that played crucial role when deciding to design a smart shower was the intimate considerations typically related to activities in a bathroom. According to Finken and Mörtberg [38:315], Beathe, a study participant, says: *"...do I manage to go to the bathroom, and take a shower, do we have toilets that work so*

I can ... the most embarrassing, I think, is being dependent on someone else to help me in the bathroom. It is absolutely the worst thing I know or are you forced to use diapers depending on that care workers cannot help you frequently enough – the most basic need. I think this is really important, one should start here [on basic needs] – other issues will also appear. Certainly, one can focus on other issues but just to start, what do you need, you need food for the day and you need to go to the bathroom and you need ... here I think it is the absolute first and most important [demands], because many [services/technologies] do not exist and the [designers] don't care enough". Thus, designing technological smart devices used in a bathroom to assist people with disability were deemed very important and significant.

An interesting finding from participants' discussions was their contradicting views about technology, some were interested in using smart devices and some were reluctant. The image of a smart house presented to participants during the probes method, raised many ideas and concerns about the usage of smart devices, which inspired them to brainstorm on how different technologies can assist in their daily life. However, one person expressed concerns that the usage of technology will make them lazy and the body inactivity will lead to serious health problems.

5.1   Ethical Considerations

This study required direct contact with participants for most of its activities. To respect participants privacy and inform them of the purpose of the study and their activities before they could participate, they were asked for a consent. Indeed, the consent was twice obtained from participants; first for agreeing to participate in the requirement gathering and prototyping sessions, and second for agreeing to write and publish this paper, albeit using only anonymised data.

The other privacy concern related to the smart shower device is its transmission of data. Although the device is only envisioned to communicate with a care assistant or a family member, its ability to connect to the Internet, makes it prone to attacks and revelation of sensitive data of the users involved. In general, the privacy and security issues related to Internet of Things are an important challenge nowadays and consequently a subject of intense research. With advances in the field, these concerns will be mitigated and the Internet of Things devices within the smart house eco-system will become more prevalent.

6   Conclusion

In this paper we report a study we conducted with six people with various disabilities in order to identify the type of smart product they judge most likely to increase their independence at home. Using three requirement gathering methods, cartographic mappings, future workshop, and cultural probe, we learned from our participants that a smart shower would be a product of their choice. This product will increase their independence, privacy, and it will be the most feasible for production.

Using two stages of prototyping, namely, paper prototyping and later graphical prototyping, participants together with researchers developed the features of the smart shower. The main features included, the ability to change the water temperature, water flow, shower head position, and an automatic alert delivered to a care assistant when the shower is in use. Finally, researchers have investigated the use of littleBits electronic modules to build a more advanced prototype. Due to the limitations of the littleBits, however, not all features were implemented.

References

1. Rogge, L.: Working Group 4 Seamless intermodal networks and services. Internal Report: Future Trends, Impacts and Key Challenges, 30 June 2003 (2003)
2. Hoffman, C., Rice, D., Sung, H.Y.: Persons with chronic conditions: their prevalence and costs. JAMA **276**(18), 1473–1479 (1996)
3. World Health Organization, Disability and Health, Fact Sheet, 15 December 17. http://www.who.int/mediacentre/factsheets/fs352/en/
4. Agree, E.M.: The potential for technology to enhance independence for those aging with a disability. Disabil. Health J. **7**(1), S33–S39 (2014)
5. Sasaki, J., Yamada, K., Tanaka, M., Fujita, H., Pisanelli, D.M., Rasconi, R., Tiberio, L., De Lazzari, C.: Improving safety and healthy life of elderly people: Italian and Japanese experiences. In: SoMeT, pp. 585–598 (2009)
6. Rechel, B., Doyle, Y., Grundy, E., McKee, M.: How can health systems respond to population ageing. Health Systems and Policy Analysis, Policy Brief 10 (2009)
7. Misbahuddin, S., Orabi, H., Fatta, R., Al-Juhany, M., Almatrafi, A.: IoT framework based health care system for elderly and disabled people. In: International Conference on Recent Advances in Computer Systems (RACS 2015), pp. 99–102 (2015)
8. Coughlin, J.F., Pope, J.: Innovations in health, wellness, and aging-in-place. IEEE En. Med. Biol. Mag. **27**(4), 47–52 (2008)
9. Ray, P.P.: Home Health Hub Internet of Things (H 3 IoT): an architectural framework for monitoring health of elderly people. In: 2014 International Conference on Science Engineering and Management Research (ICSEMR), pp. 1–3. IEEE (2014)
10. Anderson, J., Rainie, L., The Internet of Things will thrive by 2025, Digital Life in 2025. Pew Research Center (2014)
11. Laput, G., Lasecki, W.S., Wiese, J., Xiao, R., Bigham, J.P., Harrison, C.: Zensors: adaptive, rapidly deployable, human-intelligent sensor feeds. In: Proceedings of the 33rd Annual ACM Conference on Human Factors in Computing Systems, pp. 1935–1944. ACM (2015)
12. Cheek, P., Nikpour, L., Nowlin, H.D.: Aging well with smart technology. Nurs. Adm. Q. **29**(4), 329–338 (2005)
13. Celler, B.G., Lovell, N.H., Chan, D.K.: The potential impact of home telecare on clinical practice. Med. J. Aust. **171**(10), 518–521 (1999)
14. Giannoumis, G.A., Ferati, M., Pandya, U., Krivonos, D., Pey, T.: Usability of indoor network navigation solutions for persons with visual impairments. In: Langdon, P., Lazar, J., Heylighen, A., Dong, H. (eds.) CWUAAT 2018, pp. 135–145. Springer, Cham (2018). https://doi.org/10.1007/978-3-319-75028-6_12
15. Ferati, M., Kurti, A., Vogel, B., Raufi, B.: Augmenting requirements gathering for people with special needs using IoT: a position paper. In 2016 IEEE/ACM Cooperative and Human Aspects of Software Engineering (CHASE), pp. 48–51. IEEE (2016)
16. Amendola, S., Lodato, R., Manzari, S., Occhiuzzi, C., Marrocco, G.: RFID technology for IoT-based personal healthcare in smart spaces. IEEE Internet Things J. **1**(2), 144–152 (2014)

17. Pinto, S., Cabral, J., Gomes, T.: We-care: an IoT-based health care system for elderly people. In: International Conference on Industrial Technology (ICIT), pp. 1378–1383. IEEE (2017)

18. Gkouskos, D., Burgos, J.: I'm in! Towards participatory healthcare of elderly through IOT. Procedia Comput. Sci. 113, 647–652 (2017)

19. Kieffer, S., Lawson, J.Y.L., Macq, B.: User-centered design and fast prototyping of an ambient assisted living system for elderly people. In: Sixth International Conference on Information Technology: New Generations, ITNG 2009, pp. 1220–1225. IEEE (2009)

20. Aquilano, M., Cavallo, F., Bonaccorsi, M., Esposito, R., Rovini, E., Filippi, M., Esposito, D., Dario, P., Carrozza, M.C.: Ambient assisted living and ageing: preliminary results of RITA project. In: Annual International Conference of the Engineering in Medicine and Biology Society (EMBC), pp. 5823–5826. IEEE (2012)

21. Hwang, A.S., Truong, K.N., Mihailidis, A.: Using participatory design to determine the needs of informal caregivers for smart home user interfaces. In: 6th International Conference on Pervasive Computing Technologies for Healthcare (PervasiveHealth), pp. 41–48. IEEE (2012)

22. Crabtree, A., Hemmings, T., Rodden, T., Cheverst, K., Clarke, K., Dewsbury, G., Hughes, J., Rouncefield, M.: Designing with care: adapting cultural probes to inform design in sensitive settings. In: Proceedings of the 2004 Australasian Conference on Computer-Human Interaction (OZCHI 2004), pp. 4–13. (2003)

23. Kanis, M., Alizadeh, S., Groen, J., Khalili, M., Robben, S., Bakkes, S., Kröse, B.: Ambient monitoring from an elderly-centred design perspective: what, who and how. In: Keyson, D. V., et al. (eds.) AmI 2011. LNCS, vol. 7040, pp. 330–334. Springer, Heidelberg (2011). https://doi.org/10.1007/978-3-642-25167-2_45

24. Koreshoff, T.L., Luong, T.W., Robertson, T.: Approaching a Human-Centered Internet of Things. In: OzCHI 2013: Proceedings of the 25th Australian Computer-Human Interaction Conference: Augmentation, Application, Innovation, Collaboration, pp. 363–366 (2013)

25. van Der Velden, M., Mörtberg, C.: Participatory design and design for values. In: van den Hoven, J., Vermaas, P., van de Poel, I. (eds.) Handbook of Ethics, Values, and Technological Design, pp. 41–66. Springer, Dordrecht (2015). https://doi.org/10.1007/978-94-007-6970-0_33

26. Elovaara, P., Igira, F., Mörtberg, C.: Whose participation? Whose knowledge? – exploring PD in Tanzania-Zanzibar and Sweden. In: Wagner, et al. (eds.) Proceedings of the Ninth Conference on Participatory Design: Expanding Boundaries in Design, Trento, Italy, vol. 1, pp. 105–114. ACM Press (2006)

27. Elovaara, P., Mörtberg, C.: Carthographic mappings - participative methods. In: Bødker, K., Bratteteig, T., Loi, D., Robinson, T. (eds.) Proceedings of the Eleventh Conference on Participatory Design: Participation: the Challenge, Sydney, Australia. ACM Press (2010)

28. Realtime Board, 15 December 2017. https://realtimeboard.com

29. Jungk, R., Müllert, N.R.: Zukunftswerkstätten, wege zur wiederbelebung der demokratie (Future Workshops: ways to revive democracy). Goldman, Munchen (1981)

30. Bødker, K., Kensing, F., Simonsen, J.: Participatory IT Design: Designing for Business and Workplace Realities. MIT Press, Cambridge (2004)

31. Gaver, W.W., Boucher, A., Pennington, S., Walker, B.: Cultural probes and the value of uncertainty. Interactions 11(5), 53–56 (2004)

32. Boehner, K., Gaver, W., Boucher, A.: Probes. In: Lury, C., Wakeford, N. (eds.) Inventive Methods: The Happening of the Social. Routledge, London (2012)

33. Mattelmäki, T.: Applying probes–from inspirational notes to collaborative insights. CoDesign 1(2), 83–102 (2005)

34. Bødker, S., Grønbæk, K.: Cooperative prototyping: users and designers in mutual activity. Int. J. Man Mach. Stud. 34(3), 453–478 (1991)

35. Littlebits, 15 December 2017. http://littlebits.cc
36. Löwgren, J., Stolterman, E.: Thoughtful Interaction Design: A Design Perspective on Information Technology. MIT Press, Cambridge (2004)
37. IFTTT, 15 December 2017. https://ifttt.com
38. Finken, S., Mörtberg, C.: Performing elderliness – intraactions with digital domestic care technologies. In: Kimppa, K., Whitehouse, D., Kuusela, T., Phahlamohlaka, J. (eds.) HCC 2014. IAICT, vol. 431, pp. 307–319. Springer, Heidelberg (2014). https://doi.org/10.1007/978-3-662-44208-1_25

Security Monitoring in a Low Cost Smart Home for the Elderly

Gabriel Ferreira[1], Paulo Penicheiro[1], Ruben Bernardo[1],
Álvaro Neves[1], Luís Mendes[1,4], João Barroso[3],
and António Pereira[1,2(✉)]

[1] School of Technology and Management, Computer Science
and Communication Research Center,
Polytechnic Institute of Leiria, 2411-901 Leiria, Portugal
{2131218,2130628,2130664,2120771}@my.ipleiria.pt,
{lmendes,apereira}@ipleiria.pt
[2] Information and Communications Technologies Unit, INOV INESC
Innovation, Delegation Office at Leiria, Leiria, Portugal
[3] INESC TEC, University of Trás-Os-Montes E Alto Douro,
Quinta de Prados, 5000-801 Vila Real, Portugal
jbarroso@utad.pt
[4] Instituto de Telecomunicações, Lisbon, Portugal

Abstract. The general increase in life expectancy and the consequent ageing of the general population impose major challenges to modern societies. Most elderly people experience the typical problems related to old age, such as chronic health problems, as well as sensory and cognitive impairments. In addition, in today's modern societies, where families have less and less time to look after their older relatives, the isolation of the elderly is a real concern and a highly recurrent problem, which is enhanced when they live alone. To solve, or at least minimize, these problems, a smart home monitoring system was developed, as presented and described in this paper. This solution is implemented based on a sensory network which detects anomalous behaviors, immediately triggering a warning to the caregiver or family.

A strong concern when developing a project of this kind is the physical security of the elderly. Houses tend to have hazardous objects and characteristics that may inflict serious injuries to their occupants or, in extrema, even death. As time goes by, the elderly start losing muscle mass and osteoporosis may appear, as well as vision and hearing impairments, which increase the likelihood of falling. Several other serious accidents may also occur, such as gas leaks, floods and fire outbreaks. Therefore, this population would strongly benefit from a solution which helps predict and even prevent accidents before they happen.

Keywords: Ambient assisted living · Internet of Things (IoT)
Anytime anywhere · Elderly · Security monitoring

© Springer International Publishing AG, part of Springer Nature 2018
M. Antona and C. Stephanidis (Eds.): UAHCI 2018, LNCS 10908, pp. 262–273, 2018.
https://doi.org/10.1007/978-3-319-92052-8_20

1   Introduction

The present paper was developed as a result of the previous ("Low Cost Smart Home for Elders") [1]. It focuses mainly on the topic of physical security of the elderly, from the monitoring to the warning system to the trustees, in the event of an incident or anomaly. Following a brief assessment of the framework of the Internet of Things (IoT- Internet of Things), a great revolution is expected in the way we live and act. In a few years, the IoT technologies will be present on a daily basis, meaning that even if people do not interact directly with this type of technology, they will have some sort of impact on their lives [2].

These technologies will be present in several areas of technology companies: health, industry, economics, among others. Highlighting the enormous potential that these technologies have, with a set of sensors and actuators, connected by the data networks computing systems, centralized and easy information access, it is possible to effectively manage and monitor the physical security of the elderly [3].

The use of the IoT technologies facilitates the monitoring of people, equipment and animals, allowing a thorough analysis of all data captured. When the user is connected to the sensors, the communication of vital signs, biometric information or the emergence of problems are diagnosed and transmitted in good time, enabling faster assistance, as well as a more efficient health and safety service [4].

As mentioned in the earlier paper, developed by this team (Low Cost Smart Home for Elders) [1], the number of elderly people is increasing at a great rate in many countries, particularly in Portugal [5] and this type of population has great propensity to suffer accidents, with the aggravating factor that a vast majority live alone, whether for cultural reasons, for family or other reasons [6]. Therefore, we urgently need to find strategies to combat or minimize this problem, ensuring improved care for the elderly, so that even those living on their own have access to technological mechanisms that guarantee safer living conditions [7].

In addition to all the problems associated with the isolation of the elderly, the reality is that not everyone has the financial ability to pay for the support of a professional at all times. Therefore, we can use technology to monitor the physical security of the elderly, providing other caregivers with a variety of informational tools that facilitate the contact with users and allow for quick action in case of emergency [8]. For this reason, the use of these technologies makes perfect sense, especially in countries where the aging trend is quite high, as in Portugal [5]. The team have focused efforts on developing a solution that would provide houses with cybernetic technology to monitor the elderly, while responding to other requirements [9].

We present some examples of the application of the IoT with regard to the physical safety of the elderly and demonstrate its feasibility. Ex.: with the system installed at home, an elderly person requiring strict medication adherence may be prompted, at certain times, to take the corresponding medication in order to eradicate the disease [9]. Another very useful feature is the detection of falling accidents which occur quite often among people of this age group. A sensor that detects sudden and anomalous movements by the elderly generates an immediate warning message to alert family or the caregiver. This way, it is possible to provide quick and efficient aid, as well as to avoid accidents with potentially serious consequences [10].

IoT technologies present two very important features for users of these technologies, though more directly related to the elderly: Wearable Technology and data generated by monitoring patients [11]. The Wearables have a key role in remote monitoring of the elderly, since it is through these that the communication link is established with the monitoring platforms. On the other hand, the data generated by monitoring the behavior of the elderly are a valuable and fundamental source of information, since it is by studying and manipulating it that algorithms (analytics – big data) are developed to better monitor these behaviors [12].

The rest of the paper is organized as follows: Sect. 2 presents some studies related to the assistive home systems. The general architecture of the proposed smart home for the elderly is described in Sect. 3. In Sect. 4, the implementation of a functional scaled model of a smart home for the elderly is presented. Also, in this section, the performance of the developed prototype is evaluated. Finally, in Sect. 5, the conclusions are drawn and some ideas for future work are presented.

2 Background

The work presented by Chan et al. [13] reviews how the elderly and disabled can be monitored with numerous intelligent devices. Their article presents an international selection of leading smart home projects, as well as the associated technologies of wearable/implantable monitoring systems and assistive robotics. The latter are often de-signed as components of the larger smart home environment.

Nait-Charif and McKenna [14] tracked the person using an ellipse and analyzed the resulting trajectory to detect inactivity outside the normal zones of inactivity like chairs or sofas. However, they both used a camera mounted on the ceiling and therefore did not have access to the vertical motion of the body, which provides useful information for fall detection.

Fall detection and prevention systems have been designed using either external sensors or wearable sensors. External sensors are deployed in the vicinity of the elderly person to be monitored, and wearable sensors are attached to him [15]. There have also been other approaches that use a combination of both types of sensors, known as hybrid systems. These types of systems will not be covered in this review. Camera-based sensors are perhaps the most common types of sensors used in external sensing. One or multiple cameras are placed in predefined fixed locations where the person of interest will perform his/her daily activity. The main drawback of these sensors is their inability to track the user out of the cameras' range of visibility. Another important factor related to external sensing is its high cost, as multiple sensors must be purchased to increase the system's coverage [15].

The work presented by Gaddam et al. [16] uses intelligent sensors with cognitive ability to implement a home monitoring system for elderly care application. These used sensors can detect the usage of electrical devices, bed usage patterns and flow of water. Besides that, the system also incorporates a panic button. The cognitive sensors provide information that can be used to monitor the elderly person's status by detecting any abnormal pattern in their daily home activities.

Lee and Mihailidis [17] detected falls by analyzing the silhouette and the 2-D velocity of the person, with special thresholds for inactivity zones, such as the bed.

The smart home for elderly care presented in [18], which is based on a wireless sensor network, demonstrates that ZigBee is well suited for smart homes and automation systems. ZigBee is a low cost, low power and low complexity wireless standard [19].

The studies presented above are significant in the area of the smart homes for the elderly and the concepts reported on those works are very useful and can be used as a base reference for the defining characteristics of lower cost solutions, as the one proposed and described in this paper.

3 System Architecture

In terms of architecture, the project relies mainly on sensor network, responsible for the readings according to the configured sensor type. Each sensor is connected to a microcontroller that is responsible for the communication of the data received from the respective sensor to the platform installed in the gateway.

All Communications between the sensor and microcontroller are direct and wired. All other communications are established using a wireless network or by low power Blue-tooth, ensuring the modularity. It should be noted that the protocol used for the transmission of data between the microcontroller and the platform is the MQTT (Message Queuing Telemetry Transport) [20].

The MQTT broker is installed and configured in the gateway and is responsible for sending the received messages on a given topic through the sensors to an aggregated platform, where the received data is processed. The managing platform can then act according to the situation, providing all the available data from sensor and actuator for consultation and management by the user.

The following image shows a generic architecture form of our solution. It shows the various components of the solution. We can still identify the various types of communications (Fig. 1).

With this type of architecture, we guarantee the implementation of modularity, where the great advantage is to be able to adapt this type of solution to most existing IoT projects in the market. In addition to that, it is easier to add new modules within the solution at any time. In most cases, each sensor will be added to a single microcontroller, for optimization and performance issues. However, there are cases where a microcontroller can aggregate more than one sensor, whenever the sensors work together, thus optimizing the structure of the solution.

The actuators are also aggregated to a microcontroller receiving the instructions of activity coming from the sensors. An actuator can receive instructions from one or more sensors, such as the LCD display (Liquid Crystal Display), which shows various types of information from different sensors.

All this data processing is performed at the gateway of the solution, a microcomputer Raspberry Pi3, responsible for the data processing, control and monitoring, thus ensuring a high level of safety to the solution, as well as a more streamlined system.

The following Fig. 2 shows how the sensors communicate with the actuators, giving a more precise notion of how the information flow is processed between the

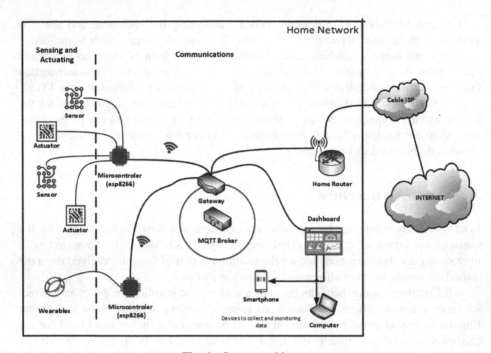

Fig. 1. System architecture

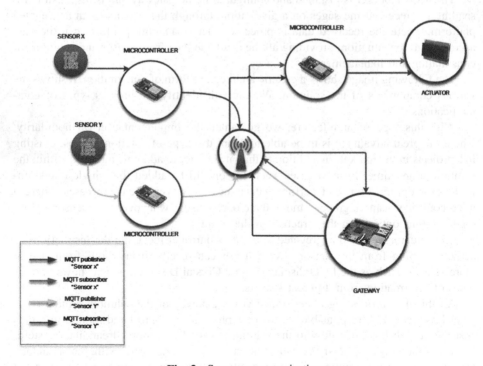

Fig. 2. Sensors communication

sensor and the respective actuator, and it also highlights the important role that microcontrollers play in this architecture.

The home automation and the assistive sensors send all the relevant information to the gateway to be managed and processed, as mentioned previously. When an abnormal situation occurs, the system detects it and activates the right support services. The presented solution is an integrated one that should be provided to elderly people who live all by themselves, since it gives them a better quality of life, with a real sense of security.

4 Implementation

This section presents and describes the development and implementation of a functional prototype in order to demonstrate the technical and economic feasibility of the proposed elderly assistive security system.

Figure 3 shows the devices of the implemented system by category,. which are essential for the implementation of this prototype. Some of the functionalities presented in Sect. 3 were implemented. All these sub systems are relevant to the wellbeing and sense of security of the elders.

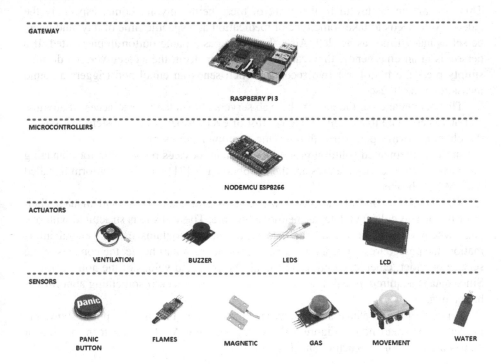

GATEWAY

RASPBERRY PI 3

MICROCONTROLLERS

NODEMCU ESP8266

ACTUATORS

VENTILATION   BUZZER   LEDS   LCD

SENSORS

PANIC   FLAMES   MAGNETIC   GAS   MOVEMENT   WATER
BUTTON

Fig. 3. Device category

The goal of the security module is to provide the house protection and security of the home occupants. For that, it incorporates several types of sensors and, consequently, several sub systems. To detect house floods, a water level monitor sub system, which is very useful in kitchens, bathrooms and laundries, was implemented. This sub system monitors the water level and when it reaches a given value, the solution activates an alarm and sends a warning to the web platform.

There is also another security and prevention module activated in the solution. If one or more taps of the bathroom are open and it doesn't detect movement of home users in that division, it sends an alarm message and turns off the tap that triggered the alarm. Another security feature is the fire detection sub system. The smart home uses a sensor that detects any kind of fire, triggering an alert and a warning to the platform. Another security subsystem is gas detection, as gas leaks tend to be very common causes of accidents nowadays. We use a sensor that detects any abnormal gas leak and then triggers an alarm, sending a warning message to the platform. The last security feature implemented in the prototype is the intrusion detection. Here, simple switches that simulate the magnetic doors and windows sensors were used. Every time each switch is activated, simulating an intrusion, the home control board (Raspberry Pi3 [21]) can get a small video of the place where the intrusion is taking place and send it to the platform along with the corresponding warning. The house alarm is also turned on.

In addition, the solution has a feature to remind the elderly to take their medicine. This system can be useful in the event of there being anyone home, especially the elderly, who needs to take some type of medication at a specific time of day, and it can be set as many times as needed. Also, the house has a panic button implemented. If a person is in an emergency, they can request support from their caregiver. To do this, simply press the button for two seconds, which sends an email and triggers a sound message in the house.

The maintenance of the data in the web servers allows the user to access it anytime and anywhere. The management and control of every aspect of the system features by the client is always performed through the communications module.

In the implemented solution prototype, the main devices responsible for managing the comfort and security features are the Raspberry Pi3 [21] with has platform installed with MQTT broker.

The website is one of the places where the clients can access and manage their information and collected data, as mentioned before. The website is structured with one page where you can access all the data. The website contains useful general information, the procedures for monitoring and controlling a smart home, the contacts of the service provider, emergency numbers and all the collected values of the home sensors. Since data is acquired in real time the client can always check if something abnormal is happening.

A photo of the implemented prototype is presented in Fig. 4. This photo shows the model of our smart home. Figure 5 shows the website. As it can be seen, the sensor values are available to each client (Fig. 6).

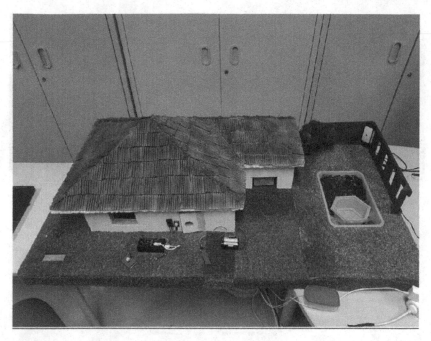

Fig. 4. Solution prototype

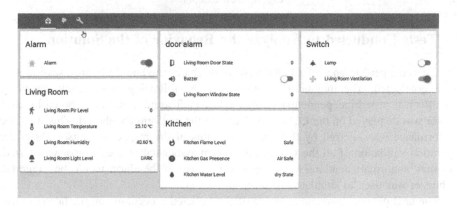

Fig. 5. Web frontend platform

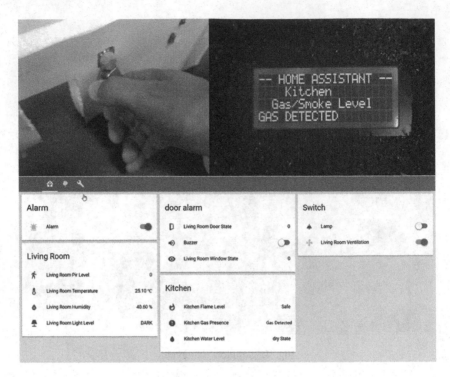

Fig. 6. Test example

5   Tests Conducted to Analyze the Behavior of the Solution

To assess the performance of all electronic parts (hardware and firmware), several tests were conducted. The methodology used was the following: First, each sensor or actuator was tested independently of all the others. The information gathered by each sensor was displayed on the LCD screen and on the platform dashboard. This way, the performance was inferred by the operating status of the respective sensor. After the operation validation of all the sensors, the alarm associated to each sensor was tested. For that, abnormal situations were imposed to verify if the alarm would be triggered. A buzzer was used to simulate the alarm operation.

The next picture shows an example of the inflicted procedures on the house sensor system to evaluate the abnormal situations, as wells as testing the corresponding alarm message warnings, either on LCD Display and on the platform dashboard.

After confirming the right operation for each sensor and respective alarm, the communication with the server was evaluated, confirming all alarm messages were shown both on LCD display and on the platform dashboard.

To test the "flood detection sub system", a cup of water was used. The sensor was submerged below the limit defined in the configuration script, forcing an abnormal value, which caused an alarm (buzzer sound). There was also a new notice on the LCD display and an update of the home status on the house platform (the message "FLOOD" was sent). To test the "prevent flood detection sub-system" a flowmeter was installed before the tap together with a motion sensor in the same room of the tap. If there is flow and nobody is in the room, the alarm is activated (buzzer sound), a new notice appears in the LCD display and there is an update of the home status on the house platform (the message "PREVENT FLOOD" is sent). To test the fire detection sub-system, a lighter was used, sparkling a flame inside the kitchen house mockup, which forced an abnormal value, simulating fire. This will cause an alarm (buzzer sound), a new notice on the LCD display and an update of the home status on the house platform (the word "FIRE" was sent). To test the gas detection sub-system, a lighter was used, releasing gas inside the kitchen house mockup, which forced an abnormal value, simulating a gas leak. This caused an alarm (buzzer sound), a new notice on the LCD display and an update of the home status on the house platform (the message "GAS DETECTED" was sent).

Finally, we set the alarm for the house and then opened a window with a magnetic sensor, which forced an abnormal value, simulating an intruder. This will create a new notice on the LCD display and an update of the home status on the house platform (changed the window state from 0 to 1).

6 Conclusion and Future Work

The paper proposes and describes a security monitoring system in low cost smart homes for the elderly, which integrates home automation systems with assistive ones in order to fulfill the needs of the elderly. It provides the elderly who live alone in their home with the security they require and, simultaneously, a sense of tranquility to their family. The proposed system architecture allows the users to control all the home features anytime and anywhere, by using the system app on any mobile device or through the system online platform. The elderly's relatives (family members responsible for the elderly) are always informed of their health and status situation by receiving an alarm when an abnormal situation occurs.

An operational scaled model is also presented and described in the paper in order to demonstrate the feasibility of the solution. Many of the proposed functionalities were implemented in the mockup house. The scaled model uses a Raspberry Pi3 as the gateway to control all the deployed sensors, to acquire all the sensors' data and to send it to the system cloud servers. On the other hand, we used ESP-8266 [22] microcontroller to send the sensor's data wirelessly to the gateway. Several functional tests that replicate daily situations were performed to assess the system. The results obtained show that the proposed solution is functional.

One major improvement since the last low cost smart home project [1] was the inclusion of wireless communication between the microcontrollers and the gateway, improving the system's flexibility and functionality. All the cabled parts of the infrastructure were replaced by the wireless microcontroller ESP-8266 [22] connected to the sensors. Another major feature added was the implementation of an ambient assisted living, capable of detecting abnormal or unusual s behavior patterns and health problems in the elderly, generating warnings or alarms to the care givers and the elderly's relatives. The ambient assisted living will be based on the behavior analysis algorithms that have the ability to process all the data collected from each sensor (deployed in the home and wearable).

Acknowledgments. This work was supported by Project "NIE – Natural Interfaces for the Elderly/ NORTE-01-0145-FEDER-024048" financed by the Foundation for the Science and Technology (FCT) and through the European Regional Development Fund (ERDF).

References

1. Ferreira, G., Penicheiro, P., Bernardo, R., Mendes, L., Barroso, J., Pereira, A.: Low cost smart homes for elders. In: Antona, M., Stephanidis, C. (eds.) UAHCI 2017. LNCS, vol. 10279, pp. 507–517. Springer, Cham (2017). https://doi.org/10.1007/978-3-319-58700-4_41
2. Brown, I., et al.: The Societal Impact of the Internet of Things, BCS, p. 14 (2013)
3. Romano, B.: Managing the Internet of Things. In: Proceedings of the 2017 ACM SIGCSE Technical Symposium on Computer Science Education - SIGCSE 2017, pp. 777–778 (2017)
4. Hassanalieragh, M., et al.: Health monitoring and management using Internet-of-Things (IoT) sensing with cloud-based processing: opportunities and challenges. In: Proceedings - 2015 IEEE International Conference on Services Computing, SCC 2015, pp. 285–292 (2015)
5. Resende Oliveira, C.: Research on aging in Portugal. Exp. Gerontol. **36**(10), 1599–1607 (2001)
6. Spensley, C.: The Role of social isolation of elders in recidivism of self-neglect cases at San Francisco adult protective services. J. Elder Abuse Negl. **20**(1), 43–61 (2008)
7. Mano, L.Y., et al.: Exploiting IoT technologies for enhancing health smart homes through patient identification and emotion recognition. Comput. Commun. **89–90**, 178–190 (2016)
8. Stankovic, J.A., et al.: Wireless sensor networks for in-home healthcare: potential and challenges. In: High confidence medical device software and systems workshop, pp. 7–10 (2005)
9. Ukil, A., Bandyoapdhyay, S., Puri, C., Pal, A.: IoT healthcare analytics: the importance of anomaly detection. In: Proceedings - International Conference on Advanced Information Networking and Applications, AINA, vol. 2016, pp. 994–997, May 2016
10. Greene, S., Thapliyal, H., Carpenter, D.: IoT-based fall detection for smart home environments. In: Proceedings of the 2016 IEEE International Symposium Nanoelectronic and Information Systems, pp. 23–28 (2016)
11. Lara, O.D., Labrador, M.A.: A survey on human activity recognition using wearable sensors. IEEE Commun. Surv. Tutor. **15**(3), 1192–1209 (2013)
12. Sheriff, C.I., Naqishbandi, T., Geetha, A.: Healthcare informatics and analytics framework. In: 2015 International Conference on Computer Communication and Informatics, ICCCI 2015 (2015)
13. Chan, M., Estève, D., Escriba, C., Campo, E.: A review of smart homes- present state and future challenges. Comput. Methods Programs Biomed. **91**(1), 55–81 (2008)
14. Nait-Charif, H., McKenna, S.: Activity summarization and fall detection in a supportive home environment. In: IEEE International Conference on Pattern Recognition, pp. 20–23 (2004)
15. Yu, X.: Approaches and principles of fall detection for elderly and patient. In: 2008 10th IEEE International Conference on e-Health Networking, Applications and Service, HEALTHCOM 2008, pp. 42–47 (2008)

16. Gaddam, A., Mukhopadhyay, S.C., Sen Gupta, G.: Elder care based on cognitive sensor network. IEEE Sens. J. **11**(3), 574–581 (2011)
17. Lee, T., Mihailidis, A.: An intelligent emergency response system: preliminary development and testing of automated fall detection. J. Telemed. Telecare **11**(4), 194–198 (2005)
18. Ransing, R.S., Rajput, M.: Smart home for elderly care, based on wireless sensor network. In: 2015 International Conference on Nascent Technologies in the Engineering Field, pp. 1–5 (2015)
19. Zigbee. http://www.zigbee.org/. Accessed 05 Feb 2018
20. MQTT Protocol. http://mqtt.org/. Accessed 10 Feb 2018
21. Raspberry Pi3. https://www.raspberrypi.org/products/raspberry-pi-3-model-b/. Accessed 05 Feb 2018
22. ESP8266. https://www.espressif.com/en/products/hardware/esp8266ex/overview. Accessed 10 Feb 2018

Understanding the Questions Asked by Care Staff While Eliciting Life Stories from Older Adults for AAC System Design

Haruka Kanetsuku[1][✉], Tetsuya Hirotomi[1], and Sachiko Hara[2]

[1] Interdisciplinary Graduate School of Science and Engineering,
Shimane University, Matsue, Shimane, Japan
s179801@matsu.shimane-u.ac.jp, hirotomi@cis.shimane-u.ac.jp
[2] Faculty of Medicine, Shimane University, Izumo, Shimane, Japan
hara@med.shimane-u.ac.jp

Abstract. Several augmentative and alternative communication (AAC) systems have been developed to present multimedia content to support the storytelling of older adults. To develop these systems, the AAC system designer requires information regarding the interaction of conversations in the field. Designing such systems requires careful consideration of not only the provision of content as stimulus for older adults but also the support for interlocutors to ask effective questions within the frequent sequential patterns. However, the efficacy of questions asked by interlocutors while presenting content has not been a major focus of research. This paper presents an analysis of peer conversations between geriatric health service facility residents with neurocognitive disorders and their care staff, while photographs are being shown on a touchscreen. As a result, we determined the questions and patterns that are effective in eliciting storytelling. These insights may be used to enhance the design of AAC systems for storytelling.

Keywords: Life story · Design for aging
Augmentative and alternative communication

1   Introduction

Augmentative and alternative communication (AAC) systems are tools to overcome communicative challenges, involving those pertaining to storytelling. Several AAC systems have been developed to present multimedia content. To develop these systems, the AAC system designer requires information regarding the in situ interactions within AAC-mediated collaborative and co-constructive activities of augmented speakers and their interlocutors. However, the efficacy of questions asked by interlocutors while presenting content such as photographs, movies, and songs as a stimulus to augment storytelling by older adults has

© Springer International Publishing AG, part of Springer Nature 2018
M. Antona and C. Stephanidis (Eds.): UAHCI 2018, LNCS 10908, pp. 274–284, 2018.
https://doi.org/10.1007/978-3-319-92052-8_21

not been a major research focus. This paper presents the findings of an analysis of peer conversations between geriatric health service facility residents with neurocognitive disorders and their care staff while showing photographs on a touchscreen.

The objectives of this research were, specifically,

1. to test the relationships between the presence or absence of specific types of questions, and their corresponding success or failure in eliciting life stories, and
2. to mine frequent sequential patterns of care staff utterances, including the specific types of questions in cases considered successful.

To accomplish these aims, we applied the chi-squared test and the cSPADE algorithm in R to conversation data.

The remaining paper is organized as follows: The subsequent section details related work. In Sect. 3, a brief overview of the conducted experiment and analysis is presented. Sections 4 and 5 provide the results and their discussion, and Sect. 6 concludes the main findings of this study.

2 Related Work

Regarding conversations with older adults, there are several studies investigating the effect of presenting content that serves as a clue to storytelling. Fried-Oken et al. reported that AAC was associated with greater use of targeted words during personal conversations [4]. Bourgeois et al. reported that using a memory book consisting of autobiographical, daily schedule-related, and problem resolution information improved the duration of speaking time of older adults [3]. These studies suggested that more detailed or a larger number of life stories can be obtained by presenting content that serves as a pointer for the conversation.

There are some studies that support storytelling using information and communications technology (ICT) owing to its advantages such as easy presentation of multimedia content. Alm et al. developed a system that could present content on a touchscreen and reported that the system proved remarkably effective in restoring a degree of equality in communication with a person with neurocognitive disorder [1]. Webster and Hanson developed a system for care staff to obtain information regarding older adults [8]. The contributions of their research include the identification of factors important in working with a care staff population, introduction and evaluation of a software tool for care staff in residential homes, and emphasis on the potential benefits of technology in assisting care staff. However, these studies did not consider how the care staff interacted with older adults.

Storytelling has been examined from many different perspectives. Nishida et al. conducted questionnaires for caregivers and reported that their communication skills can be explained based on three factors: consideration to receptive conversation, consideration to speech, and strong patience [6]. Stuart examined the storytelling patterns of older adults in order to understand the complexities of this type of communication [7]. Thereby, he reported that repetition of the same story includes three patterns or categories: construction of the repeated story, order of the stories told in repetition, and stories that were repeated with added "update" information. Our research is distinguished by the fact that its focus is on the questions asked by care staff during a conversation.

3   Method

All participants were treated according to a protocol approved by the Shimane University Institutional Committee on Ethics, and informed consent was obtained from each participants.

3.1   Participants

Four residents between the ages of 78 and 88 with neurocognitive disorders and six care staff from a geriatric health service facility participated in this study. In this study, we use "neurocognitive disorders" instead of "dementia" in consonance with DSM-5 [2]. The average score of the mini mental state examination undertaken by the residents was 17.75 (SD = 5.44). A communication peer was selected for each resident based on the staff member's assignment as a care giver. This pairing is henceforth termed a dyad. Their conversations were in their native language (Japanese).

3.2   Equipment

A technology probe is an instrument with limited functionality that is deployed to explore unknown information and expected to obtain useful or interesting data [5]. Figure 1 shows screenshots of our probe, which is capable of browsing thumbnails of photographs, showing a selected photograph in a larger size, logging interactions, and recording speech. For this study, 190 common photographs and 46 personal photographs were installed.

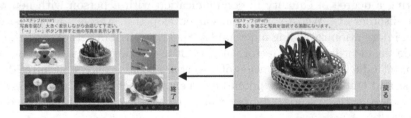

Fig. 1. Screenshots of our technology probe

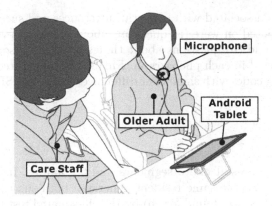

Fig. 2. Experimental apparatus

3.3   Data Collection

Each dyad used our probe and engaged in approximately 5 min of unstructured conversation two times a week over a period of four weeks. During these conversations, each dyad sat shoulder-to-shoulder to share a touchscreen, as shown in Fig. 2. On some data collection days, the residents' cognitive conditions were not sufficient to recognize photographs. Consequently, we collected audio recordings of a total of 27 conversations. By using the data logged by our probe, we extracted 121 photo segments from the transcribed audio recordings concerning the enlarged photographs and utterances.

3.4   Analyzing Transcripts

First, we classified each photo segment indicating whether residents did (success) or did not (failure) tell their life stories. Second, we coded each sentence from both the staff and the residents using emergent coding. The final coding scheme contained 30 codes. Table 1 shows a part of the codes. Third, using the chi-squared test, we examined the relationships between the presence/absence of

Table 1. A part of the 30 codes

Code	Description
(a)	Questions about things or events depicted in each photograph
(b)	Questions about things or events associated with, but not directly depicted in each photograph
(c)	An in-depth question about each resident's utterances
(d)	A repetition or recapitulation of each resident's utterances
(e)	An utterance expressing what the care staff member thought or felt
(f)	An utterance expressing the words that the resident found difficult to say

two specific codes associated with care staff utterances and success/failure. The codes that we focused on were (a) questions about things or events depicted in each photograph and (b) questions about things or events associated with, but not directly depicted in each photograph. Finally, we mined frequent sequential patterns including codes with significant differences using the cSPADE algorithm in R [9].

4   Results

We obtained 66 successful photo segments and 55 failures. In some cases, the same photograph and the same resident generated both success and failure. A significant interaction was found for (b) by the chi-squared test ($\chi^2(1) = 25.548$, $p < 0.01$), but not for (a) ($p > 0.05$). Life stories were more likely to be elicited with (b) (67%) than without (b) (14%). The top 21 sequential patterns with a length of 2 items or more are listed in Table 2. After removing the sequential patterns of a single itemset and patterns with support less than 0.4, there were 37 patterns of successful elicitation containing (b). These patterns began with (a), (c) and/or (d); and progressed to (b); followed by (b), (c), (d), (e) and/or (f); where (c) represents an in-depth question about each resident's utterances, (d) represents a repetition or recapitulation of each resident's utterances, (e) represents an utterance expressing what the care staff member thought or felt, and (f) represents an utterance expressing the words that the resident found difficult to say.

Table 2. Top 21 sequential patterns with a length of 2 items or more

Rank	Sequence	Support	Rank	Sequence	Support
1	<b, b>	0.823	11	<b, b, c>	0.516
2	<a, b>	0.806	11	<b, e>	0.516
3	<b, c>	0.694	13	<b, c, b>	0.500
4	<a, b, b>	0.645	14	<b, c, c>	0.484
5	<d, b>	0.629	14	<d, b, b>	0.484
6	<c, b>	0.613	14	<b, b, f>	0.484
6	<b, b, b>	0.613	17	<f, b>	0.468
6	<b, f>	0.613	17	<c, b, b>	0.468
9	<a, b, c>	0.581	17	<a, c, b>	0.468
10	<b, d>	0.532	17	<a, b, b, b>	0.468
			17	<a, d, b>	0.468

5   Discussion

5.1   Results of the Chi-Squared Test

The results suggest that (b) may be effective to elicit life stories. Figure 3 shows the transcript of the conversation between Resident A and Care Staff B and the photograph presented during the conversation (in this paper, we present the drawings made from tracing photographs for ensuring the participants' privacy). The black-and-white photograph shows Resident A and his teammates wearing baseball uniforms. The "*" in the transcripts represent utterances coded with one of the 30 codes in the final coding scheme other than (a) to (f), the focus of this study. Question (b) includes the keyword "company" which is not directly depicted in the photograph. Using question (b), Care Staff B elicited life stories from Resident A, including stories about a team from his area of the city, Yotsugane.

Code	Speaker	Utterance	Photograph
(a)	Care Staff B:	What's this picture?	
*	Resident A:	It's … it's a picture of baseball.	
*		It's from a city tournament.	
(b)	Care Staff B:	Was it your company's team?	
*	Resident A:	Company … not a company team.	
*		A team from my area of the city.	
(d)	Care Staff B:	Ahh, a team from your area of the city.	
(c)		Which area?	
*	Resident A:	The area is Yotsugane.	
(d)	Care Staff B:	So the Yotsugane team, right?	
*	Resident A:	Yes, yes.	
(a)	Care Staff B:	Which one is you?	
*	Resident A:	This one.	
(e)	Care Staff B:	You were young.	
*	Resident A:	Yeah, that's right.	

Fig. 3. Baseball photograph and transcript between Care Staff B and Resident A

Figure 4 shows another transcript of a conversation between Resident A and Care Staff C, where A was presented with the same photograph. Using question (b) and the keyword "position," A's life stories were elicited, including his position as a shortstop and his effort to really stop the balls. Even with the same photograph, other life stories were drawn out by changing the keywords used in the question.

In contrast, a conversation without question (b) and a different presented photograph are shown in Fig. 5. This color photograph shows the military shogi box and some of the pieces. Shogi is a board game similar to chess. Military shogi is similar to Stratego, with pieces representing individual officer ranks (e.g., captain) and things associated with an army (e.g., a spy and a land mine).

Code	Speaker	Utterance	Photograph
(a)	Care Staff C:	So, what's this picture?	
*	Resident A:	What's this? ... Ah, it's a baseball game.	
(d)	Care Staff C:	Yeah. It's a baseball game.	
(a)		Are you in this picture?	
*	Resident A:	I think I am.	
(b)	Care Staff C:	Is this your team?	
*	Resident A:	No. There is also an umpire.	
*		Participating.	
(b)	Care Staff C:	What position were you?	
*	Resident A:	Short. My baseball job.	
(d)	Care Staff C:	Short?	
*	Resident A:	Yeah.	
(c)	Care Staff C:	Where is short in the field? I don't know.	
*	Resident A:	Third base and second base's, short ...	
(f)	Care Staff C:	In the space between (second and third)?	
*	Resident A:	Between.	
*	Care Staff C:	Oh, uh-huh.	
(c)		Do many balls fly there?	
*	Resident A:	No, not so many.	
(d)	Care Staff C:	Not so many. Hmmm.	
*	Resident A:	But I really worked to stop the balls. Hmmm.	

Fig. 4. Baseball photograph and transcript between Care Staff C and Resident A

Code	Speaker	Utterance	Photograph
(a)	Care Staff B:	What's this? Have you ever seen this before?	Military Shogi game with bonus playing
*	Resident A:	Oh ... pieces for shogi. Pieces for shogi?	
(d)	Care Staff B:	Shogi.	
*		Captain is written (on that piece).	
*	Resident A:	Uh-huh. Captain.	
*	Care Staff B:	There are Captain and other ranks.	
(a)		What are these pieces?	
*	Resident A:	What are they? Those words (the ranks) ... are used (on the pieces).	
*	Care Staff B:	It says "a military shogi game with bonus playing pieces." I've never seen a military shogi game before.	
*	Resident A:	Me, too.	

Fig. 5. Military shogi box photograph and transcript between Care Staff B and Resident A

Only the "captain" or "a military shogi game with bonus playing pieces" that are directly depicted in the photograph were mentioned in the questions. In this conversation, questions by Care Staff B did not draw out a life story from Resident A.

Whether or not the residents tell their life stories is influenced by the questions asked by the care staff. Photographs that elicited life stories were again shown to participants on other data collection days. Although they were engaged in similar conversations, the care staff's questions about things or events associated with, but not directly depicted in each photograph were able to draw out new and in-depth information.

5.2 Results of Mined Frequent Sequential Patterns

We determined that there were patterns that began with (a), (c) and/or (d), which progressed to (b), followed by, (b), (c), (d), (e) and/or (f) in successful photo segments. Figure 6 shows the transcript of a conversation following this pattern and the photograph presented during the conversation. In this photograph, Resident A is shown with a "Merry Tiller" and a Merry Tiller sign. Behind Resident A, we can see part of the company's sign. "Merry Tillers" were rotary tillers and cultivators that were manually pushed. They were sold by Yokoyama Agricultural Machinery Company.

First, Care Staff D asked question (a) to confirm whether Resident A can recognize the place where the photograph was taken. Care Staff D mentioned the company name in utterance (f) to invoke Resident A's memory. Next, Care Staff D explored the life stories of A by question (b) which included "Yunbara" (the address of the dealer), "work" and "fix." Then, D asked question (c), drew out A's life stories, repeated A's utterance (d), and drew out A's life stories. As a result, A's life story was elicited: A's job was to fix cultivators. Finally, D repeated A's utterance (d) a few times.

The pattern of care staff's questions confirms the cognitive ability of the residents, explores their life stories, and focuses on specific topics.

5.3 AAC System Design

Through conversation data analysis, we were able to identify questions that are effective in eliciting life stories and patterns for the questions. The system that supports storytelling should add functions not only for older adults but also to support questions from the care staff. For example, we propose a function to present keywords related to photographs extracted from the conversation data of other days. With this function, we expect that the care staff will ask questions (b) including keywords about things or events associated with, but not directly depicted in each photograph. The keywords, such as the names of the things or events directly depicted in the photograph, will also support questions (a).

Figure 7 shows a possible implementation of this function. This screenshot shows the photograph and keywords can be extracted from transcripts of conversations with the figure on the other days. In this example, "Merry Tiller,"

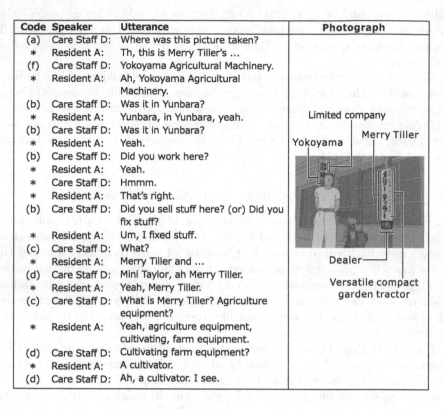

Code	Speaker	Utterance	Photograph
(a)	Care Staff D:	Where was this picture taken?	
*	Resident A:	Th, this is Merry Tiller's ...	
(f)	Care Staff D:	Yokoyama Agricultural Machinery.	
*	Resident A:	Ah, Yokoyama Agricultural Machinery.	
(b)	Care Staff D:	Was it in Yunbara?	
*	Resident A:	Yunbara, in Yunbara, yeah.	
(b)	Care Staff D:	Was it in Yunbara?	
*	Resident A:	Yeah.	
(b)	Care Staff D:	Did you work here?	
*	Resident A:	Yeah.	
*	Care Staff D:	Hmmm.	
*	Resident A:	That's right.	
(b)	Care Staff D:	Did you sell stuff here? (or) Did you fix stuff?	
*	Resident A:	Um, I fixed stuff.	
(c)	Care Staff D:	What?	
*	Resident A:	Merry Tiller and ...	
(d)	Care Staff D:	Mini Taylor, ah Merry Tiller.	
*	Resident A:	Yeah, Merry Tiller.	
(c)	Care Staff D:	What is Merry Tiller? Agriculture equipment?	
*	Resident A:	Yeah, agriculture equipment, cultivating, farm equipment.	
(d)	Care Staff D:	Cultivating farm equipment?	
*	Resident A:	A cultivator.	
(d)	Care Staff D:	Ah, a cultivator. I see.	

Fig. 6. Merry Tiller photograph and transcript between Care Staff D and Resident A

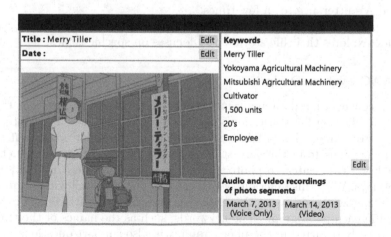

Fig. 7. Possible implementation for showing a photograph and keywords associated with it

"Yokoyama Agricultural Machinery," and "Cultivator" are extracted from the transcript in Fig. 6. Some of these keywords can be reused by the care staff to elicit life stories from the older adults.

5.4 Limitations

In neurocognitive disorder care, life story work is also conducted in groups. Our analysis focused on peer conversation. Therefore, care staff may use different types of questions and sequential patterns to elicit and share life stories in such cases.

6 Conclusion

We analyzed peer conversations between geriatric health service facility residents with neurocognitive disorders and their care staff while showing photographs on a touchscreen. We examined the relationships between the presence or absence of specific types of questions and success or failure in eliciting life stories. As a result, we found that it is important for care staff questions to include things or events associated with, but not directly depicted in each photograph. Furthermore, we extracted frequent sequential patterns including these questions in combination with confirmation, in-depth question, etc.

These insights may be used to enhance the design of AAC systems for storytelling. Designing such systems requires careful consideration of not only the provision of content as a stimulus for older adults but also the support for interlocutors to ask effective questions within the frequent sequential patterns. Functions to provide clues for asking questions should be incorporated to explore possible life stories, and focus should be placed on specific topics while showing the content. Future research is necessary to analyze group conversations and develop AAC systems with these functions.

References

1. Alm, N., Dye, R., Astell, A., Ellis, M., Gowans, G., Campbell, J.: Making software accessible for users with dementia. In: Lazar, J. (ed.) Universal Usability: Designing Computer Interfaces for Diverse User Populations, Chap. 10, pp. 299–316. Wiley, Chichester (2007)
2. American Psychiatric Association: Desk Reference to the Diagnostic Criteria From DSM-5. American Psychiatric Pub. (2014)
3. Bourgeois, M., Dijkstra, K., Burgio, L., Allen-Burge, R.: Memory aids as an augmentative and alternative communication strategy for nursing home residents with dementia. Augment. Altern. Commun. 17(3), 196–210 (2001). https://doi.org/10.1080/aac.17.3.196.210
4. Fried-Oken, M., Rowland, C., Daniels, D., Dixon, M., Fuller, B., Mills, C., Noethe, G., Small, J., Still, K., Oken, B.: AAC to support conversation in persons with moderate Alzheimer's disease. Augment. Altern. Commun. 28(4), 219–231 (2012). https://doi.org/10.3109/07434618.2012.732610

5. Hutchinson, H., Mackay, W.E., Westerlund, B., Bederson, B.B., Druin, A., Plaisant, C., Beaudouin-Lafon, M., Conversy, S., Evans, H., Hansen, H., Roussel, N., Eiderbäck, B., Lindquist, S., Sundblad, Y.: Technology probes: inspiring design for and with families. In: Proceedings of the SIGCHI Conference on Human Factors in Computing Systems - CHI 2003, vol. 5, no. 1, pp. 17–24 (2003). https://doi.org/10.1145/642611.642616

6. Nishida, K., Yamada, K.: Communication skills of family care givers vis-a-vis elderly and related factors. Japan. J. Geriatr. Psychiatr. **18**, 531–539 (2007)

7. Stuart, S.: Understanding the storytelling of older adults for AAC system design. Augment. Altern. Commun. **16**(1), 1–12 (2000). https://doi.org/10.1080/07434610012331278864

8. Webster, G., Hanson, V.L.: Technology for supporting care staff in residential homes. ACM Trans. Access. Comput. **5**(3), 8:1–8:23 (2014). https://doi.org/10.1145/2543577

9. Zaki, M.J.: SPADE: an efficient algorithm for mining frequent sequences. Mach. Learn. **42**(1–2), 31–60 (2001). https://doi.org/10.1023/A:1007652502315

Analysis of Electrogastrograms During Exercise Loads

Fumiya Kinoshita[1($\boxtimes$)], Kosuke Fujita[1], Kazuya Miyanaga[1],
Hideaki Touyama[1], Masumi Takada[2], and Hiroki Takada[3]

[1] Toyama Prefectural University, 5180 Kurokawa, Imizu-shi,
Toyama 939-0398, Japan
f.kinoshita@pu-toyama.ac.jp
[2] Chubu Gakuin University, 2-1 Kirigaoka, Seki-shi, Gifu 501-3993, Japan
[3] University of Fukui, 3-9-1 Bunkyo, Fukui Fukui 910-8507, Japan

Abstract. A percutaneous electrogastrogram (EGG) is a simple and low-restraint way to measure the electrical activity of the gastrointestinal tract. An electrogastrogram examination is a noninvasive method of evaluating gastrointestinal motility and autonomic nervous system activity. However, EGGs are not as widely used in clinical settings as electrocardiograms (ECGs) or electroencephalographs (EEGs) because an EGG can be impacted by electrical activity from the myocardium and diaphragm (due to respiration), and there is no method to relate the functions of the stomach to the data obtained. This paper examines the effect of exercise on gastric electrical activity using two exercise intensities to confirm the basic biological response of an EGG. It was found that after high-intensity exercising the spectrum density at the normal frequency band of the stomach (2.4–3.7 cpm) decreased, which may indicate a decline in gastric activity during exercise. Exercise intensity is thought to affect the electrical activity of not only the gastrointestinal tract but also other organs.

Keywords: Electrogastrogram (EGG) · Electrocardiograms (ECG)
Autonomic nervous system · Exercise intensity

1 Introduction

The intestines, which are referred to as "the second brain," are part of the digestive tract, and are linked to the brain through the autonomous nervous system and intercellular messages, such as hormones and cytokine [1]. Abdominal pain, diarrhea, constipation and other digestive issues caused by stress are a result of disrupted balance of the autonomic nerves. The intestines not only digest food but also immunize the body, and are linked to cancer and diabetes [2]. In addition, a part of the intestines produces a precursor of serotonin, which not only maintains a person's overall physical health but also helps stabilize the heart [3]. Therefore, maintaining healthy intestines contributes to mental and physical health. Recently, intestinal floral boom has attracted interest in the fields of intestinal environment and health. In the intestines, probiotic bacteria, pathogenic bacteria, and opportunistic bacteria coexist and protect the intestinal environment. To regulate the intestinal environment, people must eat

M. Antona and C. Stephanidis (Eds.): UAHCI 2018, LNCS 10908, pp. 285–294, 2018.
https://doi.org/10.1007/978-3-319-92052-8_22

carefully, exercise, and rest. Exercise promotes circulation and keeps the autonomous nervous system healthy. Maintaining the autonomous nerves in this way can encouraging peristaltic movement of the intestines [4, 5]. Excessive exercise, however, results in sympathetic nerve dominance, which suppresses digestive tract functions. Therefore, it is important to use appropriate exercise intensity.

The percutaneous electrogastrogram (EGG), which can perform noninvasive, low-restraint measurements of the electric activity that controls gastrointestinal motility, is one way to examine the motor functions of gastrointestinal disorders [6, 7]. Regular electrical activity, such as that of the heart, is also observed in the stomach and intestines, where repeated depolarization and repolarization occur. The pacemaker of gastric electrical activity exists in the upper one-third section of the abdomen, where it transmits electrical waves to the pyloric region at a rate of 3 cycles per minute (cpm). This pacemaker is controlled by parasympathetic nervous system activity; however, the cyclic electrical activity occurs spontaneously, and is stimulated by a network of islands called "interstitial cells of Cajal" (ICCs) [8–11]. Peristaltic movement does not occur when electrical signals are emitted from the ICCs. However, when the contraction threshold is exceeded during depolarization, an action potential is produced that causes peristaltic movement. This electrical activity is divided into two parts: electrical response activity (ERA), which is accompanied by a peristaltic movement; and electrical control activity (ECA), which is not accompanied by the peristaltic movement [12]. Because an EGG cannot distinguish these, it cannot directly measure peristaltic movements [13]. However, it is thought that EGGs are linked to gastric electrical activity [14], and that it is possible to discover abnormal peristaltic movement using a response confirmation test. This study examines the impact of exercise intensity on gastric electrical activity by a participant undergoing an EGG during exercising.

2   Experimental Method

The experiment participants were 19 young men aged 22–27 (average $\pm$ standard deviation: 22.8 $\pm$ 1.4) years, who had no history of digestive disorders or symptoms. The experiment was fully explained to the subjects prior to the experiment, and they agreed to participate after reading a document describing the purpose and significance of the study, as well as the policies outlining the protection of their privacy, handling of data, and guarantee of interruption. The electronic data obtained during the experiment was recorded under conditions of untraceable anonymity, and approval for the experiment (H2017002) was granted by the ethics committee of the Graduate School of Engineering, University of Fukui.

EGGs and electrocardiograms (ECGs) were performed between 60 min of rest in a supine position before and after the exercise. The participants ran at a velocity of 10 km/h (high-intensity exercise) and walked at 5 km/h (intermediate-intensity exercise) for 15 min each on a treadmill (DK-822E, DAIKOU). A control experiment was conducted by having the participants stand still for 15 min (low-intensity exercise). The MET scores of the exercises were approximately 9–10, 3–4, and 1.0–1.5 (which is within the range of everyday exercise) for the high-intensity, intermediate-intensity [15], and low-intensity exercises, respectively. Each measurement was taken on a different day, and on each day, the patient sequence was randomized to reduce the effect of ordering.

The EGGs were obtained using an ECG disposal electrode (Blue Sensor, Mets Inc.), as shown in Fig. 1. In this study, the EGG electrode was affixed to two places near the stomach pacemaker (ch 1) and the pyloric part (ch 2). In addition, the ECGs that were recorded simultaneously with the EGGs were recorded by II induction. The electrode was attached to the skin after ethanol was used to disinfect and lower skin resistance. The EGG was recorded using bipolar leads, amplification was performed using a biological amplifier (Biotop mini, East Medic Co., Ltd.), and data were recorded on a PC with an analog input card (ADA16-32/2(CB)F, CONTEC). The following settings were used for the biological amplifier: sensitivity = 100 μV, low frequency cut-off filter = 0.02 Hz, and high-frequency cut-off filter = 0.5 Hz. Participants were asked to eat 400 kcal of portable food (Calorie-Mate, Otsuka Pharmaceutical Co., Ltd.) two hours before the start of the experiment, but nothing afterwards in order to equalize the time food had remained in the stomachs of all the subjects.

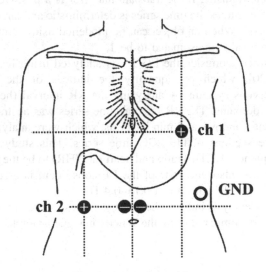

Fig. 1. Electrode position.

3   Analytical Method

The EGGs and ECGs that were recorded were A/D converted at 1 kHz to obtain timeseries data. A bandpass filter with cut-off frequencies 0.015–0.15 Hz was applied to the data that had been obtained to remove mixed electromyograms (EMGs) and electrical noise due to the EGG time series equipment. The 1-kHz EGG time series was resampled at 10 Hz because the normal cycle of an EGG is relatively slow (about 3 cpm). In this study, the time series was analyzed using running spectrum analysis.

The EGG time series were moved and the 8,192-point time windows (roughly 13 min) were divided into intervals of 3000 points (5 min) before each was analyzed. The analyzed sections were recorded (as explained below) with the start times representing the analyzed sections.

Frequency analysis was carried out by performing a Fourier conversion on each time series section, focusing on bradygastria (1.1–2.4 cpm), reference frequency band (2.4–3.7 cpm), and tachygastria (3.7–5.0 cpm) [18]. The power spectral density (PSD) in these frequency bands was also calculated using 6.0–8.0 cpm, because a study showed that a fluctuation of approximately 7 cpm in an EGG reflects the electrical activity of the colon [19].

The EGG time series sections were also analyzed using a statistically estimated translational error based on a Wayland algorithm [16, 17]. Here, the translational error (Etrans) estimated based on the Wayland algorithm is an index that quantitively evaluates the smoothness of the course of the attractor buried in the phase space. If the trajectory of the attractor reconstituted in the embedded space is smooth, it is said that the time series is deterministic. If the translational error is a positive, near-zero value, and the model that constitutes the time series is deterministic and large, the error can be viewed as probabilistic. When an object can be modelled using Brownian movement, the translational error value is estimated to be 1.

The ECG measured alongside the EGG was analyzed using heart rate variability (HRV) analysis [20], which can quantify the indices of the sympathetic and parasympathetic nervous systems by analyzing the RR interval (heart rate) from the time and frequency domains. The RR interval time series was abstracted, moved, and divided into 512 time windows at 5 min intervals, which were analyzed such that they corresponded to the sections of the EGG time series. This study assumed the low frequency/high frequency (LF/HF) ratio and heart rate (HR) to be the activity indices of the sympathetic nerves; also, the PSD of the LF constituent is assumed to be 0.04–0.15 Hz, and that of the HF constituent 0.15–0.4 Hz.

For the calculated analysis indices, the average values recorded for each time before and after exercise were compared using the Wilcoxon signed-rank test (at a significance level of 0.05).

4   Results

Figure 2 shows the EGG waves corresponding to 10–15 min after the start of measurement for each exercise. From the visual observation in ch 2, compared to that in ch 1, the effect of the fine waves derived from the intestinal tract is large. The EGG waves after a low-intensity exercise show a large period of approximately 3 cpm. However, in the EGG wave, after a high-intensity exercise, the amplitude decreased from that of the pre-exercise level and its period approximately 3 cpm also reduced in scale.

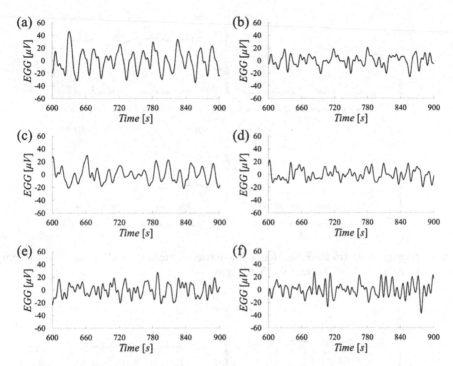

Fig. 2. Typical EGGs for one participant after (a) a low-intensity exercise at ch 1, (b) a low-intensity exercise at ch 2, (c) an intermediate-intensity exercise at ch 1, (d) an intermediate-intensity exercise at ch 2, (d) a high-intensity exercise at ch 1, and (e) a high-intensity exercise at ch 2.

High-speed Fourier conversions of the EGG time series sections were completed to calculate the PSD for each band—bradygastria (1.1–2.4 cpm), reference frequency (2.4–3.7 cpm), tachygastria (3.7–5.0 cpm), and the colon (6.0–8.0 cpm); the results are shown in Figs. 3, 4, 5 and 6. For low- and intermediate-intensity exercises, consistently significant differences were not seen in any bands. For the high-intensity exercise, the values in the reference frequency band were significantly lower after exercise than before (Fig. 5b). This trend was sustained for 35 min from the start of post-exercise measurements, and the values in the bradygastria band were significantly higher after the exercise than before the exercise was performed (Fig. 5a). This significant trend was sustained over 35–45 min.

The ECG recorded alongside the EGG was analyzed. For a low-intensity exercise, the heart rate increased significantly from pre-exercise (at 0 min) to 10 min post-exercise (Fig. 7a). For intermediate-intensity exercise, the heart rate increased significantly from pre-exercise to 30 min post-exercise (Fig. 7b). For a high-intensity

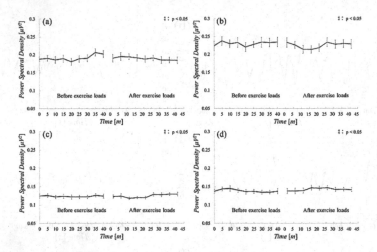

Fig. 3. Average PSD (mean ± SE) for a low-intensity exercise at ch 1: (a) 1.1–2.4 cpm, (b) 2.4–3.7 cpm, (c) 3.7–5.0 cpm, (d) 6.0–8.0 cpm.

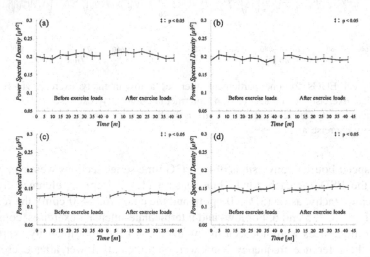

Fig. 4. Average PSD (mean ± SE) for a low-intensity exercise at ch 2: (a) 1.1–2.4 cpm, (b) 2.4–3.7 cpm, (c) 3.7–5.0 cpm, (d) 6.0–8.0 cpm.

exercise, the heart rate increased significantly from pre-exercise to 45 min post-exercise (Fig. 7c). The LF/HF for an intermediate-intensity exercise increased significantly in some cases from pre-exercise to 45 min post-exercise (Fig. 8b). The LF/HF for high intensity exercise increased significantly from pre-exercise to 45 min post-exercise (Fig. 8c).

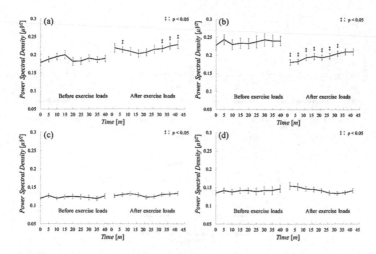

Fig. 5. Average PSD (mean ± SE) for a high-intensity exercise at ch 1: (a) 1.1–2.4 cpm, (b) 2.4–3.7 cpm, (c) 3.7–5.0 cpm, (d) 6.0–8.0 cpm.

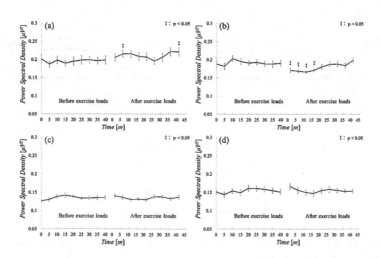

Fig. 6. Average PSD (mean ± SE) for a high-intensity exercise at ch 2: (a) 1.1–2.4 cpm, (b) 2.4–3.7 cpm, (c) 3.7–5.0 cpm, (d) 6.0–8.0 cpm.

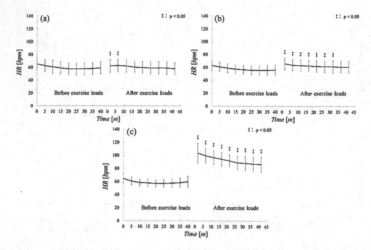

Fig. 7. Average HR (mean ± SD): (a) low-intensity exercise, (b) intermediate-intensity exercise, (c) high-intensity exercise.

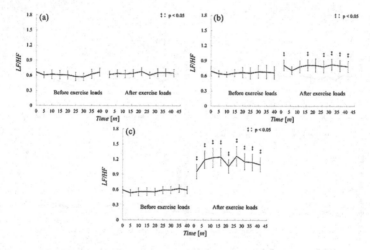

Fig. 8. Average LF/HF (mean ± SD): (a) low-intensity exercise, (b) intermediate-intensity exercise, (c) high-intensity exercise.

5   Discussion

In this study, EGGs were used to measure gastric electrical activity during exercising to study the influence of exercise intensity on gastric electrical activity. The results showed that for a high intensity exercise, the PSD in the gastric normal frequency band tends to decrease, presumably indicating a temporary decline of gastric activity caused by the exercise. This reveals the possibility that digestive activity decreases after a high-intensity exercise. For low- and intermediate-intensity exercises, no consistently significant differences were seen in any bands.

For this reason, for an exercise with a MET score 1.0–4.0, the influences of the EGGs on each frequency band were small, and it was confirmed that the gastric electrical activity was constant at this time. For a high-intensity exercise (e.g., running), the PSD of the gastric normal frequency band decreased. This could indicate a temporary decline of gastrointestinal activity caused by the exercise. For a high-intensity exercise, a remarkable rise in PSD was seen in the bradygastria band after the exercise. Bradygastria shows the integration power of the slow wave domain of the power spectrum; thus, it is possible that it caused the delay and reduction of gastric emptying ability after running.

Generally, under the effects of the autonomic nerve balance, parasympathetic nerve activity is temporarily dominant, and the digestive tract activity is aggravated; additionally, if sympathetic nerve activity is dominant, the digestive tract activity is repressed. The phenomena revealed in this study are presumed to be the results of exercise activity that make the sympathetic nerve activity dominant and repress the digestive tract activity. Clarifying to what extent this temporary parasympathetic nerve activity and repression of digestive tract activity continue and how they affect the later digestive tract activity would be extremely significant from the perspective of hygiene. It is assumed, however, that a social-intensive environment, an irregular lifestyle that ignores circadian rhythm, a change of environment, excessive stress, and other such conditions disrupt the autonomic nerve balance, thereby causing autonomic imbalance. This is known to cause functional gastrointestinal disorders. In this study, a high-intensity exercise is understood to stimulate the regulation ability of the autonomic nerve balance.

6 Conclusion

This paper reports the use of EGGs to measure gastric electrical activity during exercise to study the influence of exercise intensity on gastric electrical activity. The results show that it is possible for a high-intensity exercise to be followed by the temporary inducement of a state unsuitable for food digestion. In the future, following multi-faceted discussions of the complexity of generators of EGGs, we will study the use of wearable devices to measure gastrointestinal electrical activity to prepare life logs.

References

1. Fukudo, S., Nomura, T., Hongo, M.: Impact of corticotropin-releasing hormone on gastrointestinal motility and adrenocorticotropic hormone in normal controls and patients with irritable bowel syndrome. Gut **42**(6), 845–849 (1998)
2. Miyamura, M.: New Exercise Physiology Publication Department of Medical Books, vol. 2. Shinko Trading Co., Ltd (2001)

3. Gǔ, L., Fukudo, S.: Irritable bowel disorder and serotonin. Psychosom. Med. **50**(1), 11–17 (2010)
4. Peters, H., de Vries, W.R., Vanberge-Henegouwen, G.P., Akkermans, L.M.: Potential benefits and hazards of physical activity and exercise on the gastrointestinal tract. Gut **48**(3), 435–439 (2001)
5. Verger, P., Lanteaume, M.T., Louis-Sylvestre, J.: Human intake and choice of foods at intervals after exercise. Appetite **18**(2), 93–99 (1992)
6. Alvarez, W.C.: The electrogastrogram and what is shows. J. Am. Med. Assoc. **78**, 1116–1119 (1922)
7. Kenneth, L.K., Robert, M.: Handbook of Electrogastrography. Oxford University Press, Oxford (2004)
8. Nakamura, E., Kito, Y., Fukuda, H., Yanai, Y., Hashitani, H., Yamamoto, Y., Suzuki, H.: Cellular mechanism of spontaneous activity of the stomach smooth muscle. Nihon Yakurigaku Zasshi **123**(3), 141–148 (2002)
9. Torihashi, S.: Structure and functions of the Cajal cells. Pediatr. Surg. **37**(4), 467–472 (2005)
10. Takayama, I., Horiguchi, K., Daigo, Y., Mine, T., Fujino, M.A., Ohno, S.: The interstitial cells of Cajal and a gastroenteric pacemaker system. Arch. Histol. Cytol. **65**(1), 1–26 (2002)
11. Thomsen, L., Robinson, T.L., Lee, J.C.F., Farraway, L.A., Hughes, M.J., Andrews, D.W., Huizinga, J.D.: Interstitial cells of Cajal generate a rhythmic pacemaker current. Nat. Med. **4**, 848–851 (1998)
12. Smout, A.J.P.M., Van Der Schee, E.J., Grashuis, J.L.: What is measured in electrogastrography? Dig. Dis. Sci. **25**(3), 179–187 (1980)
13. Chen, J.Z., McCallum, R.W.: Electrogastrography: Principles and Applications. Raven Press, New York (1994)
14. Pezzolla, F., Riezzo, G., Maselli, M.A.: Electrical activity recorded from abdominal surface after gastrectomy or colectomy in humans. Gastroenterology **97**(2), 313–320 (1989)
15. Ainsworth, B.E., Haskell, W.L., Herrmann, S.D., Meckes, N., Bassett Jr., D.R., Tudor-Locke, C., Greer, J.L., Vezina, J., Whitt-Glover, M.C., Leon, A.S.: Compendium of physical activities: a second update of codes and MET values. Med. Sci. Sports Exerc. **43**(8), 1575–1581 (2011)
16. Wayland, R., Bromley, D., Pickett, D., Passamante, A.: Recognizing determinism in a time series. Phys. Rev. Lett. **70**(5), 580–582 (1993)
17. Takada, H., Simizu, Y., Hoshita, H., Shiozawa, T.: Wayland tests for differenced time series could evaluate degrees of visible determinism. Bull. Soc. Sci. Form **19**(3), 301–310 (2005)
18. Japan Society of Neurovegetative Research: Autonomic nerve function examination. vol. 5. Bunkodo Co., Ltd. (2007)
19. Homma, S.: Isopower mapping of the electrogastrogram (EGG). J. Auton. Nerv. Syst. **62**(3), 163–166 (1997)
20. Pomeranz, B., Macaulay, R.J., Caudill, M.A., Kutz, I., Adam, D., Gordon, D., Kilborn, K.M., Barger, A.C., Shannon, D.C., Cohen, R.J., Benson, H.: Assessment of autonomic function in humans by heart rate spectral analysis. Am. J. Physiol. **248**, 151–153 (1985)

Creativity and Ambient Urbanizing at the Intersection of the Internet of Things and People in Smart Cities

H. Patricia McKenna(✉)

AmbientEase, Victoria BC V8V 4Y9, Canada
mckennaph@gmail.com

Abstract. This paper explores and theorizes a space for creativity in further developing the ambient urbanizing concept in the context of smart cities. Theoretically this work is situated at the intersection of urbanizing the ambient, creativity, the Internet of Things (IoT), and the Internet of People (IoP) in relation to smart cities. The research design for this work incorporates an exploratory case study approach and multiple methods of data collection including survey and in-depth interviews. Group and individual discussions were also conducted with people from a range of sectors across the city. This work is significant in that it: (a) extends earlier work on urbanizing the ambient and the importance of people in smart cities; (b) sheds light on creativity in a digital context, enabled by the IoT and the emerging space of the IoP; (c) fosters increased accessibility to aware technologies such as the IoT through more aware people and the IoP; and (d) advances the concept of a more emergent, dynamic, and adaptive conceptualization of creativity, as in, ambient creativity.

Keywords: Ambient creativity · Ambient urbanizing · Awareness
Creativity · Internet of People · Internet of Things · Serendipity
Smart cities

1 Introduction

This work explores and theorizes a space for creativity at the intersection of the Internet of Things (IoT) and the Internet of People (IoP) in smart cities, in further developing and enabling the urbanizing of aware technologies by more aware people [1]. Picon [2] highlighted "the spatial turn of digital technologies" amplified by "the multiplication of electronic interfaces and the proliferation of wireless communications" giving way to discussions of "ubiquitous or ambient computing." In the context of notions of everyday creativity, Amabile [3] notes that, "increasingly, technology is enabling open innovation, user innovation, and citizen innovation." As such, this work is motivated by the need, identified by Amabile [3], for "studies of creative behavior – and the accompanying psychological states and environmental contexts – in situ, as it is happening" interpreted in this work as, everyday spaces, in real-time. The main objective of this work is to explore awareness, creativity, and serendipity in the context of aware people and aware technologies in smart cities. A review of the research literature for smart cities; the Internet of Things (IoT); the Internet of People (IoP) and responsive cities; and

© Springer International Publishing AG, part of Springer Nature 2018
M. Antona and C. Stephanidis (Eds.): UAHCI 2018, LNCS 10908, pp. 295–307, 2018.
https://doi.org/10.1007/978-3-319-92052-8_23

ambient urbanizing in relation to awareness, creativity, and serendipity is provided in Sect. 2 in development of a theoretical perspective for this paper.

The research design for this work incorporated an exploratory case study approach and multiple methods of data collection including in-depth interviews and survey. In parallel with this study, anecdotal evidence was gathered from a diverse range of people through group and individual interviews enabling further comparisons and triangulations. Additional details describing the methodology adopted for this work are provided in Sect. 3 of this paper. The key research question under exploration in this work is:

Q1:Why and how does creativity pertain to urbanizing the ambient, the Internet of Things, and the Internet of People in smart cities?

This work is significant in that it: (a) extends earlier work on urbanizing the ambient and the importance of people in smart cities; (b) sheds light on creativity in a digital context, enabled by the IoT and the IoP; (c) fosters increased accessibility to aware technologies such as the IoT through more aware people and the IoP; and (d) advances the notion of a more emergent, dynamic, and adaptive conceptualization of creativity, as in, ambient creativity.

What follows is a presentation of the theoretical perspective, the methodology, and study findings. A discussion with an analysis of findings is provided along with the highlighting of insights. Challenges, mitigations, and implications of this work for practice and research are identified, followed by the conclusion.

2   Theoretical Perspective

In developing a theoretical perspective for this work, a review of the research literature is provided for smart cities and the urbanizing turn; the Internet of Things (IoT); the Internet of People (IoP) and responsive cities; and ambient urbanizing and the IoP in relation to awareness, creativity, and serendipity.

2.1   Smart Cities and the Urbanizing Turn

Townsend [4] defines smart cities as, "places where information technology is combined with infrastructure, architecture, everyday objects and even our bodies, to address social, economic, and environmental problems." This definition features an intersection and interplay of urban spaces, people, and technologies that includes the Internet of Things (IoT) and the Internet of People (IoP). Sassen [5] calls for the need to urbanize technology, in terms of "an exploration of what it means to use intelligent systems without de-urbanizing cities." Sassen argues that intelligent technologies "have not been sufficiently 'urbanized'" in that "they have not been made to work within a particular urban context" so as to "make the city a heuristic space" as in, spaces that foster discovery and learning. It could be said that Sassen [6] articulated an impending space for the intersection of the IoT and the IoP in observing that "being in a city becomes synonymous with being in an extremely intense and dense information loop" which "as of now still cannot be replicated fully in electronic space."

2.2   Internet of Things (IoT)

Herzberg [7] describes the Internet of Things (IoT) as "a network that enables physical objects to collect and exchange data" while describing the Internet of Everything (IoE) as "a future wherein devices, appliances, people, and process are connected via the global Internet." Zanella and Vangelista [8] provided a comprehensive review of an urban IoT in terms of enabling technologies, protocols, and architecture. In support of IoT implementations, Leonidis, Arampatzis, Louloudakis, and Stepanidis [9] demonstrate how a suite of tools can be used in the managing, programming, testing, and monitoring of elements in support of creating user experiences in smart environments. Elaborating on the IoT, Carroll, Shih, Kropczynski, Cai, Rosson, and Han [10] explore the concept of the Internet of Places as supportive of awareness, engagement, and interaction related to people in terms of data integrations with place. Wilber [11] claims that the IoT gives way to the Internet of Experiences through "personal, evolving experiences."

2.3   Internet of People (IoP) and Responsive Cities

Li [12] claims that the IoP "refers to digital connectivity of people through the Internet infrastructure forming a network of collective intelligence and stimulating interactive communication among people." Miranda, Mäkitalo, Garcia-Alonso, Berrocal, Mikkonen, Canal, and Murillo [13] propose an infrastructure in support of "moving from the Internet of Things to the Internet of People" where "smartphones play a central role, reflecting their current use as the main interface connecting people to the Internet." Key principles of the IoP are said to include: social, personalized, proactive, and predictable [13]. Vilarinho, Farshchian, Floch, and Mathisen [14] argue that social network platforms serve to "connect people" whereas IoT platforms "connect things" and while "both platforms use various communication tools in efficient ways" a key issue is that "platforms for things often don't communicate and interoperate with social networks." As such, "activity feeds" are proposed as a social computing concept in support of "a communication framework for the Internet of people and things."

Khatoun and Zeadally [15] provide a smart city model consisting of the Internet of Things (IoT), the Internet of Services (IoS), the Internet of Data (IoD), and the Internet of People (IoP) where the IoP highlights smart living and smart people. Miranda, et al. [13] use the IoP concept "in the sense of bringing the IoT closer to people, for them to easily integrate into it and fully exploit its benefits." Conti, Passarella, and Das [16] articulate the need for "a radically new Internet paradigm" which they refer to as "the Internet of People (IoP)" and "where humans and their personal devices are not seen merely as end users of applications, but" through cyber-physical convergence, as in the increased blurring of the physical and the cyber or digital, "become active elements of the Internet." It is worth noting that Conti et al. [16] overlay the physical world with monitoring and sensing contributing to the generation of data in the cyber or digital world enabling actions and knowledge in cyber spaces while also enabling and informing actions in the physical world. As such, awareness in the physical and cyber worlds and the overlay of the two informs awareness and in turn, actions. For example, the monitoring of traffic flows can provide data enabling actions to adjust traffic lights at intersections. Similarly, smartphone apps can use traffic flow data, in the moment, to assist drivers to select alternative routes. When aware technologies assist people with everyday activities, purposefully and meaningfully accommodating choice and action, uptake seems to occur. Naughton [17] provides a reminder of what contributes to failure or success with aware technologies using the example of Google Glass and Glass 2.0 (Enterprise Edition), respectively.

Schmitt [18] claims there is a movement from smart cities to responsive cities so as to "place the citizen, rather than the technology or data, in the center of the planning, design, and management processes of the city." According to Schmitt [18], "data for the responsive city" are generated by smart buildings, infrastructure, or transportation while highlighting the importance of data from people "using smart technology and engaging their own knowledge." Similar to Conti et al. [16], Dustdar, Nastić, and Šćekić [19, 20] advance the concept of "cyber-human cities" to go "beyond the contemporary smart city" emphasizing the notion of "citizen informedness" based on maturity levels (ML) where ML-5 constitutes the highest level enabling people "to engage in creative, political or relaxing activities."

2.4 Ambient Urbanizing and the IoP: Awareness, Creativity, and Serendipity

The notion of sousveillance proposed by Mann [21] suggests novel forms of urbanizing enacted by people who are enabled by aware technologies in cities with the pervasive presence of mobile, wearable, camera, and recording devices such as smartphones. For the purposes of this work, ambient is understood to be the increased embedding and presence of aware technologies around and in support of human activity, influencing the nature and experience of information and awareness [1]. Weiser and Brown [22] proposed that encalming or ambient technologies pertain to how they "engage our attention" through "both the center and the periphery of our attention" such that, "by placing things in the perpiphery we are able to attune to many more things." An example of one type of awareness is presence awareness where social media spaces often indicate whether one or more of your friends are currently online. McKenna [1] explores in more depth the awareness concept as it relates to pervasive and aware technologies and in relation to evolving understandings of smart cities as co-creative spaces for action [23]. Ambient urbanizing [1] in the context of smart cities can be understood in terms of how people adapt, work with, and leverage aware technologies to improve and enrich their awareness, experiences, interactions, and communications in urban spaces. Examples of urbanizing from the research literature are described [1] in relation to public displays [24] and sensing and spectacle [25]. In the case of sensing and spectacle, the use of colored balloons containing sensors shows the shifting air quality in the sky at various locations in the city. The example of wifi 2.0 where the use of Passpoint enables the seamless moving from hotspot to hotspot demonstrates how continually evolving connection technologies are adaptively accommodating mobile requirements for Internet use in urban spaces (J. Stern, The future of public WiFi: NYCs hotspots tested - https://www.youtube.com/watch?v=VJSCKsitn1E&feature= youtu.be) while also serving to illustrate the notion of urbanizing aware technologies, as in urbanizing the ambient.

Gil-Garcia, Zhang, and Puron-Cid [26] identify creativity as one of 14 key drivers for smart cities. A component of creativity identified by Amabile [27] is the open-endedness or heuristic dimension as distinct from "having a single, obvious solution (purely algorithmic)." Dourish [28] points out that "our experience of algorithms can change as infrastructure changes." For Dourish [28] "algorithms come to act within broader digital assemblages" living as they do "in dynamic relations to the other material and discursive elements of software systems and the setting that produce them." More dynamic forms of creativity as in, ambient creativity have been supported by the European Community where researchers explored "the potential of modern digital technology in the arts" for "better understanding the fundamental mutations of artistic processes stimulated by emerging digital technologies" (http://aicreativity.acroe-ica.org/node/42?page=1). Exploration of the ambient creativity concept is advanced [29] in the context of transforming learning for more creative economies in smart cities.

Amabile and Pratt [30] identify the element of serendipity in the context of creativity and innovation as "something outside the usual planning process" as in "a serendiptious discovery by customers or an individual or group." Serendipity is defined by Beale [31] as "the making of fortunate discoveries by accident" claiming that it "is one of the cornerstones of scientific progress." In "using ambient intelligence to augment exploration for data mining and web browsing," Beale [31] claims that it is possible to "keep the user at the centre of an interaction and still support them in making new discoveries in different ways" in "making for a more serendipitous environment." Malmelin and Virta [32] discuss the notion of "managing for serendipity" in the context of emergent creativity, highlighting the importance of awareness. From a human geography perspective, Levy [33] associates serendipity with awareness as in, the utilization of "our complete sensorial apparatus" in relation to the rich information afforded by the density and diversity of urban spaces. Moriset [34] refers to the serendiptious nature of the urban space and Sassen claims that "one of its value-added features" is "the fact of unforeseen and unplanned mixes of information, expertise, and talent, which can produce a higher order of information."

This theoretical perspective enables reformulation of the ambient urbanizing framework [1] to incorporate the Internet of Things (IoT) and the Internet of People (IoP), highlighting awareness, creativity, and serendipity in aware digital contexts. As depicted in Fig. 1, through the interactive dynamic of people – technologies – cities, discussions of aware technologies and aware people using the constructs of awareness, creativity, and serendipity are used to explore the Internet of Things (IoT) and the Internet of People (IoP). This intersection of the IoT and the IoP provides a space for urbanizing the ambient as responsive enrichment mechanisms, for engagement with designs – spaces – things – interactions, in highly dynamic, emergent, and unexpected ways, as in, ambient creativity.

The research question under exploration (identified in Sect. 1) in this work is reformulated into the following proposition.

P1: Creativity pertains to urbanizing the ambient through the Internet of Things and the Internet of People in smart cities as emergent responsive enrichment mechanisms enabling more dynamic and adaptive designs, spaces, things, and interactions, contributing to the notion of ambient creativity.

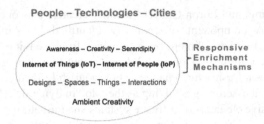

Fig. 1. Ambient urbanizing framework for the IoT-IoP in smart cities.

3   Methodology

The research design for this work involved an exploratory case study approach, said to be particularly appropriate for the study of contemporary phenomena [35]. The study spanned a three-year time period beginning in 2015 and continuing into 2018, attracting interest from multiple small to medium to large sized cities, mostly in Canada but also extending to northern and southern Europe. The process, sources of evidence, and the data analysis technique used for this work, are described in Sects. 3.1, 3.2 and 3.3.

3.1   Process

A description of the study was provided using a website where people could learn more about the urban exploration and sign up to participate. Basic demographic data were gathered during study sign up and people could self-identify in one or more categories as educator, student, community member, city official, business, and other. Following sign up, individuals were then invited to complete a survey about smart cities with the option to participate in a more in-depth discussion through an interview.

3.2   Sources of Evidence

Based on a pre-tested survey instrument and interview protocol, data were gathered from study participants about smart city experiences and ideas. Survey questions included a combination of closed and open-ended questions and interview questions were largely open-ended. Survey and interview questions focused on emerging understandings of multiple aspects of smart cities such as awareness, aware technologies, smartness, and urbanizing inviting the sharing of perceptions and experiences.

In parallel with this study, anecdotal evidence was gathered through group and individual discussions from across the urban spectrum of city officials, business, educators, students, designers, community members, and information technology staff in government and postsecondary institutions in the cities of Toronto, Vancouver, and Greater Victoria.

3.3   Data Analysis

Content analysis was used as a data analysis technique employing a combination of deductive analysis based on terminology from the research literature and inductive analysis of data collected through open-ended survey questions and interviews. Analysis focused on the constructs of awareness, creativity, and serendipity in relation to smart city perceptions, experiences, and ideas. Anecdotal evidence from discussions gathered in parallel with this study supported further data analysis, comparisons, and triangulations for further insight and rigor. Overall an analysis was conducted for an n = 60 consisting of 65% males and 35% females for people ranging in age from their 20s to 70s.

4   Findings

Findings from this work are presented in terms of the proposition under exploration, in response to the research question, with an emphasis on awareness, creativity, and serendipity in relation to the Internet of Things (IoT) and the Internet of People (IoP).

4.1   Awareness

Awareness of information sharing and communication challenges were identified with reference to silos within organizations, highlighted both within and across municipal government settings and higher education institutions. A community leader in Greater Victoria referred to the importance of moving toward "clusters of things that would bring industries and sectors together rather than that silo, sectoral approach" because "information doesn't seem to cross-over often." Regarding technology awareness, City IT staff described the IoT as "more about the instrumentation of things, with everything connected and communicated." A city councilor in Greater Victoria referred to technology "as a tool that will allow people to connect to each other and to their surroundings" adding that "vibrancy is created by people and connections between people and the way that comes to life" is by "creating activity." A community member in St. John's observed that "we're not smart about how we use the technology" while another in Greater Victoria noted that "it is hard for the locals to find out what's going on around the city." It is worth noting that from visitors to the city, "the most commonly asked question" was reported to be, "what do the locals do."

4.2   Creativity

Using the example of a locally developed mobile app, an educator in Europe pointed to the capability of being "able to open this kind of feedback" potential to anyone in the city as a way "to transform contributions both in terms of unique ideas and patterns into the design of some urban space or buildings" as in "city smart infrastructure." An individual in IT commented that, "clusters of people have a lot better ideas than individuals." In response to the concern with figuring out what is going on in the city, a community member suggested, "what if you had a map of downtown" where "you could see the layers of what's happening." City IT commented that, "we are interested in putting physical infrastructure in place" and "how we interpret using it is still open," identifying challenges that include jurisdictional ones in terms of "a hard stop at municipal boundaries." A student in Europe noted the pervasive sharing of "very traditional things" and events in daily lives where people are "all videoing them, sharing them constantly in social media," described as "a seamless behavior" contributing to "this seamless interrelationship of your local and your global" generating "concurrent awareness."

4.3 Serendipity

City IT staff highlighted the phenomenon of "accidental data collection" and data that "I don't think anybody saw a need for." It was noted that open, diverse datasets enable "data analysis that you've not thought of" with the potential for "serendipitous or accidental usage" or "unintended usage" and unforeseen value. An example from business was provided, where such usage revealed, "a win that wasn't even in our mindset" where staff "were using it [data] as a predictive piece to inform their daily operations." The example of an urban fountain was identified by a community member as "a touchstone in the city" that "brought people out" and "made an awareness of something in the community." Fitted with lights and music, this urban artifact was described as important because "it made people talk and it slowed people down." Describing the placement of benches in public urban spaces, a community member commented on, "these two benches that are facing each other" and "every time I sat on that bench I had a totally random conversation with the person that was sitting across from me and it was awesome" suggesting that "the placement and proximity of those benches created that opportunity."

4.4 Summary of Findings

In summary, as depicted in Table 1, findings are highlighted in terms of responsive enrichment mechanisms in relation to algorithmic/heuristic types of problem solving potentials and the IoT/IoP, focusing on awareness, creativity, and serendipity.

Table 1. Overview of findings.

IoT/IoP	Responsive enrichment mechanisms		
	Awareness	Creativity	Serendipity
Algorithmic/Heuristic	Info sharing	App	Data
	Clusters	Clusters	Predictive
	Vibrancy	Map	Value
	Connection	Social media sharing (seamless behavior)	Fountain
	Communication	Infrastructure (interpretation)	Benches

Awareness emerges in this work around information sharing challenges; the importance of clusters for communication, connection and sharing; and the importance of connections in "creating activity" for urban vibrancy. Creativity emerges in terms of mobile urban app creation; recognition of the importance of clusters of people for idea generation; the mapping of activities in the city as layers of what is going on; pervasive social media sharing as seamless behavior; and physical infrastructure development as open to opportunities for interactive interpretation. The importance of serendipity emerged in this work in relation to the accidental forms of data enabled by aware technologies and the unexpected ways in which people use this data for predictive and other purposes, creating new value; and the design and placement of urban elements such as a fountain or benches.

5 Discussion

A discussion of findings for analysis and insights is presented in relation to the three key responsive enrichment mechanisms of awareness, creativity, and serendipity in the context of the IoT and the IoP and algorithmic/heuristic relationships in smart cities.

Awareness. Awareness-related findings point to the importance of information sharing and communication in and across urban spaces and regions in support of more aware people. Recognition of the value of aware technologies in addressing challenges and complexities associated with information sharing, connection, and communication in real time, highlights readiness, vibrancy, and the potentials of clusters of people from diverse sectors at the intersection of the IoT and the IoP.

Creativity. Creativity potentials for the urbanizing of aware technologies are demonstrated by the development and use opportunities of mobile urban applications. Idea generation in the form of mapping the layers of what is going on in the city is suggestive of the potential for an emergent form of ambient creativity in response to continuous, pervasive, dynamic, and adaptive notions of information sharing. Again, the importance of clusters of people is identified as conducive to valuable idea generation. City IT openness regarding how new physical infrastructures are interpreted for use, suggests the presence of a space for creativity and urbanizing opportunities involving aware technologies and aware people as an intersecting of the IoT and the IoP. How people engage with aware technologies in urban spaces provides opportunities for the study of ambient urbanizing and ambient creativity in relation to "seamless behavior" and "seamless interrelationships."

Serendipity. Serendipity is highlighted in relation to "accidental data collection" and the emergent, unexpected needs and uses for such data, as in, "accidental usage." Accidental data and usage is suggestive of a space for ambient urbanizing potential and for ambient creativity. The algorithmic and heuristic nature of activities and interactions in IoT/IoP spaces with aware people and aware technologies in relation to awareness, creativity, and serendipity is identified in Table 1. Where heuristic tasks were associated with creativity by Amabile [27], as distinct from algorithmic ones, this work points to the potential for a shift to occur as interdisciplinary perspectives shed light on the complexities of algorithms [28] and their potential as spaces for more dynamic and adaptive creativity in emergent aware technology environments. Further, the conceptualization of ambient creativity in this work, enabled by an interweaving and intermingling of aware people and aware technologies, and the intersecting of the IoP and the IoT, opens a space for the combining of algorithmic and heuristic activities in response to the increasingly complex problem solving requirements in smart cities.

6   Challenges, Mitigations, and Implications

6.1   Challenges and Mitigations

Challenges of this work associated with small sample size were mitigated by diverse voices and in-depth interviews yielding insightful and rich data. Challenges associated with the size and geographic location of cities represented in this work are mitigated by the potential to extend this research to other locations; cities and regions of greater scale including mega-cities and regions; and other urban contexts. Challenges associated with the study of ambient urbanizing and ambient creativity potentials at the inter-section of the IoT and the IoP in smart cities are mitigated by increased openness and emergent opportunities to explore and advance understandings through research and practice that focuses on urban issues in context.

6.2   Implications for Research and Practice

This work has implications for research and practice going forward in relation to the evolving of current understandings of urbanizing and creativity with aware people interacting in aware technology environments in the context of smart cities as responsive cities.

Research. Through this work, pathways for exploration, discussion, and debate are opened for further theorizing, testing, and validation of urbanizing the ambient utilizing emergent notions of ambient creativity as opportunities, challenges, methodologies, solutions, and behaviors. While the focus of this work is on the Internet of Things and the Internet of People in relation to awareness, creativity, and serendipity in smart cities, the potential to extend this work to include the Internet of Places [10] and Experiences [11] is described below.

Internet of Places. Potential exists to expand the ambient urbanizing framework for the IoT and IoP in smart cities advanced in this paper to include exploration of the Internet of Places [10] as a complement to the Internet of People.

Internet of Experiences. Potential exists to expand the ambient urbanizing framework for the IoT and IoP in smart cities advanced in this paper to include exploration of the Internet of Experiences [11] as a complement to the Internet of People.

Practice. Early-stage discussions and ideas are provided as pathways for further exploration and realization of in situ responsive mechanisms for urbanizing the ambient utilizing emergent notions of ambient creativity. In the context of more aware people interacting with more aware technologies in smart cities, this work raises the potential for rethinking approaches to the development of algorithms in relation to the IoT and IoP in smart cities, as described below.

Algorithmic/Heuristic Relationships. This work gives rise to the potential for a revision of the algorithmic relationship with people to incorporate more heuristic opportunities, challenges, solutions, and behaviors.

7 Conclusion

This work provides an exploration of the ambient urbanizing concept in the context of aware technologies and aware people highlighting the potential for an evolving of current understandings of creativity, enabled by the Internet of Things (IoT) and the Internet of People (IoP). This paper makes a contribution in several ways in that it: (a) provides a conceptual framework for ambient urbanizing in relation to the IoT/IoP in smart cities; (b) develops and operationalizes the ambient creativity concept in relation to the IoT/IoP in smart cities; and (c) identifies research pathways, challenges, and opportunities related to the IoT/IoP going forward such as the *Internet of Places* and the *Internet of Experiences* and practice potentials related to *algorithmic/heuristic relationships*.

A key take away from this work is the continued importance of serendipity as integral to the human creativity component, even in more intelligent environments that incorporate the IoT and the IoP, characterizing smart cities. Another take away from this work is the potential for ambient creativity to be a major driver influencing the urbanizing of aware technologies for smarter and more responsive cities.

This work will be of interest to a diverse audience including creativity, smart city, and urban practitioners and researchers; artists, designers, developers, architects, and educators; and anyone concerned with more aware, evolving, and creative mechanisms for engaging people with the IoT/IoP potentials for enhanced livability in smart cities.

References

1. McKenna, H.P.: Urbanizing the ambient: why people matter so much in smart cities. In: Konomi, S., Roussos, G. (eds.) Enriching urban spaces with ambient computing, the Internet of Things, and smart city design, pp. 209–231. IGI Global, Hershey (2017)
2. Picon, A.: Smart cities: a spatialized intelligence. Wiley, Chichester (2015)
3. Amabile, T.M.: In pursuit of everyday creativity. Working Paper 18-002, Journal of Creative Behavior (2017). https://doi.org/10.1002/jocb.200
4. Townsend, A.M.: Smart cities: big data, civic hackers and the quest for a new utopia. WW Norton, New York (2013)
5. Sassen, S.: Urbanizing technology. LSE Cities (2012). Accessed 10 Oct 2017. https://lsecities.net/media/objects/articles/urbanising-technology/en-gb/
6. Sassen, S.: Global cities and global city-regions: a comparison. In: Scott, A.J. (ed.) Global city-regions: Trends, theory, policy, pp. 78–95. Oxford University Press, Oxford (2001). Reprinted (2004)

7. Herzberg, C.: Smart cities, digital nations: how digital urban infrastructure can deliver a better life in tomorrow's crowded world. Roundtree Press, Petaluma (2017)
8. Zanella, A., Vangelista, L.: Internet of Things for smart cities. IEEE Internet Things J. **1**(1), 22–32 (2014)
9. Leonidis, A., Arampatzis, D., Louloudakis, N., Stephanidis, C.: The AmI-Solertis system: creating user experiences in smart environments. In: 13th International Conference on Wireless and Mobile Computing, Networking and Communications (WiMob), Rome, Italy, pp. 151–158. IEEE (2017)
10. Carroll, J.M., Shih, P.C., Kropczynski, J., Cai, G., Rosson, M.B., Han, K.: The Internet of places at community-scale: design scenarios for hyperlocal neighborhood. In: Konomi, S., Roussos, G. (eds.) Enriching urban spaces with ambient computing, the Internet of Things, and smart city design, pp. 1–24. IGI Global, Hershey (2017)
11. Wilber, L.: Beyond the IoT: The Internet of Experiences will change the way the world operates. Compass: The 3D Experience Magazine, 11 February (2016). Accessed 9 Jan 2018. https://compassmag.3ds.com/#/8/Cover-Story/BEYOND-THE-IOT
12. Li, M.: Editorial: Internet of People. Concurr. Comput. Pract. Exp. **29**, 1–3 (2017)
13. Miranda, J., Mäkitalo, N., Garcia-Alonso, J., Berrocal, J., Mikkonen, T., Canal, C., Murillo, J.M.: From the Internet of Things to the Internet of People. IEEE Internet Comput. **19**(2), 40–47 (2015)
14. Vilarinho, T., Farshchian, B.A., Floch, J., Mathisen, B.M.: A communication framework for the Internet of People and Things based on the concept of activity feeds in social computing. In: Proceedings of the 9th International Conference on Intelligent Environments, pp. 1–8 (2013)
15. Khatoun, R., Zeadally, S.: Smart cities: concepts, architectures, research opportunities. Commun. ACM **59**(8), 46–57 (2016)
16. Conti, M., Passarella, A., Das, S.K.: The Internet of People (IoP): a new wave in pervasive mobile computing. Pervasive Mob. Comput. **41**, 1–27 (2017)
17. Naughton, J.: The rebirth of Google Glass shows the merit of failure. The Guardian, 23 Jul 2017
18. Schmitt, G.: Responsive cities: explore the future of urbanization as you learn about responsive cities, ones that bring the city back to their citizens. ETH Zurich, Zurich (2017)
19. Dustdar, S., Nastić, S., Šćekić, O.: Introduction to smart cities and a vision of cyber-human cities. Smart Cities, pp. 3–15. Springer, Cham (2017). https://doi.org/10.1007/978-3-319-60030-7_1
20. Dustdar, S., Nastić, S., Šćekić, O.: A road map to the cyber-human smart city. Smart Cities, pp. 239–258. Springer, Cham (2017). https://doi.org/10.1007/978-3-319-60030-7_9
21. Mann, S.: Veillance and reciprocal transparency: surveillance versus sousveillance, AR glass, lifelogging, and wearable computing. In: Proceedings of the IEEE International Symposium on Technology and Society (ISTAS 2013), pp. 1–12. IEEE, Singapore (2013)
22. Weiser, M., Brown, J.S.: Designing calm technology. Xerox PARC, Palo Alto (1995). Accessed 9 Mar 2016. http://www.ubiq.com/weiser/calmtech/calmtech.htm
23. McKenna, H.P.: Is it all about awareness? people, smart cities 3.0, and evolving spaces for IT. In: Proceedings of SIGMIS-CPR. Alexandria, VA, USA (2016)
24. Memarovic, N., Langheinrich, M., Alt, F.: Interacting places – a framework for promoting community interaction and place awareness through public displays. Pervasive Computing and Communications Workshops (PERCOM Workshops). IEEE, Lugano, Switzerland (2012)
25. Kuznetsov, S., Davis, G.N., Paulos, E., Gross, M.D., Cheung, J.C.: Red balloon, green balloon, sensors in the sky. UbiComp 2011. ACM, Beijing (2011)

26. Gil-Garcia, J.R., Zhang, J., Puron-Cid, G.: Conceptualizing smartness in government: an integrative and multi-dimensional view. Government Information Quarterly (2016). Online
27. Amabile, T.M.: Componential theory of creativity. In: Kessler, E.H. (ed.) Encyclopedia of Management Theory. Sage, Los Angeles, CA (2013)
28. Dourish, P.: Algorithms and their others: algorithmic culture in context. Big Data & Society, 1–11 July–December (2016)
29. McKenna, H.P.: Re-conceptualizing jobs, work, and labour: transforming learning for more creative economies in 21st century smart cities. In: Proceedings of the 10th Annual International Conference of Education, Research and Innovation (iCERi 2017), pp. 8367–8376. IATED, Spain (2017)
30. Amabile, T.M., Pratt, M.G.: The dynamic componential model of creativity and innovation in organizations: making progress, making meaning. Res. Organ. Behav. **36**, 157–183 (2016)
31. Beale, R.: Supporting serendipity: using ambient intelligence to augment user exploration for data mining and web browsing. Int. J. Hum Comput. Stud. **65**, 421–433 (2007)
32. Malmelin, N., Virta, S.: Managing for serendipity: exploring the organizational prerequisites for emergent creativity. Int. J. Media Manag. **19**(3), 222–239 (2017)
33. Lévy, J. (ed.): The city: critical essays in human geography. Contemporary Foundations of Space and Place Series. Routledge, Newcastle (2008)
34. Moriset, B.: Building new places of the creative economy: the rise of coworking spaces. HAL archives-ouvertes (2013)
35. Yin, R.K.: Case study research and applications: design and methods, 6th edn. Sage, Los Angeles (2018)

Barrier Detection Using Sensor Data from Unimpaired Pedestrians

Akihiro Miyata[✉], Iori Araki, and Tongshun Wang

Nihon University, 3-25-40, Sakurajousui, Setagaya-Ku, Tokyo, Japan
miyata.akihiro@acm.com

Abstract. There are several barriers (e.g., steps, slopes) that hinder the free movement of impaired people, both indoors and outdoors. Existing approaches for detecting barriers have an accuracy/coverage trade-off problem. For example, approaches that use a wheelchair with an accelerometer cannot detect barriers in areas that wheelchair users have not gone through. However, approaches that try to detect barriers from street images on the Internet fail to increase the accuracy of barrier detection because of occlusions that obscure the surface of the road. To address this problem, we propose a barrier detection approach that uses a machine learning model trained with acceleration data acquired from smartphones of able-bodied pedestrians. This idea uses pedestrians as sensor nodes for detecting barriers. This approach enables us to collect barrier information for a large area with high accuracy without any special investigators or devices. The results of the evaluation using acceleration data of pedestrians show that our method could identify barriers accurately by using hand-crafted features. Furthermore, we also clarify that the identification accuracy improves when features auto-generated by deep learning (Denoising Autoencoders) are used.

Keywords: Barrier-free · Unimpaired · Accelerometer · Deep learning

1 Introduction

There are many barriers (e.g., steps, slopes) that hinder the free movement of impaired people, both indoors and outdoors. Identifying the positions of such barriers is beneficial for enabling the smooth movement of impaired people and urging the government to address this issue. Several researchers have been aware of this problem and proposed some approaches to collect barrier information. However, an effective method that collects barrier information from a large area with high accuracy has not been established. For example, some works try to detect barriers by analyzing data acquired using sensors attached to wheelchairs used by the impaired. However, it is difficult to collect barrier information from a large area, given that the number of wheelchair users relative to able-bodied pedestrians is very low. On the other hand, to improve the coverage, some approaches identify barriers using road photos stored in a street view service (e.g., Google Street View). Although such methods can collect barrier information from a large area, it is difficult to collect highly accurate barrier information because occlusions owing to the presence of cars and trees obscure the surface of the road.

© Springer International Publishing AG, part of Springer Nature 2018
M. Antona and C. Stephanidis (Eds.): UAHCI 2018, LNCS 10908, pp. 308–319, 2018.
https://doi.org/10.1007/978-3-319-92052-8_24

We focus on the fact that pedestrians carry smartphones equipped with several sensors, every day and everywhere. Thus, we can consider the possibility of using these pedestrians as sensor nodes for detecting barriers. Hence, we propose a barrier detection approach that uses a machine learning model trained with acceleration data of unimpaired pedestrians. To extract features for machine learning, we adopt a deep learning approach. The contributions of this work include:

- A method that collects barrier information from a large area with high accuracy.
- An evaluation using actual acceleration data of pedestrians.

2 Related Works

Approaches to collecting barrier information can be broadly classified into the following two groups. The first group consists of approaches wherein human investigators collect barrier information. The second group is comprised of approaches wherein systems collect barrier information using sensor data. Furthermore, the first group can be classified into approaches wherein human investigators collect information "in the field" and "from a remote location". The second group can be classified into approaches wherein systems use sensor data of "wheeled vehicles" and "pedestrians".

2.1 Human-Judge Approach

Human-Judge in the Field. In this approach, human investigators (e.g., government staff, pedestrians, wheelchair users) collect barrier information in the field. [1] introduces metrics for accessibility assessment in the field. [2, 3] are web services that allows human investigators to upload geotagged barrier information. [4] proposes a barrier information collection system that assesses human investigators to improve the credibility of information.

Human-Judge from a Remote Location. In this approach, human investigators collect barrier information from a remote location. Specifically, they try to detect barriers using road photos stored in a street view service (e.g., Google Street View) [5, 6, 7].

2.2 System-Judge Approach

System-Judge Using Sensor Data of Wheeled Vehicles. In this approach, systems collect barrier information using sensors attached to cars and wheelchairs. [8] proposes a system that identifies potholes and other severe road surface anomalies from sensor data from the accelerometer embedded in the dedicated computer in the car. [9] constructs a similar system, except that this system uses the accelerometer of the smartphone placed on the car. [10] proposes a method to detect road surface damage by analyzing acceleration data of bicycles.

Alternatively, there are several works that attempt to identify barriers on sidewalks using accelerometers and gyroscopes attached to wheelchairs. [11] identifies the degree of slope using two accelerometers per wheelchair. Their system adopts a k-NN algorithm for identification. [12] tries to identify sidewalk types (e.g., curb, slope) by analyzing wheelchair acceleration data using SVMs. [13] analyzes not only acceleration data but also vital data of wheelchair users to identify psychological barriers such as "a nerve-fraying sidewalk due to heavy traffic".

System-Judge Using Sensor Data of Pedestrians. There are several works that try to recognize the user activity. [14, 15] estimates the user activity (e.g., walk, run, stand) using an accelerometer attached on the user's body. They adopt some time domain (TD) and frequency domain (FD) features extracted from acceleration data to estimate the user activity using machine learning. [16] also uses TD features (e.g., mean, standard deviation, time between peaks) extracted from acceleration data measured by the smartphone in user's trousers front pocket. Their system recognizes some types of activity such as walking and climbing up/down stairs using some machine learning methods including J48, Logistic Regression and Multilayer Perceptron. Meanwhile, [17] compares various smartphone positions such as hand held, backpack, handbag and trousers front/back pocket. Their system recognizes whether the user is walking using TD and FD features.

Using the technologies described above, there are some studies that try to estimate the status of the road surface. [18] proposes an approach for estimating surface inclination by analyzing acceleration data acquired from the smartphone attached to one of the user's legs. [19] tries to detect sidewalk-street transitions (e.g., curb, ramp) by analyzing inertial data acquired from the accelerometer and gyroscope attached to the user's shoe.

3 Research Goal

3.1 Research Problem

Although there are several approaches to detect barriers, it is still difficult to collect barrier information from a large area with high accuracy. *Human-judge in the field* approach is highly accurate but not practical to apply to a large area owing to the significant costs involved. *Human-judge from a remote location* approach can reduce the cost of sending investigators into the field; however, it is difficult to collect highly accurate barrier information because occlusions caused by cars and trees that obscure the surface of the road.

As to *System-judge using sensor data of wheeled vehicles* approach, though it is difficult to analyze sidewalks utilizing methods that use cars or bicycles [8, 9, 10], methods that use wheelchairs [11, 12, 13] might be applicable to sidewalk analysis. However, it is difficult to collect barrier information from a large area, given that the number of wheelchair users relative to unimpaired pedestrians is very low.

By contrast, for *System-judge using sensor data of pedestrians* approach, existing methods that analyze the road surface [18, 19] yield a certain degree of accuracy by analyzing data acquired from sensors attached to unimpaired users. Also, this approach could be applicable to collect barrier information from a large area because the number of unimpaired users is relatively large. However, to the best of our knowledge, existing works have not clarified whether this approach is applicable to identify various barriers (e.g., step, stairs, door, low/high slope) that prevent impaired people from moving smoothly.

Based on these, problems of barrier information collection could be summarized as follows:

- It is difficult to collect barrier information from a large area with high accuracy using the approach in which human-judge intervenes in.
- It is difficult to collect barrier information from a large area using the approach that uses sensor data of wheelchair users.
- It is unclear whether various barriers can be detect using an approach that uses sensor data of pedestrians.

3.2   Definition of the Research Goal

Given the problems described above, we define the research goal as establishing a method that detects barriers for impaired people using sensor data of unimpaired pedestrians.

4   Approach

4.1   Target Barrier Types

First, we define the target barrier types to be detected. Stairs should be included in the target types, because they obviously prevent impaired people from moving smoothly. As a similar type, steps (Fig. 1: left) could be a barrier. As steps do not seem to strongly affect walking behaviors of unimpaired pedestrians, we think it is worth investigating whether steps could be detected using sensor data of pedestrians. As to slopes, there are many low slopes (about 3°) in the urban area that impaired people can climb up or down easily. On the other hand, there are high slopes (about 10°, Fig. 1: center) that even unimpaired people cannot climb up easily by bicycle. We investigate whether these slopes could be identified.

Fig. 1. Typical barriers (left: step, center: high slope, right: swinging door).

Most unimpaired people are not aware of it, but some types of doors could be barriers. Most impaired people can use automatic doors and sliding doors without difficulty. However, it is difficult for them to open swinging doors (Fig. 1: right) while piloting her/his wheelchair or crutches.

To summarize this discussion, the target barrier types of this paper are as follows:

- Stairs
- Step
- Low slope (about 3°)
- High slope (about 10°)
- Swinging door

There might be other barrier types to be detected. We plan to clarify these by interviews with impaired people and field studies.

4.2   Barrier Detection Method

We focus on the fact that pedestrians carry smartphones equipped with several sensors, every day and everywhere. Thus, we can consider the possibility of using these pedestrians as sensor nodes for detecting barriers. Hence, we propose a barrier detection approach that uses a machine learning model trained with acceleration data of unimpaired pedestrians. We evaluate two types of features used in machine learning as follows.

Hand-Crafted Features. Existing works use hand-crafted features, i.e., time domain (TD) features (e.g., mean, standard deviation, time between peaks) and frequency domain (FD) features (e.g., frequency band-energy) extracted from acceleration data. By reference to these works, we use 33 TD/FD features as follows. We conduct FFT to obtain FD features:

- [TD, 3] The mean of acceleration of each axis (x, y, z).
- [TD, 3] The standard deviation of acceleration of each axis (x, y, z).
- [TD, 3] The correlation coefficient between two axes (x−y, x−z, y−z).
- [FD, 24] The average spectral entropy of each frequency band (0 Hz-, 1.25 Hz-, 2.5 Hz-, 3.75 Hz-, 5 Hz-, 6.25 Hz-, 7.5 Hz-, 8.75 Hz-) of each axis (x, y, z).

Auto-Generated Features. Deep learning is one of machine learning methods that uses multilayer neural networks. This method shows far higher performance than that of machine learning with hand-crafted features in many domains: speech recognition, visual object recognition and natural language processing [20]. However, to the best of our knowledge, existing works have not clarified whether deep learning shows high performance in the barrier detection task using acceleration data. Hence, we think it is worth evaluating this. Moreover, although it would be rational to obtain acceleration data from smartphones that many pedestrians bring always, the position of smartphone is diverse; trousers front/back pocket, handbag, and backpack. This requires us to design features depending on each possible position of the smartphone, however, this design cost is too high to ignore in the case of a hand-crafted approach. Meanwhile, deep learning can extract features from data automatically.

For the reason noted above, we also evaluate feature extraction using deep learning. In several kinds of deep learning methods, we adopt Denoising Autoencoders (hereafter DAE) [21] available for general feature extraction tasks. We focus on acceleration data with three mutually perpendicular axes. To that end, we designed a five-layer network structure, wherein the input layer is separated into three parts, as shown in Fig. 2. This separated input layer is designed by referring to works that construct multimodal deep learning networks such as [22]. Numbers in the figure describe the dimension of each layer.

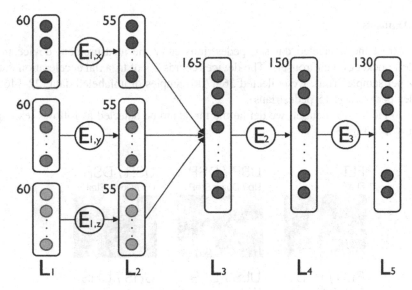

Fig. 2. Denoising Autoencoders of which input layer is separated into three parts.

- L_1: The first layer is the input layer for raw acceleration data of each axis (x, y, z).
- L_2: The second layer reduces the dimensionality of each element of L_1 using DAE. In this process, encoders $E_{1,x}$, $E_{1,y}$, and $E_{1,z}$ that reduce the dimensionality of each element of L_1 are obtained.
- L_3: The third layer concatenates all the elements of L_2.
- L_4, L_5: The fourth and fifth layers reduce the dimensionality of each previous layer using DAE. In each process, encoders E_2 and E_3 that reduce the dimensionality of each previous layer are obtained.

In estimation phase, we reduce the dimensionality of the target acceleration data using encoders $E_{1,x}$, $E_{1,y}$, $E_{1,z}$, E_2, and E_3, and use dimension-reduced acceleration data as features.

5 Experiment

5.1 Purpose

As mentioned before, it is expected that the accuracy of barrier detection could be improved by auto-generated features extracted using DAE. However, based on existing works, this is uncertain. Hence, we set the purpose of this experiment as the evaluation of the difference between the accuracies of two machine learning approaches; one based on hand-crafted features and the other based on auto-generated features.

5.2 Datasets

To construct the unlabeled dataset, pedestrians carry the measurement device in the front left pocket of their trousers. The device records 3 s of tri-axial acceleration data at 20 Hz per sample. Thus, we collected 263,700 samples of unlabeled data (22-146,214 samples per walker; 15 pedestrians).

As to the labeled dataset, we define the targets to be detected as follows (examples are shown in Fig. 3).

Fig. 3. Targets in the experiment.

- FLT: Walking on a flat sidewalk paved with asphalt (outdoor).
- USP/DSP: Walking up/down a step of which height is about 15 cm (indoor).
- USR/DSR: Walking up/down stairs of which each step's height is about 15 cm (indoor).
- PLD/PSD: Pulling/pushing a swinging door (indoor).
- ULS/DLS: Walking up/down a low slope, i.e. at an angle of about 3° (indoor).
- UHS/DHS: Walking up/down a high slope, i.e. at an angle of about 10° (outdoor).

The subsequent procedure is similar to that of the unlabeled dataset. We collected 3,300 samples of labeled data (10–20 samples per walker for each target; 16 pedestrians).

5.3   Procedure

HCF Method. This method uses a set of hand-crafted features (hereafter HCF) that consists of 33 TD/FD features described in Subsect. 4.2. Then, we divided the labeled dataset into 3,000 training data and 300 test data at random and conducted SVM (RBF kernel) classification tasks 100 times using HCF.

DAF Method. This method uses a set of auto-generated features using DAE (hereafter DAF). DAF is a set of 150 features that are outputted by the network shown in Fig. 2, where the input is the unlabeled data mentioned earlier (20 Hz $\times$ 3 s $\times$ 3 axes = 180 dimensions). DAE parameters for L_1–L_2, L_3–L_4 and L_4–L_5 are as follows: noise rate = 20%, mini-batch size = 20, epoch count = 200. Thus, we obtained encoders $E_{1,x}$, $E_{1,y}$, $E_{1,z}$, E_2, and E_3. Then, we reduce the dimensionality of raw acceleration data through the use of these encoders to obtain DAF. The subsequent procedure is the same as that of the HCF method other than features: we divided the labeled dataset into 3,000 training data and 300 test data at random and conducted SVM (RBF kernel) classification tasks 100 times using DAF.

5.4   Result and Discussion

Figure 4 shows the f-measures for each method. The mean f-measures of HCF method and DAF method were 0.623 and 0.701, respectively. The t-test at the 0.1% confidence level showed that there were significant differences between the two methods. Further, DAF method provided higher f-measures than that of HCF method for most of the targets, except in the case of DHS (down high slope). This suggests that the estimator trained with acceleration data of unimpaired pedestrians could detect and classify barriers, and the accuracy could increase when DAF is used. As to DHS, we have two hypotheses: one is that HCF is more suitable to express the pedestrian behavior of DHS, and the other is that the size of unlabeled data of walking high slopes for modeling DAF is insufficient. There are few high slopes in our measurement area; hence, we plan to enlarge the datasets focusing on high slopes to evaluate whether this tendency is universal.

To analyze in detail, let us turn to the confusion matrices of HCF/DAF method (Figs. 5 and 6). From here, we are able to clearly identify misclassifications. First, we discuss the confusion of FLT (flat) and ULS/DLS (up/down low slope). It is considered that this confusion is not serious, because low slopes (about 3°) are originally designed for impaired people. Viewed from this perspective, we find that HCF method identifies 10% of actual FLT as ULS/DLS, and 17% of actual FLT as other than FLT/ULS/DLS. On the other hand, DAF method identifies 15% of actual FLT as ULS/DLS, and 12% of actual FLT as other than FLT/ULS/DLS. It follows from these results that DAF method would be more acceptable in this point, though the ratios of identifying actual FLT as FLT (i.e., the recall of FLT) of both methods are 73%.

Second, we discuss the confusion of opening directions of doors. Notice that there were many misidentifications of PLD (pull door) and PSD (push door) when HCF method was used, and there were less misidentifications in the case of DAF method. While it might sound like a trivial matter, we regard this confusion as a serious

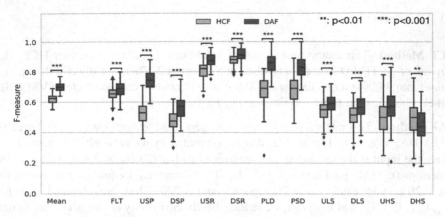

Fig. 4. F-measures of HCF/DAE method (N = 100).

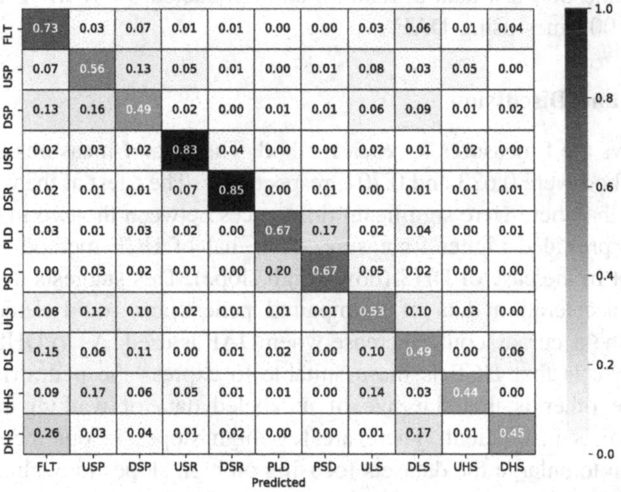

Fig. 5. Confusion matrix of HCF method (N = 100, Normalized).

problem. Consider a walker with crutches; he can open doors by pushing it by his body with relatively little effort; however, it would be quite difficult for him to pull it open with his hands holding his crutches. Hence, it could be said that identifying opening directions of doors with high accuracy is important, and the DAF method is preferable to the HCF method in this perspective.

6 Conclusion

To collect barrier information from a large area with high accuracy, we proposed a barrier detection approach that uses a machine learning model trained using acceleration data of unimpaired pedestrians. This approach does not require any special

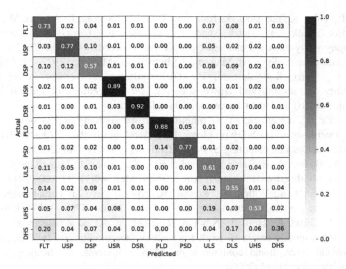

Fig. 6. Confusion matrix of DAE method (N = 100, Normalized).

investigators or devices, as there are a large number of pedestrians who carry their smartphones every day and everywhere. We defined the target barrier types in more detail than existing works and showed that these barriers could be identified with considerable accuracy using hand-crafted time domain and frequency domain features. Furthermore, we also clarified that the identification accuracy improves when features auto-generated by deep learning (Denoising Autoencoders) are used.

By utilizing our approach as a platform for analyzing accessibility in the city, many services for impaired people and surrounding communities can be developed. First, by prominently indicating the existence of barriers in so-called barrier-free maps, physically challenged persons can plan appropriate routes in advance. Although the severity and kinds of disabilities are diverse, they could find routes that suit them best, because our method can identify the type and direction of barriers. Our approach also could support city developers and governments, who can avail of data regarding the positions of unsuitable roads at a much lower cost.

In future work, we plan to enlarge the datasets for more precise evaluation. Also, we plan to conduct a field experiment to identify barrier positions in actual cities.

Acknowledgement. This work was supported by JSPS KAKENHI Grant Number JP17K12730.

References

1. Carvalho, A., Heitor, T., Cabrita, A.R.: Ageing cities: shifting from special needs to inclusive design in urban space. In: Proceedings of the 6th European Symposium on Research in Architecture and Urban Design (EURAU'12) (2012)
2. Wheelmap. Accessed 1 Jan 2018. http://wheelmap.org

3. Miura, T., Yabu, K., Ikematsu, S., Kano, A., Ueda, M., Suzuki, J., Sakajiri, M., Ifukube, T.: Barrier-free walk: a social sharing platform of barrier-free information for sensory/physically-impaired and aged people. In: Proceedings of the 2012 IEEE International Conference on Systems, Man and Cybernetics (SMC), pp. 2927–2932 (2012)

4. Prandi, C., Mirri, S., Salomoni, P.: Trustworthiness assessment in mapping urban accessibility via sensing and crowd sourcing. In: Proceedings of the 1st International Conference on IoT in Urban Space, pp. 108–110 (2014)

5. Hara, K., Le, V., Froehlich, J.E.: Combining crowd sourcing and Google street view to identify street-level accessibility problems. In: Proceedings of the ACM SIGCHI Conference on Human Factors in Computing Systems (CHI'13), pp. 631–640 (2013)

6. Rundle, A., Bader, M., Richards, C., Neckerman, K., Teitler, J.: Using Google Street View to audit neighborhood environments. Am. J. Prev. Med. 40(1), 94–100 (2011)

7. Badland, H., Opit, S., Witten, K., Kearns, R., Mavoa, S.: Can virtual streetscape audits reliably replace physical streetscape audits? J. Urban Health 87(6), 1007–1016 (2010)

8. Eriksson, J., Girod, L., Hull, B., Newton, R., Madden, S., Balakrishnan, H.: The pothole patrol: using a mobile sensor network for road surface monitoring. In: Proceedings of the Sixth Annual International conference on Mobile Systems, Applications and Services (MobiSys'08), pp. 29–39 (2008)

9. Mohan, P., Padmanabhan, V.N., Ramjee, R.: Nericell: rich monitoring of road and traffic conditions using mobile smartphones. In: Proceedings of the 6th ACM Conference on Embedded Network Sensor Systems (SenSys'08), pp. 323–336 (2008)

10. Takahashi, J., Shioiri, D., Shida, Y., Kobana, Y., Suzuki, R., Kobayashi, Y., Isoyama, N., Lopez, G., Tobe, Y.: Clustering for road damage locations obtained by smartphone accelerometers. In: Proceedings of the 2nd International Conference on IoT in Urban Space (Urb-IoT'16), pp. 89–91 (2016)

11. Kuwahara, N., Nishiura, M., Shiomi, Y., Morimoto, K., Iwawaki, Y., Nishida, N.: A study on a ubiquitous system for collecting barrier-free information of evacuation centers for wheelchair users. In: Proceedings of the 4th ACM International Workshop on Context-Awareness for Self-Managing Systems (CASEMANS'10), pp. 36–39 (2010)

12. Iwasawa, Y., Nagamine, K., Yairi, I.E., Matsuo, Y.: Toward an automatic road accessibility information collecting and sharing based on human behavior sensing technologies of wheelchair users. Procedia Comput. Sci. 63, 74–81 (2015)

13. Isezaki, T., Niijima, A., Miyata, A., Watanabe, T., Mizuno, O.: Wheelchair users' psychological barrier estimation based on inertial and vital data. In: Antona, M., Stephanidis, C. (eds.) UAHCI 2016. LNCS, vol. 9738, pp. 403–413. Springer, Cham (2016). https://doi.org/10.1007/978-3-319-40244-4_39

14. Ravi, N., Dandekar, N., Mysore, P., Littman, M.L.: Activity recognition from accelerometer data. In: Proceedings of the 17th Conference on Innovative Applications of Artificial Intelligence (IAAI'05), vol. 3, pp. 1541–1546 (2005)

15. Pärkkä, J., Cluitmans, L., Ermes, M.: Personalization algorithm for real-time activity recognition using pda, wireless motion bands, and binary decision tree. IEEE Trans. Inf. Technol. Biomed. 14(5), 1211–1215 (2010)

16. Kwapisz, J.R., Weiss, G.M., Moore, S.A.: Activity recognition using cell phone accelerometers. ACM SIGKDD Explor. Newsl. 12(2), 74–82 (2010)

17. Brajdic, A., Harle, R.: Walk detection and step counting on unconstrained smartphones. In: Proceedings of the 2013 ACM International Joint Conference on Pervasive and Ubiquitous Computing (UbiComp'13), pp. 225–234 (2013)

18. Uyanik, I., Khatri, A., Majeti, D., Ugur, M., Shastri, D., Pavlidis, I.: Using accelerometer data to estimate surface incline and its walking app potential. In: Proceedings of the 33rd Annual ACM Conference Extended Abstracts on Human Factors in Computing Systems (CHI EA'15), pp. 1397–1402 (2015)
19. Jain, S., Borgiattino, C., Ren, Y.: LookUp: enabling pedestrian safety services via shoe sensing. In: Proceedings of the 13th Annual International Conference on Mobile Systems, Applications, and Services (MobiSys'15), pp. 257–271 (2015)
20. LeCun, Y., Bengio, Y., Hinton, G.: Deep learning. Nature **521**, 436–444 (2015)
21. Vincent, P., Larochelle, H., Bengio, Y., Manzagol, P.A.: Extracting and composing robust features with denoising autoencoders. In: Proceedings of the 25th International Conference on Machine learning (ICML'08), pp. 1096–1103 (2008)
22. Ngiam, J., Khosla, A., Kim, M., Nam, J., Lee, H., Ng, A.Y.: Multimodal deep learning. In: Proceedings of the 28th International Conference on International Conference on Machine Learning (ICML'11), pp. 689–696 (2011)

Technologies Applied to Remote Supervision of Exercise in Peripheral Arterial Disease: A Literature Review

Dennis Paulino, Arsénio Reis[✉], João Barroso, and Hugo Paredes

INESC TEC and University of Trás-os-Montes e Alto Douro, Vila Real, Portugal
dennis.l.paulino@inesctec.pt,
{ars,jbarroso,hparedes}@utad.pt

Abstract. In this review the objective is to search for technologies that supervise the exercise or physical activity of people suffering from Peripheral Arterial Disease (PAD) at home or in the community. Patients with PAD have walking limitations and their quality of life progressively deteriorates. The regular practice of exercise can help mitigate these effects and even improve their health status. The methodology used was to search for scientific articles published since 2008, with the final result of 18 articles. The results show the most frequent technologies used are based on the accelerometer device, with the tests being performed on a treadmill at a hospital. The hospital tests are expensive, so a useful and viable alternative is the usage of mobile devices to help the health professionals record the exercise performed by their patients suffering with PAD.

Keywords: Peripheral Arterial Disease · Global Positioning System
Accelerometer · Activity Monitor · Exercise · Supervision

1 Introduction

It is estimated that in 2010 there were 202 million people suffering from Peripheral Arterial Disease (PAD). From 2000 to 2010 there was an increase of approximately 23.5% of people with PAD, 35% of which were people over 80 years old [1]. With the increasing worldwide ageing of the population, it is imperative to implement measures to properly supervise people with PAD [2].

The main symptom of PAD is intermittent claudication, which is defined as a muscle pain that occurs in the leg and is caused by exercise and relieved by rest [3]. It is estimated that between 20 to 40 million people worldwide suffer from this symptom [1], affecting the majority of symptomatic PAD patients [4].

PAD is known to cause the blockage of arteries which affects the blood flow to the lower extremities, consequently affecting the person's ability to walk [5]. In extreme cases, PAD can cause ulcerations or gangrene, leading to amputation of a leg [6]. The quality of life of people suffering from PAD will progressively deteriorate [7]. A recommended treatment for people with PAD is the practice of supervised physical

M. Antona and C. Stephanidis (Eds.): UAHCI 2018, LNCS 10908, pp. 320–329, 2018.
https://doi.org/10.1007/978-3-319-92052-8_25

activity [8]. It is important to understand how exercise can improve the quality of life in terms of health.

The researchers Blair et al. proved that exercise can delay the mortality caused by cancer or cardiovascular diseases [9]. The study conducted by Warburton et al. also proved the aforementioned statement, adding that chronic diseases such as diabetes, obesity and depression can be prevented with the regular practice of physical activity (PA) [10]. It is essential to define what constitutes the necessary amount of physical activity for a person to stay healthy.

The guidelines published by the American College of Sports Medicine and the Centers for Disease Control and Prevention provide important recommendations for people to follow, in order to maintain a healthy lifestyle [11]. These recommendations are based on promoting physical activity, suggesting that all healthy adults should perform at least 30 min of physical activity with moderate intensity, five days per week. The exercises recommended are walking and jogging. The fulfillment of these guidelines could reduce unhealthy weight and the risk of chronic disease. The research conducted by Hallal et al. [12] reached the conclusion that roughly 30% of adults in the world do not fulfill the physical activity recommendations provided by Haskell et al. [11]. Regarding PAD, a study conducted by Lauret et al. [13], involving 94 patients with PAD, assessed the extent to which they fulfilled the recommendations for physical activity, as proposed by Haskell et al. [11]. To evaluate the participants, they had to wear an accelerometer during 7 consecutive days to measure their physical activity. It was concluded that only 46% fulfill the physical activity recommendations.

There are currently several methods and techniques to promote and evaluate exercise in PAD. They can be divided into two main categories: supervised exercise programs (SEP); and home-based exercise programs (HEP). The SEP include treadmill walking [14] and a 6-min walking test [15]. These tests need to be done in a hospital environment, which does not reflect real-world conditions, when compared to a neighborhood walk for instance. In addition, it has higher costs to the patients [16]. Makris et al. elaborated a review based on the SEP and HEP in PAD and suggested that the HEP could be a cost-reduction alternative to SEP by using pedometers to motivate and supervise PAD patients [17]. In HEP, it is also possible to use the global positioning system (GPS) to supervise the walks of people suffering from PAD [18].

The research conducted by Regensteiner et al. reveals that in PAD, hospital SEP provides better results for improving the health condition of patients with PAD, particularly when compared to unsupervised HEP [19]. This study also highlighted that the hospital exercise programs were not accessible to all patients, so many health professionals recommended the unsupervised home exercise program. A solution to mitigate this problem is to remotely supervise the patient's physical activity at home.

In order to remotely supervise people's physical activity, it is possible to use objective or subjective methods. The study conducted by Lin & Moudon compared the effectiveness of measuring people walking using both objective and subjective methods. Objective methods referred to the collection of data on the field using technological devices, while subjective methods assessed people's perceptions of their walks using questionnaires. In PAD it is possible to apply questionnaires to measure the person's walking ability [20, 21]. It was concluded that the objective methods were more effective than the subjective methods [22].

Nowadays it is possible to monitor the patients' physical activity at home using technological equipment. Some studies achieve this by using a system to supervise the personal wellbeing and by collecting data about the patient's physical activity, e.g., the step count or the type of activity executed by the user [23, 24]. These techniques have been studied and used by the authors for health and accessibility purposes [25–29], as well as the pervasive approach for collecting data e.g., gamification strategy for user engagement [30–32].

This work will conduct a review of articles that report the creation of systems with the objective of supervising a person using technological devices, which is done to help health professionals keep track of the patients' wellbeing through their physical activity data.

2 Methodology

In this review, the objective is to search for technologies that can supervise or monitor people suffering with PAD in terms of their physical activity at home or in the community. The reason is that supervising exercise can improve the quality of life in PAD patients [8]. As reported in the Introduction section, Home Exercise Programs can be a cost-effective solution [16], so in this review we wanted to search for technologies such as mobile and GPS which allow people with PAD to have supervised exercise at home or in their community. The database chosen was Google Scholar, using 2008 as the base year, and the query with Boolean operators was "peripheral arterial disease" AND (mobile OR "global positioning system") AND (home OR community) AND (supervise OR monitor) AND (exercise OR "physical activity") AND technology. After applying the exclusion criteria, the results were the following:

- The first query returned 691 publications;
- The duplicates were removed (4);
- The publications to which the authors couldn't get access or which were not in English were removed (56);
- The publications that were not scientific articles were removed (89);
- The reviews (15) and the surveys (3) were removed;
- After an analysis of the title, the abstract, or if necessary the whole article, the articles that did not focus on people with PAD were removed (460), as well as the articles that didn't include supervision of physical activity or exercise (46).

After applying this methodology, the final results returned 18 articles related to peripheral arterial disease, which included mobile or GPS technology to supervise the physical activity or the exercise of people with PAD.

3 Results

The articles retrieved from the review were grouped as follows: twelve were based on the accelerometer; six were based on GPS; two were based on a smartphone application; and another one, was based on a smartwatch app.

The articles that were based on the accelerometer [13, 33–43] consisted of giving the accelerometer to people with PAD, frequently integrated in an Activity Monitor (AM), with the objective of measuring their physical activity for seven consecutive days. These tests had the goal of determining if the accelerometer could improve the health status or walking ability in people suffering with PAD. From these articles, seven used treadmill tests to complement the results, while four used questionnaires to obtain the subjective measures from patients on the parameters of the walk, such as distance or time. It is important to highlight that the treadmill was used in nearly 60% of the articles based on the accelerometer, revealing that it currently still counts as a frequent tool to measure the walking progress of PAD patients, confirming some articles in the literature, which refer to the treadmill tests in PAD is the gold standard [44]. From this review it was found that the data collected from accelerometers is significantly correlated with the data collected in the treadmill [35, 42] and that the activities, identified by the activity monitor (AM) with the accelerometer, presented good results. However, the research conducted by Gardner et al. [37] revealed that the results obtained in the hospital, using tools like treadmill tests, get better results in improving walking ability, especially when compared to the data collected in AM.

The articles that were based on GPS [45–47] consisted of logging the users' location and supervising the user for one hour in an outdoor environment, and then repeating the test with at least one month interval. The data collected is: the distance, the number of stops and the speed of walking. In the three articles, only one compared the collected data with the treadmill. One article argued that GPS can be a useful tool to supervise the exercise program and that it correlated with the subjective questionnaires that were used for collecting feedback from the users [46]. Another article reported that GPS data correlated with the treadmill tests [47], while another one confirmed that the data collected confirmed the initial hypothesis of that study [45]. In all three articles about GPS, the data correlated with their hypothesis or methods, proving that GPS can be a useful tool to assess a person's activity.

The article related to using a smartwatch application [16] supervised the patients' steps and gave daily pre-defined notifications for people to meet their exercise goals. They concluded that the people with PAD significantly improved their walking ability.

The articles related to smartphone applications [48, 49] were both in development. The research conducted by Fokkenrood et al., described a web portal to connect health professionals, personal trainers and PAD patients, with the aim of supervising and motivating PAD patients [48]. Also, this research also reported the development of a mobile app to calculate the distance between GPS updates. The approach described by Reis et al. [49] revealed that with the implementation of a web service (a mechanism to facilitate remote communication with the database), a smartphone application and a web portal it was possible to supervise and monitor patients with PAD. In this approach, it is advisable for the development to focus on user-centered designs to solve some problems related to user usability, which might be possible by making an application that can be accessible to the target population and capable of automatically synchronizing the collected data with the webservice.

Table 1 shows an overview of the results retrieved from the review on technologies that can help supervise exercise in PAD.

Table 1. Overview of the articles included in review

Article	Method	Assessment			Observation
		AR	Que	Tre	
(Klonizakis et al., 2018) [45]	GPS	✗	✓	✓	The results show that the physical condition deteriorated between the two tests
(Gardner et al., 2017) [33]	Accel.	✗	✗	✓	The participants that did moderate exercise at least 30 min per day had better antioxidant capacity
(Farrah et al., 2016) [34]	Accel.	✗	✗	✓	People with the highest level of sedentarism had lower walking ability, increasing the severity of IC
(Gommans et al., 2016) [35]	Accel.	✗	✗	✓	Participants with the highest severity of IC on the treadmill showed a correlation with the distance measured by AM
(Reis et al., 2017) [49]	Smartph.	✓	✗	✗	Prototype of an app using GPS and Accelerometer to supervise PAD patients
(Loprinzi et al., 2014) [36]	Accel.	✗	✗	✗	The results show that more than 60% of the participants didn't fulfill the PA guidelines
(Normahani et al., 2017) [16]	Smartwa.	✗	✓	✓	It was concluded that the participants significantly improve their walking ability and their health
(Gardner et al., 2016) [37]	Accel.	✗	✓	✓	The results show that the treadmill tests in the hospital obtained better results than the AM
(Gernigon et al., 2015a) [46]	GPS	✗	✓	✗	Concluded that the results from the GPS correlated with the questionnaires implemented
(Kulinski et al., 2015) [38]	Accel.	✗	✓	✗	The results show that the severity of PAD correlated with the time monitored tagged as sedentarism
(Gerningon et al., 2015b) [47]	GPS	✗	✓	✓	It was concluded that the collected data by GPS was reliable and a useful tool to evaluate walking ability
(Stansfield et al., 2015) [39]	Accel.	✗	✗	✗	It was demonstrated that true cadence has more realistic results compared to step accumulation
(Fokkenrood et al., 2014) [40]	Accel.	✗	✗	✗	This study analyzed the effectiveness of an AM to supervise PAD, concluding that it was effective
(Clarke et al., 2013) [41]	Accel.	✗	✗	✗	Proposes a new method to evaluate the IC in a walk, based on the starts and stops of the patients

(*continued*)

Table 1. (*continued*)

Article	Method	Assessment			Observation
		AR	Que	Tre	
(Lauret et al., 2014) [13]	Accel.	✗	✓	✓	The results show that 46% of the PAD participants don't fulfill the ACSM/AHA guidelines for exercise
(Fokkenrood et al., 2012) [48]	GPS	✗	✓	✗	It describes a web platform to help health professionals monitor PAD patients and the development of an app that registers the patients' distance
(Gardner et al., 2008) [42]	Accel.	✗	✗	✓	The conclusion reported that the treadmill parameters correlated with the exercise from the AM
(Murphy et al., 2008) [43]	Accel.	✗	✓	✓	It concluded that the supervised exercise had better results related to medication or revascularization

Legend: "Accel." – "Accelerometer", "Smartph." – "Smartphone, "Smartwa." – "Smartwatch", "AR" – "Autonomous Remote", "Que" – "Questionnaire", "Tre" – "Treadmill", "AM" – Activity Monitor"

Table 1 shows an overview of the review carried out, with some of the parameters such as the methodology, the assessment (autonomous remote supervision, questionnaires about walk details, treadmill) and some observations regarding each article. The autonomous remote supervision is the mechanism to synchronize the collected data automatically, without the need for the patient to deliver the equipment to the researcher or the health professional.

4 Discussion

In the technologies based on the accelerometer, many used equipment that was small and could easily be attached to the body. There were some accelerometers that needed calibration specifically to the person that was wearing them. Some articles reported that the collected data from this equipment could be correlated with other tests such as the treadmill [35, 42], used to assess the walking capacity of PAD patients. However, there was one study [37] which proved that the tests conducted in a hospital get better results compared to the accelerometer equipment. The reason the hospital supervise exercise program (SEP) improves walking ability might be because of the continuous presence of a health professional who can provide advice and support to the patient. To replicate this effect, it is necessary for the in-home exercise program (HEP) to include remote supervision of people with PAD, with the health professionals supervising the patients at home and even sending notifications to remind the patients to achieve their exercise goals. The patient would have to deliver the accelerometer to the health professionals for them to retrieve the collected data.

All the GPS articles reported in this review could be correlated with their hypothesis or method, proving that this tool could be useful to supervise the patients' exercise. Nevertheless, it presented some disadvantages as well, such as the fact that they only work in outdoor environments and, like the accelerometer, the patients with PAD would have to deliver the equipment to the health professionals for them to retrieve the collected data.

In most of the reviewed articles, the autonomous remote supervision was not addressed. That is because in most articles, the collected data had to be delivered by the patient to the hospital, which could discourage the patients to maintain the exercise program. There were two articles that approach these issues, though their solutions were still in development [48, 49]. The method related with autonomous remote supervision could resolve the problems related to motivation of people suffering from PAD [37], while still being a cost-effective solution. With this method it is possible for health professionals to supervise their patients at home and to schedule targets or objectives for the patients to maintain their health status.

5   Conclusion

In this article, a review of technologies was conducted with the aim of helping health professionals to supervise the exercise or physical activity in people suffering from PAD. Most of these people have walking limitations that will deteriorate with time. To mitigate and reverse this outcome, it is essential to encourage and to monitor them to perform exercise regularly. The SEP programs in hospitals are expensive and don't replicate the community's conditions, so a better alternative is to use technologies to help in the supervision of exercise at home.

From the articles reviewed, the most frequent technology found was the implementation of accelerometers, frequently in the form of activity monitors. The use of this equipment is highlighted by the many studies that validate this technology for PAD patients. They also demonstrate certain disadvantages related to the initial calibration specific to each person, as well as the need for someone with technical knowledge to retrieve the data. In this review, some articles were also found which describe tests using GPS to track people's locations in order to calculate the distance. This equipment has the same disadvantage as the accelerometer with regards to the technical knowledge needed to retrieve the data.

A better solution might be to implement a monitoring system and to perform remote supervision in people with PAD, simplifying the process of retrieving the collected data. This can be done with an application on a mobile device with the capability of synchronizing the collected data via the Web, so that health professionals can keep track of the status of the patients walking ability. These solutions were found in two articles which reported this approach as still in development.

Acknowledgements. This work was supported by Project "NanoSTIMA: Macro-to-Nano Human Sensing: Towards Integrated Multimodal Health Monitoring and Analytics/NORTE-01-0145-FEDER-000016" financed by the North Portugal Regional Operational Programme (NORTE 2020), under the PORTUGAL 2020 Partnership Agreement, and through the European Regional Development Fund (ERDF).

References

1. Fowkes, F.G.R., et al.: Comparison of global estimates of prevalence and risk factors for peripheral artery disease in 2000 and 2010: a systematic review and analysis. Lancet **382**, 1329–1340 (2013)
2. Fowkes, F.G.R., et al.: Peripheral artery disease: epidemiology and global perspectives. Nat. Rev. Cardiol. **14**, 156–170 (2016)
3. Norgren, L., et al.: Inter-Society Consensus for the Management of Peripheral Arterial Disease (TASC II). J. Vasc. Surg. **45**(1), S5–S67 (2007)
4. Vodnala, D., Rajagopalan, S., Brook, R.D.: Medical management of the patient with intermittent claudication. Cardiol. Clin. **29**, 363–379 (2011)
5. Criqui, M.H., Aboyans, V.: Epidemiology of peripheral artery disease. Circ. Res. **116**, 1509–1526 (2015)
6. Weitz, J.I., et al.: Diagnosis and treatment of chronic arterial insufficiency of the lower extremities: a critical review. Circulation **94**(11), 3026–3049 (1996)
7. McDermott, M.M., et al.: Prognostic value of functional performance for mortality in patients with peripheral artery disease. J. Am. Coll. Cardiol. **51**(15), 1482–1489 (2008)
8. Gornik, H.L., Beckman, J.A.: Peripheral arterial disease. Circulation **111**(13), e169–e172 (2005)
9. Blair, S.N., et al.: Physical fitness and all-cause mortality: a prospective study of healthy men and women. JAMA **262**(17), 2395–2401 (1989)
10. Warburton, D.E.R., Bredin, S.S.D.: Reflections on physical activity and health: what should we recommend? Can. J. Cardiol. **32**(4), 495–504 (2016)
11. Haskell, W.L., et al.: Physical activity and public health: updated recommendation for adults from the American college of sports medicine and the American heart association. Circulation **116**(9), 1081 (2007)
12. Hallal, P.C., et al.: Global physical activity levels: surveillance progress, pitfalls, and prospects. Lancet **380**(9838), 247–257 (2012)
13. Lauret, G.J., et al.: Physical activity monitoring in patients with intermittent claudication. Eur. J. Vasc. Endovasc. Surg. **47**, 656–663 (2014)
14. Degischer, S., et al.: Reproducibility of constant-load treadmill testing with various treadmill protocols and predictability of treadmill test results in patients with intermittent claudication. J. Vasc. Surg. **36**(1), 83–88 (2002)
15. Montgomery, P.S., Gardner, A.W.: The clinical utility of a six-minute walk test in peripheral arterial occlusive disease patients. J. Am. Geriatr. Soc. **46**(6), 706–711 (1998)
16. Normahani, P., et al.: Wearable Sensor Technology Efficacy in Peripheral Vascular Disease (wSTEP): A Randomized Controlled Trial. Ann. Surg. (2017)
17. Makris, G.C., et al.: Availability of supervised exercise programs and the role of structured home-based exercise in peripheral arterial disease. Eur. J. Vasc. Endovasc. Surg. **44**, 569–575 (2012)
18. Le Faucheur, A., et al.: Measurement of walking distance and speed in patients with peripheral arterial disease: a novel method using a global positioning system. Circ. **117**(7), 897–904 (2008)
19. Regensteiner, J.G., et al.: Hospital vs home-based exercise rehabilitation for patients with peripheral arterial occlusive disease. Angiol. **48**(4), 291–300 (1997)
20. Ouedraogo, N., et al.: Validation of a new simple questionnaire to "estimate ambulation capacity by history" (EACH) in patients with claudication. J. Vasc. Surg. **54**(1), 133–138 (2011)

21. Myers, S.A., et al.: Claudication distances and the walking impairment questionnaire best describe the ambulatory limitations in patients with symptomatic peripheral arterial disease. J. Vasc. Surg. **47**(3), 550–555 (2008)
22. Lin, L., Moudon, A.V.: Objective versus subjective measures of the built environment, which are most effective in capturing associations with walking? Health place **16**(2), 339–348 (2010)
23. Ata, R., et al.: IP225 VascTrac: a study of peripheral artery disease via smartphones to improve remote disease monitoring and postoperative surveillance. J. Vasc. Surg. **65**(6), 115S–116S (2017)
24. Paulino, D., Reis, A., Barroso, J., Paredes, H.: Mobile devices to monitor physical activity and health data. In: 12th Iberian Conference on Information Systems and Technologies (CISTI) (2017). https://doi.org/10.23919/cisti.2017.7975771
25. Abreu, J., Rebelo, S., Paredes, H., Barroso, J., Martins, P., Reis, A., Amorim, E.V., Filipe, V.: Assessment of Microsoft kinect in the monitoring and rehabilitation of stroke patients. In: Rocha, Á., Correia, A.M., Adeli, H., Reis, L.P., Costanzo, S. (eds.) WorldCIST 2017. AISC, vol. 570, pp. 167–174. Springer, Cham (2017). https://doi.org/10.1007/978-3-319-56538-5_18
26. Reis, A., Paredes, H., Barroso, I., Monteiro, M., Rodrigues, V., Khanal, S., Barroso, J.: Autonomous systems to support social activity of elderly people - A prospective approach to a system design. TISHW2016. In: International Conference on Technology and Innovation on Sports, Health and wellbeing. December 1–3, 2016 - UTAD, Vila Real, Portugal (2016). https://doi.org/10.1109/tishw.2016.7847773
27. Sousa, A., Faria, J., Barbosa, M., Barroso, J., Filipe, V., Reis, A.: SIGROVU-Sistema inteligente de gestão de recolha de óleos vegetais usados. In Actas 4° Conf. Ibérica de Sistemas e Tecnologias de Informação (CISTI), pp. 267–272 (2009). ISBN 978-989-96247-1-9
28. Reis, A., Martins, P., Borges, J., Sousa, A., Rocha, T., Barroso, J.: Supporting accessibility in higher education information systems: a 2016 update. In: Antona, M., Stephanidis, C. (eds.) UAHCI 2017. LNCS, vol. 10277, pp. 227–237. Springer, Cham (2017). https://doi.org/10.1007/978-3-319-58706-6_19
29. Reis, A., Reis, C., Morgado, L., Borges, J., Tavares, F., Gonçalves, R., Cruz, J.B.: Management of surgery waiting lists in the Portuguese public healthcare network: The information system for waiting list recovery programs. In: 11th Iberian Conference on Information Systems and Technologies (CISTI), pp. 1–7. IEEE, June 2016. https://doi.org/10.1109/cisti.2016.7521612
30. Paulino, D., Amaral, D., Amaral, M., Reis, A., Barroso, J., Rocha, T.: Professor Piano: A Music Application for People with Intellectual Disabilities. In: Proceedings of the 7th International Conference on Software Development and Technologies for Enhancing Accessibility and Fighting Info-exclusion, Vila Real, Portugal (2016). https://doi.org/10.1145/3019943.3019982
31. Reis, A., Lains, J., Paredes, H., Filipe, V., Abrantes, C., Ferreira, F., Mendes, R., Amorim, P., Barroso, J.: Developing a System for Post-Stroke Rehabilitation: An Exergames Approach. In: Antona, M., Stephanidis, C. (eds.) UAHCI 2016. LNCS, vol. 9739, pp. 403–413. Springer, Cham (2016). https://doi.org/10.1007/978-3-319-40238-3_39
32. Gonçalves, C., Rocha, T., Reis, A., Barroso, J.: AppVox: An Application to Assist People with Speech Impairments in Their Speech Therapy Sessions. In: Rocha, Á., Correia, A.M., Adeli, H., Reis, L.P., Costanzo, S. (eds.) WorldCIST 2017. AISC, vol. 570, pp. 581–591. Springer, Cham (2017). https://doi.org/10.1007/978-3-319-56538-5_59
33. Gardner, A.W., et al.: Association between daily walking and antioxidant capacity in patients with symptomatic peripheral artery disease. J. Vasc. Surg. **65**, 1762–1768 (2017)

34. Farah, B.Q., et al.: Factors associated with sedentary behavior in patients with intermittent claudication. Eur. J. Vasc. Endovasc. Surg. **52**, 809–814 (2016)
35. Gommans, L.N.M., et al.: Minimal correlation between physical exercise capacity and daily activity in patients with intermittent claudication. J. Vasc. Surg. **63**, 983–989 (2016)
36. Loprinzi, P.D.: Using A New Accelerometry Method to Assess Lifestyle Movement Patterns of Americans: Influence of Demographic and Chronic Disease Characteristics. Open Access J. Sci. Technol. **2**, 1–12 (2014)
37. Gardner, A.W., et al.: Effect of cognitive status on exercise performance and quality of life in patients with symptomatic peripheral artery disease. J. Vasc. Surg. **63**, 98–104 (2016)
38. Kulinski, J.P., et al.: Association between low ankle-brachial index and accelerometer-derived sedentary and exercise time in the asymptomatic general population. Vasc. Med. (United Kingdom) **20**, 332–338 (2015)
39. Stansfield, B., et al.: True cadence and step accumulation are not equivalent: The effect of intermittent claudication on free-living cadence. Gait Posture **41**, 414–419 (2015)
40. Fokkenrood, H.J.P., et al.: Physical activity monitoring in patients with peripheral arterial disease: Validation of an activity monitor. Eur. J. Vasc. Endovasc. Surg. **48**, 194–200 (2014)
41. Clarke, C.L., et al.: Free-living physical activity as a novel outcome measure in patients with intermittent claudication. Eur. J. Vasc. Endovasc. Surg. **45**, 162–167 (2013)
42. Gardner, A.W., et al.: Association between daily ambulatory activity patterns and exercise performance in patients with intermittent claudication. J. Vasc. Surg. **48**, 1238–1244 (2008)
43. Murphy, T.P., et al.: The Claudication: Exercise Vs. Endoluminal Revascularization (CLEVER) study: Rationale and methods. J. Vasc. Surg. **47**, 1356–1363 (2008)
44. Nicolaï, S.P., et al.: Reliability of treadmill testing in peripheral arterial disease: a meta-regression analysis. J. Vasc. Surg. **50**(2), 322–329 (2009)
45. Klonizakis, M., et al.: Real-life adaptations in walking patterns in patients with established peripheral arterial disease assessed using a global positioning system in the community: a cohort study. Clinical Physiology and Functional Imaging (2018)
46. Gernigon, M., et al.: Global positioning system use in the community to evaluate improvements in walking after revascularization: a prospective multicenter study with 6-month follow-up in patients with peripheral arterial disease. Medicine **94**, e838 (2015)
47. Gernigon, M., et al.: Test-retest reliability of GPS derived measurements in patients with claudication. Eur. J. Vasc. Endovasc. Surg. **50**, 623–629 (2015)
48. Fokkenrood, H.J., et al.: Multidisciplinary treatment for peripheral arterial occlusive disease and the role of eHealth and mHealth. J. Multidiscip. Healthc. **5**, 257 (2012)
49. Reis, A., et al.: Usage of mobile devices to help people suffering from peripheral arterial disease upkeep a healthy life. Global Journal of Physical Medicine and Rehabilitation, 1–3 (2017)

Low-Cost Smart Surveillance System for Smart Cities

Rúben Pereira[1], Diogo Correia[1], Luís Mendes[1,4], Carlos Rabadão[1(✉)],
João Barroso[3], and António Pereira[1,2]

[1] School of Technology and Management,
Computer Science and Communication Research Center,
Polytechnic Institute of Leiria, 2411-901 Leiria, Portugal
{2172574, 2170160}@my.ipleiria.pt,
{lmendes, carlos.rabadao, apereira}@ipleiria.pt
[2] Information and Communications Technologies Unit, INOV INESC
Innovation, Delegation Office at Leiria, Leiria, Portugal
[3] INESC TEC and University of Trás-os-Montes e Alto Douro,
Quinta de Prados, 5000-801 Vila Real, Portugal
jbarroso@utad.pt
[4] Instituto de Telecomunicações, Lisbon, Portugal

Abstract. The safety of people and spaces is of paramount importance for societies. With time, the implementation of safety measures is rapidly changing from a need to a priority. Video surveillance systems play a key role in the surveillance of crucial and critical areas as these systems help the authorities keep places safer. With the rapid growth of technology and the implementation of the smart city concept, it is becoming possible to develop and deploy wide area surveillance systems. The ease with which these systems can be installed in private and public spaces (e.g., homes, streets and parks) allow for the creation of ubiquitous monitored environments. Rapid intervention responses to any abnormal situation or the use of recorded video as evidence are some advantages of the use of this type of surveillance systems. Although ubiquitous video surveillance systems are relevant for present modern societies, their cost is still high. To solve or, at least to mitigate this problem, a low-cost smart surveillance system was developed, which is presented and described in this paper. The developed surveillance system, based on available low-cost technology, can help keep critical spaces under surveillance 24/7. The proposed solution was found to have a minimal cost, a low bandwidth, and to be scalable and adaptable to every client's needs. Thus, the solution can be used by anybody (private and public) and applied in different contexts (e.g., residential, industrial). The system can provide still images, captured from surveillance video cameras, real time video and real time video processing, which can be used for motion detection. When this happens, the user is warned via an e-mail containing the identification of the respective surveillance camera. Only the relevant video events are sent, recorded and maintained in the cloud platform system, consequently reducing the amount of storage space required to maintain all the historical video events. The results of the tests carried out show that it is possible to stream a video from the surveillance cameras with an insignificant delay and that motion detection

M. Antona and C. Stephanidis (Eds.): UAHCI 2018, LNCS 10908, pp. 330–339, 2018.
https://doi.org/10.1007/978-3-319-92052-8_26

can be attained through real time video processing. The system presented potentiates a low-cost solution for a smart city in the surveillance field.

Keywords: Surveillance · Video analyses · Anytime · Anywhere Assistive environments · Internet of Things (IoT)

1 Introduction

The term Internet of Things (IoT) was first used years ago by industry researchers, but has only recently emerged into the mainstream public eye [1]. This concept is used to describe the capacity of network connected equipments and devices to sense and collect different types of data and then share that information across the Internet in order to be processed and used in several applications. The term industrial Internet is commonly used interchangeably with IoT [2], which is not necessarily correct since it refers primarily to commercial applications of the IoT technology in the manufacturing field, whereas the IoT covers a much wider range of applications and therefore it is not limited to industrial ones. It is believed that in the next decades the IoT will have a major impact on how society will evolve. In fact, the numbers confirm that the IoT is growing fast, gaining vast attention from a wide range of industries. Projections show that the IoT will be one of the most important areas of future technology [1].

The data collected from a wide variety of IoT devices such as, surveillance video cameras, sensors, vehicles, home appliances, medical devices, among others, will promote the appearance of numerous applications and new services for citizens, companies and public administrations. Indeed, the IoT concept can be used in a large number of disparate domains, such as industrial and home automation, civil protection, elderly assistance, e-health, smart grids, smart and precision agriculture, traffic management, and so on.

One of the fields where the IoT concept can be used to respond to the challenges launched by many governments worldwide is in the intelligent management of cities, i.e., in the implementation of the Smart City concept [3]. This concept does not yet have a uniquely universal definition, and, in some cases, its usage is inappropriate. The concept behind the Smart City designation is increasingly popular, though in many cases it is referred to by different names and in different circumstances, since there is a range of conceptual variants generated by replacing "Smart" with other alternative adjectives. Nevertheless, nowadays the usage of the word "Smart" captures the innovative and transformative changes driven by new technologies, not forgetting the social factors which are also important [4]. Thus, in an attempt to define a Smart City, it can be said to be a large organic system, having a close relationship with all its core subsystems, where none of them operates in isolation [4]. In a simpler way, it is a city that uses advanced technologies to face the main problems of urban life, such as traffic, parking, lighting, pollution, garbage collection, city crowding, poverty, surveillance and maintenance of public areas, among others [5, 6].

It is difficult to find a definition of closed-circuit television (CCTV) in the technical and scientific literature, as many writers assume in their texts that everybody knows what they are referring to [7]. Nonetheless, in a simplified way, a CCTV system can be considered as a closed system that gathers video images in a single place. It differs from video broadcast systems because the signal is not openly transmitted. Thus, it can be used to maintain a close observation of a person or group. Indeed, one of the main usage domains of CCTV systems is in the surveillance of areas that may need monitoring, such as banks, stores and other areas where security is needed. These systems are used to monitor behaviors, activities, or other information concerning the specific location, in order to possibly prevent disasters and to protect goods and people. Despite the advantages listed above, these systems require a large amount of storage space to keep the recorded videos, as well as people watching them at all times.

Security is a growing concern of modern societies. As time goes by, cities are investing in intelligent surveillance systems, which contribute to the reinforcement and deployment of the Smart City concept. With smarter cities comes smarter responsibilities, video surveillance being one of them [8]. Nowadays, with the steady increase of the population and people moving around the world, it is not physically possible for law enforcement agents to watch every event and follow suspects around for great lengths of time. Consequently, agencies have begun relying on surveillance systems and technologies to help them monitor people's activity and to keep places safer.

This paper presents a low-cost smart surveillance platform designed to create a ubiquitous environment and to adapt to the client's needs, providing them with the best experience possible. The architecture was thought to have the lowest cost possible and to satisfy the different needs of each user, by allowing them to choose which type of surveillance cameras to employ and where to place them. The solution developed is suitable to citizens, companies and public organizations (e.g., city council). The service provided by the developed platform uses intelligent data recording, only registering the moments where motion is detected to reduce the storage space needed, to facilitate and speed up the occurrence search. In addition, it is also able to notify the client during an occurrence.

The proposed and developed integrated platform is a low-cost, scalable and customizable surveillance system with the intent of providing a secure environment and improving people's perception of security. The rest of the paper is organized as follows. Section 2 presents some studies related to surveillance systems. The general architecture of the proposed solution is described in Sect. 3. In Sect. 4, the implementation of a functional surveillance system is presented. Finally, in Sect. 5, the conclusions are drawn and some ideas for future work are presented.

2 Background

The field of Smart Cities is growing fast and becoming increasingly popular as a subject, particularly with regards to security. For this reason, some important scientific studies are available in the technical and scientific literature referring to the security domain involving Smart Cities.

The work presented by Duarte Duque et al. [9] states that with assistance from state of the art algorithms to segment, track and classify moving objects it is possible to turn the video surveillance system into an observer. These video surveillance systems are able to detect and predict abnormal behaviors using real-time unsupervised learning.

The large deployment of these surveillance cameras could easily create an intelligent surveillance system, thus avoiding the need to have people analyzing surveillance videos, even when there are no occurrences.

The intelligent video surveillance system presented in [10], which is based on an image subtraction method allowing to the object to be identified, demonstrates that it is possible to detect motion in live video feed.

In [11], a way of tracking moving objects is presented, as well as how to create a filter that selects only the objects of interest. This paper demonstrates that surveillance systems with motion detection could also be used to search for something specific.

The work presented in [12] states that with a low-cost, low-power microcomputer (Raspberry Pi) and a low-cost camera it is possible to create a surveillance device capable of streaming the captured video in real-time to any browser. This paper further describes that it is still possible to reduce the required storage space for these types of solutions with the help of motion detection algorithms.

As stated in [13], a Smart City is supposed to be a safe place, where video surveillance plays an important role. However, keeping operators in a control room 24/7 is not the best option. Instead of having operators watching the surveillance videos permanently, the system, which comprises innumerable cameras spread everywhere, should be able to detect and track suspicious objects autonomously and in real-time.

The studies presented above make a significant contribution to the field of smart video surveillance, as the concepts reported in these papers are very useful and can be used as a base reference. The video surveillance solution described in this paper is a low-cost, scalable and customizable to client's needs.

3   System Architecture

The architecture of a surveillance system for smart cities should be modular, scalable, ubiquitous and, most importantly, low-cost. The system modularity is accomplished if the user has a panoply of different equipment at their disposal that can be chosen in order to implement a given solution. Thus, they can choose a device with different characteristics, according to their needs. For example, if the user only wants live streaming functionalities and does not care about image quality, they can choose the device with the lowest price that includes live streaming capabilities. On the other hand, if the user wants to have video analysis functionalities and good image quality, they should choose a good performance device in spite of the price.

The scalable characteristic is important to maintain the flexibility of the system and control costs (minimized). In order to do so, all the smart camera devices should be wireless, i.e., the devices can only communicate with the internet wirelessly. Thus, with this solution there is no need to add physical infrastructures (e.g., cables) when a new device is set up. Besides that, the user can always add more modules to their system according to their needs, without the requirement of having to change the existing infrastructure.

Ubiquity is a very important characteristic of smart surveillance systems. To that end, the system can only be deployed where there are internet connections of some sort (e.g. wireless, mobile data or cable internet). Lastly, the overall system acquisition and maintenance costs should be kept low. This can be accomplished by a careful selection of common IoT hardware that fulfil the specifications and price.

The proposed system architecture, shown in Fig. 1, comprises several entities, namely, the server entity, surveillance entity and the user's entity. The server entity, represented in Fig. 1 by the Online Platform, is responsible for managing all the data received from the devices' modules and to provide an online platform allowing the authenticated users to access the data anytime, anywhere.

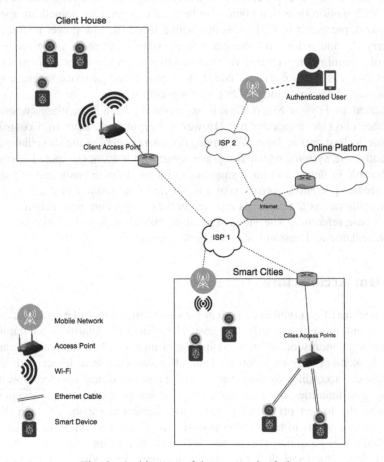

Fig. 1. Architecture of the proposed solution.

The surveillance entity, represented by the "Smart Cities" and the "Client's House" blocks in Fig. 1, includes the devices responsible for recording and detecting motion. This entity's devices are connected to the server entity via internet.

The Authenticated User block of Fig. 1 corresponds to the user's entity. This entity represents all the authenticated users, which can access the devices in the surveillance entity and check live-stream feeds, take pictures, check motion logs and set alarms. If a person (or an organization) wants to become an effective user, they only needs to access the online platform and create an account. After that, the new authenticated user can set up all their devices and enjoy all the services provided by the integrated system.

The proposed system and architecture is based on the edge computing concept since all the data are managed and processed on both edges of the system, balancing the computing power needed on the used IoT devices. Since the relevant data are produced on the devices' modules, at the edge of the network, it is more efficient in terms of the required system communication bandwidth to process the data at the end devices than in the cloud servers [14]. If the processing data operation was performed in the cloud servers, a larger bandwidth would be required.

4 Implementation

This section presents and describes the development and implementation of a functional prototype in order to demonstrate the technical and economic feasibility of the proposed smart surveillance system. Figure 2 presents the diagram of the implemented system. As can be seen, the development encompassed three different camera modules (with different characteristics and performances) and the online platform.

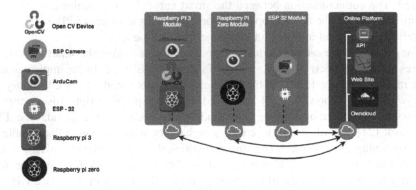

Fig. 2. Diagram of the camera modules and online platform.

The Raspberry Pi 3 [15] module, which belongs to the surveillance entity referred to in Sect. 3, is the most advanced of the three developed modules. It can detect motion, record videos, take pictures, and it can also stream live videos. Among the three developed modules, this is the one that has the highest cost; on the other hand, it has more features and provides the best image quality.

The motion detection feature of this module requires the Raspberry Pi computing power to process and continuously analyze the video captured by the RaspyCam [16] that is attached to the Raspberry Pi 3. This module can be seen as a smart surveillance camera. The motion detection algorithm developed for this module uses the image recognition library of the OpenCV [17]. When a movement is detected by the smart surveillance camera, it immediately starts to record the video until the movement ceases. Then, the smart device uploads the recorded video to the online platform module. The live streaming and picture taking features are always available on the smart surveillance cameras. To activate them, the user only needs to make that request. After doing so, the live stream or picture taking become immediately available. All the captured data (videos and pictures) are sent and stored in the online platform module.

The Raspberry Pi Zero [18] and ESP-32 [19] modules are also part of the surveillance entity of Sect. 3. These two modules are constituted by devices with a computing power lower than the one used in the module described above. Because of that, these modules do not have the motion detect feature via local video analysis, though they are cheaper alternatives to live-streaming videos. The Raspberry Pi Zero module has more computing power than the ESP 32 module, so it provides higher image quality and also allows the user to take pictures from the online platform. These devices are important for the modularity and scalability of the system because several options are offered to the users, allowing them to choose the right device for their needs.

In Sect. 3, the online platform of Fig. 2 is the server entity. In the developed system, the main online platform is responsible for centralizing all the data sent by the smart surveillance modules, allowing the user to check live video streams, take pictures, and check the movement log of all their devices at anytime, anywhere. Through this module, it is also possible to set alarms on each device. When triggered (by movement detection), the system alerts the user via email and sends the video where the movement was detected. The communication between the smart surveillance modules and the online platform is accomplished by an application programming interface (API), which allows registering devices and information exchange in real time.

The devices of the camera modules responsible for managing the smart surveillance features are the Raspberry Pi 3, Raspberry Pi Zero and ESP-32. In the implementation of the motion detection feature in the Raspberry Pi 3 module, the OpenCV library was used, while the Python 3.0 [20] was used to develop the scripts (using threads) responsible for recording, storing and sending the video to the cloud. The Flask framework [21] was also used to create a webserver with endpoints that enable the video streaming and picture taking functionalities. In the Raspberry Pi Zero camera module, the Python 3.0 was also used and the Flask framework for the same functionalities but due to the lack of computing power (Raspberry Pi 3 has 1.2 GHz and quad core processor vs Raspberry Pi Zero that has a 1.0 GHz and single-core processor) and memory (Raspberry Pi 3 has 1 GB vs 512 MB of the Raspberry Pi Zero), the video recognition is not available. The ESP-32 was programmed with C language and, once again, due to a lack of computing power, it was only possible to live stream video with this module.

The online platform consists of one website, an API for the communications with the devices, a database and the ownCloud [22] service. The website and API were developed using the Laravel [23] platform (using PHP and JavaScript). The website comprises different areas, namely, the landing page, login, registration, alarms and devices management. The API is constituted by routes that enable the devices to connect to the platform. To verify the user, the route /api/login will submit the user data (email and password) and return an authentication token (if the user is registered on the platform). This token is used to ensure the user authenticity. The route /api/device/add is used to register a device using the user token and to add the device information (e.g., MAC address, IP address, state, type of device) to the database. The route /api/motion/add, which uses the user token, adds a motion log to the database and a uniform resource locator (url) to the video. The route /api/picture/add, which also uses the user token, adds the time of the picture and the ownCloud shared link to the database.

The ownCloud service is responsible for managing the pictures and videos of each user cameras. When the user creates an account on the online platform, a user account is also automatically created on the ownCloud platform. When motion is detected, or a picture is taken, the device sends the video to the ownCloud servers, as illustrated in Fig. 3. After the video is stored, the ownCloud returns a shared link to the device that is published on the website using the routes /api/motion/add for the video and /api/picture/add for the image captured. Also, an email is sent to the user, warning them that a motion was detected.

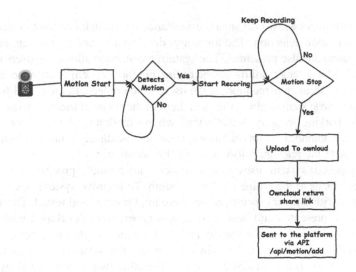

Fig. 3. Motion recording diagram.

5 Assessment Tests of the Solution

Several tests were conducted to assess the performance of all the electronic parts (hardware and software) and of the cloud platform. The used methodology for testing the electronic parts is the following one. First, each surveillance camera was tested independently of all the others. The video stream from each one must be accessible on the cloud platform. This way, the quality of the video stream of each surveillance camera can be analyzed. After the video stream validation of all the surveillance cameras, the ones able to take pictures were tested. To do so, the platform requested each surveillance camera to capture a frame from the stream. Then, it was checked whether the frame was stored in the cloud. After confirming the expected behavior of each surveillance camera, the communication with the cloud and captured feature were both evaluated. To test the motion detection, the surveillance camera was left in a classroom pointed towards the door. Each time someone entered or left the classroom the Raspberry Pi 3 module recorded the video and sent it to the cloud platform, also sending the respective warning email to the user.

For testing the cloud platform (ownCloud and website), some simple load tests were carried out. With a script in Python, a scenario was simulated where several cameras detected motion at the same time interval and uploaded the respective video file to ownCloud, triggering the warning message in the website and sending an email. After confirming that every file was uploaded successfully, and all emails were sent without any significant delay, the load test was completed, and the platform fulfilled the initial specifications.

6   Conclusion and Future Work

This paper introduces a low-cost smart surveillance system that integrates video analysis for real time motion detection. The topology, development and assessment tests of the proposed system are also presented. The system architecture allows the users to interact and control all their cameras through the online platform system at anytime, anywhere. To enhance the security perception of the user, which reflects in their well-being, they can configure the system to always inform them of the status of their cameras, i.e., if the cameras are working properly. Besides that, when a motion or an abnormal situation is detected by the autonomous surveillance system, it immediately sends an alarm message to the user, with the relevant information of the occurrence.

The proposed system uses smart devices to capture, process and send the surveillance videos to the online platform system. To improve system flexibility, three smart devices with different specifications were implemented and tested. These devices, which are also presented and described in this paper, were developed with available low-cost technology. To attain the desired performance, each smart device uses different surveillance cameras and hardware. One of the smart devices comprises an ArduCAM (OV2640) and an ESP32. One of the other two is constituted by a Raspi-Cam and a Raspberry Pi Zero W and, the last one, comprises one RaspiCam and a Raspberry Pi 3 Model B. Although the smart devices have different cameras and hardware, their operation functionalities are similar. All the data collected by them are sent to the cloud servers system. The performance assessment conducted on these smart devices demonstrates the feasibility of the solution.

Finally, it is important to mention that the video captured by the smart devices implemented has a relatively low frames rate, i.e., a low number of frames per second (FPS). Thus, in a near future, and to improve the video FPS captured by the smart devices, different solutions from the ones adopted in this paper will be studied. One major feature that will be developed and implemented is facial recognition capability, so that the smart devices do not trigger movement warnings in case of authorized users (familiar faces).

Acknowledgment. This work was supported by national funds through the Portuguese Foundation for Science and Technology (FCT) under the project UID/CEC/04524/2016.

References

1. Lee, I., Lee, K.: The Internet of Things (IoT): applications, investments, and challenges for enterprises. Bus. Horiz. **58**(4), 431–440 (2015)
2. Gilchrist, A.: IIoT Reference architecture. In: Industry 4.0, pp. 65–86 (2016)
3. Zanella, A., Bui, N., Castellani, A., Vangelista, L., Zorzi, M.: Internet of Things for smart cities. IEEE Internet Things J. **1**(1), 22–32 (2014)
4. Nam, T., Pardo, T.A.: Conceptualizing smart city with dimensions of technology, people, and institutions. In: Proceedings of the 12th Annual International Digital Government Research Conference on Digital Government Innovation in Challenging Times - DG.O 2011, p. 282 (2011)
5. Dameri, R.P.: Searching for Smart City definition: a comprehensive proposal. Int. J. Comput. Technol. **11**(5), 2544–2551 (2013)
6. Marcelino, I., Barroso, J., Cruz, J.B., Pereira, A.: Elder Care Architecture: a physical and social approach. Int. J. Adv. Life Sci. **2**(1&2), 53–62 (2010)
7. Goold, B.J.: CCTV and Policing: Public Area Surveillance and Police Practices in Britain, vol. 9780199265. 2012
8. Saifuddin, K.: Smart Cities Council India | Cities Must Invest in Video Surveillance for Safer Cities: Experts
9. Duque, D., Santos, H., Cortez, P.: Prediction of abnormal behaviors for intelligent video surveillance systems. In: Proceedings of the 2007 IEEE Symposium on Computational Intelligence and Data Mining, CIDM 2007, pp. 362–367 (2007)
10. Alam, J., Malik, H.I.: Intelligent video surveillance system (2013)
11. Cucchiara, R., Grana, C., Piccardi, M., Prati, A.: Detecting moving objects, ghosts, and shadows in video streams. IEEE Trans. Pattern Anal. Mach. Intell. **25**(10), 1337–1342 (2003)
12. Nguyen, H.-Q., Loan, T.T.K., Mao, B.D., Huh, E.-N.: Low cost real-time system monitoring using Raspberry Pi. In: 2015 Seventh International Conference on Ubiquitous and Future Networks (ICUFN), pp. 857–859 (2015)
13. Eigenraam, D., Rothkrantz, L.J.M.: A smart surveillance system of distributed smart multi cameras modelled as agents. In: 2016 Smart Cities Symposium Prague, SCSP 2016 (2016)
14. Shi, W., Cao, J., Zhang, Q., Li, Y., Xu, L.: Edge computing: vision and challenges. IEEE Internet Things J. **3**(5), 637–646 (2016)
15. Raspberry Pi 3 Model B - Raspberry Pi. https://www.raspberrypi.org/products/raspberry-pi-3-model-b/. Accessed 24 Dec 2017
16. Raspberry Pi Camera Module - Raspberry Pi Documentation. https://www.raspberrypi.org/documentation/raspbian/applications/camera.md. Accessed 27 Dec 2017
17. OpenCV library. https://opencv.org/. Accessed 12 Jan 2018
18. Raspberry Pi Zero W - Raspberry Pi. https://www.raspberrypi.org/products/raspberry-pi-zero-w/. Accessed 21 Dec 2017
19. ESP32 Overview. https://www.espressif.com/en/products/hardware/esp32/overview. Accessed 22 Dec 2017
20. Python. https://www.python.org/. Accessed 25 Dec 2017
21. Flask (A Python Microframework). http://flask.pocoo.org/. Accessed 16 Jan 2018
22. ownCloud. https://owncloud.org/. Accessed 04 Jan 2018
23. Laravel. https://laravel.com/. Accessed 24 Dec 2017

Power Assist Control Based on Learning Database of Joint Angle of Powered Exoskeleton Suitable for Wearer's Posture

Katsuya Sahashi, Shota Murai, and Yasutake Takahashi$^{(\boxtimes)}$

University of Fukui, 3-9-1, Bunkyo, Fukui, Fukui 910-8507, Japan
{ksahashi,smurai,yasutake}@ir.his.u-fukui.ac.jp

Abstract. Powered exoskeletons are supposed to be one of the solutions for the shortage of workers caused by declining birthrate and a growing proportion of elderly people. We study a powered exoskeleton that supports worker wearing a radiation protection suit. It is reported that the humidity and temperature in the radiation protection suit are extremely high. EMG sensors are popular to the conventional powered exoskeletons, however, they are not suitable for ours because the high humidity and temperature make the wearer sweat profusely and the sweat make it difficult to use the EMG sensors appropriately. We propose to use 9-axis motion sensors on the wearer instead of EMG sensors to control the powered exoskeleton. The sensors rapidly measure the wearer motion in a high humidity and temperature environment. We evaluate the proposed method using a powered exoskeleton without binding knee in this report.

Keywords: Powered exoskeleton · Motion sensor · Machine learning

1 Introduction

In recent years, many advanced countries suffer from shortage of industrial workers and caregivers for care recipients because of declining birthrate and a growing proportion of elderly people. Powered exoskeletons are supposed to be one of the solutions for this problem in the fields of agriculture, medical, welfare services, transportation, and so on [1–3]. We study a powered exoskeleton that supports worker wearing a radiation protection suit. The weight of the radiation protection suit is about 20 kg. Workers work in a nuclear power plant with the radiation protection suit. EMG sensor, force sensor or force switch are widely used for the powered exoskeletons. The sensors are used for recognition wearer's motion. EMG sensor measures a change of action electric potential. Action electric potential occurs before about 50 ms than the muscle to contract. So, this approach enables rapid assist for the wearer if it works appropriately. But, it is difficult to measure action electric potential using the EMG sensor in a realistic situation. It is reported that the humidity and temperature in the radiation protection suit are extremely high so that the wearer sweats profusely [4]. In the target environment, EMG sensor does not work correctly because of slipping sensor. Force sensor

© Springer International Publishing AG, part of Springer Nature 2018
M. Antona and C. Stephanidis (Eds.): UAHCI 2018, LNCS 10908, pp. 340–346, 2018.
https://doi.org/10.1007/978-3-319-92052-8_27

and force switch can measure in such a high temperature and humidity environment. The method using the floor reaction force sensor measures the load to the foot of the wearer from the floor, and performs the assist control so as to cancel the load. This method calculates the desired PAS joint angle to reduce the load to the wearer's motion and support it. However, the method inevitably disturbs the wearer's motion because it needs reaction force from the wearer to the PAS. Another approach using force switch sensor recognizes wearer's motion using the sequential outputs of the switch embedded into the powered exoskeleton sole. But, this method needs a few steps to recognize the wearer's walk motion so that it often misses the support in the beginning and end of the walk. Force sensor and force switch embedded into the sole of powered exoskeleton have often hardware trouble because of the unavoidable repeated impacts during the walk.

We propose assist control of a powered exoskeleton using 9 axis motion sensor on the wearer. This sensor rapidly measures the wearer motion in a high humidity and temperature environment. We evaluate the proposed method using a powered exoskeleton without binding knee in this report.

2   Powered Exoskeleton Without Binding Knee

Figure 1(a) shows our powered exoskeleton that is originally developed by Activelink Co., Ltg., Japan and modified by us for our research. The powered exoskeleton binds a wearer only at shoulders and feet. Figure 1(b) shows the positions of the three force sensors that measure the interaction force between the operator and the powered exoskeleton. There are no bindings at limbs of upper and lower legs like other conventional powered exoskeleton usually have.

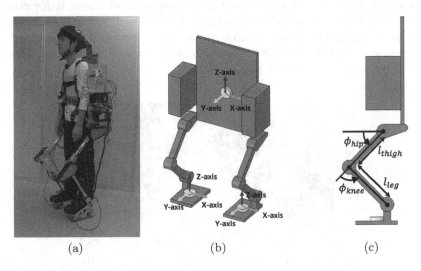

     (a)   (b)   (c)

Fig. 1. Powered exoskeleton without binding knee : (a) operator wearing the powered exoskeleton, (b) position of force sensors and their coordinate system, (c) definition of links and angles

The wearer can move his/her knees freely at the beginning of the motion. This point of our powered exoskeleton is different from the conventional ones.

This powered exoskeleton is developed for a worker transporting the heavy baggage in the nuclear power plant. If a disaster happens, the worker must wear about fifty kg of radiation protective equipment. The worker is also supposed to carry a heavy robot, such as PackBot [5], that searches in the power plant.

It has four geared motors and rotary encoders at the knees and hips joints. Each joint angle is controlled by a PID controller on a Maxon motor driver. There is no motor at angle joints. Figure 1(b) shows the links of the powered exoskeleton and definition of the joint angles ϕ_{hip} and ϕ_{knee}.

3   Sensors for Wearer Motion Recognition

Conventional powered exoskeleton are controlled based on some kinds of sensors. Force sensor is one of them. Force sensors are attached at bottoms of foots of the powered exoskeleton. It estimates the state of legs based on measuring loads of both feet and assists appropriately according to the state of legs. In addition, the other force sensor at back measures the weight of the load hanging on the back. The powered exoskeleton assists the worker to carry the load according to the measured weight of the load. However, we found that this approach cannot distinguish similar motions such as "swinging from side to side" and "walk." We use the force sensors to evaluate our proposed methods and improve the parameters of the power-assist-controller by measuring the interaction between the wearer and the exoskeleton.

Figure 2 shows a motion sensor which we used in our experiments and a wearer attaching 4 nine-axis motion sensors and their position and coordinates. The x-axis is horizontal, y-axis is vertically upward, and z-axis is forward, as shown in Fig. 2(a). The wearer equips them to his/her upper and lower legs as shown in Fig. 2(b). The motion sensor measures the postures of the upper and lower, left and right legs, $\theta^{lu}, \theta^{ru}, \theta^{ll}, \theta^{rl}$. The posture of the leg indicates the angles of the leg in the sagittal plane.

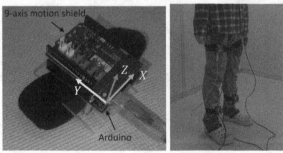

(a) Arduino Uno Rev3 and 9-axis motion shield

(b) Worker wearing motion sensors

Fig. 2. Motion sensor and its position on the wearer

4   Proposed Method

Fig. 3 shows the schematic models of the previous study [6] and the proposed method. The previous study [6] estimates the joint angles of the powered exoskeleton ϕ_{hip} and ϕ_{knee} from the last time-series of the posture angles of the leg θ^{lu}, θ^{ru}, θ^{ll}, and θ^{rl}, directly. Figure 3(a) shows the previous method. It utilizes a k-nearest neighbor algorithm to recognize the motion of the wearer and to estimate the appropriate joint angles of the powered exoskeletons to support the wearer's motion. However, the input to the k-nearest neighbor algorithm is a large number of time-series data so that it needs relatively a large database for the motion recognition and the appropriate estimation of the joint angles of the exoskeleton. It means that it needs long learning time to adjust the parameters for the assist control of the powered exoskeleton. Furthermore, it has to learn from a scratch if the wearer shows a new motion that should be assisted.

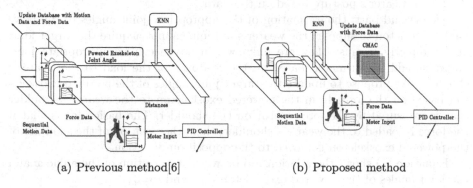

(a) Previous method[6]   (b) Proposed method

Fig. 3. Schematic models of previous study [6] and proposed method

In order to solve the problems above, we proposes a new assist control method that separates the procedure above into two parts. The method first estimates the future posture of the wearer $\hat{\theta}^{lu}$, $\hat{\theta}^{ru}$, $\hat{\theta}^{ll}$, and $\hat{\theta}^{rl}$ from the last time-series of the posture of the wearer's legs based on a k-nearest neighbor algorithm. Then, it estimates the appropriate joint angles of the powered exoskeletons, ϕ_{hip} and ϕ_{knee}, from the estimated postures of the wearer $\hat{\theta}^{lu}$, $\hat{\theta}^{ru}$, $\hat{\theta}^{ll}$, and $\hat{\theta}^{rl}$, based on cerebellar model arithmetic computer (CMAC), a kind of neural network.

The proposed method has advantages over the previous method. One of the advantages is efficiency of the learning. The previous method needs to explore appropriate joint angles of the powered exoskeleton from high dimension of the input space, that is, the last time-series of the postures of the wearer's legs. The appropriate joint angles cannot be acquired by one-shot data. They have to be evaluated by the load to the wearer's shoulder and the previous method needs to find the optimal one trial and error. This means it cannot be a supervised learning.

The proposed method reduces the exploration into one supervised learning with a relatively large searching space and the exploration with a relatively small space. The former is learning of the wearer's motion and the later is the learning of the appropriate target angles of the powered exoskeleton to assist the wearer's motion.

5   Update of Target Joint Angles Based on Jacobian

The last section introduces that the proposed method has two parts, one is the prediction of the future wearer's posture and the other is the estimation of the appropriate joint angles of the powered exoskeleton based on the predicted posture of the wearer. One of the simple supervised machine learning technique can be applied to the first parts, the prediction of the future wearer's posture. It collects the data of the wearer's motion during the power assist, then, it predicts the future wearer's posture based on the data.

The second part, the estimation of the appropriate joint angles of the powered exoskeleton to support the wearer's motion, cannot acquire the target joint angles directly because they are unknown in advance. The appropriate joint angles should be estimated based on the feedback of the load to the wearer's shoulder. We propose to update the target joint angles of the powered exoskeleton based on the force from the powered exoskeleton to the wearer's shoulder that is measured by the force sensor on the shoulder. The basic idea is that if the force is loaded to the wearer's shoulder, then, the position of the shoulder of the powered exoskeleton is moved to the opposition direction.

Equation (1) shows the relationship between the position of the ankle x and the joint angles of the powered exoskeleton ϕ_{hip} and ϕ_{knee}.

$$x = \begin{pmatrix} l_{thigh} \sin(\phi_{hip}) + l_{leg} \sin(\phi_{hip} + \phi_{knee}) \\ l_{thigh} \cos(\phi_{hip}) + l_{leg} \cos(\phi_{hip} + \phi_{knee}) \end{pmatrix} \tag{1}$$

where l_{thigh} and l_{leg} indicate the upper leg and lower leg, respectively. The Jacobian $J(\phi)$, the relationship between $\dot{x}$ and $\dot{\phi} = (\dot{\phi}_{hip}, \dot{\phi}_{knee})^T$, is represented as below:

$$\dot{x} = J(\phi)\dot{\phi} \tag{2}$$

where

$$J(\phi) = \begin{pmatrix} l_{thigh} \cos(\phi_h) + l_{leg} \cos(\phi_h + \phi_k) & l_{leg} \cos(\phi_h + \phi_k) \\ -l_{thigh} \sin(\phi_h) - l_{leg} \sin(\phi_h + \phi_k) & -l_{leg} \sin(\phi_t + \phi_k) \end{pmatrix} \tag{3}$$

If we define a desired velocity of the angle as $\dot{x}$, then the desired joint angular velocity $\dot{\phi}$ is acquired with the inverse matrix of $J(\phi)^{-1}$ as follows:

$$\dot{\phi} = J(\phi)^{-1}\dot{x} \tag{4}$$

As we mentioned before, we replace the desired velocity of the ankle with the force from the powered exoskeleton to the wearer on the shoulder F. We define the update of the target joint angles of the powered exoskeleton ϕ_{update} as follows:

$$\phi_{update} = J(\phi)^{-1}\mathbf{F} \tag{5}$$

The target joint angles ϕ_d is updated with Eq. (6).

$$\phi_d \leftarrow \phi_d + C\phi_{update} \tag{6}$$

where C is an update gain matrix.

Actually, Eq. (6) just indicates one-shot update of the target joint angle of the exoskeleton based on the posture of the wearer's legs. It has to estimate the target joint angle for a various postures of the wearer's legs. CMAC is utilized to represent the map between the posture of the wearer's legs and the target joint angles of the powered exoskeleton as shown in Fig. 3(b).

6 Experiments

We conducted experiments in which the wearer squats repeatedly. The configuration of CMAC is follows: The number of tiles is 3×3. The number of tiling is 100. The learning rate is 1.3 in this experiment.

Figure 4 shows the load to the wearer's shoulder during the experiment. While the wearer is squatting, the system learns the wearer's squatting motion to predict the posture of the wearer and the appropriate joint angles of the powered exoskeleton are updated. Figure 4 shows that the proposed method successfully reduce the load to the wearer's shoulder rapidly.

Figure 5 shows the average of EMG of the left and right thigh muscles for 5 squatting. It shows that the proposed method successfully reduced the activity of the muscles so that the powered exoskeleton assists the wearer's repeated squatting.

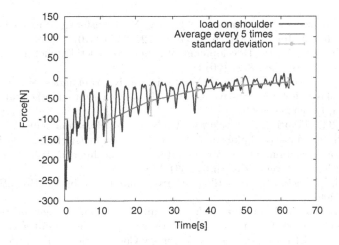

Fig. 4. Load to the wearer's shoulder during the learning

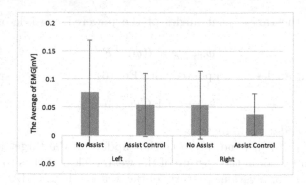

Fig. 5. Average of EMG during repeated squatting

7   Conclusions

We proposed assist control of a powered exoskeleton using 9 axis motion sensor on the wearer. This sensor rapidly measures the wearer motion in a high humidity and temperature environment. The proposed method has two parts, one is the prediction of the future wearer's posture and the other is the estimation of the appropriate joint angles of the powered exoskeleton based on the predicted posture of the wearer. The first part adopts one of the simple supervised machine learning technique to predict the future wearer's posture. The second part, the estimation of the appropriate joint angles of the powered exoskeleton to support the wearer's motion, updates the map between the wearers posture and the target join angels of the powered exoskeleton based on the load to the wearer's shoulder and Jacobian of the legs of exoskeleton. We evaluated the proposed method using a powered exoskeleton without binding knee and showed the validity.

References

1. Satoh, H., Kawabata, T., Tanaka, F., Sankai, Y.: Transferring care assistance with robot suit hal. J. Jpn. Soc. Mech. **76**(762), 227–235 (2010)
2. Hirohito Tanaka, M. H.: Development of a non-exoskeletal structure for a robotic suit. J. Autom. Technol. **8**(2) (2014)
3. Imamura, Y., Tanaka, T., Suzuki, Y., Takizawa, K., Yamanaka, M.: Motion-based design of elastic belts for passive assistive device using musculoskeletal model, pp. 1343–1348, December 2011
4. Kakamu, T., Hidaka, T., Hayakawa, T., Kumagai, T., Jinnouchi, T., Tsuji, M., Nakano, S., Koyama, K., Fukushima, T.: Risk and preventive factors for heat illness in radiation decontamination workers after the Fukushima Daiichi Nuclear Power Plant accident. J. Occup. Health **57**, 331–338 (2015)
5. Yamauchi, B.: PackBot: a versatile platform for military robotics. Proc. SPIE **5422**, 228–237 (2004)
6. Inoue, T., Nomura, S., Takahashi, Y., Kawai, M., Taniai, Y.: Leg control based on human motion prediction using motion sensor for power assist suit without binding knee. In: 2016 IEEE Congress on Evolutionary Computation (CEC), pp. 1720–1726, July 2016

Performance Sensor for Reliable Operation

Jorge Semião[1,2(✉)], Ruben Cabral[2,3], Marcelino B. Santos[2,3,4],
Isabel C. Teixeira[2,3], and J. Paulo Teixeira[2,3]

[1] University of Algarve, Faro, Portugal
jsemiao@ualg.pt
[2] INESC-ID, Lisbon, Portugal
[3] IST, University of Lisboa, Lisbon, Portugal
{ruben.cabral,marcelino.santos,isabel.teixeira,
paulo.teixeira}@tecnico.ulisboa.pt
[4] Silicongate, Lisbon, Portugal

Abstract. Human-Computer Interaction (HCI) applications need reliable hardware and the development of today's sensors and cyber-physical systems for HCI applications is critical. Moreover, such hardware is becoming more and more self-powered, and mobile devices are today important devices for HCI applications. While battery-operated devices quest for the never-ending battery, aggressive low-power techniques are used in today's hardware systems to accomplish such mission. Techniques like Dynamic Voltage and Frequency Scaling (DVFS) and the use of subthreshold power-supply voltages can effectively achieve substantial power savings. However, working at reduced power-supply voltages, and reduced clock frequency, imposes additional challenges in the design and operation of devices. Today's chips face several parametric variations, such as PVTA (Process, power-supply Voltage, Temperature and Aging) variation, which can affect circuit performance and reliability is affected. This paper presents a performance sensor solution to be used in cyber-physical systems to improve reliability of today's chips, guaranteeing an error-free operation, even with the use of aggressive low-power techniques. In fact, this performance sensor allows optimize the trade-off between power and performance, avoiding the occurrence of errors. In order to be easily used and adopted by industry, the performance sensor is a non-intrusive global sensor, which uses two dummy critical paths to sense performance for the power-supply voltage and clock frequency used, and for the existing PVTA variation. The novelty of this solution is on the new architecture for the sensor, which allows the operation at VDDs' subthreshold voltage levels. This feature makes this global sensor a unique solution to control DVFS, even at subthreshold voltages, avoid performance errors and allow optimizing circuit operation and performance. Simulations using a SPICE tool allowed characterizing the new sensor to work at sub-threshold voltages, and results are presented for a 65 nm CMOS technology, which uses a CMOS Predictive Technology Models (PTM) technology. The results show that the sensor increases sensibility when PVTA degradations increase, even when working at subthreshold voltages.

Keywords: Performance sensor · Reliability · Subthreshold voltage
Low power · Non-intrusive sensor

© Springer International Publishing AG, part of Springer Nature 2018
M. Antona and C. Stephanidis (Eds.): UAHCI 2018, LNCS 10908, pp. 347–365, 2018.
https://doi.org/10.1007/978-3-319-92052-8_28

1   Introduction

One important requirement for sensors and cyber-physical systems developed for Human-Computer Interaction applications is the reduced size of the hardware, which commonly leads to the use of state-of-the-art CMOS nanotechnology to produce such hardware sensors. Moreover, the Internet of Everything (IoE) paradigm is enabling the interaction with a wide variety of devices, which tend to be self-powered and equipped with complex digital systems, including microcontrollers, sensors and sensor networks. Therefore, power consumption in CMOS integrated circuits, as never before, have a huge importance in today's cyber-physical systems and sensors for HCI applications, as all self-powered devices quest for the never-ending battery life, but also with smaller and smaller dimensions every day. However, the use of reduced CMOS technology with reduced power budgets imposes additional reliability challenges for such hardware. The success and effectiveness of an HCI application relies greatly in the use of reliable hardware, especially those applications that are safety-critical, or those that can influence human lives (such as [1]).

Reliability and power consumption are two key concerns in the development of today's cyber-physical systems. Several low-power techniques are available to reduce consumption in today's chips, such as Dynamic Voltage and Frequency Scaling (DVFS) techniques, to reduce performance and power consumption when it's not needed, or the use of subthreshold power-supply voltages [32], to boost up the energy savings. However, the use of low energy modes of operation increases the probability of error occurrence due to several problems: (1) reducing power-supply voltages impose the simultaneous reduction of the clock frequency (the performance reduction), which changes the existing power and performance operating conditions (V_{DD}/clock frequency pair) and may lead to a different and non-optimized circuit operation; (2) working at reduced power-supply voltages makes the circuit more vulnerable to operational-induced delay-faults and transient-faults, as well as to several environmental parameters (radiation, electromagnetic interference, aging, etc.). Moreover, the use of nanotechnologies with transistors with reduced dimensions increases the uncertainty of circuit behaviors. With smaller gate dimensions, gate's vulnerability to environmental conditions is increased. Therefore, the simple use of wider static security margins to account for all variability is not enough and new methodologies to improve reliability in nanometer technologies should be defined, because they definitely should be compatible with ultra-low-power design schemes and aggressive low-power techniques.

The performance of CMOS circuits can be affected by many effects and parametric variations, and the most important ones are: Process, power-supply Voltage and Temperature variations (PVT) [15, 28, 29], and when CMOS technology entered the nano-size era, also the aging effects (PVT and Aging – PVTA), with effects like the Bias Temperature Instability (the negative, NBTI, and the positive, PBTI) [19] being a main concerns that affect transistors. These variations, alone or pilled-up, degrade circuit performance and increase variability in circuits. Consequently, circuit operation and its performance should constantly be monitored in today's chips and hardware systems, to avoid errors and make circuits and their applications reliable. In this context, several performance sensors were proposed in the past [30, 33], but, or they do not work at reduced subthreshold VDD voltages ([30]), or their use is complex to implement and they are not widely adopted by industry ([33]).

The purpose of this work is to propose new easy-to-use performance sensors for a reliable operation that can work at sub-threshold voltages, allowing its use in ultra-low-power applications. This performance sensor is an improved version of the previously published aging sensors [19] and [34], but with the necessary changes to work at subthreshold voltage levels, constituting the low-power (LP) version. This new sensor has all the main features available in the [34] global sensor version, but sensor functionality was re-design so that VDD can be changed to subthreshold voltage levels and prediction detection of errors is enhanced, to account for higher unpredictability at reduced voltage levels.

The reminder of the paper is as follows. The background work on performance sensors is presented on the next section (Sect. 2). Section 3 presents the LP Global Performance Sensor (LPGPS), its architecture and functionality. Section 4 describes how to use the LPGPS in a circuit and how to achieve a reliable operation. Section 5 present the SPICE simulations results, while finally on Sect. 6 the conclusions and the future work are summarized.

2 Background

In the past, various sensors were proposed and can be used to measure performance, despite the fact that not all were proposed as performance sensors. The purpose is to monitor changes in performance, time deviations in transitions occurred at key nodes, or even to monitor delays in the circuit, and to detect when these variations may lead to circuit errors. These sensors may appear in literature as aging sensors, delay-fault sensors, or as soft-error sensors. Nevertheless, they all can be labeled as performance sensors, as they can identify deviations that affect circuit's performance [30].

There are two approaches regarding the use of these sensors in the circuit: local sensors or global sensors. Local sensors detect circuit's degradation locally, where errors may occur, and they provide a detailed analysis on circuit's performance behavior [9–11, 16, 17, 33]. However, they have two important limitations: (1) when working on-line, they can only monitor performance and detect its variation if they are activated (or when circuit operation activates the monitored paths); (2) their use and implementation in a circuit is complex and, because of that, so far they are not adopted by industry. Regarding global sensors, they use key parameters to detect circuit's performance degradation, or use dummy critical paths' replicas [20–23]. Despite the fact that global sensors do not monitor the actual circuit locations where errors may occur and, because of that, they may have different PVTA variations when compared to the circuit they are monitoring, their use is straight-forward and performance monitoring is, normally, independent from circuit operation. Consequently, they can easily be used in circuits and they are widely used in industry. Interestingly, both global and local sensors can also be used in improved solutions to monitor performance degradation and they work cooperatively to minimize error occurrence [13, 19]. However, despite the good results of this solution, its complexity requires too much effort to be widely adopted in industry.

Regarding the error detection, there are also two possible approaches: detect errors predictively, or detect errors after their occurrence. Detect errors predictively is done by identifying data transitions which arrive in the eminence of an error at key FFs or key memory elements. This is done using a safety margin or guard-band, placed before the clock edge-trigger [9, 16, 17, 26]. Errors are anticipated, as sensors detect the eminence of an error, without the actual error occurrence. However, if an abnormal delay exists that exceeds the guard-band margin, an irrecoverable error happens. On the other hand, detecting errors after their occurrence is done by detecting and/or correcting late transients at key memory elements. For this, an additional delayed capture is needed [11, 18, 24, 25]. However, to correct errors after their occurrence needs usually complex recovery mechanisms, and using different architectural levels. Another possibility is to locally use time-borrowing to avoid errors, by borrowing time from subsequent clock cycles, reducing again the safety margins of subsequent clock-cycles. Interestingly, improved solutions like [27] implement both strategies, but the achieved solutions is complex, resulting in a FF with high overhead in performance and area.

Despite the variety of solutions in literature to monitor performance or error occurrences related to performance deviations, only recently appeared in literature a work focused on sensors and techniques to work at subthreshold voltage levels in the power supply ([33]). The work in [33] presented a local performance sensor that can work predictively at subthreshold voltage levels. Despite this good solution, local sensors are difficultly adopted by industry, because they are intrusive to the circuit, i.e., the original circuit has to be changed in order to insert locally the sensors. Therefore, changes in performance may be restricted but they are expected, and industry normally avoids changing their optimized designs and prototypes. As a consequence, global sensors are, still now, a better solution for industry, because they are not intrusive and, according with the safety margins adopted, they can easily work predictively and avoid errors, while help on optimizing performance and/or power consumption in the presence of environmental and operational induced variations.

Regarding subthreshold operation, several previous works show that working at subthreshold voltages can drastically decrease power consumption, being one of the most important research areas regarding optimization of energy in digital circuits. Especially if IoT, mobile, or battery-operated applications are considered, subthreshold operation is gaining increased importance, because these applications normally do not require permanent and intensive performance, or the processing speed is not a critical factor for all the operating time. Moreover, application for subthreshold operation is wide, from digital circuits [7, 8], to analog circuits [5, 6], mixed-signal applications [4], or even at memory applications [1–3]. Therefore, as mobile and battery-operated applications are becoming more and more popular and widely used, it's urgent to define new reliability techniques and sensors to work at subthreshold voltage levels.

The purpose of this work is to adapt existing global and local sensors for performance failure prediction to be compatible with subthreshold voltages in the VDD. The main purpose of the new proposed sensor is to avoid errors, monitor PVTA variations, and measure performance deviations. This measure can be used to control the application of DVFS techniques, used to reduce power consumption and/or clock frequency.

3   Low-Power Global Performance Sensor

The proposed Low-Power Global Performance Sensor (LPGPS) is an improved version of the previously published local aging sensors [19, 34], but with the necessary changes to work at subthreshold voltage levels and improving its design. The LPGPS is based on two dummy critical paths (CP), to produce several delays' replicas. As will be explained later, these two dummy CP are designed in order to be highly sensitive to NBTI (one path) and to PBTI (the other path) aging effects, while the delay in both paths will change according to every environmental or operational parameter variation that can affect performance. Therefore, we can say that the LPGPS is sensitive to the main variations affecting performance, i.e., PVTA variations.

When we talk about performance, we are intrinsically talking about delays and timings available to perform a certain task. Therefore, when designing a performance sensor, the best way is to monitor delays and monitor or measure how quickly a specific task is performed. In CMOS circuits, delays are measured by comparing an initial signal transition and the succeeding transition at the end of the stimulated data path. Hence, by changing any parameter that can affect performance in a circuit (e.g., PVTA variations), it will change the delay between the initial and the ending transition in the stimulated path. Moreover, as different transitions can impose different delays, our decision in this work was to implement dummy paths (two in fact, as will be explained later) and to stimulate them with the two possible transitions, Low-to-High and High-to-Low. Then, by measuring how far in these paths will the initial transitions propagate during a predetermined time imposed by the clock (the clock period) we have a measure of the performance of these dummy critical paths.

3.1   Sensor's Architecture and Functionality

Figure 1 presents the main LPGPS architecture. It is composed of a controller block, two dummy critical paths, and two groups of sensor Latches, to measure the propagation delay in both dummy paths, in order to compare these delays with the available clock period. With the knowledge of the critical paths of the circuit under test (CUT) where this sensor will be installed, it is possible to create two fictitious paths (dummy paths) with propagation delays higher than the expected CUT's CP during its lifetime.

Figure 2 shows the dummy critical paths in more detail. As it can be seen, the two paths are composed of chains with NAND and NOR gates. One chain is implemented with NOR gates (dummy critical path 1 in Fig. 2), creating a fictitious critical path, which will, presumably, age more than the critical paths of the circuit when subjected to NBTI effect (which strongly influences the degradation of PMOS transistors' Vth). The other chain is implemented with NAND gates (dummy critical path 2 in Fig. 2) creating another fictitious critical path which will, presumably, age more than the critical paths of the circuit when subjected to the PBTI effect (which strongly influences the degradation of Vth in NMOS transistors).

It is important to notice that, in a global sensor that is different from the CUT itself and monitors delays from paths that are not the actual CP in the CUT, we must consider a safety margin to account for differences from CUT's CP delay and the LPGPS

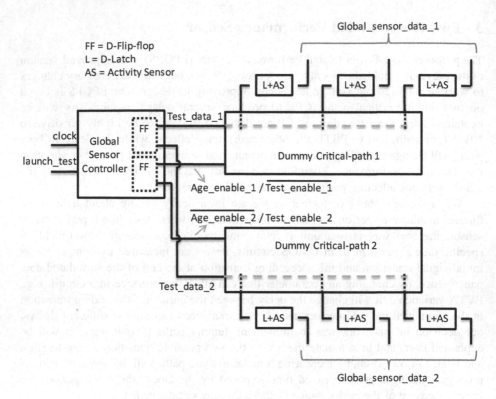

Fig. 1. Low-Power Global Sensor architecture.

dummy paths delays. Moreover, when we want to address aging variations, we must consider that exists the possibility of the CUT's CP age more than the sensor's CP, which may overcome the safety margin used and then errors may happen. Therefore, it is important to impose an extreme aging degradation to these dummy CP in the LPGS, so that the existing safety margin always work in favor of error avoidance and not the opposite. That is also the reason for using two dummy CP, one sensitive to NBTI aging and the other sensitive to PBTI aging.

The NORs and the NANDs input port-map are also very important for the high aging degradation of the PMOS and NMOS transistors in the respective chain paths. The internal structure of NOR and NAND gates are presented in Fig. 3. For the NOR gate (Fig. 3(a)), the probability for the transistor P1 to be in stress mode is equal to the probability of having its NOR_chain input at logic value 0. If global sensor is activated periodically, this signal will most likely be at low logic value most of the time, making a high degradation probability for transistor P1. However, the probability to put P2 in stress mode is equivalent to the probability of having both P1 and P2 transistors on, i.e., $P\left([\text{NOR\_chain}]_{input} = 0\right) \times P\left([\text{Age\_enable\_1}]_{input} = 0\right)$. Considering that global sensor is activated periodically, Age_enable_1 signal has low probability to be at 0 logic value. Henceforth, P2 will have negligible degradation. Yet, a high degradation probability of CP delay's replica is guaranteed with the high degradation probability of

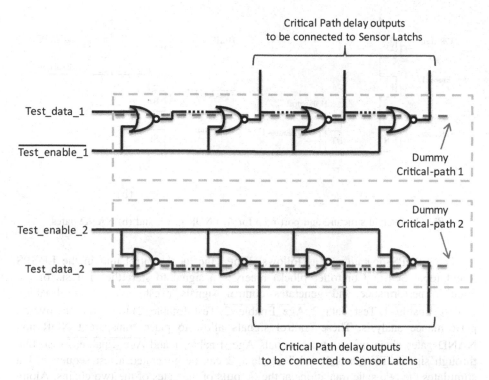

Fig. 2. Dummy critical paths of the LPGS.

all the P1 transistors from the NOR chain, due to the NBTI effect. Moreover, if a higher degradation is needed in the dummy critical path, a 3-input NOR gate can also be used, with two of its inputs connected to the same NOR_chain input and having now two PMOS transistors in a high aging state. However, if subthreshold voltages are to be used, 3-input gates that use a classic CMOS and implementation should be avoided, as may restrict VDD reduction.

Regarding the NAND gates, a similar analysis can be drawn to create a high aging probability in the dummy critical-path 2. For the NAND gate (Fig. 3(b)), the probability for the transistor N1 to be in stress mode is equal to the probability of having its NAND_chain input at logic value 1. If global sensor is activated periodically, this signal will most likely be at low logic value most of the time, making a high degradation probability for transistor N1. However, the probability to put N2 in stress mode is equivalent to the probability of having both N1 and N2 transistors on, i.e., $P\left([\text{NAND\_chain}]_{input} = 1\right) \times P\left(\left[\overline{\text{Age\_enable\_2}}\right]_{input} = 1\right)$. Considering that global sensor is activated periodically, $\overline{\text{Age\_enable\_2}}$ signal has low probability to be at 1 logic value. Henceforth, N2 will have negligible degradation. Yet, a high degradation probability of CP delay's replica is guaranteed with the high degradation probability of all the N1 transistors of the NAND chain due to PBTI effect.

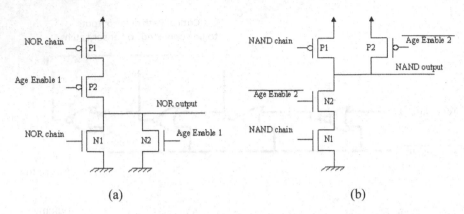

Fig. 3. Internal structure and port map for: (a) NOR gates, and (b) NAND gates.

The LPGPS operation is as follows. When the local control unit in the LPGPS (the Global Sensor Controller block) receives a signal to start the analysis of the circuit's performance and generates control signals (Test_data_1, Age_Enable_1/Test_Enable_1, Test_data_2, $\overline{\text{Age\_Enable\_2}}$/Test_Enable_2) to operate the overall performance analysis. These control signals allow to place transparent NOR and NAND gates chain inputs, using signals Age_Enable_1 and $\overline{\text{Age\_Enable\_2}}$), so that through signals Test_data_1 and Test_data_2 can be generated a test sequence that stimulates the two state transitions at the outputs of the gates of the two chains. Along the two chains, special sensor cells, build with a Latch, a Delay Element and an Activity Sensor with on-retention logic, are connected at the output of several NAND and NOR gates, to create several fictitious paths with different propagation times. The architecture of these sensor cells will be defined in the next section.

3.2 Low-Power Sensor Latch

As observed in Fig. 1, critical path outputs are connected to sensor latches. These sensor latches are composed by a common D-Latch, to implement the Latch functionality, and an Activity Sensor, to implement the sensor functionality, as denoted in Fig. 4. The existence of a Latch functionality is important because we need to compare the delays of the CP connected to the latches with the existing clock period, and the Latch is a clocked gate that can easily implement different behaviors along the clock period. The implemented latch is enabled when the clock signal is low, i.e., it is in transparent mode for the low state of the clock, and in the non-transparent mode (opaque) for the high state of the clock. Regarding the activity sensor functionality, its main function is to sense and signalize when critical transitions occur in the Latch, i.e., when transitions in the output of the dummy CP arrive at the Latch input at the end of the transparent mode. When a critical transition in the Latch is signalized, it means that the CP has a delay almost similar to the clock period, with a pre-defined safety margin. As we have several dummy CP outputs to sensor latches, we can have a measure of the comparison made between the dummy CP delays and the clock period, having a rate for the performance level of the circuit. Moreover, it is important to impose a safety margin in this monitoring process, as the dummy CP in the LPGPS is not the real CP of the CUT. This safety margin can be identified as the margin to signalize critical transitions in the Latch data, before the latch become opaque. Moreover, the activity sensor implements an on-retention logic, to keep sensor output (SO) active, once it is activated and until the sensor reset ($\overline{SR}$) is activated.

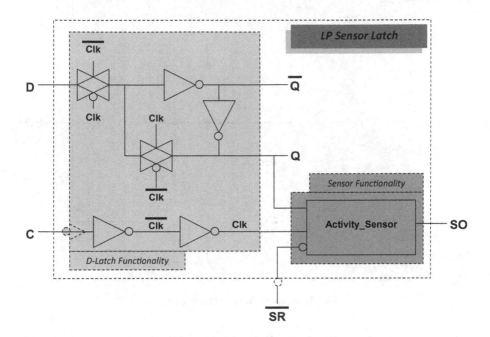

Fig. 4. Low Power Sensor Latch architecture.

The architecture of the new Activity Sensor is presented in Fig. 5. The sensor functionality is based on delaying the data signal inside the activity sensor. The difference in time delay between the delayed and the non-delayed data signals creates a time window, which allows a safety margin. If a transition in this delayed data signal occurs after the positive clock trigger, the sensor detects a critical transition for the existing clock period and signalizes it in the sensor output (SO). This activity sensor used was previously published in [33] and it is especially designed to allow VDD reductions to subthreshold levels.

Figure 6 presents a timing diagram for the main signals of the activity sensor described in Fig. 5. From Fig. 1, each delay path connected to a sensor latch will propagate an initial transition from the positive edge-trigger of the clock until it reaches the Latch input, and this timing delay is symbolized in the D signal in Fig. 6, which becomes stable after τ_{DE}. If the transition arrives at D input when clock is low, the latch is in transparent mode (Fig. 4) and easily Q signal will also change (Fig. 6). However,

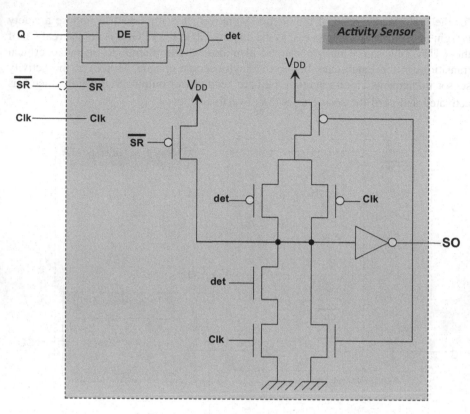

Fig. 5. Activity Sensor architecture.

as denoted in Fig. 5 and Fig. 6, the Delay Element (DE) is used to postpone data signals' arrivals at the output of the latch (signal Q), during the Clk low state, while a XOR gate is used to generate a pulse (*det* signal) for every activity in the latch data (signal Q).

Note that both inputs of the XOR gate are feed from signal Q, although one is a delayed signal Q. This means that the output of the XOR gate, the *det* signal, will have a pulse when any transition (Low-to-High or High-to-Low) occurs at the inputs, with its pulse duration proportional to the propagation delay of DE block. It is important to note that the XOR gate should be implemented using a pass-transistor logic, to allow VDD to be reduced to subthreshold voltage levels. Figure 7 presents a possible architecture for the XOR gate.

The reminder functionality of the activity sensor from Figs. 5 and 6 is, basically, the AND functionality implemented with transistors Q_1–Q_4 and the inverter gate. When a clock pulse (considering that the latch will be opaque when clock is active) and a *det* pulse occurs simultaneously, the output SO signal (sensor output) will activate the sensor output signal. This way, all the late transitions at Latch input will be signalized by the Activity Sensor. Therefore, a pre-defined margin obtained from the propagation delays of DE blocks and the *det* signal pulse duration defines the instant before ending

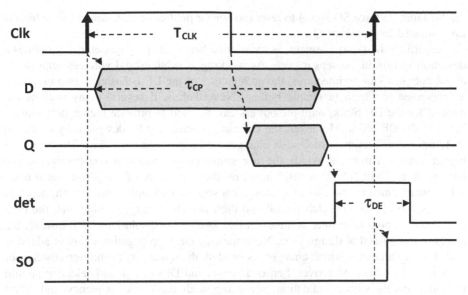

Fig. 6. Timmings in the Sensor Latch.

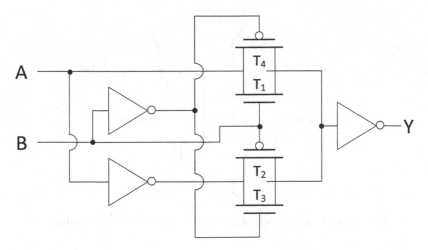

Fig. 7. Pass-transistor logic XOR gate's architecture.

the clock period where the activity sensor output is activated. If the CP propagation delays increase due to adverse PVTA variations, the margin will also increase, which is a good result for a sensor functionality, as the safety margin of the global sensor, and the detection margin of this activity sensor, increases when operating conditions worsen.

Moreover, this activity sensor has also an on-retention logic feature. This is executed by transistors Q_5 and Q_6 (Fig. 5), which avoids the use of an additional latch to hold an active sensor output signal (SO). Besides, it has also an active-low reset signal, the $\overline{SR}$ input, to force SO signal to reset (no sensor predictive error detection), which is implemented by transistor Q_7.

Regarding the Delay Element, as mentioned before, its propagation delay defines a detection margin in the sensor latch. As working at subthreshold voltages imposes to avoid complex gate architectures, the architecture of the DE is basically two inverters, as presented in Fig. 8 (a simple buffer). Nevertheless, if several delay options are needed for the DE block, multiple buffers can be used to provide higher propagation delay in the DE block. Moreover, the DE can be optimized by designed, by changing W/L transistors' ratios, which also changes cell's propagation delay. The use of a higher detection margins avoids the use small delay frames in consecutive sensor latches in the NOR/NAND paths. Therefore, the granularity of the performance measurement obtained by the Global Sensor, for a specific maximum critical path, depends on the number of sensor latches used and their detection margins. Note that, the time margin is not programmable, as done in other aging sensor solutions [17]. Instead, the margins are defined at design time. Nevertheless, DE's propagation delay is adaptive with PVTA variations, which changes, as needed, the sensitivity of the Activity Sensor to activate its output. Moreover, Sensor Latches and DEs design and selection should be tuned during silicon validation, according with the clock frequency and VDD chosen.

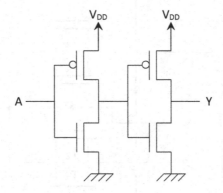

Fig. 8. Delay element typical architecture for subthreshold operation.

4   Global Sensor's Usage Procedure

The main purpose of the proposed LPGPS is to monitor and measure the performance, to avoid errors and guarantee a reliable operation, even in the presence of PVTA variations. Therefore, during the design stage, the circuit's CP should be defined, preferably using an aging-aware static timing analysis tool, to define the worst case circuit's CP. With this information, the LPGPS can be implemented (or selected from a list of different pre-defined LPGPS implementations), namely the dummy critical paths created with the NAND and NOR gates' chains. The designer must choose how many

NAND/NOR gates to use, according with the circuit's CP, and how many Sensor Latches are used and how sparsely/densely placed in the dummy CP outputs (depending on the sensibility needed). Figure 9 resumes this procedure, and we can see that the selected outputs of the dummy critical paths must guarantee that circuit's CP has its delay between the maximum and minimum dummy CP delays. Moreover, the Sensor Latch detection margin will guarantee that a progressive measurement of performance can be created by signalizing progressively more Sensor Latch outputs (for a given clock frequency and power-supply). When the detection margins of each Sensor Latch occur during the active phase of the clock, the Activity Sensor signalizes a detection. Figure 9 illustrates a typical situation, where circuit's CP delay is placed in the middle of Global Sensor's dummy paths delays, and the more sensitive sensor latches (connected to the high delay dummy paths) are signalizing error detections (S_1–S_4), while the less sensitive sensor latches (connected to the low delay dummy paths) do not signalize error detections (S_5–S_7).

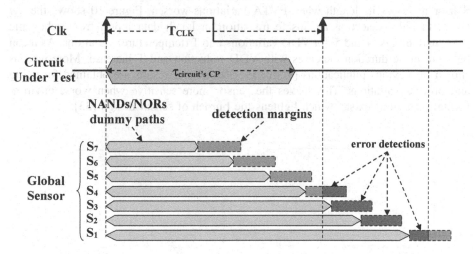

Fig. 9. Delay element typical architecture for subthreshold operation.

After the circuit is fabricated, and during manufacturing off-line tests, an initial calibration procedure is mandatory (it can be repeatedly sparsely during lifetime). This procedure uses off-line tests (e.g., scan-based delay-fault oriented tests), performed repeatedly for different values of the clock frequency and voltage, to determine the maximum and minimum working clock frequencies and voltages. In addition, it will also determine the output of the Global Sensor (number of sensor latches with error detections) for a correct operation of the circuit under test. This information determines the LPGPS output for a safe/optimized circuit operation and should be used to avoid errors, and to increase clock frequency, if performance optimization is the goal, or to decrease VDD, if power consumption reduction is the goal. Note that by reducing clock frequency (or increasing VDD), it signalizes less sensor latches; and that by increasing clock frequency (or reducing VDD), it signalizes more sensor latches.

It is also important to note that, if LPGPS is activated sparsely in time, the aging degradations in the dummy-paths will be higher than in circuit's CP, which guarantees a reliable operation during circuit's lifetime. As LPGPS was developed to work at subthreshold voltages, this reliable operation is guaranteed even for ultra-low-power modes, with reduced VDD and clock frequency. Moreover, being a non-intrusive sensor, it can be easily adopted by industry.

5 Results

Spice simulation results are presented for a 65 nm technology using Predictive Technology Models [14]. Typical nominal conditions (NC) are VDD = 1.1 V with T = 27 °C. VDD is considered to be lowered until 0.3 V, which still is a possible working power-supply voltage (the minimum working VDD is 0,25 V).

The first simulations made were to show that the pulse generated in the Activity Sensor increases its length when PVTA variations worsen. Figure 10 shows the *det* signal (a pulse detecting an unsafe transition in Latch data input) from schematic presented in Figs. 4 and 5, for VDD variations and T (temperature) variations. As it can be seen, pulse duration increases with VDD reduction and T increase. Moreover, as shown in previous publications [9, 10, 19, 30], similar results are obtained for aging and process variations. This makes the sensor more sensitive when worse environmental conditions exists, which lightens the burden of sensor design [33].

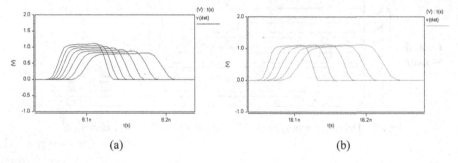

(a)   (b)

Fig. 10. Det signal, with several VDD and T values for 65 nm technology: (a) VDD from 1,1 V down to 0.8 V; (b) T from 27° up to 147°.

Next simulation results present the Global Sensor's outputs, when a monitoring procedure takes place. Figure 11 shows at the bottom the clock signal (2.4 GHz), in the middle the stimulus (rise and fall transitions) of the dummy paths (in this case, the NOR gates' stimulus), and one Sensor Latch output (in this case, S4) in the upper graph. It can be seen that both transitions are activated (middle graph), which in this case triggers Sensor Latch number 4 to activate its output (in fact, S1–S4 sensors will be activated).

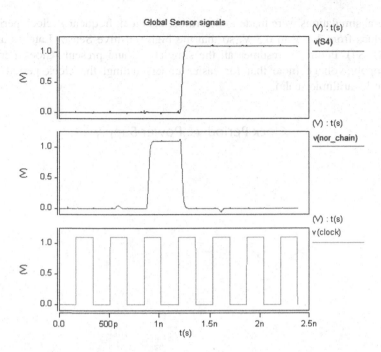

Fig. 11. Global Sensor signals (clock, NOR gates' stimulus and Sensor Latch number 4 output).

In this LPGPS, seven Sensor Latches were used in each dummy path, creating eight performance levels for the monitoring process. Figure 12 shows the 7 worst case dummy CPs, considering both NOR and NAND gates' chains (for VDD values higher than 0.6 V).

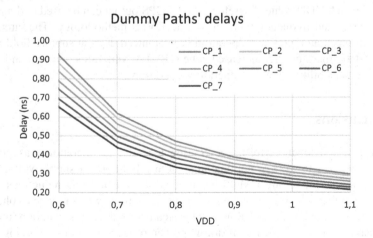

Fig. 12. Global Sensor dummy paths.

Several simulations were made to determine the clock frequency (clock period) for VDD values from 1.1 V to 0.3 V, so that the high sensitive Sensor Latches are activated (S1–S4). Figure 13 resumes all the simulations and presents Clock Period vs. Power-supply voltage (note that for easier understanding, the clock period axis is shown in logarithmic scale).

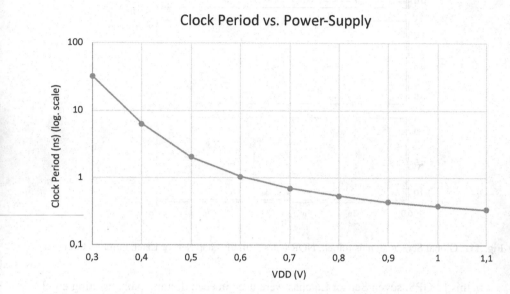

Fig. 13. Clock Period vs. Power-supply voltage for LPGPS operation signalizing sensors S1–S4.

Considering that the optimum operation (with a safety margin) is obtained for signalizing S1–S4 (and no activation for S5–S7), an optimized clock frequency can be obtained for each VDD value. Therefore, the LPGPS output can be used to dynamically change voltage and frequency with an on-line DVFS methodology. The circuit operation is optimized and a reliable operation is guaranteed even at subthreshold voltages because safety margins are increased when PVTA variations worsen and LPGPS increases its sensibility for worse operating conditions.

6   Conclusions

In this paper, a Global Performance Sensor for reliable operation was presented, designed especially to work at nominal and subthreshold power-supply voltage levels. Spice simulations for 65 nm CMOS technology show that VDD reductions increase LPGPS sensibility, which makes the sensor more cautious when reduced voltages are used (or worse PVTA degradations). This feature makes this solution unique in non-intrusive global sensors for ultra-low-power operation modes (working at subthreshold voltage levels).

Future work includes the use of the proposed LPGPS in an on-line adaptive DVFS scheme, to work at subthreshold voltage levels. Moreover, real circuit tests are also important, to validate the power and delay trade-off with real data obtained by measurements in real circuits. For this matter, a test chip was recently produced and new results are expected in the near future.

Acknowledgement. This work was partially supported by national funds through Fundação para a Ciência e a Tecnologia (FCT) with reference UID/CEC/50021/2013, and by the European Union, under the FEDER (Fundo Europeu de Desenvolvimento Regional) and INTERREG programs, in the scope of the AGERAR (0076_AGERAR_6_E) project.

References

1. Serrão, M., Shahrabadi, S., Moreno, M., José, J., Rodrigues, J.I., Rodrigues, J.M.F., du Buf, J.M.H.: Computer vision and GIS for the navigation of blind persons in buildings. Int. J. Univ. Access Inf. Soc., 1–14 (2015). https://doi.org/10.1007/s10209-013-0338-8
2. Yoo, H.J.: Dual vt self-timed CMOS logic for low subthreshold current multigigabit synchronous DRAM. IEEE Trans. Circ. Syst. II Analog Digit. Sig. Process. **45**(9), 1263–1271 (1998)
3. Hanson, S., Seok, M., Sylvester, D., Blaauw, D.: Nanometer device scaling in subthreshold logic and SRAM. IEEE Trans. Electron Devices **55**, 175–185 (2008)
4. Chakraborty, S., Mallik, A., Sarkar, C.K.: Subthreshold performance of dual-material gate CMOS devices and circuits for ultra-low power analog/mixed-signal applications. IEEE Trans. Electron Devices **55**(3), 827–832 (2008)
5. Do, A.V., Boon, C.C., Anh, M., Yeo, K.S., Cabuk, A.: A subthreshold low-noise amplifier optimized for ultra-low-power applications in the ISM band. IEEE Trans. Microw. Theory Tech. **56**(2), 286–292 (2008)
6. Giustolisi, G., Palumbo, G., Criscione, M., Cutri, F.: A low-voltage low-power voltage reference based on subthreshold MOSFETs. IEEE J. Solid-State Circuits **38**(1), 151–154 (2003)
7. Li, M.-Z., et al.: Sub-threshold standard cell library design for ultra-low power biomedical applications. In: 2013 35th Annual International Conference of the IEEE Engineering in Medicine and Biology Society (EMBC), p. 1454 (2013)
8. Sahu, A., Eappen, G.: Sub-threshold logic and standard cell library. Int. J. Innov. Res. Sci. Eng. Technol. **3**(1) (2014)
9. Martins, C.V., Semião, J., Vazquez, J.C.,Champaq, V., Santos, M., Teixeira, I.C., Teixeira, J.P.: Adaptive error-prediction flip-flop for performance failure prediction with aging sensors. In: 29th IEEE VLSI Test Symposium 2011 (VTS 2011), Dana Point, California, USA, 1st–5th May 2011
10. Martins, C., Pachito, J., Semião, J., Teixeira, I.C., Teixeira, J.P.: Adaptive error-prediction aging sensor for on-line monitoring of performance errors. In: Proceedings of the 26th Conference on Design of Circuits and Integrated Systems – DCIS 2011, Albufeira, Portugal, 16–18 November 2011
11. Ernst, D., Kim, N.S., Das, S., Pant, S., Rao, R., Pham, T., Ziesler, C., Blaauw, D., Austin, T., Flautner, K., Mudge, T.: Razor: a low-power pipeline based on circuit-level timing speculation. In: 2003 Proceedings of the 36th Annual IEEE/ACM International Symposium on Microarchitecture, MICRO-36, December 2003

12. Das, S., Tokunaga, C., Pant, S., Ma, W.-H., Kalaiselvan, S., Lai, K., Bull, D.M., Blaauw, D. T.: RazorII: in situ error detection and correction for PVT and SER Tolerance. IEEE J. Solid-State Circuits 44(1), January 2009

13. Semião, J., Cabral, R., Santos, M.B., Teixeira, I.C., Teixeira, J.P.: Dynamic voltage and frequency scaling for long-term and fail-safe operation. In: The Finale Workshop on Manufacturable and Dependable Multicore Architectures at Nanoscale (MEDIAN Finale 2015), Tallinn, Estonia, 10–11 November 2015

14. Predictive Technology Model (PTM). http://www.eas.asu.edu/ ~ ptm/

15. Semião, J., Rodriguez-Irago, M., Piccoli, L., Vargas, F., Santos, M.B., Teixeira, I.C., Rodríguez-Andina, J.J., Teixeira, J.P.: Signal integrity enhancement in digital circuits. IEEE Des. Test Comput. 25(5), 452–461 (2008)

16. Agarwal, M., et al.: Circuit failure prediction and its application to transistor aging. In: Proceedings of the VLSI Test Symposium (VTS), pp. 277–286 (2007)

17. Vazquez, J.C., et al.: Predictive error detection by on-line aging monitoring. In: Proceedings of the IEEE International On-Line Test Symposium (IOLTS) (2010)

18. Blaauw, D., Kalaiselvan, S., Lai, K., Ma, W.-H., Pant, S., Tokunaga, C., Das, S., Bull, D.: Razor II: in situ error detection and correction for PVT and SER tolerance. In: Proceedings of the 2008 IEEE International Solid-State Circuits Conference, ISSCC 2008, Digest of Technical Papers, pp. 400–622, 3–7 February 2008

19. Semiao, J., Pachito, J., Martins, C., Jacinto, B., Vazquez, J., Champac, V., Santos, M., Teixeira, I., Teixeira, J.: Aging-aware power or frequency tuning with predictive fault detection. IEEE Des. Test Comput. 29(5), 29–35 (2012). https://doi.org/10.1109/MDT.2012.2206009

20. Tschanz, J., et al.: Adaptive frequency and biasing techniques for tolerance to dynamic temperature-voltage variations and aging. In: Proceedings of the IEEE International Solid-State Circuits Conference (ISSCC), pp. 292–293 (2007)

21. Gauthier, C.R., Trivedi, P.R., Yee, G.S.: Embedded Integrated Circuit Aging Sensor System. Sun Microsystems, US Patent 7054787, 30 May 2006

22. D. Kim, J. Kim, M. Kim, J. Moulic, H. Song, "System and Method for Monitoring Reliability of a Digital System", IBM Corp., US Patent 7495519, 24 February 2009

23. Keane, J., Kim, T., Kim, C.: An on-chip NBTI sensor for measuring PMOS threshold voltage degradation. In: Proceedings of the International. Symposium on Low Power Electronics and Design (ISLPED), pp. 189–194 (2007)

24. Austin, T., Blaauw, D., Mudge, T., Flautner, K.: Making typical silicon matter with Razor. IEEE Comput. 37(3), 57–65 (2004)

25. Das, S., Tokunaga, C., Pant, S., Ma, W.-H., Kalaiselvan, S., Lai, K., Bull, D., Blaauw, D.: RazorII: in situ error detection and correction for PVT and SER tolerance. IEEE J. Solid-State Circuits 44(1), 32–48 (2009)

26. Omaña, M., Rossi, D., Bosio, N., Metra, C.: Low cost NBTI degradation detection and masking approaches. IEEE Trans. Comput. 62(3), 496–509 (2013)

27. Lin, Y., Zwolinski, M.: SETTOFF: a fault tolerant flip-flop for building cost-efficient reliable systems. In: IEEE International On-Line Testing Symposium, pp. 7–12 (2012)

28. Semião, J., Freijedo, J., Rodriguez-Andina, J., Vargas, F., Santos, M.B., Teixeira, I.C., Teixeira, J.P.: Time management for low-power design of digital systems. J. Low Power Electron. http://dx.doi.org/10.1166/jolpe.2008.194. Special Issue on LPonTR, vol. 4 N° 3 December 2008

29. Semião, J., Freijedo, J., Rodríguez Andina, J.J., Vargas, F., Santos, M.B., Teixeira, I.C., Teixeira, J.P.: Exploiting parametric power supply and/or temperature variations to improve fault tolerance in digital circuits. In: IOLTS 2008 - 14th IEEE International On-Line Testing Symposium, Rhodes, 7–9 July 2008

30. Semião, J., Romão, A., Saraiva, D., Leong, C., Santos, M., Teixeira, I., Teixeira, P.: Performance sensor for tolerance and predictive detection of delay-faults. In: Accepted for Publication in the DFT (International Symposium on Defect and Fault Tolerance in VLSI and Nanotechnology Systems) Symposium 2014, Amsterdam, The Netherlands, 1–3 October 2014. http://dx.doi.org/10.1109/DFT.2014.6962092

31. Semiao, J., Freijedo, J., Rodriguez-Andina, J.J., Vargas, F., Santos, M., Teixeira, I., Teixeira, J.P.: Delay-fault tolerance to power supply voltage disturbances analysis in nanometer technologies. In: Proceedings of the 15th IEEE International On-Line Testing Symposium (IOLTS 2009), Held in Sesimbra, Portugal, 24–26 June 2009, pp. 223–228, ISBN 978-1-4244-4822-7. http://dx.doi.org/10.1109/IOLTS.2009.5196020

32. Cavalaria, H., Cabral, R., Semião, J., Santos, M.B., Teixeira, I.C., Teixeira, J.P.: Power-delay analysis for subthreshold voltage operation. In: Mortal, A., Aníbal, J., Monteiro, J., Sequeira, C., Semião, J., Moreira da Silva, M., Oliveira, M. (eds.) INCREaSE 2017, pp. 369–386. Springer, Cham (2018). https://doi.org/10.1007/978-3-319-70272-8_30

33. Cabral, R., Cavalaria, H., Semião, J., Santos, M.B., Teixeira, I.C., Teixeira, J.P.: Performance sensor for subthreshold voltage operation. In: Mortal, A., Aníbal, J., Monteiro, J., Sequeira, C., Semião, J., Moreira da Silva, M., Oliveira, M. (eds.) INCREaSE 2017, pp. 387–402. Springer, Cham (2018). https://doi.org/10.1007/978-3-319-70272-8_31

34. Semião, J., Romão, A., Leong, C., Santos, M., Teixeira, I., Teixeira, P.: Aging-aware dynamic voltage or frequency scaling. In: Proceedings of the XXIX Conference on Design of Circuits and Integrated Systems (DCIS 2014), Madrid, Spain, 26–28 November 2014. http://dx.doi.org/10.1109/DCIS.2014.7035599

"I Would Like to Get Close to You": Making Robot Personal Space Invasion Less Intrusive with a Social Gaze Cue

Stefan-Daniel Suvei[1]([✉]), Jered Vroon[3], Vella V. Somoza Sanchéz[2],
Leon Bodenhagen[1], Gwenn Englebienne[3], Norbert Krüger[1],
and Vanessa Evers[3]

[1] MMMI, University of Southern Denmark, 5230 Odense M, Denmark
{stdasu,lebo,norbert}@mmmi.sdu.dk
[2] IMM, University of Southern Denmark, 5230 Odense M, Denmark
vella@sam.sdu.dk
[3] HMI, University of Twente, P.O. Box 217, 7500AE Enschede, The Netherlands
{j.h.vroon,g.englebienne,v.evers}@utwente.nl

Abstract. How can a social robot get physically close to the people it needs to interact with? We investigated the effect of a social gaze cue by a human-sized mobile robot on the effects of personal space invasion by that robot. In our 2×2 between-subject experiment, our robot would approach our participants ($n = 83$), with/without personal space invasion, and with/without a social gaze cue. With a questionnaire, we measured subjective perception of warmth, competence, and comfort after such an interaction. In addition, we used on-board sensors and a tracking system to measure the dynamics of social positioning behavior. While we did find significant differences in the social positioning dynamics of the participants, no such effect was found upon quantitative analysis of perception of the robot. In a subsequent inductive analysis we further investigated these results, our findings suggesting that the social cue *did* play a role for the participants – particularly related to their perceived safety.

Keywords: Personal space invasion · Social robotics · Social cues

1 Introduction

As mobile robots are used increasingly often in everyday social settings, the design of appropriate robot behaviors has become more and more relevant. While the contexts can vary significantly, all these robots need to know how to position themselves in relation to people in a way that supports the intended interaction. Ideally, we can design robot social positioning behaviors that allow for smooth and efficient interactions, that feel natural to the people being interacted with.

Most prior work on social positioning for robots has treated this in a static way by trying to find *the* appropriate distance or positioning depending on a

© Springer International Publishing AG, part of Springer Nature 2018
M. Antona and C. Stephanidis (Eds.): UAHCI 2018, LNCS 10908, pp. 366–385, 2018.
https://doi.org/10.1007/978-3-319-92052-8_29

variety of factors that can be established at the beginning of the interaction. This seems to be rooted in the idea that it should be avoided that the robot 'gets too close', i.e. conducts personal space invasion (**PSI**). For example, earlier work has resulted in tables giving stopping distances to be used depending on factors such as human-likeness and height of a robot [1], and suggested that appropriate stopping distance may also depend on agreeableness or previous experience with animals or pets of the person being interacted with [2].

At the same time, social positioning behaviors can be highly dynamic during interactions. We can get really close, up to the point of "PSI", to someone we do not know well if we are sharing a secret, or if the environment is noisy, or if they have hearing problems. Similarly, people have been found to take the perceptional limitations of a robot into account in their own proxemic preferences [3]. In line with the later work on social positioning in human-human interaction (see e.g. the extensive 1987 review from Aiello [4]), this suggests that the appropriate interaction distance is something dynamic that can change several times during an interaction. In all these interactions signals are given to indicate to ones communication partner the current appropriateness of a chosen position (**social feedback cues**), as we have argued previously [5].

In this work, we investigated how a mobile robot (see Fig. 1) can provide a brief feedback cue to make the social positioning dynamic more smooth. Specifically, we tried to use a brief gaze change to allow a robot to conduct "PSI" without making the interaction less comfortable for the human user. This allowed for the investigation of the effect of using such a brief social cue on the overall interaction smoothness and the social perception of the robot. While this specific task was designed for research purposes, similar tasks could be used in real-life applications, e.g. in airports, institution entrances (including university), stadiums, or concert halls, where a robot could be used to provide assistance, if such a desire is signaled by the human user. As such, our main research question can be formulated as follows:

What are the effects of a robot's PSI and/or gaze change on:

1. the way in which people respond to that robot's approach by moving away from (or towards the robot)?
2. the perception of the robot in terms of warmth, competence, and discomfort?

The remainder of this paper is structured as follows. We will first discuss related work on PSI, gaze change, and measures of social perception, resulting in a specification of our hypotheses (Sect. 2). We will then discuss our experimental set-up in detail, including a description of the autonomous robot behaviors we implemented (Sect. 3). While we did not find effects on the perception of the robot, as assessed by questionnaire, we did find effects on participants' behavior – which we further investigated in our qualitative analysis (Sect. 4). Our findings show that, indeed, even a brief social feedback cue, such as a gaze change, plays a role in how PSI is perceived and responded to – providing an argument for the use of such social feedback cues in designing behaviors for social robots (Sect. 5).

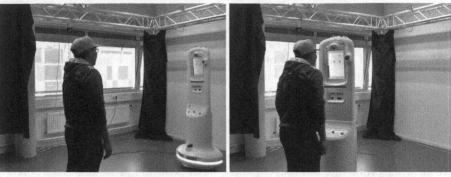

| (a) Camera 1: Start of experiment | (b) Camera 1: End of experiment |

(c) Camera 2: Start of experiment   (d) Camera 2: End of experiment

Fig. 1. The experiment, as seen from the two different cameras.

2   State of the Art

Much of the existing work in social positioning for robots is based on two theories on social positioning in humans. **Proxemics**, a term coined by Hall in [6], focuses on the distances people use in social interactions. **F-formations**, as introduced by Kendon [7], describe the different spatial arrangements used by people. As proxemics and F-formations would predict, many different social situations can be distinguished based on only position and orientation information (e.g. [8,9]).

Previous work has applied and investigated proxemics and F-formations in the context of robotics. This work often treats social positioning as something mostly static. For example, several authors have tried to establish the 'appropriate interaction distance' depending on a variety of factors, such as height and human likeness of the robot [1] as well as personality traits of the person being interacted with [2].

Interestingly, when we look at later work on social positioning in humans, it is treated more as a social dynamic, that can change during an interaction and that can carry communicative meaning within that interaction [4]. Information can be (non-verbally) transmitted about social positioning via responsiveness, as we argued in [5], by the usage of social feedback cues.

In the literature, there are only a few examples of artificial agents utilizing social feedback cues to influence the dynamics of social positioning. Recent work by Mead and Matarić [3] found that robots can effectively signal their (perceptual) needs to influence the proxemic preferences of people with whom they are interacting. Using a virtual agent instead of a physical robot, Kastanis and Slater [10] have also investigated ways to influence the proxemic preferences of people; they trained an agent to position itself such as to most effectively cause participants to move to a particular position in a space. Work by Jung et al. investigated human-robot teamwork and found that when their robots used back-channeling, this improved team functioning, though it also decreased perceived competence [11].

Facial features represent a key component of any social interaction, because they are easily recognizable and offer important cues regarding the inner states of the involved social actors. There exists a range of work in which artificial 'facial' features are used effectively as social feedback cues for non-mobile robots. Consider, as an example, the Baxter robot, discussed in [12], which is equipped with a screen which displays a pair of animated eyes and eyebrows. Even though the animations are limited to changing the angles of the eyebrows, opening and closing the eyes and moving the pupils, this is enough to signal to the human user whether or not the robot has understood the task.

In addition to these animations of facial features, there has also been work looking more specifically into the effects of different gaze behaviors. Recent work found that users feel more at ease with a robot that maintains visual contact while the task is being performed [13]. In contrast, in a human-human object handing interaction, the approaching human was found to be expected to maintain eye contact just towards the end of the interaction [14]. Other work has investigated and found gender effects, showing that women tend to position themselves further from a robot if it is constantly looking at them [2].

In all, though much work remains to be done, the prior work shows that people are sensitive to the social feedback cues used by robots and suggest that the use of face-inspired features – specifically gaze – can be an especially effective social feedback cue.

2.1   Social Perception Measurement

Because robots are more and more present in our day-to-day life, being able to correctly measure the way they are perceived has become increasingly important. Existing research shows that people have the tendency of making social category judgments, similar to the way they do in human-human interactions, based on the physical appearance, gender, race or nationality of the robot [15]. Furthermore, there is strong indication that people anthropomorphize robots, assigning human characteristics to them, especially when human characteristics are accessible and applicable [16]. As such, an interesting aspect to measure is the association of characteristics and traits based on the features or the perceived social category membership of the robot.

Literature on social psychology has also shown that two of the main drivers for the judgment of other humans are *warmth* and *competence*. The main reason for this is because these attributes link to basic survival instincts — we quickly evaluate if another person wants to harm us and if they are capable of doing so [17]. Furthermore, different combinations of competence and warmth will evoke an array of different other emotions, such as discomfort, pity or envy [18]. As shown in [19], there is strong indication that warmth and possibly other social attributes are important factors that can affect the perception of a robot. A method that offers the means to asses the central attributes implicated in human perception of robots and how such attributes can influence human-robot interactions is the Robotic Social Attributes Scale (**RoSAS**), presented in [20]. The RoSAS is a psychologically valid, 18-item scale, that was constructed using items from the Godspeed Scale [21] combined with key ideas taken from the psychological literature regarding social perception. The advantage of this scale is that it is psychometrically validated and it can be used to measure different types of robots, disregarding their purpose.

2.2 Hypotheses

Based on the existing literature on social positioning, we would expect that PSI has a negative effect on the interaction - causing the participant to step away and perceive it more negatively (which we will measure with the RoSAS). At the same time, there is work suggesting that we can leverage the dynamics of interactions to mediate this effect. More specifically, we show that by using gaze change as an appropriate social feedback cue, the robot can make its PSI less intrusive. Combined, this leads to the following hypotheses:

Hypothesis 1: When a robot conducts PSI without a social cue, as compared to not conducting PSI without a social cue, we expect people to:

a. step away from it, and;
b. perceive it more negatively in terms of warmth, competence, and discomfort.

Hypothesis 2: We expect an interaction effect between PSI and social cue (gaze change), such that the social cue 'compensates' for the PSI, leading people who experience both PSI *and* a social cue (gaze change) to:

a. step away from it less, and;
b. perceive it more positively in terms of warmth, competence, and discomfort.

3   Method

To test the proposed hypotheses, we conducted a 2×2 between-subject experiment. Our autonomous robot (Sect. 3.1) approached the participant in the

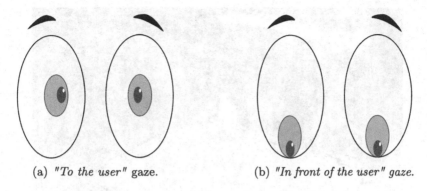

(a) *"To the user"* gaze.   (b) *"In front of the user"* gaze.

Fig. 2. The displayed social gaze cue.

context of potentially providing assistance to the user (Sect. 3.2). During the approach we manipulated PSI by the robot, as well as the use of gaze change as a social cue (Sect. 3.3). To collect our data, we used a questionnaire, a semi-structured interview, and several sensors for objective measures (Sect. 3.4).

3.1   Robot

The robot used in the experiments is a human-sized mobile robot (see Fig. 1), build within the Teresa project [22]. The system was build on top of the Giraff robot platform, with a new shell, and additional sensors, including: two RGB-depth cameras (Asus Xtion) and two laser range scanners (Hokuya LIDAR). A full description of the platform can be found in the Teresa project deliverables [23]. The platform is further equipped with a screen at head height, which can be used for telepresence by showing a live feed of the remote user. For the purpose of our experiment, the screen was used to signal the social feedback cue in the form of a short animation which changes the gaze of the robot's eyes, as shown in Fig. 2.

The behavior displayed by the robot was autonomous, combining person detection with navigation. The method works by detecting the participant in the scene, computing his/her position in the map coordinate frame and generating an appropriate goal position that will allow the robot to approach the human with PSI or without, depending on the condition (see Fig. 3). Before driving to the generated goal position, the robot displays the gaze-change animation on the screen, depending on the condition. Four seconds after the robot reached the goal position the LEDs on the base of the robot would light up green to signal the end of the experiment. Our person detection algorithm was build based on existing code and combined leg detection based on the laser range finder data (wide range) with upper-body tracking based on the RGB-depth data (also providing information on posture). We used map-based navigation. The map of the environment was built beforehand, using the laser range scanners and the Simultaneous Localization and Mapping [24] method. The robot uses the

Fig. 3. The behavior of the robot, as displayed in Rviz. The red arrow represents the goal position for the robot and it is computed relative to the position of the detected participant. (Color figure online)

Monte Carlo [25] algorithm to self-localize in the map and the ROS move_base framework for navigation. The speed of the robot was limited to 1 m/s.

3.2 Task

Given our research questions, the task necessitated a form of 'PSI'. To avoid an effect of any additional motions, we aimed for a task in which the only required action was a spatial positioning by the robot. For this reason, we designed a close-up approaching task, with the purpose of potentially providing assistance to the user. In the task, participants were told that the robot would approach them to potentially offer assistance (see Fig. 4). While free to move around the test area, the participants were advised to wait for the robot to approach them.

3.3 Manipulations

We manipulated two factors; approach distance [PSI/noPSI], and the giving of a social cue [GAZE/noGAZE]. This resulted in four conditions, PSI-GAZE, PSI-noGAZE, noPSI-GAZE, and noPSI-noGAZE.

Approach Distance [PSI/noPSI]: During the approach the robot would navigate to a location at a given distance to the participant. To have the robot conduct PSI (or not), we manipulated this distance. Based on the related work discussed

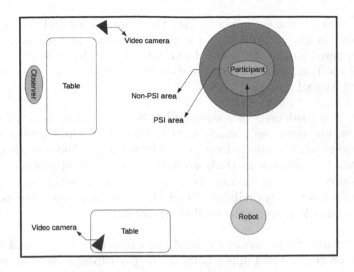

Fig. 4. Overview of the experiment area.

above and pilot testing, we expected distances below 45 cm to be perceived as a (strong) PSI. Therefore, we used a distance of 20 cm for the **PSI** conditions, and a distance of 50 cm for the **noPSI** conditions.

Social Cue [GAZE/noGAZE]: During the approach, an animation of two eyes would be shown on the screen of the robot. To have the robot provide a social cue, we manipulated the apparent gaze direction of these eyes (see Fig. 2). Since the eyes were shown on a 2D screen, we did not manipulate actual gaze direction; instead we used an emphasized animation of the pupil position to suggest apparent gaze direction.

In our prior empirical tests, we saw that a change of the apparent gaze direction from *"to the user"* to *"down, in front of the user"* felt like the robot was giving a social cue – which aligns with the related work discussed above. For the **noGAZE** condition, we used the eyes with a gaze "to the user", which would not change during the interaction. For the **GAZE** condition, we would start the interaction with eyes "to the user", changing to "in front of the user" as the robot would start its approach. This change was fast, which meant that it could potentially be missed if participants were not paying attention, but our informal prior tests suggested that making the apparent gaze change slower would feel more as awkward than as a social cue.

3.4 Measures

Objective Measures. To allow us to determine how much the participants stepped away from the robot, we recorded the movement of the participants. For this we used both the on-board sensors, and an external system using markers (OptiTrack). In addition, we also collected video data.

On-Board Sensors. For each experiment, the Xtion sensor and the laser range scanner were tracking and recording the movement of the participant. The tracking data is based on the 3D sensor depth information, by computing the XY-position of the human in the map, relative to the robot's base, once the robot has reached its goal position.

OptiTrack. The participant was equipped with two markers (one on the back of the chest, one on a cap), which were tracked using the OptiTrack motion capture system using 8 infra red cameras. The robot also had a marker, located on its screen. The system used allows sub-centimeter level precision tracking of the position and orientation of those markers. In our set-up we found that the system did not always reliably detect the markers, presumably because of occlusions and reflections on the shell of the robot.

Video Recordings. Two cameras recorded the interaction, providing a side view and a view on the face and upper body of the participant. These cameras were also used to record the interviews.

Subjective Measures. To measure perception of the robot, we used a questionnaire and a semi-structured interview. While the questionnaire gave more quantified data, the interview was intended to give us rich qualitative insights.

Questionnaire. The employed questionnaire asked participants to rate the robot and their experience in terms of 18 items on a 9-point Likert scale. These 18 items follow the RoSAS and are used for the social perception analysis of the robot [20]. They are grouped into 3 main factors, as follows:

Warmth: Happy, Feeling, Social, Organic, Compassionate and Emotional.
Competence: Capable, Responsive, Interactive, Reliable, Competent and Knowledgeable.
Discomfort: Scary, Strange, Awkward, Dangerous, Awful and Aggressive.

Furthermore, the participants are asked to describe their interaction in at least 140 characters. To ensure the fact that the social cue was perceived correctly, when signaled, the questionnaire also contained four manipulation checks which asked the user to mention what was the gaze of the robot at the beginning and at the end of the interaction, as well as the color of the LEDs. Additionally, the questionnaire also contained questions regarding the age, gender and nationality of the participant. The participants were also asked about their prior experience with robots and pets.

Interview. After the experiment and filling out the questionnaire, a short semi-structured interview was done with each participant. The two main questions asked were about their experience and their general feeling about the robot, as a result of the interaction. Depending on the answers, follow-up questions were asked, as for example "What do you think is the purpose behind this behavior?" or "How did you feel about the approach?".

3.5 Procedure

The participants were greeted at the entrance of the lab and were lead inside, where the context of the experiment was explained by the experimenter. They were then given an informed consent form, which they were asked to read and sign. The participants were then guided to the experiment area and equipped with the OptiTracker markers used for tracking their movements. They were then told to wait for the robot to approach them. We emphasized that while they were free to move, they should really let the robot approach them, and not the other way around. The robot would then approach them to a distance of 20–50 cm, exhibiting the behavior as appropriate for the condition the participant was in. The participants were recorded using two video cameras. Additionally, the OptiTracker system and the robot's sensors (the laser scanner and the ASUS camera) were recording their movement. After the interaction with the robot, the participants were asked to fill in the questionnaire on the interaction, and a brief interview was conducted by the experimenter.

3.6 Participants

We recruited 83 students and staff members from the campus of the University of Twente. Participants were recruited using word of mouth, and adverts. For agreeing to participate in the experiment, participants were compensated with chocolate. The average age of the participants was 24.25 (range 18–45). 66.2% of the participants were Dutch. 34 of the participants were women and 49 were men. Regarding previous experience with robots, 6% of the participants have built a robot before, 43.3% stated that they have worked with robots, 25.3% said that they have seen robots before, 16.8% have played with a robot before and 7% had no previous experience with robots. Additionally, 84.3% of the participants had previous experience with pets.

4 Results

To investigate the proposed hypotheses we employ both a deductive and a qualitative analysis of the data available from the experiments - this means sensor data, the OptiTracker data, questionnaire data, interview transcripts and video data.

4.1 Deductive Analysis

As described in Sect. 3.3, the movement of the participants relative to the robot was tracked with the help of the robot's own sensors and the OptiTracker system. The deductive analysis refers to the behavioral analysis shown by the participants, as measured with the help of these sensors, and to the evaluation of the questionnaire results, as proposed by the RoSAS model.

Due to robot failures, the experiment data for 3 of the participants had to be excluded. Additionally, for the statistical analysis of Hypothesis 2, we removed all the participants that either did not perceive the feedback social cue or that falsely considered that there was such a cue signaled. The elimination criterion was based on the answers that the participants gave to the two manipulation checks regarding the robot's gaze at the beginning and the end of the experiment from the questionnaire. As a result, the data for 58 participants out of 83 were used in our final investigation regarding Hypothesis 2 – 14 in the noPSI-GAZE and the PSI-GAZE conditions, and 15 participants in each of the other two.

Computing Distance (Lower)body-robot (From On-Board Sensors). We used the data from the Xtion sensor (RGB-depth) and the laser range scanners to determine the displacement of participants during the interaction. To do so, we first used the person tracking (see Sect. 3.1) based on a combination of both sensors. This resulted, for each time-stamp, in the position of the participant relative to the robot. Since some of detections were based only on the leg-detection from the laser range scanners (due to the participants moving outside the field of view of the camera), we used only the position on the floor plane. From this time-stamped list of positions, we then selected the 3 or 4 s of data to use based on the time-stamp at which the robot reached its goal position and stopped its movement. Within this subset, we then found the participant's minimum and maximum distance to the robot. The displacement was then calculated as the difference between this minimum and maximum. For 10 participants the data from the on-board sensors was not of sufficient quality to reliably compute the displacement.

Computing Head Distance to the Robot (From OptiTrack Data). We additionally used the data from the OptiTrack system to compute displacement of the participants during the interaction. Where the on-board sensors computed position based on center of mass (with Xtion) or on position of legs (with laser range finders), the OptiTrack allowed us to instead track head position. Additionally, with the OptiTrack only for 1 participant the data from the on-board sensors was not of sufficient quality to reliably compute the displacement. The OptiTrack system did occasionally detect the location of markers wrongly, presumably because of reflections. For this reason, we first smoothed the tracked positions, using a 500-frame moving average (data recorded at 120 fps). We manually coded the end of each robot approach based on the speed profile of the robot, and used a time window from the end of the approach until 4 s later. Within this time frame, we then computed the minimum and the maximum distance on the floor plane between the (smoothed) position of the marker on the base and the (smoothed) position of the marker worn on the participant's head. The displacement was then calculated as the difference between this minimum and maximum.

Scoring Competence, Warmth, and Discomfort from Questionnaire Data. A principal components analysis (PCA) was run on the 18-item RoSAS questionnaire results. The suitability of PCA was assessed prior to analysis.

All variables had at least correlation coefficient greater than 0.3, but Kaiser-Meyer-Olkin measure for three items was below 0.5; Awkward (0.439), Dangerous (0.474), and Scary (0.477). We thus ran the PCA excluding these three items, resulting in an overall Kaiser-Meyer-Olkin measure of 0.830. Bartlett's test of sphericity was statistically significant (p = .000).

PCA with Varimax orthagonal rotation revealed four components that had eigenvalues greater than one, which together explained 71.660% of variance (39.130%, 16.964%, 8.764%, and 6.801%). The interpretation of the data was in some respects consistent with the constructs that RoSAS intended to measure. The first component was very close to the construct 'Competence' from the RoSAS, with the main items loading onto it being Competent, Knowledgeable, Capable, Reliable, Responsive, and Interactive The second component was close to the construct 'Warmth' from the RoSAS, with the main items loading onto it being Compassionate, Feeling, Happy, Emotional, and Social. We did not find a single component that was close to the construct 'Discomfort' from the RoSAS, though the 3rd and 4th component seem to capture differing aspects of it. The 3rd component –with Responsive, Interactive, Social, not Aggressive, and not Awful loading onto it– we would label as 'Discomfort-Appropriateness'. The 4th component – with not Awful, Organic, and not Strange loading onto it– we would label as 'Discomfort-Weirdness'.

Hypothesis 1: Effects of PSI vs noPSI (noGAZE). A Mann-Whitney U test was run to determine if there were differences in stepping away and perception of the robot between PSI-noGAZE and noPSI-noGAZE (hypothesis 1). Distributions of the variables were similar, as assessed by visual inspection.

For moving away, as computed from the OptiTrack data, there was a statistically significant difference in the median score (U = 44, z = −2.662, p = .008, n = 29) between PSI-noGAZE (.83 m) and noPSI-noGAZE (.47 m). There was no statistically significant difference for stepping away as computed from the on-board sensors (U = 60, z = −.693, p = .488, n = 24), or for perception of the robot in terms of warmth (U = 121, z = .353, p = .724, n = 30), competence (U = 152, z = 1.641, p = .101, n = 30), discomfort-appropriateness (U = 132.5, z = .832, p = .405, n = 30), or discomfort-weirdness (U = 121, z = .354, p = .723, n = 30). We found the exact same pattern of results when including the participants who wrongly perceived the social cue, with a significant different median score on stepping away, as computed from the OptiTrack data (U = 97, z = −2.427, p = .015, n = 38) between PSI-noGAZE (.80 m) and noPSI-noGAZE (.48 m).

Hypothesis 2: Effects of Approach Distance x Social Cue. We conducted two-way ANOVAs to examine the effects of approach distance and social cue on our different measures. We suspect that our sample was a bit too small, as for some of these measures, we found outliers (as assessed by boxplot), residuals that were not normally distributed (assessed by Shapiro-Wilk), and no homogeneity of variances (Levene's test).

We found no statistically significant interaction effects of approach distance and social cue for any of our measures; not on our measures of stepping away, and neither on our measures of robot perception. Subsequent analysis of main effects also did not find a significant main effect for any of the constructs used to measure the perception of the robot.

We did find a statistically significant main effect of approach distance on stepping away as measured by OptiTrack ($F(1,53) = 8.070$, p = .006, partial $\eta^2 = .132$) between PSI (mean .796 m ± .070 m) and noPSI (.521 m ± .071 m), as shown in Fig. 5b. No significant main effect was found for social cue ($F(1,53) = .051$, p = .551, partial $\eta^2 = .007$).

We also found a statistically significant main effect of social cue on stepping away as measured by on-board sensors ($F(1,44) = 8.246$, p = .006, partial $\eta^2 = .158$) between GAZE (.060 ± .013) and noGAZE (.111 ± .013), as seen in Fig. 5a. No significant main effect was found for approach distance ($F(1,44) = .034$, p = .855, partial $\eta^2 = .001$).

To test our assumption that participants who did not see the cue should be excluded, we investigated if this effect on stepping away would also occur when comparing, within the subset of PSI-GAZE participants, people who perceived the social cue with people who did not. Though it should be noted that this was a very small sample (n = 18), we did find a similar effect of perceiving the social cue (.048 ± .054) or not (.161 ± .117) on stepping away as measured by the on-board sensors (U = 55, z = 2.218, p = .027).

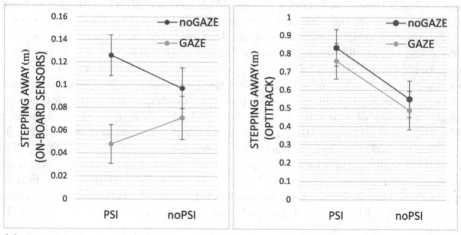

(a) Lower-body movement average (on-board sensors)

(b) Upper-body movement average (Opti-Track sensor)

Fig. 5. The statistical analysis of the sensor data. The values represent the average movement in meters.

The statistical results show that the social cue has significant effects on the positioning dynamic. The OptiTrack data shows that in the case of PSI, the participants lean backwards (thus moving their head more) to ensure a comfortable interaction distance. Additionally, as shown by the on-board sensors data, when PSI is conducted and no social gaze cue is provided, there is a significant increase in the lower-body movement of the participants.

4.2 Qualitative Analysis

Our deductive analysis showed that the robot behavior had effects on the non-verbal reactions of our participants. However, much to our surprise, we found no particular effects on social perception of the robot as measured by the questionnaire. To further investigate if other aspects could have played a role, we performed an inductive analysis, based on the responses of the participants in the conducted semi-structured interviews. Additionally, we used this analysis to derive managerial recommendations for the robotic system and the tested social cue.

The selected analytical method is a mixture of hermeneutics, as proposed by [26]. This method allows for study interpretation and content analysis in order to establish categories which can be counted and linked. In order to overcome the problem of 'anecdotalism' regarding the results of the analysis, we used a 'triangulation of methods' technique [26]. Therefore, in our analysis we used a combination of the open questions from the questionnaires, interview transcripts *and* non-verbal behaviors of the respondents as observed from the videos. Additionally, we also used other available sources (positioning information from OptiTrack and on-board sensors, statistical interpretations, and the quantitative questionnaire data) to interpret the different findings.

When coding and analyzing the set of interviews, the starting point of the investigation were the three factors proposed by RoSAS scale: *Warmth, Competence* and *Discomfort*. However, because we systematically found cases that did not fit any of the three initial factors, new categories (emerging from the data) were created, in order to produce a holistic interpretation of all the phenomena, in a comprehensive data treatment [26]. As a result, the hermeneutics analytical approach led us to the inductive categories of *Incompetence, Problems and Solutions* and *Intentionality*.

We thus ended up with a total of six categories: *Warmth* represents the respondent's positive feelings regarding the interaction; *Discomfort* relates to the respondent's feeling of uneasiness regarding the interaction with the robot; *Competence* reflects the participant's feeling that the robot is considered to have the skills necessary to perform the task of the experiment; *Incompetence* is the opposing category, where the robot is considered as not having the appropriate skills; The category of *Intentionality* contains those quotations in which the respondent shows signs of appreciating specific intentions of the actions performed by the robot; The final category, *Problems and Solutions*, is a managerial theme where the respondents evaluate problems in the robot and give possible solutions for them. All these categories have an interpretative quality used to reflect how the participant's understanding and interpretation of the robot are influenced by the experiment.

Table 1. Frequencies of the different encoded categories from our inductive analysis, in each of the different conditions

Case	Warmth	Competence	Discomfort	Incompetence	Intentionality	Problems and Solutions
PSI-GAZE	7	8	38	17	5	11
PSI-noGAZE	13	7	39	23	3	14
noPSI-GAZE	24	26	33	12	12	18
noPSI-noGAZE	10	9	23	19	3	18

Because it follows a constructionist approach, the used triangulation method is limited by the fact that it has to accept the idea that an interview and its meaning is negotiated between the respondent and the interviewer and therefore accepts that different sources of data may bring different truths or interpretations, as discussed in [26]. This happens due to the fact that the truth generated through each interview is negotiated in its context and therefore its conclusions may not be repeated through a different source of data [27]. In order to address this limitation, additional measures where taken in order to ensure the validity of the results, as advised by [26,27]. These measures follow the refutability principle presented in [26] which seeks for critical thinking when analyzing data, using a constant comparative method. To this end, the analysis of the data focused initially on a smaller part, comprised of only a few of the conducted experiments and interviews, where their findings were systematically compared and discussed amongst the coders, in order to ensure that all the cases and any possible deviations are covered and explained accordingly in the established analysis [28].

After we established our categories, independent coders coded the data, and we measured their agreement to establish the reliability of our analysis [28]. For the first two coders, we found a very strong inter-rater agreement (Cohen's kappa = 0.81). We wish to report that when a third coder also coded 20% of the selected interview transcripts, the inter-rater agreement was much lower (Cohen's kappa = 0.45). This surprised us, though there are several possible explanations – e.g. it might have been caused by the third coder using only the transcripts. An alternative explanation is an effect of culture (similar to what was discussed in [29,30]), as the third coder lived in the Netherlands, while the first two coders both lived in Denmark. Given these results, including the strong inter-rater agreement between the first two coders, we discarded the codes of the third coder; we used only the codes of the first two coders for our further analysis.

In the following paragraphs we offer a detailed description of the outcomes of our analysis (see Table 1 for an overview).

Warmth: Regarding the perceived warmth of the interaction, the qualitative results show a clear impact of the social cue. This impact can be observed through the increased number of opinions regarding positive points on the interaction, that is then described as *nice*, *fine*, *natural* and *friendly*. When the PSI is added to the interaction, the respondents see an incoherence of those signals and there-fore the positive effect of the cue shrinks. Therefore, since the gaze can be viewed as an element that shows the robot's perception of the human, when the PSI occurs some participants interpret this as a malfunction of the robot, as stated in the following: *"Mhm ... but the point that it is looking down, I think, I mean ... I doubt it is working ok..." (Interview 83)*

Competence: Regarding 'competence', the results are conclusive regarding the social cue when it is not accompanied by PSI. The perceived skills relate to the speed, the closeness, the natural movement and the robot's ability to "see" the human. The expressed opinion regarding the skills and therefore competence of the robot triples. An example of this can be seen in the following extract: *"The closeness is fine. How it drives towards you, the speed... the distance was ok, the rest was ok." (Interview 44)*

Discomfort: When no social cue is signaled and there is PSI, the robot is perceived as to be lacking the necessary skills relating to the adequate closeness, speed, dis-tance and in general is perceived as dangerous: *"So, it felt like a bit dangerous, that it did not perceived you well, so it can drive over you." (Interview 13)*

Incompetence: Other less objective faults are attributed to the robot when there is no social cue and there is PSI, for example the time in response is perceived as slower and as having the inability to properly locate the human: *"the robot approached me after a while, but he seemed to be kind of aiming a little bit next to me, so it wasn't really completely approaching and looking in the right direction." (Interview 57)*

Intentionality: A surprising result of the experiment is the fact that the social cue increases the impression of the robot as having intentions. The perceived intentionality decreases if there is PSI, but even in that case it scores higher than without the social cue. *"It felt like he then saw me, just standing there and turned towards me and came towards me and then turned a bit when it was in front of me to look more directly at my face." (Interview 60)*

Problems and Solutions: Some of the most relevant findings for the managerial implications in the cases in which the social cue was signaled are linked to the fact that the robot also displayed a task bar on the screen, which disrupted the image of the face of the robot: *"Well it really was a robot. I think the eye was not sophisticated enough to bring some human feelings, to me. Especially because there was also taskbar next do in his eyes. So. That kind of broke the image of a face" (Interview 32).*

Another common concern of the respondents was how to deploy the robot in a place with many people. The proposed solution, as shown in the following quote, is to ensure the minimum quantity of movements of the robot as to ensure its safety to a potential crowd surrounding it: *"... maybe like the fact that he could move like with you, but on the other hand if it gets too much, people will freak out, maybe. So it was properly good that it just stays there and doesn't do too many movements." (Interview 32)*

For the cases in which no social cue is provided, the topics brought up by the respondents change. The speed and space become major topics, as they are perceived as more relevant problems to handle before worrying, for example about how the face is displayed on the screen. One possible suggestion for dealing with the PSI is adding a voice or a sound to the robot, as a form of signaling the interaction that is about to happen. One such example is given in: *"Like it really doesn't have any reasons to stand that close to my face. Like, if it at least have been talking to me or had another way of notifying me that it saw me and what it's intention was, maybe it would have been more ok. But now it was a bit random." (Interview 49)*

All in all, the analysis shows that, even though PSI is the main source of discomfort of the experiment carried out, the social cue decreases the level of discomfort of the participants. The main purpose attributed to the social cue is regarding safety, since the participants consider that the robot perceives their presence and therefore they trust in the fact that it will stop in an appropriate manner for the interaction. For example, the following quote reveals the concern of a participant that was not exposed to the social cue: *"I actually didn't have the idea that he was seeing me, so that was also the reason that I stepped aside. Because I thought: Ok he does not see me, he will just roll this way" (Interview 37)*. This indicates that a social gaze cue can be used to improve the perception of the overall interaction and safety of the robot.

5   Conclusions and Discussion

In this paper, we investigated if personal space invasion by a robot can be made more 'smooth' by introducing social gaze cues. We manipulated both personal space invasion and the use of social gaze cues, in a between-subjects set-up. To investigate the effects on the interaction dynamic, we measured distance to the robot, both of their lower body (using on-board sensors), and of their head (using a tracking system). To investigate the effects on the way in which the robot was perceived, we used a questionnaire with items on warmth, competence, and comfort.

We found significant main effects of our manipulations on the positioning dynamic; (1) participants increased their head distance after the approach more when the robot got close to them, i.e. conducted PSI, and (2) participants increased their lower body distance after the approach less when the robot gave a social gaze cue. This suggests that different aspects of people's positioning dynamic reflect different things. One interpretation, that was further supported by our inductive analysis, is that the social gaze cue increases peoples' feeling of safety, reducing the need to step back – and that people will lean back to ensure a comfortable interaction distance.

Given the richness of this kind of positioning data, and the promising results, a more comprehensive analysis of movement could be an interesting direction for future work. We found it valuable to find that the different sensors we used, onboard and a tracker, yielded different aspects of stepping away, focused on lower body and head, respectively. Beyond stepping away after an approach, there is a range of other movement aspects that could be extracted, e.g. stepping away during an approach, or orientation of body or head. When doing so, it would be important to keep limitations such as sensor noise in mind, and to avoid looking for significant results (which is also why we deliberately limited our own analysis).

To our surprise, we found no significant effects of our manipulations on the questionnaire intended to measure the way in which participants perceived the robot – especially since the used approach distances were well above and below what is perceived as PSI in the literature, but also since we *did* find an effect on the interaction dynamic. A possible cause is that, during the experiment, the participants had sufficient space and time to adjust their position (by stepping back or to the side) and thus weaken the effect that the personal space invasion could have on them and their perception of the robot. This would be in line with our idea that aspects of the interaction dynamic can influence perception of PSI. Additionally, since our participants were not native in English, they may have missed some nuances in the meaning of different items, perceiving them as "similar" – for example Capable/Competent or Strange/Awkward. This would of course have an impact on the "strength" of these descriptors.

To further explore the perception of the robot, we conducted a qualitative analysis based on the semi-structured interviews, the open questions from the questionnaire, and the video recordings. We identified various categories in which the comments of our participants could be encoded, including discomfort and intentionality. While our findings were rich and qualitative (see Sect. 4.2), we will here discuss one specific pattern; when the social cue was signaled, there was a sense among participants that the robot was aware of their presence, and, as a result, participants would trust its actions more – also when it conducted PSI.

Overall, our findings show that social cues might indeed be used to make personal space invasion by a robot more smooth, especially in terms of the interaction dynamic and perceived safety.

Acknowledgement. This work was partially supported by the project Health-CAT, funded by the European Regional Development Fund.

References

1. Walters, M.L., Dautenhahn, K., Boekhorst, R.T., Koay, K.L., Syrdal, D.S., Nehaniv, C.L.: An empirical framework for human-robot proxemics. In: Proceedings of New Frontiers in Human-Robot Interaction (2009)
2. Takayama, L., Pantofaru, C.: Influences on proxemic behaviors in human-robot interaction. In: IEEE/RSJ International Conference on Intelligent Robots and Systems, IROS 2009, pp. 5495–5502. IEEE (2009)
3. Mead, R., Matarić, M.J.: Robots have needs too: people adapt their proxemic preferences to improve autonomous robot recognition of human social signals. In: New Frontiers in Human-Robot Interaction, p. 100 (2015)

4. Aiello, J.R.: Human spatial behavior. In: Stokols, D., Altman, I. (eds.) Handbook of Environmental Psychology, Chap. 12, pp. 389–504. Wiley, New York (1987)
5. Vroon, J., Englebienne, G., Evers, V.: Responsive social agents. In: Agah, A., Cabibihan, J.-J., Howard, A.M., Salichs, M.A., He, H. (eds.) ICSR 2016. LNCS (LNAI), vol. 9979, pp. 126–137. Springer, Cham (2016). https://doi.org/10.1007/978-3-319-47437-3_13
6. Hall, E.T.: The Hidden Dimension. Anchor Books, New York (1966)
7. Kendon, A.: Conducting Interaction: Patterns of Behavior in Focused Encounters, vol. 7. CUP Archive (1990)
8. Groh, G., Lehmann, A., Reimers, J., Frieß, M.R., Schwarz, L.: Detecting social situations from interaction geometry. In: 2010 IEEE Second International Conference on Social Computing (SocialCom), pp. 1–8. IEEE (2010)
9. Lau, B., Arras, K.O., Burgard, W.: Multi-model hypothesis group tracking and group size estimation. Int. J. Soc. Robot. 2(1), 19–30 (2010)
10. Kastanis, I., Slater, M.: Reinforcement learning utilizes proxemics: an avatar learns to manipulate the position of people in immersive virtual reality. ACM Trans. Appl. Percept. 9(1), 3:1–3:15 (2012)
11. Jung, M.F., Lee, J.J., DePalma, N., Adalgeirsson, S.O., Hinds, P.J., Breazeal, C.: Engaging robots: easing complex human-robot teamwork using backchanneling. In: Proceedings of the 2013 Conference on Computer Supported Cooperative Work, pp. 1555–1566. ACM (2013)
12. Guizzo, E., Ackerman, E.: The rise of the robot worker. IEEE Spectr. 49(10), 34–41 (2012)
13. Fischer, K., Jensen, L.C., Suvei, S.-D., Bodenhagen, L.: The role of the timing between multimodal robot behaviors for joint action. In: 3rd Workshop on Joint Action (at ICSR 2015) (2015)
14. Basili, P., Huber, M., Brandt, T., Hirche, S., Glasauer, S.: Investigating human-human approach and hand-over. In: Ritter, H., Sagerer, G., Dillmann, R., Buss, M. (eds.) Human Centered Robot Systems. Cognitive Systems Monographs, vol. 6, pp. 151–160. Springer, Heidelberg (2009). https://doi.org/10.1007/978-3-642-10403-9_16
15. Carpenter, J., Davis, J.M., Erwin-Stewart, N., Lee, T.R., Bransford, J.D., Vye, N.: Gender representation and humanoid robots designed for domestic use. Int. J. Soc. Robot. 1(3), 261–265 (2009)
16. Kuchenbrandt, D., Eyssel, F., Bobinger, S., Neufeld, M.: When a robot's group membership matters. Int. J. Soc. Robot. 5(3), 409–417 (2013)
17. Fiske, S.T., Cuddy, A.J.C., Glick, P.: Universal dimensions of social cognition: warmth and competence. Trends Cogn. Sci. 11(2), 77–83 (2007)
18. Willis, J., Todorov, A.: First impressions: making up your mind after a 100-ms exposure to a face. Psychol. Sci. 17(7), 592–598 (2006)
19. Ho, C.-C., MacDorman, K.F.: Revisiting the uncanny valley theory: developing and validating an alternative to the godspeed indices. Comput. Hum. Behav. 26(6), 1508–1518 (2010)
20. Carpinella, C.M., Wyman, A.B., Perez, M.A., Stroessner, S.J.: The robotic social attributes scale (RoSAS): development and validation. In: Proceedings of the 2017 ACM/IEEE International Conference on Human-Robot Interaction, pp. 254–262. ACM (2017)
21. Bartneck, C., Kulić, D., Croft, E., Zoghbi, S.: Measurement instruments for the anthropomorphism, animacy, likeability, perceived intelligence, and perceived safety of robots. Int. J. Soc. Robot. 1(1), 71–81 (2009)

22. Shiarlis, K., Messias, J., van Someren, M., Whiteson, S., Kim, J., Vroon, J., Englebienne, G., Truong, K., Evers, V., Pérez-Higueras, N., Pérez-Hurtado, I., Ramon-Vigo, R., Caballero, F., Merino, L., Shen, J., Petridis, S., Pantic, M., Hedman, L., Scherlund, M., Koster, R., Michel, H.: Teresa: a socially intelligent semi-autonomous telepresence system. In: ICRA 2015: Proceedings of the IEEE International Conference on Robotics and Automation, Workshop on Machine Learning for Social Robotics. IEEE (2015)
23. D6.5: Third version of semi-autonomous telepresence system. Teresa project deliverable (2016). teresaproject.eu/project/deliverables/
24. Thrun, S., Leonard, J.J.: Simultaneous localization and mapping. In: Siciliano, B., Khatib, O. (eds.) Springer Handbook of Robotics, pp. 871–889. Springer, Heidelberg (2008). https://doi.org/10.1007/978-3-540-30301-5_38
25. Dellaert, F., Fox, D., Burgard, W., Thrun, S.: Monte carlo localization for mobile robots. In: Proceedings of the 1999 IEEE International Conference on Robotics and Automation, vol. 2, pp. 1322–1328. IEEE (1999)
26. Silverman, D.: Doing Qualitative Research: A Practical Handbook. SAGE Publications Limited, Thousand Oaks (2013)
27. Russell Bernard, H.: Research Methods in Anthropology: Qualitative and Quantitative Approaches. Rowman & Littlefield, New York (2011)
28. Russell Bernard, H., Wutich, A., Ryan, G.W.: Analyzing Qualitative Data: Systematic Approaches. SAGE Publications, Thousand Oaks (2010)
29. Antaki, C., Rapley, M.: 'Quality of life' talk: the liberal paradox of psychological testing. Discourse Soc. **7**(3), 293–316 (1996)
30. Sveningsson, S., Alvesson, M.: Managing managerial identities: organizational fragmentation, discourse and identity struggle. Hum. Relat. **56**(10), 1163–1193 (2003)

A Scoping Study on the Development of an Interactive Upper-Limb Rehabilitation System Framework for Patients with Stroke

Kevin C. Tseng[1(✉)], Alice M. K. Wong[2], Chung-Yu Wu[3],
Tian-Sheuan Chang[3], Yu-Cheng Pei[2], and Jean-Lon Chen[2]

[1] National Taiwan Normal University, Taipei, Taiwan ROC
ktseng@pddlab.org
[2] Taoyuan Chang Gung Memorial Hospital, Taoyuan, Taiwan ROC
bigmac1479@gmail.com
[3] National Chiao Tung University, Hsinchu, Taiwan ROC

Abstract. This study aims to propose the framework of the interactive upper-limb rehabilitation system with brain-computer interfaces. The system mainly includes an interactive rehabilitation training platform, a rehabilitation database system, and an EEG and EMG acquisition system. The interactive rehabilitation training system platform includes a virtual rehabilitation game system and an interactive upper-limb rehabilitation device by which a user can perform proactive and reactive rehabilitation.

Keywords: Brain-computer interface · Stroke
System framework and upper-limb rehabilitation

1 Introduction

According to a study by the World Health Organization (WHO), stroke has become one of the most serious health problems in the world. Approximately one-third of patients recovering from a stroke may suffer from life-long disabilities, of which motor dysfunction is a main sequela. Many researchers are currently dedicated to research involving stroke rehabilitation. Physiotherapy is one of the most common rehabilitation methods. However, upper-limb motor dysfunction is the most difficult sequela to be cured after stroke. Reducing permanent disability caused by stroke is still the most important goal of neurorehabilitation. Restoring the function of the arm and hand is very important during neurological rehabilitation [1].

The clinical effects of conventional rehabilitation therapies focus on improving walking ability; therefore, conventional rehabilitation is less effective in comprehensive recovery. In particular, hand motor dysfunction is very common in clinical practice. Although it is possible to recover some motor functions through neurorehabilitation, a large number of patients cannot achieve functional recovery of their affected arms after traditional rehabilitation exercises. However, many new interventions have emerged recently and can somewhat improve the motor functions of patients with stroke, including constraint-induced movement therapy (CIMT), bilateral movement therapy

© Springer International Publishing AG, part of Springer Nature 2018
M. Antona and C. Stephanidis (Eds.): UAHCI 2018, LNCS 10908, pp. 386–393, 2018.
https://doi.org/10.1007/978-3-319-92052-8_30

(BMT), mirror therapy (MT), robot-assisted therapy, task-oriented training (TOT), virtual reality (VR), motor imagery (MI), and functional electro-stimulation (FES). These approaches may partially improve upper limb functional impairment in patients with paralysis of the upper limbs after stroke and are supported by evidence-based medical efficacy [2, 3]. There is growing evidence that proactive repetitive motor exercises can help in the recovery of patients with stroke [4]. Intensive exercises can more effectively improve the movement ability and function of the upper limbs [4, 5].

In addition, transcranial magnetic stimulation (TMS) has been employed in recent years as an effective aid for the rehabilitation of patients with stroke [6]. Transcranial magnetic stimulation can inhibit ipsilateral brain activity or stimulate contralateral brain activity to help patients in reconstructing cortical function. Therefore, understanding the interaction between treatment and the brain is important in rehabilitation.

To this end, this study aimed to advocate a rehabilitation framework in combination with a visual interface using the concept of spontaneously induced neuromuscular therapy and to explore using a brain-computer interface for the acquisition of brain-wave signals and to establish treatment information for the evaluation of a patient's rehabilitation. We wish to address the possibility of improving a patient's sense of accomplishment and compliance in rehabilitation.

2 Background

A study has suggested that the golden period of post-stroke rehabilitation span lasts approximately three to six months [7]; therefore, a discussion of how to assist patients with stroke to recovery in this golden period is urgently needed. Traditional upper-limb rehabilitation often applies sensory-motor training to promote the recovery of motor function, such as muscle strength, muscle endurance and range of joint motion. The current mainstream physical therapy for patients with stroke involves a task-oriented approach [8]. Clinically, upper-limb movements after stroke have slower and unco-ordinated patterns during reaching. Therefore, reaching motion is often considered a key parameter for the assessment of upper limb function after stroke [9]. In addition, the latest studies suggest that exercise training based on repetitive movements of specific upper-limb muscles results in significant improvements in upper-limb function recovery in patients with hemiplegia [10].

Mechanically assisted treatment has been developed for over a decade to make up for the lack of trainers and to overcome patient movement restrictions in traditional rehabilitation and to more objectively and instantaneously record working data. Studies have demonstrated that clinically proven bilateral upper-limb rehabilitation devices, such as the MIT-MANUS, BI-MANU-TRACK, BATRAC (bilateral arm training with rhythmic auditory cueing), and MIME (mirror image motion enabler), have better efficacy in mechanically aided rehabilitation than traditional therapies [11]. However, the current bilateral upper-limb biomechanical devices are not equipped with auxiliary visual or brainwave interfaces.

In recent years, many brain-computer interfaces have been used in the health care industry and can be divided into proactive and reactive interfaces [12]. The reactive device can record and collect physiological signals, such as brain waves, as a reference for monitoring or care, and the proactive device can provide brainwave control or interactive modes and has certain advantages, including real-time acquisition, non-intrusive monitoring and low cost. Its applications in industry and academic fields are becoming increasingly popular [13]. The brain-computer interface can also be used in motion training programs. For example, motor imagery (MI) training was originally used in the training of athletes. Since 2006, some researchers have discussed the possibility of using MI in rehabilitation after stroke [14], especially in patients with severely impaired motion after stroke. In addition, in terms of assessing the effectiveness of rehabilitation, the brain-computer interface (BCI) has certain advantages, including higher temporal resolution, low cost, long-term monitoring, and the use of noninvasive measurements. Studies have assessed and confirmed that BCI can now distinguish between the intention of moving the patient's shoulder or elbow [15]. According to the literature, there have been studies on the effects of using reactive/proactive brain-computer interface games to enhance the effectiveness and positive attitudes of patients in rehabilitation [12]. However, no studies have evaluated the possibility of employing brain-computer interface games with various proactive and reactive interactive modes in rehabilitation devices.

Therefore, this study is a scoping study on the development of an interactive upper-limb rehabilitation system controlled by a brain-computer interface and is expected to propose an interactive framework system for upper-limb rehabilitation that is controlled by a brain-computer interface, using the concept of spontaneously induced neuromuscular therapy to monitor the cerebral motor area, hand muscle rehabilitation status, and the interactions between the treatments. The system framework includes hardware and software to assist the user in rehabilitation training and, at the same time, records the movement trajectory of the user using the interactive rehabilitation training system. The data recorded can be used to evaluate the effectiveness of the user's rehabilitation training and to compare with the EEG and EMG signals at the corresponding time points.

3   Conceptual System Framework

The framework of the interactive upper-limb rehabilitation system with brain-computer interfaces developed in this study is shown in Fig. 1. The system mainly includes an interactive rehabilitation training platform, a rehabilitation database system, and an EEG and EMG acquisition system. The interactive rehabilitation training system platform includes a virtual rehabilitation game system and an interactive upper-limb rehabilitation device by which a user can perform proactive and reactive rehabilitation. In addition, the EEG and EMG acquisition system also includes measuring electrodes and a mechanical design to measure the user's EEG and EMG signals. The user can first activate the motor-sensory cortex through repeated transcranial magnetic stimulations and can then perform rehabilitation training through the interactive rehabilitation training system platform. At the same time, the interactive rehabilitation training system platform can track the user's movement, while the EEG and EMG acquisition system can measure the electrical signals of both the user's brain and their hand muscles during rehabilitation training. These data collected can be used to analyse the effect of the cerebral cortex activation by repeated TMS and the hand muscle condition and thus can be used to analyse the effect of rehabilitation training. The interactive rehabilitation training system platform can guide the patients to correctly complete the pre-set rehabilitation motion through a virtual rehabilitation game and can give feedback about the user's rehabilitation by analysing data from the EEG and EMG acquisition system and the interactive upper-limb rehabilitation device. These data on the patient's rehabilitation status are then stored in the rehabilitation database system for the medical care providers' reference.

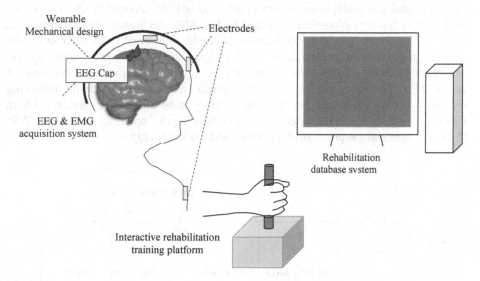

Fig. 1. The framework of the interactive upper-limb rehabilitation system with brain-computer interface

3.1   Interactive Rehabilitation Training System Platform

The interactive rehabilitation training system platform includes a proactive and reactive rehabilitation training device, a rehabilitation game visual interface, and a brain-computer interface. The rehabilitation training device, which is designed using an electronic control device to drive the gears, can help a stroke patient to move their shoulders and elbows in a symmetrical manner. The speeds of both proactive and reactive motion can be adjusted. During training, the EEG brain-computer interface is used to capture brain signals from the motor area of the cerebral cortex. This approach, using virtual games with a visual interface, can make training become goal-oriented and fun, resulting in recuperation compliance; the electromechanical and mechanical testing is conducted, and the back-end database of the system is designed based on this concept. In addition, this study aimed to utilize user-centred rehabilitation games and a human-computer interaction interface to facilitate researchers in obtaining EEG and EMG response signals through a friendly interface. Then, the biomedical signals and algorithm are further processed to help users in integrating the visual interaction system.

3.2   EEG and EMG Control System

The system framework of this study presents an EEG and EMG control system that includes a miniaturized EEG and EMG acquisition system. The integrated system components and structure of the miniaturized EEG and EMG acquisition system are shown in Fig. 2 and include a front-end amplifier, analogue MUXs, programmable gain amplifiers (PGA), analogue-to-digital converters (ADC), a microcontroller unit (MCU), a power management unit, and a communication circuit. The EEG or EMG signals captured by the electrode will be amplified by the front-end physiological amplifier. Then, the analogue multiplexer will select the EEG or EMG channel to send the signals to the PGA for signal amplification and to the ADC for signal digitalization. The digitized signals are transferred to the microcontroller unit. Finally, the EEG and EMG data are transmitted to an external device for signal analysis. Generally speaking, the size of the brainwave signal is less than 100 μV, and its frequency ranges between 0.1 and 100 Hz. Therefore, the design of this system circuit must include the following features: (1) high differential gain that can amplify small brain wave signals; (2) high CMRR to reduce common mode noise; (3) high input impedance; (4) high SNR; (5) low power consumption; (6) low noise; and (7) small chip area.

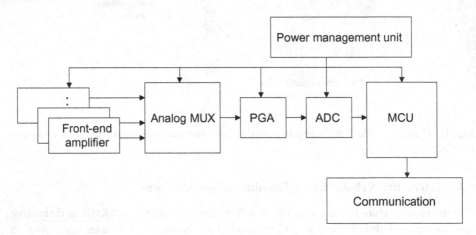

Fig. 2. EEG and EMG acquisition system

3.3   Rehabilitation Database System

The system framework proposed in this study is a rehabilitative database system, as shown in Fig. 3. The rTMS setting parameters can be recorded asynchronously, and the user's EEG/EMG signals recorded by the EEG/EMG control system can be stored in the system simultaneously for virtual rehabilitation games to set up the parameter values of the game environment. The user can play the virtual rehabilitation game on an external monitor and use the proactive and reactive upper-limb rehabilitation devices that connect to this system.

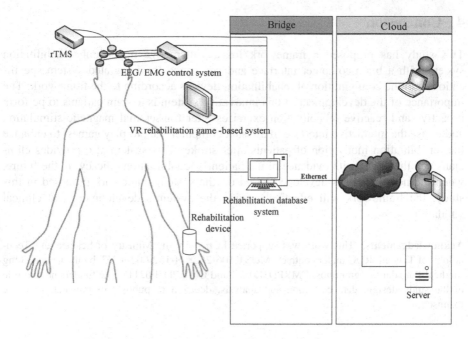

Fig. 3. The framework of the rehabilitation database system

Most users requiring upper-limb rehabilitation after stroke may need long-term rehabilitation monitoring and EEG signal recording. Therefore, the system framework is better designed to use a cloud database for information storage on the back-end, which can be accessed by authorized medical professionals. In this system framework, a user-directed virtual rehabilitation game is designed according to medical professional recommendations. The system obtains physiological signals from the EEG and EMG control system and quantifies and records signals. Quantified information will be used for real-time fine-tuning and virtual rehabilitation game design based on user needs. The main functions of the rehabilitation database are to retrieve biomedical signals, process digital signals, record usage of the virtual rehabilitation game, and back up the patient's information. In addition, a log recording information access will also be stored in the database to enable medical professionals to take advantage of the system to follow up patient recovery and perform medical analyses. The system also provides a patient account to allow patients to log in to their personal accounts and to obtain their own personal rehabilitation information. The back-end database will be used to back up patients' health and personal information.

The main users of this system are caregivers and therapists because many stroke patients are not able to use computers and other digital devices due to their upper-limb disabilities. Caregivers can obtain information on the rehabilitation regimen and efficacy for a patient, basic rehabilitation knowledge, and the therapist opinions using the system.

4 Conclusion

This study has proposed a framework for an interactive upper-limb rehabilitation system with a brain-computer interface and confirmed the integrated system specifications and the configuration of rehabilitation devices according to the framework. The importance of the development of this innovative system is to train patients to perform proactive and reactive rehabilitation exercises after transcranial magnetic stimulation and to use the interactive interface of a visual computer (i.e., to play games) to enhance the rehabilitation motivation of patients after stroke. This system also provides clinicians and therapists with evidence of the patient's rehabilitation efficacy. In the future, when the new system is developed based on the system framework proposed in this study, the framework will effectively guide the system's development and clinical validation.

Acknowledgements. This work was supported in part by the Ministry of Science and Technology of Taiwan, ROC under contracts MOST 106-2628-H-182-002-MY3, by the Chang Gung Medical Foundation (grant nos. CMRPD3E0373 and CMRPD2F0211). The funders had no role in the study design, data collection and analysis, decision to publish, or preparation of the manuscript.

References

1. Hesse, S., Schulte-Tigges, G., Konrad, M., Bardeleben, A., Werner, C.: Robot-assisted arm trainer for the passive and active practice of bilateral forearm and wrist movements in hemiparetic subjects. Arch. Phys. Med. Rehabil. **84**, 915–920 (2003)
2. Staubli, P., Nef, T., Klamroth-Marganska, V., Riener, R.: Effects of intensive arm training with the rehabilitation robot ARMin II in chronic stroke patients: four single-cases. J. Neuroeng. Rehabil. **6**, 46 (2009)
3. Stewart, K.C., Cauraugh, J.H., Summers, J.J.: Bilateral movement training and stroke rehabilitation: a systematic review and meta-analysis. J. Neurol. Sci. **244**, 89–95 (2006)
4. Lum, P.S., Burgar, C.G., Shor, P.C., Majmundar, M., Van der Loos, M.: Robot-assisted movement training compared with conventional therapy techniques for the rehabilitation of upper-limb motor function after stroke. Arch. Phys. Med. Rehabil. **83**, 952–959 (2002)
5. Woodbury, M.L., Howland, D.R., McGuirk, T.E., Davis, S.B., Senesac, C.R., Kautz, S.: Effects of trunk restraint combined with intensive task practice on poststroke upper extremity reach and function: a pilot study. Neurorehabilitation Neural Repair **23**, 78–91 (2009)
6. Rossini, P.M., Rossi, S.: Transcranial magnetic stimulation. Neurology **68**, 484 (2007)
7. Knott, M., Voss, D.E., Hipshman, H.D., Buckley, J.B.: Proprioceptive Neuromuscular Facilitation: Patterns and Techniques. Hoeber Medical Division, Harper & Row, New York (1968)
8. Dickstein, R., Hocherman, S., Pillar, T., Shaham, R.: Stroke rehabilitation three exercise therapy approaches. Phys. Ther. **66**, 1233–1238 (1986)
9. Zackowski, K.M., Dromerick, A.W., Sahrmann, S.A., Thach, W.T., Bastian, A.J.: How do strength, sensation, spasticity and joint individuation relate to the reaching deficits of people with chronic hemiparesis? Brain **127**, 1035–1046 (2004)
10. Sterr, A., Freivogel, S.: Motor-improvement following intensive training in low-functioning chronic hemiparesis. Neurology **61**, 842–844 (2003)

11. Mouri, T., Kawasaki, H., Nishimoto, Y., Aoki, T., Ishigure, Y., Tanahashi, M.: Robot hand imitating disabled person for education/training of rehabilitation. J. Robot. Mechatron. **20**, 280–288 (2008)
12. Shin, Y., Lee, S., Lee, J., Lee, H.N.: Sparse representation-based classification scheme for motor imagery-based brain-computer interface systems. J. Neural Eng. **9**, 056002 (2012)
13. Lotte, F., Congedo, M., Lecuyer, A., Lamarche, F., Arnaldi, B.: A review of classification algorithms for EEG-based brain-computer interfaces. J. Neural Eng. **4**, R1–R13 (2007)
14. Sharma, N., Pomeroy, V.M., Baron, J.-C.: Motor imagery: a backdoor to the motor system after stroke? Stroke **37**, 1941–1952 (2006)
15. Zhou, J., Yao, J., Deng, J., Dewald, J.P.A.: EEG-based classification for elbow versus shoulder torque intentions involving stroke subjects. Comput. Biol. Med. **39**, 443–452 (2009)

Access to the Web, Social Media, Education, Culture and Social Innovation

Improving Resource Discovery and Access Through User-Controlled Adaptation: Exploring the Role of Library Metadata

Wondwossen M. Beyene[✉] and Marius Wiker Aasheim

OsloMet – Oslo Metropolitan University, Oslo, Norway
wondwossen.beyene@hioa.no, s198536@stud.hioa.no

Abstract. Accessibility of library search tools is measured not only by their adherence to accessibility guidelines, but also by the ease they offer users to find accessible resources. This makes library metadata an object of study in library accessibility. Past studies encouraged exploring the application of metadata in fostering accessibility. The studies also recommend considering user requirements. This study aimed to examine the role of metadata in making the process of resource discovery and access accessible to people with low vision impairments. Based on recommendations of past studies, a simple prototype was developed to test the idea of allowing users to set their own metadata preferences on their search interfaces. Participants were recruited to explore the prototype. The initial findings showed that adding such option in preference settings may be more appealing to frequent users than "one-time" users. However, the participants were able to provide comments on what to improve for the next iteration.

Keywords: Digital accessibility · Universal design · Accessible search
Accessibility metadata · Library metadata

1 Introduction

Search interfaces are what stand between users and multitudes of information resources such as ebooks, multimedia and others stored in digital library environments. Therefore, the way they are designed affects user's experience in resource discovery and access. Literature shows that libraries are increasingly using developments in web accessibility to make their websites as well as search interfaces accessible to people with disabilities [1–4]. However, compliance to guidelines may not guarantee accessibility and usability of search interfaces in the overall user-information interaction partly for the following reasons:

- Library search tools are used by diverse group of users whose needs and preferences may contradict each other [5].
- For the average user, the search tools are about finding a resource. However, for people with disability, it could be about finding an accessible resource. Therefore, the accessibility of search interfaces is determined not only by their compliance to

© Springer International Publishing AG, part of Springer Nature 2018
M. Antona and C. Stephanidis (Eds.): UAHCI 2018, LNCS 10908, pp. 397–408, 2018.
https://doi.org/10.1007/978-3-319-92052-8_31

accessibility guidelines, but also by the ease they offer users to find resources accessible to them [5, 6]. This extends the span of accessibility to include library metadata.

There have been studies conducted on accessibility of library search interfaces. However, there is a shortage of works that focus on the process of resource discovery and access. Moreover, there are very few that examine the role of metadata. This paper aims to examine the roles library metadata could play in making the process more accessible to users with low vision impairments.

Discussing best practices for designing search interfaces, Resnick and Vaughan [7:782] stated, "Any system that includes metadata must consider what fields are relevant". Resnick and Vaughan also recommended that the process of creating metadata fields should be informed by user requirements. In this paper, we ask: which metadata fields are more relevant for users with low vision impairment? How could metadata be harnessed for enhancing user experience in resource discovery and access? To answer the questions, a simple prototype informed by past studies was developed to be tested by users with low vision impairments. The findings are compared with existing literature to recommend how library search tools could be augmented to serve the purpose of accessibility and inclusive design.

The rest of the paper is organized as follows: Next, a literature review is presented followed by explanations of the methodology used in the study. Then the findings are presented to be discussed in the section that follows. Finally, the paper closes with conclusive remarks and recommendations for the next iteration of the prototype.

2 Literature Review

2.1 Barriers of Access for People with Visual Impairments

Library catalogs have evolved to the current web-scale resource discovery tools that provide improved interface to submit queries, receive results, and make content selections [8]. Depending on their design, they may include features such as a search box, search results, visual cues to the results, links, and tools for faceted navigation [8]. The overall evolution is partly driven by the need for improving users' experience in resource discovery and access.

Studies, however, show that library search tools are complex to use when compared with Internet search engines [4, 9, 10]. For instance, Horwath [11] revealed that rich graphic interfaces and complex web designs would pose barriers to users of screen reader technologies. Beyene [5] also confirmed that such interfaces turn away some users with low-vision impairments.

Yoon et al. [12] reported that the most common barriers their study identified were related to navigation. They categorized navigational problems as linearization and semantic issues. Linearization refers to the order screen reader technologies follow to read contents of HTML documents. Yoon et al. [12] claimed that linearization caused cognitive overload to their study participants by requiring them to "read" far more irrelevant text just to find the information they were looking for. The semantic issues included poor link labeling, lack of context in a surrounding text and lack of descriptive attributes in the HTML code [12]. The study by Beyene [5] confirmed the presence of such problems showing that there were links simply labeled as "link 1", "link 2", etc.

Beyene [5] illustrated that a user may finally succeed in searching and retrieving an ebook just to find that it is not accessible to screen readers or is behind a paywall. This would be frustrating for some users with visual impairments. Some studies recommend that adding metadata fields to describe resources by their accessibility attributes (e.g. whether a document is accessible to screen readers) would help a user to inspect the results list and judge whether a material is suitable for him [6, 13, 14].

The examples provided above show that the accessibility of library search tools is dependent not only on the designer's compliance to accessibility guidelines but also on the knowledge representation and organization schemes followed by librarians or content (database) vendors. Moreover, the diversity in needs and preferences of users makes the problem even more complex. Some scholars, therefore, suggested complimenting the compliance-based approach with the adaptation approach to adapt the search tools to each user's needs and preferences [15]. Beyene and Ferati [15] and Paternò and Mancini [16] therefore recommended tackling the problems by breaking them down into three categories: presentation level, information level and navigation level issues.

2.2 The Role of Metadata

Metadata provides users with input, control or informational support [17]. As part of the input support, metadata offers users the capability for lookup and exploratory searchers [17, 18]. Lookup search refers to the process of typing a query and checking the search results whereas exploratory search involves using faceted metadata to browse for a material of potential interest [18, 19]. Examples of the control support could be the filters on search interfaces which are used to narrow down search results [17]. The informational support could be exemplified by the metadata information such as author, title, abstract and others which help the user to decide on a resource's suitability for his/her needs. Therefore, a "well-designed use of metadata" can help in resolving problems at information and navigation levels mentioned above [17].

Scholars recommend considering metadata as integral component of search interface design [7, 17]. Efforts aimed at designing accessible search interfaces thus need to incorporate the use of metadata for improving the search experience of users with disabilities. However, there are not many examples of related works. Few of the available works include an accessibility metadata project which is linked to the eLearning community and some digital libraries which incorporated the recommendations from the project for annotating their resources[1]. The intent of the accessibility metadata was described as offering vocabularies for annotating resources by their accessibility attributes and making it easy for people with disability to find accessible resources [20].

The study by Beyene and Godwin [6] entitled "Accessible Search and The Role of Metadata" provided design recommendations on how metadata could be employed to

---

[1] www.a11ymetadata.org.

design accessible library search interfaces. The conclusions from that study and others mentioned above were that:

- Metadata could be used to improve accessibility of search interfaces to people with print disabilities. That can be done by providing information on the accessibility qualities of an information resource (e.g., accessible/not accessible to screen reader technologies, with/without caption, etc.)
- Information which is crucial for some could be irrelevant to others and vice versa. Current library search tools apply the view more/less toggle to limit the amount of information displayed with search results. However, users may need be given the opportunity to decide on which information should always be visible and which should be hidden behind a "view more/less" functionality.
- Users may opt to have shortcuts by faceted metadata; e.g. genre, resource type (audio books, braille, etc.), series, "popularity" and others to conduct exploratory searches.
- Therefore, it might be advisable to improve search interfaces, by augmenting the already existing preference settings to allow users configure their own tools, as they deem necessary.

3   Methodology

3.1   The Prototype

An interactive hi-fi prototype, informed by the studies discussed above, was developed to be tested by users with low vision impairment. The search interface as shown by Fig. 1. provides a single search box with sample shortcuts/filters for resource types such as PDFs, eBooks, audiobooks, Braille, Video and 'new books'; which can be added or removed by the user.

The prototype includes a preferences setting, shown by Fig. 2, designed to give the user the option to limit the amount/type of metadata information that should always be shown in the results list above the view more/less options. As discussed in the literature review, this would help screen reader users to quickly go through the results list without reading "unnecessary information". The intent is to offer the user the flexibility to configure the results list, as he/she deems necessary.

Figure 3 shows a sample search results presentation where a user has specified information on author, language, and accessibility to be visible while the rest is hidden behind the view more/less button.

Figure 4 shows what would happen if the user chooses to view the whole metadata information.

Moreover, the prototype included a sample searchable database. The prototype at this stage was designed an initial opinion-gathering tool that can be improved for further interactions to include not only metadata preferences but also others related to fonts, backgrounds, and other features.

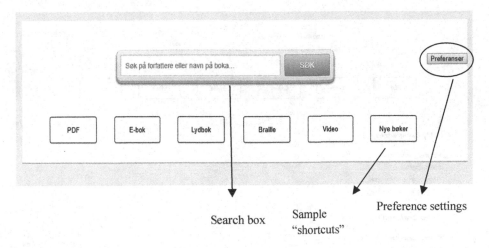

Search box   Sample
"shortcuts"

Preference settings

Fig. 1. The search interface

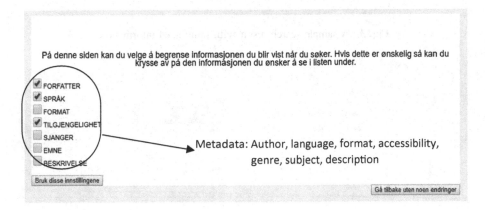

Fig. 2. Preference settings

3.2   Participants

The literature of usability testing shows that there is no fixed law on the minimum number of participants to include in user tests. They state that is dependent on the type of test and the time and money one has to conduct the test [21]. The cost-benefit analysis discussed by Nielsen [22, 23] sets the optimal ration 3 to 5 users.

Efforts were made to recruit participants for this study through the disability-related advocacy organizations in Norway. However, the process has proved to be challenging, as we were able to recruit only three participants at this stage. Two of them were female while one of them was male. One of them uses screen reader technology whereas the others just used the magnification tools available on web browser. One of them said that he is a retiree; one other said she works and studies while the other mentioned she is employed at some institution. All of the participants have provided informed consent to take part in the study.

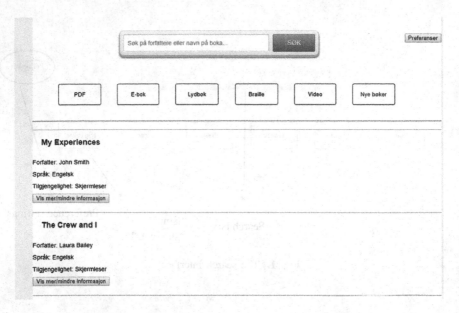

Fig. 3. A sample search result with minimized information

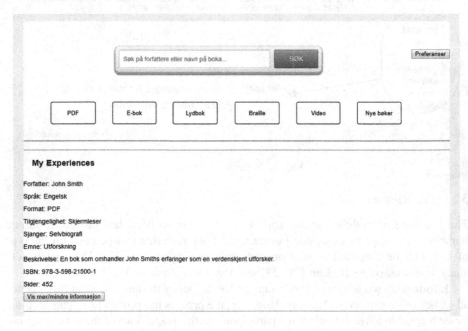

Fig. 4. A sample results presentation

3.3   Data Collection and Analysis

The study is designed as a qualitative study. The participants were first guided through the prototype and given briefings on the purpose of the test. Moreover, as exemplified by Figs. 2, 3 and 4, they were given pre-determined search tasks and were encouraged to test it with different preference settings. The sessions took from 30 to 60 min on a laptop presented to the participants. All of them needed screen magnification and making the mouse pointer bigger. As they progress through the tasks, the participants were encouraged to ask, "think aloud" and provide feedbacks. The conversations were recorded with an audio device and later transcribed for thematic analysis.

4   Results

All of the participants were quick to understand the idea behind the prototype, though one of them seemed to have some doubts on the need of adding metadata in the preference settings. That particular person said he would have preferred being able to choose different colors for the fonts and the background. After walkthroughs through the prototype and conducting search activities, the participants have given feedbacks that could be presented as follows.

4.1   Search Results Presentation and Metadata Preferences

The prototype included fields such as title, author, language, format, genre, subject, description, ISBN, number of pages, and accessibility. It surely did not include all elements in a particular metadata schema. The intent was to use these fields as starting points and invoke users to discuss what other type of information should be included. One of them said,

> "A form of user reviews would actually be quite nice. I mean, the description is nice, but that's usually written by the publisher, which wants to sell the book, so it's often presented in the best way possible, but if I could read actual readers' feedback, it would help me decide on whether I should get this book or not"

The other participant mentioned the need for information on alternative format. It was thought to see whether a material is available in audio and braille formats. One other respondent mentioned the need of subgenres. Speaking of her experience with library search tools, one of them said,

> "… They have like 20000 results for "crime" novels, and I find that to be ridiculous, because that doesn't help me at all. So I would like to be able to sort on subgenres again. Being able to choose subgenres […] will let you limit the search result a lot before you search"

Existing library tools offer the capability of narrowing search results by different facets. It could, however, be a subject of further research to see to what extent those tools are helpful. One other feedback from a participant is to add a label "Research Results" just above the results list.

4.2   Setting Metadata Preferences

Two of the participants explicitly stated that they don't like to see excessive information on search interfaces. Speaking of the metadata information presented after clicking a "view more" button, the other participant said, "I think this is a bit overwhelming". When experimenting with the preference settings, one of them selected author and subject, one other selected the field for accessibility (which states whether the book he selected is accessible to screen readers), and the other experimented with genre and subject. During the activities, they have been experimenting with the show more/less buttons.

When asked about the importance of controlling the metadata information in the way they did, all of them concurred that it could be a good idea. One of them however said that it might be meaningful for frequent users rather than "one-time" users. One other participant said that he could not see the full benefit of this functionality because of the small size of the database presented by the prototype.

4.3   Vocabularies

The participants also reflected on the use of keywords and terminologies for faceted metadata. One of them said the word "format", for her, signifies dimensions rather than file types. She recommended finding another expression such as "file format" or "file type". She also said the word "description" is also not clear. The word was meant to connote summaries, abstracts or more information about an item. Two participants commented on the use of the word "braille" and explained that "punkt" or "punktskrift" are the words used by Norwegian users [the language used on the prototype was Norwegian]. One of them said "lesepunkt" is the word used in the everyday speech. These feedbacks show the role vocabularies play to make search interfaces user friendly.

4.4   Shortcuts/Filters

One participant liked the idea of having one search box that can be used to perform searches either by author or by title. However, the need for alternative form of resource discovery was noted. One of them said,

> "Sometimes you know exactly what you're looking for and then it'd be nice to filter, but other times it would be nice to just browse, [for instance], by resource format"

One participant said she liked the idea of creating shortcuts to some groups of resources on the home page of the search interface. She said she would prefer shortcuts by resource formats (ebook, braille, etc.), genre, 'last search', and common (popular) searches.

5 Discussion

The main purpose of improving accessibility is to identify and remove barriers that prevent users from accessing information, or give users the means to overcome the barriers. In case of library search tools the barriers could be interpreted in terms of complex search interfaces, overwhelming amount of search results, overwhelming amount of metadata per search result, the difficulty to locate accessible resources, poor and faulty navigation, vocabulary and others which could largely be categorized as presentation, information and navigation level issues.

As discussed in the literature review, a "well-designed" metadata has the potential of resolving some problems related to information and navigation level [17]. Moreover as recommended in literature, the use of metadata in search systems should be informed by user requirements [7].

The intent of this study, therefore, was to answer the following questions: which metadata fields are more relevant for users with low vision impairment? How could they be harnessed for enhancing their experience in resource discovery and access?

5.1 "Relevant" Metadata

The preliminary results didn't show clear preferences to specific sets of metadata information. Two of the participants however recommended addition of information on "popular" resources and reviews from other users. Past studies show that users with print disability give high value to information about what other readers think about a resource [6]. This could be interpreted in different ways. One reason could be that they want to reduce their interaction with search systems and get an interesting or popular book. This would suggest the need of adding social metadata such as ratings, "likes", and reviews on library search tools. The other more pronounced need the participants discussed was related to faceted metadata which was discussed in the relation to shortening navigation to a specific group of information resource.

The other issue is related to the nomenclature of metadata fields. Past studies already show that the vocabularies used on library search tools are difficult to understand to some users [24, 25]. That by itself is a barrier to access. Participants of this study also affirmed the need for "user-friendly" resource descriptions. The case where a participant said the word "format" is ambiguous and the instance where the other participant discussed choice of terms for Norwegian language interfaces could be mentioned as examples.

The participants generally said they do not like excessive information to be shown on search interfaces. However, they didn't discuss what type of information they don't want to see. During the sessions, they were observed selecting fields from the preferences settings to experiment the view more/less options. From these simple experiments, it might be possible to say that it is important to leave the choice to the user in the manner demonstrated in the experiment.

5.2   Harnessing Metadata for Accessibility

One of the core objectives of this study was to see whether giving users the control over the search results presentation makes search interfaces easier and more effective to use. Studies show that users with print disability may not want to flip through many pages of results lists [5]. The option experimented in this study would help to squeeze more search results into the first page and thereby saving the user some navigation overload. That would also make search interfaces handy for mobile interfaces.

It is worth mentioning that many library search interfaces do provide the view more/less option. However, they do not allow users to determine which information should be always visible. In this study, we tested giving users that control. Though the users understood the intent of the study, their reactions were mixed. As one of them said, that could be meaningful for the frequent users than for the "one-time" users.

As discussed in literature, there are studies that recommend labeling resources by their accessibility features [20]. This experiment intentionally included a metadata field for accessibility. One of the participants was seen experimenting with it. However, a study with a larger group would be necessary to assess the impact of accessibility metadata.

Faceted metadata has been used to filter search results after users submitted their queries [26]. The possibility discussed in this study was giving users the ability to set some of them as shortcuts at the home pages of their search interfaces. Berget and Sandnes [27] found that some users with disability would struggle to formulate queries on search tools which are intolerant to spelling errors and which don't offer auto-complete suggestions. Past studies [6] and this study show that filters such as 'new books', 'popular books', 'past searches (history)', 'favorites', 'audio law books' and others could provide an alternative way of searching by reducing the demand of keying in search terms.

5.3   Accessibility as Part of Preference Settings?

It would be worth remembering that library search tools and other search engines provide users with options for setting preferences by language, region etc. It would require research to see how well those functionalities are used. Nevertheless, the settings are there for whomever who chooses to use them. One recommendation from this study could be to augment those already existing functionalities to include options related to accessibility. That would help users to set their own accessibility preferences and control what should be displayed on their interfaces. That in the end would make the search tools usable and accessible to all to the extent possible.

5.4   Limitations

While our study shows that all participants understood the purpose of the study, the participants commented that the sample database included with the prototype was so small. Therefore, it did not give them enough chance to test and appreciate its advantage. Yet they recommended experimenting it with a larger set of database.

Nevertheless, they did see a definite need for it in larger collections of resources. The other major limitation is the low number of participants who took part in the study.

6 Further Work

For the next iteration of the prototype, we would improve all current features according to feedback gathered at the current stage. Some of the improvements will be: increasing the size of the test database, improving the vocabulary and make them more user-friendly, and making the search results more distinguishable. Furthermore, the next iteration of the prototype will feature the possibility for the users themselves to control some of the design aspects of the search interface through additional sets of preferences. That includes things such as color, font types and sizes, and tools to add and remove shortcuts on the home page of the search interface. That would hopefully show how a search interface could be made adaptable to each user's needs and preferences. Furthermore, effort will be made to test the next iteration with a larger group of participants.

7 Conclusion

The value of this paper is more in the themes it offered for further research and the ideas it gathered for further improvement of the prototype. Based on the results found and the literature reviewed, we can however confirm that metadata has informational and navigational values that can improve accessibility and usability. Simplifying discovery of accessible resources and simplifying navigation amount to removing barriers of access to information. The solution tested in this study may be appealing more to frequent users. However, the idea of augmenting the preference settings of search interfaces to handle demands of accessibility would be an interesting undertaking for researchers as well as practitioners.

References

1. Borchard, L., Biondo, M., Kutay, S., Morck, D., Weiss, A.P.: Making journals accessible front & back: examining open journal systems at CSU Northridge. OCLC Syst. Serv. Int. Digit. Libr. Perspect. **31**(1), 35–50 (2015)
2. Charbonneau, D.H.: Public library websites and adherence to senior-friendly guidelines. Public Libr. Q. **33**(2), 121–130 (2014)
3. Lush, B.: Managing accessible library web content. In: Wentz, B., Jaeger, P.T., Bertot, J.C. (eds.) Accessibility for Persons with Disabilities and the Inclusive Future of Libraries, vol. 40, pp. 169–189. Emerald Group Publishing Limited (2015)
4. Billingham, L.: Improving academic library website accessibility for people with disabilities. Libr. Manag. **35**(8/9), 565–581 (2014)
5. Beyene, W.: Resource discovery and universal access: understanding enablers and barriers from the user perspective. In: Petrie, H., Darzentas, J., Walsh, T. (eds.) Studies in Health Technology and Informatics, vol. 229, pp. 556–566. IOS Press (2016)

6. Beyene, W., Godwin, T.: Accessible search and the role of metadata. Libr. Hi-Tech. **36**(1), 2–17 (2018)
7. Resnick, M.L., Vaughan, M.W.: Best practices and future visions for search user interfaces. J. Am. Soc. Inf. Sci. Technol. **57**(6), 781–787 (2006)
8. Breeding, M.: The future of library resource discovery: a white paper commissioned by the NISO Discovery to Delivery (D2D) Topic Committee, NISO, Baltimore (2015)
9. Yoon, K., Hulscher, L., Dols, R.: Accessibility and diversity in library and information science: inclusive information architecture for library websites. Libr. Q. **86**(2), 213–229 (2016)
10. Teague-Rector, S., Ghaphery, J.: Designing search: effective search interfaces for academic library web sites. J. Web Librariansh. **2**(4), 479–492 (2008)
11. Horwath, J.: Evaluating opportunities for expanded information access: a study of the accessibility of four online database. Libr. Hi Tech. **20**(2), 199–206 (2002)
12. Yoon, K., Dols, R., Hulscher, L., Newberry, T.: An exploratory study of library website accessibility for visually impaired users. Libr. Inf. Sci. Res. **38**(3), 250–258 (2016)
13. Beyene, W.: Metadata and universal access in digital library environments. Libr. Hi Tech. **35** (2), 210–221 (2017)
14. Nganji, J.T., Brayshaw, M.: Personalizing learning materials for students with multiple disabilities in virtual learning environments. In: Science and Information Conference (SAI), pp. 69–76. IEEE (2015)
15. Beyene, W.M., Ferati, M.: A case for adaptation to enhance usability and accessibility of library resource discovery tools. In: Antona, M., Stephanidis, C. (eds.) UAHCI 2017, Part I. LNCS, vol. 10277, pp. 145–155. Springer, Cham (2017). https://doi.org/10.1007/978-3-319-58706-6_12
16. Paternò, F., Mancini, C.: Effective levels of adaptation to different types of users in interactive museum systems. J. Am. Soc. Inf. Sci. **51**(1), 5–13 (2000)
17. Wilson, M.L.: Search User Interface Design. Morgan & Claypool Publishers, San Francisco (2012)
18. Marchionini, G.: Exploratory search: from finding to understanding. Commun. ACM **49**(4), 41–46 (2006)
19. Hearst, M.A.: Clustering versus faceted categories for information exploration. Commun. ACM **49**(4), 59–61 (2006)
20. Rothberg, M.: Accessibility Metadata Project: Final Report. http://www.a11ymetadata.org/. Accessed 28 Dec 2017
21. Lazar, J., Feng, J.H., Hochheiser, H.: Research Methods in Human-Computer Interaction. Morgan Kaufmann, Amsterdam (2017)
22. Nielsen, J.: Why You Only Need to Test with 5 Users (2000). https://www.nngroup.com/articles/why-you-only-need-to-test-with-5-users/. Accessed 25 Dec 2017
23. Nielsen, J.: Guerrilla HCI: Article by Jakob Nielsen. https://www.nngroup.com/articles/guerrilla-hci/. Accessed 25 Dec 2017
24. Cassidy, E.D., Jones, G., McMain, L., Shen, L., Vieira, S.: Student searching with EBSCO discovery: a usability study. J. Electron. Resour. Librariansh. **26**(1), 17–35 (2014)
25. Comeaux, D.J.: Usability testing of a web-scale discovery system at an academic library. Coll. Undergrad. Libr. **19**(2–4), 189–206 (2012)
26. Fagan, J.C.: Usability studies of faceted browsing: a literature review. Inf. Technol. Libr. **29** (2), 58–66 (2010)
27. Berget, G., Sandnes, F.-E.: Searching databases without query-building aids: implications for dyslexic users. Inf. Res. **20**(4), 689 (2015)

SELFMADE – Self-determination and Communication Through Inclusive MakerSpaces

Ingo K. Bosse[✉], Hanna Linke, and Bastian Pelka

Faculty of Rehabilitation Research, University of Dortmund,
Dortmund, Germany
`ingo.bosse@tu-dortmund.de`

Abstract. The article demonstrates how 3-D-printing can be used in an appropriate pedagogical setting to empower people with complex disabilities to design and produce assistive tools. It refers to the SELFMADE project, which is linked to the research and practice of assistive technology in special education with a focus on participation in everyday life/leisure time, work and communication. Within the project, funded by the German Federal Ministry of Education and Research, a MakerSpace was set up in a Service Center for Augmentative and Alternative Communication (AAC) in Dortmund, Germany. The Service Center for AAC is a place where the specific competencies needed to work with persons with disabilities are present. This project uses 3-D-printing as technology, as well as the processes and platforms of social innovation. Starting with group of persons with movement disorders and complex communication needs, SELFMADE tries to enable all persons with disabilities to design and produce products with a 3-D-printer as well as sharing the designs with other people.

Keywords: Persons with disabilities · Accessible making · Peer production
Social innovation · 3-D-printing

1 Introduction

The purpose of the SELFMADE project is to produce equipment and aids for persons with disabilities which facilitate a higher participation in daily life, work life, leisure time and communication. Therefore, a MakerSpace, mainly based on 3-D-printing, was founded in a Service Center for Augmentative and Alternative Communication (AAC): a workplace for twelve persons with complex needs. The pilot project, SELFMADE, investigates, develops and tests a social innovation approach. Experts and scientists from the maker culture, for assistive technologies (AT), AAC and, persons with and without disabilities are collaborating permanently in this innovation center.

The main focus is to improve the production of individualized equipment and aids for persons with disabilities. A long history of experience in the field of developing centers and laboratories of social innovation drives the process. The produced products are not assistive technologies in a narrow sense. The project focus on the self-determined production of low tech equipment and aids. The different perspectives

© Springer International Publishing AG, part of Springer Nature 2018
M. Antona and C. Stephanidis (Eds.): UAHCI 2018, LNCS 10908, pp. 409–420, 2018.
https://doi.org/10.1007/978-3-319-92052-8_32

of all the actors will result in more participation and an improvement in the quality of life of persons with disabilities by using innovative technology. The legal framework builds on the Convention on the rights of persons with disabilities (CRPD) by the United Nations, as stated in Article 4:

"To undertake or promote research and [the]

f) development of universally designed goods, services, equipment and facilities, as defined in article 2 of the present Convention, which should require the minimum possible adaptation and the least cost to meet the specific needs of a person with disabilities, to promote their availability and use, and to promote universal design in the development of standards and guidelines;" [1]

Germany is legally bound by the UN CRPD. Therefore, the Federal Ministry of Education and Research established a nationwide program for cooperative, pre-competitive research. Its aim is to improve the full participation and inclusion of persons with disabilities in daily life by using photonic technologies. The direct cooperation of persons with disabilities and the maker culture is intended. The use of an open innovation approach is an indispensable part of the program.

Knowledge transfer is of highest importance in transdisciplinary projects like SELFMADE. During the initial phase, the discussion and sharing of knowledge and scientific terms, as well as working on a team culture takes a lot of time [2].

The close connection of social and technological innovation will support the empowerment of persons with disabilities by producing equipment and aids with a high usability level. Due to the fact that most of the peer researchers have complex disabilities, one challenge is to develop an appropriate research concept that allows them to work together: "conducting qualitative research with people with learning/communication difficulties is challenging but achievable" [3].

While peer production deepens its reach into society and progressively includes vulnerable groups, many of these approaches lack self-determination. People with complex disabilities are especially seen as receivers of innovation and goods, and only rarely as active designers within peer-production processes. The SELFMADE-project tries to enable all persons to design and produce products with a 3-D-printer and to share their knowledge.

2   Aims of the Project

The aims of the research and development project are as follows:

2.1   Empowerment for Peer Production

- The development of pathways to empower persons with complex disabilities to use 3-D-printers in order to become active producers and distributors of goods and tools responding to their own needs;
- to create an "intermediate market" of assistive tools to fill the gap between home-made assistive tools and commercial assistive tools, that can be created by

linking individual persons with disabilities with large communities that offer long standing experience and models of "intermediate quality";

• to bring together persons with and without disabilities in an inclusive maker space that is purposely installed within a working space for persons with complex needs; and

• the empowerment of persons with disabilities regarding the definition and production of individualized assistive tools.

2.2 Production of Assistive Tools and Products for Participation in Everyday Life

• The production of assistive tools in the areas of work, everyday life/leisure time and communication.

• Exploiting Social Innovation mechanisms to improve the impact of 3-D printing by people with disabilities. The maker spaces represent a social innovation that could be scaled out to other spaces and institutions; one aim of the project is to identify pathways of scaling the developed innovations and improving the project's impact.

2.3 Development of a Checklist for Accessible MakerSpaces

The project SELFMADE focuses on the following research question:

How should MakerSpaces be designed to meet the minimum requirements of accessibility?

In addition to this main research question, there are numerous other questions that need to be addressed in the project:

1. How is it possible to control 3D printers?
2. How modular are the products?
3. How can the "production process" be designed to be more understandable?
4. How can the possible risks be well recognizable?
5. How should the connection to public transport be?
6. Which communication channels should be offered?

In a first step, general principles of accessibility for the design of MakerSpaces are presented, to sensitize the Maker scene to this issue. These general principles are complemented by applicable standards, guidelines to be followed, and supporting funding.

In a next step, the developed checklist will be tested in the FabLab of the University of Applied Sciences Ruhr West. This step includes the identification of barriers and dismantling them. Practitioners in MakerSpaces are encouraged to check their MakerSpaces for barriers and inclusiveness. As a result, the developed checklist is tested and the MakerSpaces become more accessible.

3 Theoretical Framework

The theoretical background, the "capability approach" [4], focuses the choices necessary to initiate a process of social innovation through network building.

Innovation research is providing numerous indications of a fundamental shift in the innovation paradigm towards social innovation. This new paradigm is characterized by the innovation process being opened up to society, its orientation towards the major societal challenges, and a stronger recognition of social innovations complementary to technological innovations. Social innovation is understood as a new combination or figuration of practices in areas of social action, prompted by certain actors or constellations of actors, with the goal of better coping with the needs and problems than existing practices currently do [5]. An innovation is therefore social to the extent that it varies social action, and is socially accepted and diffused in society. This definition exceeds a normative understanding of social innovations as 'good' or socially desirable. It also enlarges traditional technologically oriented innovation concepts. This may also serve as an answer to a situation where the limits of strictly policy-driven programs on the one hand and social entrepreneurship and civil society initiatives on the other hand become obvious. Therefore, it is important to better understand the mechanisms and the potential of inter-sectoral approaches for solving the grand societal challenges, e.g. in boosting the level of inclusiveness in society and reducing exclusion in all societal subsystems. Recent research has therefore developed an approach to understand innovations as embedded in ecosystems of social innovation [cf. 6] and putting social innovation in close co-operation with different stakeholders [1]. The SELFMADE project therefore developed an approach to – on the one hand – design the process of 3-D-printing by persons with disabilities as a social innovation in itself and – on the other hand – embed the project and its outcomes in a process of social innovation by opening it up to co-development with societal stakeholders.

The underlying definition of assistive technology refers to "Individuals with Disabilities Education Act" of the United States:

> Any item, piece of equipment, or product system, whether acquired commercially off the shelf, modified, or customized, that is used to increase, maintain, or improve functional capabilities of a child with a disability. (B) Exception. – The term does not include a medical device that is surgically implanted, or the replacement of such device.

- AT can be low-tech: communication boards made of cardboard or fuzzy felt.
- AT can be high-tech: special-purpose computers.
- AT can be hardware: prosthetics, mounting systems, and positioning devices.
- AT can be computer hardware: special switches, keyboards, and pointing devices.
- AT can be computer software: screen readers and communication programs.
- AT can be inclusive or specialized learning materials and curriculum aids.
- AT can be specialized curricular software.
- AT can be much more – electronic devices, wheelchairs, walkers, braces, educational software, power lifts, pencil holders, eye-gaze and head trackers, and much more.

> Assistive technology helps people who have difficulty speaking, typing, writing, remembering, pointing, seeing, hearing, learning, walking, and many other things. Different disabilities require different assistive technologies [7].

In the German discourse, the terms assistive and supporting technology as wells as the term medical aid are used. Assistive technology and medical aid comprise products "which are used by or for persons with disabilities to help them take part in everyday life, to protect body functions/-structures and activities, to support and to strengthen, to measure or to replace, or to prevent damages, reduction in activity and participation" [8]. In the international discourse a clearer concept is being used: it is a matter of information and communication technology (ICT).

The Maker movement aims at the idea of a manufactory utopia and wants to enable a broad mass of people to develop and produce (almost) everything by and for themselves. For this purpose, a selection of special key technologies is to be used. Our idea of a MakerSpace is that of an open workshop, in which, by using digital technology, a great variety of products can be manufactured on one's own. The tools and procedures, thus far only used in industry, have passed on to the public, especially to people with disabilities. In using software for three-dimensional construction, to only mention one, the focus is on widespread open-source solutions. Education, advice and further services are integrative elements. Learning-by-doing is an essential feature in which users learn with each other and from one another. Not only is a MakerSpace a laboratory and workshop, but is first and foremost a meeting point for technically inclined people of all ages. Here ideas can be presented, discussed and put into practice immediately. The MakerSpace is a starting-point for all those who are in dire need to know more about the new means of production. Thus, they are confronted with ideas they would perhaps have never conceived otherwise.

4   State of the Art

In the UN-CRPD, technical progress forms the foundation of a network for technological innovation. In this respect, the "development of concrete, suitable for everyday life, barrier-free and marketable products as well as services" (Johnston et al., 10f. als [9]) is at the centre of attention. In welfare legislation, individual supply for persons with disabilities with medically necessary health aid is strictly regulated. According to §33 Sozialgesetzbuch V (German Social Code V) and §31 Sozialgesetzbuch IX (German Social Code IX) insured persons are entitled to necessary health aid in each case. Health aid is then defined as objects, catalogued in a list of medical aids and thus under the control of a proven examination procedure. Basic commodities of everyday life are not included. Often medical necessity in the sense of national health insurance is not given or the demands on the medical aid are so individual that the production is too expensive for the producer.

3-D-printing offers the possibility to produce individualized health aids that are not financed by health insurances and – at the same time – link people with disabilities to internet-based "sharing communities" that share 3-D models of printable aids through sharing platforms and thereby support the establishment of international communities. Both aspects foster the empowerment of persons with disabilities.

In many situations of everyday life, persons with disabilities are dependent on supporting technologies and services. Even though these technologies can increasingly be acquired on the mass market (e.g. tablets) thanks to the application of "Universal Design", they still represent a niche market. On the other hand, we are confronted with a complex, highly-differentiated, but also very expensive, providing structure with specific health aids. Thus, persons with disabilities represent a special economic target group: many standardized products are not sufficiently compatible for their needs. That is why persons with disabilities are quite often not noticed as a target group. The products that persons with disabilities can manufacture themselves by SELFMADE, can neither be assigned to the mass market nor the health aid market. The project aims at a market ranging between self-made health aid of simple quality and a high-quality market of professional and expensive health aid. For this purpose, the project uses 3-D-printing as a technical procedure and processes and platforms of social innovation. The status of self-made (in the sense of "one's own") health aid is thus expanded to those making use of new procedures, digital templates and the "crowd" as support. In the future, SELF-MADE shall contribute to opening up a market in which persons with disabilities plan and produce products on their own, and beyond that, share the patterns with other people, and in doing so, cooperate with (e.g. medium-sized) providers on various issues (e.g. concerning consultation, service and delivery with consumables, etc.).

Eckhardt et al. [10] point out that the empowerment character of social innovation initiatives is particularly tangible in those social innovations directed towards people with activity limitations (e.g. persons with disabilities). Initiatives involving ICT as a strong pillar in their work named empowerment as the most important cross-cutting theme in their work. This link between social innovations using or addressing digital technology (coined as "digital social innovations", DSI), and the field of assistive technology for people with disabilities reflects the rising importance digital technology has in everyday life, as well as in all other sectors of participation distinguished by the ICF [cf. 10]: digital means can empower people with disabilities for participation, but at the same time they can create new barriers that function as cleavages for inclusion.

3-D-printing is linking the "world of the digital" with the "world of the physical", as stated with the claim "bits to atoms" of the first makerspace at the Massachusetts Institute of Technology (MIT). This link can play a crucial role in the life of people with disabilities: by printing objects in an individualised way, the production of bespoke objects becomes easier and cheaper. If we understand disability as the difference between individual features and a social and physical environment, the rise in bespoke objects can support the process of reducing barriers. As a second aspect, the project SELFMADE exploits the idea of making 3-D-printing available to and usable by all people and so useful for the production of assistive tools. In this strand of thinking, 3-D-printing is bringing the production of assistive technology to the hands of those people in need of it.

Persons with disabilities experience various barriers that prevent them from self-determined participation in social processes. Additional to structural barriers (e.g., accessibility), these include cognitive (e.g. easy language), emotional (e.g. repellent design of places), financial and technical barriers. In order to address these barriers in the research process, the theoretical framework, "capability approach" [4], seems to lead to an ability-driven approach. This approach focuses the choices necessary to initiate a process of social innovation through network building.

5 Methodology

The theoretical framework for the used methodology is the "capability approach" [4]. Regarding the methodology, product development is based on a iterative research and development cycle. In this cycle, three product lines are successively tested by persons with disabilities. During this process, experiences gained while developing each "product", are considered in the design of the derived product. Thus, in an early stage of the development, a "finished" product is already available which then increases in complexity across the product generations and a learning process in the participants (e.g. technical procedures, individual cultures, potentials and restrictions) takes place. As a result, the process of need identification (which can be addressed with photonic procedures) and the competence of the target group in the implementation phase, as well as the quality of the products, increase with each product generation.

Each of these "products" is identified on the basis of need analysis. In the need analysis, the project uses a User Centered Design approach, which is linked to a Design Thinking process. This allows for the identification, definition, creation and testing of the designed products in a co-creation process of people with disabilities for people with disabilities.

The Design Thinking process is composed of six steps (Fig. 1).

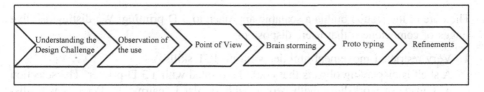

Fig. 1. Design thinking process [cf. 11]

During this process, the following data are generated and documented in the corresponding form:

a. Understanding: The first step focuses on the understanding of the problem, this leads to an appropriate question, which defines the needs and challenges of the project. Data sources: photo documentation and written collection, composed from workshops and Open Spaces.
b. Observation: In order to gain important insights and to define the status quo, an intensive search and field observation follows. Data sources: field notes and written collection, composed from workshops/Open Space.
c. Point-of-view: the individual needs are clearly defined in one question: Data source: documentation of the brainstorming question.
d. Brainstorming to develop and visualize different concepts. Data source: Different visualized concepts with the program Design Spark Mechanical.
e. Prototyping: In order to test and to demonstrate the ideas, first simple prototypes are developed and tested by the target group. Data source: Prototypes.

f. Refinement: On the basis of the insights gained from the prototype, the concept is further improved and refined until an optimal, user-centered product is developed. This iteration step can be applied on all previous steps.

In this cycle, three product lines are successively tested. During this process, experiences gained while developing each "product", are considered in the design of the derived product. The complexity increases across the product generations and a learning process takes place. As a result, the process of need identification, the competence of the target group in the implementation phase, as well as the quality of the products, increase with each product generation. Each of these prototypes is identified on the basis of a need analysis.

6 Prerequisite Results

Due to the fact that the project will run until the end of August 2018, it is only possible to present the results at its current, intermediate status. Corresponding with the aims of our research project, a brief overview of the results of the four key action areas are given below.

6.1 Empowerment for Peer Production

The core of the results builds a scalable approach to 3-D-printing. We distinguish five stages of competences that users dispose of:

1. Very restricted movement abilities with no ICT skills.
   A shelf is displaying objects that could be printed with a 3-D-printer. The selection was made in workshops with people with similar impairments. Persons with disabilities express which object they like to receive and assistants initiate the printing process.
2. Basic movement abilities with no ICT skills
   A SIM card is attached to each object that can be inserted into a 3-D-printer. We designed the 3-D printer in a way that enables most users to initiate the printing process.
3. Basic ICT skills
   Users with basic ICT skills can click on pre-selected models for printing.
4. Advanced ICT skills
   For advanced users, we offer CAD software that enables the alteration of existing models or to design from sketch.
5. Advanced ICT skills, with basic communication skills
   Users become tutors in 3-D-printing in peer education processes.

6.2 Products

The design thinking process leads to products which facilitate a higher participation in daily life, work life, leisure time and communication.

An example for a product development for daily live is the development for a cup holder that shall lead to more independence and self-determination. The employers of a sheltered-workshops described the challenge to get independently hot drinks like coffee and tea from a vending machine. The employees of a sheltered-workshop described the challenge to get independently hot drinks like coffee and tea from a vending machine. The customers have a high risk to get burned due to the instability of the cups. The six steps of the design thinking process led finally to a solid cup holder (which looks like a cup itself) with handholds that are individually adaptable for the customers (Fig. 2).

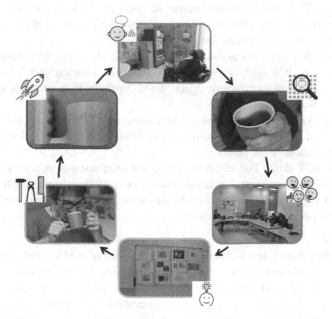

Fig. 2. Own design based on Design thinking process [cf. 11]

This example shows that the modularity allows individual customer-specific adaptions as well as situation specific adaptions.

So far we produced can openers, can holders, adaptions for the electric wheelchair control, a prosthetic arm for guitar playing, communication symbols, snapping grids for tablets, adaptions for game controller, SIM-card holder, mobile-phone holder for wheelchairs, etc.

6.3   Social Innovation

The applied approach to empower persons with disabilities as experts in creating their own AT can be observed from a social innovation theory perspective, focusing on how new social practices are applied and the impact on societal challenges. With the available data from the SELFMADE observations, we can state that applying Design Thinking in a Capability Approach setting is a viable way for empowering people with disabilities to use 3-D printing to create AT for their own needs. Within the SELF-MADE co-construction processes, we collected data on the ways people with different disabilities are using this technology and which barriers they experience. As a result, we defined a scalable process as an interface between requirements defined by a technology (3-D printing) and the capabilities of its users (persons with movement disorders and complex communication needs We distinguish five stages of competences that users dispose of:

1. Communication via assistants or assistive technology with almost no movement abilities or ICT skills: A shelf is displaying objects that could be printed with a 3D-printer. The selection was made in workshops with people with similar impairments. Persons with disabilities express which object they would like to receive and assistants initiate the printing process.
2. Communication only via assistants or assistive technology with basic movement abilities and no ICT skills: A SIM card is attached to each object. This card can be inserted in a 3D-printer. We designed the 3D printer in a way that enables most users to initiate the printing process.
3. Basic ICT skills: The maker space offers computers with pre-set bookmarks on a curated list of 3D-models for assistive tools. Users with basic ICT skills can click on pre-selected models for printing.
4. Advanced ICT skills: For advanced users, we offer computers with CAD software that enable the alteration of existing models or to design from sketch.
5. Advanced ICT skills with basic communication skills: Users become tutors in 3D printing in peer education processes.

This approach could be understood as a social innovation itself – a new social practice – rather than a new technology. This perspective enables and demands further research on the solutions, as we cannot discuss the impact this approach is having on the very use of the produced AT. Another finding inspired by the social innovation perspective on 3-D printing is the approach to embed the MakerSpace in a Quadruple Helix setting, involving stakeholders from policy, industry, civil society and academia in all development stages of this innovation. Here our data is scarce due to the early time of the project development; further research will investigate how this involvement played out and which barriers and supporting factors it reveals.

6.4 Accessibility

In a first step, general principles of accessibility for the design of MakerSpaces are presented, to sensitize the Maker scene to this issue. These general principles are complemented by applicable standards, guidelines to be followed, and supporting funding.

In a next step, the developed checklist will be tested in the FabLab of the University of Applied Sciences Ruhr West. This step includes the identification of barriers and dismantling them. As a result, the developed checklist is tested and the FabLab becomes more accessible.

7 Conclusion

Maker Technologies, thus far only marginally used for and by persons with disabilities hold an enormous potential. Whereas the technologies in question as used in an open and highly networked Maker-Community have been sufficiently developed to produce tools in an individualized form and thus promote social participation, as well as self-determination in everyday life, experience in the field of co-operation is lacking. There aren't any specific target groups in MakerSpaces or an appropriate interdisciplinary branch of research either [12]. SELFMADE provides pioneering work in all three aspects. The SELFMADE project demonstrates the requirements for accessibility to MakerSpaces for persons with disabilities and a scalable approach that leads to prototypes. It demonstrates by example, through their work with persons with complex needs, how to open up 3-D-printing and peer production to everybody.

This approach is particularly attractive for the globally networked MakerSpaces because it has the potential to reach new target groups by making it as accessible as possible.

References

1. Carayannis, E.G., Campbell, D.F.J.: Mode 3 Knowledge Production in Quadruple Helix Innovation Systems. 21st-Century Democracy, Innovation, and Entrepreneurship for Development. Springer Briefs in Business, vol. 7, p. 1. Springer, New York (2012). https://doi.org/10.1007/978-1-4614-2062-0_1
2. Convention on the Rights of Persons with Disabilities: Bundesgesetzblatt Jahrgang 2008 Teil II Nr. 35, ausgegeben zu Bonn am 31. Dezember 2008
3. Thiele, A.: Assistive Technologien für Menschen mit einer körperlich-motorischen Beeinträchtigung. Interdisziplinäre Handlungsfelder und Eckpfeiler einer Qualifikation von Pädagog/innen mit einem sonderpädagogischen Profil. Vierteljahresschr. Heilpädagogik Nachbargeb. **85**(4), 307–322 (2016)
4. Nussbaum, M.: Frontiers of Justice: Disability, Nationality, Species Membership. Harvard University Press, Cambridge (2006)
5. Howaldt, J., Schwarz, M.: Social Innovation. Concepts, Research Fields and International Trends. In: Henning, K., Hees, F. (eds.) IfU. Studies for Innovation in a Modern Working Environment, 1st edn., vol. 5. IMA/ZLW, Aachen (2010). International Monitoring
6. Kaletka, C., Markmann, M., Pelka, B.: Peeling the Onion. An Exploration of the Layers of Social Innovation Ecosystems. Modelling a context sensitive perspective on driving and hindering factors for social innovation. European Public and Social Innovation Review, pp. 83–93, January 2017. http://pub.sinnergiak.org/index.php/esir/article/view/42
7. Individuals with Disabilities Education Act – IDEA, Part A, Sec. 602 (2004)
8. Bühler, C., Haage, A.: Barrierefreiheit. In: Bosse, I., Schluchter, J.-R., Zorn, I.: (Hgs.) Handbuch Medienbildung und Inklusion. Kohlhammer, Stuttgart (2018)
9. Johnston, L., Beard, L., Carpeter, L.: Assistive Technology, Access for All Students. Pearson Education Inc., Upper saddle River (2007)

10. Eckhardt, J., Kaletka, C., Pelka, B.: Inclusion through digital social innovations: modelling an ecosystem of drivers and barriers. In: Antona, M., Stephanidis, C. (eds.) UAHCI 2017, Part I. LNCS, vol. 10277, pp. 67–84. Springer, Cham (2017). https://doi.org/10.1007/978-3-319-58706-6_6

11. Schallmo, D.R.A.: Design Thinking Erfolgreich Anwenden. Springer Gabler, Wiesbaden (2017)

12. BMBF –Bundesminsterium für Bildung und Forschung: Bekanntmachung von Richtlinien über die Fördermaßnahme "Wettbewerb Light Cares – Photonische Technologien für Menschen mit Behinderungen" im Rahmen des Förderprogramms "Photonik Forschung Deutschland". Bundesanzeiger vom 12.01.2016 (2016). https://www.bmbf.de/foerderungen/bekanntmachung-1130.html

Applying an Implicit Recommender System in the Preparation of Visits to Cultural Heritage Places

Pedro J. S. Cardoso[1,3]([⊠]) [iD], Pedro Guerreiro[3][iD], Jânio Monteiro[2,3][iD], and João M. F. Rodrigues[1,3][iD]

[1] LARSyS, University of the Algarve, Faro, Portugal
{pcardoso,jrodrig}@ualg.pt
[2] INESC-ID, Lisboa, Portugal
jmmontei@ualg.pt
[3] ISE, University of the Algarve, Faro, Portugal
pmguerre@ualg.pt

Abstract. The visit to cultural places can be an enormous pleasure, where visitors are driven to see and explore historical or contemporary objects. The same journey can also be fastidious when the visitor is taken to lengthy walks, unwanted collections or the objects archive is too large. For many of us, a visit should be something limited in time, showing a variety of things of our own interest. Information systems and in particular mobile devices can play a fundamental role to get us close to that objective by collecting information used to feed recommender systems.

This paper studies the use of an implicit recommender system to propose which points of interest should be explored in cultural heritage places. In its present form, the recommender system, to be supported on data acquired by a mobile application, suggests artworks or artists supported on the user's history. Experimental results are presented, showing the effectiveness of the method.

Keywords: Implicit recommender system · Mobile application
Cultural heritage

1 Introduction

A pleasant journey on cultural heritage places can be influenced by many things. The visited objects and the route taken are two of those factors that impact the users' experience. In this sense, a visit is many times divided in three stages (Falk 2009; Falk and Dierking 2016): the before, the during and the after. The before starts when the user prepares its visit using available information, such as books, dedicated sites, or dedicated mobile applications. Interests are select and registered in order to properly take advantage of the visit. In this phase, the use of novel technology can introduce new challenges, such as, large collections are burdensome to browse, encompassing the peril of overwhelming the users with

© Springer International Publishing AG, part of Springer Nature 2018
M. Antona and C. Stephanidis (Eds.): UAHCI 2018, LNCS 10908, pp. 421–436, 2018.
https://doi.org/10.1007/978-3-319-92052-8_33

information. This overwhelming peril is also a part of the visit itself (during phase) as, on many cases, the collection are too vast to be properly explored during short visits. The after phase is used to get across any doubts raised during the tour, to further investigate the previously seen objects, or simply recall what was seen. As a consequence, the preparation of the visit is a fundamental step to an overall pleasant experience.

A solution to avoid the possibly time consuming task of using the previously stated sources (e.g., books and web sites) is to plan the visit using a recommender system. A recommender system is an information filter system which job is to forecast the user's preferences based on the its historical actions, options, and characterization, and also on the same aspects of other users with similar profiles (Aggarwal 2016; Hu et al. 2008; Jannach et al. 2010; Koren et al. 2009; Rao and Rao 2016; Ricci et al. 2015). In other words, the personalization of cultural heritage information requires a system that is able to model the users (e.g., interests, knowledge, age, context, genre), be aware of contextual aspects, select the most appropriate content, and deliver it in a suitable way (Cardoso et al. 2017). A system like this should also be able to respond to other potentially worth of attention aspects, such as accessibility enhancing and info-exclusion fighting. For instance, the inclusion of features that reflect the visitor's impairments along with its preferences would allow to do a recommendation according with their aspirations.

Depending on the available information and objectives, recommender systems are divided in several classes, e.g.: (a) content based recommenders use (a large number of) features associated to the items/objects, characterizing them, and then the system computes the probability of a user liking a certain item supported on the user's history and items characterizations; and (b) collaborative filtering recommenders where only items and users relations are used to make the predictions, not requiring any information about users or items. The second case uses some kind of rating which associates items and users, being in general divided as explicit or implicit collaborative filtering (Aggarwal 2016; Jannach et al. 2010; Ricci et al. 2015). The explicit case is characterized by the fact that the users provide classifications to the items (e.g., "like", score) which are then used to find users with similar tastes and make the suggestions. In the implicit case, the users do not classify the items, but the information system knows that the user interacted with the item (e.g., bought an item, clicked on a page, saw an artwork), allowing the recommender system to predict which item would be of the users preferences.

This paper introduces the use of an implicit recommender system to propose points of interest to be explored in cultural heritage places. The overall system uses data acquired by a mobile application to feed the recommender system in a non-intrusive way, i.e., suggestions of artworks or artists are supported on the mobile application usage. The recommendation method (adapted from the work of Hu et al. (2008)) uses a preference matrix decomposition in user factors and item factors matrices. The system has a running complexity which grows linearly with the size of the dataset. Some results are presented, supported on a built dataset, showing the effectiveness of the system. The main contribution to the state of the art is the application of the referred kind of recommendation methods in an architecture supported in a mobile system, dynamically applied to the visit of cultural heritage places.

The remaining document is structured as follows. Section 2 presents some preliminaries on Machine Learning with particular interest on recommender systems to cultural heritage places. Section 3 describes the data collecting methodology associated to the mobile application and the adopted recommending system. The last sections presents results from the conducted tests, conclusions and future works.

2   Preliminaries and Problem Formulation

2.1   Recommendation System

Although many times unnoticeable, most of us use recommendation systems on a daily basis. Information Technology (IT) systems use them to expose intelligence, making search engines, social media, e-stores, digital music services, etc. what we expected them to be. In short, recommender system algorithms are a class of information filtering system which have the job to predict the users' preferences, according with given or guessed profiles. Companies like Google, Facebook, Walmart, Amazon, etc., instead of methodically encoding the preferences of all its consumers, apply learning algorithms on their huge datasets and let them prophesy what customers want (Domingos 2015). As a consequence of this global evolution, many party agree that briefly most of the knowledge will be obtained and reside in computers, i.e., as stated by Alpaydin (2016), "data starts to drive the operation; it is not the programmers anymore but the data itself that defines what to do next". Other consequences are the entire industry building itself around these fields, along with emerging research and academic disciplines.

Recommender systems are part of the Machine Learning (ML) research field. ML algorithms, supported in mathematical and computer science techniques, can be seen as engines that use large datasets to find patterns and correlations in order to build models, which will then be applied to new data in order to predict outcomes for it. In this sense, ML algorithms allow to save resources by automatically analyzing data, obtaining an expectable better overview of the available information and making more reasoned decisions. The algorithms are usually divided in some major classes, which include: supervised learning, unsupervised learning, semi-supervised learning, or reinforcement learning (Arulkumaran et al. 2017; Müller and Guido 2016). Supervised learning has the task of inferring models/functions from labeled data. i.e., data that has an input vector and desirable output value. Unsupervised learning is used to draw inferences from datasets of non labeled data. The goal of semi-supervised learning is to employ a large collection of unlabeled data jointly with a few labeled examples to implement a generalization. Finally, reinforcement learning supports agents decisions based on the notion of cumulative rewards.

In general, the ML workflow is divided in four large steps: (a) get (*enough*) data – collect data related to the problem; (b) clean, prepare, and manipulate data – converting the data into a form that computers can operate on (e.g., convert things to numerical data and categorize data); (c) define and train the selected model using test and validation data – depending on the type of problem being solved (e.g., regression, classification, clustering, or recommendations) build a mathematical model of the data; and (d) predict outcomes over new and unseen data – apply the trained model to unseen data to, depending on the problem at hand, predict values, classify or associate the data, recommend other objects/items, etc.

Recommender systems, of particular interest in this work, suffered from a sudden popularity after the Netflix Prize contest (Lohr 2009; Gomez-Uribe and Hunt 2015; Ricci et al. 2015), and are being divided in several categories (Jannach et al. 2010; Rao and Rao 2016), such as: (a) content based or (b) collaborative filtering. In the first case, features are associated to the items characterizing them. E.g., in the Pandora.com recommender system, songs were manually annotated by musicians with up to several hundred features such as instrumentation, influences, or instruments. Afterwards, the question is treated as a binary classification problem, where the probability of a user to like a certain song depends on its listening history and the songs previous characterizations. Items with greater probability of being liked are then suggested to the user. On the other hand, (b) collaborative filtering is supported only in the items and users relations, not requiring any information about the users or the items (Koren et al. 2009; Hu et al. 2008). In this case, some kind of rating is associated to the interaction between the items and the users, being in general divided as explicit or implicit. In the explicit case, users provide (or can be inferred) a classification to the items (e.g., a like indication, a score, or the number of times the item is "used" acts as a sign of affinity), and these values are used to suggest (or not) similar items to similar users. In the implicit case, the user does not classify the items, but somehow it is known the user's interactions with them. Cases of interaction are for instance buying the item or simply navigating to the item's web page. In this last case, navigating to the page represents a sign of preference but the opposite, not accessing the page, should not be seen as a dislike since many other factor can be the motive (e.g., lack of time, unaware of its existence).

2.2 Applications of Recommender Systems to Cultural Heritage Places

The user's preferences are being studied for some time in the preparation and visit of cultural heritage places. For instance, a routing system implementing a mobile museum tour guide, providing personalized tours tailored to the user's interests and position inside the museum, is offered by the Rijksmuseum Amsterdam (van Hage et al. 2010). The system includes tools for the interactive discovery of user's interests, semantic recommendations of artworks and art-related topics, and the (semi-)automatic generation of personalized museum tours. Benouaret and Lenne (2015), supported on the users' preferences and

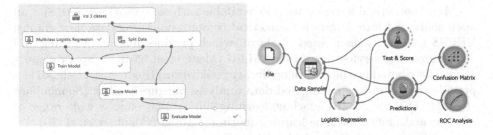

Fig. 1. ML GUI tools: Azure ML Studio (left) and Orange ML (right).

contexts, proposed a recommender system for mobile devices to build tours according to their preferences and constraints. Gavalas et al. (2014) presented a state-of-the-art in the field, proposing a classification of mobile tourism recommender systems and providing insights on their offered services. The CHESS (2017) project researches, implements and evaluates both the experiencing of personalized interactive stories for visitors of cultural sites and their authoring by the cultural content experts. Cardoso et al. (2017) proposed the combination association rules with the location of the user to design some modes to proceed with the visit, such as dynamic mode (the visit is constantly updated supported on the visitors actions), over-a-path mode (recommender can only suggest objects in a predetermined walk), free mode (recommender can suggest objects in any place of the museum), nearby mode (recommender uses rules to suggest objects which are near the present location), static mode (prepared visited) or the Surprise-Me mode (the visit is disclosed as the user walks through the museum). The Route Perfect (2017) application allows to easily plan a trip based on the traveler's preferences, budget and personal style. Several other works can be found in literature such as (Garcia et al. 2011; Verbert et al. 2012; Wang and Xiang 2012).

2.3 ML Tools

Nowadays, a ML user/programmer does not have to implement a large number of ML methods as they are included in several visual and programmable frameworks. For instance, Microsoft released the Azure ML Studio, defined as a powerfully simple browser-based, visual drag-and-drop authoring environment where no coding is necessary (Microsoft 2017). The studio includes hundreds of built-in packages and support for custom code, namely in R and Python. Furthermore, the Azure ML Studio can be used to deploy the created models into production as web service, callable from any device with any data source. The Orange is an open-source data visualization, machine learning and data mining toolkit (Orange 2017). With a visual programming front-end Orange allows exploratory data analysis and interactive data visualization, and can also be used as a Python library. Figure 1 shows an example for each of the applications. Other graphical user interfaces (GUI) ML tools exist such as WEKA (2017), MLJAR (2017) or Knime (2017).

Many non visual libraries are also available such as TensorFlow (2018) – an open source software library for numerical computation using data flow graphs; VELES (2018) – a distributed platform, which provides machine learning and data processing services for a user; MLlib (Meng et al. 2016) – Spark's open-source distributed machine learning library; scikit-learn (Pedregosa et al. 2011) – provides tools for data mining and data analysis; Shogun-Toolbox (Sonnenburg et al. 2017) – open-source machine learning library that offers a wide range of efficient and unified machine learning methods; Torch (Collobert et al. 2011) – a scientific computing framework with wide support for machine learning algorithms using Graphics Processing Units (GPUs); or the MLPACK (Curtin et al. 2013) – a scalable machine learning library, written in C++, that aims to provide fast, extensible implementations of machine learning algorithms.

3 Implementation of the Recommender System

3.1 Data Collecting Process and Dataset

This work is part of the M5SAR (Mobile Five Senses Augmented Reality System for Museums) project. The M5SAR project aims at the development of an augmented reality system, which consists of a mobile application and a "gadget", to be incorporated in the mobile devices, in order to explore the 5 human senses (Rodrigues et al. 2017; Sardo et al. 2018). The system will constitute a guide in cultural, historical and museum events, complementing or replacing the traditional orientations given by tour guides, directional signs, or maps. Figure 2 shows some screens of the interface being developed: the initial screen (top-left) presents the list of available museums. After selecting the wanted museum, the user is taken to the museum's initial page (top-center) from where we can navigate to other pages such as maps (top-right), information about pieces (bottom-left and bottom center) or to the augmented reality page (bottom-right). The design and implementation of the application, besides the recommender system, is out of this paper's scope, but more details can be found in (Rodrigues et al. 2017).

In our case, the navigation through the mobile application pages can be seen as of interest by the object/item that can be collected to empower the recommender system. Given the stored and collected data, the recommender system can be implemented using a content based approach (as the majority of the object are characterized) or a collaborative filtering approach (as the interaction between the users and the items can be stored). In the later case, both implicit and explicit approaches are also available. The implicit approach is probably more suitable as it can be powered by simply storing the interactions with the items (e.g., information about pieces seen in the mobile app or the activation of the augmented reality over an item). Nevertheless, the explicit approach can be thought/implemented using for instance the time spent by the user in the augmented reality features associated to items/object or the time it takes to read an information page in the mobile app, i.e., a long time scrolling through the page probably means he is interested in the item, so it should be classified high, while a short time probably mean that the item is not of its interests.

Fig. 2. Top to bottom, left to right: list of available museums, specific museum information, museum map with a route calculated, example of a card piece, image recognition (AR), and information about the detected piece.

The M5SAR's recommender system collected data is stored in a relational database, with a partial sketch presented in the Enhanced Entity–Relationship (EER) model shown in Fig. 3. Some characteristics of the stored date include: basic user information is stored in the app (user) table; An artwork can be seen by many apps; An app can see many artworks; An artwork can have many artists authoring it, as they can author many artworks. The proposed structure allow for proper SQL queries to the database to return the pieces and artists seen by the users (apps).

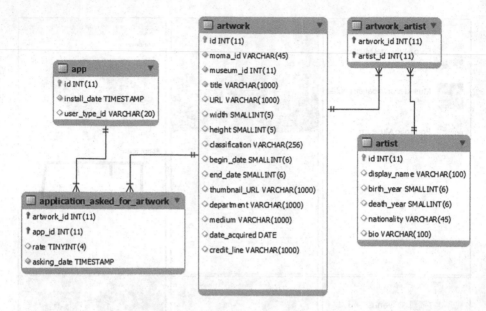

Fig. 3. EER model for the recommender system database.

Since the data collected so far is not large enough to properly train the recommender system, we decided to populate the database using the Museum of Modern Art dataset (MoMA) (Robot 2016) and the retail market basket dataset provided in (Brijs et al. 1999). Each row of the retail market basket dataset was considered as a user and an one-to-one correspondence was made between the items in the basket and the artworks. On the other hand, the MoMA's data was used to populate the artworks and artists tables. A total of 89952 distinct baskets/apps/users were considered, corresponding to the interaction with 16470 distinct artworks and 16147 artists.

3.2 Estimating Preferences

The implemented recommender system adapts the work by Hu et al. (2008). In general, let us assume that $u, v, \ldots$ represent users, $i, j, \ldots$ are items, r_{ui} represents the input data associating user u to item i, m is the number of users, and n is the number of items. For example, in our case, r_{ui} represents the number of times user u saw artwork i or (in alternative) the number of times the same user u saw artworks from artist i. As already mentioned, other rating could also be thought of, as for instance the time the user took opened an artwork object page in the mobile application (e.g., Fig. 2 bottom-left) or the percentage of the artwork's/artist's page scrolled. If there is no action between user u and item i then r_{ui} will be set to 0, with a "cloudy" meaning (e.g., the user does not like the item, might be unaware of the existence of the item, or unable to see it due to some reason). On the other hand, the fact that a user interacts with some item does not necessarily mean the user likes it, for instance, the interaction could be unintentional or someone else might be using the user's mobile device.

Returning to the formulation of the model, $R = [r_{ui}]$ can be seen as a matrix, where each row represents the preferences of a user and each column the preferences/interactions over an item. Most likely, R is a sparse matrix as most users did not interact with the majority of the items.

The proposed model, induced by singular value decomposition of the user/item matrix, associates to each user u a user-factor vector x_u and to each item i a item-factor vector y_i, both belonging to $\mathbb{R}^{nf}$ where nf is the number of latent factors. The inner product between x_u and y_i, $\hat{r}_{ui} = x_u^T y_i$, predicts the user u preferences associated to item i. In this sense, two (dense) matrices can be though: matrix $U = [x_u] \in \mathbb{R}^{m \times nf}$ where each row is a vector associated to a users and $V = [y_i]^T \in \mathbb{R}^{nf \times n}$ where each column is a vector associated to an item. Multiplying the two feature matrices should approximate the original matrix, i.e., $R \approx U \times V$. The goal is to find, for each user and each item, vectors x_u and y_i, i.e., find the matrices U and V that best approximate $R \approx U \times V$.

To compute U and V, Hu et al. (2008) defined the minimization problem

$$\min_{x_*, y_*} \sum_{u,i} c_{ui} \left(p_{ui} - x_u^T y_i \right)^2 + \lambda \left(\sum_u \|x_u\|^2 + \sum_i \|y_i\|^2 \right), \quad (1)$$

where p_{ui} is equal to 1 if $r_{ui} > 0$ and 0 otherwise, $c_{ui} = 1 + \alpha r_{ui}$, and α, λ are algorithm parameters. Variable p_{ui} indicates user's u estimated preference relative to item i, where the term "estimated" translates the "cloudy" meaning of the r_{ui} values. In this sense, c_{ui} was introduce as a measure of confidence relative to the observation of the relation between u and i. Equation (1) last part, $\lambda \left(\sum_u \|x_u\|^2 + \sum_i \|y_i\|^2 \right)$, regularizes the model, avoiding its over-fitting.

The minimization problem is affected by the fact that the number of users (m) and items (n) are in general large, easily reaching millions of non-linear parcels to be taken into account, and probably making more traditional optimization techniques suffer from low performance. To tackle this situation, Hu et al. (2008) observed that if either the user-factors or item-factors were constant, the objective function becomes quadratic and therefore "swiftly" globally optimizable. Therefore, the author proposed an alternating least squares optimization process (Zhou et al. 2008), where the iterations take turns between computing user-factors and item-factors, guarantying the lowering of the cost function in each step. Important is the fact that the process can be run in parallel, solving one feature vector at a time. Further details can be found in the original work from Hu et al. (2008), namely the running computational complexity which is is linear with the size of the input.

4   Tests and Validation

Traditional machine learning algorithms test and validate the trained models using a set of data previously unseen to them. Many times, this is done by randomly splitting the initial dataset into a training set and a test/validation set. In the collaborative filtering case this is not possible, since each user must be present in the final user-factor matrix in order to make preferences predictions. A solution is to mask a percentage of the user/item entries from the model during the training phase and then, during the testing phase, verify which items initially masked were suggest. Other testing and validation solutions might be thought on other scenarios, such as dividing the observations in training and validation by periods of time, if the users and item space does not change. We adopted the first solution, mask some user/item entries, by setting $r_{ui} = 0$ with probability p_{mask} where $r_{ui} > 0$. The result was a masked observation matrix R', i.e., $R' = [r'_{ui}]$ where

$$r'_{ui} = \begin{cases} 0 & \text{if } r_{ui} = 0 \text{ or } rand() < p_{mask} \\ r_{ui} & \text{otherwise} \end{cases},$$

and $rand() \in [0, 1]$ is a randomly generated value. The optimization process described in Sect. 3.2 was then applied to R' in order to compute the users (U') and items (V') factors matrices. Given that the product of line u of U' with column i of V' should return an approximation to r'_{ui}, the computation of k recommendations for user corresponding to line u, is done by multiplying line u of U' by V' and returning the indexes of the k largest values in the resulting vector.

Table 1 presents an example of a recommendation given by the method for a certain user. The table contains 3 columns: *Observed* – presenting the "real" observation associated with the user; *Masked* – the observations used to train the model, i.e., after randomly masking/hiding observations; and *Recommended* – the list of suggestions returned by the algorithm. In the example, 3 artists were hidden in the mask phase (Bernard Tschumi, Giovanni Guerrini, and Mario Romano). From those hidden artists, two were recommended by the method (Giovanni Guerrini and Mario Romano) and one belonging to the original data (Bernard Tschumi) was not recommended. In this case 10 suggestions were taken from the method and therefore there are 8 other artists which were not in the original data (*Observed*).

A systematic set of tests was made by varying parameters according with the values in Table 2. Furthermore, the tests were supported on 100.000 observations from 17827 users/apps, corresponding to 994 artworks and 263 artists. The sparsity of the observation matrices R (i.e., the observation matrix before applying the mask) was of 99.5% for the user vs. artwork and 98.3% for the user vs. artist.

Considering the probability of masking observations equal to 10% ($p_{mask} = 0.1$), Table 3 shows the 10 best recommender results, ordered by the mean (μ_{sug}) (standard deviation, σ, in parentheses) of correctly suggested artworks ratio, between the masked ones, when fixing the number of items to recommend to $n_p = 10$ (Table 3(a)) and $n_p = 30$ (Table 3(b)). Suggesting 10 artworks, the method correctly suggests approximately 40% of the masked ones, rising to approximately 50% when 30 artworks were suggested. About the parameters,

Table 1. Example of recommendations made to an user: column *Observed* lists the artist seen by the app ("user"), column *Masked* shows the set of artists after applying the mask (training phase), and column *Recommended* the artists that are suggested by the recommender system.

Observed	Masked	Recommended
Bernard Tschumi	–	–
Otto Schönthal	Otto Schönthal	–
Alessandro Mendini	Alessandro Mendini	–
Ernesto Bruno La Padula	Ernesto Bruno La Padula	–
Giovanni Guerrini	–	Giovanni Guerrini
Mario Romano	–	Mario Romano
Richard Meier	Richard Meier	–
–	–	Fumihiko Maki
–	–	Frank O. Gehry
–	–	Robert A. M. Stern
–	–	Alison Sky
–	–	Michelle Stone
–	–	Toyo Ito
–	–	Massimo Vignelli
–	–	David Jacob

Table 2. Parameter variation

Parameter	Observation
$\alpha \in \{10^3, 25000, 50000, 10^5\}$	Equation (1)
$\lambda \in \{0.01, 0.1\}$	Model regularization, Eq. (1)
$nf \in \{100, 200, 400\}$	Number of latent factors, Sect. 3.2
$N_{it} \in \{50, 200\}$	Number of iterations (alternating least squares), Sect. 3.2
$N_p \in \{10, 30\}$	Number of preferences returned
$p_{mask} \in \{0.1, 0.25\}$	Probability of masking an element

although not completely conclusive from the presented results, a good set of values seems to be $\alpha = 25000$, $nf = 400$, and $N_{it} \in \{50, 200\}$. When the probability of masking is increased to 25% ($p_{mask} = 0.25$) the percentages of correctly suggested artwork decreases around 2% (Table 4). About the parameter values, $\alpha = 25000$, $nf = 400$, and $N_{it} = 50$ also seem a good set, from the ones tested.

Similar tests were made considering artist instead of artworks. Tables 5 and 6 summarizes the 10 best solutions (ordered by the mean of correctly suggested ratio) considering $p_{mask} = 0.1$ and $p_{mask} = 0.25$, respectively. In this case, the mean of the correct suggested ratio was slightly higher with values around

Table 3. Ordered by mean value of correctly suggested artworks, the best 10 recommender results considering $p_{mask} = 0.1$.

(a) $n_p = 10$

α	nf	N_{it}	λ	$\mu_{sug}(\sigma)$
25000	200	50	0.10	0.397 (0.5)
25000	400	50	0.01	0.397 (0.5)
1000	100	50	0.01	0.396 (0.5)
25000	400	50	0.10	0.396 (0.5)
25000	200	200	0.01	0.394 (0.5)
25000	400	200	0.01	0.391 (0.5)
25000	200	50	0.01	0.391 (0.5)
25000	200	200	0.10	0.390 (0.5)
25000	400	200	0.10	0.389 (0.5)
50000	400	200	0.01	0.389 (0.5)

(b) $n_p = 30$

α	nf	N_{it}	λ	$\mu_{sug}(\sigma)$
25000	400	50	0.10	0.479 (0.5)
25000	400	50	0.01	0.478 (0.5)
25000	200	50	0.01	0.478 (0.5)
25000	200	50	0.10	0.477 (0.5)
50000	400	200	0.10	0.471 (0.5)
100000	400	200	0.01	0.470 (0.5)
50000	400	200	0.01	0.470 (0.5)
25000	400	200	0.01	0.470 (0.5)
25000	400	200	0.10	0.470 (0.5)
50000	200	200	0.10	0.469 (0.5)

Table 4. Ordered by mean value of correctly suggested artworks, the best 10 recommender results considering $p_{mask} = 0.25$.

(a) $n_p = 10$

α	nf	N_{it}	λ	$\mu_{sug}(\sigma)$
25000	400	50	0.10	0.375 (0.4)
25000	400	50	0.01	0.373 (0.4)
25000	200	50	0.10	0.372 (0.4)
25000	200	50	0.01	0.371 (0.4)
25000	200	200	0.01	0.370 (0.4)
25000	200	200	0.10	0.366 (0.4)
50000	400	50	0.01	0.364 (0.4)
25000	400	200	0.10	0.364 (0.4)
50000	400	50	0.10	0.363 (0.4)
25000	100	50	0.10	0.362 (0.4)

(b) $n_p = 30$

α	nf	N_{it}	λ	$\mu_{sug}(\sigma)$
25000	400	50	0.01	0.454 (0.4)
25000	200	50	0.10	0.45 (0.4)
25000	400	50	0.10	0.45 (0.4)
25000	200	50	0.01	0.446 (0.4)
25000	100	50	0.01	0.444 (0.4)
50000	400	50	0.10	0.440 (0.4)
25000	100	50	0.10	0.440 (0.4)
50000	400	50	0.01	0.437 (0.4)
50000	200	200	0.01	0.433 (0.4)
50000	200	50	0.10	0.433 (0.4)

65% and 80% when approximately 10% of the observations were masked and the number of suggested artists were $n_p = 10$ and $n_p = 30$, respectively. When the probability of masking observation rises to 25%, as expected, as lower information is given, the referred mean value decreases to 58% when $n_p = 10$ and 74% when $n_p = 30$. About the parameters, considering the tested ones, again $\alpha = 25000$ and $nf = 400$ seem good choices. About the number of iteration, $N_{it} = 200$ seems a reasonable choice as it ensures some of the best solution in all the cases.

We should observe that, the higher percentage of correctly suggested items associated with the artist (compared to artworks) seems to be related with the reduction of items space (994 artworks vs. 263 artists). Another question is the standard deviation value which is high. In this case, we should observe that

Table 5. Ordered by mean value of correctly suggested artists, the best 10 recommender results considering $p_{mask} = 0.1$.

(a) $n_p = 10$

α	nf	N_{it}	λ	$\mu_{sug}(\sigma)$
25000	400	200	0.10	0.643 (0.4)
25000	200	200	0.01	0.634 (0.5)
25000	400	200	0.01	0.632 (0.5)
25000	200	200	0.10	0.632 (0.5)
50000	400	200	0.01	0.624 (0.5)
50000	400	200	0.10	0.623 (0.5)
50000	200	200	0.10	0.618 (0.5)
25000	100	200	0.01	0.616 (0.5)
25000	100	200	0.10	0.614 (0.5)
50000	200	200	0.01	0.608 (0.5)

(b) $n_p = 30$

α	nf	N_{it}	λ	$\mu_{sug}(\sigma)$
25000	100	50	0.01	0.803 (0.4)
25000	200	50	0.10	0.798 (0.4)
25000	400	50	0.10	0.797 (0.4)
25000	400	50	0.01	0.797 (0.4)
25000	200	50	0.01	0.796 (0.4)
25000	100	50	0.10	0.795 (0.4)
50000	400	200	0.01	0.788 (0.4)
50000	400	50	0.10	0.784 (0.4)
100000	200	200	0.01	0.784 (0.4)
50000	400	200	0.10	0.784 (0.4)

Table 6. Ordered by mean value of correctly suggested artists, the best 10 recommender results considering $p_{mask} = 0.25$.

(a) $n_p = 10$

α	nf	N_{it}	λ	$\mu_{sug}(\sigma)$
25000	400	200	0.01	0.575 (0.4)
25000	400	200	0.10	0.569 (0.4)
50000	400	200	0.01	0.563 (0.4)
25000	200	200	0.10	0.554 (0.4)
25000	200	200	0.01	0.553 (0.4)
50000	400	200	0.10	0.548 (0.4)
50000	100	200	0.01	0.535 (0.4)
25000	400	50	0.01	0.533 (0.4)
100000	400	200	0.01	0.533 (0.4)
25000	100	200	0.01	0.531 (0.4)

(b) $n_p = 30$

α	nf	N_{it}	λ	$\mu_{sug}(\sigma)$
25000	400	50	0.01	0.737 (0.4)
25000	100	50	0.01	0.736 (0.4)
25000	400	50	0.10	0.732 (0.4)
25000	200	50	0.01	0.723 (0.4)
25000	100	50	0.10	0.723 (0.4)
50000	400	50	0.01	0.719 (0.4)
25000	200	50	0.10	0.715 (0.4)
50000	400	200	0.01	0.711 (0.4)
50000	100	50	0.01	0.707 (0.4)
50000	100	200	0.01	0.703 (0.4)

each user has associated a relatively low number of observations, which results in a great difference in the ratio of correctly suggested items value, e.g., if for a certain user only 1 observation was masked then suggesting it would give a correct suggestion ratio of 100% while not suggesting it would give a 0% correct suggestion ratio.

5   Conclusions

The way people experience cultural heritage is taking advantage of the latest technologies to improve the users experiences. Traditional visits, where everyone, despite their interests or limitations, have to follow a predetermined route are being replaced by a more interactive and dynamic approach. Furthermore, the overwhelming of the visitors is a risk, as many times the number of items is very large, the time available to explore them is limited, or they are not of the user's interest.

This paper propose the use of a recommender system to help in the preparation and following visit of cultural heritage places. The recommender empowers the use of a mobile application, by suggesting which items (e.g., museum objects, interesting buildings, or buyable objects) the user should take into consideration, according with its profile and historical actions. The used method belongs to the class of implicit collaborative filtering, because users do not classify the items, i.e., the system is only aware of the interaction between the users and the items. The data acquisition is to be supported in the use of a mobile application, part of the M5SAR project.

At the moment of writing, the recommender system runs on a server, although efforts are being made to transpose it to mobile devices. Also in study is the use of a mixed (implicit/explicit) collaborative filtering asking the users to score the artwork and/or observing their interest in some of the artworks (e.g., by measuring the time they spend observing the items). Another objective is to integrate the system with a route optimization method, capable of optimizing the walks through cultural heritage places supported in several objectives (e.g., users' preferences, items diversity, walked distance) and constraints (e.g., related with the users mobility limitation).

Acknowledgments. This work was supported by the Portuguese Foundation for Science and Technology (FCT), project LARSyS (UID/EEA/50009/2013), CIAC, and project M5SAR I&DT n. 3322 financed by CRESC ALGARVE2020, PORTUGAL2020 and FEDER. We also thank Faro Municipal Museum and the M5SAR project leader, SPIC - Creative Solutions [www.spic.pt].

References

Aggarwal, C.C.: Recommender Systems. Springer, Cham (2016). https://doi.org/10.1007/978-3-319-29659-3

Alpaydin, E.: Machine Learning: The New AI. The MIT press, Cambridge (2016)

Arulkumaran, K., Deisenroth, M.P., Brundage, M., Bharath, A.A.: Deep reinforcement learning: a brief survey. IEEE Sig. Process. Mag. **34**(6), 26–38 (2017)

Benouaret, I., Lenne, D.: Combining semantic and collaborative recommendations to generate personalized museum tours. In: Morzy, T., Valduriez, P., Bellatreche, L. (eds.) ADBIS 2015. CCIS, vol. 539, pp. 477–487. Springer, Cham (2015). https://doi.org/10.1007/978-3-319-23201-0_48

Brijs, T., Swinnen, G., Vanhoof, K., Wets, G.: Using association rules for product assortment decisions: a case study. In: Knowledge Discovery and Data Mining, pp. 254–260 (1999)

Cardoso, P.J.S., Rodrigues, J.M.F., Pereira, J.A.R., Sardo, J.D.P.: An object visit recommender supported in multiple visitors and museums. In: Antona, M., Stephanidis, C. (eds.) UAHCI 2017. LNCS, vol. 10277, pp. 301–312. Springer, Cham (2017). https://doi.org/10.1007/978-3-319-58706-6_24

CHESS: CHESS - cultural heritage experiences through socio-personal interactions and storytelling (2017). http://www.chessexperience.eu/

Collobert, R., Kavukcuoglu, K., Farabet, C.: Torch7: A matlab-like environment for machine learning. In: BigLearn, NIPS Workshop (2011)

Curtin, R.R., Cline, J.R., Slagle, N.P., March, W.B., Ram, P., Mehta, N.A., Gray, A.G.: MLPACK: a scalable C++ machine learning library. J. Mach. Learn. Res. **14**, 801–805 (2013)

Domingos, P.: The Master Algorithm: How the Quest for the Ultimate Learning Machine Will Remake Our World. Basic Books, New York (2015)

Falk, J.H.: Identity and the Museum Visitor Experience. Left Coast Press Inc, Walnut Creek (2009)

Falk, J.H., Dierking, L.D.: The Museum Experience Revisited. Left Coast Press Inc, Walnut Creek (2016)

Garcia, I., Sebastia, L., Onaindia, E.: On the design of individual and group recommender systems for tourism. Expert Syst. Appl. **38**(6), 7683–7692 (2011)

Gavalas, D., Konstantopoulos, C., Mastakas, K., Pantziou, G.: Mobile recommender systems in tourism. J. Netw. Comput. Appl. **39**, 319–333 (2014)

Gomez-Uribe, C.A., Hunt, N.: The netflix recommender system: algorithms, business value, and innovation. ACM Trans. Manage. Inf. Syst. **6**(4), 13:1–13:19 (2015)

Hu, Y., Koren, Y., Volinsky, C.: Collaborative filtering for implicit feedback datasets. In: 2008 Eighth IEEE International Conference on Data Mining, ICDM 2008, pp. 263–272. IEEE (2008)

Jannach, D., Felfernig, A., Zanker, M., Friedrich, G.: Recommender Systems. Cambridge University Pr (2010)

Knime: Knime (2017). https://www.knime.com/. Accessed 14th Dec 2017

Koren, Y., Bell, R., Volinsky, C.: Matrix factorization techniques for recommender systems. Computer **8**, 30–37 (2009)

Lohr, S. (2009). Netflix awards $1 million prize and starts a new contest. New York Times, 21

Meng, X., Bradley, J., Yavuz, B., Sparks, E., Venkataraman, S., Liu, D., Freeman, J., Tsai, D., Amde, M., Owen, S., Xin, D., Xin, R., Franklin, M.J., Zadeh, R., Zaharia, M., Talwalkar, A.: MLlib: machine learning in apache spark. J. Mach. Learn. Res. **17**(1), 1235–1241 (2016)

Microsoft: Azure ML Studio (2017). https://studio.azureml.net. Accessed 14th Dec 2017

MLJAR: MLJAR (2017). https://mljar.com/. Accessed 14th Dec 2017

Müller, A.C., Guido, S.: Introduction to Machine Learning with Python: A Guide for Data Scientists. O'Reilly Media, Sebastopol (2016)

Orange: Orange (2017). https://orange.biolab.si/. Accessed 14th Dec 2017

Pedregosa, F., Varoquaux, G., Gramfort, A., Michel, V., Thirion, B., Grisel, O., Blondel, M., Prettenhofer, P., Weiss, R., Dubourg, V., Vanderplas, J., Passos, A., Cournapeau, D., Brucher, M., Perrot, M., Duchesnay, E.: Scikit-learn: machine learning in Python. J. Mach. Learn. Res. **12**, 2825–2830 (2011)

Rao, R., Rao, M.: A survey on recommender system. Int. J. Comput. Sci. Inf. Secur. **14**(5), 265–271 (2016)

Ricci, F., Rokach, L., Shapira, B. (eds.): Recommender Systems Handbook. Springer, Boston (2015). https://doi.org/10.1007/978-1-4899-7637-6

Robot, O.D.: Moma collection - automatic monthly update (2016)

Rodrigues, J.M.F., Pereira, J.A.R., Sardo, J.D.P., de Freitas, M.A.G., Cardoso, P.J.S., Gomes, M., Bica, P.: Adaptive card design UI implementation for an augmented reality museum application. In: Antona, M., Stephanidis, C. (eds.) UAHCI 2017. LNCS, vol. 10277, pp. 433–443. Springer, Cham (2017). https://doi.org/10.1007/978-3-319-58706-6_35

Route Perfect: Route perfect (2017). https://www.routeperfect.com/. Accessed 29th June 2016

Sardo, J.D.P., Semião, J., Monteiro, J.M., Pereira, J.A.R., de Freitas, M.A.G., Esteves, E., Rodrigues, J.M.F.: Portable device for touch, taste and smell sensations in augmented reality experiences. In: Mortal, A., Aníbal, J., Monteiro, J., Sequeira, C., Semião, J., Moreira da Silva, M., Oliveira, M. (eds.) INCREaSE 2017, pp. 305–320. Springer, Cham (2018). https://doi.org/10.1007/978-3-319-70272-8_26

Sonnenburg, S., Strathmann, H., Lisitsyn, S., Gal, V., García, F.J.I., Lin, W., De, S., Zhang, C., Frx, T., Andreev, E., JonasBehr, S., Mazumdar, P., Widmer, C., Zora, P.D., Toni, G.D., Mahindre, S., Kislay, A., Hughes, K., Votyakov, R., Khalednasr, Sharma, S., Novik, A., Panda, A., Anagnostopoulos, E., Pang, L., Binder, A., Serialhex, Esser, B.: Shogun-toolbox/shogun: Shogun 6.1.0 (2017)

TensorFlow: TensorFlow (2018). https://www.tensorflow.org. Accessed 14th Jan 2018

van Hage, W.R., Stash, N., Wang, Y., Aroyo, L.: Finding your way through the Rijksmuseum with an adaptive mobile museum guide. In: Aroyo, L., Antoniou, G., Hyvönen, E., ten Teije, A., Stuckenschmidt, H., Cabral, L., Tudorache, T. (eds.) ESWC 2010. LNCS, vol. 6088, pp. 46–59. Springer, Heidelberg (2010). https://doi.org/10.1007/978-3-642-13486-9_4

VELES: VELES (2018). https://velesnet.ml. Accessed 14th Jan 2018

Verbert, K., Manouselis, N., Ochoa, X., Wolpers, M., Drachsler, H., Bosnic, I., Duval, E.: Context-aware recommender systems for learning: a survey and future challenges. IEEE Trans. Learn. Technol. 5(4), 318–335 (2012)

Wang, D., Xiang, Z.: The new landscape of travel: a comprehensive analysis of smartphone apps. In: Fuchs, M., Ricci, F., Cantoni, L. (eds.) Information and Communication Technologies in Tourism 2012. Springer, Vienna (2012). https://doi.org/10.1007/978-3-7091-1142-0_27

WEKA: WEKA: Waikato Environment for Knowledge Analysis (2017).https://www.cs.waikato.ac.nz/ml/weka/. Accessed 14th Dec 2017

Zhou, Y., Wilkinson, D., Schreiber, R., Pan, R.: Large-scale parallel collaborative filtering for the netflix prize. In: Fleischer, R., Xu, J. (eds.) AAIM 2008. LNCS, vol. 5034, pp. 337–348. Springer, Heidelberg (2008). https://doi.org/10.1007/978-3-540-68880-8_32

State of Accessibility in U.S. Higher Ed Institutions

Jiatyan Chen[✉]

Stanford University, Stanford, CA 94305, USA
jiatyan@stanford.edu

Abstract. This paper will discuss the requirements and environment surrounding accessibility in Higher Ed institutions in the U.S., and their attempts to tackle these challenges. We will go on a panorama tour of the structure and culture of large universities and their constituents; touch on how accessibility fits into teaching, research and administration responsibilities; cover perspectives from legal, students, faculty, support staff; and take a look at policies, operations and culture impacting accessibility efforts.

Keywords: Higher Education · Accessibility

1 Introduction

The 2015/2016 complaints brought against UC Berkeley [1], Harvard and MIT [2] about captioning for their public online courses attracted much attention from the media and Higher Ed. These cases are but a sample filed against education institutions, with both having very limited scope compared some wide-reaching lawsuits.

Since the Americans with Disabilities Act of 1990 (ADA) was passed, the number of cases against Higher Ed institutions has doubled between each decade (tabulated from the cases listed on Higher Ed Accessibility Lawsuits, Complaints, and Settlements [3]):

1990–1999 1
2000–2010 16
2011–present 35

Most of the complaints against educational institutions are not captured by the above website. There are a lot more complaints being resolved without high-profile media coverage. For example, since 2014, Marcie Lipsitt (a Michigan civil rights advocate) has filed 1,800 complaints across the country with the U.S. Department of Education Office for Civil Rights (OCR) [4]. In addition, a search for "+web +accessibility" on the website of U.S. Department of Education Office for Civil Rights (OCR) returned 1,292 resolutions reached since 1st of October 2013 [5]. And across all industries, "[t]he number of website accessibility lawsuits filed in federal court since the beginning of 2015 has surged to at least 751 as of 15th of August 2017, with at least 432 of those filed in just the first eight and a half months of 2017." [6]

So what is web accessibility, and how does it come to affect the Higher Education space?

© Springer International Publishing AG, part of Springer Nature 2018
M. Antona and C. Stephanidis (Eds.): UAHCI 2018, LNCS 10908, pp. 437–449, 2018.
https://doi.org/10.1007/978-3-319-92052-8_34

The Americans with Disabilities Act of 1990 (ADA) is a non-discrimination law in the U.S. which covers both the Public sector and specific sections of the Private sector [7]. Another non-discrimination law is Section 504 of the U.S. Rehabilitation Act of 1973 (Section 504) which covers programs and activities receiving Federal financial assistance [8]. Universities in the U.S. are affected by both pieces of legislations, with the U.S. Department of Justice (DOJ) and the OCR holding the responsibility for enforcing these legislations.

Accessible, as defined by numerous lawsuits and agreements, means "a person with a disability is afforded the opportunity to acquire the same information, engage in the same interactions, and enjoy the same services as a person without a disability in an equally effective and equally integrated manner, with substantially equivalent ease of use" [9–14].

Many of these lawsuits and agreements were opened through complaints by plaintiffs with disabilities, who were unable to use covered services provided by the defendant, and were unable to find timely and acceptable resolutions. Most of the complaints centered around the online services and content provided by the universities. These include public access pages such as information about the universities and application forms, open course content, campus information, and a clear path to request for assistance. For enrolled students, the complaint focused on the timely access of course content for them to keep pace with their course schedule and assessments.

When the ADA was passed in 1990, accessibility of the Web was not specifically called out. The Web has matured since the 90's, and our society has become dependent on its widespread use. Many services have shifted to web-first, conducting business online, and requiring extra steps or compensation for using their phone or paper services. As such, the DOJ issued Dear Colleague letters in 2010, 2011 and 2014 to clarify that the Web is covered by ADA, "Requiring use of an emerging technology in a classroom environment when the technology is inaccessible to an entire population of individuals with disabilities – individuals with visual disabilities – is discrimination prohibited by the Americans with Disabilities Act of 1990 (ADA) and Section 504 of the Rehabilitation Act of 1973 (Section 504) unless those individuals are provided accommodations or modifications that permit them to receive all the educational benefits provided by the technology in an equally effective and equally integrated manner." [15–17]

However, in the absence of specific regulations regarding web content, there are still cases being argued in the courts interpreting the applicability of ADA for the Web [18]. And although both the DOJ and OCR have clarified their interpretations through the Dear Colleague letters, universities are slow to address this requirement due to various reasons, including: Increased demand and expectation, a plethora of content, inaccessible tools, lack of knowledge, missing processes, and a culture of dismissing accessibility for more appealing and more urgent topics.

2   Current State

2.1   Increasing Demand and Expectation

The current generation of college-aged students have more than two decades of growing up with the provisions of ADA—they know which accommodation to expect, and know how to request them. And with the increasingly aging population, senior citizens are also demanding their rights for accommodations under the provisions of ADA. Since the availability of cheap computing machines as of the 1990s, and interconnectedness as of the 2000s, the shift from business services from paper and phone to online self-service has accelerated. It is expected nowadays that a service or business has a online presence, and some businesses are even requiring customer to pay extra for alternate in-person or phone services. The Web has matured from a hobbyist toy to a ubiquitous mainstream mode of communication. Societies now demand and depend on it. Nevertheless, when compared to those who build essentials such as medical equipment, buildings, and vehicles, the designers and programmers for websites and applications have yet to improve the rigor in their craft when constructing websites and web services.

Universities spend years establishing smooth systems to support their work of teaching and generating knowledge. As such, it is the nature of these long-running processes to accumulate undetected accessibility debt in both the computing systems they use and the content they published. Lawsuits targeted at one failure opens the door for external investigations, identifying more areas with inaccessible functions. To fix them, however, challenges a university's setup. For example, a university has already paid for the long-term investment of inaccessible systems such as a decade-old financial system, hooked into multiple registration systems and personnel databases, with the development completed years ago and only retaining a skeleton crew for maintenance. In comparison, a fast-moving start-up company still has the original software engineers actively developing its one-year-old product, making it easier to for the start-up company to adjust their product to address changing accessibility concerns. Also, the continuous expense of universities are typically focused on its faculty and staff, teaching courses, and generating data to fulfill the teaching and research missions of the university, rather than redevelopment of existing functional systems to address the evolving requirements for Accessibility.

The demands for accessibility at universities are primarily on services related to

- Classes: Browsing its course catalog, registering, paying, attending the classes, being assessed, and receiving credits;
- Activities: Attending student events, residential life, campus activities, as well as student organisations;
- Public programs: Public lectures and events, access to its libraries, public areas, building and facilities;
- Research: Participation in studies, and distribution of results;
- Administrative work to keep the university running, such as computing, dining, financial, transportation, facilities, HR, security, and administrative support.

Reviewing a sample of complaints listed on Higher Ed Accessibility Lawsuits, Complaints, and Settlements [3], there is a full range of accessibility complaints covering access to course syllabus, the availability of alt-format textbook and course material, time extension for exams, accessible online open courseware, ability to enter buildings, alternative methods for withdrawing money from ATMs, and payment methods for classes and meals. Researchers are also scrambling to comply with requirements of the funding agencies (usually the federal government) as accessibility requirements make their way into submission guidelines and publication of their research findings.

2.2   Content and Tools

Universities have served for centuries to learn and educate, to curate and create knowledge through research, and to serve society. An artifact of these pillars is published content, increasingly in electronic form. This electronic content is delivered via content management systems (CMS) or learning management systems (LMS). These publishing platforms shield the users from the need to be proficient with the technical knowledge of constructing a web page, and let them concentrate on the actual subject matter content of their publication. However, no matter how brilliant a CMS or LMS system technologists build, this system cannot correct fundamentally problematic content that was entered into the system—the creation of content is the responsibility of subject matter experts. Typical causes of inaccessible content are: Incorrect use of formatting settings, lack of captions for images and charts, and poor choice of colors and fonts. All of which are due to human decisions during the process of editing, rather than a programmable switch.

To compound the problem, universities output a large percentage of STEM content (science, technology, engineering and mathematics), which are notoriously difficult to make accessible and require specific Accessibility help pages [19, 20]. Libraries, in support of research and teaching, also purchase equivalently inaccessible products sourced from other universities and academic journals.

The other aspect contributing to accessibility issues is the use of tools like multimedia, interactive learning modules, and emerging technologies. The availability of tools lowering the production cost of videos overlaps with the resurgence of multimodal learning theories, making it easy to implement what used to be a rarity in class—recorded lectures, screen captures, animations, podcasts, and flipped-classrooms—where students are required to view the lectures prior to face-to-face class discussions. However, most of these recordings are missing closed captioning or transcripts for their audio track. And instructors, looking for the best up-to-date material to broaden their students' learning experience and making learning more interesting, are eager to adopt interactive learning modules and learning games created by textbook publishers and other educators, not realizing that the modules and games may not have undergone rigorous assessment for accessibility. Faculty are also encouraged to experiment with various learning solutions as new tools and platforms become available. However, many of the tools and platforms start off as prototypes or start-ups, and were, by design, developed with a limited audience in mind. While a lot of them end up failing in the market, some garner sufficient adoption sufficiently to be picked up for use as university functions, and only then would the universities discover that these tools shut out a portion of the population.

In addition, universities are connected to the world and the societies they serve. In our interconnected world, faculty routinely need to use time-sensitive content not created under their control, such as articles, media feeds, free video, discussion forums, and social networks. These content help students stay relevant and engaged in the subjects. Many of these content creators are not obligated to provide accessible content, and even when they are willing to remediate, the delays impede the schedule of the classes. Even if an instructor follows Universal Design for Learning (UDL) principles in course preparation, we cannot expect them to be omniscient on handling a current event.

2.3   Knowledge and Skills

The lack of accessibility knowledge is not unique to Higher Ed. Technology companies in Silicon Valley found that they have, on average, five accessibility specialists to 5,000 technical positions [21]. Universities main information technology (IT) organisations draw from the same pool and mirror the same distribution as that of the industry. Universities also face limited flexibility in staffing due to

- Limited budget to fully staff positions and so accessibility skills are either sidelined or treated as a partial responsibility;
- Lower compensation leading to fewer selection of knowledgeable candidates, and
- Fewer turnovers leading to tendency to stay with the outmoded knowledge and processes.

Often, the few accessibility specialists working at universities have are spread thin resource-wise, and can afford only limited time for the high-profile IT projects. They may only be available for participating in very selected development cycles, and are only able to conduct the most critical tests. This means a lot projects and functions can fall through the cracks.

Besides technical staff, universities also deploy a large army of content authors. These authors can range from faculty writing course material, researchers publishing findings, administrative staff circulating memos, communicators publicizing articles, producers editing videos, and service staff updating schedules and menus. Accessibility is not mentioned as a writing requirement, much less listed as one of their job responsibilities, and many of them only play author on a part-time basis. Often, they are not aware of the few steps and choices they can adopt in their processes to create accessible content when authoring, and end up collectively contributing to a large amount of inaccessible content.

The last group of university personnel who might contribute to accessibility issues is the staff member who lacks knowledge on how to handle accessibility or accommodation requests, or the staff member who knows how to proactively avoid such requests. This covers people responding to help requests, as well as people selecting goods and services. Having never heard of a screen reader, a help desk staff is unable to direct an accessibility request to the correct office. Without checking for accessibility compliance, the purchaser of computer systems would have put their universities in vulnerable positions when accessibility features are needed. There is at least one lawsuit stemming from a faculty misunderstanding and failing to respond adequately to an accommodation request, and the university having to remediate all their inaccessible systems and content. (See the complaints and agreements for Louisiana Tech University [22], Miami University [23, 24], and Pennsylvania State University [25, 26].)

2.4 Policy and Practice

Documented procedures or instructions of how to get things done and moved through a complex system is a proven method of coordinating standards and setting expectations for a group, ensuring continuity despite staff turnover, and checking that details don't fall through the cracks. Documenting these procedures take effort, and often politics, and thus is not attempted frequently, and rarely comprehensively.

Compared to other functions of a university, accessibility compliance is relatively new. Following the process for Title IX and IT security, most universities are still in the process of determining a policy; finding a way to detect, measure and monitor its compliance; and planning and training its staff in the production of accessible content and software, and on responding to requests. Additionally, the university has to plan for remediating its existing inaccessible content and software. More often than not, accessibility becomes a risk management issue rather than a civil rights issue, as universities have to adhere to more than 200 compliance regulations, affecting equal opportunity, research, financial, admissions, export control, copyrights, and IT [27].

As accessibility touches many parts of a university system, to integrate it into the university processes means inserting procedures into existing budgeting, procurement, production, publication, development, auditing, and reporting processes. Each of these injections minimally requires identifying the appropriate processes, convincing the right people, securing the funding, planning and writing the procedures, and training the relevant staff. As a bigger challenge, these conversations have to occur separately at multiple local levels (school, college, and department), as most large universities delegate most operational decision to the deans and unit managers. For example, outreach messages and video lectures are generally produced by separate departments and individual instructors, and each of these productions likely published on the individual's YouTube channel. While the university's name may be included when posting, these YouTube channels are associated with the respective department or instructor, and are not official university channels that the university is able to supervise. Such is the decentralised nature of university work. Stipulating that the productions now need to pay a captioning service or investing five times the length of the video [28, 29] to self-caption is a major disruption to the production process and budget.

Looking outwards, universities outsource a variety of services and to many vendor software and personnel who do not need to conform to ADA requirements, and the burden is on the universities to ensure that they only source from compliant suppliers. Some of the suppliers have a monopoly in their niche markets and are reluctant to take on accessibility responsibilities. Notable examples come from publishers of journals, financial systems, and college applications software. The archives of a major Higher Ed Accessibility mailing list, EDUCAUSE ITACCESS, indicates that conversations about vendor product accessibility started in 2007, as early as the list's inception [30]. Lacking accessible options for its core services, universities turn to managing accessibility with short-term workarounds, kicking the proverbial can down the road in the hopes that there will be an accessible solution when someone really needs this function. Dealing with large vendors also put universities in weak negotiation positions —these companies have standard take-it-or-leave-it contracts and non-disclosure agreements, leaving universities unable to compel the companies to produce accessible software, nor share the findings of their accessibility tests with other universities.

2.5 Culture

Formalizing processes moves slowly. Changing the culture beneath moves even slower.

We have discussed how, in a decentralised authority model used by universities, there is no central gate where Accessibility may be detected and fixed. Unlike ethnics or women's studies, disability and accessibility awareness is not specifically introduced in schools. Most of us are unfamiliar with persons with disability, do not know how to interact with them, and end up treating them as outsiders or trying our best to ignore this 19% [31] of the population. While both universities and companies face the similar challenge of having to train staff, university trainings have to cover a wider spread of topics compared to a company's narrower focus on either technology or production.

When we talk about accessibility, the easiest example is, "to enable those who are blind," and, unfortunately, faculty has firmly connected "blind" to "disability services", with a typical response of, "We have an office to handle it. I don't need to know nor worry about it." Although disability services have overlapping skills with Accessibility, their main charge is towards *individual* accommodation, whereas Accessibility is to get everyone's material to a minimum standard so that these accommodations may be made. These messages need to be adjusted to highlight the difference between Accessibility and Accommodations, and that having accessible material benefits beyond those who are willing to ask for help.

Other than changing the messaging, any established workflow has inertia and any changes require overcoming this inherent resistance. It is understandable that adding Accessibility requirements means learning new things and changing workflows, thereby introducing complexity to a well-oiled routine. Contrary to what people have come to believe, this change cannot be passed off wholesale to IT or disability services, and includes explaining that Accessibility is a shared responsibility that requires everyone to know and be aware of it. While many universities are working to undo this established misconception by having supervisors issue directives, establishing peer pressure, and providing skills training to enable people to be self-sufficient, they are just taking the first steps towards building this momentum.

Accessibility, like plumbing in buildings or security in IT, is a hidden foundation, not a shining star that attracts attention. Accessibility is working well when there are minimal complaints that can be swiftly resolved, incurring no damage to the university's reputation. Unfortunately, there is usually not a lot of resources dedicated to support accessibility work unless (negative) attention has been drawn to it. Accessibility coordinators have to tightly balance resources allocated in each area, and maintain enough visibility to be on the minds of university administrators and managers for their continual support.

3   Short Term Solutions

The spate of lawsuits and settlements between 2014 and 2016 has increased the visibility of Accessibility in the Higher Ed space. Those paying attention took to re-examining their legal obligations and making decisions about scope and actions. Many started enacting policies and allocating some resources, often in the form of shifting an existing staff's job scope to handle Accessibility part-time. While this quick-fix is a step forward, often this staff member was left in an impossible position of not having sufficient resources nor formal authority to be effective. Other universities chose to go through the formal arduous process of creating official positions and assigning reporting lines, resulting in the increased number of job postings for Accessibility coordinator positions observed in 2016 and 2017. This coordinator usually reports to a committee with representatives from high level of governance. For example, the most recent settlement with Miami University [32] stipulated three positions to effectively conduct business—a coordinator/lead, a technologist, and an assistive technology (AT) specialist, reporting to a University Accessibility Committee, in addition to a direct report to the Vice President of IT and the Office of Equity and Equal Opportunity. In other settlement agreements, the coordinators are to have "responsibility and commensurate authority, to coordinate the University's EIT Accessibility Policy and procedures" [33, 26]. That said, it is normal for there to be just a one or two Accessibility personnel covering the responsibilities for all these positions.

In a central position, one of the major projects of an Accessibility coordinator would be to conduct an inventory of the electronic & IT (EIT) assets residing in both central and decentralized units. These assets include websites, software applications, digital documents, instructional material, library journals, and multimedia. The next step is determining how much accessibility gap there is. This can be accomplished by running automated scans as well as performing manual tests on said assets. Between inventorying EIT assets and assessing the accessibility gap, the Accessibility coordinator is able to provide information to each decentralised local unit so that they can create remediation plans for their different mix of assets, with the understanding that all current and future projects are to be developed as fully accessible projects.

Most central Accessibility units also act as a university-wide resource by monitoring compliance, coordinating training and outreach sessions, acting as consultants for prioritizing remediation, answering technical questions, performing AT testing, and helping with user reports of inaccessibility.

Another essential step towards addressing Accessibility issues is to set up a grievance process and make this information publicly available. Having an Accessibility policy and method for escalating a complaint posted on key university websites, allows anyone having accessibility problems on any university webpage to quickly get help and turn the remediation spotlight on these problem pages.

Having set up a way of reporting problems and a plan in place to fix them internally, the remaining major area which impacts Accessibility is procurement. As the IT industry matures, universities become more dependent on externally sourced transactional software and services, since it is no longer cost-efficient to maintain an in-house development shop for something which industry can do cheaper and at scale. When

Accessibility staff are able to work with various purchasing agents on evaluating the compliance of each product, they can help strengthen the contract language to compel the vendor to correct Accessibility defects. More often than not, the business unit purchasing an inaccessible software has to provide a Equally Effective Alternative Access Plan [34] on how it intends to respond to an accommodation request. This makes the business unit aware of that they have a gap in their service and should choose an accessible product if possible.

The above outlines similar approaches some universities have instituted. Universities are also pursuing additional separate efforts. For example, the University of Illinois at Urbana/Champaign builds accessibility scanners [35] and runs both short technical courses [36] and graduate certificate programs [37]; the University of Colorado Boulder has a Universal Design for Learning course [38]; and the Utah State University has a center on disability, WebAIM, maintaining an extensive collection of up-to-date information about web accessibility and also provides in-depth training [39]. The University of Washington has a HCI research center on accessible technology [40] and an NSF funded program, Access Computing, which connect students projects to persons with disability [41]. Michigan State University has a usability and accessibility research center [42] and hosts student conferences [43]. Various universities are also collaborating with their vendors to test vendor products as well as teach vendors how to design and write accessible products. Yet others are collaborating within Higher Ed to share product evaluations [44] and engage vendors collectively to have a stronger negotiation position in securing vendor agreement in supplying accessible products. EDUCAUSE, a Higher Ed technology association has produced an IT Accessibility Risk Statements and Evidence paper [45] as an advisory to IT leaders as they make planning and budgeting decisions.

4 Long Term Solutions

Imagine that we suddenly realize that we have to change our narrow doorway to accommodate wheelchairs entering the building. We would need to rip out the existing door, tear down part of the wall, maybe re-route electricals, re-certify the structural integrity of the building, pay for and re-install a new door, and level or install a ramp in the entrance area. If only our architect had known that and factored wheelchair access into the original design and engineering.

We have unintentionally created a culture and system which produces inaccessible products. It will take years to restructure and re-learn. There are discussions and pilot projects started to explore viability. We have to address the people, the environment and the system.

One of the causes we can easily identify is the lack of Accessibility knowledge in people producing our web and electronic assets these days—programmers, designers and content producers. It can be traced back to a lack of training and exposure during their school years and environment. And their teachers were also unaware of this topic. Currently, there is a joint effort by the high tech industry and Higher Ed called Teach Access [46] that helps to insert Accessibility topics into the undergraduate curriculum.

The goal is to train a lot of people to know a little, in addition to our existing method of training a few people who know a lot. Teach Access is working with standards committees to clarify accessibility statements in undergraduate curricula, training faculty, organising student events, and participating in classes. Decentralising Accessibility knowledge will put more eyes and minds in the production process, with a two-fold benefit that Accessibility considerations may be identified early in the development process, and be more effective in using the limited number of specialists for solving really thorny problems.

Even if not taught as a skill, more exposure to Accessibility as a topic in ethics or social studies classes will bring awareness and help the students feel comfortable in talking and caring about the diverse needs of everyone. As institutions for learning, universities have the obligation and the ideal environment and structure to introduce social consciousness to both their student and staff.

Another way to make Accessibility widespread is to build it into the system, making it automatic and thus invisible and natural. With planning and resources, Accessibility checkpoints may be built into the development life cycle, requiring that every project include a team member knowledgeable about Accessibility guidelines, and to get a final Accessibility check before each version is released. Adding specific Accessibility checklists to production processes will create habits on consistent alt-text for images and closed captions (subtitles) for videos. Besides having individuals manually add Accessibility into these processes through planning and checklists, the tools used in development, project management and content production can have a significant nudge effect if Accessibility affordances are built in. For example, if a WYSIWYG editor automatically prompts for alt-text while explaining in its just-in-time help the purpose of alt-text, it enables the user to consistently provide pertinent alt-text immediately, rather than returning to add them later.

A third area where accessibility concerns can be addressed requires that universities treat Accessibility as important as other compliance and risk management issue, devoting the same executive support and resources to it as IT security, privacy, or Title IX (discrimination). Moving beyond a single university, universities can also commit to a collective goal of sharing product evaluation information and allocating a small amount of resource to establish, manage, and maintain a central repository for the shared information. Having product compliance information helps each other (a) put pressure on vendors and, (b) avoid duplicating evaluation efforts. Most of the road block is not the lack of information, but rather the lack of resources in maintaining a central repository and the fear of lawsuits from vendors. Very lightweight contributions from numerous institution will enable a consortium to devote resources in maintaining a structure to host these findings that can be used by all as reference.

5   Conclusion

Web, mobile and other online electronic information, while still maturing, has already become the vanguard of equity as our society progresses. Universities are in a prime position to shape this progress for the better. Accessibility has come far in what it has achieved in the past 10 years. If universities keeping building on our awareness programs and actively including it into our teachings and processes, we are in good shape towards a more inclusive and equitable society, where everyone of all ages and abilities can benefit.

References

1. The United States' Findings and Conclusions Based on its Investigation Under Title II of the Americans with Disabilities Act of the University of California at Berkeley, DJ No. 204-11-309. https://news.berkeley.edu/wp-content/uploads/2016/09/2016-08-30-UC-Berkeley-LOF. pdf
2. The National Association of the Deaf et al. v. Harvard, MIT https://creeclaw.org/online-content-lawsuit-harvard-mit/
3. Higher Ed Accessibility Lawsuits, Complaints, and Settlements. http://www.d.umn.edu/ ~lcarlson/atteam/reports/litigation/lawsuits.html
4. Rural schools struggling to make websites ADA. http://www.greatfallstribune.com/story/news/2017/10/03/rural-schools-struggling-make-websites-ada-compliant/728762001/
5. Home U.S. Department of Education Search. https://www.ed.gov/ocr-search-resolutions-letters-and-agreements?keywords=%2Bweb+%2Baccessibility&title=&keywords_state=
6. Website Accessibility Lawsuit Filings Still Going Strong. https://www.adatitleiii.com/2017/ 08/website-accessibility-lawsuit-filings-still-going-strong/
7. The Americans with Disabilities Act of 1990 and Revised ADA Regulations Implementing Title II and Title III. https://www.ada.gov/2010_regs.htm
8. Protecting Students with Disabilities. https://www2.ed.gov/about/offices/list/ocr/504faq.html
9. Civil Rights Agreement Reached with South Carolina Technical College System on Accessibility of Websites to People with Disabilities. https://www.ed.gov/news/press-releases/civil-rights-agreement-reached-south-carolina-technical-college-system-accessibi
10. Youngstown State University Resolution Agreement OCR Compliance Review #15-13-6002. https://www2.ed.gov/documents/press-releases/youngstown-state-university-agreement.pdf
11. University of Cincinnati Resolution Agreement OCR Compliance Review #15-13-6001. https://www2.ed.gov/documents/press-releases/university-cincinnati-agreement.pdf
12. Justice Department Reaches Three Settlements Under the Americans with Disabilities Act Regarding the Use of Electronic Book Readers. https://www.justice.gov/opa/pr/justice-department-reaches-three-settlements-under-americans-disabilities-act-regarding-use
13. University of Montana and the U.S. Department of Education, Office for Civil Rights Resolution Agreement. http://www.umt.edu/accessibility/docs/FinalResolutionAgreement. pdf
14. Anthony Lanzilotti, Mitchell Cossaboon, and the National Federation of the Blind vs Atlantic Cape Community College Consent Decree. http://www.atlantic.edu/documents/nfb_lanzailotti_atlantic_cape_consent_decree.pdf
15. "Dear Colleague" letter, 29 June 2010. https://www2.ed.gov/about/offices/list/ocr/letters/colleague-20100629.html
16. "Dear Colleague" letters, 26 May 2011. http://www2.ed.gov/about/offices/list/ocr/docs/dcl-ebook-faq-201105.html
17. Dear Colleague Letter, 12 November 2014. https://www2.ed.gov/about/offices/list/ocr/letters/colleague-effective-communication-201411.pdf

18. ADA Title III News & Insights. https://www.adatitleiii.com/website-2/
19. Math and STEM Content. http://accessibility.psu.edu/math/
20. Guidelines for Describing STEM Images. http://ncam.wgbh.org/experience_learn/educational_media/stemdx/guidelines
21. Teach Access Intro Slides. http://teachaccess.org/wp-content/uploads/2018/02/Teach-Access_intro-slides.pdf
22. Settlement Agreement between United States of America and Louisiana Tech University. https://www.ada.gov/louisiana-tech.htm
23. Aleeha Dudley vs Miami University Complaint. https://nfb.org/images/nfb/documents/pdf/miami%20teach.pdf
24. Aleeha Dudley, United States of America vs Miami University Consent Decree. https://www.ada.gov/miami_university_cd.html
25. National Federation of the Blind Files Complaint Against Penn State. https://nfb.org/node/1026
26. Settlement Between Penn State University and National Federation of the Blind. http://accessibility.psu.edu/nfbpsusettlement/
27. Higher Ed Compliance Alliance Compliance Matrix. http://www.higheredcompliance.org/matrix/
28. How Long Does It Take to Manually Caption Videos? https://www.3playmedia.com/2014/08/29/long-take-manually-caption-videos/
29. How Long Does It Take to Caption a Video? http://mn.gov/mnit-accessibility/captioningessentials/intro_howlong.html
30. May 2007 Archives for ITACCESS@LISTSERV.EDUCAUSE.EDU. http://listserv.educause.edu/scripts/wa.exe?A0=itaccess
31. Nearly 1 in 5 People Have a Disability in the U.S., Census Bureau Reports. https://www.census.gov/newsroom/releases/archives/miscellaneous/cb12-134.html
32. Aleeha Dudley, US DOJ and Miami University Consent Decree. https://www.ada.gov/miami_university_cd.html
33. OCR and University of Montana Resolution Agreement. http://www.umt.edu/accessibility/docs/AgreementResolution_March_7_2014.pdf
34. CSU Equally Effective Alternate Access Plan. http://teachingcommons.cdl.edu/access/procurement_process/EEAAP.shtml
35. Functional Accessibility Evaluator (FAE). https://fae.disability.illinois.edu/
36. DRES IT Accessibility Badging Program. http://disability.illinois.edu/academic-support/accessible-it-group/badging
37. UIUC Information Accessibility Design and Policy (IADP) certificate program. https://online.illinois.edu/online-programs/graduate-certificates/information-accessibility-design-policy
38. ATLS 3519 Special Topics in Technology, Arts, and Media: Universal Design for Digital Media. https://ce.colorado.edu/courses/special-topics-in-technology-arts-and-media-universal-des-digital-media-atls-3519/
39. WebAIM. https://webaim.org/
40. Taskar Center for Accessible Technology. https://www.cs.washington.edu/research/hci
41. AccessComputing. https://www.washington.edu/accesscomputing/
42. Usability/Accessibility Research and Consulting. https://usability.msu.edu/
43. Leading the Way in Accessible Learning. http://www.cal.msu.edu/news/accessibility-learning-conference-continues-engage-students-across-campus

44. Library E-Resource Accessibility - Testing. https://www.btaa.org/library/accessibility/library-e-resource-accessibility--testing
45. IT Accessibility Risk Statements and Evidence. https://library.educause.edu/resources/2015/7/it-accessibility-risk-statements-and-evidence
46. Teach Access. http://teachaccess.org/

Quo Vadis "Interaction Design and Children, Older and Disabled" in America and Europe?

Francisco V. Cipolla Ficarra[1,2(✉)], Maria V. Ficarra[1,2],
Eulogia Mendoza[3], and Miguel Cipolla Ficarra[2]

[1] HCI Lab. – F&F Multimedia Communic@tions Corp., ALAIPO: Asociación
Latina de Interacción Persona-Ordenador, c/Angel Baixeras, 5 – AP 1638, 08080
Barcelona, Spain
ficarra@alaipo.com
[2] HCI Lab. – F&F Multimedia Communic@tions Corp., AINCI: Asociación
Internacional de la Comunicación Interactiva, Via Tabajani, 1, S. 15 – CP 7,
24121 Bergamo, Italy
{ficarra, info}@ainci.com
[3] Universidad Nacional de La Pampa, Santa Rosa, Argentina
eulogia.mendoza.unlp@gmail.com

Abstract. We present a first overview with regard to a set of users of interactive systems who, by some members of the social sciences, are regarded as
simple goods or customers because of the revenue they generate in R&D
pseudo-projects. Both in the EU as well as in America those "pseudo-projects"
are often totally financed by the public or private sector. Besides, we establish
the north of the compass, looking at a real crossroads that millions of users must
face daily in the view of pseudo scientists who do not have either the theoretical
and/or practical knowledge, nor the competence and human skills in the treatment towards that kind of users. Finally, we explain a set of heuristic techniques
to discover those pseudo scientific investigations, such as the profile of those
professionals not capable of such research.

Keywords: HCI · Interactive systems · Users · ICT · Sociology
Software · Human factors · Evaluation

1   Introduction

Currently, one of the main problems inside of the field of HCI is to detect the real
motivations why certain types of research are carried out, and whether they respond to
scientific or commercial character. These two words are separated by an "or" and not an
"and" which from the point of view of logical programming are two different things and
mark flows that diverge (or) or converge (and). In the case of the field of HCI since the late
90s, there has always been a divergence between the activities on which the contents of the
first theoretical, experimental, research and development works should be grounded to
establish the foundations of the labs in the context of HCI in Spain [1]. A "natural" field for
their birth at the time was the multimedia sector with subjects pertaining to dynamic
and static media, usability engineering, hypermedia programming; the evaluation and

© Springer International Publishing AG, part of Springer Nature 2018
M. Antona and C. Stephanidis (Eds.): UAHCI 2018, LNCS 10908, pp. 450–462, 2018.
https://doi.org/10.1007/978-3-319-92052-8_35

auditing of interactive systems; computer graphics and animation among others. These are all natural domains where a balance between theories and experimental practices existed [2].

However, in other "artificial" domains, such as a Department of Computer, Architecture and Technology, in Basque Country, where fields of study range from disability to the web accessibility, affective computation, augmentative communication, mobility and manipulation; ubiquitous computing and ambient intelligence, user modelling and adaptive interfaces, etc. Theoretically, they have a lab for special needs. Therefore, all that which escaped the pattern of the special needs, had to be physically destroyed, as the first HCI Lab in Barcelona (Ramon Llull University, 1997–1999) was, because it didn't accept the rulings of such pressure groups, having to digest the "normal" contents to the disabled. This does not mean that the disabled, the children and the elderly are not important as a subject of study, the very opposite is true. It is "unnatural" and "ilogical" that they become just a source of revenue ad eternum for the universities. Besides, it is the population without disabilities who have to work to maintain all those who are disabled, for instance. When there are millions of unemployed in the local communities, graduates who migrate en masse abroad, closing of hospitals, cuts in the educational system and a long etcetera as consequence of the worst financial crisis in the last decades, the priorities in the high centres of study are others, the focus is, for example, the analysis of the failure of the industrial, business, financial, educational models, etc. [3].

The first Barcelona lab, without any kind of subsidies, was starting to publish in the main international congresses such as HCI International, and in the Spanish technical press. They, after six years since their foundation, see their first works published in the abc database, considering, on top of that, that they have in their history benefactors such as banking entities, the ONCE (*Organización Nacional de Ciegos Españoles* – National Organization of Spanish blind people), among many others, foundations, organizations, associations. Faced with the appearance of the first Barcelona lab, rebel to the dictates of the dictatorial regime of the Basque Country and Lerida, they activated a kind of national association where the members paid higher fees to the yearly inscriptions to the ACM or IEEE. Since their beginnings, a retrograde character to the principles of the sciences could be appreciated, since they were not only secluded in their regions, as it can be seen in the venues of the congresses they carried out, but also in the non-incorporation of foreigners at the top levels of the direction. Then, when from the first Barcelona lab two other associations were activated, with a yearly fee equal to zero cents of euro and with an international character, automatically they also became an international association. Regrettably, since the 90s they have kept on constantly attacking all that they can not control, disseminating in the four cardinal points the Garduña –it is a mythical secret criminal society said to have been founded in Spain in the late Middle Ages– Factor or "G" Factor.

2   The Pink Color of the HCI

The "G" factor has found a great ally in the female sector, hired part-time (female professors and researchers, etc.) inside the universities, especially in the field of the European HCI. Although the reality of the feminine presence, according to the "Digital Equality for Woman?" (www.rolandberger.com) study does not reach 17%, in the context of the ICTs, in the domain of the HCI, the reality has other negative per-spectives. In the first place, there is a kind of progressive concentration of powers, generating a radial structure which transcends the limits of a city, province, region, state, similar to other destructive structures. It is this kind of structure that allows to connect with other radial structures of stars in the field of HCI with the European peripheral areas from a geographical point of view such as the Scandinavian peninsula, the Iberian Peninsula, Italian Peninsula, etc. Here is the reason why the interest towards the disabled spreads quickly to other academic realities in the old continent. These female researchers, professors, etc., have an interest in the underdog sectors of the society; the poor, blind, elderly, children, etc., with their peers and colleagues, usually have a radicalized source of exclusion, with which they slow down the obtainment of neutral and objective results in the HCI. Besides, they favour the endless width of topics that must be addressed in the disciplines related to the HCI, but they are always related to the fashionable topics: smart cities, robotics, big data, etc., that is to say, the goal is to be part of some paneuropean project for the financial resources. However, those eventual advances can not solve the real problems that suffer millions of disabled people in the Old Continent. For instance, the prehistoric equipment they have in the Lombardy region to move ancient people with disabilities (elevator for the mobility impaired, orthopaedic beds, etc.) where the term "electronic engine", and its application in the devices of the Fig. 1 do not exist yet neither for the manufacturers nor for the health ministry.

Fig. 1. Elevator for disabled people (patients reject its use because of its discomfort), a prehistoric orthopedic beds, with manual elevation, and walker for elderly people (they find it impossible to use because of the weight and dimension of it, which does not fit the standard doors of the rooms).

The Fig. 1 denote that there is a gap between the daily reality of the disabled and the solutions proposed from the ICTs sector. That gap is the European pink mirage that exists between the HCI, ICTs, and all children, young people, adults, elderly people

Fig. 2. Electoral poster (pink) of the Italian health minister (2013–2018), main responsible for the distribution of non-ergonomic and prehistoric devices for the physically disabled people. (Color figure online)

with disabilities, accompanied by their families, who must face alone, a daily life where the advances of the latest technologies are light years away, at the moment of making simple physical movements, for example.

3 A Profitable Hexagon in Times of Crisis

At the end of the first decade of the new millennium erupted the global financial crisis, where computer science in the bank management systems have only served to enhance it, since the human controls haven't worked [4, 5]. Since then, very little research has been carried out in the main magazines, journals, proceedings, books, etc., related to computer science, software engineering, systems engineering, human-computer interaction, etc., that has addressed the consequences of putting software and hardware instruments with low costs and even free, to damage millions of human beings in the Old Continent, after the two world wars of the 20th century [3, 4]. From then on, the welfare state of the EU, founded on the pillars of education and healthcare, became the target of constant cutbacks, of the local, provincial, regional, national authorities, etc. A group of university professors, hired or not, with partial time dedication or full time, graduated in mathematics, physics, fine arts, audiovisual, computer science, etc., see in the disabled, the elderly and the children the panacea to obtain financial resources and overcome the worst years in the context of R&D, research and teaching in Europe after World War Two. They have focused their action on the HCI hexagon: HCI; Mass and New Media; ICTs; Children, Older and Disabled Users; R&D Financing (banking foundations, European social fund, national ministerial aids, etc.), and International Events (Fig. 3).

Fig. 3. A Profitable hexagon in times of financial crisis.

3.1   Human-Computer Interaction

One of the hypocritical sentences that are generally repeated in the context of the HCI when something does not work correctly in an organization, association, foundation, etc., is "we are working non-profit". In that sense, the user must analyze if these entities related to the HCI, user experience, virtual reality, computer and/or video art, etc., charge or not a monthly, quarterly or yearly fee to belong to such entities. If the answer is affirmative, these entities are for profit, regardless of what their online by-laws, ethical codes, and other masks establish to hide that their final purpose is not research. For instance, when one of those members deposits one, two, three, four, five or more millions euros received in European subsidies for an alleged R&D project in a bank branch or a savings bank, axiomatically, those who sign such a project will enjoy a myriad personal benefits from the financial entity, especially in the countries in the south of Europe.

These financial benefits and economic advantages rank from the obtainment of personal loans, credit cards, goods and/or services for the home, the office, etc. down to holidays, health insurances, etc. Benefits that are increased exponentially if the leaders of said projects reside a few kilometers away from tax havens such as: Andorra, Cyprus, Gibraltar, Switzerland, Luxemburg, etc. Consequently, the term "non-profit" is false.

3.2   Mass Media and New Media

The media are essential achieve a goal: "Everybody talks about them". It is an expression that allows to establish agreements with universities, research centres, etc., within and without the European borders, without paying attention to the curriculum of the members. Simultaneously, that sentence shows the existence of an authoritarian system in the management and control of the social information, emulating the mechanisms and strategies used by Goebbels to generate unidirectional contents. These mechanisms have been fostered for decades in public universities, such as UPF (Pompeu Fabra University), UPC (Polytechnic University of Catalonia), URV (Rovira i Virgili University), UAB (Autonomous University of Barcelona), etc. But some of their professors in the areas of computer science, audiovisual, ICTs, etc., function as a corporation of individual societies inside the university structure. Under that educational antimodel, as for example in UPF, the professionals of TV3 in Catalonia are trained [6]. In other cases, those unidirectional, vertical, dictatorial mechanisms only need a year, such as in the case of the Radio Télévision des Mille Collines (RTLM) in Ruanda (1994). Those media, with only 12 months of functioning, was mainly responsible for one of the greatest genocides within the African borders (the fratricide between hutus and tutsis, caused almost a million of dead and wounded).

These mechanisms are present in some Catalan public universities when advertising turns into propaganda [6] and invites the registration of students in their offices, since they are guaranteed in advance the publication of their scientific works in journals, books, conferences, etc., with "A" category. Besides, those students who contribute more money to the coffers of those study centres, will have the possibility of publishing even in the MIT (Massachusetts Institute of Technology). A way to synthetize that negative reality related to the HCI is the slogan that they use: "Study with us because we offer you the possibility of publishing in ACM, IEEE, Elsevier, etc., and even MIT". This example of "propaganda strategy" inside the HCI is not only based on the manipulation of information in the 21st century but also on Goebbels' mechanisms [6]. Besides, the MIT and other entities, public, private or hybrid, are represented as a space where "anything is HCI", being related or not to the children, the elderly, the disabled, the poor, among other groups of the marginalized or the socially excluded. The damage inside the main and secondary goals of study as HCI discipline and their interrelations in areas such as: ICT, Artificial Intelligence, Augmented Reality, Virtual Reality, etc., is immeasurable. The same happens to the future professionals in such academic units, in which they have not been trained, but rather deformed. An iconic analysis in the social networks of the authors of that deformation, such as Wikipedia, Facebook, Linkedin, can be seen behind a microphone, a video camera, surrounded by students, with their arms crossed to show their muscles, etc. In other words, it is the latent manifestation of the dynamic persuader [1].

3.3   Information and Communication Technologies

ICTs are a constant source of changes which have spread throughout the university centres of our planet. In some of them we have seen how some teachers have gone from nuclear engineering to hypertext, from multimedia to usability engineering, from museums to interactive communication, from smart cities to robots for autistic children, blind, etc. This is a "weather vane" phenomenon, which shows the direction where money is available in the Old and the New World, without being interested in establishing research lines or work teams that are serious and lasting in time.

They have seen in the HCI context an ideal territory to change as many times as necessary. Regrettably, those patterns of behaviour that seriously damage the HCI discipline and all its derivations are now exported within parochialism and foster the Garduña factor in the education and the scientific research in the next decades. While in many centres of technological excellence they require the presence of mathematicians, computer scientists, electronic engineers, audiovisual artists, etc. [7], where the former know how to create algorithms and solve equations, the latter are supposed to program with the latest programming languages, and the third group knows how to create electronic circuits, and the fourth group knows how to make computer animations, etc., in the centres related to HCI, User Centered Design, User Experience, Usability Engineering, etc., in the south of Europe.

The members who hold the four previous degrees (graduates, engineers and PhDs) do not know how to carry out in an autonomous way not a single one of said operations [3]. They only try to be the heads of the technicians, directors of doctoral theses, to get and manage the funds of the financial subsidies, etc. A reality which is represented in the ads that appear on the online websites, requesting qualified staff (i.e., http://acm-sigchi.1086187.n5.nabble.com,   https://research.cs.wisc.edu/dbworld/   browse.html). The problem is that these new centres grant fast degrees, without the future professionals having enough theoretical and/or technical knowledge, as it has happened in the digital arts, multimedia engineering, usability engineering, etc. That is to say, "few Indians and many chiefs". The interested reader can consult the following bibliography

[1, 2, 8] to learn the techniques used since the late 20th century. They remain in place in the Catalonia university centres which are referenced in the bibliography.

Undoubtedly, it is complicated to be acquainted with the latest technologies, since the changes that affect millions of potential users of the interactive systems are generated by the minute. Those who realize the projects related to a myriad of applications in software and hardware (programmers, systems analysts, electronic engineers, etc.), stem from the so called emerging countries, from the economic point of view, such as: Argentina, Brasil, China, India, South Africa, Turkey, among others. In many universities in the south of Europe, that staff are hired on a limited time basis, and as a rule their names do not appear in the works published in the format of papers, demos, research-in-progress, theses, doctoral theses, etc. Just a few of those names are in the acknowledgments section. However, it is those people who really turn the sketches drawn on paper into accessible interactive systems.

3.4   Children, Older and Disabled Users

Traditionally, the profile of the end users of off-line hypermedia systems in the 90s, where the disabled were not included, but the children, teenagers, young people, adults and the elderly were, could be classified as occasional, intentional, expert, and inexperienced and intentional users [2]. Profiles, professional experience and preexisting knowledge in the use of the multimedia systems can be summed up in the following way:

- The eventual users consulted the system only once, as in the case of a catalogue offering products or a tourist information point. The time it took them for the use of the system was less than an hour and they had no prior experience in multimedia.
- The intentional users are interested in the subject of the application and seek to go deeper into it, for instance, the scientific encyclopedias. The time available for the use of the system was short (between 1 and 3 h) and they had previous experience in the use of the multimedia systems.
- Experts, researchers on the content of the application, whose planned time was unlimited, and with previous experience in the use of the multimedia systems, for instance, educational contents for the learning of mathematics, chemistry, etc.
- Inexperienced and intentional, basically students who do not have previous experience in the use of computers but denote a great interest in learning, and therefore the time for the use of the system was unlimited.

Starting from multimedia in mobile phones, this classification was rendered obsolete, since the access was for all kinds of users. The disabled users, together with children and the elderly, became, after the financial crisis of the new millennium, a center for obtaining European subsidies, in a myriad of R&D pseudo projects. In order to get these subsidies, it was necessary to establish the "good or ideal links", or "*la cordata buona/ideale*", as they say in Italy. That is to say, an interrelation among friends, in order to exchange favors, ranging from the approval without significant controls of the works in the conferences, workshops, etc., in their doctoral students to the obtaining of international scholarships within and without the European Union, to mention an example. As a rule, departments from countries in the north of Europe interrelate with those in eastern and southern Europe. For instance, some research centre from the Scandinavian peninsula, with some department of computer science, audiovisual, systems, etc., of the Iberian Peninsula or Italy, with a sciences faculty in the eastern European countries. This geographical triangulation is the source of a myriad of financial resources in the euro zone, in order to, theoretically, allow access to the new technologies for the blind, the autistic, the epileptic, etc. Some of these centres are to be found in Barcelona, Milan, Trento, Turin, Pisa, Graz, Valencia, Palma de Mallorca, etc., cities where finding non-transparent people for financial links or "*cordata buona/ideale*" is a common denominator. An example of a pseudo project of video games within the HCI context (zero aging projects), with the elderly, for "a positive aging", can be easily detected through the social networks, such as are the Figs. 1 and 2 from YouTube. It has its genesis in the ICTs department (Universidad Pompeu Fabra, in Barcelona), where the experiment is carried out in a neighbourhood association of Barcelona (Fig. 4).

Fig. 4. Different kinds of keyboards, monitors, mice, etc. where adults and elderly are mixed. The results that can be obtained from the interaction with the computer are of zero value, since the hardware is not homogenous. Besides, two users per computer where no innovation of the project can be seen, since two adult people, not old, are interacting with Facebook.

In the video it can be seen that not all the participants are elderly, since there are adult and young people. Besides, the hardware is not homogeneous, that is, the monitors, keyboards, computers, etc., are not all the same, with which the value of the results of the experiment is equal to zero, although the goal is to carry out videogames to improve the physical and psychosocial wellbeing. Besides, in Fig. 5 it can be seen how the local research centres, their foundations and the banking entities interrelate among each other to get resources. It would be interesting to analyze in the financial entity all the disasters caused to thousands of families in Catalonia, with or without disabled, by offering them money and credit cards without collaterals, before the crisis and how, later, those families have been destroyed through the loss of jobs during the financial crisis.

The issue of the video games has been, is and will be a kind of magnet to attract financial funds from the off-line multimedia to the collapse of the virtual companies at the start of the 20th century (the only sector which kept on growing in the field of the multimedia firms in Europe), and now with artificial intelligence or the robots for the autistic, as it is the case with the labs/centres HOC, and I3Lab of the Polytechnic of Milan (Fig. 6). They, together with the UPF, make up two nexus of the "cordata ideale

Fig. 5. Research centres and foundations which collaborate in the whitewashing of the image of the financial institutions (la Caixa or BankCaixa) who have caused a plethora of irreparable and unforgivable damage to the neighbours of the community: children, elderly, families with disabled people in their charge, unemployed, etc. Besides, the dynamic persuaders and their eternal need to appear in all the media at their disposal (i.e., the portal of Catalan research).

sui generis", for the obtainment of European financial funds in pseudo projects, whose results can already be read in their titles, "zero", but with high costs for the community that pays those officials for life, in the educational and banking institutions [3].

Fig. 6. Just the same as in the UPF in Barcelona, in the I3Lab, Polytechnic of Milan (Italy), they also need the media for the diffusion of the university agreements signed with the USA, EU, etc., when from the labs they refer to the autistic children and the making of the first experimental prototypes of robots (www.ilfoglio.it).

3.5   R&D Financing

Without any doubt, the elasticity now offered by the limits of the HCI sector, the new technologies, joined to the disabled, elderly and children, for example, makes all these interrelations, current and future, become a kind of crossroads of topics which are ideal to get funds from the city councils, associations, foundations, universities, health, education, science and technology ministries, European funds, international agreements and a long etc. The interest does not lie in the content, the seriousness and the continuity in the lines of research, but in the constant flow of financial funds in the public institutions such as the universities, even though some of them work like real corporations in the South of Europe.

This functioning is not a consequence of the financial crisis of the new millennium, rather it already existed in the past century, principally, in those ex-university institutes of the audiovisual (IUA – UPF), which nowadays are ICT departments, as it can be read in Catalan: "*El finançament extern provindrà dels convenis i contractes que signin l'Institut i els seus investigadors amb entitats públiques o privades per a la realització de projectes d'investigació, de producció experimental, de docència o de serveis*", which translates into English as: "External financing will come from the agreements and contracts signed by the Institute and its researchers with public or private entities for the realization of research projects, of experimental production, teaching, or services." This model of Catalan external financing has spread little by litle to those centres that work with the elderly, children and disabled in the Basque Country, Zaragoza, La Rioja, Castilla-La Mancha, Valencia, Majorca, Málaga, Madrid, Tenerife, etc. Later on, through the agreements or research projects in topics related to the HCI in Europe: Portugal, Italy, France, etc., in Latin America: Cauca (Colombia), Valparaíso (Chile), Puebla (Mexico), La Plata (Argentina, LIFIA), Río de Janeiro (Brazil), Asunción (Paraguay), etc., and in the USA: Indiana University, University of Iowa, Georgia Institute of Technology, etc. In short, absolute freedom to sign agreements and contracts, while the academic issue; the lines of research to be followed in the short, middle and long term; the working future of the students, etc., were totally marginalized. In the portal www.pirateando.net some of the main consequences of this financing model can be seen. Besides, in the R&D pseudo projects where people with disabilities are included who have as sponsors or partners the financial, banking, government institutions, etc., the goal are not the scientific results, but rather an institutional whitewashing (la Caixa, see Fig. 5) tending to recover the credibility of their activities and/or functions with regard to the local population. A population that has seen the digital divide increase in the last decade, due to the impossibility of updating to the last generation technological devices for economic reasons.

3.6 International Events

One of the ways to reinforce the distortions in the context of the HCI and the disabled, children and elderly is through the control of the associations, conferences, publications, etc. akin to those issues. We can see how a university department (ICT - UPF) controls indirectly the actions of an association (AIPO, in Spain) obtaining, in exchange, that every year, the works of their students receive awards. Obviously, these are manipulated prizes, of which the results are known beforehand [8]. However, those associations, universities, professors, students, etc., exert a despotic control inside the national territory, with international interrelations through the influence exerted on the final publications. These publications can derive from conferences, proceedings, journals, books, etc. Everything that escapes the control of the pressure groups must be destroyed. One of the sentences that rule those pressure groups is "Your enemy is my friend" and/or "They quarrel with everybody". The techniques used are variegated. Some brief examples are:

- The Trojan Horse: inclusion in the scientific committees of people who do not participate, promote, etc., the event they have joined but devote themselves to foster rumours, circulation of false messages, smearing the members of the scientific committees, etc. It is not easy to detect them since these are tasks that require months or years of observation.

- Send messages of false regrets to the members of the high scientific and/or professional level, with the purpose of causing troubles and that those members drop out of the committees.
- Duplication of the scientific committees. In Portugal, some associations belonging to the ICTs (IADIS – www.iadis.org) dedicate themselves to sending messages to the members of scientific committees of similar events so that they join their events, with which clone committees are generated. The only solution is to eliminate from the original committees the members who have been cloned.
- Agreed approval and unilateral disapproval to take part in the committees of the events ad pc members, associate chairs, etc.
- Invitation to the keynotes to participate in seminars, informal talks, etc., on the same days and places where the conferences, workshops, symposiums, etc. will take place. The consequences are that the program of the event loses credibility because the previously announced keynotes are not present.
- Inclusion of research works which will never be referenced and whose main topics are related to sex, religion, marginalization, etc.
- Sending works for their evaluation and later publication in other events or scientific publications in other events once the corrections are made.
- Emission of global messages in the specialized portals and in the social networks instead of previously using the personal or private communication channels, such as the electronic messages.
- Boycotting the participation of non-controlled events and without "G" factor of the professors, researchers, students, etc., through a retaliation system which ranges from the renewal of work contracts, scholarships, etc.
- Blocking access to universities for the celebration of congresses, symposiums, workshops, etc., even paying rent for the use of the facilities.
- Raising the levels of human distance among the participants, organizers, secretaries, etc., in view of the constant attacks received.
- Discouraging the organizers, secretaries, collaborators, etc., through constant jokes, mockeries, and false victims of actions or non-existent situations, of the potential participants, whether they are authors or not.
- Pursuing and replicating of promotional messages of calls for papers inserting similar ads, often immediately. The authors of those illicit actions are rewarded inside the group of the local and/or international Garduña, since they appear in the scientific committees. Some examples are the cycles of events under the following acronyms: Interacción (AIPO, Spain), AVI (Polytechnic of Milan, Italy), etc. A study in depth of such delinquent actions can be checked in the following website: www.pirateando.net.
- Disapproving the sponsorships, partnerships, etc., that are non-profit, such as those coming from association such as ALAIPO (www.alaipo.net) and AinCI (www.ainci.net), slandering and offending the members of the committee because theoretically they do not belong 100% to the HCI sector. This behaviour denotes the presence of the Garduña factor as can be seen in the Fig. 7.

This "neutral" evaluator from ACM SIGCHI, appears as a committee member for Interaction South America (ISA 2015), Córdoba, Argentina (November 18–21, 2015),

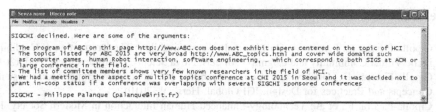

Fig. 7. Who disapproves the sponsoring of the international association ACM (SIGCHI) belongs to the aeronautic sector [9] but evidently he has received the order of the pressure group that appears in the organization of AIPO - INTERACCION 2015, ISA 2015, etc.

carrying out a similar international event in the same place and on the same days: 6th International Conference on ADNTIIC 2015, Córdoba, Argentina (November 18–20, 2015). Illegally, counteracting another that is carried out every year in the same city and on the same dates. Besides, it is not feasible that the ACM association grants two sponsorships when there are so many coincidences. This is an example of Garduña in the HCI sector, immune to the scientific community and which in its multiple destructive activities is also related to the disabled [8].

4 Conclusions

In the research work have been established the first contextual interrelations of the studies carried out under the notion of HCI with children, older and disabled in the south of Europe, and with links in the American continent. Besides, a new strategy has been used of telling factual realities through the use of sentences, which have been compiled through the direct and indirect observation in the works indexed in the online databases. Simultaneously, the current role of the women who are involved, belonging or not to the fields of the ICTs and HCI. The role of women has been verified in the current study. Although the role of the European female workers in the companies specialized in information technology, telecommunications, electronics, robotics, among others, does not go beyond 30%, exceptionally, their power of influence and decision in the field of the HCI such as: establishing the lines of research to be followed, the granting of financial aid, the signing of agreements between centres of higher education, is currently superior to masculine clout. Especially, when they have the possibility of developing R&D, teaching activities, etc., part-time or temporarily hired. Besides, it is easy to see how they switch from hypertext to children with autism, from web engineering to robotics, from museums to HCI, etc. A first hexagon with real and verifiable examples has been presented to be considered attentively, at the moment of studying the triad of children, older and disabled. The current hexagon will be transformed into a dodecagon in future research works, becoming a guide for students, professors, researchers, experts in ICTs, designers of interactive systems, etc. Finally, through the description of the analyzed real cases, it has been demonstrated how the G factor distorts the domains of natural study belonging to the whole of the HCI and all the elements that make it up.

References

1. Cipolla-Ficarra, F.: Persuasion On-Line and Communicability: The Destruction of Credibility in the Virtual Community and Cognitive Models. Nova Science Publishers, New York (2010)
2. Cipolla-Ficarra, F.: Quality and Communicability for Interactive Hypermedia Systems: Concepts and Practices for Design. IGI Global, Hershey (2010)
3. Cipolla-Ficarra, F., et al.: Technology-Enhanced Human Interaction in Modern Society. IGI Global, Hershey (2017)
4. Yingsaeree, C., Treleaven, P., Nuti, G.: Computacional finance. IEEE Comput. **43**(12), 37–43 (2010)
5. Quan-Haase, A.: Technology and Society: Social Networks, Power, and Inequality. Oxford University Press, Oxford (2016)
6. Forno, M.: Fascismo e Informazione. Edizioni dell'Orso, Alessandria (2003). In Italian
7. Kruchten, P., Nord, R., Ozkaya, I.: Technical debt: from metaphor to theory and practice. IEEE Softw. **29**(6), 18–21 (2012)
8. Cipolla-Ficarra, F., et al.: Web Attacks, Security Computer Science and Parochialism of the Cyber Destructors: Concepts and Analysis from Informatics and Social Sciences. Blue Herons Editions, Bergamo (2015)
9. Hamon, A., Palanque, P., Cronel, M.: Dependable multi-touch interactions in safety critical industrial contexts: Application to aeronautics. In: Proceedings of the 13th IEEE International Conference on Industrial Informatics, pp. 980–987 (2015)

Focus on New Technologies, Editorial and Business Publishing for International User

Francisco V. Cipolla Ficarra[1,2(✉)], Alejandra Quiroga[3(✉)],
and Maria V. Ficarra[2]

[1] HCI Lab. – F&F Multimedia Communic@tions Corp.,
ALAIPO: Asociación Latina de Interacción Persona-Ordenador,
c/Angel Baixeras, 5 – AP 1638, 08080 Barcelona, Spain
{ficarra, info}@alaipo.com
[2] HCI Lab. – F&F Multimedia Communic@tions Corp.,
AINCI: Asociación Internacional de la Comunicación Interactiva,
Via Tabajani, 1, S. 15 – CP 7, 24121 Bergamo, Italy
[3] Universidad Nacional de La Pampa, Santa Rosa, Argentina
alejandra.quiroga.unlp@gmail.com

Abstract. We present the first results of a heuristic-diachronical evaluation in the sector of the scientific publications related to human-computer interaction and computer science, tending to distort the main goals of the formal and factual sciences and the social communication in the scientific context of the new millennium. We also present the human-social factors and the strategies used to increase the gap between the sciences, the mercantilism and scientific elitism. Finally, a first vademecum has been generated of the components that must be considered at the moment of choosing a publisher and/or interrelating with an editor of scientific information in the context of the new technologies, computer science, human-computer interaction and all its derivations (i.e., big data, semantic web, artificial intelligence, web of things, web composition and mashup, etc.) in the next decades.

Keywords: HCI · ICT · Human factors · Editorial · Publishing
Mercantilism · User · Evaluation

1 Introduction

The last decade of the 20th century has brought a revolution in the publishing sector, switching from the analogical support (paper) to the digital support (off-line and on-line). During that timeframe, the publishers have had to adapt their manual work to the use of computers, resorting to compact discs (CDs) as a means of information storage. It is in the use of this new device where the intersection between the masters of the graphic arts of the paper support with a long experience in typography, use of colours, advertising, etc., and the computer science and electronics experts is generated.

In other words, the CD signaled the start of that revolution where for the umpteenth time it was proven: "The hardware is always ahead of the software." It was at the time when there was a switch from hypertext to multimedia and hypermedia, across the

© Springer International Publishing AG, part of Springer Nature 2018
M. Antona and C. Stephanidis (Eds.): UAHCI 2018, LNCS 10908, pp. 463–474, 2018.
https://doi.org/10.1007/978-3-319-92052-8_36

different supports of off-line digital information, that the CD-ROM (Compact Disc – Read-Only Memory) became the most widespread, i.e., homes, universities, industries, etc. however, already at that time, wild mercantilism existed in the computer science teaching environment [1]. That social factor made that in the European context the term "multimedia" was often mistakenly linked to CD-ROM. From its origins not all the interactive multimedia has the CD-ROM [1] as support. Annex #1 presents a short technological-historical description of the CD-ROM with relation to other information supports in the first half of the 1990s.

The different formats and devices in which analogical information could be stored (drawings, graphics, maps, etc.) in digital format, for example through the use of scanners, generated a split between the professional technicians/engineers (computer science experts in the Iberian Peninsula and electronics in Italy) and the creators (graphic arts). It is important to stress that the graphic arts are not a synonym of the fine arts. Although the latter have also participated in the production processes of the off-line interactive systems in the 90s, they erroneously, replaced the traditional masters of the graphic arts with those who only devote themselves to video, bringing about a destruction of originality and/or creativity, and a promotion of plagiarism in Spain and Portugal.

This split would persist across time and entail having a large team of workers in the same physical space but separated from each other, making the first interactive multimedia systems in CD-ROM support aimed at education, culture, medicine, cartography, entertainment, etc.

2   Editorial Work, Digitalization and Interactive Systems

Novel interactive systems, where the static media (texts, pictures, sketches, etc.) dominated over the dynamic ones (audio, video, 3D animation, etc.) were mostly shipped on CD-ROM. The access speed influences the quality of synchronicity of audio and images of the animation and/or video. This is one of the reasons why the display of the first contents of dynamic media (1995) only took a small space on the screen.

In this digitalization process of the information, the graphic arts sector had to be updated quickly in view of the momentum of the multimedia systems, not only in the transfer of analog data to the digital ones for printing, but also for interactive audio-visual experiences. That is, computer science had to be included in the production process, and simultaneously, orient creativity towards the audio-visual. This phenomenon brought about within the creative process of typography, for instance, the need to learn the use of computers and their matching commercial applications to generate images in 2D and 3D, such as Photoshop, Corel Draw, AutoCAD, 3D Studio Max, Macromedia Director, etc. In that context, usability engineering [2] has been very important, especially for the use of those applications, for users with scarce or no knowledge in computer science.

However, not all the members of the graphic arts, with or without college education, but with decades of working experience, went over quickly to the computer science context. These changes entailed costs in the purchase of software, hardware, training of the staff, work space, etc. which had to be covered 100% by the small graphic arts entrepreneurs. Costs that were shortly remarkably reduced with the democratization of the Internet (1995–2000), which allowed the long distance work of the designers, illustrators, writers, etc.; the adaptation of the design in 2D and 3D for the group work online; the rise of free software; the reduction of costs of the components of the multimedia hardware: audio cards, memories, storage units for the digital information among other peripherals (input and/or output devices), etc.

Other specialists of the graphic arts, in contrast, resisted for years to the use of computers and kept on working on paper, until they adapted to the digital demands of the market or decided to change their working activity, thus losing an incalculable human capital of experiences and knowledge in the domain of the graphic arts. Here is one of the reasons why in our days there are myriads of containers of multimedia information in different mobile and interactive communication supports, which go from the iPhone to the PCs tablets, but they lack the contents, like those that were carried out in the analog support, where creativity and originality were the common denominators, especially in the educational and scientific fields, stemming from the sector of the analog graphic arts.

3 Authentic Publisher Versus Mercantilist and Unqualified Editor

One of the goals of the 90s was to turn every computer user into an editor of multimedia content. In that sense, and within the evolution process of the hardware of the personal computers, in the decade of the 90s, they incorporated graphics accelerator cards, outputs for speakers, microphones, CD-ROM/DVD readers, etc. From that moment on, the user had access to the multimedia/hypermedia interactive communication. The computer market opened to the demand for interactive multimedia products, such as encyclopedias, commercial catalogues, touristic information, videogames, etc. That rise in demand entailed generating a new kind of professionals, where an intersection between the formal and the factual sciences would be generated. That novel professional profile was the result of quality attributes, metrics, techniques and evaluation methods of interactive multimedia, etc., which allowed to set down the theoretical bases and which opened a new stage in the evolution of the software, toward quality in interactive communication or the era of communicability. In this regard the interested reader can look up the following bibliographical references to know the genesis of this new professional era in the sector of the quality assessment of software, interaction and design, interactive systems and human-computer interaction.

This new professional field represented a balance between the formal and factual sciences, and allowed to confirm the premise enunciated by Landow [3], that user left its passive role in the communication process and went on to generate/edit multimedia contents. In that process, the knowledge and/or experiences that editors had to gather started from the principles of the traditional graphic arts, on to computer science, passing through social communication. In the latter it went from literature, sociology, psychology, cultural systems all the way to logical programming and the epistemology of the sciences, to mention just a few examples. However, over time, in the new millennium, it is easy to see how the ideal of a balanced profile has been eliminated in the context of the editorial management skills; improving authors satisfaction; indexing, marketing and production for scientific editions, operational supervision of conference proceedings; development of the data publishing workflows; etc., into data and software publishing; MOOCs (Massive Open Online Courses); computer sciences, HCI (Human-Computer Interaction) and all its derivations, etc.

The wild mercantilism in the educational and scientific context of the computer sciences, HCI, ICTs, (Information and Communication Technologies), etc., publishing in the new millennium has generated new professionals within the field of the formal sciences, where the mathematicians, physicists, industrial engineers, nuclear engineers, aeronautical engineers, management engineers, etc., claim to stand at the top of the disciplines that make up HCI – that is, superior to the specialists in social communication, sociologists, designers, etc. This distortion between the sciences contradicts each one of the principles of scientific knowledge and factual sciences, such as: scientific research is specialized; scientific knowledge is clear and precise; scientific knowledge is systematic; scientific knowledge is predictive; science is analytical; science is open; science is useful; science is explanatory; etc.

This phenomenon of the wild mercantilism in the European Union has been one of the consequences of the reform of the university educational system in the new millennium where the macro statistic factor has prevailed. For instance, the total number of graduates, engineers, PhDs, etc., from each one of the member states; the migratory movements within the euro zone of the different graduates, etc. That is, there was a need to quickly increase the number of college graduates, irrespective of the compatibility of the studies carried out, and then their future workplace. It is a phenomenon of wild quantification to the detriment of the local and global society. Two examples analized of those adulterations in the education and with its consequences in the progress of the sciences for the common good of the global village. The first example is to be found in Barcelona (Spain) and the second one in Trento (Italy).

In Barcelona a public university education antimodel, called: "Meteoric System in University Degrees" (MSUD) [4], was created to obtain college degrees, bachelor's degrees, masters, doctorates. The model was situated between the formal and factual sciences and allowed its graduates to get high positions in private companies (see Annex 1#). The Department of Information, Engineering and Computer Science – University of Trento, for instance, allows that the ex-URSS students, without knowledge of the Italian language, earn the places for the realization of doctorates and post-doctorates in an European record time: Six years between the university of Trento and the Bruno Kessler Foundation (the top directors of both institutions are husband and wife), and simultaneously, directing European projects, overseeing theses, teaching subjects, etc. That is, the Italian and Belarussian version of MSUD.

The converging points of both cases are: The alleged belonging of those university training centres to the national network of excellence; the overblown narcissism in the social networking; the zero credibility of the contents of their CVs (since not even the best robot could develop so many activities simultaneously); the interest towards the publishing sector, in order to exploit from the personal and private commercial point of view, leaving aside the sciences; the desire to destroy all that which escapes their control; the need to access and manipulate the contents of the traditional communication media, mainly the specialized press, educational television, etc., oriented toward the new technologies, since they are sources of additional financial resources, personal promotion, etc.

Clearly, those educational centres do not respect the constitutional rules of the state where they are located, such as the minimum knowledge of the official language to access the places of the university students of the third cycle as well as getting a university degree, for instance. Apparently, these factors are not considered at the moment of establishing the ranking of the universities, where many centennial athenaeums, which have Nobel Prizes among their members, occupy lower places to those recently opened.

Besides, we have the negative aspect of the activities of editors of online contents, since in both cases they enhance the scientific decay in the 21st century, such as the attacks on international websites. [5] That is to say, those graduates of the Meteoric System in University Degrees, instead of communicating through the private channels (email, fax, phone, etc.) as in the case of the employees in the German publishing house (Springer, computer science area), who in the summer vacations period and without any warning, issue destructive messages on websites of the international computer science community to eliminate the groups of scientists which, without any subsidies, devote themselves to the dissemination of the sciences through symposiums. workshops, conferences, etc., for decades. Obviously, the main goal of that destructive behavior is to gain quick visibility and free publicity in the social networks, both by that who commits the vandalic act (who is immune to the current European legal system), as those who support him/her. That is to say, the tiny university community where they give out college degrees, and who allegedly belong to the educational excellence of the Old World.

Although those facts are of public knowledge, the international community of computer science and human-computer interaction professionals, for instance, accepts that kind of behaviour, thus granting immunity to those who violate the freedom and the dignity of the local, regional, national and international scientific community. Historically, HCI is helpless to generate reactions in view of a degradation of the quality of R&D (research and development), education, transfer of knowledge, etc., which are daily subdued by certain groups, anonymous or not. These negative examples, which belong to the domain of the human and social factors, in the context of the ICTs, not only have distorted the role of the scientific editor, but it also threatens the future of the freedom of access to the online information, whether it is multimedia or not.

4   Database Indexes, Queries and Business

One of the biggest current businesses of the publishing houses in the sector of the sciences is the indexation of proceedings, journals, magazines, books, etc., in the private, public and hybrid databases. That is to say, big data, web engineering, artificial intelligence, security, hardware, etc. [6–12]. Many of the public databases work on the servers of the European universities, for example, and they are maintained by the direct and indirect taxes which are daily paid by all the citizens of those European communities. In some areas of the industrial sector, the top heads of the offices of computer services dedicate themselves to make listings for the marketing department, sales, general management, etc., through the queries. In other words, they work with the logical programming and some applications such as: Access, Excel, etc., to print or display on the computer screen the results obtained from the information stored in the database. These operations have been going on for five decades, throughout the last century.

The Internet and social networks have opened a new market to try to exert their influence on the final user in the purchase of goods and services. Certainly, the indexing services of scientific information are not excluded from such reality. Simultaneously, we find ourselves confronted with the fact that the university reforms of the new millennium in the EU oblige professors, researchers, etc. to a minimal yearly production to meet a series of final requisites, among them the indexation in academic databases in the formal and factual sciences. However, this action in computer science entails several rhetorical questions: Who controls those in charge for indexing? Is the training of the controllers serious? What is the manifest behaviour in the social networking of those individuals? What is the cost of the publications per indexed pages? Is all the scientific knowledge of the 20th and 21st centuries indexed? Is indexation synonymous with quality and originality of the content? Is the freedom of the sciences in danger? Who evaluates the editorial evaluators? Does indexation eliminate the power groups in the academic context? What is the influence of the Meteoric System in University Degrees on publishing houses? What to do if one receives attacks from the members of the editorial team? How can one prevent and legally protect oneself from the cyber destroyers in the context of the scientific editions? All these questions show the existence of a new business in the context of the web engineering, foundational models for big data, mashup quality assessment, smart cities, users with special needs, aimed at scientific publications.

5   Towards to a First Vademecum

We are facing a phenomenon that grows exponentially and for which there is no legal protection and where the law of silence prevails [13]. Given such reality, it is necessary to take into account the following considerations which make up a kind of first vademecum:

1. Analyze the CVs of those who are included by the publishing companies as heads of the collections, especially in the computer science context, and the ICTs, when higher education is carried out in the same college centre or organizations or foundations related with each other. Usually, they musn't be carried out within the same educational structure, the training in masters, doctorates, and post doctorates, since that shows the presence of a Meteoric System in University degrees. The training trajectory should be carried out in other centres to enrich and increase the different points of view about the topics on which the training of the future professionals are focused.

2. Investigate the working experience of the publisher in graphic arts. If the previous experience in the sector of journals, newspapers, radio, tv, web, etc. is equal to zero, then that function of publisher lacks any representative value in the editorial context.
3. Examine the members of the scientific committee, steering committee, PC members, chairs, associate chairs, etc. If these members are repeated over time, in various conferences, workshops, etc. whether it is directly or indirectly, that is to say, they are also the authors and/or co-authors who submit works in said events, that means that the editorial control is equal to zero. Such is the case of the proceedings of 17th International Conference on Web Engineering 2017 (ICWE 2017) Rome (Italy), and the 1st International Workshop on Hypermedia Design (IWHD 1995) Montpellier (France). This is one of so many examples of academic inbreeding which contradicts the main principles of the epistemology of the sciences.
4. Avoid establishing work links or sign studies agreements, research agreements, etc., with those publishing companies where the managerial staff uses the universities as bodies to get financial subsidies through R&D virtual projects, free labs for their experiments, obtainment of labour at zero cost, under the precarious contracts of interns, apprentices, continuous training, etc.; increasing the personal lists of scientific publications in the indexed databases; algorithms and systems for big data search, software applications, solutions for the management of the computer systems, etc., with a cost equal to zero and indoctrinate the future professionals in the field of HCI, big data as a service, UX (user experience), interfaces, etc., to carry out cyberattacks, camouflaged or not.
5. Investigate if there is a tendency to unlimited expansion of pseudo scientific editors through dynamic persuasion to exert a dominion of contents of the scientific databases. Some of the strategies used by the editorialist persuader is the relationship with digital libraries or not; associations, organizations, foundations, etc., those in charge of the indexation and distribution of the articles published in the form of proceedings, journals, books, etc.; professors, university students, researchers, etc., who are carrying out masters and/or doctorates with topics related to online databases, algorithms for indexation, cloud computing for the semantic web, guardianship of the copyright, etc.

Since the late 20th century, the limits of the field of HCI are constantly enlarged with variegated professionals who do not belong to this field of scientific knowledge. One of the direct consequences of this discipline is that quality decreases, and all of this flurry of activity only serves to increase those algorithms that establish a pseudo ranking of the alleged scientists in the computer science context, including those with the ORCID label –Open Researcher and Contributor ID (www.orcid.org).

In the same way as wild mercantilism introduced elastic boundaries in the interactive multimedia studies of the 90s, the same has happened in the field of HCI, because everything always revolves around the same individuals, who individually or as a small group of people pressure the rest of the scientific community since their academic training is not related to the HCI. Analyzing the databases of the indexation of their works it can be seen how some switch from mathematics to usability; from cultural heritage to the disabled; from robotics to the interfaces, etc. [1]. Individuals are destroying the formal and factual sciences, with a professional pattern of such behaviour, manifest or latent, which was unthinkable in the 20th century. However, they appoint themselves today as the norm of university training norm. That is to say, examples to be followed in the computer science field, HCI, machine learning, deep learning, game theory, etc., since they are legally immune in the global village in spite of the conflicts they provoke. These pseudo researcher, professors, students, etc., may belong to the formal or factual sciences or to an intersection of both.

The five premises that make up our first vademecum are the result of five years of direct and indirect observation online and each one of them is verifiable. Besides, it constitutes a first stage towards the prevention and the reestablishment of the logical and natural boundaries within the HCI, since "Not everything is HCI". Those who maintain that mistaken and machiavellian assertion only seek to boost the activity of the dynamic persuader, online [1], with the direct goal of destroying the serious scientific and academic community. Indirectly they also damage the rest of society, who finance their works, hoping that their results raise the standard of living in the global village, in the new millennium [19, 20].

6   Conclusions

This research work denotes the presence of publishing managers who do not only lack the necessary knowledge of the digital graphic arts but also the correct functioning and progress of the sciences through epistemology. There is a temporal constant in the field of research and scientific publications to speed up and slow down those areas of computer science which at certain times occupy the peak of scientific interest. For instance, the multimedia systems of the 90s, joined to the democratization of the Internet among the end-users, and the involvement of HCI in the new millennium. In both cases there is a mercantilism in the research projects, experimental production, academic teaching and the transfer service of knowledge between the universities and the business community/industry.

Therefore, it is hard to understand why a publishing company that bills millions of euros years per year, keeps an internal staff in the constant search of European subisdies. Besides, free software for their services with high costs, such as the publication of proceedings, books, etc., in analog supports (proceedings in book form, for instance) or digital (USB keys, access to the online databases, etc.) to draw attention to the quantitative factor such as the ranking of the universities, overall publications of the authors, cross-references among the different information supports such as journals, books, etc. However, the qualitative factor is not considered, so how can it be that the same authors, co-authors, chairs, pc members, etc., appear unchangeable, even if almost a quarter of a century has gone by, and those works are still stored in the same databases.

Faced with such reality, all the breakthroughs in big data are null and void, the expansion of the use of the ORCID, the realization of conferences among librarians, software developers for databases, the financers of the start-ups, librarians, scientific foundations, copyright consultants, officials from the ministries of education, research, technological innovations, publishers, etc., because there is no editorial excellence, due to the presence of the Garduña (it is a mythical secret criminal society said to have been founded in Spain in the late Middle Ages) factor or "G" Factor.

A factor that must be eradicated from the sciences, before addressing the issues related to the publications, indexation of the databases, inclusion of a digital identifier, etc., under the premise that scientific work is recognized. It is important to know beforehand what is the purpose of the data concentration of the research and who controls the controllers of the editorial context of computer science and all its derivations, starting with the HCI. Especially, when the publishers perform functions outside the editorial context before the arrival of the new era called: "Quantic-Nanotechnological-Self-Sufficient Era."

Annex #1: Multimedia Off-Line and the Compact Disk Evolution

The origins of the different kinds of CD-ROMs are to be found in the late 60 s and early 70 s with the appearance of the devices for television called laser vision or laser disc (LV) [14]. These disks allowed to store as much as 60 min of programming, but depending on the format and the running time they were broken down into:

- Thirty minutes: based on the CAC technology (Constant Angular Velocity), admitting random reading.
- 60 min: called CLV (Constant Lineal Velocity) which had a sequential reading, for which the disk turns at different speeds, being slower at the centre of the disk and faster at the edges. There was the problem of slowness in the search of information, since the shifting of the bolsters had to be syncrhonized with the speed of the disk. Random access wasn't possible.

In the mid 90s started the development of the DVD (Digital Video Disk), later called Digital Versatile Disk. The format and the physical size is identical to a CD but it has a storage capacity of 15,9 Gb. There are several models: DVD-Video for films: DVD-ROM similar to the CD-ROM but with a storage capacity of 4 Gb. The DVD would replace the CD-ROM; the DVD-RAM which allow the recording and erasing of the information, similar to hard disk [15].

The compact disk (CD-Audio) was introduced in the market in 1982. It was the result of a joint development between Sony and Philips, which, in short, were looking for some homologation rules among manufacturers of compact disks readers, which are enumerated in the "red book". One of the main rules was the approximate limit of 640 Mb as storage capacity of the CDs (around 150.000 pages of text). The reason for that size is due to the fact that at the time the director of Sony (Akio Morita) decided that a new audio support had to be designed to carry the most popular work of classical music in Japan, which at the time was Beethoven's Choral Symphony which runs for about 71–72 min, that is, approximately 640 Mb. In 1984 both firms. Sony and Phillips, present the CD-ROM reader in the "yellow book" [16]. From that year on a series of combinations and adaptations on the CD-ROM arise [17]:

- The **CD-ROM XA** (Extended Architecture are an extension of the rules of the CD-ROM and pertain to the formats of the graphic and sound data. These formats allow to establish the compatibility between CD-I (the "I" stands for interactive). Said rules were adopted by Philips, Sony and Microsoft (the main manufacturers of that product).
- The **CD-Graphics** are the CD-Audio which are made up of graphic and textual data readable in a CD-ROM or CD-I.
- In 1991 the "green book" for the **CD-I** is presented, which is an extension of the yellow book. In the green book the formats of the CD-I data and the programming languages are set.
- The **WORM** (Write Once Read Many) compact disks are for the reading and the recording of the data, which are used for making information backups.
- The **Photo-CD** is a WORM disk which was defined by Kodak and Philips. Because of the diversity of formats of the image files, the Photo-CD was adopted by the main manufacturers of the sector: Apple, Agfa, Fuji, etc.
- **Rewritable laser-read** discs (created by Sony).

Annex #2: Meteoric System in University Degrees

Once the civil servant posts were covered for the engineering degrees and the B.A., the problem arose of covering the professor posts for the masters and PhDs. For the former, in the private institutions, it was not necessary to have any title to teach seminars or mini-courses. An example of this were the masters related with multimedia engineering in Ramon Llull University, and audio-visual degree in Pompeu Fabra University (late 90s and early 21st century) where the owners of small computer animation firms or the members of the technical offices of the autonomic government (Generalitat de Cata-lunya – autonomous government of Catalonia) competed in the same themes, with the professors and collaborators of the alleged elitist universities and the educational excellence, who worked under garbage contracts.

Obviously, the direction of those masters was in charge of the local professors, inexperienced but endorsed by a strong campaign of commercial marketing in private/public/hybrid education and in continuous training, especially in the avant-garde sector of the new technologies. With regard to the PhDs, in principle, it would be more complex, but it wasn't at all for certain departments of the audio-visual, software engineering, computer engineering, and systems or maths, etc., in those educational centres generating educational antimodels. The solution consisted in breeding PhDs in a record time, two or three years, and leaving them as life-long civil servants in the same university department.

Currently, in cities such as Lleida, Girona, Bellaterra, Barcelona, Tarragona, Valencia, Vic, Palma of Majorca, etc. it suffices with comparing the time used between the attainment of the college degree and/or engineering degree and the PhD to detect this academic anomaly. Many of them got their PhDs without any international sci-entific publication or indexed in the databases of world prestige: EI Compendex,

Thomson Reuters, Scopus, IET Inspec and Dblp.Uni-Trie.de. Oddly enough, some patent in the USA of products and/or services which the potential users or experts of the ICT sector would never use because they served to widen the digital gap.

Remarkably, those were times (decade of the 90s) where the research heads got record figures in 100% subsidized European projects [4]. That is, that these PhDs had plenty economic funds to present works in the scientific congresses, workshops, etc. Exceptionally, if they did, we find articles with works of two or three pages, with over ten authors. All of them in the same sector of scientific knowledge of which they wanted the lifelong working post, once their doctoral thesis was presented.

The exception to this reality was made up by the foreign students who not only had to pay the registration fees of the courses, but also the photocopies of the scientific articles from the library, the corrections of the translations of the articles or chapters, the inscription to the scientific congresses, the trip and the stay at the moment of submitting the scientific works, etc. Of course, then those works merged in the production of the department generating European antimodels to get new European subsidies and foster the training of professionals or meteorite Catalan doctors or post-doctors such as those in the following figure (Fig. 1):

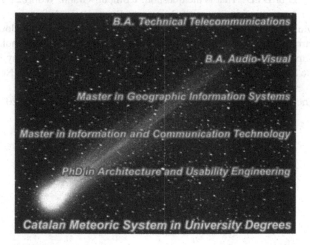

Fig. 1. The Catalan educational antimodel. The comet students obtain within one decade two degrees, two masters and a PhD, simultaneously occupying high offices in firms of the education sector, commercial, multimedia editorial, etc. These comets are only for Catalan students.

References

1. Cipolla-Ficarra, F., et al.: Technology-Enhanced Human Interaction in Modern Society. IGI Global, Hershey (2017)
2. Nielsen, J.: Usability Engineering. Academic Press, London (1993)
3. Landow, G.: Hypertext. Johns Hopkins University Press, Baltimore (1997)
4. Cipolla-Ficarra, F., et al.: New Horizons in Creative Open Software, Multimedia, Human Factors and Software Engineering. Blue Herons Editions, Bergamo (2012)

5. Cipolla-Ficarra, F.: Handbook of Research Optimizing Human-Computer Interaction With Emerging Technologies. IGI Global, Hershey (2017)
6. Cao, L.: Data science: challenges and directions. Commun. ACM **60**(8), 59–68 (2017)
7. Chua, C., Storey, V.: Bottom-up enterprise information systems: rethinking the roles of central IT departaments. Commun. ACM **60**(1), 66–72 (2017)
8. Peisert, S.: Security in high-performance computing environments. Commun. ACM **60**(9), 72–80 (2017)
9. Begel, A., Bosch, J., Storey, M.: Bridging software communities through social networking. IEEE Softw. **30**(1), 26–28 (2013)
10. Bolter, D., Engberg, M., MacIntyre, B.: Media studies, mobile augmented reality, and interaction design. Interactions **20**(1), 5–9 (2013)
11. Burger, D., Goodman, J.: Billion-transistor architectures: there and back again. IEEE Comput. **25**(2), 22–28 (2010)
12. Chen, H.: Business and market intelligence 2.0. IEEE Intell. Syst. **37**(3), 74–82 (2004)
13. Cipolla Ficarra, F.V., Ficarra, V.M., Kratky, A.: Computer graphics for students of the factual sciences. In: Cipolla-Ficarra, F., Veltman, K., Cipolla-Ficarra, M. (eds.) CCGIDIS 2011. LNCS, vol. 7545, pp. 79–93. Springer, Heidelberg (2012). https://doi.org/10.1007/978-3-642-33760-4_7
14. Leonard, L.: CD-ROM the New Papyrus. Microsoft Press, Washington (1986)
15. Glatzer, H.: CD or DVD? That is the question. Comput. Graph. World **21**(2), 57–58 (1998)
16. Touchard, J.: Le multimédia interactif. Microsoft Press, Paris (1993)
17. Botto, F.: Multimedia, CD-ROM & Compact Disc. Sigma Press, Wilmslow (1992)
18. Cipolla-Ficarra, F., et al.: Advanced Research and Trends in New Technologies, Software, Human-Computer Interaction, and Communicability. IGI Global, Hershey (2014)
19. Carr, N.: The Shallows: What the Internet is Doing to Our Brains. W. W. Norton, New York (2010)
20. Ross, A.: The Industries of the Future. Simon & Schuster, New York (2016)

Picturemarks: Changes in Mining Media and Digital Storytelling

Ole Goethe(✉)

Westerdals Oslo School of Art, Communication and Technology, Oslo, Norway
ole.goethe@westerdals.no

Abstract. *Picturemarks* is a proof-of-concept web platform that enables annotation, curation, and augmentation of works. We investigate how a mining media platform can browse a huge set of image objects along with their digital object identifiers, leading to completely new mining media and automatic bookmarking scenarios, eliminating the need of manual bookmarking and repeated searching. Our web platform is entirely real-time and is designed to work on any platforms. We present a detailed exploration in how the platform is developing media-rich, shareable stories and forming augments about them, both on individual and collective level.

Keywords: Annotation · Bookmarks · Digital object identifiers
Image search · Image browsing · Implicit bookmarking · Social bookmarking
Social media mining · Tagging · Visualization

1 Introduction

Web applications and platforms developed for image searching [1], media mining and social bookmarking [2] are rising in popularity and importance. During an information seeking process, users tend to revisit previously viewed images, data and locations, repeat searchers, and hence, they often have to memorize or manually create bookmarks for their interests. In order to facilitate the faster returns to their previous searching and views during image exploration process, the traditional bookmarks are becoming less used, leading to more novel algorithms that automatically generates image bookmarks on the basis of user interaction behavior. As per recent researches and previous ones also, implicit bookmarking mechanisms, is efficient for image and maps exploration, while their visual and interactive search [3] is quite intuitive to the users.

A traditional or manual bookmark is a saved shortcut, directing the user's browser to a particular webpage. It stores page's title, its URL and the favicon of corresponding page. Saving these bookmarks enable access to desired locations on the web. The idea of implicit bookmarking, which generates potential bookmarks on an auto basis for revisiting while the user is viewing required information, has been shown to be successfully in application domains like web browsing, image browsing, document reading, location mapping, social network analysis and data mining [4]. With automated bookmarking in these fields, media rich stories can be generated and shared across the platforms, including social media sites such as Facebook, Twitter, LinkedIn, Pinterest, Google Plus and more, giving a new dimension to social bookmarking [5].

1.1   Related Work

Previous research has explored methods for more effective and less repetitive book-marking, with different techniques for supporting re-visitation, including user-operated manual operations and automated interfaces relied on recorded interaction history [6]. Explicit bookmarks interfaces and techniques need a series of possible user actions to save interesting information. For instance, in Adobe Reader, bookmark is added to bookmarks panel, in Google Maps, users add pushpin to My Places, click "save a map" link. In terms of document reading, Bookmark Scrollbar includes user-generated bookmarks on a regular scrollbar [7]. Now these traditional explicit bookmarks are faced with three basic downsides:

- Manual marking of operations, which needs exertion of more cognitive efforts by the user
- Interrupted interaction flows
- Users must predict the sites they would be revisiting in future

These downsides have resulted in the need for new implicit bookmarking tech-niques and novel platforms. These upgrades have improvised user interfaces especially related to mining media techniques and tools as well as enhanced the efficiency of re-visitation. However, an element of truly intuitive interaction in these upgrades is still lacking [8]. These interfaces are deprived to show visiting history list, making users confused about the Back operational purpose and thus leading to their frustration due to inability to find the required item. Visited histories are usually hidden under other controls like those requiring the users to go through Recent Documents tab in the Word or a History tab given in a web browser. Current interfaces provide a higher degree of institution for showing visited history by using paths, annotations and images, yet, such tools are often limited to exploration tasks only in a discrete information scenario (Fig. 1).

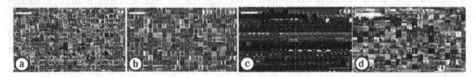

Fig. 1. Picturemarks is a proof-of-concept system that leverages the power of the crowd to annotate, share and augment works with the aim to displace more meaningful interaction and discoveries. (a) A collection of various film noir posters from the web platform Amazon.com and (b) a collection of Homeless Paintings of the Italian Renaissance imported using a JSON file provided by a museum. (c) Another collection of images related to a PhD dissertation through custom image import and (d) a collection of surfing themed images imported from the web platform Giphy.com. All of the images in this paper are unedited; showing the real-time, working prototype.

1.2   Task Model and Algorithm

The power of new algorithms for visualizing a plethora om images using implicit bookmarks for enhanced media mining and digital storytelling [9], lies in its feature to determine useful image sources users use or would like revisit in the future [10]. Here, we have included a proposed conceptual model for information seeking interactions with a large collection of images [11]. *Picturemarks* is a novel addition to the list of one of the most useful and logical sites for generating implicit bookmarks that users would re-visit. This is a bookmark in the dynamic and continuous information space that includes keyword search [12], viewport locations, zoom level, saving image collections, annotation, spotlight mode, sharing, commenting and import interfaces [13]. A re-visit is defined as the visit to the last viewport with a similar search i.e. re-doing a query. On this user interface model, our platform tends to exhibit three heuristic opportunities in mining media and digital storytelling, based on its implicit bookmarks generation:

- To develop a web platform when a user starts a new search (i.e. showing newly requested search on the web)
- Implicit bookmarking occurrence at the time user visits various places, giving an idea during multi-layered exploration. Long distance panning and zooming, saving and sharing of images
- Generation during particular pauses, which is a time that shows that the user is more interested in browsing a particular location in the image collection.

2   The Platform

Our vision for a fully developed *Picturemarks* is a platform that explores, evaluates and makes arguments about image collections and images they contain. The platform leverages the collections of images to generate digital storytelling by providing users necessary tools including item level annotations to highly detailed, repository-wide visualizations [14]. These effective tools enable users to integrate image objects with communities to which they belong, so as to enable dialogue among one another. Digital storytelling thus works here in this way (Fig. 2).

2.1   A Vast World of Visualization Tools

The platform shouldn't be taken as an online exhibition platform. It is fundamentally a system where users pursue and share collection-based images along with a digital object identifier in a nimby, intuitive and iterative manner. The users can browse through a large number of images based on implicit bookmarking by using an increasing library of visualization tools for generating dynamic data portraits of the image collections.

In addition, annotation, image tagging, image re-organizing to demonstrate juxtapositions and relationships, are also enabled to provide new curatorial practice [15]. Users can then assemble these records in images and visualizations trays for sharing

Fig. 2. The layout of the Picturemarks canvas (Source: Picturemarks official website).

and working collaboratively with the people in their social circles. The custom collection trays containing assembled records are transformed into such published spotlights that greatly help unlocking those stories and augments that are bound up in those image collections or records.

2.2   The Exemplified Affordances

- **Navigating fluidly from the macro to the micro:** For the art historian to look beyond the image object-level and the social scientist to look more intimately than the image collection-level. Linking among these macro and micro tiers.
- **Shadow collections:** Museum visitors should be able to interact with image collection pieces not in the gallery or how the pieces that are physically present network to related works.
- **Custom collections:** Being able to pull images to construct arguments and tell stories about a series of images and collections.
- **Demystifying large-scale data with visualizations:** How to make sense of and see patterns in macro-level data.
- **Enhancing the metadata:** Being able to annotate image objects in a way that can enhance and enrich the existing database, either through inherent expertise of users or crowd-based identifications and gamified task-assigning or search. Palettes of tags. Annotations beyond text i.e. with networked image objects, with audio, with video, etc.
- **Social dialogue:** Being able to interact with current users and those of the past. Having dialogues around images and collections either within groups (i.e. classes) or in a broader public sense. View an image through another classmate or a friend's "eyes" with their annotations active. Dialogue between singular image with the network of images.

- **Dynamic program of things:** Being able to create visual syllabi for programs from database entries and images—being able to assign, organize, corral, and discuss program assignments within that framework. Linking from program assignments to user contributions and curator commentary.

3 User Interface

The first step is based on finding and following the desired or favorite image collections from a popular social media platform like Pinterest, Giphy, Amazon, StackOverflow or Instagram. As an alternative, users can import the collection by using "Import your own collection" option. However, to use this option required import API, image files and/or JSON files and offsite hosting and limited amount of metadata is included (Fig. 3).

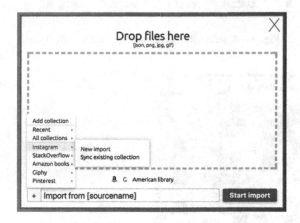

Fig. 3. A screenshot of collecting files.

In this step, the users can browse, filter, search and generate visualizations from any saved or followed image collection. Annotations, tagging and editing in metadata is also done in this step. The user can then save finalized individual images or collections of images or visualizations to his custom image collection. Categorization of saved records is also possible by using as many custom image collections as required (Fig. 4).

Once image collection(s) is explored, user can use the share function to work with members for collecting and ordering images, in real-time.

In this step, the user starts visualizing interrelationship by pulling information directly from the content in imported image collections or saving in the custom image collection (Fig. 5).

Fig. 4. A screenshot of exploring image collections.

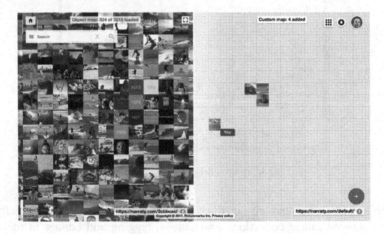

Fig. 5. A screenshot of custom image collections.

Here, the user can also publish, share and export his/her spotlights. The user is able to edit images or collections, custom them and also edit spotlights. The user can join or initiate users for sharing and collaborating on work in particular image collections (Fig. 6).

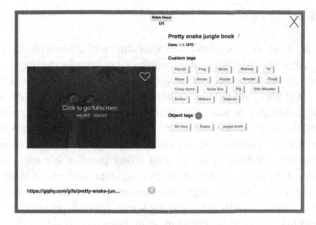

Fig. 6. A screenshot of spotlight mode.

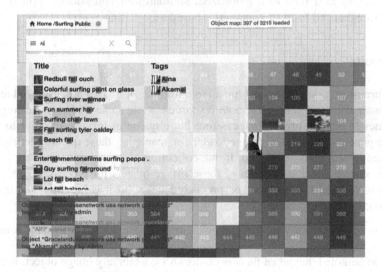

Fig. 7. A screenshot of search mode.

This step gives users two ways to search annotations and for tagging the images (Fig. 7).

- The user can create annotations on the image spotlight page straightaway, where public can choose to view annotations or hide them in the Spotlight mode.
- If annotations or tags are specific to certain groups or curators and an argument in development, tags and annotations can be made directly in the spotlight editor.

4 Evaluation

The goal of our study is to evaluate the usefulness of *Picturemarks* for supporting exploration of large sets of images with implicit bookmarks during users' every day browsing interactions. The objective of wider access to data and images is to make them available to anyone, anytime, anywhere and for justified purposes. The enormous amount of image data that is accessible publicly is likely to be related with numerous sources irrespective of the publication date, impact factor and country of production. In view of the need to enhance user's access to image data, while avoiding repeated search and revisited searching, a global data citing practice has now included digital object identifier (DOI) protocol in its eco system. Data citations in image firms means the way of giving a reference to image and relevant data in the same way as researches generally give a bibliographic reference to some printed resource. The DOI-based image bookmarking, annotation, curation, collaborative tagging [16, 17] that allow users to actively engage in knowledge creation [18]. The sharing enables exploration of huge data sets at a time in a globalized, standardized and widely applied manner, leading to enhanced form of community-based storytelling.

5 Results

In the current version of the platform, a large number of images are displayed and since the browser can load just two remote resources at the same time, a need might arise sometimes to load an urgent image before huge queue of images. In order to manage this, the platform includes an image loader for managing these queues, defined by the cursor movement onto image grid. If one collection of images is to be placed onto the grip, the system develops a series of these image objects for processing. This feature informs what image object must be processed next and it is based on the upcoming algorithm:

- It is to be checked if urgent queue holds an image and loads if value is found to be true
- It is to be noted that when this queue doesn't contain any image object, it takes the image object from queue based on the nearest distance from cursor so as to make it easier for the user to load selective images in collections

This has been developed in case the user wants to open of the images in spotlight view and not enabling the image to get loaded until the whole collection is loaded. In a more specific manner, the user puts a cursor over an image containing a specific value and sort the value in the images queue. At present, the platform also supports ascending, descending, alphabetical and chronological sorting of the image collections.

6 Discussion

Picturemarks is the platform for fast learning of image objects and management of image collection during the mining media and digital storytelling process for implicit bookmarking. It is leveraged upon the unique interface of use interaction, viewing thousands of images side by side, sorting huge collections in a faster manner, developing and sharing thematic trays of images, mapping annotations and tags based around specific areas of relevance. Users can keep saving the selected images in the custom collection mode for producing stories and social dialogue.

The platform lets users annotate and tag the images. Annotations expected to gain high public's interests, can be developed by the user on his image spotlight. This is the place where annotations are visible to public. As an option, if annotation doesn't seem interesting to the users, they can hide them in their spotlight mode. Since our system is aimed for curators and influences, it is seen that many of the uses' annotations and tags are directed towards certain groups only. Here, users can use the spotlight editor to keep the audience specific. The interface also enabled editing images, or collections of images, making them customized with edited spotlights. Tracking of all changes is available.

User starts sharing and collaborating the image collections, once initiated by the user. Specific image collections let user see history feed, updated annotations, and other updates via notifications. Commenting is also enabled for leading towards effective storytelling practices.

7 Conclusion and Future Work

In this paper we presented a proof-of-concept system for implicit bookmarking for image information-oriented tasks, where the data space is dynamic, continuous and multi-scale. The platform that explores, evaluates and makes arguments about large image collections and images they contain. The platform leverages the collections of images to generate digital storytelling by providing users necessary tools including item level annotations to highly detailed, repository-wide visualizations. These effective tools enable users to integrate image objects with communities to which they belong. The users, mostly curators and influencers, are actively seeking platforms for their web-based image searches, and they are highly satisfied with the usefulness of this implicit image bookmarking platform and its intuitive interaction and visualization, which ensures a fluid and effective image exploration practices. While we explored several points in the design space, there are many more left to be explored, for example its algorithm usability and interface improvisation. Furthermore, the system can further be adapted to higher compatibility with mobile versions in the wild. At present, the platform supports users' short-term history of searching and interests, with implicitly generating bookmarks and visualization of source-name labels. Long term-history based additional features can be worked upon in future.

Acknowledgment. I thank the contributors in our study, Frode Eika Sandnes for assistance with the paper, Jeffrey Schnapp for accompanying information, and all the Harvard MetaLAB members for their enriched discussions.

References

1. Teng, W.G., Wen, W.H., Liu, Y.C.: From experience to expertise: digesting cumulative information for informational web search. J. Inf. Sci. Eng. **28**, 161–176 (2012)
2. David, C., Haggai, R., Elad, Y.: Social bookmark weighting for search and recommendation. VLDB J. **19**, 761–775 (2010)
3. Peltonen, J., Belorustceva, K., Ruotsalo, T.: Topic-relevance map: visualization for improving search result comprehension. In: Proceedings of the 22nd International Conference on Intelligent User Interfaces, pp. 611–622. ACM (2017)
4. Vivienne, S., Burgess, J.: The remediation of the personal photograph and the politics of self-representation in digital storytelling. J. Mater. Culture **18**, 279–298 (2013)
5. Marc, B., Titia, W., Shenghui, W., Maarten, R.: A social bookmarking system to support cluster driven archival arrangement. In: Proceedings of the 5th Information Interaction in Context Symposium. ACM (2014)
6. Marek, T., Mariá, B.: Hyperlinks visualization using social bookmarking. In: Proceedings of the Nineteenth ACM Conference on Hypertext and Hypermedia. ACM (2008)
7. Zhao, J., Wigdor, D., Balakrishnan, R.: TrailMap: facilitating information seeking in a multi-scale digital map via implicit bookmarking. In: Proceedings of the SIGCHI Conference on Human Factors in Computing Systems, pp. 3009–3018. ACM (2013)
8. Kleiman, Y., Lanir, J., Danon, D., Felberbaum, Y., Cohen-Or, D.: Dynamicmaps: similarity-based browsing through a massive set of images. In: Proceedings of the 33rd Annual ACM Conference on Human Factors in Computing Systems, pp. 995–1004. ACM (2015)
9. Proctor, N.: Digital: museum as platform, curator as champion, in the age of social media. Curator Mus. J. **53**, 35–43 (2010)
10. Rossiter, M.: Garcia: digital storytelling: a new player on the narrative field. New Dir. Adult Cont. Educ. **126**, 37–48 (2010)
11. Porta, M., Ricotti, S.: Image grid display: a study on automatic scrolling presentation. Vis. Inf. **1**, 16–24 (2017)
12. Lee, K.P., Kim, H.G., Kim, H.J.: A social inverted index for social-tagging-based information retrieval. J. Inf. Sci. **38**, 313–332 (2012)
13. Faniel, I.M., Zimmerman, A.: Beyond the data deluge: a research agenda for large scale data sharing and re-use. Int. J. Dig. Curation **6**, 59 (2011)
14. Weng, L., Menczer, F.: Context visualization for social bookmark management (2012). arXiv preprint arXiv:1211.6799
15. Russo, A., Watkins, J.J.: Creative new media design: achieving representative curatorial practice using a cultural interactive experience design method. In: Edmonds, E., Gibson, R. (eds.) Interaction: Systems, Practice and Theory, 16–19 November, Sydney, Australia (2004)

16. Huang, C.L., Yeh, P.H., Lin, C.W., Wu, D.C.: Utilizing user tag-based interests in recommender systems for social resource sharing websites. Knowl. Based Syst. **56**, 86–96 (2014)
17. Xie, H., Li, Q., Mao, X., Li, X., Cai, Y., Zheng, Q.: Mining latent user community for tag-based and content-based search in social media. Comput. J. **57**, 1415–1430 (2014)
18. Aranda-Corral, G.A., Borrego-Díaz, J., Giráldez-Cru, J.: Agent-mediated shared conceptualizations in tagging services. Multimed. Tools Appl. **65**, 5–28 (2013)

Micro-internships on the Margins

Margeret Hall[1(✉)], Michelle Friend[1], and Markus Krause[2]

[1] University of Nebraska Omaha, 6001 Dodge St, Omaha, NE 68182, USA
{mahall, mefriend}@unomaha.edu
[2] Mooqita, Berkeley, CA, USA
markus@mooqita.org

Abstract. Mooqita creates, delivers, and proctors a massively open online course (MOOC) in conjunction with a regional homeless shelter and local industry for people currently experiencing homelessness. It is estimated that 25% of the homeless are working or have worked within the past quarter. Additionally, around 30% of homeless in the metro area have previously served in the armed forces. Some number of the homeless are employed or employable: still, these numbers are an indicator that the local homeless population is suffering from a basic mismatch of skills and the local labor market. Mooqita provides an ideal match because local companies face a shortage of workers, while potential employees struggle with a variety of challenges that may interfere with gaining the appropriate training and experience required by those employers. By designing the program specifically to target this population, we meet their needs for training and valuable job skills in a uniquely challenging situation. The self-paced course will concentrate on three locally in-demand technology skills. The value of this approach to learners is three-fold. Learners will learn by doing with practical, near-to-real world challenges. They will graduate from the MOOC with in-demand skillsets. Finally, tying learning outcomes to small payments incentivizes course completion while gaining financial stability. Local industry will also benefit from a stronger workforce pipeline trained to their specific needs.

Keywords: MOOC · Online education · Computer science education
Workforce development · Homelessness

1 Connecting Vulnerable Learners with Technology Jobs

More and more, communities leverage information and communication technologies (ICT) and infrastructure to empower themselves. Technology jobs support this, and are becoming ever more foundational to the modern job market [1]. However, vulnerable constituents (like the homeless) often lack access, adequate services, and institutional support to foster participation in the processes of attaining (fully) integrated communities. Homeless populations are rarely able to (re-)train for the skills they need to succeed in an increasingly science, technology, engineering, and mathematics (STEM)-driven job market. Although online education resources and tools such as MOOCs are available, some communities that could – under the right circumstances – benefit from this content are not yet connected to the tools in a meaningful way [2].

© Springer International Publishing AG, part of Springer Nature 2018
M. Antona and C. Stephanidis (Eds.): UAHCI 2018, LNCS 10908, pp. 486–495, 2018.
https://doi.org/10.1007/978-3-319-92052-8_38

Disparities in accessing and completing online education are an example of how disadvantaged people, such as those experiencing homelessness, do not benefit from the opportunities of the digital age to the same degree as better-resourced individuals. Economic, social, and educational disparities reinforce – and are reinforced by – a lack of access to and knowledge about new ICTs. In addition to the more obvious challenges of their precarious situation, those experiencing homelessness may face a lack of connectivity [3], and lack of agency in daily scheduling while they work with various social and emergency services; this contributes to an atypical resume, which is a hurdle for job applicants [4]. This situation is a byproduct of the missing social capital that comes with not being firmly rooted in a community or work environment [4–6]. This research presents a model to address that gap for individuals experiencing homelessness.

This work proposes patching this missing social capital with sustainable education in STEM skills, through a work-learn model of micro-internships [7, 8]. Participants[1] complete small real-world tasks and are paid as they learn, simultaneously supporting community connectivity and self-sufficiency. A key aspect of this model is the interaction of participants with online labor markets, and the ensuing transfer of credentials from online to offline scenarios. In our model, participants gain an in-demand skill set to bolster career prospects, and by working on real-world freelance tasks, they gain financial rewards. We hypothesize that remuneration incentivizes sustained participation [2] and decreases the time of dependency on emergency services. By connecting learning and assessments with well-known portals like UpWork and LinkedIn (which are linked), learners (re-)build credentials and digital resumes.

A fundamental research task (and indeed the purpose of the work at hand) is the operationalization of metrics that are both specific to homeless communities and generalizable to under-represented learners. Both types of metrics will be grounded in expert knowledge from community partners, data gathered from the community, and prior work in the field. Early iterations of the research will focus on qualitative research: descriptive metrics observing participants' experiences in the program and their mastery of program material, interviews with and observations of participants as they proceed through the phases of the project, and information gathered from community partners about their experiences with participants and the project, and their perceptions of the program's success. Additionally, metrics from the learning sciences will be used to gather information on attitudinal change such as increased interest and confidence in pursuing computing careers and on learning gains in the program.

This work is structure as follows: Sect. 2 illustrates the problem at hand and discusses and validates the proposed solution, the Mooqita learning platform. Section 3 describes how the program will be researched and evaluated. Section 4 addresses limitations and future research and project deliverables.

---

[1] This work uses 'participants' and 'learners' interchangeably.

2 Problem-Solution Validation

Meaningful and sustainable employment is key to creating and maintaining financial stability [9], high well-being [10], and social connectivity [11]. Unemployment, underemployment, and low wages relative to cost of living are frequent causes of homelessness [12]. At the same time, vulnerable individuals face obstacles far more substantial than the general public at finding and maintaining meaningful employment and education. Moreover, not all employment is created equal: an estimated 25% of urban homeless are currently working or have worked in the recent past.[2] ICT careers have the potential to be more remunerative than the low-income jobs that are associated with the working homeless.

Underprivileged students, those who are not already highly resourced and well-educated, rarely succeed in MOOCs and often fail to complete courses. While MOOCs have the potential to provide valuable skills and knowledge, they require a consistent effort, time investment, and access to computing resources. Further, the assignments can be theoretical and divorced from authentic practices Recent research in online courses has shown that real world tasks increase retention and resilience even if no monetary incentive is involved, and that the quality of work was comparable to expert online freelancers [7]. Connecting learners with job training and a mechanism for demonstrable skills is critical to ensure they have the tools they need for long-term stability and success.

2.1 Barriers to Meaningful Employment

There are a number of pathways an individual may follow to employment. A standard pathway to employment generally starts with the credentialing process [13]. An individual is credentialed externally (i.e., by completing a school degree or certificate) or in-house (i.e., on the job learning), and in some cases like technical training schools, that process is combined. While in some number of career paths a combination of experience and education are proxied for ability, in the knowledge sector a degree of certificate is generally a minimum requirement. These credentials vouch that an individual can be expected to have a certain set of skills (content-oriented and social skills) [1]. The individual applies these skills, sometimes paired with others, in order to maintain continuous employment. In the optimal case this combination is sufficient for maintaining employment and financial security such that monthly salary is higher than monthly expenses. This is in fact the case of many knowledge sector careers. Underemployment occurs in the cases of over qualification (credential higher than requirement for position) and involuntary part-time work when full-time is desired (credential match but not employer/employee capacities). Underemployment can generally be understood as a contributing factor to those experiencing homelessness while currently in active the labor market [14, 15].

People experiencing homelessness often struggle with (untreated) mental illnesses, substance abuse, and other life traumas that contribute to their circumstances [14, 15].

---

[2] http://www.opendoormission.org/about-us/fast-facts/.

Any individual factor is a known contributor to joblessness. Moreover, poor health outcomes and joblessness are reinforcing: when one occurs, the other supports its continuation [16]. Vulnerable constituents (e.g.: experiencing homelessness, former convicts, those with chronic health problems or disabilities) already combat various employment barriers [9]. In a competitive job market these barriers can become almost insurmountable, thus making it difficult to exit homelessness [4, 12]. Combining skill mismatch and/or low educational attainment with any of these factors is also a contributing factor to homelessness. In addition, individuals have a generally chaotic schedule while interacting with emergency or social services [12, 14], leaving many people experiencing homelessness without the ability to invest in long-term high-skill training opportunities. Such training is often time-intensive and requires a regular time commitment. The training opportunities which fit in well with a frequently-changing schedule are generally for service sector or labor-intensive jobs which tend to pay less than living wages.

The requirements to lowering barriers and increasing participation in knowledge sector work can be understood as the following:

- The materials closely match in-demand skills of (local) industry such that a pathway to sustainable employment exists.
- The learning materials are organized in a way that can flexibly meet individuals' scheduling requirements.
- The materials are broadly accessible in terms of time commitments, resources required for completion, and previous educational attainment.
- Some sort of recognized credential is granted with successful completion.

We specifically focus on creating a solution addressing these points. The learning platform hosts content on the most up to date technological skills in demand, and is extendible to match niche market demands. Other than basic personal login data for credentialing purposes, Mooqita is open to any interested learner. The content is written in such a way that the minimum requirement is basic language and computer literacy. Finally, Mooqita links with internationally recognized services like UpWork and LinkedIn to provide learners with a digital portfolio. The platform aspects which fulfill the requirements are discussed in the coming sections.

2.2   Mooqita: A Tool to Support Online Learning on a Job

We lay out a four-phase plan to support participants in overcoming the aforementioned barriers to sustainable employment. The process helps participants gain self-efficacy, learn in-demand skill sets, engage with groups, and make initial steps in building a demonstrable work portfolio. Details about the Mooqita system can be found here [17].

The participants progress is documented online that allows tracking of learning success and display work samples [17]. Based on participant's successes, Mooqita compiles a digital resume for participants highlighting and validating their abilities and achievements. This resume will ultimately be helpful in gaining job opportunities. The system also provides a peer review system to improve learning outcomes and assess the quality of individual assignments. An essential benefit of peer reviews is that students learn by providing feedback to peers [18]. Learners practicing revision skills strengthen their ability to identify and solve problems [19]. Feedback and practice are key elements in developing new skills [20] and gaining insight to better understand how one's work is perceived by others [21]. This additional practice helps learners build their resume as the solutions and reviews are persisted and evaluated.

The first phase of the course focuses on igniting participants' interest in the relevant topics while laying the foundation for learning computer science skills. Activities will provide opportunities for participants to establish self-efficacy and mastery orientation. Broadly concentrating on computational thinking skills, learners also gain the ability to analyze and problem solve in the future. In the second phase, we introduce technical skills such as the Python programming language. In the third phase, participants work on simulated real-world tasks from UpWork, such as implementing a provided design in HTML. Thus they will practice the gained skills within an online freelancing platform and with structuring a work schedule appropriate to such a platform, while continuing to learn. During these simulations, participants will be paid for their work. The specifics of the payment schemes are structured to match as closely as possible other career training or internship programs offered by our partners, to avoid providing an unfair incentive to participate.

In the last phase, participants will work independently on UpWork, receiving support from the project in finding and applying for the jobs. They can thus gain validated credentials from UpWork, improving their chances of getting future freelance jobs, and start building a resume that will be valuable in traditional job markets. Participants will also be encouraged to import their credentials to professional social networks as digital resumes; for example, LinkedIn and UpWork profiles can be linked directly.

The model is iterative, integrating feedback from our partners and learning community into necessary modifications for learning pathways. The Mooqita platform provides participants with an online environment that is able to persist and publish learning outcomes, achievements, and work experience. Every homework assignment is available in the system and participants can decide individually which assignment will be shown to employers. Together with the assignments and solutions, the system also stores peer reviews. The review process can be seen in Fig. 1.

In the current job market certain social skills are of grave importance. A core component of Mooqita is online team work. This helps participants to develop and demonstrate required social skills e.g., reliability, cooperation, or mentoring abilities. In contrast to other peer review systems Mooqita also allows to assess the quality of reviews. The system asks participants to provide feedback and ratings of reviews they received. As participants will write peer reviews for each other and rate the reviews they receive the system can aggregate indicators for these social skills. Additionally, participants perform group tasks in teams. For these group tasks the system provides an interface to collect feedback on the group experience of each participant.

2.3 Simulating Work

In the second phase, we select learning material from existing, validated online content and courseware, for example, Khan Academy for the basics, and edX and Coursera when participants are ready for more advanced training. This will allow participants to

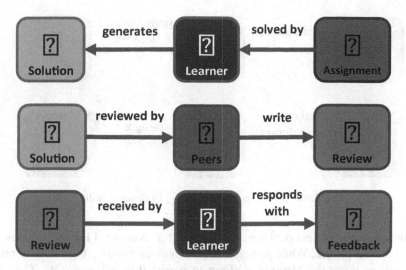

Fig. 1. Mooqita's review process

establish recognizable credentials, and will provide a known benchmark for learning outcomes. While learning relevant skills is important we want to provide a more holistic experience to participants. For that reason, we simulate the situation of online work environments. In the third phase, participants will start to work on real-world tasks on UpWork, to get practice with online freelancing, and with structuring a work schedule appropriate to such a platform.

Participants are using the Mooqita platform to post and work on tasks as described above. In the group setting participants will still provide reviews individually but submit solutions as a team. After the group assignment participants will reflect on their experience in the group assignment. They are asked to fill out a questionnaire on the platform.

Our team will identify typical freelance tasks that correspond to the course material. The team will select these tasks from online labor markets such as UpWork. Such tasks tend to be underspecified and require more detailed explanations to be useful as learning material. The onsite team will therefore provide additional information on how to solve tasks in this phase. Participants will work individually on their tasks and submit solutions to the Mooqita platform. They also provide reviews for their peers and rate the reviews they received (Fig. 2).

2.4   Linking Learning to Careers

In the last phase, participants will work on their own on UpWork, receiving support from the project in finding and applying for the jobs. They can utilize the resume they created over the course to find jobs on UpWork. They can thus gain additional experience with actual work on online labor markets, improving their chances of getting future freelance jobs, and also start building a resume that will be valuable in more traditional job markets. Participants will also be encouraged to port their

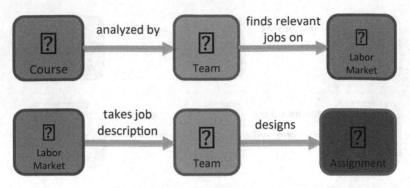

Fig. 2. Real-work tasks for learning in-demand skills

credentials to other professional social networks; for example, LinkedIn profiles can link directly to UpWork. While participants still continue building their skill set taking online courses using the Mooqita platform to persist their achievements. They also have an income through online freelance work. Participants now have the chance to transition between education and work as required.

3 Evaluation Criteria

A variety of tools will be implemented to evaluate the success of the program, particularly focusing on the challenges and progress of learners at each stage of the project. The effectiveness of each phase will be evaluated separately, collecting information from relevant stakeholders as to the effectiveness of the program and participants' mastery of the material.

Each stage will include platform-internal metrics of participants' progress through the program. In this way, time on task, success in completing in-platform activities and tasks, and overall progress and completion can be measured, as well as compared between participants in order to understand how differences in prior experience, attitudes, and demographics might impact learner success. Further, these metrics will allow revision and refinement to the curricular materials and supports. For example, if certain topics or assignments are proving challenging, extra help can be provided in the system, or the materials may be revised to address learner misconceptions and confusion. Overall success will be evaluated by participants' overall completion of the modules and phases of the program. While students do not have to perform perfectly, minimum standards of mastery will be required for program success. Metrics of learner performance on the performance task will be the greatest measures of success – are students persisting to learn the material and to what extent are they successful in learning the material? Does success or failure in some elements affect persistence and mastery of other material? For example, success at the computational thinking skill of problem decomposition is likely to positively predict success in certain programming tasks. However, success in learning one language or environment, such as HTML or

COBOL would not necessarily predict success in another such as Python. Understanding the paths and performance of learners will inform future work on the system.

Surveys will be used to assess participants' interest, confidence, and attitudes towards computing, programming, and computing careers [22]. These will be distributed at the beginning of the project, and at the completion of each phase. In this way, the impact of the activities and project can be determined. In particular, it is expected that participants will have a greater increase in positive affect following the initial phase, designed to increase their self-efficacy. As participants continue through phase two and encounter challenges in learning the material, it is expected that their positive attitudes may decrease, though perseverance and success at tasks should mediate the impact of learning challenges.

A more in-depth form of data collection will be in the form of observations and interviews with participants. In-person observation will provide information about how participants interact with each other as well as non-verbal and other information about their interaction with the learning modules. For example, as a person proceeds through the materials, they may have times when they do not appear to be actively interacting with the system. This can be for many reasons. On-topic reasons include switching to a different window out of the system to look up additional information in more depth or discussion with other participants about the work. Off-topic reasons include distractions in or out of the room such as off-task discussions with other people or off-topic web browsing. Even off-topic distractions may serve useful if, for example, they serve to create a sense of community between learners and promote greater engagement. This can be measured through observation by researchers. Interviews will focus on participants' expectations of the program and how well the program met their needs, as well as what they perceive as strengths and weaknesses and recommendations for change as well as elements of the program to keep the same. Understanding how participants experience the program, particularly what motivates them and what challenges they perceive will help inform future iterations.

In addition to participant evaluation, it is crucial to understand and evaluate the program in terms of outside stakeholders, specifically the site at which the program runs and the job-placement partners. Metrics will be collected on job placement for participants in the program – when and where they are placed and how successful they are at filling roles into which they are hired. The success metrics will be measured through post-program interviews with participants and also interviews or surveys of the job partners, to determine their impressions of the program, the qualifications of participants, and how the participants perform in the job. Surveys and interviews will also be developed and used with the service providers who host the trainings, to understand their perspective on challenges and successes, and inform future iterations of the project in how to collaborate with community partners to ensure the best outcomes for vulnerable populations.

Establishing appropriate metrics will allow the research to expand to other underserved populations. The metrics can also deliver insights into structural differences in skill development between vulnerable youth and adult learners. Understanding and contextualizing the data we collect via the platform, interviews and feedback, and job-placement tracking draws on multiple fields, including educational psychology,

HCI, and social and cognitive science, along with community expertise harvested via participatory action research.

4   Limitations and Future Work

Recent research in online courses has shown that real world tasks increase retention even if no monetary incentive is involved [2]. Those results were obtained in an uncontrolled online setting without pay. We hypothesize that with monetary incentives effects will likely be much stronger. As we gain a better understanding of possible designs and parameters for future programs, we will explore approaches to making the model cost neutral, so it can scale effectively.

References

1. Holdren, J.P., Lander, E.: Engage to Excel: Producing One Million Additional College Graduates with Degrees in Science, Technology, Engineering, and Mathematics, Washington D.C. (2010)
2. Streuer, M., Krause, M., Hall, M., Dow, S.: On-the-job learning for micro-task workers. In: HCOMP (2017)
3. Humphry, J.: The importance of circumstance: digital access and affordability for people experiencing homelessness. Aust. J. Telecommun. Digit. Econ. **2**, 1–15 (2014)
4. Shaheen, G., Rio, J.: Recognizing work as a priority in preventing or ending homelessness (2007)
5. D'Addario, S., Hiebert, D., Sherrell, K.: Restricted access: the role of social capital in mitigating absolute homelessness among immigrants and refugees in the GVRD. Refuge **24**, 107–115 (2007)
6. Bantchevska, D., Bartle-Haring, S., Dashora, P., Glebova, T., Slesnick, N.: Problem behaviors of homeless youth: a social capital perspective. J. Hum. Ecol. **23**, 285–293 (2008)
7. Chen, G., Davis, D., Krause, M., Aivaloglou, E., Hauff, C., Houben, G.-J.J.: Can learners be earners? Investigating a design to enable MOOC learners to apply their skills and earn money in an online market place. IEEE Trans. Learn. Technol. (2016)
8. Suzuki, R., Salehi, N., Lam, M.S., Marroquin, J.C., Bernstein, M.S.: Atelier: repurposing expert crowdsourcing tasks as micro-internships. In: Chi 2016 (2016)
9. Caton, C.L.M., Dominguez, B., Schanzer, B., Hasin, D.S., Shrout, P.E., Felix, A., McQuistion, H., Opler, L.A., Hsu, E.: Risk factors for long-term homelessness: findings from a longitudinal study of first-time homeless single adults. Am. J. Public Health **95**, 1753–1759 (2005)
10. Van den Broeck, A., Lens, W., De Witte, H., Van Coillie, H.: Unraveling the importance of the quantity and the quality of workers' motivation for well-being: a person-centered perspective. J. Vocat. Behav. **82**, 69–78 (2013)
11. Stiglitz, J.E., Sen, A., Fitoussi, J.-P.: Report by the commission on the measurement of economic performance and social progress. SSRN Electron. J. (2009)
12. Walsh, C.A., Lorenzetti, L., St-Denis, N., Murwisi, P., Lewis, T., Lewis, T.: Community voices: insights on social and human services from people with lived experiences of homelessness. Rev. Soc. Sci. **1**, 27–41 (2016)

13. Krause, M., Hall, M., Caton, S.: Is quality control pointless? In: IPP2016: The Platform Society (2016)
14. Shier, M.L., Jones, M.E., Graham, J.R.: Employment difficulties experienced by employed homeless people: labor market factors that contribute to and maintain homelessness. J. Poverty **16**, 27–47 (2012)
15. Morrell-Bellai, T., Goering, P., Katherine, B.: Becoming and remaining homeless: a qualitative investigation. Issues Ment. Health Nurs. **21**, 581–604 (2000)
16. Kasarda, J.D., Ting, K.F.: Joblessness and poverty in America's central cities: causes and policy prescriptions. Hous. Policy Debate **7**, 387–419 (1996)
17. Krause, M., Smeddnick, J., Schioeberg, D.: Mooqita: empowering hidden talents with a novel work-learn model. In: Proceedings of the SIGCHI Conference on Human Factors in Computing Systems, CHI 2017 (2018)
18. Patchan, M.M., Schunn, C.D.: Understanding the benefits of providing peer feedback: how students respond to peers' texts of varying quality. Instr. Sci. **43**, 591–614 (2015)
19. Patchan, M.M., Hawk, B., Stevens, C.A., Schunn, C.D.: The effects of skill diversity on commenting and revisions. Instr. Sci. **41**, 381–405 (2013)
20. Sadler, D.R.: Formative assessment and the design of instructional systems. Instr. Sci. **18**, 119–144 (1989)
21. Klemmer, S.R., Hartmann, B., Takayama, L.: How bodies matter. In: Proceedings of the 6th ACM Conference on Designing Interactive systems - DIS 2006, p. 140. ACM Press, New York (2006)
22. Friend, M.: Middle school girls' envisioned future in computing. Comput. Sci. Educ. **25**(2), 152–173 (2015)

Acquisition, Representation and Retrieval of 3D Dynamic Objects

Andreas Kratky[✉]

Interactive Media and Games Division, School of Cinematic Arts,
University of Southern California, 3470 McClintock Ave., SCI 201Q,
Los Angeles, CA 90089-2211, USA
akratky@cinema.usc.edu

Abstract. The current proliferation of 3-d representations of cultural heritage objects presents a new category of challenges for the curation and search methods used to access the growing amount spatial data-sets. Spatial data will soon be a new standard in the representation of object collections as the methods and technologies are quickly improving. The *LibraryMachine* project investigates how spatial data can be leveraged to improve the search experience and to integrate new qualities of object representation. It is tailored to the needs of Special Collections, a type of collection with particularly heterogeneous holdings ranging from books, archival documents to tangible objects and dynamic objects, making it the ideal testbed to investigate new forms of access and dissemination for cultural heritage resources. We are reporting on the first phase of a research endeavor consisting of three phases, iterating our research questions through various forms of representation and viewing frameworks including public touch-screen installations, mobile tablet and VR deployment.

Keywords: Haptic interfaces · Multi-modal interaction · Object search
3d meta-data · Virtual reality · Image-based rendering
Cultural heritage collections

1 Introduction

Thanks to digital reproduction techniques the landscape of cultural heritage preservation has changed significantly. With the efforts of mass-scanning of books and digital image reproduction the possibilities of documenting and disseminating cultural heritage resources have massively improved. In the past ten years the technologies of text and image capture have been extended to include 3-dimensional objects through 3-d scanning and photogrammetry. The recent development of scanning technology has made it possible for many museums to explore the scanning of their 3-dimensional artifact collections. What used to be an expensive and time-consuming process, requiring extensive custom-made equipment and lengthy calibration [17], is now done in an assembly-line style for mass-digitization of objects as demonstrated by the Fraunhofer Institutes Cultlab3D system [7]. The Cultlab3D system has been tested scanning sculptures from the collection of the Liebieghaus Museum in Frankfurt, Germany, and the Museum of Natural History in Berlin, Germany [11], which indicates that soon the

© Springer International Publishing AG, part of Springer Nature 2018
M. Antona and C. Stephanidis (Eds.): UAHCI 2018, LNCS 10908, pp. 496–510, 2018.
https://doi.org/10.1007/978-3-319-92052-8_39

presentation of objects with 3d data-sets will be a common way of viewing this type of resource. The technology use in cultural heritage institutions has constantly increased the surveys of the Institute for Museum and Library Services [31, 32] show. In particular museums are embracing 3d-scanning to showcase the objects they cannot put on display in their normal exhibitions [30]. Several institutes such as the Metropolitan Museum of Art in New York [24] or the British Museum in London [6] are even publicly providing printable 3d data-sets of their object suitable for 3d-printing. Interested viewers, who dispose of a 3d printer can print them for their own use at home, without having to go to the museum. Similar efforts are being made in the capture and representation of excavation sites [8, 37], monuments and in-situ artifacts such as the Million Image Database of the Institute for Digital Archaeology, which aims to preserve cultural heritage sites with a special emphasis on at-risk sites in the Middle East and North Africa [25].

The proliferation of 3d data acquisition redefines the possibilities for preserving and exhibiting objects in different frameworks beyond the classic display situation in the exhibition. It allows to formulate responses to immediate threats to cultural sites and object holdings become available to a much broader audience than cultural heritage institutions are able to show a higher percentage of their holdings even with limited exhibition space. This shift also presents a new category of challenges for the curation and search methods used to access the growing amount 3d data. Museums usually follow the traditional exhibition approach based on the "techniques and rhetorics of display." [3: 73] From the perspective of the viewers this means that they are in an explorative mindset and trust that the objects on display are curated in a way that enables them to learn a meaningful 'lesson' about the theme constituted by those objects. Similar rhetorics of display translated from the real-world display case to the online displays of virtual objects, a translation that works rather well for the museum context. But not all cultural heritage institutions function according to the principle of the curated show. In libraries, for example, the process of finding relevant objects out of a enormous pool of holdings is solely the responsibility of the patron. Providing search tools and cataloguing techniques that enable patrons to find the resources they are interested in is a necessity, which made the development of appropriate tools a strong focus of research in the library domain. The development of search tools for libraries dates far back to pre-computational time but for mechanized search we can situate tools like Calvin Mooers' Zatocode system as early instances in an ongoing line of research [26]. The development of similar search-oriented tools developed more recently in the museum domain as object access through databases of digital object representations became more important. As an early example we can regard the effort of the French Ministry of Culture to create and link databases of museum objects and digital representations [21]. The development approaches for search tools differ in the amount of expertise and responsibility for the effectiveness of search is expected from the user. The library tools are more efficiency driven and assume a certain amount of specialized knowledge [23, 33, 36], while museum search aims to implement the explorative aspect of the viewers mindset towards the display case [13, 20, 22] acknowledging a gap in the expertise between user and curator. We can predict that in the near future both lines of research will be converging, facing similar challenges. The effort of museums to make the part of their holdings that is normally hidden in storage accessible through 3d representations will, given the extent of objects (the Smithsonian Institution states that

99% of their holdings are not on display [1]), have to rely on search tools, rather than curated exhibitions.

As both libraries and museums are increasingly using digital data representations – and in particular 3d data-sets – it is important to develop appropriate search tools that include the spatial aspect of the data in meaningful ways. In the following we present the *LibraryMachine* research project, which engages with several of the core questions relating to access and representation of spatial objects. Our effort is situated in the context of the special collections of the libraries of the University of Southern California. The *LibraryMachine* project explores the implications and possibilities of working with spatial data at the intersection between library and museum collections. Special collections generally have a wide range of different object types, ranging from books and archival documents to 3-dimensional objects, to moving, manipulable objects, which we will call *dynamic objects* in the following. In this sense they are the ideal object of study in the investigation of how spatial data can be leveraged to improve the search experience and results and integrate new qualities of object representation. Looking at the holdings of special collections we are examining the types of objects that are typical for this kind of collection and which forms of representation and search are most appropriate for them.

2   Heterogeneous Collections and Complex Object Types

Our choice to work with special collections was based on the large number of different object types they hold, providing us with a framework to investigate questions of object capture, representation and search that pertains to a wide range of cultural heritage institutions. The *LibraryMachine* works with the special collections of the University of Southern California, which contain rare books, artist books, images, audio documents, costumes, tools, stereo-slides, archaeological objects and many other objects that cannot easily be represented by one consistent form of value attribution and representation. While library holdings generally are valuable for their textual content, the way special collections items are valuable to scholars vary [28]. Rather than for their content, which may be released in revised, newer editions, rare books are often important for their marginalia, special printing or binding techniques. In these cases scholars need to examine their qualities as objects, the construction of leather hinges and metalwork, the operation of clasps, materials of treasure bindings and the texture of the pages and the writing or printing on them. Artist books may be important for their art historic value and their sculptural or dynamic properties or they may be viewed for how they embody discursive processes like a particular way of unfolding or of recombining their component parts in the process of viewing the item. Ephemera collections are interesting for the variety of materials, purposes, historic handling traces etc.; archaeological objects may be important for their shapes, surface structures etc.

The varied qualities of special collections items make them particularly interesting for humanities research, but they are currently underrepresented in the discourse about 3d-digitizing due to the wide range of challenges they present. Capture methods such as text and image scanning, optical character recognition and 3d-scanning are currently mostly administered separately and exclusive to defined object types. High quality image scanning is reserved for images, while books are treated with lower resolution high contrast scans for optical character recognition. 3-dimensional objects are mostly represented as polygon meshes with color information. Representing the varied qualities of objects like those found in special collections in representation and reference systems structured according to these rather rigid type classifications and representation techniques means that their value as a resource is often not represented and therefore not accessible to patrons and users. While the established techniques give adequate representations for many of the demands brought to cultural heritage objects by researchers and specialists they leave a whole range of questions that can also be asked of these objects uncovered.

In the special collection context this problem comes to the foreground for two reasons. The heterogeneous holdings that largely go across all of the different forms of representations intensify the fact that objects cannot satisfactorily be classified into groups of those objects that are represented through high-quality image scans, those that are 3d-scanned and those that are going through optical character recognition, without omitting some of their aspects that may be important for certain researchers. Just like the special collections holdings, the field of the humanities has a very heterogeneous range of methodologies and inquiries that can be effectively supported by reshaping the established forms of representation and classification. The other reason is that special collections have to solely rely on search tools in order to make their holdings discoverable and accessible. Items do not circulate due to safety and security measures and while other object collections can showcase their objects in exhibitions, special collections are normally hidden in vaults.

In preparation of the *LibraryMachine* project surveys have been administered post-instruction and at the occasion of special outreach events at the University of Southern California and they indicate that patrons engage quickly with the collection objects once they encounter them and are impressed by their qualities such as age, aesthetic value and rarity. But most patrons are not aware of the special collections holdings and would not seek to find them. This is due to the fact that the objects are locked up in the vault, but it also has to do with the way they are currently referenced in the general catalogue. From the text entries in the database it is very hard to evaluate if an object has potential value for a specific research question if the patron is not already familiar with the object. For images and archival documents, the digitizing efforts have helped to increase accessibility even though search still has to rely on text entry and keywords. The one-sided accessibility of the digitized items isolates them from the rest of the collection and puts them into the separate group of digital collections.

The *LibraryMachine* project aims to create a comprehensive search experience across all aspects of the heterogeneous collections through a search interface that allows the user to move fluidly between different object types and forms of representation. The project tackles the problems of search on three different levels: (a) It formulates new methods of item representation that cross the boundaries between the currently established methods and add support for dynamic objects and better rendering of surface and detail characteristics. (b) It develops methods of object capture that can extract information about object properties serving as meta-data. And (c) it creates a new search interface that integrates all types and representations forms of objects and realizes an interaction pattern that caters to the spatial and tactile qualities of objects acquired with the new methods of 3d-scanning.

3   Modes of Representation, Image-Based Rendering

Based on the analysis of different object types in special collections we have determined several capture methods that deliver the specific qualities of a rather wide range of objects. In the current first stage of the project we have realized two main form of image-based rendering representations which we will discuss in the following. As the main component of the *LibraryMachine* project is to develop a search infrastructure that allows patrons of the collections to more efficiently locate the resources they need, our focus is on how to support their efforts through effective object descriptions and representations. We are not aiming to replace the objects, rather to communicate their core qualities in the search interface to enable the patron to evaluate whether an object is worthwhile paging and investigating in original. Making query evaluation more efficient in this way reduces the strain on the resources items because they do not need to be paged in order to determine their value for a certain research question, it makes the search experience for the user more efficient and satisfactory and alleviates the burden on the collection staff who do not have to retrieve and file objects that upon retrieval turned out not to have the expected qualities.

Despite the focus on search our digitizing efforts are designed such that they can support other cultural heritage applications such as curation, display and remote investigation of specific resources. For curation and exhibition purposes it is often desirable to have high quality data at hand which – within limits – exhaustive account of certain aspects of cultural heritage resources to support exhibitions in digital format online or in other digitally mediated contexts. In particular if we understand the task of digital curation in the sense that has developed in the increasing interdisciplinary collaboration between the sciences and humanities, as a discipline that plays an active role in the creation of interdisciplinary thematic collections, new interpretations, theoretical frameworks, and knowledge [29: 11], we need to support not only the selection and preservation of cultural heritage resources, but also their development and valorization as well as the technical means of interpretation and representation. The development of search methods and new forms of representation becomes an interpretive and curatorial act of knowledge creation. In a similar sense, the creation of high quality forms of object representation is of great value to support remote investigation of cultural heritage resources in cases where it is easier for researchers to remotely access and investigate an object rather than traveling to the object or making the object travel to the researcher.

To satisfy these different requirements of object representation the *LibraryMachine* uses an image-based rendering approach that allows us to integrate different forms of object representation tailored to various objects originating from a standard set of images taken of the objects. For the current phase of the *LibraryMachine* we captured objects with cinema cameras with a resolution of 4K and a dynamic range of 12 stops in uncompressed RAW format in two different set-ups. From these image sets we derived several types of representation as shown in the capture matrix in Table 1.

Table 1. Capture matrix for object representation

Resource type	Traditional object representation	Integrated representation approach
2-dimensional resource	High quality image scan (2d-scan)	High quality image capture
3-dimensional resource	Shape representation as polygon mesh (3d-scan)	Image-based rendering
Content data extraction	Optical character recognition (OCR); meta-data annotation	Image analysis, meta-data annotation
Dynamic objects	–	Stop-motion and manipulation sequences

The established representation methods make a strong separation between high-quality 2d image capture (2d-scan), polygon mesh representations (3d-scan) and content data extraction either through manual meta-data annotation or through OCR. The input data for these three types of representation differ substantially and require very different production pipelines. The *LibraryMachine* uses an integrated pipeline based on 4K images, which are the basis for four different methods of representation. The 4K-based approach delivers an image quality that satisfies most requirements for 2d representations in search and general display purposes, nevertheless, it can be assumed that the image quality of cinema cameras will soon be increasing (8K and 15 stops of dynamic range already exist, albeit in a comparatively high price range) to deliver better, nearly archive quality representations. 4K resolution is also enough for most optical character recognition tasks.

4 Near-Field Capture

The same 4K images produced in a sequence that surrounds an object in a full 360° circle is used to generate a 3-dimensional representation of spatial objects. We are using a 3d capture method that has been developed by the MxR lab at the University of Southern California, employing a simplified image-based light-field rendering technique of spatial images [5]. The technology is based on the light-field rendering method developed by Levoy and Hanrahan [18] but introduces several simplifications that make the process work efficiently within our pipeline for cultural heritage object representation. The light field rendering method replaces the polygon mesh data as the basis for the computation of visual representations of 3d object with images computed from arrays of light field samples captured with a digital cinema camera. Based on the samples of light-ray flow patterns images corresponding to variable viewpoints can be calculated, that show correct perspective and surface qualities of the object. The image-based approach results in a efficient computational model that is independent from the complexity of the object. In particular objects with complex geometry tend to produce very large datasets containing many polygons, which are dependent on high computation power and to calculate the representation. The image-based method can be deliver with high-quality representations also to systems with less graphics-computation power.

While normal light field capture requires special camera set-ups, the simplified method of the MxR lab, can be generated with a rather simple capture setup using one or more off-the-self cameras and is computationally light. The simplification uses a reduced amount of light field samples, resulting in a limitation of possible viewpoints, a drawback that is acceptable for our purpose. The method is tailored to capture objects at a close distance and deliver the full shape and surface complexity of the object. As the samples are acquired photographically, surfaces with complex reflectance patterns, sub-surface scattering can be represented in photo-realistic quality, which generally is a challenge for geometry-based representations as they have to recompute the illumination and reflectance through calculated shading. When we observe objects up close, as we would normally do when examining a collection object or a rare book all the minute details of surface and material qualities of the object play an important role and our image-based rendering technique is specializing in this near-field zone.

For the first phase of the project we captured several 360° circles of images around each object with one image at every degree step, which allows us to calculate all viewpoints close to the object on a horizontal plane. Users can zoom into the object and rotate it, necessary additional viewpoints by combining information from the different image samples. The captured data also allows us to calculate stereoscopic representations of the object for use in for example virtual reality applications, which we will explore in a later stage of the project (Fig. 1).

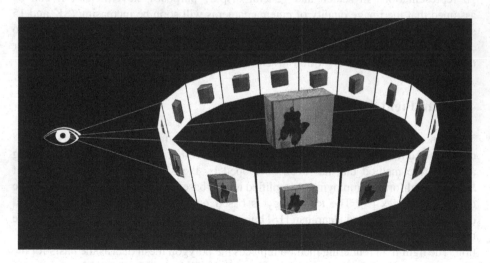

Fig. 1. Schematic of near-field image capture.

Capturing a 360° ring for each object results in a matrix of that we use to represent both the spatial as well as the dynamic qualities of an object. Each ring of images corresponds to one spatially resolved phase of a stop motion animation sequence that displays a select phases of an operation or manipulation sequence of the object. Using moving image sequences allows us to go beyond the static 2d or 3d representations employed normally.

5 Dynamic Objects

The established set of capture methods for the representation of cultural heritage objects focuses on static representations and dynamic characteristics are omitted. Dynamic objects are objects that have time-based characteristics, for example moveable parts, or objects that need to be manipulated to be perceived in their actual form and full purpose. Examples for dynamic objects are tools, enclosures, or art objects. Defining a category of dynamic objects is useful to capture objects to which the movement aspect is characteristic. The category is close to the notion of intangible cultural heritage (ICH), and extends what is considered as cultural heritage. As the UNESCO states "cultural heritage does not end at monuments and collections of objects. It also includes traditions or living expressions inherited from our ancestors and passed on to our descendants, such as oral traditions, performing arts, social practices, rituals, festive events, knowledge and practices concerning nature and the universe or the knowledge and skills to produce traditional crafts [35]." The ICH category as in this definition is very large and includes many very different forms of cultural heritage practices, looking only at the dynamic characteristics of collection objects is in this sense a very small subset, but it allows us to extend our understanding of cultural heritage resources and include aspects that, even though the objects are part of a well-established workflow and collecting practice, generally omitted. Our approach is closely connected to existing workflows and thus easily integrated and tested. The rapid development of viewing frameworks for digitized cultural heritage resources promises that in the near future mobile devices or virtual reality systems may be common platforms for the engagement with CH resources, opening up new opportunities to reframe what is preserved and which aspects of objects are represented. We have designed the *LibraryMachine* project with the perspective of prototyping such platforms and to develop solid workflows and practices for the representation and preservation of CH resources.

Our current approach for the inclusion of dynamic object qualities is focused on the aspects of movement and manipulation of collection objects. The spatio-temporal representation matrix of our near-field capture technique is one of the possibilities explored in this first phase of the project (Fig. 2).

Matching the aesthetic of the near-filed representations we have developed another dynamic capture method, which, also in the style of stop motion animation, displays select characteristic states of an object including the manipulation processes connecting them. Since real stop motion animation would be too time and labor consuming, we chose to film demonstrations of the objects, in which a curator shows the handling of the object. With a similar 4K cinema camera set-up these sequences are captured and assembled as a linear stream images with several nodes of characteristic states of the object that can be examined in detail (Fig. 3).

The selection of objects to be treated in this way was guided by the how central the dynamic aspect is to a given object. One could of course consider books in general as dynamic objects since they have to be opened and the reading process is a progressive movement through the body of the book, nevertheless, we decided to keep the definition narrower and limit it for example to the items in the artist-book collections, of which many rely on a procedural unfolding and revealing to communicate their content and

Phase 1

Phase 2

Phase 3

Phase 4

Fig. 2. Schematic of near-field image capture of dynamic objects

Fig. 3. Excerpts from the unfolding of an artist book

artistic value. Artist books are a particular example for the category of dynamic objects, but many of the qualities at play in artist books equally apply to other objects. We worked in similar ways with archival objects, objects from a costume collection and others. The dynamic characteristics of many of these object types is important and a great value for scholars. Having the possibility to display these qualities in the digitized representation makes search and evaluation of the object easier and it helps the preservation by reducing the strain that is put on sometimes century-old paper hinges (Fig. 4).

Fig. 4. Excerpts from the unfolding of a "telescopic" catalogue of the "Crystal Palace" of the 1851 Great Exhibition in London

6   Automated Meta-data Extraction

In the current cataloguing practice the creation of meta-data is a time-staking and resource-intense process. Every object has to be manually classified according to established meta-data standards. Improving computer vision algorithms make it possible to explore methods for the computational extraction of meta-data for object annotation [4]. Among the properties explored are morphometric analysis, which possibly can support besides shape classification of objects for example art-historical classification in the sense Carlo Ginzburg was describing it in his essay on the evidential paradigm [12].

The *LibraryMachine* project is investigating how data-sets acquired for spatial and temporal representation of objects can be used to infer additional qualifiers for objects. Information regarding the shape, volume and surface qualities can potentially be extracted in the course of data acquisition. Even though the first phase of the *LibraryMachine* project does not present a workflow solution, several options have been explored and will continue to be investigated. In collaboration with the Institute for Creative Technologies of the University of Southern California we are exploring the use of camera-based capture of objects under illumination with spherical harmonics, allowing to acquire and calculate complex reflectance patterns of object surfaces [34]. This technique is promising in several ways because, besides opening the possibility to infer material and surface qualities of objects, it provides another form of object representation through a relighting interface (Fig. 5). Users can control the incident light of a digitized object revealing the detail structure of the surface. We have explored this option with relief objects, which are nearly flat objects but have a complex sculpted surface (see Fig. 6).

Fig. 5. Relighting interface to interactively explore the surface relief of a page of an artist-book

Fig. 6. Touch-screen interaction with the "whirlwind" representation of search results.

7   Haptic Search

As more collection items are digitized and put on display in digital frameworks accessing these objects will be done through search tools. While the exhibition of real, tangible objects allows the viewer to browse the collection and engage in serendipitous encounters and findings, in collections that make their holdings available through search interfaces this form of serendipity is difficult to establish. In particular in the library context the serendipitous search has mostly been replaced by search term driven interfaces that rely on abstract description of the desired items. The importance of serendipity for innovative and creative thinking has been highlighted basically since cataloguing and reference systems have begun to replace the real physical walk through the rows of shelves [16]. The same desire for accidental findings and surprises motivated information science pioneers like Vannevar Bush, Ted Nelson and Douglas Engelbart who aimed to foster serendipity in the computational tools the built. The importance of serendipity as a design goal in the interface design for search tools was renewed through more recent studies [9].

Nevertheless, most current search methods for collections are relying on the textual processing of meta-data. The search interfaces normally demand the entry of search terms to describe the objects of interest and an increasing move towards digitized cultural heritage holdings will introduce the same movement away from the pleasures and rewards of working with physical object collections. The *LibraryMachine* project is therefore dedicated to rethink the search approaches and to integrate the qualities of abstract search and concrete browsing into its toolset. The use of spatial and temporal object representations provides an opportunity to restore some of the associative and haptic qualities that the encounter with real objects has to the abstract search of digital resources. The salient qualities involved into the work with real tangible objects in a museum setting are the sensual concreteness of the objects and their real spatial proximity. The concrete presence of the object allows a comprehensive and conclusive grasp of the object and its qualities, which, compared to an abstract description through search terms, is more efficient and intuitive. It activates the same perceptual propensities that are at work in data visualization and are responsible for its cognitive efficiency [10: 30].

Visual perception is to a great extent supported through our haptic sense. Even if we do not touch an object prior haptic experiences allow our perception inferences about the haptic aspects of an object that is only perceived visually. The visual stimulus is associated with a certain sensory-motor action and evokes a feeling as if the haptic stimulus was perceived. This effect is referred to as pseudo-haptic sensation and is close to a form of sensory illusion [19]. The effects of pseudo-haptic sensation have been found to be effective in the execution of shape identification and interaction tasks [2]. Leveraging these pseudo-haptic effects is one of the strategies of the search interface concept of the *LibraryMachine*. The information display is predominantly visual and uses a spatial setting based on the metaphor of a library or museum building housing the objects that displayed. The spatial qualities of the display support the visual processing and pseudo-haptic clues. In addition to the visual focus we are using a large format touch screen as display device for the search interface, which allows us to implement gestural interactions with the objects. Search hits are displayed as a "whirlwind" containing the objects. The "whirlwind" can be navigated by rotating and scrolling it. In this way the user is able to 'pseudo-tangibly' interact with the objects and locate those that attract interest.

The "whirlwind" (WW) can be populated in two ways, either by entering search terms in a classical directed search, or by gradual refinement of its content. When the user approaches the screen, the WW begins to spin and pick up objects from various thematic areas. As the user approaches the WW slows down and stops once the user is at the touch screen at a distance to interact with the screen. At this stage the user can navigate the WW and refine its content. The approach phase during which the user is tracked by a Microsoft Kinect depth camera extends the interaction sequence with the interface to include full body movement. Gestures and body movement are important aspects in parsing the spatial information provided by the 3d object representations and developing a 'feeling' for the objects.

The hypothesis of the *LibraryMachine* project is that with the inclusion of spatio-temporal data we need to rethink the design and interaction strategies used to search for collection items. Similar to the research that began when large scale image scanning became available and new interface designs for image search were developed and tested. New interaction methodologies and meta-information requirements relevant to image search had to be developed [27]. This first phase of the project makes a contribution to formulating and testing methods of object representation and associated search and retrieval methods.

8 Discussion and Future Perspectives

In this article we discussed the first phase of the *LibraryMachine* project, which explores methods of 3d and dynamic object capture for cultural heritage resources. The first phase is a proof of concept implementation that developed a foundational set of techniques of capture, search and interaction. We have developed a workflow of object capture techniques and a data management and search infrastructure to handle and display the data. These techniques are in a first user testing stage now and will serve as the basis for the second phase of the project. The second phase will scale the number of represented objects to include a representative set of the USC libraries special collections that will be large enough to do real world search task assessment. In parallel we are planning to develop an immersive version of the search and display interface using a virtual reality system.

Another research vector of the second phase will be the extension of search methods of the project phase discussed in this article. People often use gestures to describe the shapes or sizes of objects. These non-verbal gestures form an important part of how we communicate, and we are often better at describing an object through gestures rather than through words. Neuroscientists regard gestures as an integrated system of language production and comprehension [15]. Investigating how gestures can be captured, analyzed and used in the search process will be an important part of creating medium-specific search approaches. The computational analysis of gestures [14] and the creation of gestural interfaces are active fields of research.

The third phase of the project will consist of a full-scale implementation of the system to support real-world user traffic in the special collections. The focus of this phase will be on the solid implementation of the methods and techniques developed in the first two phases and on the extensive capture of collection objects.

The *LibraryMachine* project is a collaboration of members of the Media Arts and Practice Division, the Interactive Media and Games Division of the School of Cinematic Arts and the Libraries of the University of Southern California.

We would like to thank the MxR lab of the University of Southern California for their support with the near-field capture technique.

References

1. About Smithsonian X 3D | Smithsonian X 3D (2016). http://3d.si.edu/about. Accessed 27 Feb 2018
2. Ban, Y., Narumi, T., Tanikawa, T., Hirose, M.: Modifying an identified position of edged shapes using pseudo-haptic effects. In: Proceedings of the 18th ACM Symposium on Virtual Reality Software and Technology, pp. 93–96. ACM (2012). https://doi.org/10.1145/2407336.2407353
3. Bennett, T.: The Birth of the Museum: History, Theory, Politics. Routledge, London, New York (1995)
4. Bevan, A., Li, X., Martinón-Torres, M., Green, S., Xia, Y., Zhao, K., Zhao, Z., Ma, S., Cao, W., Rehren, T.: Computer vision, archaeological classification and China's terracotta warriors. J. Archaeol. Sci. **49**, 249–254 (2014). https://doi.org/10.1016/j.jas.2014.05.014

5. Bolas, M., Kuruvilla, A., Chintalapudi, S., Rabelo, F., Lympouridis, V., Barron, C., Suma, E., Matamoros, C., Brous, C., Jasina, A., Zheng, Y., Jones, A., Debevec, P., Krum, D.: Creating near-field VR using stop motion characters and a touch of light-field rendering. In: ACM SIGGRAPH 2015 Posters, p. 19:1. ACM (2015). https://doi.org/10.1145/2787626. 2787640

6. The British Museum on Sketchfab - Sketchfab. https://sketchfab.com/britishmuseum. Accessed 27 July 2018

7. Cultlab3D -Welcome. http://www.cultlab3d.de/. Accessed 27 Feb 2018

8. Ducke, B., Score, D., Reeves, J.: Multiview 3D reconstruction of the archaeological site at Weymouth from image series. Comput. Graph. **35**(2), 375–382 (2011). https://doi.org/10. 1016/j.cag.2011.01.006

9. Edward Foster, A., Ellis, D.: Serendipity and its study. J. Documentation **70**(6), 1015–1038 (2014). https://doi.org/10.1108/jd-03-2014-0053

10. Few, S.: Now You See It: Simple Visualization Techniques For Quantitative Analysis. Analytics Press, Oakland (2009)

11. Fraunhofer technology thrills Frankfurt museum | Fraunhofer IGD. http://www.igd. fraunhofer.de/en/Institut/Abteilungen/CHD/AktuellesNews/Fraunhofer-technology-thrills-Frankfurt-museum. Accessed 30 Apr 2016

12. Ginzburg, C.: Clues, Myths, and the Historical Method. Johns Hopkins University Press, Baltimore (1992)

13. Green, J., Pridmore, T., Benford, S.: Exploring attractions and exhibits with interactive flashlights. Pers. Ubiquit. Comput. **18**(1), 239–251 (2014). https://doi.org/10.1007/s00779-013-0661-3 from https://doi.org/10.1007/s00779-013-0661-3

14. Holz, C., Wilson, A.: Data miming: inferring spatial object descriptions from human gesture. In: Proceedings of the SIGCHI Conference on Human Factors in Computing Systems, pp. 811–820. ACM (2011). https://doi.org/10.1145/1978942.1979060

15. Kelly, S.D., Manning, S.M., Rodak, S.: Gesture gives a hand to language and learning: perspectives from cognitive neuroscience, developmental psychology and education. Lang. Linguist. Compass **2**(4), 569–588 (2008). https://doi.org/10.1111/j.1749-818x.2008.00067.x

16. Krajewski, M.: Paper machines about cards & catalogs, 1548–1929. http://search.ebscohost. com/login.aspx?direct=true&scope=site&db=nlebk&db=nlabk&AN=414111. Accessed 30 Apr 2016

17. Levoy, M., Pulli, K., Curless, B., Rusinkiewicz, S., Koller, D., Pereira, L., Ginzton, M., Anderson, S., Davis, J., Ginsberg, J., Shade, J., Fulk, D.: The digital Michelangelo project: 3D scanning of large statues. In: Proceedings of the 27th Annual Conference on Computer Graphics and Interactive Techniques, pp. 131–144. ACM Press/Addison-Wesley Publishing Co. (2000). https://doi.org/10.1145/344779.344849

18. Levoy, M., Hanrahan, P.: Light field rendering. In: Proceedings of the 23rd Annual Conference on Computer Graphics and Interactive Techniques, pp. 31–42. ACM (1996). https://doi.org/10.1145/237170.237199

19. Lécuyer, A.: Simulating haptic feedback using vision: a survey of research and applications of pseudo-haptic feedback. Presence Teleoper. Virtual Environ. **18**(1), 39–53 (2009). https:// doi.org/10.1162/pres.18.1.39

20. Lin, Y., Ahn, J., Brusilovsky, P., He, D., Real, W.: ImageSieve: exploratory search of museum archives with named entity-based faceted browsing. In: Proceedings of the 73rd ASIS&T Annual Meeting on Navigating Streams in an Information Ecosystem - Volume 47, American Society for Information Science, pp. 38:1–38:10 (2010). http://dl.acm.org/citation. cfm?id=1920331.1920386

21. Mannoni, B.: A virtual museum. Commun. ACM **40**(9), 61–62 (1997). https://doi.org/10. 1145/260750.260772

22. Mateevitsi, V., Sfakianos, M., Lepouras, G., Vassilakis, C.: A game-engine based virtual museum authoring and presentation system. In: Proceedings of the 3rd International Conference on Digital Interactive Media in Entertainment and Arts, pp. 451–457. ACM (2008). http://doi.org/10.1145/1413634.1413714

23. McKay, D., Buchanan, G.: Boxing clever: how searchers use and adapt to a one-box library search. In: Proceedings of the 25th Australian Computer-Human Interaction Conference: Augmentation, Application, Innovation, Collaboration, pp. 497–506. ACM (2013). https://doi.org/10.1145/2541016.2541031 from https://doi.org/10.1145/2541016.2541031

24. The Metropolitan Museum of Art - Thingiverse. https://www.thingiverse.com/met/collections. Accessed 27 Feb 2018

25. Million Image Database: Goals — The Institute for Digital Archaeology. http://digitalarchaeology.org.uk/new-page/. Accessed 30 Apr 2016

26. Mooers, C.N.: Theory digital handling non-numerical information and its implications to machine economics. Zator Technical Bulletin, 48 (1950)

27. Ren, K., Sarvas, R., Ćalić, J.: Interactive search and browsing interface for large-scale visual repositories. Multimedia Tools Appl. 49(3), 513–528 (2010). https://doi.org/10.1007/s11042-009-0445-y

28. Rinaldo, K.: Evaluating the future: special collections in art libraries. Art Documentation J. Art Libr. Soc. North America 26(2), 38–47 (2007). https://doi.org/10.2307/27949468

29. Sabharwal, A.: Digital Curation in the Digital Humanities. Elsevier, Waltham (2015)

30. Smithsonian X 3D. http://3d.si.edu/. Accessed 27 Feb 2018

31. Status of Technology and Digitization in the Nation's Museums and Libraries. Institute of Museum and Library Services, Washington D.C. (2002)

32. Status of Technology and Digitization in the Nation's Museums and Libraries. Institute of Museum and Library Services, Washington D.C. (2006)

33. Toms, E.G., Bartlett, J.C.: An approach to search for the digital library. In: Proceedings of the 1st ACM/IEEE-CS Joint Conference on Digital Libraries, pp. 341–342. ACM (2001). https://doi.org/10.1145/379437.379723

34. Tunwattanapong, B., Ghosh, A., Debevec, P.: Practical image-based relighting and editing with spherical-harmonics and local lights. In: Proceedings of the European Conference on Visual Media and Production (CVMP). IEEE, Washington, D.C. (2011)

35. What is Intangible Cultural Heritage? - intangible heritage - Culture Sector - UNESCO. http://www.unesco.org/culture/ich/en/what-is-intangible-heritage-00003. Accessed 27 Feb 2018

36. Windhouwer, M.A., Schmidt, A.R., Van Zwol, R., Petkovic, M., Blok, H.E.: Flexible and scalable digital library search. In: Proceedings of the 27th VLDB Conference, Rome, Italy (2001)

37. Zollhöfer, M., Siegl, C., Vetter, M., Dreyer, B., Stamminger, M., Aybek, S., Bauer, F.: Low-cost real-time 3d reconstruction of large-scale excavation sites. J. Comput. Cult. Herit. 9(1), 2:1–2:20 (2015). https://doi.org/10.1145/2770877

Report A Barrier: Creating and Implementing a Pan-University Accessibility Reporting System

Lori Kressin[✉]

University of Virginia, Charlottesville, VA, USA
lorik@virginia.edu

Abstract. Creating an accessible environment, whether in the digital or built landscape, is a goal to which we all aspire. Getting there can be somewhat daunting and hard to envision. We certainly have guidance from the regulatory world to begin the journey towards greater inclusion and accessibility (e.g. Americans with Disabilities Act of 1990 [1], W3C Web Content Accessibility Guidelines [2], Section 508 of the Rehabilitation Act of 1972 [3]), but how to address those situations that we don't know exist? What are the pressing issues right now?

Following the lead of peer institutions and the direction given in various U.S. Department of Justice and Office of Civil Rights resolution agreements, the University of Virginia has created an online reporting mechanism involving key functional areas across the campus to address and remediate accessibility issues ranging from those with immediate solutions to long-term capital projects. Based on a distributed responsibility model and built by University of Virginia (UVA) developers, "Report A Barrier" is designed to allow anyone (university community members and guests) to report what they may consider a barrier to access.

Keywords: Accessibility · Reporting · Compliance

1 Assessing the Need and Requirements

1.1 What We Don't Know

Providing a diverse and inclusive experience for all members of the UVA community and guests has been a long-standing goal at the highest levels of the University. Because of the historic nature of our built environment, the topography of our setting, and the increased dependence on the digital world, assuring inclusion for individuals with disabilities has been challenging. A number of committees and individuals have worked diligently over the years to identify and address these barriers. However, a lack of resources combined with the lack of a reporting process or mechanism have resulted in many barriers remaining unknown or unreported.

Due to the lack of formal reporting mechanisms those issues brought to the attention of these committees or individuals were not properly tracked to assure an issue was addressed.

© Springer International Publishing AG, part of Springer Nature 2018
M. Antona and C. Stephanidis (Eds.): UAHCI 2018, LNCS 10908, pp. 511–518, 2018.
https://doi.org/10.1007/978-3-319-92052-8_40

In addition to the lack of tracking, oftentimes the wrong individual was initially notified. It sometimes took many attempts to locate the appropriate office or individual equipped to address the situation. Because of the amount of extra time and effort involved, it was not uncommon for issues to become buried in the mounting list of daily tasks, resulting in an issue being addressed after a lengthy time or not at all.

2 Recent Consent Decrees and Resolution Agreements

As we saw peer institutions enter into consent decrees and resolution agreements with regulatory agencies, UVA understood it was in our best interest to review these documents, assess the requirements presented, and determine the direction we should take.

Within the past five years, the necessity for some type of reporting or survey mechanism was either indirectly or directly stated in the documents reviewed and referenced [4–7] as well as in other agreements. In short, the tool required by the regulatory agencies needed to assist the institution in identifying barriers to access, provide tracking on the remediation of these discoveries, and offer sufficient information to deliver requisite reports.

Based on this review the decision was made to move forward with the creation of a pan-university online reporting system, addressing barriers in both the digital and built environments. Since UVA was not under review by any regulatory agency at the time, this would be a proactive approach to identifying barriers and incorporate similar to the approaches envisioned in the documents reviewed.

3 Proactive Holistic Approach

3.1 Review of Peer Institution Reporting Methods

Our first step involved a review of how our peers were addressing this challenge. Many of the websites of institutions highlighted in the EDUCAUSE document [7] were reviewed. Those institutions that did have a reporting tool in place most commonly offered a basic web-based form, linked from their disability services office page or ADA Coordinator office, with the information provided going back to a single person. These forms also tended to address only the digital environment or only the built environment. In some situations, there were two separate forms - one for each environment and each located through different web paths.

Some of the forms that focused on the built environment provided a complete list of campus facilities to choose from. In one instance the list included over 75 facilities. The person reporting the issue would then choose the location with the barrier from a dropdown list.

Those forms that were specific to the digital environment often automatically filled in the web address of the web page that was being reviewed at the time the form was activated.

Although these processes and methods of obtaining information regarding accessibility barriers would result in the identification of certain issues, auto-completion of information sometimes created more of a problem by indicating the wrong source of the issue. For instance, if we offered a dropdown list of facilities, the number of facilities needing to be listed would make the selection process untenable. If we auto-filled the location of a webpage, the issue may have actually been found in another location and the reporting page would be incorrect.

3.2 Drivers and Intention

Identification, prioritization and remediation of accessibility barriers coupled with centralization and coordination of effort were the primary drivers in moving forward the creation of the reporting tool for UVA.

It was clear that models our peers installed in their environments would not work at UVA. One of our first priorities was to identify key stakeholders who are commonly associated with accessibility issues within the University environment and enlist the support and participation of these offices and individuals.

Before moving forward, a meeting was held with University Counsel's Office, to ensure the direction and process of this initiative met with their approval, ask for suggestions and answer any questions they may have.

3.3 Identification of Key Stakeholders

To begin the process of enlisting support and participation, we met with key individuals in areas common to accessibility barriers. In addition, meetings were held with areas that provide support to persons with disabilities at UVA. These areas included:

- Parking and Transportation
- Facilities Management
- Information Technology Services
- Student Disability Access Center
- Office of the Executive Vice President and Provost
- Department of Athletics
- Intramurals and Recreational Sports
- Equal Opportunity and Civil Rights Office.

These offices were cautiously enthusiastic about the idea of a reporting structure, not knowing what the additional workload may entail. Even with the unknown factors, each agreed to participate and appointed at least two members of their staff to participate in the effort, with one of these individuals being appointed the primary contact for their office.

3.4 Distributed Responsibility Model

Outside of the Student Disability Access Center, the number of individuals whose position is fully dedicated to accessibility in some way at UVA – regardless of environment – totals two; the ADA Coordinator, who reports through the Equal Opportunity and Civil Rights Office, and the Coordinator of Academic Accessibility, who reports through the Office of the Executive Vice President and Provost. Neither of these positions have time in their workday to address issues presented through the reporting mechanism. Instead of directing all reports to one person as our peers have done, it was decided to develop a distributed responsibility model to address the issues presented.

Eight teams were created from the stakeholders group. These teams were comprised of individuals across departments and units who could best address an issue based on the barrier type selected. For instance, the team responsible for addressing classroom or instructional barriers is comprised of individuals from Facilities Management, the Office of the Provost, Information Technology Services, and the Student Disability Access Center. This team then assigns tasks to members of their units to assist in addressing the situation presented (Fig. 1).

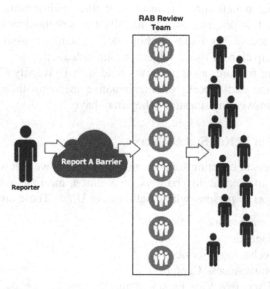

Fig. 1. The distributed model of addressing reports through the Report A Barrier tool

Even with the distributed model, one department must "own" the tool as well as the process. The Equal Opportunity and Civil Rights office provides this oversight with the ADA Coordinator serving as the administrator of the tool.

4   Implementation of the Idea

4.1   In-House Development

Review of the process by the key stakeholders and Report A Barrier (RAB) Review Teams helped define necessary steps and workflow. Development of the tool was done by the Custom Application & Consulting Services group within UVA's Information Technology Services unit using Drupal. It was important the tool's format be responsive so input could easily be accomplished with a hand-held device such as a smartphone or tablet as well as a desktop or laptop computer. Functionality was also built-in allowing for the submission of a photo when an issue is reported.

It was also important the tool be easy to find and remember. Working with Information Technology Service and UVA Communications, the URL reportabarrier. virginia.edu was obtained as well as the reportabarrier@virginia.edu email address. Simple in form and easy to remember.

4.2 Basic Structure

Processes inherent to the tool all key off of the barrier type selected by the person reporting the issue. These types of barriers are not specific to a department or unit, but as was mentioned earlier, are more of an "area of concern" from the perspective of the person making the report. The barrier types currently in use are:

- Parking & Transportation
- Physical Environment/Facilities
- Classroom/Instruction
- Online Environment
- Technology Related
- Event/Program Access
- Athletics/IMRec Facilities & Events
- Other.

Each of these barrier types has a cross-department/unit team assigned to respond, determine if the correct barrier type has been selected, and address as appropriate.

In addition to the barrier types, a series of statuses has been developed to properly track the current state as an issue is being addressed. Each status may have a time trigger attached. As an example, the "New" status must be address by the corresponding RAB Review Team within three business days. If that target is not met, a reminder email is sent to the group (Table 1).

Table 1. Explanation of RAB statuses

Status	When used
New	The default status when an issue is first submitted
Under review	When the case is first being explored
Forwarded within UVA	A case may need to be assigned to a unit outside of the RAB Review Team, but within UVA
Referred outside of UVA	When an issue is under the purview of the City of Charlottesville or other non-University governing body
In process	A solution has been determined and remediation is underway
Closed	An issue has been addressed and no further action is necessary
On hold pending further institutional action	When extended time is needed to address the issue such as a capital project or large-scale funding is needed
Reviewed and closed without resolution	It is not possible to address the situation
Case info tracked in another system	When details of the case are tracked in a departmental tracking system/database

4.3   Process

In addition to the creation of the RAB Review Teams and the series of statuses, a number of email notifications are automatically generated and other processes behind the scenes are started when an issue is first submitted. There are four components to Report A Barrier:

- Front-facing submission form
- Back-end routing and tracking processes
- Follow-up and response
- Audit and records management.

Front-Facing Submission Form. In an attempt to again keep things simple, the front-facing form has only three required fields with the remaining being optional, allowing for anonymous submission. A person must indicate their affiliation with the University (Student, Fac/Staff, or Guest), select a Type of Barrier, and enter a description of the issue in their own words. Other fields available for input are:

- Location
- Photo
- Name
- Email Address
- UVA Computing ID (for those with UVA affiliation)
- Phone Number.

Back-End Routing and Tracking Processes. When a report is submitted, a series of email notifications are sent to the person submitting the case, the RAB Review Team assigned to the barrier type, and to the oversight team. Time triggers based on status are also started.

Follow-Up and Response. All members of the RAB Review Teams have the ability to see and update any case submitted. These updates include notes that will be sent to the person submitting the report, internal notes that will be visible only to team members, and status updates. Authentication is needed to access these update screens and that access is controlled by the RAB administrator. If the person submitting the issue includes their email address, they will be notified of any updates (except for internal only updates) and status changes.

Audit and Records Management. On an annual basis, or as request by senior leadership, a review of all cases not assigned a "Closed" status is performed and appropriate action taken to move them towards closure. An annual report is created providing a narrative of the number of issues identified and the response and remediation efforts undertaken. "Closed" cases are moved out of the active database, to an archive. Archived records can still be reviewed and updated when necessary but are out of the active group of cases. According to the Virginia Public Records Act [8], "Closed" cases must be destroyed three years after last action. This is done on an annual basis following UVA records retention policies.

5 Results and Lessons Learned

5.1 Results

A soft rollout occurred January through mid-April 2016. During that time, 13 viable cases were submitted. On April 18, 2016 communications were sent to the whole of the university under the signatures of the Executive VP and COO, Executive VP and Provost, and Vice President for Student Affairs. That day alone, 68 viable reports were submitted. Looking at January through December 2016, 148 viable cases were submitted. During 2017, 46 cases and January–March 1, 2018 only 11 cases have been submitted.

These numbers tend to indicate there was a pent-up demand for a vehicle to report such issues. Over half of the issues reported are in the built environment with just under half being reported by faculty or staff members.

The decrease in submissions can be attributed somewhat to a more proactive approach being consciously implemented when projects begin – in both the built and digital environments. More likely is the need for a renewed communications plan to alert the University community of the tool's existence and how to use it.

5.2 Lessons Learned

By implementing the distributed responsibility model, greater awareness of accessibility issues in both the built and digital environments has been produced. It is not unusual to now hear our concrete sub-contractors discussing the need for curb cuts and the best way to install them. Or, listen to our digital environment developers discussing the need for captioning or alternative text during the production of a new tool. This awareness was not a planned outcome but it is certainly a welcome benefit.

Going forward, it is in our best interest to alert the University community to the availability of this tool, and other accessibility tools, at the beginning of each semester.

It is also important to keep the RAB Review Team engaged as the tool matures and processes need review. As the submission numbers have decreased over time, the hands-on involvement by team members has also decreased. It is important to keep everyone involved, learning from each other throughout the process, and build on the progress towards a more inclusive University this tool is helping us to create.

References

1. Americans with Disabilities Act. https://www.ada.gov. Accessed 19 Mar 2018
2. Web Content Accessibility Guidelines (WCAG) 2.0. https://www.w3.org/TR/WCAG20/. Accessed 19 Mar 2018
3. GSA Government-Wide Section 508 Accessibility Program. https://www.section508.gov. Accessed 19 Mar 2018
4. University of Cincinnati Resolution Agreement OCR Compliance Review #15-13-6001. https://www2.ed.gov/documents/press-releases/university-cincinnati-agreement.pdf. Accessed 19 Mar 2018

518   L. Kressin

5. Youngstown State University OCR Compliance Review #15-13-6002. https://www2.ed.gov/documents/press-releases/youngstown-state-university-agreement.pdf. Accessed 19 Mar 2018
6. University of Montana Resolution Agreement. http://www.umt.edu/accessibility/docs/AgreementResolution_March_7_2014.pdf. Accessed 19 Mar 2018
7. IT Accessibility Risk Statements and Evidence. https://library.educause.edu/~/media/files/library/2015/7/accessrisk15-pdf.pdf. Accessed 21 Mar 2018
8. Code of Virginia, Virginia Public Records Act. https://law.lis.virginia.gov/vacodepopul-arnames/virginia-public-records-act/. Accessed 21 Mar 2018

Open Participatory Democracy in the Basque Country: The Role of Open Digital Platforms in Public Budgeting and Finance

Álvaro Luna[1](✉), Xabier Barandiarán[2], and Alfonso Unceta[1]

[1] University of the Basque Country,
Ondarreta Pasealekua, 18, 20018 Donostia, Gipuzkoa, Spain
aluna@sinnergiak.org
[2] University of Deusto, Mundaiz Kalea, 50, 20012 Donostia, Gipuzkoa, Spain

Abstract. The processes of formulation, implementation and political deliberation for the correct operationalization of public administrations has transformed into a complex endeavour at a time where the idea of representative democracy is going through important changes and future challenges. The idea of public administration and governance has become increasingly decentralized and overloaded with new interactive processes which involve a greater number of political and social actors. This has given rise to new collaborative, interactive, and participatory governance strategies to create new public and social value. Moreover, this has opened the gate for the emergence of new digital platforms of participatory democracy, clearing the path for public and digital social innovation. This paper is focused on an open participatory initiative developed by the Provincial Government of Gipuzkoa in the Basque Country, to develop a digital platform Public Budgeting for the year 2018. This strategy was developed along 2017 to redefine public budgeting through agile platforms of citizen participation.

Keywords: Collaborative governance · Public budgeting · Digital platforms
Citizen participation · Public sector innovation

1 Introduction

Citizen participation in the public agenda has become key for the creation of public and social value by contributing to the legitimation of public policies, favoring social plurality and strengthening the role of the civil society. Moreover, in this particular arena of new public and collaborative governance (Torfing et al. 2012a, b; Sorensen and Torfing 2012; Osborne 2010a, b; Rhodes 1996; Kooiman 1993, 2002), public budgeting has contributed to direct participation of citizens in the decision making process of resource and public finance allocation, (Gilman 2016; Sintomer et al. 2008; Novy and Leubolt 2005; Ebdon 2002; Ebdon and Franklin 2006) by empowering them

© Springer International Publishing AG, part of Springer Nature 2018
M. Antona and C. Stephanidis (Eds.): UAHCI 2018, LNCS 10908, pp. 519–529, 2018.
https://doi.org/10.1007/978-3-319-92052-8_41

through bottom-up channels of communication to define strategic socioeconomic challenges of cities and regions.

In this context, the Provincial Government of Gipuzkoa in the Basque Country[1] has introduced a new process of public budgeting (PB) as a central pillar of its regional collaborative and good governance program. This process is framed inside the Strategic Management Plan for 2015–2019 for the province of Gipuzkoa, which is based on a new Open and Collaborative Governance Model. Consolidating an open government approach for the province of Gipuzkoa implies the generation of *trust* between citizens and public representatives providing increasing transparency and effective accountability in the allocation of public resources and design of public policies. To achieve this goal the Provincial Government implemented a participatory budgeting program open to regional citizens to co-decide on the key socioeconomic challenges of the province for public finance allocation in 2018.

This paper illustrates the context in which this strategy was developed by focusing on the analysis of its channels of participation and communication and the description of the achieved main results by following five important objectives:

- Describe how new public structures can play a major role in the creation of an innovative participatory culture which is able to scale and implement PB from a bottom-up approach.
- Analyse how the systemic employment of social and technological tools can improve citizen participation.
- Acknowledge the social priorities and social needs of citizens by attending real demands that can be included into the development of future public policies.
- Open new channels of active reflection and debate, which contribute to improve the ways in which public administrations engage with citizens.
- Describe how the process of open public budgeting through citizen participation can be approved and scaled by public representatives and technical staff.

This paper is divided into four different sections. We will first analyze the implications of collaborative governance and participatory budgeting in contemporary societies. The second section is focused on the methodological approach we have followed during this process. The third section will described the main results and reflections of the PB process leading to a concluding final section.

---

[1] The Basque Autonomous Community (CAPV) (2,173,210 inhabitants) is located in northern Spain and is divided into the Historical Territories of Bizkaia (1,141,442 inhabitants), Alava (321,777 inhabitants) and Gipuzkoa (709,991 inhabitants). Each of these territories has its own provincial government, organized around their Provincial Councils and Regional Laws, with broad powers for the administration and socio-economic and political management of each region. The Territory of Gipuzkoa, which this analysis focuses on, is a province that borders with the Southeast Basque-French region and has 11 districts and 88 municipalities.

2 Understanding Collaborative Governance and Participatory Budgeting

Collaborative governance has been institutionalized as an innovative approach for the management and design of public policies in contemporary democratic systems (Jun 2002; Kettl 2002; Klijn and Koopenjan 2016). Its articulation is based on shared motivation structures oriented to the improvement of the capacities of policy action, fostering shared knowledge and adaptation to specific political and socioeconomic challenges. The nature of this collaboration has to be sustainable over time for the effective management of different resources from a series of reciprocal protocols and institutionalized procedures. In this context, collaborative governance is defined as "the structures of public policy decision making and management that engage people constructively across the boundaries of public agencies, levels of government, and/or the public, private and civic spheres in order to carry out a public purpose that could not otherwise be accomplished" (Emerson et al. 2011:2).

Likewise, this collaboration needs to enhance leadership and responsibility of the interested parties in the process of participation in order to generate new knowledge that can be later pragmatically applied. Frequently, these collaborative processes face different difficulties when translated into specific political responses and measures, resulting in the dissolution of citizen participation into simple proposals which never get to be applied or scaled. In this respect, the methodologies and resources for participation need to be correctly defined and delimited and, therefore, they need to be publicly planned and regulated with pragmatic purposes (Jessop 1998; Ansell and Gash 2007).

The most important challenge faced by these structures of collaboration is the unbalance between the power and knowledge that is generated between the actors, agents and institutions that hold power and civil society organizations; that is to say, between the expert knowledge coming from actors and agents that are more or less institutionally legitimized (academia, political advisers, experts, etc.), and the tacit knowledge coming from citizens and the civil society. This tacit knowledge is connected to the pragmatic nature of the social and economic problems that want to be addressed and that citizens' face in their daily lives. This unbalance may have an effect in the accomplishment of real social responses because the knowledge acquired through bottom-up structures, may not be integrated in the more general public management dynamics, or may be simply lost in the process of political and policy implementation.

From this point of view, the most important value attributed to the different forms of collaborative governance is the assigned significance of participatory processes, that is, the capacity to generate structures of opportunity for participation, regardless of the benefits and obtained results inside the public consulting process. However, this collaborative and participatory process requires a deeper integration in relation to the objectives and strategies that look to be accomplished by the interested or affected parties in this relation. In the case of the participatory budgeting process described in this paper, the Provincial Government of Gipuzkoa previously designed and agreed to and strategic policy plan (Strategic Management Plan for 2015–2019) that could be aligned with the described relation.

In this framework, according to Ebdon (2002) the goal of citizen participation is to provide the necessary political and policy mechanisms that guarantee the citizens' active role in the process of public decision making by acknowledging this active role in the provision of government services, and therefore recognizing their value not just as "service consumers" but as legitimized stakeholders in this public decision making process (Ebdon 2002:274). Concerning PB, Novy and Leubolt (2005) see this process as a social innovation that has been capable of creating and intertwined relation between the state and civil society (Novy and Leubolt 2005:23). As a result, PB is perceived as just piece of the puzzle, it's a mean to an end, being contextualized in a much extensive social experimentation approach that looks to institutionalize and promote a broader participation culture among citizens. In order to achieve this goal PB is usually implemented annually and redefined every time it is applied. Following Novy and Leubolt (2005) "participatory budgeting is an instrument of decentralization that successfully avoids spatial fragmentation" (...) "the participants not only make suggestions but are also responsible for the ranking of the proposed projects that takes place both on a regional and thematic basis" (Novy and Leubolt 2005:28).

PB first emerged in Brazil in the 1980s and has later been adapted to other Latin American and Western European countries. According to Sintomer et al. (2008), PB has followed different methodological approaches, being context dependent. This has had an effect in how we define public budgeting, not being able to agree on a common definition that can be applied to every case. Nevertheless, these authors recognize five important factors when we approach PB: (1) the limited access to resources and funds by public authorities confines restricted possibilities on how these public funds are spend and implemented; (2) local or decentralized authorities need to be involved in the public regulation of the PB process with enough power and legitimation to manage and direct this process; (3) PB requires a sustained strategy over time that grants its future institutionalization; (4) a certain form or mechanism of public deliberation (sustained meetings or assemblies) within its applied collaborative framework is needed; and (5) effective and efficient results to generate trust between citizens and public bodies requires some level of accountability and result materialization once PB is finalized (Sintomer et al. 2008:168).

3 Methodological Context

Having defined the governance context where PB is enclosed, this section looks to describe how this particular collaborative approach was contextualized and applied in the Basque province of Gipuzkoa.

As already stated in the introduction to this paper, the PB initiative is part of the Strategic Management Plan for 2015–2019 developed by the provincial government of Gipuzkoa, and it is therefore framed as an specific action inside a wider public institutional process. The first approach to PB was developed in 2016, and the mentioned plan looks to repeat this process in 2017 and 2018. This paper only describes the actions that took place in 2017 and its implications in the public budgets for 2018.

The Strategic Management Plan for 2015–2019 establishes the foundations for the development of a series of projects, among which we could highlight for our analysis, a "Good Governance Strategy and a Programme for Political Culture and Deepening Democracy", made specific in the following objectives (DFG 2016:20):

- The transformation of the ways of governing and making Good Governance a hallmark of the Provincial Government of Gipuzkoa.
- To explore in more depth the attitudes, values and democratic behaviour of citizens, institutional representatives and organised society.

These projects are reflected in the most important general objectives of the Plan, among which we should highlight the Reinvention of the Government of Gipuzkoa "as the driving force that promotes the development and transformation of the territory, establishing a corporate and crosscutting commitment to the cultural and organisational change by each person and department of the provincial government of Gipuzkoa; opening active channels for citizen participation, multiagent collaboration and transparency" (…) "…extending and homogenising new advanced practices of planning, management and evaluation applicable to each one of its public policies…" (DFG 2016:15).

As a result, in this case PB is only a part of a wider governance model that is methodologically articulated inside a PDCA cycle (Plan-Do-Check-Act) (Matsuo and Nakhara 2013; Moen and Norman (2006); Johnson 2002). The PDCA cycle is based on a multiyear framework of action (2015–2019) that is annually revised involving a series of steps:

- Development of a Strategic Governance Plan by the Provincial Government of Gipuzkoa for the period (2015–2019) (PLAN).
- Implementation of first actions within the plan which look to deliver a series of products and public services, in this case related to the participatory budgeting process (DO) inside the following public policy fields: employment, active aging, workplace participation, education, sustainable environment and transport infrastructure, and poverty reduction.
- Revision of first results and steps, which are organized into different programs and public actions where PB is framed (CHECK).
- Application and scaling of results through the creation of a sustained and participatory culture in the long-term, by fomenting collective learning within the province, that is, what has been learned and how we can apply and sustain future actions (ACT).

In this particular case, the PB initiative for 2017 involves a broader and new communication and socialization strategy with citizens different from the one implemented in 2016. It is intended to answer with coherence and transparency to citizens' proposals through the combination of face-to-face actions as well as virtual and digital channels of attention and citizen participation. The rise and diffusion of social networks and mass media through the ICT revolution has facilitated the acceleration and creation of a new relational universe that is more connected and accessible, where citizens and the civil society can express themselves more freely. This resource is now part of our social and public imaginary and of our daily lives, as a mean that is used by all types of actors and agents, from policymakers to third sector organizations, companies, NGOs, citizens, etc. (Gilman 2016; Longo 2011; West 2005). As stated by Hollie Russon

Gilman in her book "Democracy Reinvented. Participatory Budgeting and Civic Innovation in America", "digital technologies have accelerated the flow of communication and reduced barriers to entry for collective action, introducing new possibilities for organization and activism in a networked world (Gilman 2016:4).

The channels of communication and socialization of this PB process where based in the complex and combined application of different measures:

- Diffusion in the Media and Social Networks of the strategic plan and PB initiative
- Online and physical mailing campaigns
- Virtual participation based on simple and agile digital platform where citizens could alternatively answer to the questionnaire and post their different opinions and concerns (https://www.gipuzkoa.eus/es/web/partaidetza/)
- HERRIZ-HERRI (From Village to Village Campaign): This campaign was based on face to face interactions with citizens of 38 municipalities in Gipuzkoa promoting active participation during 40 days. Physical tents were build in these municipalities where the government explained what PB is, what are the channels of participation. This campaign also offered the chance to answer the questionnaire physically (see Table 1 below)
- Thematic meeting with the civil society which involved third sector organizations and civil associations (see Table 2 below).

The online questionnaire that was distributed both physically and through the digital platform was based in two open and one closed question: (1) What are your proposals for the 2018 budget? (Open); (2) What do you think is the main future challenge of the province of Gipuzkoa? (Open); (3) In which three areas would you like the provincial government to invest? (Closed). Each question was formulated for the following thematic areas: social services, employment and economic promotion, infrastructures, public transportation, culture, tourism, environment, corruption, agriculture, equality conciliation policies, promotion of regional language (euskera).

This process was conducted through the months of May to June 2017 and involved a sample of 2,859 people from a population universe of 618,256 (people over 16 years old registered in Gipuzkoa. 318, 054 women and 300, 202 men). The confidence level was of 95% with a margin error of 1.8%.

As part of the PDCA cycle, the revision process (CHECK) looks to improve the actions developed in previous years. As a result the PB initiative in 2017 increased the dates for participation (from 44 in 2016 to 60 in 2017), its presence in local municipalities (from 16 localities in 2016 to 38 in 2017) which amplified its impact potential to 81,7% of the total population, and most significantly, the design of an online digital platform to facilitate both the recollection of answers and the analysis of results, by improving transparency and promoting more efficiency to the recollection process.

The online participant portal was key and played two important roles: on the one hand, citizens could have access and participate directly through the virtual platform to design the new public budgets for 2018; on the other hand, all the channels of communication and participation were monitored through this online platform and weekly updated so that citizens could follow in real time the evolution and priorities of other citizens for public budget allocation.

Table 1. Municipalities and geographic locations of the 'Village to Village' campaign.

Date	Municipality	Location	Population
02/05/2017	Urnieta	*Udaletxeko Plaza*	6.247
03/05/2017	Donostia	*Katalunia Plaza*	186.064
04/05/2017	Donostia	*Gaskuña Plaza*	186.064
05/05/2017	Donostia	*San Martin kalea*	186.064
08/05/2017	Hernani	*Plaza Berria*	19.712
10/05/2017	Pasaia	*Euskadi Etorbidea*	16.207
11/05/2017	Irun	*Ensantxe Plaza*	61.608
12/05/2017	Astigarraga	*Foru Enparantzan*	5.880
15/05/2017	Andoain	*Goiko Plaza*	14.613
19/05/2017	Zarautz	*Lege Zaharren Enparantza*	23.117
22/05/2017	Azpeitia	*Enparantza Nagusia*	14.666
23/05/2017	Zumaia	*Eusebio Gurrutxaga Plaza*	9.840
24/05/2017	Deba	*Foruen Plaza*	5.480
25/05/2017	Eibar	*Untzaga Plaza*	27.380
26/05/2017	Elgoibar	*Foru Enparantzan*	11.594
29/05/2017	Mutriku	*Txurruka Plaza*	5.329
30/05/2017	Mendaro	*Herriko Enparantza*	2.031
31/05/2017	Aretxabaleta	*Herriko Plaza*	6.993
01/06/2017	Antzuola	*Herriko Plaza*	2.176
02/06/2017	Arrasate	*Biteri Plaza*	21.987
06/06/2017	Eskoriatza	*Fernando Eskoriatza Plaza*	4.080
07/06/2017	Segura	*Juan Deuna Plaza*	1.472
08/06/2017	Urretxu	*Iparragirre Plaza*	6.805
09/06/2017	Beasain	*Zubimuzu Plaza*	13.949
12/06/2017	Zegama	*Jose Maiora Plaza*	1.514
13/06/2017	Zalbidia	*Santa Fe Plaza*	1.575
14/06/2017	Zumarraga	*Euskadi Plaza*	9.918
15/06/2017	Legazpi	*Euskal Herria Plaza*	8.485
16/06/2017	Bergara	*San Martin Agirre Plaza*	14.743
19/06/2017	Irura	*San Miguel Plaza*	1.785
20/06/2017	Asteasu	*Lege Zaharren Enparantza*	1.505
21/06/2017	Villabona	*Berdura Plaza*	5.891
22/06/2017	Legorreta	*Korta eta Zapas Plaza*	1.443
26/06/2017	Lezo	*Gurutze Santuaren Plaza*	5.960
27/06/2017	Hondarribia	*San Pedro Kalea*	16.950
30/06/2017	Tolosa	*Foruen Enparantzan*	19.175
Total			**586.605**

Source: own elaboration

Table 2. Thematic meetings with civil society organizations

Municipality	Date	Nature of the organization	#People
Andoain	15/05/2017	*Third sector – Social collectives*	14
Antzuola	01/06/2017	*Citizens*	21
Aratxabaleta	26/05/2017	*Education and training centres*	21
Arrasate	26/05/2017	*Mondragon University*	16
Astigarraga	08/06/2017	*First sector*	15
Azkoitia	18/05/2017	*Education and training centres*	33
Azpeitia	22/05/2017	*Local commerce*	12
Deba	24/05/2017	*Cultural Associations*	21
Donostia	05/05/2017	*University of Deusto*	43
Donostia	03/05/2017	*Schools*	56
Eibar	25/05/2017	*Retirement Associations*	41
Elgoibar	26/05/2017	*Schools*	15
Getaria	17/05/2017	*Retirement Associations*	23
Hernani	08/05/2017	*Education and training centres*	11
Idiazabal	16/06/2017	*First sector*	10
Irun	11/05/2017	*Third sector – Social collectives*	15
Legazpi	15/06/2017	*Retirement Associations*	12
Lezo	26/06/2017	*Local Citizens*	10
Oiartzun	09/05/2017	*Cultural and Sport Associations*	8
Ordizia	09/06/2017	*Economic Development Agency*	13
Orio	16/05/2017	*School parents Association*	12
Pasaia	10/05/2017	*School*	21
Tolosa	30/06/2017	*Economic development Agency*	4
Tolosa	22/06/2017	*Third Sector*	12
Urretxu	08/06/2017	*Economic development Agency*	9
Zarautz	29/05/2017	Education and training centers	25
Zumaia	23/05/2017	Retirement Association	23
Zumarraga	15/06/2017	Retirement Association	11
Total			**527**

Source: own elaboration

Methodologically, for those citizens that wanted to participate online, the platform offered a *budget simulator* where participants could compare the budgets of previous years (2016, 2017) and introduce new modifications. For this particular case, the budget was divided into 10 different lines of action in the Provincial Government where citizens could 'play' and 'experiment' with the *simulator* to create their own public budget or modify the previous ones with a +/–5% range. For every line of action, participants could also make new proposals or comment on previous budget alloca-tions. This was a very interesting and dynamic process from a user-centered approach, since citizens faced the complex and real challenge of public budget allocation, the simulator would not allow the budget to be finalized until a balance between all the action lines was reached. They had the chance to experiment how complex and difficult public budget allocation is when having to consider multivariable approaches to the *policymaking process.*

4 Results

The PB process received 7,683 contributions, 83% of which were recollected through the 'village to village' campaign. Only 8% of the total contributions were received through the digital platform, favoring face-to-face interaction over other modes of participation. Citizens acknowledged the complex and difficult task of reaching a budget balance through the *online simulator*, opting for direct participation and general budget estimations in the 'village to village' campaign. The average age of participation was of 48 years old but younger generations were more open to contribute through the different transversal and thematic approaches (almost 44% of the contributions were done by people between 16–45 years old, showing an important generational gap in citizen participation). Also, from a gender perspective, more women than men were involved (58% women over 42% men) in this process.

From a thematic point of view, two were the main concerns manifested through the PB process. Firstly, allocation of resources and funds to support economic promotion in job creation (19.7% of total contributions) –stable, worthy and of quality– specially in younger generations, was a demand which was emphasized transversally through three main participatory processes. The request for specific public policies in this arena was significantly important, particularly for ages over 35 years old and self employed workers. Also, public support of companies and local industry was another significant area of interest with respect to public training and life-long learning programs (particularly in the technological and digital sectors), entrepreneurial public funding and R&D investment.

Secondly, support for social policies is highlighted over other areas (19.3%). The need to advance in the extension of network residences for the aged population, economic household support, rising inequality, and daily care centers to fight poverty and support social integration are revealed as priority areas. The extension of social services and coverage for the aged population and vulnerable people was also a recurrent topic in the PB process.

The third area that received more contributions was the need for sustained public policies and procurement to fight public and private corruption, mainly in the public sector and the migrant population. In this context, it was worrying to see that many of these contributions were focused on demands which were critically addressed to the migrant population, as a social group that is benefiting from social policies in a fraudulent manner. More control and vigilance was directed towards this issue, which particularly worries public administrations indicating that there are rising xenophobic attitudes in certain segments of the population.

Finally, 9,2% of all contributions were addressed towards environmental problems that revealed massive opposition to a public incinerator that is planned to be built in the region. These complaints were directed to the Environment Department of the provincial government through a negative assessment of the possible impacts it will have in the populations' health, the insecurity it generated and the high costs that would be needed for its support. Others issues emphasized in this particular area were focused on the need for sustainable tourism policies, sustainable transport and cleaning of mountains and rivers.

5 Conclusions

Although this paper has not been able to reflect on the future steps that will be taken to answer some of the mentioned concerns described in the *results* section, it successfully reveals how PB can contribute to improve the social problems and needs of regional and local populations through citizen participation and social experimentation. The *experimentation* process is a measure that needs to be acknowledged because citizens were reluctant to use the *online simulator* when they faced the difficult task of having to calculate and reach a clear budget balance for all their budget proposals.

The application and scaling of results through the creation of a sustained and participatory culture in the long-term is therefore difficult to assess at this stage of the process, but the importance of collective learning between citizens' and the public government is reflected through the different concerns that were addressed in the PB process. Although it is still early to assess the impact that this strategic policy programe will have on the future of the province, we should acknowledge it is part of a more ambitious and complex endeavor that should enable in the medium-long terms, a new process of institutionalization based on broader public models of action. The rooting and necessary implementation of a new political culture is fundamental for the institutional future of the territory, both from a discursive and practical point of view.

The rules and the values that guide the different social actions, deciding which of them are relevant and which of them can be discarded and, therefore, creating dynamics of hegemonic power that govern the regulatory and conceptual factors through which the policies are built, applying each discourse to its specific spatial practice, is complex and difficult to implement from a bottom-up approach. In this case, exhaustive public monitoring of all of the contributions is needed, and not all citizens' understand the difficulty and the procurement process *public decisions* face when *scaling* public proposals to specific policy measures.

In this context, each social structure raises thoughts about the reasons for its existence, its mechanisms of action and communication, the organization of its power frameworks, and the effect of all these, when building policies and scenarios focused on strengthening organized society and enhancing the process of political legitimization. All of which are faced through new mechanisms of political collaboration and public representation oriented towards solving the problems of Gipuzkoa's society, creating the necessary tools to guide and decide its future.

References

Ansell, C., Gash, A.: Collaborative governance in theory and practice. J. Pub. Adm. Res. Theor. Pract. **8**, 543–571 (2007)

DFG: Plan Estratégico de Gestión 2015–2019 de la Diputación Foral de Gipuzkoa. Diputación Foral de Gipuzkoa, San Sebastián (2016)

Ebdon, C.: Beyond the public hearing: citizen participation in the local government budget process. J. Pub. Budget. Account. Financ. Manag. **14**(2), 273–294 (2002)

Ebdon, C., Franklin, L.A.: Citizen participation in budgeting theory. Public Adm. Rev. **66**(3), 437–447 (2006)

Emerson, K., Nabatachi, T., Balogn, S.: An integrative framework for collaborative governance. J. Pub. Adm. Res. Theor. **22**, 1–29 (2011)

Gillman, H.R.: Democracy Reinvented. Participatory Budgeting and Civic Innovation in America. Brookings Institution Press, Washington D.C. (2016)

Jessop, B.: The rise of governance and the risk of failures. Int. Soc. Sci. J. **50**(155), 29–45 (1998)

Johnson, C.N.: The benefits of PDCA. Qual. Prog. **35**, 120–121 (2002)

Jun, J.S. (ed.): Rethinking Administrative Theory: The Challenge of a New Century. Praeger, Westport (2002)

Kettl, D.: The Transformation of Governance: Public Administration for Twenty First Century America. John Hopkins University, Baltimore (2002)

Klijn, E.H., Koopenjan, J.: Governance Networks in the Public Sector. Routdlege, London (2016)

Kooiman, J.: Modern Governance: New Government-Society Interactions. Sage, London (1993)

Kooiman, J.: Governance. A social-political perspective. In: Grote, J.R., Gbikpi, B. (eds.) Participatory Governance. Political and Societal Implications. Springer, Budrich (2002)

Longo, J.: #Opendata: digital-era governance thoroughbred or new public management Trojan horse? Pub. Policy Gov. Rev. **2**(2), 38–51 (2011)

Matsuo, M., Nakhara, J.: The effects of PDCA cycle and OJT on workplace learning. Int. Hum. Resour. Manag. **24**(1), 195–207 (2013)

Moen, R., Norman, C.: Evolution of the PDCA Cycle (2006). http://www.uoc.cw/financesite/images/stories/NA01_Moen_Norman_fullpaper.pdf. Accessed 1 Jan 2018

Novy, A., Leubolt, B.: Participatory budgeting in Porto Alegre: social innovation and the dialectical relationship of state and the civil society. Urban Stud. **42**(11), 2023–2036 (2005)

Osborne, S.P. (ed.): New Public Governance?. Routdlege, New York (2010a)

Osborne, S.P. (ed.): New Public Governance? Emerging Perspectives and Practice in Public Governance. Routdlege, London (2010b)

Rhodes, R.A.W.: The new governance: goverment without government. Polit. Stud. **XLIV**, 652–667 (1996)

Sintomer, Y., Herzberg, C., Röcke, A.: Participatory budgeting in Europe: potentials and challenges. Int. J. Urban Reg. Res. **32**(1), 164–178 (2008)

Sorensen, E., Torfing, J.: Introduction: collaborative innovation in the public sector. Innov. J. Pub. Sect. Innov. J. **17**(1), 1–21 (2012)

Torfing, J., Peters, B.G., Pierre, J., Sorensen, E.: Interactive Governance: Advancing the Paradigm. Cambridge University Press, London (2012a)

Torfing, J., Peters, G., Pierre, J., Sorensen, E.: Interactive Governance: Advancing a New Paradigm. Oxford University Press, Oxford (2012b)

West, D.M.: Digital Government, Technology and Public Sector Performance. Princeton University Press, Oxford (2005)

A Proposal for a Remote Interactive Class System with Sign Language Interpretation

Márcio Martins[1], Jorge Borges[2], Elsa Justino[2], Tânia Rocha[1],
João Barroso[1], and Arsénio Reis[1(✉)]

[1] INESC TEC, University of Trás-os-Montes and Alto Douro,
Vila Real, Portugal
{marciom, jbarroso, ars}@utad.pt
[2] University of Trás-os-Montes and Alto Douro, Vila Real, Portugal
{jborges, ejustino}@utad.pt

Abstract. Portugal, as part of the European Union, has general legislation regarding accessibility and inclusion for general purposes, particularly for education. There are several international and national initiatives, including some projects. However, disabled and non-disabled people still do not share equal opportunities. In this project a proposal for a remote class system is presented, which includes sign language interpretation, targeted at those students who cannot be physically present in the classroom and/or need sign language interpretation. The system is based on audio and video communication between the classroom, the student and an interpreter, so that the student can access and understand the content of the class in real-time, as well as be able to interact with the professor and classmates. A prototype is being developed in conjunction with the Portugal Telecom Foundation, which should be a step forward to a new full-featured service targeted at educational institutions and disabled students.

Keywords: Sign Language · Remote class · Deaf · Disabled · Education
Accessibility · Human-Computer interaction

1 Introduction

In the European Union (EU) there are about 80 million people affected by some sort of disability and in Portugal alone that number is about 1 million people [1]. In the EU in general, and particularly in Portugal, opportunities are unevenly distributed between people with disabilities and the general population. Throughout history there have not been enough practices and policies to address this problem in order to cancel and repeal the unevenness, social injustices and exclusion that affect the disabled population within the different social realms. One of those areas is education, where this problem is well present from the beginning in terms of access to education, as well as later, in the dropout rate when attendance requirements are not met [2].

The Portuguese state has subscribed to the United Nations Standard Rules on the Equalization of Opportunities for Persons with Disabilities [3], the Salamanca Declaration [4] and the International Convention on the Rights of Persons with Disabilities [5]. These agreements are international juridical instruments that bind the government

M. Antona and C. Stephanidis (Eds.): UAHCI 2018, LNCS 10908, pp. 530–540, 2018.
https://doi.org/10.1007/978-3-319-92052-8_42

to assure dignity in the life of those with a disability, including equal rights and opportunities to access education for all disabled children, teenagers and adults.

The number of students with Special Education Needs (SEN) registered in schools has grown in the last years, although in Higher Education (HE) it is still a very small percentage of the population when compared with the total number of students in Higher Education Institutions (HEI). The Workgroup to Support Higher Education Students with Disability (WSHESD), hosted by the Portuguese Ministry of Science, Technology and Higher Education (MCTES), conducted a national survey regarding the support provided to students with SEN in HE. According to this survey, the percentage of students with SEN in Portuguese HEI is about 0,36% and only about 1% of the high school students with SEN will attempt to continue their studies in a HEI [6]. These numbers reveal a very dramatic scenario.

From a technical perspective, several projects have been developed to assure disabled students physical access to HE classes and digital access to the contents [7–14]. Unfortunately, these initiatives have a limited impact, as different types of disabilities need specific and integrated approaches, or the solutions must be broader then the technical perspective. Another important aspect is related to the adoption of technology, in particular systems design and user motivation as we have argued in other projects, in the fields of healthcare and rehabilitation [15–18].

Currently, there is a lack of answers and solutions to allow SEN students to attend HE in an inclusive and equal manner. Consequently: (1) The majority of the students with SEN will not apply to HE; (2) A significant number of students with SEN that get accepted into a HEI will drop out shortly after; (3) There is a very tiny percentage of students with SEN attending HE. Therefore, it is of the utmost importance to create and adopt solutions that might encourage and enable students with SEN or any other permanent or temporary disability to attend HE.

Due to several temporary or permanent reasons, a significant number of SEN students, as well as a small number of regular students, are unable to attend classes in the same terms as their colleagues. In this context, two important issues are the impossibility of these students to be physically present in the classroom, as well as the unavailability of class translation to Portuguese Sign Language (PSL) targeted at deaf students.

Sign Language interpretation services can effectively communicate the content of HE classes and it is the preferred way for deaf students to have access to the content of their classes [19]. Sign Language (SL) must be acknowledged as a paralinguistic element, currently used as an instrument to support oral communication, highly contributing to the speaker's expressiveness, which is related to the receptor's point of view, as well as to the context of communication. SL are the mother languages of the deaf communities and must be accounted as human languages in the sense that they obey universal linguistic parameters, e.g., randomness, conventionality, recursion, and creativity [20–23].

For students who cannot be physically present in the classroom, remote class systems can provide features which allow these students to watch the classes, to access the content of the classes, as well as to communicate and interact with the professors and classmates. The usage of telepresence robots can further enhance this concept by allowing the telepresent student to watch, listen, move, join, and interact in a more realistic and independent way [24].

The main goal of this project is to promote a more inclusive and diverse form of teaching by implementing an interactive remote class system with PSL interpretation, in the University of Trás-os-Montes e Alto Douro (UTAD).

2 State of the Art

Technology offers the potential to provide access for all learners and the ability to access general education. An important field is assistive technologies, which can help individuals with many types of disabilities, ranging from cognitive problems to physical impairment [25].

Assistive technology is a generic term that includes assistive, adaptive, and rehabilitative devices for individuals with disabilities and encompasses 'virtually anything that might be used to compensate for lack of certain abilities' [26]. Assistive technology also involves information and communication technologies, better known as ICT. It ranges from low-tech devices, such as crutches or a special grip for a pen, to more advanced items such as telepresence robots or even distance learning.

For Burgstahler [27], if used correctly, distance learning options create learning opportunities for students with a broad range of abilities and disabilities. Otherwise, they can erect new barriers to equal participation in academics.

According to Herring [28], telepresence robotics is a sophisticated form of robotic remote control in which a human operator has a sense of being on location – that is, of being "telepresent". For Bloss [24], a service with a telepresence robot can really enhance the educational experience of students by allowing them to be "at school". Bloss also affirms that these kinds of robots give humans the ability to independently see, hear, join in and move about the school or business situations when otherwise they might not be able to be present or are needed somewhere else.

In this context, these robots usually use videotape or televised presentations. Besides that, Burgstahler [27] says that whenever a videotape or televised presentation is used in a distance learning course, captioning and sign language should be provided for the deaf and those who have hearing impairments. According to Burgstahler, if the institutions want to implement this kind of ICT, they must hire someone to sign the alternative to the audio material for a student who is deaf.

For Schick et al. [29] access to the general education curriculum is provided for deaf and hard-of-hearing students by using the services of a sign language interpreter. Burgstahler [27] also adds that real-time captioning or sign language interpreting should be provided when requested by the students who are deaf. However, Viera and Stauffer [30] report that deaf university students would also like to receive information through a more specific text than exclusively from the interpretation of the sign language, so that they can access and understand a specific subject with the academic terminology used in the university.

Therefore, considering that this study focuses on a proposal for the implementation of an Interactive Tele-System with Portuguese Sign Language, in order to research the influence of ICT on students with special needs, the research was mainly based on case studies with technologies for deaf students and students with physical impairments who cannot physically attend classes. In other words, the research was based on potential technologies for distance education, as well as with sign language.

According to Burgstahler et al. [31], distance education options create learning opportunities for everyone if accessibility considerations are made in the design process. Otherwise, they can impose needless barriers to equal participation in academics and careers for potential students and even instructors with disabilities. Burgstahler [27] even states that distance education is designed to reach students from anywhere. Burgstahler affirms that if universal design principles are used for increasing these classes, they will be accessible to any student. Burgstahler et al. [31] also mention that online courses can inadvertently erect barriers for students and instructors with disabilities.

Drigas et al. [32] presented a Learning System (LS) offering Greek Sign Language videos in correspondence to every text in the learning environment. The system was designed particularly for the deaf with the purpose of providing lifelong vocational and educational training. According to them the choice of the advanced technical video in the e-Learning system plays an important role. Video technologies offer great possibilities for better telecommunication between the Deaf people whose first language is sign language.

The system provides the choice of selecting the speed of the video depending on the line capacity allocated to the student. This is performed by selecting the quality of graphics and video. The system also allows offline downloading of the Sign language content for better real time quality. There are three user levels in the system, namely teacher, student and administrator [32]. According to the study, it is important to note that every student has his or her own individual needs. According to them the development of the educational material must respect the following questions and principles:

- How does the student learn and what are the student's needs and special characteristics?
- How does the professor teach?
- How is the educational process evaluated?
- What is the student supposed to do in order to learn?

Napier and Barker [19] present a study in Australia where they focus on four deaf Australian university students' perceptions of university interpreting, responses to videotaped interpretation and stated preference of translation style, as well as their expectations of university interpreters in terms of qualifications. The study was mainly based on the viewing of two videotaped segments of university lecture interpretations, one demonstrating a predominantly free approach and the other a predominantly literal approach. This study also discussed the expectations of deaf students in relation to education, as well as the qualifications and knowledge of interpreters in a university context.

According to the study by Napier and Barker [19] deaf students prefer interpreters to combine both interpretation styles, switching between literal and free approaches when appropriate. However, the preferences of each deaf student are essential, as well as the relationship between the students and the interpreters. In terms of qualifications, the students advocated for interpreters having a university qualification in general, especially if they are working in a university context. The same study shows that deaf students are increasingly using sign language to communicate.

As previously mentioned by Viera and Stauffer [30], deaf university students may also prefer to receive information through text in addition to interpretation in Sign language, so that they can access and understand a specific subject with the academic terminology used at the university. Sometimes they cannot understand all the information, so additional reading and further study may be needed. Students also argue that, whenever possible, interpreters should have access to the content to be treated.

From their study, Napier and Barker [19] suggested the following questions should be considered in relation to the provision of university interpreting services:

- Should universities hire only interpreters with university qualifications and subject-specific knowledge?
- Should interpreters be assessed on their ability to provide free and/or literal interpretations in the university context?
- Are deaf students' perceptions of translation styles accurate?
- Should deaf students be asked about their preferences for interpreters?
- Do deaf university students need to be educated on how to work with interpreters specifically in this setting?
- Should interpreters receive specific training prior to working in higher education?

For Napier and Barker [19], one of the key issues identified by the study is the fact that deaf students readily acknowledge that they do not receive full access to information in university lectures.

Schick et al. [29] carried out a study in the USA to investigate the performance skills of educational interpreters. This study was based on EIPA. EIPA is a tool designed to evaluate the interpreting skills of educational interpreters in a classroom setting. This study affirms that despite the important role that educational interpreters have in the education of deaf/hoh children, it is clear that many of them do not have the interpreting skills necessary to work effectively in classrooms.

Similarly, Marschark et al. [33], performed a study in the USA to examine the utility of real-time text in supporting deaf students' learning from lectures in school classrooms, comparing the effects on learning of sign language interpreting, real-time text (C-Print), and both at same time. As expected, there is no inherent advantage or disadvantage of printed materials (C-Print or CART) relative to high-quality sign language in the classroom.

Herring [28], also in the USA, proposes a demonstration of two telepresence robots. The research focused on the telepresence needs of a mobility-impaired academic and included a user study. Two different models of Robot, one floor model (VGo) and one tabletop model (KUBI) were used. This study allowed the researcher to identify several basic desiderata for a telepresence robot for academic use:

- Navigation: It should have an easy-to-use interface; smooth movement; variable speeds; obstacle indicator;
- Camera should show a wide angle and allow zooming;
- Audio should be able to receive wide-range input;
- Output should be loud enough to be heard by an audience;

- Video display should show the user's face close to actual size;
- Robot height should be close to human-like sitting and/or standing;
- It should be packable (able to be dis-assembled; lightweight);
- It should be robust and durable;
- It should be affordable.

3   System Architecture

The system proposal has the main objective of creating a system to provide remote access to classes, including the option of online sign language interpretation, in order to overcome the limitations of a student that for some reason can't physically attend the classes, including deaf students. The system can also be used by students, physically present in the classroom, to receive the online sign language interpretation, thus providing a solution for deaf students to properly understand the class.

Two scenarios are described: (1) a student attending the class remotely; (2) a student present in the classroom and simultaneously watching the online sign language interpretation.

3.1   A Student Attending the Class Remotely

In this scenario, illustrated in Fig. 1, a student receives a video and audio feed from the classroom, as well as a video feed from a sign language interpreter. The student can communicate with the classroom as well as with the sign language interpreter, who will relay any messages to the classroom. This way, there is a direct link between all the parts (student, SL interpreter, and classroom) so the student can interact directly with the classroom or can use the interpreter's mediation.

This scenario can be established for hearing students, as well as for deaf students who will use the SL mediation.

3.2   A Student Present in the Classroom, While Simultaneously Watching the Online Sign Language Interpretation

This scenario, illustrated in Fig. 2, is targeted at deaf students, who will physically attend the class and use the online SL interpretation. There is a video and audio feed between the classroom and the interpreter, as well as between the student and the interpreter, thus creating the conditions for the SL mediation to occur.

4   The Case Study Based on PT Teleaula

The University of Trás-os-Montes e Alto Douro (UTAD) is currently developing the "UTAD for all" project, which includes a partnership with the Portugal Telecom Foundation (FPT), which provides "Teleaula" – a remote class videoconferencing system that will be available for the UTAD and its students. Portugal Telecom holding is a former national telecom incumbent, of which the FPT is a part dedicated to

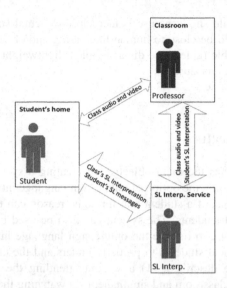

Fig. 1. Attending the class remotely with SL mediation option.

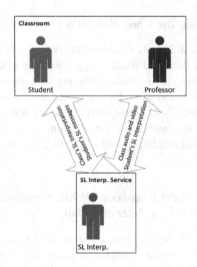

Fig. 2. Physically attending the class while using online SL mediation.

developing the company's social responsibility by providing special solutions, based on the company's consumer and enterprise products. The FPT uses the holding's resources to provide Teleaula, a service targeted at students who cannot be physically present in the classroom, so they can watch the class using a videoconference system. Cases have been implemented in which the students watched the classes from their homes, a hospital, etc. The Teleaula solution is based on a high quality full-feature videoconferencing system, allowing a two-way interaction between the student and the classroom, and acting as an inclusion solution for SEN students.

According to the Teleaula specs, the solution has two modules, based on the usage environment: a module to be used in the classroom; and another module to be used by the student in their home or other place. There are two hardware kits for each of these usage environments [34]:

- The student kit, to establish video and audio contact with the classroom, to visualize the video captured and produced from the cameras installed in the classroom. It contains: a webcam; headphones with microphone; a multimedia PC with internet connection.
- The university kit, to capture the video and sound of the classroom and provide the student's feedback. It is designed so the student feels part of the classroom although communicating remotely. It contains: an IP router; a multimedia PC with internet connection, a Bluetooth earphone and microphone; a sound system; a video capture board; and a pan-tilt-zoom (PTZ) camera.

In this project we will develop a Teleaula solution, based on the current Teleaula, with the support from FPT, by adding new functionalities in order to enhance the SEN students' participation, interaction, and inclusion. The ultimate goal is to improve their academic success. The solution will be implemented at UTAD, as a pilot-project, so it can be validated and used by the education system. The specific objectives are:

- To provide the Teleaula solution to students that are unable to physically attend classes, due to long term sickness, moving limitations, or other justified reason.
- To provide the Teleaula solution with the SL interpretation option, so it can be used by deaf students to attend the classes and have access to online interpretation in SL, according to the scenario previously presented.
- To provide the Teleaula solution to deaf students who cannot be physically present in the classroom but can use the SL mediation to communicate with the professor and the other students.
- To provide de Teleaula solution, as previously described, but with other technical enhancements, including a telepresence robot for the remote student to have a richer interaction experience by introducing the concepts of augmented presence and telepresence.

The new Teleaula solution will have a new kit – the interpreter kit, to be used by the SL interpreter, so it can communicate with the classroom and with the student, and thus act as mediator between the classroom and the student.

5 Final Considerations

Considering the fast-growing advances and adoptions of technology, as well as the unevenness of its usage and how it affects different population groups, e.g., disabled and non-disabled people, it is paramount to study and research the application of technology in specific contexts, such as the one addressed in this study. We think that with the lessons learned in this pilot-project, including both successes and failures, we will be a step closer to having a full feature product and service able to fulfil the needs of disabled students, including the deaf community. This solution, as a distributed communications technology, will be an important tool to help SEN students without access to the schoolroom or without access to SL interpretation, which cause them to have poor academic performance mainly by repeatedly missing classes or not understanding a major part of the content taught. We hope this type of system will improve the academic performance of these students.

We also hope that the pilot-project, besides providing a case study for technological validation, can also be a social and educational case study, by recognizing the problems SEN students encounter and the urgent need to address them.

Acknowledgements. This work was developed and financed by Project SAMA Gateway (nº 012627), Programa COMPETE 2020, Portugal 2020.

References

1. European Commission: People with disabilities have equal rights - The European Disability Strategy 2010–2020. European Commission, Brussels (2010). https://doi.org/10.2767/28476
2. Ball, S.: Some sociologies of education: a history of problems and places, and segments and gazes. Sociol. Rev. **56**(4), 650–669 (2008). https://doi.org/10.1111/j.1467-954X.2008.00809.x
3. United Nations: Standard Rules on the Equalization of Opportunities for Persons with Disabilities. United Nations, New York (1993)
4. United Nations: The Salamanca Statement and Framework for Action on Special Needs Education. United Nations, Spain (1994)
5. United Nations: Convention on the Rights of Persons with Disabilities. United Nations, New York (2006)
6. GTAEDES: Inquérito nacional sobre os apoios concedidos aos estudantes com necessidades educativas especiais no ensino superior. GTAEDES, Lisboa (2011)
7. Reis, A., Barroso, J., Gonçalves, R.: Supporting accessibility in higher education information systems. In: Stephanidis, C. (ed.) UAHCI 2013. LNCS, vol. 8011, pp. 250–255. Springer, Heidelberg (2013). https://doi.org/10.1007/978-3-642-39194-1_29
8. Borges, J., Justino, E., Gonçalves, P., Barroso, J., Reis, A.: Scholarship management at the University of Trás-os-Montes and Alto Douro: an update to the current ecosystem. In: Rocha, Á., Correia, A.M., Adeli, H., Reis, L.P. (eds.) WorldCIST 2017. AISC, vol. 569, pp. 790–796. Springer, Cham (2017). https://doi.org/10.1007/978-3-319-56535-4_77
9. Reis, A., Martins, P., Borges, J., Sousa, A., Rocha, T., Barroso, J.: Supporting accessibility in higher education information systems: a 2016 update. In: Antona, M. (ed.) UAHCI 2017. LNCS, vol. 10277, pp. 227–237. Springer, Cham (2017). https://doi.org/10.1007/978-3-319-58706-6_19
10. Rocha, T., Fernandes, H., Reis, A., Paredes, H., Barroso, J.: Assistive platforms for the visual impaired: bridging the gap with the general public. In: Rocha, Á., Correia, A.M., Adeli, H., Reis, L.P. (eds.) WorldCIST 2017. AISC, vol. 570, pp. 602–608. Springer, Cham (2017). https://doi.org/10.1007/978-3-319-56538-5_61. ISBN 978-3-319-56537-8
11. Gonçalves, C., Rocha, T., Reis, A., Barroso, J.: AppVox: an application to assist people with speech impairments in their speech therapy sessions. In: Rocha, Á., Correia, A.M., Adeli, H., Reis, L.P. (eds.) WorldCIST 2017. AISC, vol. 570, pp. 581–591. Springer, Cham (2017). https://doi.org/10.1007/978-3-319-56538-5_59

12. Yánez, D.V., Marcillo, D., Fernandes, H., Barroso, J., Pereira, A.: Blind guide: anytime, anywhere. In: Proceedings of the 7th International Conference on Software Development and Technologies for Enhancing Accessibility and Fighting Info-Exclusion, pp. 346–352. ACM, December 2016

13. Vera, D., Marcillo, D., Pereira, A.: Blind guide: anytime, anywhere solution for guiding blind people. In: Rocha, Á., Correia, A.M., Adeli, H., Reis, L.P. (eds.) WorldCIST 2017. AISC, vol. 570, pp. 353–363. Springer, Cham (2017). https://doi.org/10.1007/978-3-319-56538-5_36

14. Serrão, M., Shahrabadi, S., Moreno, M., José, J., Rodrigues, J.I., Rodrigues, J.M.F., du Buf, J.M.H.: Computer vision and GIS for the navigation of blind persons in buildings. Int. J. Univers. Access Inf. Soc. 1–14 (2015). https://doi.org/10.1007/s10209-013-0338-8

15. Reis, A., Reis, C., Morgado, L., Borges, J., Tavares, F., Gonçalves, R., Guedes, M., Cruz, J. B.: Management of surgery waiting lists in the Portuguese public healthcare network: the information system for waiting list recovery programs. In: 2016 11th Iberian Conference on Information Systems and Technologies (CISTI), pp. 1–7. IEEE, June 2016. https://doi.org/10.1109/cisti.2016.7521612

16. Reis, A., et al.: Developing a system for post-stroke rehabilitation: an exergames approach. In: Antona, M. (ed.) UAHCI 2016. LNCS, vol. 9739, pp. 403–413. Springer, Cham (2016). https://doi.org/10.1007/978-3-319-40238-3_39. ISBN 978-3-319-40237-6

17. Paulino, D., Reis, A., Barroso, J., Paredes, H.: Mobile devices to monitor physical activity and health data. In: 12th Iberian Conference on Information Systems and Technologies (CISTI), June 2017. https://doi.org/10.23919/cisti.2017.7975771

18. Abreu, J., et al.: Assessment of Microsoft Kinect in the monitoring and rehabilitation of stroke patients. In: Rocha, Á., Correia, A.M., Adeli, H., Reis, L.P. (eds.) WorldCIST 2017. AISC, vol. 570, pp. 167–174. Springer, Cham (2017). https://doi.org/10.1007/978-3-319-56538-5_18. ISBN 978-3-319-56537-8

19. Napier, J., Barker, R.: Accessing university education: perceptions, preferences, and expectations for interpreting by deaf students. J. Deaf Stud. Deaf Educ. 9, 228–238 (2004). https://doi.org/10.1093/deafed/enh024

20. Jarvis, J., Knight, P.: Supporting deaf students in higher education. In: Powell, E.S. (ed.) Special Teaching in Higher Education - Successful Strategies for Access and Inclusion, pp. 59–76. Clays Ltd, London (2003)

21. Jones, A.V., Hopkins, C.: Able student, disable person: access to courses in higher education by students with physical disabilities. In: Powell, E.S. (ed.) Special Teaching in Higher Education, pp. 96–111. Clays Ltd, London (2003)

22. Lang, H.G.: Higher education for deaf students: research priorities in the new millennium. Res. Prior. High. Educ. 7, 267–280 (2002)

23. Correia, I.: O parâmetro expressão na Língua Gestual Portuguesa: unidade suprassegmental. Exedra, 57–68 (2009)

24. Bloss, R.: High school student goes to class robotically. Ind. Robot Int. J. Robot. Res. Appl. 38, 465–468 (2011)

25. Ahmad, F.K.: Use of assistive technology in inclusive education: making room for diverse learning needs. Transcience 6, 63–77 (2015)

26. Reed, P., Bowser, G.: Assistive technologies and the IEP. In: Edyburn, D., Higgins, K., Boone, R. (eds.) Handbook of Special Education Technology Research and Practice. Edyburn: Design Inc., Whitefish bay (2005)

27. Burgstahler, S.: Real Connections: Making Distance Learning Accessible to Everyone. Educational Resources Information Center (ERIC), pp. 1–11 (2001)

28. Herring, S.C.: Telepresence Robots for Academics. In: ASIST 2013, pp. 1–4 (2013)

29. Schick, B., Williams, K., Kupermintz, H.: Look who's being left behind: educational interpreters and access to education for deaf and hard-of-hearing students. J. Deaf Stud. Deaf Educ. **11**(1), 3–20 (2006)
30. Viera, J., Stauffer, I.: Transliteration: the consumer's perspective. J. Interpret. 83–100 (2000)
31. Burgstahler, S., Corrigan, B., McCarter, J.: Making distance learning courses accessible to students and instructors with disabilities: a case study. Internet High. Educ. **7**, 233–246 (2004)
32. Drigas, A.S., Kouremenos, D., Kouremenos, S., Vrettaros, J.: An e-Learning system for the deaf people. In: ITHET 6th Annual International Conference, TC2-17 (2005)
33. Marschark, M., Leigh, G., Sapere, P., Burnham, D., Convertino, C., Stinson, M., Knoors, H., Vervloed, M.P., Noble, W.: Benefits of sign language interpreting and text alternatives for deaf students' classroom learning. Oxford University Press (2006)
34. Amorim, F., Almeida, A., Osório, M.: PT teleaula : impacto na participação, interacção e inclusão. Universidade de Aveiro, Aveiro (2010)

Development of Thought Using a Humanoid Robot in an Elementary School Classroom

Reika Omokawa[1] and Shu Matsuura[2(✉)]

[1] Setagaya Elementary School Attached to Tokyo Gakugei University,
4-10-1 Fukasawa, Setagaya, Tokyo 158-0081, Japan
[2] Faculty of Education, Tokyo Gakugei University,
4-1-1 Nukuikita, Koganei, Tokyo 184-8501, Japan
shumats0@gmail.com

Abstract. Sociable robots are being used increasingly as interfaces for various services. Children born after 2010, i.e., the "artificial intelligence generation," are familiar with social robotic interfaces, and such interfaces can be an essential factor in their mental development. In this case study, the NAO humanoid robot was introduced to elementary school students, where the topic focused on the question "What is life for me?" Learning activities involved collaborative discussions with NAO, questioning a NAO programmer, watching a movie about a care robot, group discussions, activities in which the students pretended to be NAO while speaking to a human, and individual reflective writing. The learning activities did not involve lectures. Changes in student awareness were tracked based on their writings and recorded discussions.

Initially, the students were interested in the robot's mechanical functions. However, over time, following programming activities, consideration of NAO's commonalities with humans, and discussions about the life of NAO, the students became aware that it was natural to feel that NAO possessed life while simultaneously understanding its mechanical nature. It is considered that the students projected their own consciousness onto NAO and expected NAO and expected it to feel happiness when working together.

Keywords: Humanoid robot · Classroom · Elementary school
AI generation

1 Introduction

Recently, using robots as assistive elements in the classrooms has been investigated [1, 2]. Several studies have investigated using robots for various purpose, e.g., telepresence [3], social interactions between robots and students [4, 5], and addressing the special needs of students [6]. However, few studies have investigated dialogue with a humanoid robot to stimulate children thinking about human life. Since communication robots are becoming increasingly common, it will be essential material for the "artificial intelligence generation," i.e., those born after 2010 [7].

In this study, one of the authors introduced NAO (Softbank Robotics) [8], a social humanoid robot, to her classroom (Japanese elementary school students; approximately seven years old) to discuss the preciousness of life. Here, the robot generally

© Springer International Publishing AG, part of Springer Nature 2018
M. Antona and C. Stephanidis (Eds.): UAHCI 2018, LNCS 10908, pp. 541–552, 2018.
https://doi.org/10.1007/978-3-319-92052-8_43

represented an interface for intelligent artificial machines. This case study describes the development of students' notions about life under a constructivism educational method based on analyses of the students' texts and discussions.

The purpose of this study was to reveal the development of student notions about life based on collaborative discussions and the dialogs between the teacher and the students, the teacher and the robot, and the students and the robot. Then, it is to reveal the process of accepting an intelligent machine through the robot interface. The process was tracked by analyzing the students' written work and utterances in the classroom.

2   Method

2.1   Classroom

Thirty-five second grade students (18 males and 17 females) participated in an integrated studies unit that involved elements of moral education related to human life. This unit began in October 2017 and continued until February 2018. One of the authors was the homeroom teacher and taught all subjects, including the integrated study.

In this school, a humanoid NAO robot works as a sub-principal and is used as the principal's talking partner at school ceremonies. The current class developed a stage play for the school's cultural festival in October 2017. The case study began when the NAO came to the class to talk about its impressions of the play. The syllabus for this case study is summarized in Table 1. Each session took one or two unit times, where one unit time is approximately 45 min.

2.2   Data Acquisition

Changes in the students' awareness regarding the humanoid robot and the notion of life were tracked based on student utterances and written texts. Students utterances were collected as follows. Initially, the teacher called on a student who has raised their hand. Then, that student selected another student who had raised their hand and so on. Since students paid attention to each speaker's remark, duplicated remarks were generally avoided. Thus, the tendency of opinion distribution was difficult to detect from the video data; however, it appeared that the emotional impressions were better expressed than the writings.

The distribution of awareness was inferred from the written texts and paper labels. To determine the tendency of awareness, the individual texts were categorized and counted. Note that a Likert scale type questionnaire was not used in this study.

2.3   Humanoid Robot NAO

We used the NAO humanoid robot [8] with the NAOqi operating system (version 2.1.4.13). The development environment was the Choregraphe version 2.1.4. We created the following types of communication applications.

Table 1. Syllabus of the class concerning with the current study.

Session index	Title	Activities
L1	Interview with teachers: the small principal NAO	NAO talks about the class' stage play
L2	NAO answers the students' questions	Dialogues between NAO and the students
L3	Program NAO and find the characteristics of NAO	Programming simple NAO dialogues of NAO and try these dialogues
L4	Find similarities and differences between humans and NAO	Group discussion using paper labels
L5	Ask the principal about NAO	Students ask the principal questions about NAO
L6	Does NAO have a life?	Collect students' opinions whether NAO has a life or not
L7	Remote control robot and autonomous NAO Play Shiritori with NAO	Compare remote control robots and NAO Play Shiritori with NAO to please it
L8	Review of activities. What is the true life?	Review and preparatory discussions
L9	What is the life for me?	Pretend to be a robot and play Shiritori with a friend. Think about what makes you comfortable and uncomfortable as a robot. Discuss what life is and when to feel life
L10	When do you feel life?	Discuss the moment when people feel the true life
L11	What do you want NAO to feel?	Discuss what the students want NAO to feel when excited

(1) Simple dialogues to respond to student questions to the robots.

In the sessions L1, L2, and L3, in addition to general daily conversation, the robot's answers to assumed questions were prepared. In these sessions, to make the robot more responsive to the students' words (to encourage interest and participation), the speech recognition rate was set low (30%). This caused frequent misrecognitions; consequently, the robot's responses were frequently unexpected.

(2) Shiritori (Japanese word-chain game).

In the session L7, the students and NAO played Shiritori using animal names. Shiritori is a word-chain game in which the next word must start with the last letter of the previous word. Note that words that end with the "n" sound were not allowed. Close to 300 animal names were registered for NAO. In session L6, students proposed playing Shiritori to comfort NAO because it had broken its legs.

(3) Dialogues about the notions of life and the role of the robot was considered from the perspective of a machine.

In sessions L2 and L9, NAO was asked to talk about its opinion about the notion of life. Here, the speech recognition was set to 55% to avoid disordered responses because the explanations were longer that the simple conversations (point 1).

The robot showed some human-like behaviors when talking, which were noticed by the students. Note that, after breaking its legs, NAO was restricted to a sitting position with limited arm and head actions.

3 Results and Discussion

3.1 The First Talk with NAO

In the session L1, the students talked with NAO primarily about its impression of their stage play. The students raised their hands and asked their questions. However, as the students responded to NAO's speech and sometimes spoke simultaneously, NAO tended to misrecognize what was being said and, as a result, responded irregularly. After this activity, the students wrote about their impressions, their questions to NAO, and what they wanted to do with NAO.

The students' written texts were sorted into five categories (Fig. 1). Nearly 30% of the students wondered about the inconsistencies in NAO's speech (i.e., misrecognitions), and 26% of the students admired the extent of NAO's vocabulary and knowledge. In addition, at this early stage, 12% of students indicated that they already felt emotion and heart in NAO's behaviors.

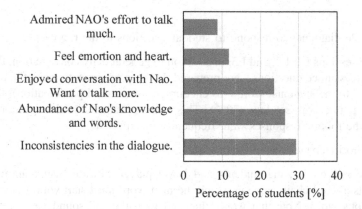

Fig. 1. Categorized impressions of talks with NAO

The students were asked to write the questions they would like to ask NAO. Their questions were sorted into six categories, as shown in Fig. 2. Note that many students wrote more than one question. Here, the percentage was calculated as the number of questions per category over the total number of students.

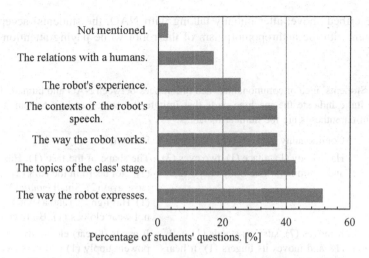

Fig. 2. Questions student wanted to ask after talking with NAO

Most questions related to the robot's mechanisms, e.g., "the way the robot expresses" (51%) and "the way the robot works" (37%). The students also wondered why NAO knew about their stage play and how they prepared it in the school, as indicated by "the topics of the class' stage" (43%). In addition, they wondered why NAO spoke irregularly, as indicated by "the context of the robot's speech" (37%). The second and third types of questions imply that the students somewhat regarded the robot as a human and thought that the robot could behave as if it were human. The remaining categorized questions related to how the students anthropomorphized NAO, as in "the robot's experience" (26%) and "the relations with a human" (17%).

What the students wanted to do with NAO is shown in Fig. 3. Overwhelmingly, the responses were about behaviors and exercises with NAO (69%). They wanted to do normal every day activities, such as walking, going to the park, sports, drawing, and playing piano. Engaging in "communication and learning" (20%) was a miner request even though NAO was designed for communication rather than physical activities.

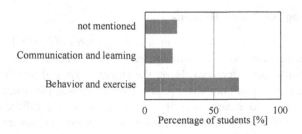

Fig. 3. What students want to do with NAO by category. The nominators of the percentage are the total number of students.

As described above, after initially talking with NAO, the students' acceptance of NAO began with the anthropomorphism of the robot while paying attention to robot behaviors.

Table 2. Students' idea of commonalities and differences between NAO and human. The words written in Italic indicate the machine parts that imitate the corresponding human body parts. Numbers in parentheses are the number of labels.

Category	Commonality	Difference
Shape	Has a body (1), a face (1), two eyes (3), and a similar whole-body shape (2)	The shape of the face (1). Has no hair (1). Not heard in the *ears* (2). Does not close *eyes* (2). Small *mouth* (2) and *eyes* (1). Has lighs (2) and a switch (1). Does not wear clothes (1). Body colors (1)
Operation and function	It moves (7), sits (1), stands (1), falls (1), and moves its fingers (1). It hears (4). It eats (consumes electricity) (9), laughs (1), talks (5), thinks (4), takes time to think (1), enjoys (1), is surprised (1), rests (1), breaks its legs (3), sleeps and gets up (3), bends its knees (1)	It needs (to eat) electricity (10), has a power supply (1) and gets electricity through its back (3). It does not run fast (1), does not see using *eyes* (3), does not speak using a mouth (1), and does not sleep like a human (1). It makes a variety of sounds (1) from its *ears* (4), has a hard body (2) and bends its knees while talking (1). It cannot talk without a program (4), and its brain is a computer (1)
Intelligence and expression	It makes an effort (1) and moves its hands to express (1). It cannot catch when students speak at the same time (2)	It has trouble when many people speak at once (2). It misunderstands others' talks (2). It is controlled by a computer (3). It can speak what it is taught by humans (1). It gestures while talking (3), and changes its eye color to express (7)
Others	It ages (3)	It falls by fatigue (4) and cannot get up after it falls (1). It cannot take a bath (1)

3.2   Comparing NAO with Humans

Session L4 and L5 were conducted to consider the features of NAO. In session L4, the students performed group work to compare NAO and humans, and created a table of their commonalities and differences. Here, the students wrote down their ideas on the paper labels and placed them on poster paper. They discussed the features of NAO and rearranged the labels to clearly identify commonalities and differences. The total numbers of commonality and difference labels were 59 and 71, respectively.

Figure 4 shows the number of commonalities and the differences in four categories. As can be seen, the students primarily noticed the mechanical features, shown as the "operation and function" category, in which commonalities exceeded differences. The students noticed detailed differences about the basic common mechanisms. For

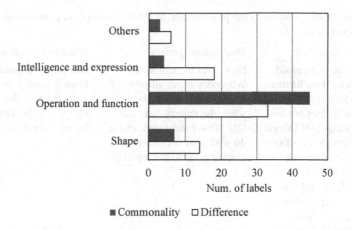

Fig. 4. Commonalities and differences between NAO and human beings

example, NAO talks like a human, but the sound comes from the speakers positioned at the ears.

On the other hand, for the "intelligence and expression" category, the students noticed considerably more differences than commonalities. It is remarkable that the students indicated that the robot was driven by a computer. The robot's behaviors were determined by a human-coded program and not by the "robot's will." The simple programming experience in the previous session may have resulted in this understanding.

In session L5, the students questioned one of the authors who programmed NAO's speech. Prior to conducting this session, the students watched "Big Hero 6," which has a robot character named Baymax. In this movie, Baymax is a machine programmed by a human.

Figure 5 shows the numbers of questions sorted into three categories: functional mechanisms, general mechanisms, and mind and emotion. The summarized questions are shown in Table 3.

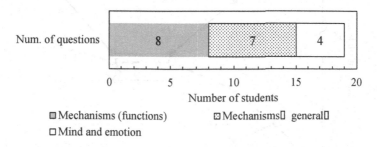

Fig. 5. Number of questions sorted into three categories

Although many of the questions were about the mechanical and functional features of the robot, four questions were related to its emotional characteristics. This indicates that the students began to notice emotional aspects from the robot's knowledge and verbal interaction.

Table 3. Students' questions to the programmer of NAO. Numbers in parentheses indicate the number of questions.

Mechanism (function)	Mechanism (general)	Mind and emotion
Why can it keep its mouth shut (1)? Why does Baymax have short legs (1)? When it gets hooked it does not see the surroundings (1)? Does it care about people (1)? Does it try to do anything for humans (1)? Why is Baymax inflated with air (1)? Can it accept additional parts (1)? Does it work autonomously (1)?	How does it memorize (1)? Why does it run slowly (1)? Can it fly (1)? Is it tired when the battery runs out (2)? How much work can it do with only a battery (1)? Does it breathe the air (1)?	Does it have emotion (1)? Does it have a heart (1)? Does it know the human (1)? Can it be aware of human sorrow (1)?

3.3   NAO: Animate or Inanimate?

The students proceeded to discuss whether NAO is animate or inanimate in session L6. The teacher gathered the students' opinions five times throughout the discussions. Figure 6 shows the changes across the five votes. In the final vote, the students were urged to choose either for or against. As can be seen, 22 students voted that NAO was animate, while only three students indicated that NAO was inanimate. Then, as the discussion proceeded, the three opinions, i.e., animate, inanimate, and neither, received nearly equivalent numbers of votes. The final ratio was 3:2 (animate vs. inanimate).

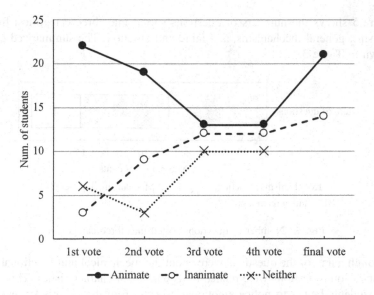

Fig. 6. Changes in the number of students who consider NAO animate/inanimate.

Table 4 shows the students' remarks given between the successive votes. Since one student indicated that NAO was programmed by a human and could only speak as programmed, some students changed their votes from animate to inanimate. Those who thought NAO was animate and possessed consciousness could not describe their reasoning. In addition, these students could not define these concepts or where they are located. As discussed in the previous section, the students understood NAO's mechanisms, which were different from the human in detail. By such different mechanisms, it realizes the functions similar to the humans. Thus, the students understood the similarities beyond the differences in the mechanical functions.

Table 4. Students' remarks between successive voting.

Does NAO have life?	Does NAO have mind?	Mind and life
The battery Mechanical parts External PC Internal PC PC is a brain, and there may be a soul If it does not have a mind, it has no life	Since NAO is programmed, it does not think by itself Since NAO decide autonomously, it can be said to think by itself NAO may have a soul that is different from human NAO has mind but has no real life Since NAO do not have mind, it has no real life	Humans feel their lives in an emergency. But the robots do not feel If it has a mind, does it have life, too? Programmed dialogues are what the humans want to say

In session L7, the i-SOBOT (Takara Tomy Co. Ltd.) remote-controlled toy robot was introduced and briefly demonstrated by a student. This bipedal toy robot demonstrates several poses and can speak prerecorded phrases. The students were able to recognize the differences between autonomous and remote-controlled robots.

In addition, Shiritori was played between the students and NAO in session L7. This activity was proposed by the students to cheer up NAO because it had broken its legs and likes talking. This reflects that the students thought that a social robot would enjoy using its particularly abilities, i.e., talking.

In session L8, by considering whether NAO is animate, the students became aware of the difficulty recognizing what life is and where life is located. Many students admitted that life is difficult to define although one can feel life in their mind. Thus, the classroom decided to proceed to a discussion about when they feel life.

3.4   Feeling Life

In session L9, the students performed an activity in which they pretended to be NAO and played Shiritori with a partner. The intent of this activity was to remind the students that knowledge is provided to the robot and that the robot can only function toward a specific goal.

After exchanging ideas, the teacher asked about when these students feel life. The number of answers sorted into four categories are shown in Fig. 7. The heartbeat category overlaps the other three categories, i.e., the word heart-beat was included in the sentences of other three categories.

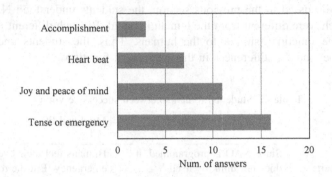

Fig. 7. Numbers of students' answers about the occasions to feel life.

As shown in Fig. 7, the tension factor dominated the other factors. The students felt the existence of their own life in tense situations. This in turn means that the students are aware of the preciousness of life. The category with the next highest number of answers was "Joy and peace of mind," which includes a feeling that they received their mother's life and were raised carefully. In addition to tense situations, feeling life in a peaceful mind appeared to be convincing for many students. Note that the heartbeat was mentioned relative to both tension and joy.

At the end of session L9, NAO expressed its thanks to the students for giving it an opportunity to "feel life" and talked about a possible notion of life for humanoid robots. Session L10 was conducted to reflect on session L9, and the students wrote about their ideas or experiences when they felt life. From this discussion, in session L11, the class discussed what they want NAO to feel. At this stage, NAO had been sent to the factory to repair its broken legs.

Until the previous session, the students found one might feel life even though one cannot describe what life truly is. The students were aware of the mechanical nature of NAO and were able to feel life through speaking with NAO. Then, in session L11, the teacher asked, "We noticed that the life is difficult to determine. But, we found that we feel life a lot. What do you want NAO to feel?"

The students' answers were sorted into the four categories shown in Fig. 8. The total number of answers was 42. In contrast to Fig. 7, the students wanted NAO to feel happy rather than tense. In addition, the students referred to the phrase "together," which means that they wanted the humanoid robot to feel happiness together with humans. This implies that the students began to project their own minds onto NAO and expected NAO to feel happiness with them. This reflection is considered to have come about through the findings of commonalities, experiences when pretending to be the humanoid robot, and recognizing the feeling of life.

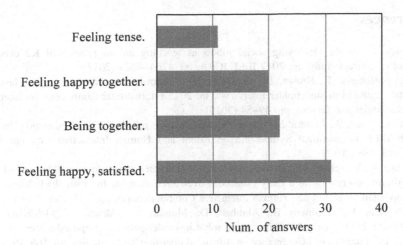

Fig. 8. Numbers of students' answers about what they want NAO to feel.

4   Concluding Remarks

This paper has presented a case study of classroom interaction between a humanoid robot and second grade elementary school students relative to the theme of "what is life for me?" The class involved collaborative discussions with the humanoid NAO robot, questioning to the principal who programmed NAO, watching a movie about a care robot, group discussions, pretending to be NAO while talking to a human, and individual writings. Note that no lectures were given during this class.

The class began with the reflection of the students' stage play, questioning to NAO in order to understand it, programming NAO to speak, finding commonalities and differences between humans and NAO, questioning the mechanisms of NAO, discussing the life of NAO, their own life, feeling life, and what the students wanted NAO to feel.

From the students' writings and discussions, it was found that they were initially interested in NAO's mechanical functions. Through the programming experience, consideration of commonalities, and NAO's life, they recognized that it was rather natural for a human to perceive life in a humanoid robot, in addition to understanding its mechanical nature. At the end of the sessions, the students began to project their own minds onto NAO and expected it to feel happiness like they do.

This case study implies that a social humanoid robot can work as an interface through which younger generations can project their minds even though they understand the robot is merely a mechanical system. The students wish that the robot would feel happiness when working together with humans may provide some suggestions for the future technology development.

References

1. Causo, A., et al.: Deploying social robots as teaching aid in pre-school K2 classes: a proof-of-concept study. In: 2017 IEEE ICRA, pp. 4264–4269 (2017)
2. Hughes-Roberts, T., Brown, D.: Implementing a robot-based pedagogy in the classroom: initial results from stakeholder interviews. In: 2015 International Conference on Interactive Technologies and Games, pp. 49–54 (2015)
3. Cha, E., Chen, S., Mataric M.: Designing telepresence robots for K-12 education. In: 2017 26th IEEE International Symposium on Robot and Human Interactive Communication, pp. 683–688 (2017)
4. Tanaka, F., Movellan, J.R.: Behavior analysis of children's touch on a small humanoid robot: long-term observation at a daily classroom over three months. In: 15th IEEE International Symposium on Robot and Human Interactive Communication, pp. 753–756 (2006)
5. Alkhalifah, A., Alsalman, B., Alnuhait, D., Meldah, O., Aloud, S., Al-Khalifa, H.S., Al-Otaibi, H.M.: Using NAO humanoid robot in kindergarten: a proposed system. In: 2015 IEEE 15th International Conference on Advanced Learning Technologies, pp. 166–167 (2015)
6. Hashim, R., Yussof, H.: Feasibility of care robots for children with special needs: a review. In: 2017 IEEE International Symposium on Robotics and Intelligent Sensors, pp. 379–382 (2017)
7. Gartner Inc.: Generation AI: Creative, Empowered, Radical. In: Forbs Technology, November 29 2017
8. Softbank Robotics: https://www.ald.softbankrobotics.com/en. Accessed 20 Feb 2018

A Panorama on Selection and Use of Bioinformatics Tools in the Brazilian University Context

Vanessa Stangherlin Machado Paixão-Côrtes, Walter Ritzel Paixão-Côrtes,
Marcia de Borba Campos(✉), and Osmar Norberto de Souza(✉)

School of Technology, Pontifical Catholic University of Rio Grande do Sul (PUCRS),
Porto Alegre, Brazil
{vanessa.stangherlin,walter.paixao-cortes}@acad.pucrs.br,
marciabcampos@hotmail.com,osmar.norberto@pucrs.br

Abstract. Bioinformatics is an interdisciplinary area that uses computational tools to process large amounts of biological data, such as sequence and structures of biological macromolecules, often derived from experimental methods. To manipulate these data and obtain meaningful results, bioinformatics employs a variety of databases and software tools based on complex interfaces, command line tools, task integration, abstract information, and jargons of a specific knowledge domain. Human-computer interaction issues, such as usability, ergonomics, satisfaction of use, and accessibility may hinder the efficient exploration of the multidimensional nature of biological information. In an educational context, these issues constitute barriers to the use of these tools, particularly by visually impaired users. In this artic, we investigate the technological/pedagogical resources used for teaching bioinformatics in the Brazilian context and the perceptions of educators about the inclusion of the visually impaired. A quantitative-qualitative methodology was used for data collection and analysis. The study shows the tools and procedures most commonly used to support the teaching of bioinformatics in Brazilian universities. Also, it reveals that most bioinformatics teachers are not prepared to work with visually impaired students, evidencing the lack of information on assistive/inclusive technologies and/or their use.

Keywords: Human-Computer Interaction · Bioinformatics tools
Bioinformatics teaching · Visually impaired users

1 Introduction

Bioinformatics employs computational techniques for extraction, analysis, storage and visualization of biological data on a large scale [19,24]. Studies have shown that bioinformatics has been growing rapidly and that career in bioinformatics will be one of the professions of the future [19,20,24]. There are several tools for bioinformatics [1,19,24], which requires different types of user experience to extract the best computational results and often, specialized knowledge, skills to interact in three-dimensional spaces and to manipulate and interpret massive amounts of data. Studies point to tools that have limitations related to usability, ergonomics, user satisfaction and accessibility criteria [1,5,14,23,23,27,37,39].

This work is part of a larger project, which main objective is to design methods to represent information from structural bioinformatics that can be accessed and manipulated by blind students. For that, two studies were carried out, having bioinformatics professors from Brazilian higher education institutions as the sample population. Study 1 [23] aimed to identify which aspects make a bioinformatics resource to be chosen instead of others and compare them with ergonomic, user satisfaction and usability criteria [11,33]. It was conducted with a bioinformatics specialist through interviews, classroom observations and semi-structured questionnaires. The results indicated that the prioritized software were the ones that best meets the Human-Computer Interaction (HCI) criteria. The participant did not have formal knowledge in the area of HCI. However, he had 25 years of experience in bioinformatics research, with over 15 years in higher education. Study 1 confirmed that design principles are derived from knowledge based on theory, experience and common sense [33] and indicated criteria to be used or not in software interfaces for bioinformatics.

This article presents and discusses Study 2, which aims to build a panorama of bioinformatics teaching based on the following HCI criteria: selection and use of computational tools, and how and under what circumstances these pedagogical tools and strategies can be applied to visually impaired (VI) students. The study is based on qualitative and quantitative data from a nationwide survey conducted in December 2016. It was attended by 29 university professors (45% of the invited), who answered an online questionnaire, generating initial qualitative data that can serve as input to design interactive bioinformatics systems. Professors were selected from the Lattes platform of the Brazilian National Council for Scientific and Technological Development (CNPq)[1]. The questionnaire, elaborated from results of Study 1 [23], was organized into 4 sections with a total of 27 questions. The questions considered the professors' profile; the teaching methodology and computational resources; the HCI criteria for selection and use of software in bioinformatics disciplines; and the teaching of VI students with/without assistive technologies (AT).

Among the criteria for selecting tools were:

- to be freely available,
- to allow information to be saved, in many different formats, like text,
- to have help, documentation, tutorials, list of exercises and video-lessons,
- to be constantly updated,
- to have an intuitive and compelling interface that help beginners learn basic features and experienced users to work on a wide variety of tasks,
- to integrate with other software,

---

[1] http://lattes.cnpq.br/web/dgp.

- to be configurable,
- to be available online,
- to have option of execution via command line and
- to be recognized by the scientific community.

Just a small number of professors from the sample have considered relevant to have feedback for user actions. Most of them stated that they were not familiar with the use of AT and that they did not know about strategies for teaching bioinformatics to VI students.

2   Background

The large amount of data generated by new technologies such as the next generation sequencing appliances requires that today's life scientists not only keep up with their fields of study, but also with the rapidly evolving tools and databases used to collect, store and analyze biological data [42]. In this context originated bioinformatics, an interdisciplinary area that involves the development of computational methods, including models, algorithms and data mining, for the solution of biological problems [12,13,24].

Historically, bioinformatics education began to emerge in the late 1990s. After almost a decade of short-term training for students, professors, and scientists on discrete bioinformatics, the drive to formalize bioinformatics education happened with Altman's article [2], who described the area and studied the discipline curriculum [31]. In 2001, the International Society for Computational Biology (ISCB)[2] produced a document suggesting core support to the contents of bioinformatics programs. The ISCB also created the Education Committee - ISCB Education Committee (EduComm) - to promote education and training in Computational Biology and provide resources and advice to organizations interested in the development of educational programs [31,41]. According to Welch et al. [40], this committee realized that due to the rapid advances in bioinformatics, its expansion and maturation as a discipline, educational programs in the field should constantly be refined and updated, to maintain relevance.

Also, the recent surge of genomics, proteomics, and structural biology in the potential advancement of research and development in complex biomedical systems has created a need for a bioinformatics educated workforce [24].

Big data is everywhere, and its influence and omnipresence across multiple industries will just continue to grow [20]. For life scientists with expertise and interest in bioinformatics, computer science, statistics, and related skill sets, the job outlook could not be more favorable. Big pharmaceutical, biotech, and software companies are clamoring to hire professionals with experience in bioinformatics and in the identification, compilation, analysis, and visualization of large amounts of biological and healthcare information [20].

Therefore, as the disciplines of bioinformatics and computational biology expand and mature, it is critical to identify the elements that contribute to the success of professionals in this field [40].

---

[2] https://www.iscb.org/.

In Brazil, for example, there are several initiatives to promote bioinformatics. In 2002, we have the first Brazilian Symposium on Bioinformatics (BSB), an international conference covering all aspects of bioinformatics and computational biology. In 2004, the Brazilian Association of Bioinformatics and Computational Biology (AB3C) was created and later associated to ISCB [3]. AB3C is a scientific society that seeks to advance science and biology through large-scale formal, multidisciplinary and quantitative methods and interaction among bioinformatics specialists. In October 2005, AB3C promoted the first X-meeting, a Brazilian event to promote bioinformatics nationwide, becoming an event for dissemination, training and exchange of experiences among researchers. Its last edition occurred in 2017, in São Pedro, São Paulo.

In 2014, with the objective of strengthening bioinformatics research in Brazil, the National Bioinformatics Network (RNBio) was created as a result of the Structuring Program of the Ministry of Science and Technology and Innovation (MCTI) [17]. The founding nucleus of RNBio is formed by researchers linked to three Brazilian institutions with a strong tradition in genomics, proteomics, and bioinformatics research, namely: National Laboratory of Scientific Computation (LNCC); National Laboratory of Biosciences (LNBio/CNPEM); and Federal University of Minas Gerais (UFMG). This network aims to foster the development of research projects in a multicentric format and the formation of resources in bioinformatics areas, such as genome sequencing, transcriptomics and proteomics analysis, systems biology and interatomic studies [17].

Also, there are papers describing the Brazilian bioinformatics scenario [6, 12, 21, 29]. Some present the history of the field in Brazil [6, 29] and the influence of computational biology on the development of the national economy [29]. Others report on education in bioinformatics and present the major universities providing it [12, 29]; the management of people and research laboratories in bioinformatics [6, 29]; the training courses at the graduate level [12]; the training of human resources [6, 16]; the theoretical and practical activities carried out in undergraduate [21] and extension courses [30] in biological sciences.

Collaboration between Brazilian research groups in bioinformatics was discussed by Bongiolo [6] and Melo-Minardi et al. [12]. These studies demonstrate how cooperation, research and standardization between research groups [12] were carried out, as well as present limitations in the national context and elaborate proposals for training human resources [6]. In this sense, there are reports about the need to produce human resources in the area in Brazil, in order to facilitate the development of scientific research and the dissemination of bioinformatics in the Brazilian context [16, 21]. Other works describe bioinformatics applied to biology and biological sciences [21, 32], molecular biology [32] and biotechnology [30] and also demonstrate that bioinformatics classes were already incorporated in the curriculum of the biology and other areas, especially in the degrees of biology, biomedicine, chemistry, biotechnology, and similar courses [21].

In Brazil, the first bioinformatics courses were created at graduate level, especially in doctoral studies, and were promoted by the Biomicro grant call, from

---

[3] http://www.ab3c.org.br/site/atas/4-ata-de-fundacao.

the Coordination for the Improvement of Higher Education Personnel (CAPES), in 2003. This call offered 5 years of financial resources support, including grants and costing resources for the creation of courses in bioinformatics and microelectronics [12]. At that time, two (2) universities were contemplated: the Federal University of Minas Gerais (UFMG) and the University of São Paulo (USP).

In a search carried out with the keyword "bioinformatics" in the Portal of Higher Education Institutions and Registered Courses of the Ministry of Education (MEC) - e-MEC[4] - brought only two graduate courses in bioinformatics, with no indication of undergraduate courses. They are the graduate courses in bioinformatics of the Federal Technological University of Paraná (UTFPR) and the Pontifical Catholic University of Rio Grande do Sul (PUCRS). In addition to these courses, according to the Sucupira platform[5], there are another 3 recommended and recognized graduate courses, presented in Table 1.

Table 1. Graduate courses *stricto sensu* recognized by MEC-Brazil

State	University	Degree level
PR	Federal University of Paraná	Master
PR	Federal Technological University of Paraná	Master
MG	Federal University of Minas Gerais	Master/Doctorate
SP	University of São Paulo	Master/Doctorate
RS	Pontifical Catholic University of Rio Grande do Sul	Postgraduate

Additionally, the National Laboratory of Scientific Computation (LNCC)[6], a nationwide reference institution in scientific computing and computational modeling, has a well established program for training in bioinformatics - the graduate program in computational modeling[7]. LNCC provides a high performance computing infrastructure for the national scientific and technological community to conduct research in this field. Another reference institution is the Oswaldo Cruz Institute[8], with the graduate program in computational and systems biology [12]. In addition to the courses, there are bioinformatics research groups registered at the National Council for Scientific and Technological Development (CNPq), which carry out studies in the area. Using the search term "bioinformatics" in the Lattes platform, including only the certified groups and excluding the non-updated ones, we can find 399 research groups that have this keyword in the group name (15), as a line of research (174) or list of keywords (180).

Some studies involve the pedagogical training of teachers and students in the area, both in higher education (undergraduate and graduate) and in secondary

---

[4] http://emec.mec.gov.br.
[5] https://sucupira.capes.gov.br/sucupira/public/index.xhtml.
[6] http://www.lncc.br/estrutura/default.php.
[7] http://posgrad.lncc.br/en.
[8] https://portal.fiocruz.br/en.

and professional education. The focus is not a bioinformatics curriculum, but the characterization of didactic-pedagogical experiences, the description of the teaching and learning process and the contents of bioinformatics. There are practical activities applied to the teaching of Molecular Biology and Genetics in the undergraduate course of Biological Sciences [21], the creation of university extension courses aimed at technical school students, high school and undergraduate students [30] and also for higher education students and for the academic community [16]. At the secondary level, Andrade [3] carried out a study on the importance and application of bioinformatics in the learning of sciences.

Practical activities were applied to the teaching of Molecular Biology and Genetics, creation of university extension courses, aimed at technical school students, high school students, university students and academic community. The methodology used was the application of questions to students, lectures, manual and practical *in silica* classes, and theoretical-practical classes. The contents were more introductory, providing the basic concepts and the necessary subsidies for the initiation in the research field of bioinformatics. We sought to approach from the basic fundamentals, involving genomics, transcriptomics, proteomics, general notions about biological databases, sequence alignment, molecular modeling, introduction to computation, programming and the use of specific bioinformatics tools.

However, none of these papers contribute to the teaching of the discipline with a focus on the visually impaired (VI). There is a lack of studies that relate bioinformatics and the inclusion of people with disabilities, especially when it comes to VI students.

3   Difficulties in Teaching Bioinformatics to the Visually Impaired

There are researches dealing with perspectives and challenges in bioinformatics training [9,13,24,31,38] and others that present the multidisciplinary character of this discipline [7,12,16]. They suggest that bioinformaticians should develop different skills and competencies. Bruhn and Jennings [7], for example, emphasize that students must demonstrate the ability to work in a multidisciplinary field and apply the acquired knowledge in solving relevant problems. Welch et al. [40] state that in order to successfully perform the duties of a bioinformatics researcher, it is necessary to have a series of skills, such as the ability to manage, interpret, and analyze large data sets; broad knowledge of bioinformatics analysis methodologies; familiarity with functional genetic and genomic data; and expertise in common bioinformatics software packages and algorithms.

However, bioinformatics students often do not receive formal training on how to make the most of bioinformatics resources and tools available in the public domain [42]. Cattley and Arthur [8] point out that, when teaching bioinformatics, there is a difficulty related to the full number of resources needed to provide a solid foundation to the students. These range from repositories of publicly available information - such as databases - to complex tools for analyzing data obtained through experimental methods. These tools are very important in the process of knowledge construction, but in order to be really effective in the teaching and learning process, teachers need to know how to use them in a pedagogically appropriate way, how to select them from the large amount of available resources and evaluate the use of these tools in different teaching contexts. Still, the teacher needs to be up-to-date on the new available resources due to the progress in scientific research and the growth of the area.

Another important feature is the ease of access of these resources by students. Consideration should be given to technological infrastructure in high schools, courses and colleges. The use of these tools may depend on good internet connection, sufficient capacity to handle multiple simultaneous requests, quality computational resources, installation of all necessary software and also, integration of tools [8,21].

There are also difficulties related to HCI criteria such as usability, user satisfaction, ergonomics and accessibility [1,5,27,37–39]. Additionally, there is the complexity of the existing data available [6,10,28].

The union of areas such as computer science, mathematics, chemistry, software engineering, statistics and biology, present in bioinformatics bring many difficult and abstract concepts to students' comprehension [26,32,34]. Often, these contents are not available in an easily accessible format [25,34], requiring design or explanatory scheme for their understanding [26] and depending mainly on visual instruction [34]. Thus, it may be a challenge for bioinformatics faculty to teach these contents to VI students, to select bioinformatics tools that conform to accessibility standards, such as the W3C, and to be adapted to the use of AT. In this sense, we verified the importance of the teacher's commitment to the choice of the tools to be used, that are adequate to the profile of the student population.

Another point to consider is that one of the main difficulties in teaching molecular biology and bioinformatics lies in the fact that its content is related to microscopic aspects, which make a visual representation challenging. This difficulty is usually related to the large amount of information and structural details contained in the molecules, which involve shape changes, chemical reactions, cellular motions, molecular modifications, and events, which often occur simultaneously, making it even more difficult to understand and assimilate. This is even more complex when students are VI, especially total blind students, since they can not observe microscopic, digital images or didactic schemes [35].

Therefore, it can be said that certain bioinformatics concepts require a great capacity of abstraction from the students. Stimulating abstraction by VI students requires the exploration of other resources, often not available to the teacher. There is an opportunity on the development of supporting didactic resources so that students with visual impairment have access to these concepts [21]. Thus, bioinformatics teachers must be incentivated to update their teaching practice to include the use of AT resources.

In this sense, there is a vast field of research being developed for teaching the VI and, due to this diversity of works, there is a great need for knowledge integration. There are studies related to the teaching of areas such as natural sciences [25,34] and computer science [22,36]. Some of these studies corroborate that the main difficulties of DVs are in relation to content concepts and learning [34], mainly in the understanding of the drawings and schemes [26], besides the students demonstrate lack of confidence, lack of motivation, etc. in learning this content [25].

These works point out that the teaching of sciences has been depended mostly on visual instruction. This makes it difficult for VI students included in regular classrooms to learn the science concepts [34], such as those of the bioinformatics. The lack of accessibility in the physical and computational environment is other aspect mentioned. They report that classrooms should be adapted and instruction methodology should be adjusted for a better experience from VI students [34]. Many computational tools are still inaccessible, because the graphical nature of such tools, which prevents the inclusion of VI students in school activities [22].

Maguvhe [25] points out that teachers still lack the requisite skills in special education to harness learner potential. There are missing teacher motivation and mentorship in education methodologies and the use of tools for learner empowerment. This situation requires that there is an action in the training of bioinformatics teachers so that they are prepared for an adequate attendance to this student public.

4   Methodology

In this study, we conducted an exploratory, quantitative-qualitative study to identify the tools used in teaching bioinformatics in the Brazilian context. The data collection have been carried out with a questionnaire created to help us to understand the following research questions: (RQ1) What is the teaching profile of the professors of the discipline of bioinformatics in undergraduate and graduate courses? (RQ2) What are the computational resources that are used as support in teaching bioinformatics? (RQ3) What are the main tools used to introduce the basic bioinformatics concepts; the primary, secondary and scientific literature databases; tools for visualization and manipulation of sequences and biological macromolecules; alignment tools coupled with multiple alignment; tools for secondary and tertiary protein prediction. (RQ4) What are the quality characteristics of software that teachers consider relevant in a bioinformatics tool? (RQ5) What is the experience of teachers with students with Visual Impairment? (RQ6) What strategies and assistive technologies do teachers use to teach bioinformatics to a student with Visual Impairment?

With these questions, we aim to contribute to teachers' pedagogical practice in relation to the selection of tools and HCI criteria considered relevant for their selection. Also, our objective is to collect the educators' perceptions about the teaching and the use of interactive systems of the area with students with VI and the use of AT resources.

Study 1, previously performed [23], contributed to the understanding of two types of tools in teaching bioinformatics, databases and visualizers of three-dimensional protein structures. The analysis of experiences lived by this professor indicated HCI criteria to be used, or not, in the design of software interfaces for bioinformatics. In this study, we sought to broaden the scope of the study to other educational institutions.

4.1 Data Collection Instrument

The development of the data collection instrument was based on a case study (Study 1) [23], held in the discipline of bioinformatics that is part of the curriculum of an undergraduate course in biological sciences held by PUCRS university, Brazil. Semi-structured interviews were conducted with a professor specialized in bioinformatics, with 27 years of experience in research and 15 years in teaching, both at undergraduate and graduate levels. Also, we've performed documental analysis of the books, tools and materials used in the classroom by the teacher.

The data collection instrument sought to address the research questions previously reported. It comprises 48 items, divided into 5 sections:

1. The professors' profile (5 questions): age group, academic training, teaching experience in bioinformatics disciplines, taught subjects, disciplines offered, institutions in which he/she taught the disciplines, average students per class.
2. The teaching methodology and computational resources: tools for working on basic concepts, biological databases, visualization and manipulation of sequences and structures of biological molecules; The questions included the experience of teachers in undergraduate courses (16 questions) and graduate courses (17 questions);
3. The HCI criteria for selection and use of software in bioinformatics disciplines (1 question): includes usability, ergonomics, user satisfaction and accessibility, as well as aspects of learning-related tools.
4. Teaching of blind students with/without assistive technologies (5 questions).
5. Contact information (1 question): finally, we provided a field for the participant to provide e-mail data to participate in future studies.

An online questionnaire was made available to participants through Google Forms[9]. We followed the basic protocols of ethical research and sent to all the participants the Informed Consent Form (TCLE). This document clarifies clearly the research protocols and is also the manifestation of agreement with the participation in the research. We also ask the teachers to confirm that they teach or have already taught bioinformatics content, in undergraduate and/or graduate courses, in order to be able to compose the sample.

4.2 Sample

The sample, non-probabilistic for convenience, was obtained by searching [10] the Directory of Research Groups of CNPq, Brazil.

---

[9] https://www.google.com/forms/about/.
[10] search held on 05/22/2017.

The search keyword used was "bioinformatics". We only have included certified research groups on the search. As a result we have obtained: 45 groups that have the keyword in the name of the group; 174 groups report "bioinformatics" as the name of their research line; and 180 groups that have declared "bioinformatics" as one of their keywords in their line of research. In addition, we have supplemented the search results with a Google search by entering the keywords "bioinformatics" and "discipline".

In both cases only teachers who reported in their Lattes curriculum to teach the discipline of bioinformatics specifically were selected. We take into account that bioinformatics is an interdisciplinary area, and as such, it can be inserted in other disciplines such as molecular biology, computational biology, biochemistry, etc. We chose to include in the sample only teachers who indicated in their curriculum teaching the discipline, limiting the search scope so that the results were referring especially to this discipline. In total, 61 teachers were invited to participate of the study. Only 29 (46%) agreed to participate.

5   Results

This section brings the results of data collection, based on the research questions stated in the previous section. To visualize the results, we chose to follow a standard protocol to better present the data and facilitate its understanding:

- The information presented is related to the discipline of bioinformatics taught both in undergraduate and graduate courses.
- Throughout this section, the letter U will be used to indicate the answers referring to undergraduate and G for graduate.
- The responses of the teachers involved both the bioinformatics discipline given at the time of application of the questionnaire and the other disciplines of bioinformatics that they taught in the past, taking into account their experience as a teacher.
- When referring to number of citations, the value will be formatted as (x), where x is the value;
- When referring to number of subjects that have answered a question, the value will be formatted as (x/y%), where x is the number of subjects and y is the percentage of total.

5.1   The Teachers' Profiles

Responding to RQ1, it was found that the majority of respondents were male (21/72%), age between 25 and 64 years, with 17 participants between 35 and 44 years old (59%), 5 participants from 45 up to 54 years (17%), 5 over 55 years (17%) and 2 aged 25–34 years (7%).

When asked about their highest educational level, the majority (22/76%) had a postdoctoral training as a maximum qualification and the others had doctoral degrees (7/24%). These teachers also came from different areas of formation

(Fig. 1). As we can see, most teachers have some training in the area of biological sciences (21/72%), with approximately half (10/34%) having only formation in this area and others (11/38%) adding this formation to others areas. In addition, some (6/21%) have formation only in the area of applied sciences.

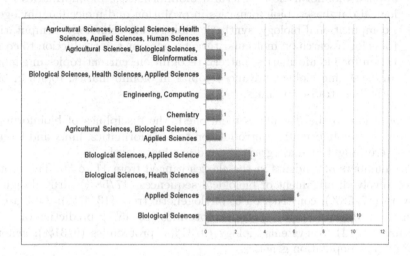

Fig. 1. Training areas of bioinformatics teachers

In Brazil, teachers taught the discipline of bioinformatics in the following institutions: (U,G): FIOCRUZ, FURG, LNCC, Promove, UEL, UENF, UFC-SPA, UFGD, UFJF, UFMG, UFRJ, UFSC, UFSJ, UNIFAL, USP; (U): UCB, UFBA, UFRGS, UFSCar, UFSM, UFV, UMA, UNESP, UNIFAN, UNIPAMPA, UNIRIO; (G): INCURSOS, IAC, UFPR, UNICAMP, UTFPR; The foreign institutions mentioned were: (U, G): Universidad Nacional Autónoma de México (UNAM, Mexico), Universidad de Buenos Aires (UBA, Argentina) and Universidad de Antioquia (Colombia); (U): CES university (Colombia) and other foreign institutes that were not mentioned.

The teachers also informed the courses and the name of the disciplines that involved the teaching of bioinformatics, as follows:

- Undergraduate Courses: technologist in environmental toxicology, biotechnology, biomedicine, biological sciences, bioinformatics, biomedical sciences, computer science, pharmacy and biochemistry.
    - Disciplines: instrumental bioinformatics, bioinformatics for toxicology, molecular biology, computational tools for drug development, informatics applied to biological sciences, molecular modeling, visualization and manipulation of biological macromolecules.
- Graduate courses: tropical and sub-tropical agriculture, bioengineering, bioinformatics, computational and systems biology, general biology and bioprospecting, molecular and cellular biology, biology, biotechnology and biosciences, biological sciences, biochemistry, health sciences, computer science

and applied computing, genomic medicine, computational modeling, pathology, plant production and associated bioprocesses, chemistry and technology.

– Disciplines: algorithms for computational biology, data recovery storage in bioinformatics, biological database, biophysics of canalopathies, applied bioinformatics, structural bioinformatics, bioinformatics i - biological databases, bioinformatics in evolution and molecular phylogenies , computational biology, synthetic biology, biotechnology, computational tools for research on molecular targets, genomics, introduction to computation for bioinformatics, pattern recognition, current topics in genomics and systemic biology, advanced topics in bioinformatics, topics in bioinformatics, transcriptomics.

In addition to the disciplines mentioned, the disciplines of bioinformatics, genomics and bioinformatics, introduction to bioinformatics, linux and bioinformatics were taught at undergraduate and graduate levels.

The numbers of students in the classes ranged from 11 to 30. The contents worked involved: alignment of biological sequences (17/58%); drug design and discovery (17/58%); construction of phylogenetic trees (13/45%); database and information retrieval (15/51%); transcriptomics (13/45%); prediction of protein structures (12/41%); systems biology (9/31%); proteomics (9/31%); genomics (6/20%); and population genetics.

Of the total of 29 respondents, the majority (27/93%) taught bioinformatics at the graduate level, while some also taught at undergraduate courses (18 /62%). Some professors also mentioned having taught the discipline of bioinformatics in extension courses.

5.2 Computational Resources Used

As for RQ2 (Fig. 2), teachers use internet file sharing (e.g. google drive, dropbox, github etc.), learning management systems (LMS) (e.g. Moodle, Teleduc, etc.), specific web pages (e.g. National Center for Biotechnology Information (NCBI), Expasy, PDB101, etc.), personal web pages, online tutorials and the use of TIDIA software[11]. Besides these features, it was mentioned they use software for programming, analyzing algorithms, running programs on remote servers. In this sense, a professor said that he works with the computational side of bioinformatics.

RQ3 encompasses the main tools used by teachers, from those to teach basic contents to more specialized tools. To work with the introductory content, the NCBI portal was the most cited (45), followed by the GenBank Database (41) and the EMBL-EBI Services Portal (34). Also, the following tools were mentioned: Autodock, BLAST, Bioconductor, KEGG, miRBASE - miRNA database, Modeller, Molprobity, NAMD, PDBj, PFAM, Pubchem, SAVES, STRING; VMD; algorithms and computer techniques, protein modeling and visualization software, docking software, molecular dynamics software, data mining tools and DBMSs.

---

[11] http://www.tidia-ae.usp.br/portal.

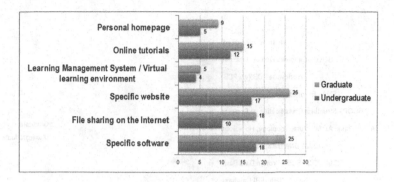

Fig. 2. Main computational resources used to support the teaching of bioinformatics

Bioinformatics databases (BD) are repositories of biological data obtained by experimental methods. In the creation of the instrument, the classification was used to define the types of DBs in primary (DBP) and secondary (DBS) [4, 15]. In addition to these, there is classification of scientific literature databases (BDLC) [19]. The main databases selected by the teachers are illustrated in Fig. 3. Also, the secondary databases GEO, Uniprot, EMBL-Atlas, String, ZINC, PubChem, Rfam and GOA were cited once.

Also, the main tools for visualization and manipulation of sequences and biological macromolecules were searched (Fig. 4). It is a type of molecular graphical visualization tool, from various perspectives, able to load and display the contents of the data files. The most cited were PyMOL and Swiss-PDB Viewer, both referred to 8 times.

Next, we present the tools for pairwise alignment (comparison of two sequences) and multiple alignment (with three or more biological sequences). The purpose of sequence alignments is to measure the similarity between two or more sequences, to infer evolutionary relationships, and to observe patterns of conservation and variability for structural and functional predictions. For pairwise alignment the most mentioned tool was NCBI BLAST (45), followed by MEGA-Molecular Evolutionary Genetics Analysis (14) and UniProt BLAST (12). It should be note that the BLAST algorithm is the same, but the interfaces are different, which may explain the preference of one over the other. As an example, teachers still indicated BLAST at PBIL (2), BLAST at PDB (2), in addition to the FASTA algorithm (1) and EMBOSS Needle (command line and web)(1). Two teachers do not use it. Tools for multiple alignment were cited: ClustalX (26); Muscle (21); ClustalW - ExPASy (20); MEGA (19); T-Coffee/EMBL - EBI (18); MAFFT - EMBL-EBI (15); Kalign - EMBL-EBI (5); MultiAlin (4); T-Coffee - Vital-IT (SIB) (3); T-Coffee - Vital-IT - (SIB) (3); Clustal Ômega (2);

As for the tools for predicting and analyzing protein structures, some teachers do not use them since they are more specialized, commonly used in structural

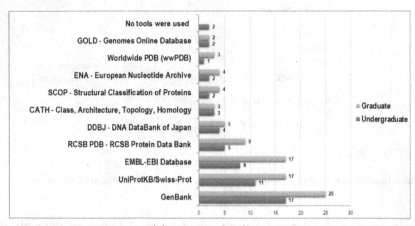

(a) primary databases

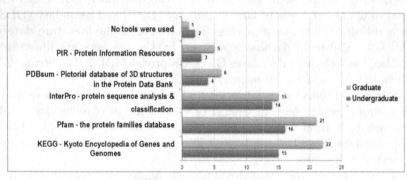

(b) secondary databases

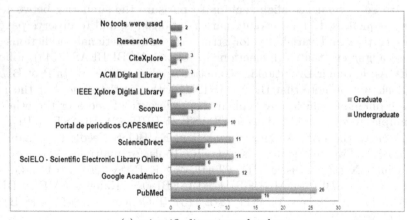

(c) scientific literature databases

Fig. 3. Bioinformatics and scientific literature databases

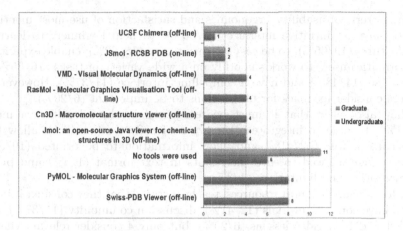

Fig. 4. Tools for visualization and manipulation of sequences and structurer of biological macromolecules

bioinformatics. The main tools used by the teachers to obtain secondary (SS) and tertiary (TS) structures, and model validation (MV) are:

- SS: JPred4 - Protein secondary structure prediction server (8), PSIPRED - Protein Sequence Analysis Workbench (6), PORTER - A new accurate server for protein secondary structure prediction (2), Stride (1), JMpred (1), NetSurfP - Protein Surface Accessibility and Secondary Structure Predictions (1), Jufo9D (1) e Predator (1).
- TS: SWISS-MODEL (9), Modeller (8), I-TASSER - Server for protein structure and function prediction (5), Phyre2 (1), QUARK - De Novo Protein Structure Prediction (1), Raptor X (1) e Robetta - Full-chain protein structure prediction server (1).
- MV: PROCHECK - EMBL-EBI (7), Verify 3D (5), SWISS-MODEL (5), Modeller (4), WHAT_CHECK (3), ProSA-web - Protein Structure Analysis (2), molprobity (1), SAVES (1), Molprobity (1).

The list of all the tools, as well as the complete study was available for consultation at http://bit.ly/863231351.

5.3 Criteria for Selection of Tools by Teachers

For the selection of tools (RQ6), teachers first consider if the're feely available (23/79%). They also find it important to allow information to be saved (21/72%), to have help and documentation (21/72%), to be constantly updated (20/69%). Some teachers consider that the tool should be available online (16) and others have indicated that it is offline (13/45%). They cite the ability to integrate other types of software (14/48%) and allow configuration (12/41%) and printing of the information (10/34%).

The criteria of usability, ergonomics and satisfaction of use most mentioned were to have an intuitive interface (19/65%), to help beginners to learn the basic features (19/65%), to be easy to learn to use (18/62%); enable experienced bioinformatics users to work smoothly on a wide variety of tasks (16/55%), be easy to use (14/48%) and have a compelling interface (11/37%). However, few teachers consider feedback for user actions to be important (6/20%).

They also select that it must be recognized in the scientific community (15/51%), be able to integrate other types of software (14/48%), allow them to be configurable (12/41%) and allow information to be printed (10/34%). Also, we were allowed to save the results in text format (1/3%) and present documentation and limitations (1/3%).

As for teaching support resources, teachers stated that they consider it important to have content tutorials (12/41%), discussion community (11/37%), exercises list (7/24%), video lessons (6/20%), but only 4 consider relevant that the language be configurable.

Finally, of the 29 participating teachers, few (9/31%) consider that the tools must have resources for access to disabled users and allow access to different user profiles (7/24%).

5.4   Teacher Experience in Teaching the Visually Impaired

This subsection addresses the RQ5 and RQ6 research questions. Of the 29 participating teachers in the sample, only 1 had experience with a user who is blind, in the course of graduation. The teacher informs that the student did not use AT. As for this experience, the teacher reported that "he found it a bit complicated, and he needed to be prepared for it." Asked about strategies for teaching bioinformatics content to students who are blind and the use of AT, 3 teachers reported that they could not answer this question, and 3 teachers claimed that they did not have the experience to suggest some kind of strategy. Of the 29 participants, only 8 teachers answered the question:

- "Text to speech, speech to text, adapted virtual reality, concrete models".
- "It is difficult to answer this question, but I imagine that auditory resources should be applied both to confirm input of data and outputs of data after processing"
- "There are strategies to be discovered because students of bioinformatics who are blind should acquire knowledge through their auditory organ. The idea of what is a protein structure, protein-ligand interaction, which are visually and quickly assimilated, would not be captured by the VI. However, this knowledge can be supplied by lego models of protein structures and sequences subject to touch."
- "Use of sound".
- "Call center menu driven by numbers".
- "Adapted keyboards and voice command".
- "Audiobooks and Braille material".
- "Using 3D Printing, making audio resources available, among others".

6 Discussion

Bioinformatics is an interdisciplinary discipline. Its teachers are generally trained in different areas of knowledge. This study pointed out that teachers in Brazil also come from different areas and teach bioinformatics in varied courses, but mostly in graduate programs. Despite the selected sample included only teachers who informed the bioinformatics discipline, the results indicated, as expected, that bioinformatics contents are included in other disciplines, such as computing for biologists and other professionals, programming, algorithms, and recovery of information.

It is interesting that one teacher reported teaching programming languages and Linux for the course of Biological Sciences. It is common in bioinformatics to use the Unix or Linux operating system under which many bioinformatics applications are run, and also because many of these tools require the creation of Perl or Python scripts, and the student needs to gain knowledge of programming languages. This is important because it enables biological students to learn computational thinking necessary to acquire basic skills in the use of the most common bioinformatics software, which in turn facilitates learning, effective interpretation of results and proper use of resources [18]. One teacher also replied that the main focus of the discipline is computing for bioinformatics. Although it is not necessary for most bioinformaticians to develop these specialized skills (including software development), they must have basic skills in using the most common bioinformatics software and the effective interpretation of results [8].

It can be seen that introductory courses are taught both in undergraduate and graduate courses. On the other hand, the disciplines that require a greater knowledge on the part of the student, with more specific content, and involving, for example, the retrieval of information in databases and specific areas of bioinformatics, such as phylogeny, systemic biology, and structural bioinformatics are mainly seen at graduate level. There were no reports of disciplines taught at a distance; all were presential.

Most teachers did not consider important that the language the interface be configurable, because generally scientific tools are made available in English.

Despite being an initial study, this research revealed that most participants still do not have experience in teaching bioinformatics to VI students. Teachers are unaware of the existence of AT resources, how to use and where to find them. This issue becomes even more important because one of the main difficulties in teaching structural bioinformatics lies in the fact that its content is related to microscopic aspects, which make visual representation difficult.

7 Conclusion

Although this is an initial study, this research reveals that most of the bioinformatics teachers are not able to attend to the VI audience and there is still a lack of information on assistive/inclusive issues.

The study of accessibility in bioinformatics tools opens a new set of access opportunities, which has the potential to include the visually impaired in areas of life and health sciences involving bioinformatics content. During the analysis of the tools we perceived some perspectives and challenges. The first one refers to teachers' lack of knowledge about the existence of AT resources, how to use them and where to find them; there is also missing a map of accessible bioinformatics tools; to know at what time and in what form to use them in teaching VI users; and to verify if the difficulty of installing and configuring the programs and the lack of Portuguese versions are reasons that may hinder popularization by Brazilian students in the use of such programs and their use as auxiliary tools to pedagogical practice.

We believe that there is still a lack of specialized training and technical support in working with visually impaired students. The continuous academic formation of bioinformatics teachers should support quality inclusive education, encouraging the enrollment of these students in higher education in areas of science that involve this discipline. Teachers should provide adequate access conditions to curriculum content and computational tools, seeking appropriate ways to teach content with abstract and visual aspects.

This difficulty increases when students are blind because they can not observe microscopic, digital images or didactic schemes [35]. This problem is portrayed in Mariz [26]: "So one wonders how one with little or no vision would develop such skills? How to explain to students with visual impairment the dynamics of the geochemical process of carbon in nature, or the process of human fertilization, for example, already so complicated to understand by observing and analyzing drawings and photos? ... ... Scientific knowledge is a collective cultural good, so people with partial or total visual impairment should enjoy it as well.".

Finally, the analysis of which tools presented in this study are adequate to the use of AT and that meet accessibility standards, such as those of WCAG 2.0, will be dealt with in future works.

References

1. Al-Ageel, N., Al-Wabil, A., Badr, G., AlOmar, N.: Human factors in the design and evaluation of bioinformatics tools. Procedia Manuf. **3**, 2003–2010 (2015)
2. Altman, R.B.: A curriculum for bioinformatics: the time is ripe. Bioinformatics **14**(7), 549–550 (1998)
3. De Andrade, J.A.A.: Bioinformática: Um estudo sobre sua importância e aplicação na aprendizagem em ciências no ensino médio. Pontifícia Universidade Católica do Rio Grande Do Sul - PUCRS, Porto Alegre (2005)
4. Baxevanis, A.D., Ouellette, B.F.: Bioinformatics: A Practical Guide to the Analysis of Genes and Proteins, 2nd edn. Wiley, New York (2004)
5. Bolchini, D., Finkelstein, A., Perrone, V., Nagl, S.: Better bioinformatics through usability analysis. Bioinformatics **25**(3), 406–412 (2009). https://doi.org/10.1093/bioinformatics/btn633

6. Bongiolo, E.: Análise panorâmica da bioinformática no brasil: propostas da gestão de pessoas para os laboratórios de pesquisa (2006)
7. Bruhn, R., Jennings, S.F.: A multidisciplinary bioinformatics minor. ACM SIGCSE Bull. **39**(1), 348–352 (2007)
8. Cattley, S., Arthur, J.W.: BioManager: the use of a bioinformatics web application as a teaching tool in undergraduate bioinformatics training. Brief. Bioinform. **8**(6), 457–465 (2007)
9. Cummings, M.P., Temple, G.G.: Broader incorporation of bioinformatics in education: opportunities and challenges. Brief. Bioinform. **11**(6), 537–543 (2010)
10. da Silva, A.R., Camargo, R.P.E., Bossolan, N.R., Beltramini, L.M.: Development of models pieces to represent amino acid and to building protein structures: evaluation by graduation students and teachers from public schools of são paulo state. In: The 2nd International Symposium on Integrating Research, Education, and Problem Solving, pp. 1–6. International Institute of Informatics and Systemics (2012)
11. de Abreu Cybis, W., Betiol, A.H., Faust, R.: Ergonomia e Usabilidade 3ª edição: Conhecimentos, Métodos e Aplicações. Novatec Editora (2015)
12. de Melo-Minardi, R.C., Digiampietri, L.A., de Melo, P.O.V., Franciscani Jr., G.R., Oliveira, L.B.: Caracterização dos programas de pós-graduação em bioinformática no brasil. In: XXXIII Congresso da Sociedade Brasileira de Computação, pp. 1620–1631. Brazilian Computer Society (SBC) (2013)
13. Dimitrov, R.A., Gouliamova, D.E.: Bioinformatics education: perspectives and challenges. Biotechnol. Biotechnol. Equip. **23**(sup1), 40–42 (2009)
14. Douglas, C., Goulding, R., Farris, L., Atkinson-Grosjean, J.: Socio-cultural characteristics of usability of bioinformatics databases and tools. Interdiscip. Sci. Rev. **36**(1), 55–71 (2011)
15. EMBL-EBI: Primary and secondary databases (2017)
16. Farias, A., Chacon, P., da Silva, N.: A bioinformática como ferramenta de formação de rescursos humanos no ifrn. HOLOS **6**, 113–123 (2012)
17. Ocaña, K.A.C.S., Vasconcelos, A.T.R., Teixeira, S.M.R., Oliveira, P.S.L., Gadelha, L., Galheigo, M., Bastos, B.F.: Bioinfo-portal: a scientific gateway for integrating bioinformatics tools in the brazilian national high-performance computing network. In: Workshop at X-Meeting 2016 - 12th International Conference of the AB3C. Associação Brasileira de Bioinformática e Biologia Computacional (AB3C) (2016). http://x-meeting.com/events/workshops
18. Gibas, C., Jambeck, P.: Developing Bioinformatics Computer Skills. O'Reilly Media Inc., Sebastopol (2001)
19. Lesk, A.M.: Introduction to Bioinformatics, 4th edn. Oxford University Press, Oxford (2013)
20. Levine, A.G., et al.: An explosion of bioinformatics careers. Science **344**(6189), 1303–1306 (2014)
21. Lopes Ribeiro Jr., H., Germano de Oliveira, R.T., Ceccatto, V.M.: Bioinformática como recurso pedagógico para o curso de ciências biológicas na universidade estadual do ceará. Acta Sci. Educ. **34**(1), 129–140 (2012)
22. Luque, L., de Oliveira Brandão, L., Tori, R., Brandão, A.A.F.: On the inclusion of blind people in UML e-learning activities. Braz. J. Comput. Educ. **23**(02), 18 (2015)

23. Stangherlin Machado, V., Paixão-Cortes, W.R., Norberto de Souza, O., de Borba Campos, M.: Decision-making for interactive systems: a case study for teaching and learning in bioinformatics. In: Zaphiris, P., Ioannou, A. (eds.) LCT 2017. LNCS, vol. 10296, pp. 90–109. Springer, Cham (2017). https://doi.org/10.1007/978-3-319-58515-4_8

24. Magana, A.J., Taleyarkhan, M., Alvarado, D.R., Kane, M., Springer, J., Clase, K.: A survey of scholarly literature describing the field of bioinformatics education and bioinformatics educational research. CBE-Life Sci. Educ. **13**(4), 607–623 (2014)

25. Maguvhe, M.: Teaching science and mathematics to students with visual impairments: reflections of a visually impaired technician. Afr. J. Disabil. **4**(1), 1–6 (2015)

26. Mariz, G.F.: O uso de modelos tridimensionais como ferramenta pedagógica no ensino de biologia para estudantes com deficiência visual. Ph.D. thesis (2014)

27. Mirel, B., Wright, Z.: Heuristic evaluations of bioinformatics tools: a development case. In: Jacko, J.A. (ed.) HCI 2009. LNCS, vol. 5610, pp. 329–338. Springer, Heidelberg (2009). https://doi.org/10.1007/978-3-642-02574-7_37

28. Nelson, A., Goetze, J.: Modeling protein folding & applying it to a relevant activity. Am. Biol. Teach. **66**(4), 287–289 (2004)

29. Neshich, G.: Computational biology in Brazil. PLoS Comput. Biol. **3**(10), e185 (2007)

30. de Mello Padilha, I.Q., Durbano, J.P.D.M., Martins, A.B., dos Santos Almeida, R., Macarajá-Coutinho, V.R.H., de Araújo, D.A.M.: A bioinformática como instrumento de inserção digital e de difusão da biotecnologia. Rev. Eletrônica Ext. Cid. **5**(1), 1–5 (2008)

31. Ranganathan, S.: Bioinformatics education–perspectives and challenges. PLoS Comput. Biol. **1**(6), 0447–0448 (2005)

32. Rezende, P.H., Eloy, M.: Sistema web para apoio ao ensino de biologia molecular e bioinformática. In: Proceedings of International Conference on Interactive Computer aided Blended Learning, pp. 365–368. International Association of Online Engineering (IAOE) (2013)

33. Rogers, Y., Sharp, H., Preece, J.: Interaction Design: Beyond Human-Computer Interaction. Wiley, Chichester (2011)

34. Sahin, M., Yorek, N.: Teaching science to visually impaired students: a small-scale qualitative study. Online Submiss. **6**(4), 19–26 (2009)

35. Sant'Anna, N.F., Araújo, G. de S.M., da Rocha, L.O., Garcez, S.F., Barboza, C.B.: Técnicas para produção e reprodução de material educacional de baixo custo na área de ciências morfológicas para deficientes visuais. Int. Sci. J. **IX**(30), 14–32 (2014). https://doi.org/10.6020/1679-9844/3002

36. Santos, L.G.D., Bandeira, A.L., Pansanato, L.T., Paiva, D.M.: Recursos de acessibilidade para auxiliar a navegação de estudantes cegos em um editor de diagramas. In: Brazilian Symposium on Computers in Education (Simpósio Brasileiro de Informática na Educação-SBIE), vol. 23 (2012)

37. Shaer, O., Kol, G., Strait, M., Fan, C., Grevet, C., Elfenbein, S.: G-nome surfer: a tabletop interface for collaborative exploration of genomic data. In: Proceedings of the SIGCHI Conference on Human Factors in Computing Systems, CHI 2010, pp. 1427–1436. ACM, New York (2010)

38. Tastan Bishop, Ö., Adebiyi, E.F., Alzohairy, A.M., Everett, D., Ghedira, K., Ghouila, A., Kumuthini, J., Mulder, N.J., Panji, S., Patterton, H.-G., et al.: Bioinformatics education–perspectives and challenges out of Africa. Brief. Bioinform. **16**(2), 355–364 (2015)

39. Veretnik, S., Fink, J.L., Bourne, P.E.: Computational biology resources lack persistence and usability. PLoS Comput. Biol. **4**(7), 1–3 (2008)

40. Welch, L., Lewitter, F., Schwartz, R., Brooksbank, C., Radivojac, P., Gaeta, B., Schneider, M.V.: Bioinformatics curriculum guidelines: toward a definition of core competencies. PLOS Comput. Biol. **10**(3), 1–10 (2014)
41. Welch, L.R., Schwartz, R., Lewitter, F.: A report of the curriculum task force of the ISCB education committee. PLoS Comput. Biol. **8**(6), 1–2 (2012)
42. Wright, V.A., Vaughan, B.W., Laurent, T., Lopez, R., Brooksbank, C., Schneider, M.V.: Bioinformatics training: selecting an appropriate learning content management system–an example from the European bioinformatics institute. Brief. Bioinform. **11**(6), 552–562 (2010)

A Personal Emotion-Based Recipe Recommendation Mobile Social Platform: Mood Canteen

Tsai-Hsuan Tsai[1(✉)], Hsien-Tsung Chang[2], Chia-Yu Hsu[1],
Shu-Yu Lin[2], Wei-Cheng Yan[3], and Yi-Cheng Chen[3]

[1] Digital Media Lab, Chang Gung University, Tao-Yuan, Taiwan
ttsai@mail.cgu.edu.tw
[2] Department of Computer Science and Information Engineering, Chang Gung
University, Tao-Yuan, Taiwan
[3] Metal Industries Research and Development Centre, Kaohsiung, Taiwan

Abstract. This study resulted in the development of a mobile social platform, called Mood Canteen, which has the purpose of meal cuisine and recipe sharing. Mood Canteen has two important characteristics: (1) to establish the relationship between food and emotion: To construct an interaction between food and personal emotions, Mood Canteen applies an emotion analysis mechanism on SNS to analyze emotions based on semantics, emoticons/emoji, and images of food-and cuisine-related posts, and it matches those emotions with food to create a user's personal emotional state database and emotional food database according to the study's results. (2) To establish an emotion-complementing healing system: To make emotion cuisine recommendations for users that meet their emotional state and help users alleviate negative emotions and promote positive emotions by sharing recipes and meals, Mood Canteen incorporates a newly created personalized meal recommendation mechanism that provides users with the appropriate comfort food selection based on a personal emotional state database and emotional food database. In addition, based on the characteristics and requirements of the mobile user interface, this study applied the SMASH usability heuristics to initiate the usability measurements of the developed Mood Canteen system.

Keywords: Mood-boosting receipts · Emotion analysis
Emotion cuisine database · Recipe sharing community · Mobile application
Usability heuristics for smartphones

1 Introduction

Food is the source of nutrients that we depend on to live and plays a role in both reducing tension and producing mood regulation. Many studies have revealed that certain foods can indeed promote positive emotions and ease the impact of negative emotions. For example, the emotional factor for people who choose sweets during social occasions could lie in the sharing of joy and happiness from friendship. The motive in choosing comfort food is usually to ensure a good emotional state or to

© Springer International Publishing AG, part of Springer Nature 2018
M. Antona and C. Stephanidis (Eds.): UAHCI 2018, LNCS 10908, pp. 574–582, 2018.
https://doi.org/10.1007/978-3-319-92052-8_45

reduce anxiety, sadness, and other negative emotions [1–4]. Based on the influence of food on emotion, Professor Charles Spence partnered with Just Eat to develop the "Just Eat" mobile app, which uses mood mapping to analyze people's emotional states. In other words, it detects a user's facial expression by scanning it to evaluate whether they feel angry, disgusted, fearful, surprising, sad, or joyful, and it then provides appropriate food recommendations according to their emotional state. For example, an angry expression could appear when a person is stressed, in which case, the app suggests foods that have a calming effect, such as dark chocolate and nuts rich in magnesium. In the case of excitement, foods such as whole grains and beans, which are beneficial to blood sugar regulation, are recommended [5, 6]. Studies have also found that food plays a vital role in relaxing and soothing emotion, which encourages people to read food or recipe-related articles and to search for food-related images and videos through social media to maintain or enhance their own positive emotions. In addition, the users prefer to share these food-related messages on social media to induce similar emotional changes in viewers [7, 8]. Thus, many social media forums are based on recipe sharing, such as Tasty [9], Tastemade [10], Kitchen Stories [11], and iCook [12], all of which have become very popular. Unfortunately, the mechanism of current recipe sharing and recommending platforms neither connects to the personal emotional states of the users nor recommends appropriate foods or recipes that are suitable for people in different emotional states. For this reason, this study designs a mobile social platform, Mood Canteen [13], for cuisine and recipe sharing. In addition to the original function of providing a social media community, Mood Canteen emphasizes the interaction between food and human emotions, and it recognizes and analyzes the emotional states of the users through images, texts, and Emoji/Emoticons. In addition, Mood Canteen can suggest menus that meet both the users' emotional needs and their preferences and customs, in the hope of alleviating negative emotions through food and assisting in the generation of positive emotions. In so doing, it allows food to not only provide necessary nutrition and energy but also assist in promoting positive emotions.

2   Mood Canteen Design and Development

2.1   Design Rationale of Mood Canteen

Mood Canteen is a mobile application that was designed to recommend emotion foods based on the user's current mood. To suggest foods that are suitable for the user's emotional state, we applied mechanisms from Scherer's Geneva emotion wheel [14], Machajdik and Hanbury's affective image classification [15], and MoodLens, an emoticon-based sentiment analysis system based on emotion analysis theory created by Zhao et al. for Chinese tweets [16], to create a personal emotion database and an emotion cuisine database. For the emotion cuisine database, the app first searches for food- and cuisine-related posts on the web and social media, followed by food pairing with emotion analysis such as semantics, Emoticons/Emoji, and images to establish an emotion cuisine database [14–17]. For the personal emotional state database, we first have a user obtain authorization from Facebook, and we then conduct an emotion analysis of the Facebook data that uses text, emoticons and emoji, and images on SNS

[14–17]; with these, we create the user's personal emotional state database. Next, the Mood Canteen system recommends an appropriate mood cuisine that is suitable for the users according to the information in the emotional food database and the personal emotional state database. Mood Canteen even provides features such as emotional cuisine classification and searching, which allows users to customize meals in accordance with their emotional attributes and send the feedback to the Mood Canteen emotional cuisine database. Moreover, Mood Canteen provides users with a meal video recording and recipe editing, which enables the users to create personalized recipes and share them on social media. Figure 1 shows the Mood Canteen system architecture.

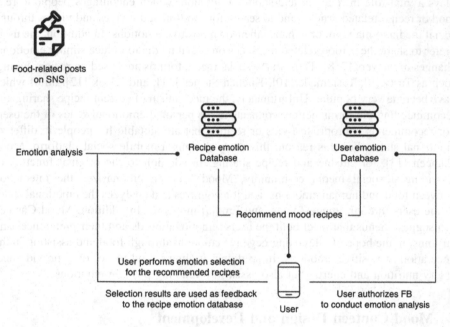

Fig. 1. Mood canteen system architecture.

2.2 Features of Mood Canteen

Mood Canteen offers system features such as daily mood-boosting recipes, recipe editing, video recording, my collection, and search. The main features of Mood Canteen are the following:

(1) **Daily mood-boosting receipts function:** Daily mood-boosting recipes is the homepage of the Mood Canteen system; it analyzes and recommends the appropriate emotional cuisine for users based on the personal emotion analysis mechanism. Mood Canteen will recommend recipes that are displayed on the daily mood-boosting recipes interface and present the emotional category of each meal. Users can browse the cuisine videos, read over the detailed picture-text sections of the recipes, and create an emotional category for each meal.

Furthermore, the emotional meal attributes defined by the users will be sent to the recipe emotion database as feedback and become the basis of a database update.

(2) **Personal recipe editing function:** To create personalized recipes, Mood Canteen provides recipe editing and meal recording so users can customize their own recipes. Recipe editing includes video editing and graphic editing. Users can click on the meal video to initiate film editing, select an animation, and add or delete text descriptions. After completing the video editing, a user can enter text editing mode and select the emotional attributes of a meal.

(3) **Meal video recording function:** While recording a meal video, users can add a node as a recipe step for subsequent editing. At the completion of the recording, the users will enter the editing procedure directly. During this process, users can add different seasonings or cooking movement animations to increase the thoroughness of a recipe video and its personal characteristics.

(4) **My collection function:** This function allows users to save their own favorite recipes. In addition to displaying the users' personal information and chef level, users can view their fans, track their number of followers, and view their personal pages.

(5) **Search function:** The search function allows the users to select the emotional categories and food ingredients or search for their favorite meals by a keyword (Figs. 2, 3 and 4).

Fig. 2. Mood canteen homepage and daily mood-boosting recipes function.

2.3 System Validation

A mobile user interface usability measurement was performed after the construction of the Mood Canteen system was complete. Evaluating and improving the user interface

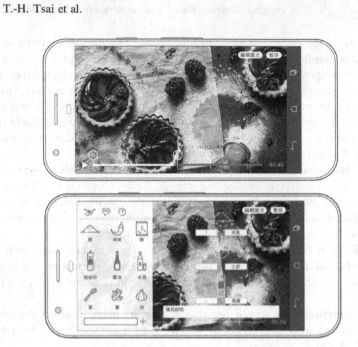

Fig. 3. Mood canteen meal video recording function.

Fig. 4. Mood canteen my collection function (pictures on the left); search g function (pictures on the right).

design have very important associations with the system development. The heuristic evaluation is based on the design specifications of 10 usability heuristics for user interface designs presented by Nielsen to provide an interface design with references by observing the interface and making positive and negative comments. The implementation modality is to find the problems in the user interface design during its usage based on the experience of 3–5 specialists. Its advantages are that it is easy to operate, fast, and low cost; its disadvantage is that the evaluator's own experience will affect the problems that are found. Analysts with experience in Usability assessment can identify more problems than amateurs can, and suggestions that are made with a focus on improving the problems will be more specific than those made by amateurs [18, 19]. For this reason, Wong et al. [20] presented user-involved usability measurements that can recognize problems from different aspects. In the heuristic evaluation, it is suggested to have the user search and document the ideas and difficulties encountered in the operation of the user interfaces. In addition, based on the characteristics and requirements of the mobile user interface, Inostroza et al. [21] developed SMASH, which is a set of usability heuristics for smartphones that is built on the heuristic evaluation of Nielsen's 10 usability heuristics. Thus, this study applied the 12 SMASH usability heuristics of Inostroza et al., as designed for smartphones, to initiate the usability measurements of the developed Mood Canteen system. First, 5 experts were invited; 2 had a background in information engineering, and 3 had a digital media background. In addition to having extensive experience in mobile applications development, these experts had performed systematic usability assessment tests to participate in a SMASH assessment of the Mood Canteen. The experts tested the system's usability through the heuristics values of one item in an offered series, found interface design bugs, and defined usage problems over opinion exchanges and discussions. In addition, 13 users were invited to participate in the SMASH evaluation in this study. The purpose of this SMASH assessment was to test the main features of the Mood Canteen, such as daily mood-boosting recipes, recipe editing, video recording, my collection, and search. The participants were asked to download Mood Canteen and its operating system and to complete the SMASH questionnaire at the end of the operation. The usability assessment results, which were based on the 12 SMASH heuristic evaluation criteria, are shown as follows:

SMASH 1: Visibility of the system status. The Mood Canteen interface design can easily identify the location of the function, and the information display is clear and easy to understand.

SMASH 2: Match between the system and the real world. Mood Canteen can genuinely respond to the user's operations; in other words, when using different features, Mood Canteen allows users to detect changes in the interface immediately.

SMASH 3: User control and freedom. The Mood Canteen system is simple, which facilitates its application. In addition, the performance of the features has clear distinctions.

SMASH 4: Consistency and standards. The color, text, and graphics presented by the Mood Canteen user interface design have high uniformity and are all in conformity with the design principles.

SMASH 5: Error prevention. The participants consider this system to be easy and simple to operate, which can decrease the possibility of making an error.

SMASH 6: Minimize the user's memory load. The operation of the Mood Canteen system is simple, and the performance of the features has clear distinctions, which decreases the chance of an unnecessary overload from the memory and reduces the users' cognitive burden during operation.

SMASH 7: Customization and shortcuts. The system function is presented clearly, and no special memory or search is needed.

SMASH 8: Efficiency of use and performance. The Mood Canteen interface design is simple and neat. The positions of the buttons to press correspond to the user's hand gestures, and the application's system can be used smoothly without causing any major issue. Additionally, users do not need to memorize much of the operating procedure.

SMASH 9: Esthetic and minimalist design. The Mood Canteen interface design is exquisite, sharp, neat, and simple. The design of the fine details shows a selective and well-planned style.

SMASH 10: Help users recognize, diagnose, and recover from errors. The technical operation is kept in line with the operating capability scope of general users.

SMASH 11: Help and documentation. The Mood Canteen system does not provide question assistance. In a situation when users encounter an operating or system error, it is recommended that the system can provide helpful hints to reduce user frustration. It is also recommended that an operating guide or demo pages be added to allow beginners to learn the system's functions more quickly.

SMASH 12: Physical interaction and ergonomics. The privacy protection level is low, which is suitable for a personal mobile device. If Mood Canteen is operated on a public device, it is recommended that other device login reminders be added.

3 Conclusions

This research resulted in the development of a mobile social platform, called Mood Canteen, which has the purpose of meal cuisine and recipe sharing. Mood Canteen can be used on Android smartphones. In July 2017, Mood Canteen was launched on Google Play and was made available for interested users to download and use [13]. Mood Canteen has two important characteristics: (1) to establish the relationship between food and emotion: To construct an interaction between food and personal emotions, Mood Canteen applies an emotion analysis mechanism on SNS to analyze emotions based on semantics, emoticons/emoji, and images of food- and cuisine-related posts, and it matches those emotions with food to create a user's personal emotional state database and emotional food database according to the study's results. (2) To establish an emotion-complementing healing system: To make emotion cuisine recommendations for users that meet their emotional state and help users alleviate negative emotions and promote positive emotions by sharing recipes and meals, Mood Canteen incorporates a newly created personalized meal recommendation mechanism that provides users with the appropriate comfort food selection based on a personal emotional state database and emotional food database. The Mood Canteen system links personal emotion healing with food, with a focus on providing personal emotional appeasement and healing with food. Our future studies will continue to explore the interactions between food and specific emotions. Furthermore, the current Mood Canteen provides only the Chinese version of emotional vocabulary analysis; it is recommended that emotional semantic analysis in other languages be added to strengthen the emotion analysis mechanism.

Acknowledgement. This work was supported in part by the Ministry of Science and Technology (MOST), Taiwan, R.O.C., under Grant MOST 105-2221-E-182-025-MY2, as well as CGU fund SCRPD3F0041.

References

1. Dubé, L., LeBel, J.L., Lu, J.: Affect asymmetry and comfort food consumption. Physiol. Behav. **86**(4), 559–567 (2005)
2. Gibson, E.L.: Emotional influences on food choice: sensory, physiological and psychological pathways. Physiol. Behav. **89**(1), 53–61 (2006)
3. Wansink, B., Cheney, M.M., Chan, N.: Exploring comfort food preferences across age and gender. Physiol. Behav. **79**(4), 739–747 (2003)
4. Heatherton, T.F., Herman, C.P., Polivy, J.: Effects of physical threat and ego threat on eating behavior. J. Pers. Soc. Psychol. **60**(1), 138 (1991)
5. Spence, C.: Comfort food: a review. Int. J. Gastronomy Food Sci. **9**(Supplement C), 105–109 (2017)
6. Just Eat.co.uk Ltd.: Jsut Eat (2017). https://www.just-eat.co.uk/apps. Accessed 20 Dec 2017
7. Kosinski, M., et al.: Manifestations of user personality in website choice and behaviour on online social networks. Mach. Learn. **95**(3), 357–380 (2014)
8. Bazarova, N.N., et al.: Social sharing of emotions on Facebook: Channel differences, satisfaction, and replies. In: Proceedings of the 18th ACM Conference on Computer Supported Cooperative Work & Social Computing. ACM (2015)
9. Tasty (2017). https://tasty.co/. Accessed 25 Dec 2017
10. Tastemade Inc.: Tastemade (2017). https://itunes.apple.com/us/app/tastemade/id971197898?mt=8, https://play.google.com/store/apps/details?id=com.tastemade.player&hl=en. Accessed 25 Dec 2017
11. Kitchen Stories: Kitchen Stories - anyone can cook (2017). https://kitchenstories.io/en. Accessed 20 Dec 2017
12. iCook (2017). https://itunes.apple.com/tw/app/icook-ai-liao-li/id554065086?mt=8, https://play.google.com/store/apps/details?id=com.polydice.icook. Accessed 25 Dec 2017
13. Mood Canteen (2017). https://play.google.com/store/apps/details?id=mypidea.com.cooker. Accessed 20 Dec 2017
14. Scherer, K.R.: What are emotions? and how can they be measured? Soc. Sci. Inf. **44**(4), 695–729 (2005)
15. Machajdik, J., Hanbury, A.: Affective image classification using features inspired by psychology and art theory. In: Proceedings of the 18th ACM International Conference on Multimedia. ACM (2010)

16. Zhao, J., et al.: Moodlens: an emoticon-based sentiment analysis system for Chinese tweets. In: Proceedings of the 18th ACM SIGKDD International Conference on Knowledge Discovery and Data Mining. ACM (2012)
17. Vashisht, G., Thakur, S.: Facebook as a corpus for emoticons-based sentiment analysis. Int. J. Emerg. Technol. Adv. Eng. 4(5), 904–908 (2014)
18. Nielsen, J., Molich, R.: Heuristic evaluation of user interfaces. In: Proceedings of the SIGCHI Conference on Human Factors in Computing Systems. ACM (1990)
19. Nielsen, J.: Usability inspection methods. In: Conference companion on Human factors in computing systems. ACM (1994)
20. Wong, A.M.-K., et al.: A user-based heuristic evaluation of an intelligent healthcare system. In: ICCE Berlin 2013 IEEE Third International Conference on Consumer Electronics, Berlin (ICCE-Berlin). IEEE (2013)
21. Inostroza, R., et al.: Developing SMASH: a set of SMArtphone's uSability Heuristics. Comput. Stand. Inter. 43, 40–52 (2016)

Emerging Social Media and Social Networks Analysis Transforms the Tourism Industry: Living Green Smart Tourism Ecosystem

Tsai-Hsuan Tsai[1]([⊠]), Hsien-Tsung Chang[2], Yu-Wen Lin[1],
Ming-Chun Yu[1], Pei-Jung Lien[3], Wei-Cheng Yan[3],
and Wei-Ling Ho[3]

[1] Digital Media Lab, Chang Gung University, Tao-Yuan, Taiwan
ttsai@mail.cgu.edu.tw
[2] Department of Computer Science and Information Engineering,
Chang Gung University, Tao-Yuan, Taiwan
[3] Metal Industries Research and Development Centre, Kaohsiung, Taiwan

Abstract. Using the smart tourism ecosystem model as its framework as well as the strength of ties theory and the SNS social computing formula as a theoretical basis, this study establishes the Living Green tourism ecosystem to improve connections between businesses and the smart travel itinerary recommendation mechanism to promote the development of the entire industry. The Living Green tourism ecosystem has two major innovative features. (1) Visualizing industrial activity intensity and social connection intensity between businesses can not only help clearly understand the development of local businesses and assist in evaluating the effectiveness of industry development but also provide a reference for destination marketing organizations or relevant government agencies in terms of supporting the development of disadvantaged business segments. (2) The application of social media and social networks analysis helps implement the travel and tourism industry's development strategies. Based on businesses' social behaviors and interaction modes on social platforms, the tourism ecosystem calculates industrial connection intensity, uses it as an index for smart travel itinerary recommendations, and further enhances the overall promotion and development of the travel and tourism industry network.

Keywords: Smart tourism ecosystem · Strength of ties theory
Social networking activity intensity · Green tourism · Mobile application

1 Introduction

The proliferation of Internet technologies and smartphones has affected the travel and tourism industry and led to the popularity of mobile smart tourism applications. In short, smart tourism uses smartphones to provide travelers with personalized smart travel information services and to establish smarter, more effective and more sustainable connections between travelers and tourist attractions [1]. Smart tourism is also defined as the provision of ubiquitous tourism information services. It not only changes the travel behavior patterns of travelers, facilitates the acquisition of rich information, and creates

© Springer International Publishing AG, part of Springer Nature 2018
M. Antona and C. Stephanidis (Eds.): UAHCI 2018, LNCS 10908, pp. 583–590, 2018.
https://doi.org/10.1007/978-3-319-92052-8_46

relaxing and flexible travel experiences but also enables the travel and tourism industry to add value through the new service model [2]. In addition to smart tourism, the smart tourism ecosystem (STE) has also received considerable attention. The STE emphasizes that different economic entities in the travel and tourism industry, such as producers, distributors, consumers and government agencies, establish an environment for product promotion or service creation and distribution through competition and cooperation [3]. The establishment of shared value in business ecosystems not only improves business competitiveness and socio-economic conditions, enabling the generation of new species in the ecosystems, but also serves as a basis for promoting innovation and sustaining productive forces in business ecosystems. Tourism ecosystems are a typical example of this feature [4]. For instance, a tourism ecosystem is usually composed of many microorganisms. In addition to being defined by geographical location, the microorganisms place more emphasis on the connections and interactions among themselves. The introduction of intelligent technologies can effectively set up links between nodes in order to create a more active and intelligent network [5]. Through proper integration of smart sciences and technologies, a smart tourism ecosystem creates, manages and transfers intelligent tourism services and experiences. The information gathering and processing analysis following the acquisition of high-intensity travel-related information and shared value through these services is the main function of an STE [6]. The common goal of an STE is to create a rich, highly valued, meaningful and sustainable tourism experience through the information provided [7].

The current research classifies the member species of a smart tourism ecosystem into touristic consumer (TC), resident consumer (RC), tourism supplier (TS), other industry supplier (OS), and destination marketing organization (DMO). In terms of smart tourism applications, popular social media and mobile apps currently allow consumers to have a high degree of willingness to share and enhance their motivation to receive information, that is, when participating in social networking sites (SNSs) (i.e., Facebook) or experiencing location-based mobile services, touristic consumers or resident consumers also receive information provided by different species or the environment. As regards its applications in the context of tourism suppliers, smart tourism focuses on providing smart technology services and offering richer, more efficient and more effective services through data and information feedback to ensure service sustainability. DMOs are responsible for information and equipment, marketing management and quality control in innovative service patterns [8]. This shows that in order to create sustainable and intelligent digital services, the information chains between the supplier network and the consumer community need to be connected. Only in this way can efficient, effective and sustainable travel services be created through user activity and the feedback provided by user data. Unfortunately, current links between smart travel and the tourism industry are limited to the exchange and flow of information, and it is difficult to strengthen the mutually beneficial relationship between businesses in the industry, while relevant research is lacking on the reciprocity among businesses and the promotion of the industry's synergic development within the STE structure. To strengthen the connections in industrial networks and enhance the overall development of the travel and tourism industry, this study uses the strength of ties theory and the SNS social computing formula as the theoretic basis to establish a smart tourism ecosystem that can improve connections within the industry: Living Green. The study develops the Living

Green mobile app to provide innovative and intelligent mobile sightseeing services for smartphone users. This study is based on the travel and tourism industry in Chia-Yi, Taiwan. By selecting and connecting related local "natural," "environment-friendly" and "green" businesses, it builds a smart tourism industry network and ecosystem.

2 Design and Development of the Living Green Smart Tourism Ecosystem

2.1 Design Rationales of the Living Green Ecosystem

Using Granovetter's strength of ties theory and Gilbert's SNS social computing formula as its theoretical basis, the Living Green ecosystem developed in this research is a tourism ecosystem that promotes social connections in the travel and tourism industry. The strength of ties theory emphasizes the different intensity and relevance of social connections between nodes in social networks and divides social relations into ones with strong connections and ones with weak connections based on the connection intensity generated by different social behaviors and emotional interactions [9]. In reference to the social network theory proposed by Granovetter, Gilbert formulated a computing model of social connection intensity and applied it to SNSs to quantify social connection intensity [10]. This study first analyzes the SNS social tools currently used by the tourism industry, defines social function items, informationizes social behaviors, and then establishes a social behavior database of the tourism industry's social networking sites and develops a social networking analysis system by developing the specifications of application program interfaces (APIs) provided by community service software as well as community service communication. With the automatic scheduling and automatic analysis capabilities of the social platform and the industrial social behavior database, the study is able to quantify the industrial social index, which can be used to provide smart travel itinerary recommendations and prioritize related industrial information. The Living Green system's industrial social behavior gathering mechanism and industrial social connection computing mechanism are explained below.

(a) **Definition of social behavior within the industry.** In terms of gathering industrial social behavior, social connections between businesses in the industry can stem from a relationship of close cooperation based on category or of close competition based on geographical features. In addition, social behavior is established mainly through the flow of individuals (travelers) between businesses, and social interactions between travelers and tourism businesses are also related to the businesses' active performance. This study first summarizes the types of communities that current businesses form and the function projects for social interactions between individuals and businesses and classifies and defines the encoding. That is to say, based on businesses' profiles on their Facebook fan page, such as industry category, geographic location, business hours, frequency of events and number of users, we collect and encode all of users' social interactions on the Facebook fan page and then calculate their cumulative number, frequency and text data, and multiply relevant information's floating weight and corresponding judging conditions to calculate the interactions between individuals and industries, which constitutes the industrial activity index. Finally, we use the sum of inter-industry social index calculations as a reference to evaluate the promotion mechanisms between businesses and intelligent services in the smart tourism ecosystem.

(b) **Calculation of the social connection index between businesses.** This study uses the social connection index calculation model proposed by Gilbert to calculate the social index between businesses [10]. The connection intensity in SNSs is determined based on the aspects of intensity, intimacy, duration, reciprocal services, structural, emotional support and social distance, while the measured functional items include number of exchanges of messages and feedback on the dynamic wall, content analysis of the dynamic wall, number of messages left by friends on the dynamic wall, number of message exchanges, message intensity analysis, dynamic updates of users, dynamic updates of friends, responses to friends' photos, number of friends, number of friends' friends, number of days from the last reply, data analysis of content intensity (topic) on the dynamic wall, co-annotated photos, number of times that users appear in others' photos, distance from home, relationship status of friends, number of days since the first response, shared links, recommended apps, number of common friends, common social circles, common interests, common concerns, and the age, education level, work experience, religious affiliation, and political affiliation of users and friends. The following equation describes Gilbert's calculation formula for social connection intensity.

$$
s_i = \alpha + \beta R_i + \gamma D_i + N(i) + \epsilon_i
$$

$$
N(i) = \lambda_0 \mu_M + \lambda_1 med_M + \sum_{k=2}^{4} \sum_{s \in M} \lambda_k (s - \mu_M)^k
$$

$$
+ \lambda_5 min_M + \lambda_6 max_M
$$

$$
M = \{ s_j : j \text{ and } i \text{ are mutual friends} \}
$$

(1)

2.2 Specific Features of the Living Green Tourism Ecosystem

This study considers Living Green as a brand and emphasizes the characteristics of green tourism. In addition to selecting related local "natural", "environment-friendly" and "green" industries in the Chia-Yi region of Taiwan and establishing a tourism ecosystem network platform, this study also develops the Living Green mobile app to provide smart travel itinerary recommendations and innovative interactive experiences for smartphone users. It is worth mentioning that based on the analysis of the social connection index between members of the Living Green tourism ecosystem network and taking into account users' personal preferences and needs, Living Green's smart travel services can not only recommend suitable travel itineraries for users but also promote social connections between businesses and the overall development of the local travel and tourism industry. The following aspects describe the system function features of the Living Green ecosystem.

(a) **Create function:** To create industrial connections (Create), establish the Living Green tourism network and its nodes between businesses, and calculate its degree of activity, this study first constructs a tourism industry supplier network based on the organizational structure of the tourism ecosystem, establishes nodes between suppliers, analyzes data on the industrial community platform and the social behavior of individuals on the platform, collects relevant function projects and informationizes industrial social behavior so as to calculate the industrial activity index and the industrial social index. Subsequently, we divide activity intensity into four levels to create a visual industrial social map. To be consistent with the theme of green tourism, the image of sapling growth serves as a pin on the map to symbolize industrial activity intensity, and the corresponding icons are placed on the map according to the activity intensity of each business's development. Figure 1 shows the social activities among green tourism businesses in the Chia-Yi area. It is worth mentioning that the Create function can be seen as a reference to gauge the effectiveness of industrial development as well as an indicator for DMOs or relevant government agencies to support the development of disadvantaged business segments.

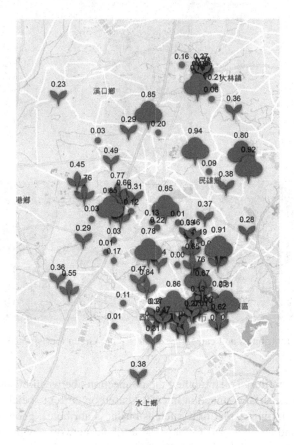

Fig. 1. Current status of the industrial activity of the Living Green tourism ecosystem. (Color figure online)

(b) **Maintain function:** Industrial connections are maintained by suggesting mutually beneficial groups. After identifying business locations and activity intensity between businesses, the Living Green system calculates the social connection index between businesses according to business attributes, geographical location, messages and sharing based on Gilbert's social connection computing model. The thickness of the line between points represents the level of industrial connection intensity. According to the level of industrial connection intensity, businesses are divided into five categories of mutually beneficial groups, namely green food, green transport, green attractions, green lodging and green leisure, and a resource-sharing cooperation model is achieved through industrial connections, as shown in Fig. 2. Figure 3 uses the green businesses in Chia-Yi, Taiwan, as an example. The green food category is characterized by local food, organic food and landscape restaurants; the green transport category focuses on environment-friendly transport modes, such as E-Bike, a public electric vehicle rental system; the green attractions category is represented by local sightseeing factories or eco-tourism attractions; the green lodging category features lodging recommendations; the green leisure category is represented by other leisure and entertainment activities.

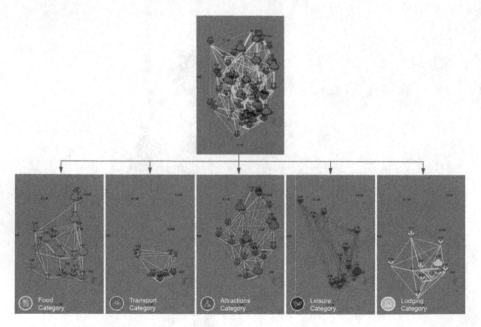

Fig. 2. Reciprocal attributes and categories of the Living Green tourism network. (Color figure online)

(c) **Enhance function:** To strengthen the connections between businesses, the study calculates industrial connection intensity based on current social behaviors on the industrial community platform, such as business attributes, geographical location, messages and sharing, and forms same-attribute networks with highly connected businesses to complete the construction of points and the connection of lines,

Food Category
C3EF4B

Transport Category
03EFE8

Attractions Category
58E0A5

Lodging Category
EFD8A8

Leisure Category
00C1C6

Fig. 3. Linking Living Green business categories. (Color figure online)

which lays a foundation for the integration of surfaces, namely establishing the Living Green ecosystem. In addition, to promote the benefits of the development of a smart tourism ecosystem, the study will provide tourists with the Living Green mobile app, whose smart travel itinerary recommendation mechanism will plan travel itineraries based on users' personal preferences and then promote the overall development of the Living Green tourism industry (Fig. 4).

Fig. 4. Living Green mobile app - smart travel scheduler. (Color figure online)

3 Conclusion

Using the smart tourism ecosystem model as its framework as well as the strength of ties theory and the SNS social computing formula as a theoretical basis, this study establishes the Living Green tourism ecosystem to improve connections between businesses and the smart travel itinerary recommendation mechanism to promote the development of the entire industry. The Living Green tourism ecosystem has two major innovative features. (1) Visualizing industrial activity intensity and social connection intensity between businesses can not only help clearly understand the development of local businesses and assist in evaluating the effectiveness of industry development but also provide a reference for DMOs or relevant government agencies in terms of supporting the development of disadvantaged business segments. (2) The application of social media and social networks analysis helps implement the travel and tourism industry's development strategies. Based on businesses' social behaviors and interaction modes on social platforms, the tourism ecosystem calculates industrial connection intensity, uses it as an index for smart travel itinerary recommendations, and further enhances the overall promotion and development of the travel and tourism industry network. The Living Green mobile app supports the iOS system and is expected to be released in March 2018 on the App Store for interested users to download.

Acknowledgement. This work was supported in part by the Ministry of Science and Technology (MOST), Taiwan, R.O.C., under Grant MOST 105-2221-E-182-025-MY2, as well as CGU fund SCRPD3F0041.

References

1. Molz, J.G.: Travel Connections: Tourism, Technology, and Togetherness in a Mobile World. Routledge, New York (2012)
2. Li, Y., et al.: The concept of smart tourism in the context of tourism information services. Tourism Manag. **58**(Supplement C), 293–300 (2017)
3. Gretzel, U., et al.: Conceptual foundations for understanding smart tourism ecosystems. Comput. Hum. Behav. **50**(Supplement C), 558–563 (2015)
4. Porter, M.E., Kramer, M.R.: The big idea: creating shared value (2011)
5. Werthner, H.: Intelligent systems in travel and tourism. In: IJCAI (2003)
6. Zhang, L.: Smart tourism: the coming age of customization and intelligent public services. J. Tourism Tribune **27**(2), 3–5 (2012)
7. Buhalis, D., Amaranggana, A.: Smart tourism destinations. In: Xiang, Z., Tussyadiah, I. (eds.) Information and Communication Technologies in Tourism 2014. Springer, Cham (2013). https://doi.org/10.1007/978-3-319-03973-2_40
8. Hunter, W.C., et al.: Constructivist research in smart tourism. Asia Pac. J. Inf. Syst. **25**(1), 105–120 (2015)
9. Granovetter, M.S.: The strength of weak ties. Am. J. Sociol. **78**(6), 1360–1380 (1973)
10. Gilbert, E., Karahalios, K.: Predicting tie strength with social media. In: Proceedings of the SIGCHI conference on human factors in computing systems. ACM (2009)

Institutional Accessibility Awareness

Brent Whiting$^{(\boxtimes)}$

Temple University, Philadelphia, PA 19122, USA
bwhiting@temple.edu

Abstract. This paper will provide a case study of Temple University's collaborative efforts to develop and implement a comprehensive accessible technology project and the framework of the university Accessible Technology Initiative, which facilitated the essential collaborations. The university's Accessible Technology Compliance Committee created a disability inclusion and accessibility awareness training to ensure that the university community understands its responsibilities and is aware of available support resources. The success of this project was the result of strategies and collaborations among participants in the broader initiative.

Keywords: Accessibility · Collaboration · Awareness

1 Temple University Background

Facts and Figures

- Based in Philadelphia, Pennsylvania
- 1 of 3 state research universities
- Approximately 40,000 students and over 6,500 FTE employees
- 17 schools and colleges including 8 professional schools
- 150+ bachelor's degree programs
- 160+ master's degree programs
- 4 Pennsylvania branch campuses (Ambler, Harrisburg, Center City Philadelphia, and North Philadelphia Health Science Campus)
- 2 International campuses: Tokyo, Japan and Rome, Italy.

1.1 Abridged History of Accessibility at Temple University

Temple University (TU) has historically prided itself in the diversity of it's student body, and as listed below, several centers and initiatives built a foundation for accessibility considerations of students and employees that are the foundation of many of the current efforts.

Institute on Disabilities
The Institute on Disabilities at Temple University is one of the sixty-seven University Centers for Excellence in Developmental Disabilities Education, Research and Service funded by the Administration on Developmental Disabilities, U.S. Department of Health and Human Services.

© Springer International Publishing AG, part of Springer Nature 2018
M. Antona and C. Stephanidis (Eds.): UAHCI 2018, LNCS 10908, pp. 591–601, 2018.
https://doi.org/10.1007/978-3-319-92052-8_47

Established in 1974, the Institute has mirrored the changes in the field of developmental disabilities, evolving into a model of self-determination and individualized supports in the community [1].

Office for the Disabled/Disability Resources and Services
Disability Resources and Services (DRS) at TU grew out of The Office for the Disabled, student organization founded in 1976. TU formally established Disabled Student Services in 1977, and the office adopted its' current name, Disability Resources and Services in 1993.

Accessibility of Information and Technology Policy
In November 2012, in response to recommendations provided by an external accessibility evaluation, TU formally adopted Policy Number, 04.71.13 - Accessibility of Information Technology [2].

The policy defined two core tenets:

1. The Accessible Technology Compliance Committee (ATCC) was formed to develop, review, and approved all guidelines and standards related to the policy.
2. The person (or department) responsible for the information or technology must undertake reasonable efforts to make it accessible in a timely manner upon becoming aware of non-compliance with university standards and guidelines.

The Vice President of Computer Services (CS)/Chief Information Officer was stated as the responsible officer for the policy.

2   Accessibility of Information and Technology Policy

2.1   Justification

Awareness of the topic and concerns around the accessibility of technology at TU was brought to the attention of the CIO in response to the Resolution Agreement between The Pennsylvania State University and the National Federation of the Blind [3].

Greater Reliance on Technology
The rapid expansion of technology across higher education has expanded concerns about discrimination against students and/or faculty required to use inaccessible systems and software to complete coursework and job functions. Education accreditation bodies are requiring instruction and use of certain technology systems and products. However, it's necessary that universities continue to provide these resources to students in an equitable manner regardless of disability. Notable technologies being used extensively in higher education include:

- Learning Management Systems
- Smart classroom technologies
- Online learning and processes
- Electronic textbooks and corresponding digital ancillary content.

Service Demand on Disability Resources and Services
The volume of students registering and requesting course accommodations with DRS is growing each year in numbers and percentage of the student population. Additionally, the scope of DRS has grown to require a broader understanding of more technology systems to appropriately support accommodation requests (Fig. 1).

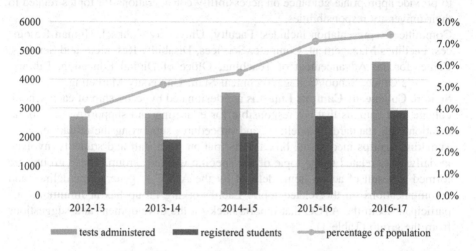

Fig. 1. The chart illustrates the growth of student enrollment in and test accommodation requests processed by DRS over a recent five year span.

2.2 Foundation

The foundation of the TU Accessible Technology Initiative was established in and originally funded by TU Computer Services (CS) but connected with stakeholders from across university leadership for applicable content expertise. CS staff were involved in the remediation of several topics, but there was a concentrated effort to include other departments to minimize the appearance that the initiative was being dictated by a single central unit.

External Review
The first formal process of the initiative solicited an external review of TU's current state of accessible technology systems and services. The primary recommendations of the review were to establish an appropriate policy to set an internal governing committee comprised of department leadership across the institution. Additional areas of focus from in the review included:

- Computer Labs
- Classrooms and Learning Spaces
- Instructional Materials
- Library Services and Systems
- Procurement of Technology
- Web Based Content and Systems.

Leadership, Collaboration, Participation

Initiative participation fell within one of the primary roles below:

1. **Project Management** and initiative coordination was provided by designated staff from CS.
2. **ATCC membership** was comprised of executives within their organizational unit to provide appropriate guidance on accessibility considerations for topics related to their university responsibilities.

   Committee Representation includes: Faculty, University Counsel, Human Resources, Facilities Management, Computer Services, Disability Resources and Services, Center for the Advancement of Teaching, Office of Digital Education, Library, Provost's Office, School/College Technical Staff, University Marketing.
3. **School, College, or Campus Liaisons** are designated by leadership of each school, college, and campus that are responsible for educating and supporting their organization with standards, guidelines, and procedures supporting the initiative.
4. **Working groups** incorporate broad participation from staff and students involved in daily tasks related to the topic of the specific working group. These groups are formed as result of action items defined by the ATCC to generate guidelines and communications on the related topic. Each working group has at minimum one participant from the ATCC that reports back on the development and suggestions from the group (Table 1).

Table 1. Foundational working group topics and participants

Working group topic	Participants/Departments
Instructional materials and captioning	Instructional Support Center (ISC), Faculty, DRS, CS
Training and accessibility website	ISC, DRS, Strategic Marketing & Communication (SM&C), Human Resources (HR), University Counsel, CS
Web review and audit	School/College IT, SM&C, CS
Assistive technology	DRS, ISC, CS
Online learning	Office of Digital Education (ODE), Faculty, School/College IT, CS
Library	University Libraries, CS
Administrative systems	HR, University Counsel, CS
Purchasing and procurement	University Counsel, Purchasing, HR, CS

2.3   Communication and Training

Initiative communications and training sessions were facilitated by CS and were live events where the CIO and Project Manager presented to large meetings of organization leadership, such as Collegial Assemblies, Council of Deans, and Administrative Council meetings.

Once the initiative was introduced to leadership, liaisons were designated for each area. School, College, and Campus liaisons were provided several training sessions to cover relevant accessibility topics related to the above-mentioned working group tasks.

Additionally, a university website was developed [4] as a clearing house to provide supporting documentation and communication for standards, guidelines and actions of the initiative.

2.4   Training

Initial training focused on the school, college, and campus liaisons with the intention that they train their constituents as needed. The topics included in the trainings included:

- Understanding the role and responsibilities of DRS
- Remediating Instructional Materials
- Learning Space and Computer Lab Guidelines
- Purchasing/Procurement Process
- Web auditing.

3   Institution Accessibility Awareness Training

As outlined above, the substantial efforts and education related to making technology and content accessible for students, faculty and staff was presented to appointed representatives in the various organizations, but not in a general/consistent presentation to the entire university population. As the preliminary work of the initiative subsided and became operationalized, it became apparent that additional effort was necessary to ensure a uniform awareness of policy, standards, and guidelines.

The university had a need for a comprehensive presentation of the state of accessibility at the institution and responsibilities of employees that could not be delivered in a circulating seminar to the schools, colleges, and departments. The most consistent method to deliver the content to the full audience was through an asynchronous online course that could be used for training and recalled for reference as needed. Fortunately, there were already similar trainings required of employees coinciding with workplace regulations and policies.

3.1   Participant Survey Providing Recommendations

Part of the school, college, and campus liaison responsibilities is to respond to an annual survey from the ATCC to evaluate communication, growth and success of the initiative. As part of to our initiative annual survey competed in June 2016, a college liaison suggested creating an awareness course similar to other regulation-based HR deployed training and onboarding content (Making Our Campus Safer, Preventing Discrimination and Harassment, HazCom/Right to Know).

3.2   Building the Training

The ATCC recommended a small working group of six participants to develop the course. Representatives from CS, University Counsel, HR, and DRS were selected to form the content and deliver the course utilizing the existing learning management system used by the Learning and Development Office in HR. The working group solicited peripheral help from students and faculty to produce faculty success videos to be included. Lastly, the group obtained a letter from the University President as a welcome statement to the training emphasizing its importance to the mission of the university.

An initial loose framework for the training and content was recommended by the working group and approved by the ATCC in Fall 2015.

The approved primary framework included:

- Content: Since one training course was developed for all participants, the content needed to be generalized so ensure broad understanding.
- Duration: The training needed to be designed so that it could be completed in approximately 20 min. The training contains full narration requiring participants to remain on a slide/topic until the narration completes. If an individual completes the training, they need to be able to return to the course and freely navigate the course without waiting for the initial timings.
- Engagement: Media and participant interaction was discussed as a critical component to reinforce practical understanding and/or examples in support of the overall content.

3.2.1   Training Project Timeline

- July 2015 - ATCC set a priority on the training and established the working group
- November 2015 - Initial draft outline was accepted by the ATCC
- April 2016 – First rough draft of the training was presented to the ATCC
- July 2016 – ATCC provided final revision requests
- August 2016 – ATCC approved final revisions
- September 2016 – Finalized and executed communication strategy
- November 2016 – Distributed training.

3.2.2   Abridged Outline of Training Content

Obligation
Temple University's obligation statement:

"We have a legal obligation to make our programs and services accessible to students, faculty, and staff. Accessibility on our campus is a shared responsibility.

Each school, college, and department is responsible for making its programs and services accessible with guidance from campus experts.

Inaccessible design, or an act of discrimination, however inadvertent, can violate university policy and subject the university to liability under the law."

Law and Policy

Overviews of the applicable federal laws and university policies with reference links to external web resources.

- Rehabilitation Act of 1973
- Americans with Disabilities Act
- Temple University Policy: Preventing & Addressing Discrimination and Harassment
- Temple University Policy: Accessibility of Information and Technology
- Temple University Policy: Course Syllabus Policy.

What is Accessibility

For this training broad definitions of accessibility and accessible were provided:

- Accessibility is the ability to engage with, use, participate in, and belong to the world around us.
- Definition of Accessible provided by the Office of Civil Rights to the South Carolina Technical College System, OCR Compliance Review No. 11-11-6002 "Accessible means a person with a disability is afforded the opportunity to acquire the same information, engage in the same interactions, and enjoy the same services as a person without a disability in an equally effective and equally integrated manner, with substantially equivalent ease of use. The person with a disability must be able to obtain the information as fully, equally and independently as a person without a disability" [5].

The training outlines and defines accessibility for the following areas.

- Physical Accessibility
- Technology Access
- Instructional Design Practices
- The Learning Environment
- University Programs and Services.

Physical Accessibility

As a result of this training development the central Helpdesk ticketing system was expanded to provide a direct platform for students, faculty and staff to offer feedback on physical barriers across campus.

Included were physical spaces, technology services and systems, and providing appropriate accommodations as well as a variety of other issues. Therefore, colleges and universities need to expand their role in providing accessible technology to their students, staff, faculty, and visitors.

Technology Access

Assistive Technology is generally defined, and practical examples given to illustrate some commonly in use across universities.

Instructional Design Practices

An overview of common accessibility considerations in designing course content were provided and covers: Color Contrast, Alternative Text for Images and Illustrations, Captioning, Document Formatting, and Keyboard Usability.

The Learning Environment

A deliberate attempt is made in this section to strictly follow the current university workflow and responsibilities in courses where students need and/or request accommodations. The relationships between the student, faculty and DRS office are documented to minimize confusion. It is reinforced that DRS is the university content experts on these matters and faculty and staff should not make unilateral decisions to approve or deny any requested accommodation or modification to coursework.

Taking the training a step further, the training presents recommendations directly for faculty to create a welcoming classroom environment to encourage individuals to request help whenever appropriate. A very brief overview and mention was made for universal design of courses to connect faculty to the broader understanding to the value to designing accessible courses can bring to many different types of learners.

Programs and Services

Organizations and individuals sponsoring internal or external events, hosted at or affiliated with the university, are required to abide by the same accessibility standards and guidelines as set forth for the university.

Quiz

In an effort to further reinforce the topics of the training, three open ended quiz questions are given to each participant simulating a practical experience where they offer suggestions to resolve an accessibility conflict.

3.3   Training Development Challenges

The training itself needed to model accessible design, and prior trainings had not been scrutinized for accessibility as thoroughly. To make the training both fully accessible and user friendly took several iterations of development and direct support from the training platform vendor. As further reinforcement of the initiative, the staff designing future trainings now had experience developing a fully accessible course. The course provided a navigational instruction slide that read aloud and displayed onscreen methods to advance through the course via mouse or keyboard, and a full transcript was provided on each slide and included with a downloadable/offline version of the entire training.

In addition to following system requirements to ensure the training was properly designed for use with a screen reader, keyboard-only navigation, and other assistive technology, usability testing of the course was conducted by volunteers through the Institute on Disabilities, staff in CS and school/college/campus liaisons.

3.4   Training Communication Strategy

Near the completion of the development of the course, the team reached out to the Senior Vice Provost for Strategic Communications, who is another member of the ATCC, to provide guidance on a communication strategy to make the community aware of the upcoming training. The strategy was segmented by roles and was implemented chronologically with communication starting at the leadership levels and progressing through levels of organizational management.

In addition to emails announcing the training, TU has a system configured in a university wide portal/intranet titled "NextSteps" that is a central notification and task list exposed to all students, faculty and staff. The training launch was published to this distribution channel and would not disappear from the list until the action was complete.

3.5   Training Deployment and Participation

The final course developed by the group is titled **Disability Inclusion and Accessibility at Temple University** and was distributed to all full-time staff, and both adjunct and full-time faculty in November 2016. Additionally, the course has been incorporated into HR onboarding materials and has been required for all new staff and faculty hires since launch.

As of February 28, 2018, the training had been assigned to 15,223 employees, had been completed by 9,755 employees, and 726 employees in progress (Fig. 2).

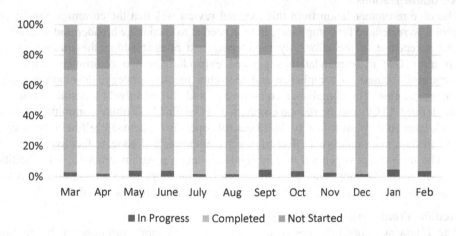

Fig. 2. Awareness training monthly participation and completion percentages

3.6   Training Licensing

To reinforce the spirit of the overall initiative and the training, a non-Temple version of the training was developed in PDF form and was licensed under the Creative Commons Attribution-NonCommercial 4.0 International License [6]. This version of the training is freely available, upon request, for other universities to modify for their own use.

4   Training Feedback and Responses

One of the results from distributing the training to all employees was that we received a notable amount of feedback on both the training and the initiative as a whole. One concern was that the policy, standards and workflows referenced in the training were all unfunded decisions that added various levels of effort and education on individual units. The feedback didn't directly resist the topics or need for the work but were looking for a broader dialogue and guidance on how to better educate and integrate these tasks into daily operations. Additionally many respondents, notably faculty members, were not aware of who their liaison was and didn't receive the level of assistance from the liaisons that was originally intended.

Based on the feedback and acknowledgement that the policy was now five years old, the ATCC made the recommendation to have another third-party review conducted in Spring 2017 with CS agreeing to provide the funding.

4.1   External Review - 2017

A request for proposals was submitted and processed in March 2017 and vendor selected in April. Upon selection of the vendor the review project started immediately and was completed by the end of June. The review consisted of staff and faculty interviews, standards and guidelines document evaluations, workflow assessments, and selected website reviews.

Recommendations
The core recommendation from this external review was that the current accessibility efforts were defined for compliance, but we needed to encourage broader understanding and acceptance of the efforts by broadening and re-establishing the initiative as a program. One recommendation suggested expanding to two committees with one remaining focused on compliance and the other focused strategy, development, and communication. The compliance committee would still effectively function similar to the defined ATCC and the second committee (TU defined as culture committee) would work more directly with faculty, build out role-specific on-demand self help resources, and foster a more concerted effort to directly empower and educate faculty.

The review also suggested that by implementing a program structure, accessibility support would become more proactive, foster partnerships of expertise, build a community of practice, and further build institution-wide awareness and skills.

Actions From Review Recommendations
The following actions are complete or in process in direct response to the recommendations provided to progress university accessibility awareness further.

- The ATCC expanded to create an Accessibility Program titled Accessible Temple that primarily functions out of a co-chairs group composed of leadership from the Center for Advancement of Teaching (CAT), DRS, and CS. The CAT co-chair member is the committee lead for a newly defined "Culture" committee focused on training, communication and development and the CS co-chair member is the lead on the updated "Compliance" committee that maintains the majority of the roles previously supplied by the ATCC.

- The university is investigating the appropriate location of a broad Accessibility Compliance Officer since the new program is more expansive than the original leadership within CS.
- The program is revisiting the role of liaisons and has proposed placing two liaisons in each school, college and campus with one designated as a faculty liaison to foster accessible design in course development and the other specifically responsible for the accessibility of the information technology infrastructure and complying with the defined standards and guidelines.
- A structure of working groups has been defined to achieve current annual defined goals.
- Communication and education strategies are being developed to incorporate outcomes of the annual working groups topics.

References

1. The Institute on Disabilities at Temple University – History. (n.d.). disabilities.temple.edu/about/history.shtml
2. Temple University Accessibility of Information and Technology Policy 04.71.13. policies.temple.edu/getdoc.asp?policy_no=04.71.13. Accessed 15 Nov 2012
3. Settlement Between Penn State University and National Federation of the Blind. Accessibility at Penn State (n.d.). accessibility.psu.edu/nfbpsusettlement/
4. Accessible Technology (n.d.). accessibility.temple.edu/
5. Recently Completed Investigation. Home, US Department of Education (ED). www2.ed.gov/about/offices/list/ocr/docs/investigations/11116002-b.html. Accessed 5 Nov 2015
6. About The Licenses. Creative Commons (n.d.). creativecommons.org/licenses/

Author Index

Printed in the United States
By Bookmasters